Matthews' American Armoury and Blue Book
by
John Mathews

A facsimile copy produced and privately printed by
The Armorial Register Limited
2016

First Published in 2016
by
The Armorial Register Limited
All rights reserved

ISBN: 978-0-9568157-7-4

British Library Cataloguing-in-Publication Data
A catalogue record of this book is available on request from
the British Library

Cover image:
George Washington copper halfpenny token dated 1795.
Reverse: The Coat of Arms of the United States of America
with legend: "LIBERTY AND SECURITY 1795"

Matthews' American Armoury
and
Blue Book.

—

1907.

LONDON, Eng :
Printed for the Editor by Chas. Mitchell,
4, West Harding Street,
Fetter Lane,
E.C.

E · PLURIBUS   UNUM

MATTHEWS'

American
Armoury
and
Blue Book

Dieu et mon droit

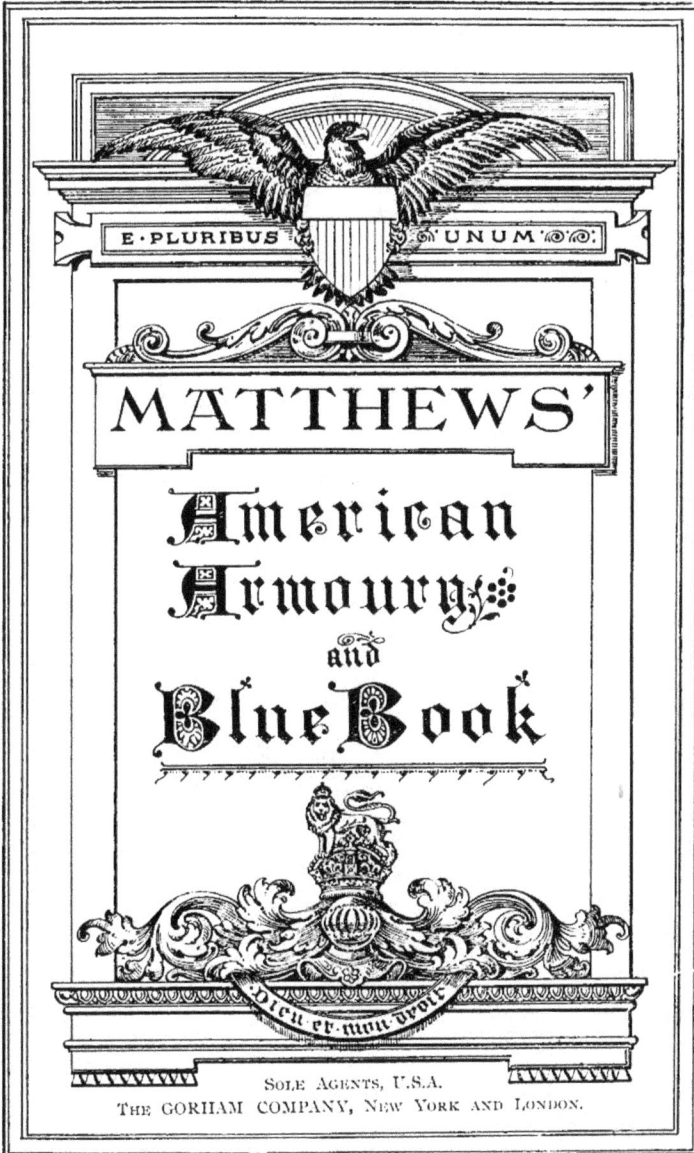

SOLE AGENTS, U.S.A.
THE GORHAM COMPANY, NEW YORK AND LONDON.

Edited and Published by JOHN MATTHEWS, 93 and 94, Chancery Lane, London, England.

PREFACE.

The **American Armoury and Blue Book** is now so well established as a time-honoured Record of Armigerous Families in the United States of America that this New Edition needs no *apologia pro vitâ suâ*, nor any statement either of its well-known attributes and aims, or of the means adopted by the Editor to render it a faithful exponent of American Ancestry and Heraldry, points which have all been dealt with at length in the Prefaces to earlier Editions.

In certain features, however, the New Edition may claim a higher place than those which have preceded it, as the Editor has given greater detail of lineage, and has added " Armorial Addenda," making the work historically comprehensive by grouping at the end of the Volume such Arms, not being in the body of the work, as are now used in America by descendants of those Armigeri to whose names, arranged in lexicographical order, the Arms are severally attached.

The Supplementary List will be of interest to a wider section of the American people than the other part of the work, and it is hoped that its inclusion in the Armoury will prompt many to supply the Editor with the necessary details of their lineage to enable him to locate them in the body of the Work.

The detailed lineage from the earliest known ancestor, now for the first time made a general feature, serves a double purpose, for it not only establishes the claim that has always been made for the Work that it is a trustworthy Record, but will doubtless often enable an enquirer seeking to elaborate his pedigree, whether on the one side of the Atlantic or the other, to recognize some ancestor among the various lineages, and so get into communication with a collateral member of his family in a position to afford him valuable information as to his own descent.

JOHN MATTHEWS,
Editor.

93 & 94, Chancery Lane,
London, W.C., England,
January, 1907.

Index.

	PAGE
ABBEY, see FREEMAN	178
ADAMS, Henry ... ... Add.	3
AGNEW, Hon. Park	202
AIKMAN, John ... ... Add.	3
AKERLY, Robert .. ... Add.	3
ALDEN, John... ... ... Add.	3
ALDIS, Owen F.	160
ALBRO, Rev. Addis	149
ALLERTON, Isaac ... Add.	4
ALLING, Roger ... ... Add.	4
ALMEY, Willey H.	207
ALSOPP, Joseph ... ... Add.	4
AMBLER, Richard ... Add.	4
AMES, Major Azel, M.D.	23
AMORY, Charles W.	161
AMORY, Jonathan ... Add.	4
ANABLE, Eliphalet N.	141
ANDREWS, John ... Add.	4
ANDREWS, John ... Add.	5
ANDRUS, John ... ... Add.	5
APPLETON, Samuel ... Add.	5
APTHORP, Charles ... Add.	5
ARNOLD, see PHILLIPS ...	76
ASHHURST, Richard ... Add.	5
ATHERTON, Humphrey Add.	5
ATKINSON, Henry M.	65
ATLEE, see CORLIES	170
ATWILL, James W.	81
AUSTIN, Col. Eugene K.	231
AUSTIN, Richard... ... Add.	6
AVERY, Frank M.	195
BACKUS, Rev. Clarence W. ...	87
BAGLEY, John ... ... Add.	6
BAGLEY, see BIGELOW	34
BAINBRIDGE, Christopher Add.	6
BAKER, Rev. William O.	96
BALCH, Thomas W.	31
BALDWIN, Edward .. Add.	6
BALDWIN, Le Roy W.	92
BALDWIN, Orville D.	131
BALDWIN, Townsend B.	153
BANGS, Edward ... ... Add.	6
BANKS, James ... ... Add.	6
BARCLAY, James .. Add.	7
BARCLAY, Sackett M.	59
BARLOW, Joel ... ... Add.	7
BARNES, Stephen ... Add.	7

	PAGE
BARRY, Llewellyn	25
BARTHOLOMEW, James H. S.	203
BARTLETT, Robert .. Add.	7
BARTLETT, Richard ... Add.	7
BARTON, Edward R.	222
BARTON, Dr. John ... Add.	7
BASCOM, George J.	66
BATT, William & Thomas Add.	8
BAYARD, Peter ... ... Add.	8
BEALL, Col. Ninian ... Add.	8
BEARE, see MICKEL - SALTON-	
STALL	224
BECKWITH, Mrs. Leonard F.	38
BEEKMAN, Lt. Wilhelmus Add.	8
BEELEN, De, see GAZZAM	142
BELCHER, Andrew ... Add.	8
BELKNAP, Henry W.	45
BELLINGHAM, Gov. Richard Add.	8
BELLOWS, Rev. Johnson M. ...	204
BENHAM, John ... ... Add.	9
BENJAMIN, John ... Add.	9
BENJAMIN, Mrs. Samuel N. ..	199
BENNETT, Daniel C.	146
BERNARD, Gov. Francis Add.	9
BETTS, Thomas ... ... Add.	9
BEVAN, Horace C.	89
BIBBY, Thomas ... ... Add.	9
BIDDLE, William... ... Add.	10
BIGELOW, Rev. Frank H. ...	57
BIGELOW, Melville, M.	34
BIRNIE, James ... ... Add.	9
BLAKE, Joseph A., M.D.	139
BLAKE, William ... ... Add.	10
BLAKE, William P.	43
BLANCHARD, Rev. Joseph N.	41
BLEECKER, Jan J. ... Add.	10
BLIVEN, Edward .. ... Add.	10
BLOSS, James O.	27
BLOSSOM, Benjamin	65
BLOUNT, see CARRITT ...	57
BOARDMAN, Albert B.	156
BOERUM, Capt. William Add.	10
BOLLES, Joseph ... ... Add.	10
BONNER, Robert E.	148
BONYTHON, Richard Add.	11
BOORAEM, Robert E.	129
BOSTON, Jacob ... ... Add.	11

PAGE

BOSTWICK, Arthur ... Add. 11
BOUTELLE, James ... Add. 11
BOWEN, Richard... ... Add. 11
BOWES, Nicholas ... ... Add. 11
BOWIE, Howard S., M.D. 108
BOYD, John ... ... Add. 12
BRADHURST, Augustus M. ... 30
BRADFORD, Gov. William Add. 12
BRADLEY, Cyrus S.... 94
BRADSTREET, Gov. Simon Add. 12
BRADSTREET, see TAYLOR ... 134
BRADSTREET, see PARTRIDGE 62
BREESE, Sydney ... ... Add. 12
BRENT, Giles .. .. Add. 12
BRENTON, Gov. William Add. 12
BRERETON, Thomas J. 32
BRETT, Francis ... ... Add. 13
BREWER, Daniel .. ... Add. 13
BREWSTER see JACKSON 116
BREWSTER, see COX... 11
BREWSTER, Harry L. 154
BREWSTER, Henry C. 225
BREWSTER, Samuel D. 123
BREWSTER, Wadsworth J. ... 109
BRICE, John ... ... Add. 13
BRIGGS, Walter ... ... Add. 13
BRIGHT, Henry ... ... Add. 13
BRISCOE, Capt. William D. ... 107
BROCKETT, Mrs. Albert D. ... 119
BROMFIELD, Edward .. Add. 13
BROOKE, George S. 189
BROOKS, Henry ... ... Add. 14
BROOKS, James G. C. 232
BROOME, George C. 206
BROTHERTON, see HOWARD... 230
BROUGHTON, John ... Add. 14
BROWN, Edward M. 205
BROWNE, John ... ... Add. 14
BROWNE, Nathaniel ... Add. 14
BROWNELL, see BURNHAM .. 29
BRUEN, see BALDWIN... 131
BRUEN, Obadiah ... ... Add. 14
BRUN, Le, see PARSONS 210
BRUNE, Frederick W. ..Add. 14
BRYANT, William S., M.D. ... 37
BULKLEY, Rev. Peter... Add. 15
BURCH, Thomas H., M.D 183
BURLEIGH, George W. Add. 15
BURNHAM, Thomas B. 29
BURRAGE, John ... ... Add. 15
BURRAGE, see MARTIN ... 16
BURROWES, William Add. 15
BURT, Stephen S., M.D. 40
BURWELL, see HAYES 160
BURWELL, Major Lewis Add. 15

PAGE

BUSH, John ... ... Add. 15
BUSHNELL, Francis ... Add. 16
BUSHNELL, see BREWSTER .. 154
BUSSEY, George ... ... Add. 16
BUTLER, Thomas ... Add. 16
BUTLER, Thomas ... Add. 16
BYINGTON, Charles S. 68

CABELL, see RUGGLES 217
CABELL, Capt. William Add. 16
CADWALADER, Charles E.,
    M.D. 184
CALHOUN, John C. 213
CALVERT, Charles B. 128
CAMPBELL, Duncan ... Add. 16
CAMPBELL, see HENDRICK ... 150
CANDEE, Zaccheus ... Add. 17
CANFIELD, Thomas ... Add. 17
CAPEN, Bernard ... ... Add. 17
CAREY, Samuel T. ... Add. 17
CARLETON, Edward ... Add. 17
CARLETON, see MOORE 216
CARPENTER, James E. 230
CARPENTER, Timothy Add. 17
CARPENTER, William ... Add. 18
CARR (KERR), William Add. 18
CARRITT, John P. 57
CARROLL, Charles ... Add. 18
CARROLL, William S. 231
CARRON, De, see READ 177
CARTER, Charles S., M.D. ... 188
CARTER, Oscar C. S.... 111
CHAFFEE, Thomas ... Add. 18
CHAMBERLAIN, R. ... Add. 18
CHANCELLOR, Capt. Richard
    Add. 18
CHANDLER, Major Job Add. 19
CHANDLER, William Add. 19
CHAPMAN, Robert ... Add. 19
CHASE, Aquala ... ... Add. 19
CHASE, William... ... Add. 19
CHASE, Walter G., M.D. 104
CHAUNCEY, Rev. Charles Add. 19
CHECKLEY, Col. Samuel Add. 20
CHENOWETH, Alexander C. ... 132
CHESTER, Leonard ... Add. 20
CHEW, John ... ... Add. 20
CHILDS, Daniel B. 103
CHOLMELEY-JONES, Edward 47
CHRISTMAS, Charles H.... ... 224
CHRYSTIE, William F. 161
CHUMASERO, William 186
CHURCHILL, William H. ... 133
CHURCHILL, Winston 192
CHUTE, Lionel ... ... Add. 20

PAGE

CLARK, John... ... ... Add. 20
CLARKE, George . ... Add. 20
CLARKSON, Matthew Add. 21
CLAIBORNE, Col. William Add. 21
CLAY, Robert ... ... Add. 21
CLEVELAND, Moses Add. 21
CLINTON, Col. Charles Add. 21
CLINTON, Charles W. 157
CLOTHIER, Isaac H. 16
COAKLEY, Dr. ... ... Add. 21
COCHRAN, Thos. & John Add. 22
COCHRANE, see BARCLAY ... 59
COFFIN, Tristram ... Add. 22
COLCOCK, Charles J. 6
COLES, Edward O. 134
COLES, Henry R. R. 196
COLEY, Samuel ... ... Add. 22
COLGATE, Bowles 182
COLGATE, William 5
COLLINS, Clarence L. 67
COLLINS, Edward ... Add. 22
COLLYNGE, see FAIRBANKS .. 107
COMSTOCK, Christopher Add. 22
COMTE, see SELLERS 7
CONE, Robert B. 129
COOK, Edward ... Add. 22
COOK, Henry F. 39
COOKE, see BLOSSOM... 65
COOKE, George .. ... Add. 23
COOKE, Jay, Jr. 71
COOPER, Henry D. 42
COPE, Porter F. 207
CORBUSIER, Lt.-Col. William
  H. 60
CORLIES, Mrs. Samuel F. 170
CORNING, Henry W. 194
CORNWALL, Edward E. 33
COSBY, Rr.-Adml. Frank C. . 106
COX, Jacob D. 11
CRADOCK, Rev. Thomas Add. 23
CRANE, Jasper ... ... Add. 23
CRANWELL, James H. 77
CROMBIE, William M. 15
CROSS, Arthur D. 163
CROSSLAND, see CALVERT ... 128
CROSSMAN, Robert ... Add. 23
CROWNINSHIELD, Johan R.
  C.... ... ... Add. 23
CUNNINGHAM, Andrew Add. 23
CURRIER, Mrs. Joseph H. A. ... 36
CURTIS, William E. 110
CURWEN, Capt. George Add. 24
CUSHING, Harry C., Jr. 218
CUTHBERT, Thomas... Add. 24
CUTLER, John ... ... Add. 24

PAGE

DACRE, see HOWARD 230
DAGGETT, Aaron ... Add. 24
DANA, Charles 48
DANCY, Frank B. 26
DALL, Horace H. 196
DAVENPORT, William B. ... 17
DAVIDSON, Sylvanus M. 203
DAVIE, John ... ... Add. 24
DAVIES, William G. 151
DAVIS, Rr.-Adml. Charles H. .. 185
DAVIS, Joseph 163
DAWKINS, Walter I. 46
DAY, Robert ... . Add. 24
DE BARRY, Adolphe 29
DE BEELEN, see GAZZAM ... 142
DE CARRON, see READ 177
DELAFIELD, John ... Add. 25
DE LA FONTAINE, Rev. Peter
  Add. 33
DELANO, Philip ... ... Add. 25
DE LA VERGNE, Col. Hughes J. 105
DELCAMBRE, Alfred P. 214
DE LUZE, Louis P. ... Add. 25
DENISON, William ... Add. 25
DENNIS, Rodney S. 204
DEVOTION, Edward ... Add. 25
DE PEYSTER, Gen. John W. ... 112
DE WITT, see SELLERS 7
DE WOLF, Edwin A. 66
DE ZENG, Frederick A. Add. 25
DIGGES, Gov. Edward Add. 26
DIODATI, William ... Add. 26
DISBROW, Samuel ... Add. 26
DODD, Edward ... ... Add. 26
DODGE, John H. P. 121
DODGE, Walter P. 50
DODGE, William E. 186
DONGAN, Gov. Thomas Add. 26
DORCY, Lt. Ben. H. 172
DORR, Edward ... ... Add. 26
DOTY, Paul A. L.... 118
DOUGHTY, Francis E., M.D. ... 205
DOUGLAS, Curtis N. 55
D'OYLEY (Marquis), John H. E. 84
D'OYLEY (Marchioness) 24
DRAKE, John... ... ... Add. 27
DRAPER, Capt. James Add. 27
DRAPER, William F. 158
DUANE, Anthony... ... Add. 27
DU BOIS, Louis ... ... Add. 27
DUDLEY, Col. Edgar S. 41
DUER, Maj.-Gen. William Add. 27
DUFFIELD, George ... Add. 27
DUKE, Richard T. W. Jr. 167
DUMARESQUE, Capt. Philip
  Add. 28

PAGE

DUMMER, Lt.-Gov. William
                Add. 28
DUNMORE, Larry ...   Add. 28
DUNNELL, Rev. William N. ... 187
DWIGHT, John ... ... Add. 28
DYER, Louis 136

EAGER, William ... .. Add. 28
EAMES, Thomas ... ... Add. 28
EARDELEY, Daniel ... Add. 29
EARLE, Henry M. 218
ECKLEY, Rev. Joseph ... Add. 29
EDDY, Charles H. 191
EDMONDS, Richard H. 18
EELLES, Major Samuel Add. 29
EGERTON, Tomas ... Add. 29
EGLESTON, Bagot ... Add. 29
ELDREDGE, Major Edward H. 206
ELDREDGE, Mrs. Edward H. ... 100
ELIOT, John ... .. Add. 30
ELLICOTT, Eugene 180
ELLIMAN, James B. ... Add. 30
ELKINS, Hon. Stephen B. 220
ELLIOT, Daniel G. 35
ELWOOD, Richard ... Add. 30
ELY, Joshua ... ... Add. 29
EMERSON, Thomas ... Add. 30
EMERY, John . ... Add. 30
EMMET, Dr. Thomas ... Add. 30
EMMONS, Samuel F. 30
EVANS, Henry 75
EVANS, James, M.D. 63
EVANS, Lott ... ... Add. 31
EYRE, George ... ... Add. 31

FAIRBANKS, Rev. Hiram F. ... 107
FAIRBANKS, Robert N. 210
FAIRFAX, Rev. Bryan Add. 31
FAIRFIELD, John ... Add. 31
FALLS, Alexander... ... Add. 31
FARMER, Robert A. ... Add. 31
FARWELL, Henry ... Add. 32
FAUNTLEROY, Thomas W.
                Add. 32
FAWCONER, Edward Add. 32
FEARN, John ... ... Add. 32
FENNER, Capt. Arthur Add. 32
FENWICK, George ... Add. 32
FENWICK, see SELLERS 7
FERGUSON, James ... Add. 33
FERRIS, Morris P. 174
FIELD, Robert ... ... Add. 33
FINDLEY, William L. 45
FISH, see BENJAMIN 199
FISKE, Louis S. 193

PAGE

FISKE, Stephen 229
FITCH, Capt. Thomas ... Add. 33
FITZGERALD, Desmond 113
FLINT, Charles R. 35
FLOYD, Charles H. 110
FONTAINE, Rev. Peter De La
                Add. 33
FOOTE, John C. 46
FORBUSH, Daniel .. Add. 33
FORSYTH, John ... ... Add. 33
FOSTER, James ... ... Add. 34
FOULKE, see MANSFIELD 11
FOULKE, William 36
FOWLER, Thomas P.... 152
FRANCINE, Albert P. 144
FRANKLIN, Dr. Benjamin, Add. 34
FRAZER, John ... ... Add. 34
FRAZER, Dr. Persifor 225
FREEMAN, see GRIFFITH ... 138
FREEMAN, Alden 178
FREEMAN, George W. 175
FRENCH, Amos T. 33
FRY, John... ... ... Add. 34
FULLER, Lt. Thomas .. Add. 34

GALLAHER, William B. 116
GALLATIN, Albert E. 93
GARDINER, Lion ... Add. 34
GARRARD, see GLENN 191
GASTON, William A. 40
GAY, John ... . Add. 35
GAYER, William ... Add. 35
GAZZAM, Edwin Van D., M.D. 142
GEDNEY, John .. ... Add. 35
GEER, Walter 154
GEORGE, Josias J. 10
GERRISH, Capt. William Add. 35
GIBBS, see LINNARD 125
GIBSON, John ... ... Add. 35
GILBERT, Charles P. H. 14
GILBERT, James H. 171
GILBERT, see POWEL... 126
GILES, Stephens W. 226
GILMAN, Daniel C. 79
GILPIN, Joseph ... ... Add. 35
GLENN, Garrard 17
GLENN, Mrs. John T. 191
GLIDDEN, Lt.-Col. John M. ... 168
GOODRICH, William .. Add. 36
GOODWIN, see MORGAN 181
GOOKIN, Col. Charles Add. 36
GORDON ... ... Add. 36
GORGE, Sir Ferdinando Add. 36
GOULD, Charles A. 179
GOVE, Edward ... ... Add. 36

	PAGE
GRANGER, Alfred H.	100
GRANT, see RICE	51
GREENE, John ... ... Add.	36
GREENLEES, William Add.	37
GREENWOOD, Miles Add.	37
GREGORY, Henry ... Add.	37
GREYSTOKE, see HOWARD ...	230
GRIFFITH, William H.	138
GRISCOM, Clement A.	96
GRISWOLD, George	214
GROSS, Capt. Samuel E.	208
GUILD, John ... ... Add.	37
HALE, Robert... ... ... Add.	37
HALE, see SHAFTER	120
HALL, George E.	140
HALL, Harry A.	94
HALLOWELL, see RICE	51
HALSEY, Frederic R.	139
HAMBLETON, William Add.	38
HAMERSLEY, William Add.	38
HAMILTON, Capt. John Add.	38
HAMILTON, Rev. Ezekiel B. ...	141
HANBURY, William ... Add.	37
HANCOCK, William ... Add.	38
HAND, John ... . Add.	38
HARE, see POWELL	126
HARE, Robert ... ... Add.	38
HARLAKENDEN, see EVANS...	75
HARRISON, Nathaniel Add.	39
HART, Henry G.	86
HARWOOD, John ... Add.	39
HASBROUCK, Abraham Add.	39
HASKELL, Frank W....	20
HASTINGS, Thomas ... Add.	39
HAWES, Edmund ... Add.	39
HAWKES, George W.... Add.	39
HAWLEY, Joseph... ... Add.	40
HAY, see COLCOCK	6
HAYES, Harry E.	160
HAYNES, Gov. John ... Add.	40
HAZARD, Thomas ... Add.	40
HENDRICK, Mrs. Calvin S. ...	150
HENDRICK, Calvin W.	176
HENRY, William H.	88
HENSHAW, Joshua ... Add.	40
HERNDON, William ... Add.	40
HERRICK, Henry ... Add.	40
HERRICK, see GRIFFITH	138
HIGGINSON, Charles H Add.	41
HILL, John P.	12
HILL, William ... ... Add.	41
HILL, Rev. William B.	53
HILLHOUSE, Francis	91
HILLHOUSE, James	159
	PAGE
HINCKLEY Samuel ... Add.	41
HINTON, Thomas ... Add.	41
HIRST, Barton C., M.D.	137
HITCHCOCK, Luke ... Add.	41
HITE, see PAINE	5
HOADLEY, William ... Add.	41
HOARE, John ... ... Add.	42
HOBART, see SMITH	209
HODGE, William .. ... Add.	42
HOFFMAN, Col. Martinus Add.	42
HOLDEN, Justinian ... Add.	42
HOLDER, Charles F.	166
HOLLINGSWORTH, Ellis ...	189
HOLLINS, William ... Add.	42
HOLMES, Edwin B.	117
HOLYOKE, Rev. Edward Add.	42
HOPKINS, Stephen .. Add.	43
HORWITZ, Miss Caroline N. ...	227
HORWITZ, Dr. Jonathan Add.	43
HOUGH, Richard... .. Add.	43
HOUGHTON, Ralph ... Add.	43
HOWARD, Abraham ... Add.	43
HOWARD, George	230
HOWARD, Thomas ... Add.	44
HOWE, Herbert M., M.D.... ...	121
HOWELL, Edward ... Add.	43
HOWES, Rev. Reuben W.... ...	59
HOWLAND, see SMITH	74
HOWLAND, Daniel W.	82
HUBBARD, ... Add.	44
HUBBELL, Richard ... Add.	44
HUIDEKOPER, Frederic W. ...	114
HUIE, William H. T.	108
HULL, George ... ... Add.	44
HUME, Robert D.	125
HUNLOCK, ... Add.	44
HUNTER, Capt. David Add.	44
HUNTINGTON, Simon Add.	45
HURD, Charles R.	172
HURRY, Edmund A.	119
HUTCHINS, John ... Add.	45
HUTCHINSON, Richard Add.	45
HYATT, Frank S.	73
HYDE, see SLADE	3
HYDE, James N., M.D.	193
IRWIN, Gen. Bernard J. D. ...	101
IRWIN, Dudley M.	3
ISHAM, Ralph	53
IVES, Chauncey	15
JACKSON, James H., M.D. ...	116
JAFFREY, George ... Add.	45
JANES, William .. ... Add.	45
JAQUET, see SELLERS	7

PAGE

JAUDON, Peter ... ... Add. 45
JEFFREY, William ... Add. 46
JEFFRIES, David . Add. 46
JENKINS, Edmund F. 50
JENNINGS, Albert G. 88
JESUP, Morris K. 70
JOCELYN, Henry... .. Add. 46
JOHNS, Richard ... ... Add. 46
JOHNSON, Edward 52
JOHNSON, John ... ... Add. 46
JOHNSON, Dr. John ... Add. 47
JOHNSON, Robert ... Add. 46
JOHNSTON, see POWELL 126
JONES, E. Clarence 64
JONES, Richmond L. 76
JONES, Walter R. T. 135
JOSSLYN, Henry ... Add. 46
JUDD, Orrin R. 47
JUDSON, see BREWSTER 154
JUDSON, William P. 73

KANE, Capt. Robert ... Add. 47
KASSON, Adam ... ... Add. 47
KAY, Nathaniel ... ... Add. 47
KEAYNE, Capt. Robert Add. 47
KELLEY, Thomas ... Add. 47
KEMPER, Andrew C., M.D. .. 194
KENDALL, Thomas 47
KENDALL, William B. 80
KERR, William ... ... Add. 18
KIMBALL, Richard ... Add. 48
KING, Major Rufus ... Add. 48
KIP, Hendrick H. ... ... Add. 48
KIPSHAVEN, see SELLERS ... 7
KITTELLE, Joachim Add. 48
KNIGHT, Edward C., Jr. 60
KNOWLTON, see GRIFFITH ... 138
KNOWLTON, Col. Thomas, Add. 48
KUHNE, Percival 150
KUNKEL, Robert S. 44

LANE, George ... ... Add. 48
LANSING, Garrit F. ... Add. 49
LA SERRE, Jean P. ... Add. 49
LATHAME, see PHILLIPS 76
LATHROP, Bryan 148
LATTING, Richard ... Add. 49
LAWRENCE, Henry ... Add. 49
LAWTON, Thomas ... Add. 49
LEARNED, Edwin J. 82
LEARNED, William L. 44
LE BRUN, see PARSONS 210
LEDYARD, John ... ... Add. 49
LEDYARD, see SARGENT 217
LEE, Col. Richard ... ... Add. 50

PAGE

LEEDS, Richard ... ... Add. 50
LEETE, Gov. William ... Add. 50
LEGGETT, Francis H. 176
LEONARD, Clarence E. 117
LEONARD, Rt. Rev. Bp. Wm. A. 75
LEVERING, Eugene 8
LEVERING, see SMITH 74
LEWIS, Clifford 223
LEWIS, Silas W. 142
LINDLY, Francis ... ... Add. 50
LINDSAY, John D. 111
LINNARD, George B. 125
LIPPINCOTT, Walter 56
LITTLE, Thomas ... ... Add. 50
LIVINGSTON, Philip 159
LIVINGSTON, Gov. William Add. 50
LLOYD, see CARRITT 57
LLOYD, see SMITH 74
LOCKWOOD, Hanford N. ... 122
LOGAN. Major John A. 13
LORD, Thomas .. ... Add. 51
LOWELL, Rev. Delmar R. ... 104
LOWNDES, Charles ... Add. 51
LUDLOW, Banyer 102
LUDLOW, Roger ... ... Add. 51
LUDWELL, Philip ... .Add. 51
LYMAN, Henry D. 184

M'CALLA, John ... ... Add. 51
McCLARY, Andrew ... Add. 51
McCLELLAND, Robert Add. 52
McCLURE, Alexander K. 118
McCLURE, see BELLOWS 204
McCULLOUGH, Capt. Benjamin ... ... Add. 52
McDOWELL, see SPITZER ... 164
MACDONALD, see D'OYLEY ... 24
MacDUFFIE, Daniel ... Add. 52
McELROY, Clayton 21
McGUIRE . .. ... Add. 52
MACKENZIE, Alexander W. ... 70
MACKENZIE, George N. 95
McCLEAN, George H. ... 153
MAGRUDER. Hon. Benjamin D. 173
MAILLET, see SELLERS 7
MAITLAND, David .. Add. 52
MANN, Edward ... ... Add. 52
MANIERRE, William R. 68
MANNING, see RICE 51
MANNING, William ... Add 53
MANSFIELD, Mrs. Walter D. 11
MANTON, see VAN SANTVOORD 2
MAPES, Charles V. 182
MARKHAM, Daniel ... Add. 53

	PAGE
MARSH, Henry D.	4
MARTIN, George C.	16
MARTIN, Robert C.	9
MASCAREN, Jean P. .. Add.	53
MATHER, Rev. Richard Add.	53
MAY, James R., M.D.	228
MAYE, John ... ... Add.	53
MENG, see SMITH	74
MEREDITH, see READ	69
MERIWETHER, Hunter M. ...	77
MERRICK, John V.	201
MERRILL, Frederick J. H. ...	211
MESIER, Louis	215
MESSINGER, Henry ... Add.	53
METCALF, Michael .. Add.	54
MICKEL-SALTONSTALL,	
Andrew H.	221
MILHAU, Cæsar M. ... Add.	54
MILLET, Josiah B.	18
MILNE, David .. ... Add.	54
MILNER, Thomas... ... Add.	54
MINER, Hon. Charles A.	86
MINOT, Jesse	6
MOFFAT, R. Burnham	83
MOFFETT, Joseph ... Add	54
MONTGOMERY, William Add.	54
MOORE, Mrs. Edwin K.	216
MORGAN, James L.	181
MORGAN, J. Pierpont	56
MORRIS, Anthony ... Add.	55
MORRIS, Richard... ... Add.	55
MORRIS, Robert C.	190
MORSE, Waldo, G.	144
MORTON, George ... Add.	55
MORTON, Henry S.	187
MOSELEY, Frank	67
MOSELEY, Rev. Samuel Add.	55
MOTT, Robert G.	190
MOWBRAY, see HOWARD... ...	230
MUMFORD, Thomas ... Add.	55
NEILL, Hon. Richard R.	171
NELSON, Thomas Add.	55
NEWBERRY, see SMITH	74
NEWHALL, Charles L.	39
NEWTON, Thomas ... Add.	56
NICHOLAS, Dr. George Add.	56
NICHOLSON, Christopher Add.	56
NICHOLSON, Robert... Add.	56
NICHOLSON, William Add.	56
NICOLL, De Lancey	140
NORRIS, Isaac	22
NORTON, George ... ... Add.	56
NOURSE, see BROCKETT	119
NOYES, James A....	124

	PAGE
OAKLEY, Samuel ... ... Add.	57
O'DONNELL, John C.	185
OFFLEY, David ... .. Add.	57
OGDEN, see SMITH	74
OLIVER, Charles A., M.D.	24
OLMSTED, James ... Add.	57
ONDERDONK, Andrew J. ...	165
O'NEILL, John ... ... Add.	57
OSGOOD, Capt. John .. Add.	57
OTIS, Edward O., M.D.	228
OTIS, John ... ... Add.	57
OVERTON, Isaac... ... Add.	58
OWSLEY, Capt. Thomas Add.	58
PAGE, Col. John . ... Add.	58
PAGET, Almeric, H.	200
PAINE, Mrs. Gordon P.	5
PAINE, Moses ... ... Add.	58
PAINE, William ... ... Add.	58
PALMER, Thomas ... Add.	58
PALMER, Walter... ... Add.	59
PALMES, Edward ... Add.	59
PARKER, Neilson, T.	2
PARKER, William ... Add.	59
PARMELE, John ... ... Add.	59
PARSONS, Albert R.	165
PARSONS, Joseph ... Add.	59
PARSONS, William ... Add.	59
PARSONS, Mrs. William E. ...	210
PARTRIDGE, Edward L., M.D.	62
PAYNE, William ... ... Add.	58
PEABODY, Francis ... Add.	60
PEASE, Robert ... ... Add.	60
PECK, George, M.D.	211
PECK, William E....	179
PELHAM, Herbert ... Add.	60
PELL, Frederick A.	10
PELL, Howland	155
PEMBERTON, Rev. D. Ebenezer Add.	60
PENHALLOW, Samuel Add.	60
PENROSE, Bartholomew Add.	60
PEPPERRELL, see SALTER ...	133
PEPPERRELL, see WHEELER ...	27
PERKINS, John ... ... Add.	61
PEROT, Jacques ... ... Add.	61
PERRINE, William ... Add.	61
PERUZZI, see ELDREDGE	100
PETER, Robert ... ... Add.	61
PETERS, William R.	173
PHELPS, John J.	71
PHILLIPS, Henry B.	76
PHILIPPIN, see SELLERS ...	7
PHIPPEN, David ... ... Add.	61
PHIPPS, see BLAKE	43, 139

PAGE

PIATT, John ... ...   Add. 61
PIERREPONT, Henry F.   ... 38
PINCHON, William ...   Add. 62
PITCHER, Andrew   ...   Add. 62
PITT, Mary   ... ...   Add. 62
PITKIN, see ROGERS 78, 229
PLACE, Barker   197
PLUMB, Henry B.   162
PLYMPTON, Gilbert M. 61
POE, John   ... ...   Add. 62
POLE, Capt. William ...   Add. 62
POLLOCK, Charles   ...   Add. 62
POMEROY, George F.   101
POND, Edwin W.   61
POOLE, Capt. Edward   Add. 63
POOR, Mrs. Edward E.   49
POORE, John   . ...   Add. 63
POPHAM, George   ...   Add. 63
PORTER, Alexander S.   156
PORTER, Hon. William W.   ... 19
PORTER, see COLES 134
POWELL, Robert J. Hare-   ... 126
PRATT, William ... ...   Add. 63
PREBLE, Abraham   ...   Add. 63
PRESTON, James   ...   Add. 63
PRICE, see CARRITT   57
PRIME, Ralph E. 52
PROVOOST, David   ...   Add. 64
PRUYN, John Van S. L.   48
PUMPELLY, Jean   ..   Add. 64
PUTNAM, John   ... ...   Add. 64
PYNCHON, William ...   Add. 62
PYNE, John ... ...   Add. 64

QUINCY, Miss Mary P. 180

RALLI, Pandia C.   92
RANDOLPH, Col. William Add. 64
RANKIN, Henry ... ...   Add. 64
READ, Charles A.   4
READ, Major Harmon P.   69
READ, Mrs. Harmon P.   177
REICHERT, Johann   ..   Add. 65
RENWICK, William C.   42
RHINELANDER, Philip 145
RHINELANDER, T. J. Oakley   99
RHOADS, John   ... ...   Add. 65
RHODES, John F.   215
RICE, Mrs. William P.   51
RICH, Thomas   ...   Add. 65
RICHARDS, Johann   ...   Add. 65
RICHARDS, Jeremiah   147
RICHARDSON, Thomas Add. 65
RICHMOND, Adelbert G.   ... 164
RIDGELEY, Henry   ...   Add. 65

PAGE

RIDGWAY, Richard ...   Add. 65
ROBBINS, John ... ...   Add. 66
ROBINSON, George ..   Add. 66
ROBINSON, Rowland   ...   Add. 66
ROCKWOOD, Charles G.   .. 132
RODES, John ... ...   Add 65
RODRIGUE, see TISDALL   ... 130
ROGERS, James .. ...   Add. 66
ROGERS, James S.   229
ROGERS, Mrs. Talbot M. 78
ROLLINS, James ... ...   Add. 66
ROOSEVELT, President Theodore   1
ROSE, see RUGGLES   217
ROSS, see READ   69
ROSS, see CURRIER   36
ROSSE, Rev. John ... ..   Add. 66
ROWLAND, Rev. Henry J.   ... 170
ROYSTER, Jacob ... ...   Add. 67
RUGGLES, Charles H.   146
RUGGLES, Mrs. Charles H.   ... 217
RUGGLES, Henry S. 20
RUGGLES, Mrs. Henry S.   ... 28
RULON-MILLER, John   208
RUSSELL, Caleb ... ...   Add. 67
RYAN, see RUGGLES 28

SACKETT, Col. Henry W.   ... 106
SALTER, William M. 133
SALTONSTALL, Dudley M.   ... 219
SALTONSTALL, see MICKLE-S. 221
SANDERS, Thomas   ...   Add. 67
SANDS, James T. 99
SARGENT, Mrs. Dudley A.   ... 217
SARGENT, William   ...   Add. 67
SATTERLEE, Capt. William
                             Add. 67
SAVAGE, Capt. Thomas   Add. 67
SCHENCK, Roelof & Jan. M.
                             Add. 68
SCHIEFFELIN, Eugene 175
SCHIEFFELIN, George R.   ... 127
SCHINDEL, Capt. Samuel J. B. 151
SCHUYLER, Philip P. van Add. 68
SCREVEN, Rev. William   Add. 68
SCUDDER, Rev. Henry T.   ... 21
SEABURY, Frederick C. 8
SEAMAN, Louis L., M.D. 19
SEARS, Richard   ...   ..   Add. 68
SELLERS, Edwin J.   7
SEWELL, Robert van V.   143
SEWELL, Wynn R.   109
SEYMOUR, Rt. Rev. Bp. Geo. F. 216
SHAFFER, Newton M., M.D. ... 120
SHAPLEIGH, Major Nicholas
                             Add. 68

PAGE

SHED, Daniel ... ... Add. 68
SHELDON, Isaac .. ... Add. 69
SHEPARD, Charles N. 158
SHERBURNE, see WHIPPLE ... 85
SHERD, Daniel ... ... Add. 68
SHERMAN, John . ... Add. 69
SHIELDS, Rev. Charles W. ... 89
SHIPPEN, Edward, M.D. 22
SHIRLEY, Rufus G. 115
SHOEMAKER, Henry F. 109
SHORT, Clement ... ... Add. 69
SHORT, see CARRITT 57
SHUFELDT, Robert W., M.D. 31
SILL, John .. .. Add. 69
SKELTON, Rev. Samuel Add. 69
SKINNER, Henry W. 222
SLADE, Mrs. William G. 3
SLAUGHTER, Francis and
  William ... ... Add. 69
SLOCUM, Anthony ... Add. 70
SLOCUM, see ROGERS ... 78, 229
SMITH, George ... ... Add. 70
SMITH, James C. 199
SMITH, Robert H. 209
SMITH, Hon. Thomas G. 74
SMITH, see RICE 51
SNELLING, Rodman P. 167
SOHIER, William D. 90
SOHIER, see BRYANT 37
SOUTHER, Charles E. 152
SOUTHWORTH, see GRIFFITH 138
SPENCER, Horatic, M.D.... ... 97
SPENCER, Selden P. 232
SPITZER. Gen. Ceilan, M. 164
SPOTSWOOD, Gen. Alexander
                           Add. 70
STANDISH, Capt. Miles Add. 70
STANLEY, James G. 166
STANSBURY, see MANSFIELD 11
STEARNS, Issac ... ... Add. 70
STEBBING, Rowland ... Add. 70
STEELE, George ... ... Add. 71
STEPHENS, John . ... Add. 71
STERLING, David ... Add. 71
STETSON, Robert ... Add. 71
STEVENS, Benjamin ... Add. 71
STEVENS, John ... .. Add. 71
STEVENS, Rev. Charles E. ... 54
STOCKBRIDGE, Henry 162
STOCKTON, Richard 227
STOCKTON, Lt. Richard Add. 71
STODDARD, Francis R. 31
STOKES, James ... ... Add. 72
STONE, Joseph 85
STONE, William ... ... Add. 72

PAGE

STONER, Stanley 202
STORRS, Samuel ... ... Add. 72
STORY, Col. Joseph G. 64
STOWE, John .. ... Add. 72
STRONG, John ... ... Add. 72
STRYKER, Thomas H. 114
STUMPF, John ... ... Add. 72
STURGIS, Edward ... Add. 73
SULLIVAN, Arthur T. 212
SUMNER, Edward A. 9
SUMNER, Rr.-Adml. George W. 58
SUSE, Frederick E. 223
SUTTON, Rev. Joseph F. 123
SUYDAM, Heyndrycke R. Add. 73
SWARTWOUT, Tomys Add. 73
SWIFT, Edwin E., M.D. 12
SYLVESTER, Nathaniel Add. 73
SYLVESTER, see SMITH 74
SYMONDS, Samuel ... Add. 73

TABER, Philip ... ... Add. 73
TAINTOR, Charles ... Add. 74
TALCOTT, Miss Mary K. 147
TALLANT, Mrs. Walter S. ... 137
TALMAGE, Thomas ... Add. 74
TAYLOR, Capt. Washington I. 134
TEACKLE, Rev. Thomas Add. 74
TEMPLE, Robert ... ... Add. 74
TEN-BROECK, Major Dirck
                           Add. 74
THACHER, Tomas & Ant. Add. 74
THAYER, William H. 183
THEOBALD, Clement Add. 75
THOMAS, Douglas H. 62
THOMAS, Isaac R. 145
THOMAS, John ... ... Add. 75
THOMAS. Ronald 181
THOMPSON, Frederick D. ... 192
THOMPSON, Henry B. 212
THOMPSON, Rev. John Add. 75
THOMPSON, Norman F.... ... 91
THORNDIKE, John .. Add. 75
TICKNOR, William ... Add. 75
TIERNAN, Charles B. 97
TILDEN, Nathaniel ... Add. 75
TILGHMAN, Dr. Richard Add. 76
TIMPSON, Thomas .. Add. 76
TISDALL, Fitzgerald 198
TISDALL, Mrs. Fitzgerald ... 130
TODD, Christopher .. Add. 76
TODD, Henry A. 83
TOMPKINS, Hamilton B. 20
TOWNE, William ... ... Add. 76
TOWNSEND, see IRWIN 3
TOWNSEND, Thomas Add. 76

	PAGE
TRACY, Thomas	Add. 76
TRENCHARD, Edward	200
TROWBRIDGE, Samuel B. P.	169
TRUMAN, Henry H.	81
TUCK, Robert	Add. 77
TUTTTE, John	Add. 77
TYLER, Edward R.	120
TYNG, Edward	Add. 77
UNDERHILL, see COLES	134
UNDERHILL, Capt. John Add.	77
USHER, Col. John... ... Add.	77
VAN CORTLANDT, Col. Olaff	
	Add. 77
VANN, Irving G.	49
VAN RENSSELAER, Kiliaen	
	Add. 78
VAN SANTVOORD, Seymour	2
VAN VORST, see SEWELL ...	143
VAN WYCK, Cornelius B. Add.	78
VASSALL, William ... Add	78
VAUGHAN, see MERRICK	201
VAUGHAN, see RICE	51
VEAZEY, Duncan	72
VEAZEY, Isaac P.	188
VERNON, Daniel ... ... Add.	78
VON SAHLER, Abraham Add.	78
VOSE, Robert... ... ... Add.	78
WADSWORTH, Chris. Add.	79
WAIT, Horatio L.	79
WALDRON, Richard .. Add.	79
WALMSLEY, Thomas Add.	79
WALTER, Thomas ... Add.	79
WALTON, Capt. William Add.	79
WALWORTH, William Add.	79
WARD, Andrew H.	219
WARD, Count Reginald H. ...	28
WARNER, Hon. John De W. ...	80
WARREN, Arthur ... Add.	80
WARREN, Charles E....	224
WARREN, see BALDWIN	131
WARREN, see HOWARD	230
WARREN, see TALLANT	137
WASHBURN, John ... Add.	80
WASHINGTON, Joseph E. ...	102
WASHINGTON, William L.	55
WATTS, see DE PEYSTR	112
WAYNE, see SELLERS... ...	7
WEAVER, Thomas ... Add.	80
WEBB, William S., M.D.	197
WEBSTER, Gov. John... Add.	80
WEED, John	157
WEED, Henry F.	177
WEIR, Robert .. .. Add.	80
WELD, Capt. Joseph ... Add.	80
WELLES, Gov. Thomas Add.	81

	PAGE
WELLS, Ebenezer Add.	81
WELLS, Edward	201
WENDEL, Civert J. ... Add.	81
WENTWORTH, William Add.	81
WEST, Robert ... ... Add.	81
WESTERVELT, Lubbert L.	
	Add. 81
WETMORE, Major William B.	135
WHARTON, Thomas .. Add.	82
WHEELER, Everett P.	27
WHEELER, Moses .. ... Add.	82
WHEELER, Gen. Joseph	226
WHEELOCK, William E., M.D.	90
WHEELWRIGHT, Rev. John	
	Add. 82
WHIPPLE, Major Charles W.	85
WHISTLER, Major .. Add.	82
WHISTLER, Lt.-Col. Garland N.	127
WHITE, see ROGERS 78,	229
WHITE, John .. .. Add.	82
WHITE, Elder John ... Add.	82
WHITELEY, Arthur ... Add.	83
WHITING, Francis ... Add.	83
WHITNEY, Drake	143
WHITON, Thomas ... Add.	83
WILBUR, Samuel .. Add.	83
WILGUS, Samuel .. ... Add.	83
WILKINS, John ... Add.	83
WILKINSON, Ogden D.	168
WILLARD, Major Simon Add.	84
WILLET, Capt. Thomas Add.	84
WILLIAMS, Gen. Otho H. Add.	84
WILLIAMS, see PHILLIPS ...	76
WILLIAMS, Robert ... Add.	84
WILLIS, George ... ... Add.	84
WILLOUGHBY, Lt. Hugh De I.	122
WILSON, Harold	124
WILSON, Rev. John ... Add.	85
WILSON, Dr. Robert ... Add.	84
WILSON, Col. William Add.	85
WISTAR, Gen. Isaac J.	209
WISTER, Rodman	25
WITT, see SELLERS	7
WOLCOTT, Hon. Roger	98
WOLCOTT, see McELROY ...	21
WOLVERTON, Charles Add.	85
WOODBURY, Andrew Add.	85
WOODFORD, Thomas Add.	85
WOODWARD, Charles Add.	85
WOODWARD, William	131
WORTHINGTON, George ...	13
WORTHINGTON, Nicholas	
	Add. 86
WRIGHT, William ... Add.	86
WRIGHT, Samuel ... Add.	86
WYATT, James ... ... Add.	86
YOUNG, Gen. Robert ... Add.	86
YOUNG, Bridget .. ... Add.	86

"ROYAL WARRANT HOLDERS," at end of Volume.

Matthews' American Armoury
and
Blue Book.

R OOSEVELT, THEODORE, President U.S.A.,
of Washington, D.C. (Son of Theodore
Roosevelt, and Martha Bulloch, a descendant of
Archibald Bulloch, the first Revol. Gov. of Georgia.
—Descended from Klaas Martensezen Van Roose-
velt, from Zeeland, Holland, settled in New
Amsterdam 1649, *m* Jannetje Samuels-Thomas).

Born at N.Y. City, Oct. 27, 1858; succeeded to the
U.S. Presidency Sept. 1901, inaugurated Mar.
4, 1905; Grad. Harvard Univ. 1880; LL.D.
Columbia Univ., 1899; LL.D. Hope College,
1901; LL.D. Yale, 1901; LL.D. Harvard,
1902; Gov. of New York, 1898–1900; Mem.
N.Y. State Assembly, 1882–83–84; Lieut. and
Capt. 8th Regt. N.G.S.N.Y., 1884–88; U.S.
Civil Commr., 1889–94; Police Commr. N.Y., 1895; Assist.-Sec. of
the U.S. Navy, 1897–98; Col. 1st Regt. U.S.V. Cavalry (Rough
Riders), Santiago de Cuba, Spanish-American War; *m* (1stly)
Oct. 27, 1880, Alice Hathaway Lee; *m* (2ndly) Dec. 2, 1886, Edith
Kermit, Carow.

Issue.
(*By 1st m.*)

i. ALICE LEE, *m* Feb. 17, 1906, Nicholas Longworth.

(*By 2nd m.*)

i. THEODORE, *b* Sept. 13, 1887.   iv. QUENTIN, *b* Nov. 19, 1897.

ii. KERMIT, *b* Oct. 10, 1889.   i. ETHEL C.

iii. ARCHIBALD B., *b* April 17, 1894.

Arms—Argent, on a mount vert, a rose bush with three roses in full bloom proper.

Crest—Three ostrich feathers per pale gules and argent.

Motto—Qui plantavit curabit.

Residences—Washington, D.C.; "Sagamore Hill," Oyster Bay, L.I.

Clubs—Union League, Republican, Century, Harvard, Seawanhaka Corinthian
Yacht, Delta Kappa Epsilon, Boone and Crockett.

Societies—N.Y. Genealogical, Holland, Military and Naval Order of the Spanish
War, Santiago, Sons of the American Revolution

VAN SANTVOORD, SEYMOUR,
of Troy (Son of Hon. George van
Santvoord, 1819-63, _m_ Elizabeth, da. of Peter van
Schaack, LL.D., _m_ Dorcas Manton, lineal descdt.
of Dr. Thos. Manton, tutor to Lord Bolingbroke;
son of Rev. Staats, 1790-1882; son of Cornelius Z.,
1757-1845; son of Zeger, 1733-1813; son of Rev.
Cornelius van Santvoord, 1686-1752, of Manhattan,
1718, Grad. Leyden Univ. Holland, _m_ Hannah
Staats, of Schenectady).

Born at Troy, N.Y., Dec. 17, 1858; Grad. Union
Coll. 1878 A.B. LL.B.; Vice-Pres. Albany
Law School; Pres. Security Trust Co.;
_m_ Jan. 4, 1888, Caroline H. Shields.

Issue.

i. GEORGE, _b_ Aug. 5, 1891. iii. RICHARD STAATS, _b_ Jan. 31, 1898.
ii. JOHN GRISWOLD, _b_ Feb. 24, 1895. iv. ALEX. SEYMOUR, _b_ Oct. 23, 1899.
i. EDITH. ii. VIRGINIA. iii. AGNES.

Arms—(Manton) Argent, on a cross engrailed azure five garbs or.
Crest—A unicorn sejant or, resting the dexter paw against a tree.

Residences—Washington Park, Troy N.Y.; "Thirteen Gables," Bennington, Vt.
Clubs—University, Reform, National Arts.
Societies—Vice-Pres. Holland Society, St. Nicholas Society.

PARKER, NEILSON TAYLOR,
of New Brunswick, New Jersey, (Son of Thos.
F. B. Parker, of N.Y., _b_ 1827, _m_ 1856, Julia Caesarine,
eldest da. of John Neilson and Anna I. (Ovington)
Taylor; son of Thos. J. W., _b_ 1794; son of Rev.
Thomas, 1753-1800, M.A., Vicar of Churcham,
Glouc.; son of Rev. Thomas, 1725-1800, M.A.,
Rector of Welsh Bicknor, Glouc.; son of John;
son of John, 1624-94; son of Richard, 1578-1642;
son of John Parker of Barnwood, Gloucestershire,
Eng.— Also descd. from Thomas Taylor, of
Littlington, Bedfordshire, Eng., _b_ 1530).

Born at Brooklyn, N.Y., June 9, 1860; _m_ (1) Oct.
10, 1888, Ellen E. Porter (decd.); _m_ (2) Nov.
21, 1905, Anna C. Benedict, of New York.

Arms—Sable, a buck passant argent between three pheons or within a bordure
engrailed of the second pellettée.

Crest—A cubit arm erect habited sable cuff argent the hand proper grasping a
stag's horn gules. _Motto_—Esto quod esse videris.

Residence—98 College Avenue, New Brunswick, N.J.
Clubs—Union, Arts Club of N.Y. _Society_—Sons of the American Revolution.

IRWIN, DUDLEY M.,
of Buffalo, N.Y. (Son of Dudley Marvin Irwin
of Fulton, N.Y.; great grandson of William Irwin
of Antrim, m —— (née Townsend) of Mass., a
descendant of Thomas, of Lynn, Mass. 1635, son
of Henry Townsend, of Gedding, Suffolk, Eng.).

Born at Fulton N.Y. June 10, 1860; Grain Commission and Shipping Agent; Graduated M.A.
Lafayette College; m December 14, 1892,
Jeannie A. Marsh.

Issue.
i. THEODORE HEYWOOD.
ii. DUDLEY M.
i. KATHERINE TOWNSEND.
ii. GWENDOLYN REEDER.

Arms—Argent, a mural crown gules between three holly leaves vert.
Crest—A dexter hand issuing out of a cloud holding a thistle proper.
Motto—Nemo me impune lacessit.
Arms (Townsend)—Azure, a chevron ermine between three escallops or.
Crest—A stag passant proper.

———

Residence—316 Summer Street, Buffalo, New York.
Clubs—Grolier of New York Country, Buffalo, University, Ellicott of Buffalo.

SLADE, Mrs. EMMA MALEEN (née HARDY),
of N.Y. City (Da. of Walter Hardy, 1815-78,
m Ruth M. Clark, 1823-1902; son of Samuel, 1781-
1852, m Mary Hardy; son of William Hardy, of
Tewkesbury, Mass., who m 1778, Hannah, da. of
Samuel Hyde, 1719-75; son of Jonathan, 1674-
1731; son of Jonathan, 1655-1731; son of Jonathan
Hyde, b 1626; d at Newton, Mass., 1711).

Born at Lowell, Mass.; Founder of the Nat. Soc.
of New Eng. Women; Pres. of the Nat. Soc.
of U.S. Daurs, of 1812; Pres. of U.S. Daurs;
Daurs. of N.Y. State; m Feb. 22, 1871,
William Gerry, son of Wm. Jennings Slade,
and Mary A., da of Thos. Gerry.

Issue.
i. HARRIET ANDERSON, m Dec. 5, 1900, William Murray Crombie.

Arms—(Hyde) Azure, on a chevron or, three fleurs-de-lis of the first, between
three lozenges voided.   Crest—A lion's head erased ppr.

———

Residence—332 West 87th Street, New York City.
Club—Woman's.
Societies—Old Planters, Founders and Patriots, Colonial Dames, Daughters of
the Amer. Rev., Daurs. of the Rev., U S. Daurs. of 1812, New Eng. Women,
Geneal. and Biogl. of N.Y., Ipswich Hist., Washington Mem. Assn., Daurs.
of Colonial Governors.

R EAD CHARLES, A.,
of Reads Island (Son of Charles A. Read
1812-82, *m* Charlotte L. Reed; son of John Reed
[Jacob Reed] 1784-1871, of Woburn; son of Amos,
1754-1812; son of Jacob 1714-1804; son of Timothy,
1678-1758; son of George, 1629-1706; son of
William Reed, 1587-1656, *b* at Newcastle-on-Tyne,
Eng., probably son of Thomas Reed, of Brocket
Hall, settled at Woburn, Mass., 1635).

Born at Boston, Mass., July 25, 1839; *m* June 30,
1882, Ellen Arvilla, da. of Anthony Jones
and Sarah Ann (Hamilton) Hatfield.

Issue.

i. CHARLES ALBERT, *b* and *d* April 6, 1886.
ii. CHARLES ALBERT, Jr. *b* June 14, 1887.
iii. NORMAN HATFIELD, *b* Jan. 17, 1891.
i. HELEN.   iii. ELLEN ELIZABETH, *b* and *d* Feb. 1895.
ii. CHARLOTTE LOUISA.

Arms—Gules, a saltire between four garbs or.
Crest—On the stump of a tree vert a falcon rising belled and jessed or.
Motto—Cedant arma togae.

Residence—Reads Island, Manchester-by-the-Sea, Mass.
Clubs—Essex County, Manchester Yacht, Appalachian Mountain, Art.
Societies—Asso. Mem. Grand Army of the Republic, Mass. Horticultural, New
Eng. Hist. and Geneal., F. and A. Soc. of Masons, J.O. of O.F., and
Nat. Geographic, &c.

M ARSH, HENRY DANIEL,
of Springfield, Mass. (Eldest son of Daniel
J. Marsh, *b* 1837, Trea. Springfield 5 Cent. Savings
Bank, Pres. Park Comn., *m* Harriet M., da. of
Noah D. Gay, of Springfield; son of Michael,
1790-1847; son of John, 1753-1817; son of Capt.
Hezekiah, 1720-91; son of Capt. John, 1668-1744;
Son of John, 1643-1727; son of John, 1618-88,
m Anne, da. of Gov. John Webster of Ct.; son of
John Marsh, 1589-1627, of Braintree, Essex, Eng.).

Born at Springfield, March 15, 1865; Mem. of the
City Gov., 1896-1901; six years Treasurer of
Springfield Canoe Club; *m* (1) March 16,
1896, Anna F. Lillis; *d* 1898; *m* (2) May 20,
1903, Edith S. Hall.

Issue.

i. JOHN ATHERTON, *b* Jan. 7, 1897.
i. Elizabeth, *b* Dec. 16, 1904.

Arms—Gules, a horse's head couped between three cross-crosslets fitchée argent.
Crest—A griffin's head argent, ducally gorged and chained, primrose in beak or.
Motto—Nil desperandum.

Residence—9 Buckingham Place, Springfield, Mass.
Clubs—Nayasset, Springfield Country, Springfield Canoe, American Canoe Assn.
Societies—Colonial Wars, Sons of the American Revolution, Loyal Legion.

PAINE, Mrs. EMMA VAUGHN (*née* THOMPSON),
of Baltimore, Md. (da. of Joseph Hamilton
Thompson of Nashville, Tenn. [descended on the
maternal side from William, Duke of Hamilton,
1215, and also from Gerret Van Sweringen, who
settled at New Castle, Del. 1657], *b* 1853, *m* Ella,
d 1896, da. of Michael Vaughn, 1829-97, son of
David Vaughn, 1772-1836, who *m* Sarah, da. of
Joshua Thomas, *d* 1794, who *m* Nancy, da. of John
Overall [lineal descendant of the father of John
Overall, Ld. Bishop of Norwich, 1618], who
m Sarah, da. of Paul Froman of Penna, 1732, who
m Elizabeth, da. of Baron Jost Hite (Heydt), 1685-
1760, who settled at the New Platz region of New
York, 1732, having secured a grant of 140,000 acres
of land, becoming the first settler of the Schenan-
doah Valley, Virginia).

Born at Nashville, Tenn. ; *m* May 5, 1897, Gordon Paxton Paine, of
Baltimore, Md.

Issue.

i. GORDON PAXTON, Jr., *b* March 4, 1903.
Arms—(For Hite) Argent, two bars azure charged with three millrinds.
Crest—A garb of wheat.

Residences—200 E. Preston Street, Baltimore, Md. ; Nashville, Tenn.

COLGATE, WILLIAM,
of N.Y. City (Son of George Colgate, of
N.Y. City, *b* November 2, 1797, *d* May 14, 1842,
m December 29, 1824, Jane, *b* February 20, 1830,
d September 22, 1866, daughter of Cornelius and
Elizabeth (Thompson) Cauldwell, of Birmingham,
England, and later of New York ; son of Robert
Colgate, of Filston, Seven Oaks, Kent, England,
b September 11, 1758, *d* in America, July 20,
1826, *m* Sarah Bowles, *b* March 26, 1780,
d December 16, 1847 ; son of John Colgate, of
Seven Oaks, *b* December 18, 1727, *d* January 13,
1801 ; son of Stephen Colgate of Horsham,
County Sussex, England, *b* 1703, *d* 1764, his wife
Martha, *b* 1701, *d* 1776).

Born at New York City, March 27, 1841.

Arms—Argent, a chevron between three escallops sable.
Crest—A demi-wolf rampant holding in the dexter paw a sword proper
Motto—Omne bonum desuper.

Residences—5 East 82nd Street, New York ; Litchfield, Connecticut.
Clubs—Metropolitan of New York ; Sanctum and Litchfield, Connecticut

COLCOCK, CHARLES JONES,

of Charleston S.C. (Son, by 2nd w., of Char'es
J. Colcock, 1820-91, originator of Charleston and
Savannah R.R., Col. 3rd S.C.Cav. in C.S.A.,
m (1) Mary C. Heyward, m (2) Lucy F. Horton,
m (3) Agnes Bostick: son of Thomas H., 1797-1851,
m Eliza M., grand-da. of Col. A. H. Hay; son of
Chas. Jones, 1771-1839, Judge of the Court of
Appeals of S.C., m Mary Woodward Hutson, [5th
in descent from Dr. H. Woodward, 6th from Col.
John Godrey and James Stanyarne, 4th from Henry
Gigniliat]; son of Hon. John Colcock 1744-82,
Sec. of the Privy Council, m Millicent, da. of
Joseph Jones; son of Capt. John Colcock, b Essex,
Eng., of Charleston 1730, d 1756).

Born at Bonnie Doon, S.C., Jan. 17, 1852; Principal of The Porter Mil.
Acad.; a Phi Beta Kappa of Union Univ. N.Y.; Grad., 1875, C.E.;
m Dec. 5, 1883, Patti Lee, da. of Samuel Hay of Barnwell, S.C.

Issue.

i. Samuel Hay, b 1884, d 1885.   ii. Errol Hay.

Arms:—(Hay) Argent, three inescutcheons within a bordure nebulé gules.
Crest—A hand proper holding an ox yoke bows gules.

Residences—The Porter Mil. Acad , Charleston ; Boiling Springs Barnwell, Co.,S.C.
Club—Commercial.   Societies— S.C. Historical, Sons of the Revolution.

MINOT, JESSE,

of Asbury Park (Son of Capt. Jonathan
Minot, of Asbury Park, b July 18, 1838, m Helen,
da. of David Berry and Jane A. (Owens) Beatson,
of N.Y.; son of Jonathan, 1797-1876; son of Jesse,
1759-1828; son of Jonathan, 1723-1806; son of
Jonathan ; son of Jonathan ; son of James, b 1659;
son of James Minott, 1628-76, of Dorchester.
Mass., m 1653, Hannah, da. of Colonel I. Stoughton,
son of George, b 1594, settled at Dorchester; son
of Thomas Minot, of Saffron Walden, Essex).

Born at N.Y. City, June 21, 1870; Assist. Cashier
Asbury Park and Ocean Grove Bank;
m Jan. 1, 1895, Lela V., da. of Gould D. and Marg. A. (Long) Jelliff.

Arms—Azure, two chevronels dancetté argent, in chief a label of three points gules.

Crest—A cross and three stars gules.

Motto—Ad astra per aspera.

Residence—Asbury Park, Monmouth Co., N.J.

Society—Sons of the American Revolution.

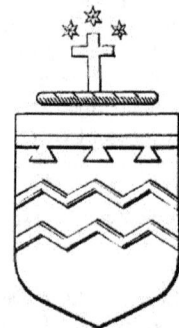

SELLERS, EDWIN JAQUETT,

of Phila. (Son of David Wampole Sellers, of the Phila. Bar, and Anna Francis Jaquett.—Descd. from Philipp Henrich Söller, of Weinheim, Germany, who settled in Penna., 1727 ; François Jaquet, of Geneva, Switzerland, Mem. of the Council of Two Hundred, 1546-72 : Jean Paul Jaquet, of Nüremberg, Governor of Delaware, 1655-57; Lieut. Joseph Jaquett, of New Castle Co., Dela., killed at the battle on Long Island, Aug. 27, 1776 ; Rev. Joseph Jaquett, d 1869 ; Jean Philippin, of Geneva, Switzerland, Syndic, 1535-52 ; Dr. Tymen Stidham, of Hammell, Sweden, who came to Delaware 1654 in the expedition of Governor Rising ; Dr. Francis Joseph Pfeiffer, of Germany, d at Phila., 1804 ; Henry Stretcher, M. of Col. Assembly ; Thos. Fenwick, Registrar of Wills, H. Sheriff, Judge ; Simon Kollock, Judge, H. Sheriff and M. of Col. Assembly ; Hercules Shepheard, Judge and M. of Col. Assembly ; John Avery, Cap. of Infy. and Pres. Judge ; Alexr. Draper, M. of Col. Assembly ; John Kipshaven, Judge and M. of Col. Assembly ; and Capt. Anth. Wayne, grandfather of General Anthony Wayne).

Born at Phila. July 25, 1865 : A.B., Univ. of Penna., June 15, 1886, A.M. and LL.B., June 5, 1889 ; admitted to the Phile. Bar June 15, 1889 ; m June 6, 1894, Blanche Bingham, da. of Michael Ehret, of Phila.

Issue.

i. Ellen Jaquett.

Arms—Quarterly : 1st, coupé, au 1 d'azur a une colombes ess, d'argent, posé sur un tertre de sin ; au 2 d'or plein demassé (Jaquet de Nüremberg) ; 2nd, d'azur au chev. acc. en chef de deux etoiles (5) en p. d'un croiss., le tout d'argent (Jaquet of Geneva) ; 3rd, gules a un tertre de trois coupeaux de sin, sommé de deux palmes adossees d'argent (Philippin) ; 4th, d'argent a deux pals se gules, une bande d'azure brochante sur le tout, au chef d'azur chargée de trois étoiles (5) d'argent (Comte) ; 5th, d'argent a un cœur enflamme a dextre, soutenu d'an échafaudage, et une main, mouv. de la p., brandissant un marteau dans la direction du cœur, le tout au nat. (Maillet) ; 6th, de sin. a un lievre courant, poursuivi d'un lévrier, tous deux en chef, et un chien braque courant en p., levant la tête vers le lièvre, le tout d'argent (De Witt) ; 7th, gules, a phœnix argent in flames proper (Fenwick) ; 8th, d'or au saut alésé de sable, les extrémités arrondies (Kipshaven) ; 9th. gules, a chevron ermine, botween three inside gauntlets or (Wayne).

Crest—Cq. cour. un homme, iss., barbu et portant moustaches, hab. d'un écartelé d'azur et d'or, au rabat d'argent, coiffé, d'un bonnet pointu d'azur retr. d'or, tenant de sa main dextre étendue un sabre en pal, son poing gauche repos sur la hanche. Mantling—D'or et d'azur.

Residence—1830, Pine Street, Philadelphia.

Clubs—Racquet, Univ., Univ. Barge, Phila. Country Club, Country of Atlantic City.

Societies—Colonial of Pa., Desedts. of Colonial Govs., Founders and Patriots of Am., Cincinnati, Sons of the Rev., Am. Wars, Loyal Legion, Hist. of Pa., Genealogical of Pa., Buffalo Hist., Pa. German, etc.

SEABURY, FREDERICK CHANDLER,
of Brooklyn (Son of Alexander Seabury of
Brooklyn 1821-96, m 1848, Lydia Briggs 1826-96,
da. of Abraham and Lydia (Shaw) Manchester of
Westport Mass.; son of Capt. Benjamin 1776-1857;
son of Capt. Gideon Seabury 1747-1827; son of
Capt. Benjamin 1708-73; son of Lieut. Joseph
1678-1755; son of Dr. Samuel 1640-81, of Duxbury
Mass., Dep. Gov. and Asst. of Plymouth Colony,
m Martha Pabodie, grand-da. of John Alden and
Priscilla Molines, passengers on the "Mayflower"
1620; son of John Seabury, from Devonshire to
Boston, 1630, d in Barbadoes).

Born at Brooklyn N.Y. July 2, 1849; Grad. Polytechnic Inst. Brooklyn
1869; m April 23, 1885, Sarah Augusta, da. of Col. Andrew A.
Bremner and Maria, da. of David Case of Goshen N.Y.

Arms—Argent, a fesse engrailed between three ibexes passant sable.
Crest—An ibex as in Arms.   *Motto*—Supera alta tenere.

Residences—414 Grand Avenue, Brooklyn, N.Y.; Westport Harbor, Mass.
Clubs—Crescent Athletic, Lincoln, Young Republican, Royal Arcanum, Poly-
technic, Union League.
Societies—Mayflower Descendants, Colonial Wars, Sons of the Am. Revolution,
Baronial Order of Runnemede.

LEVERING, EUGENE,
of Baltimore, Md. (Son of Eugene Levering,
1819-70, m Ann S., da. of Joshua Walker of
Baltimore. — Descended from Wigard Levering,
b at Gemen, Germany, 1648, settled in Roxborough,
Pa., 1685; son of Rosier Levering, of Mulheim,
Germany, and Elizabeth Van de Walle. The
family descend from John de Leveryng, b 1250, at
Leverington, Cambridgeshire, Eng.).

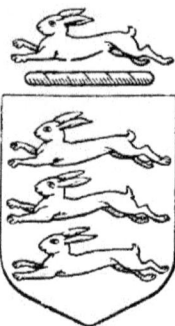

Born at Baltimore, Md., Sept. 12, 1845; Prest.
National Bank of Commerce; Mem. of the Bd.
of Trustees of John Hopkins Univ.; m Jan.
23, 1868, Mary E. Armstrong of Baltimore.

Issue.

i. EUGENE, Jr., b July 13, 1869, m Nov. 14, 1895, Adelaide Gary.
i. MARY ARMSTRONG, m March 15, 1905, Rev. Jos. H. Robinson.
ii. ETHEL.

Arms—Azure, three hares in pale argent.   *Motto*—Ducit amor patriæ.
Crest—A hare as in Arms.

Residence—1308 Eutaw Place, Baltimore, Maryland.
Club—Baltimore Country.

SUMNER, EDWARD ARTHUR,
of N.Y. City (Son of John A. Sumner, 1825,
m Helen, 1831-72, da. of Merrit and Mary (Moulton)
Brooks, of Rome, N.Y.—Descd. from Wm. Sumner,
who served throughout Revol. War, and from
Wm. Sumner, of Dorchester, Mass., Dep. Gen.
Ct., 1666.—Also on the maternal side from Baron
John Moulton, *temp* William 1st).

Born at Rome, N.Y. Nov. 3, 1856 ; Grad. Wesln.
Univ. B.A. 1878, M.A. 1880 ; Grad. Yale
Univ. 1902, M.A.; 5 yrs. Principal Gilder-
sleeve Prep. Sch.; Mem. of N.Y. Bar, 1885 ;
Adm. to U.S. Sup. Ct., 1888 ; *m* Jan. 29, 1885,
Martha Dickenson.

Issue.

i. ROBERT BROOKS, *b* Nov. 3, 1888 (*deceased*).
ii. RICHARD ERLE, *b* June 13, 1891.   i. MARGARET HELEN.

Arms—Ermine, two chevrons gules.
Crest—A lion's head erased argent, ducally gorged or.
Motto—In medio tutissimus ibis.

Residence—2131 Broadway, New York City.
Clubs—N.Y. Yacht, N.Y. Athletic, W. S. Republican, Yale, Sachems' H'd'Yacht.
Societies—Sons of the Am. Revol., New Eng. of N.Y., N.Y. State Bar Assn., Grant
    Monument Assn., Psi Upsilon, Am. Bar Assn., Amer. Geographical.

MARTIN, ROBERT COATES (*deceased*),
of N.Y. City (Son of Benjamin Martin
1797-1852, of Knox, N.Y., *m* Sarah 1799-1882, da.
of Robert and Miriam (Blodgett) Coates, of Knox ;
son of Thomas 1759-1830, served in Revol. War ;
son of Benjamin 1734-1814; son of John 1674-1757 ;
son of John Martyn *b* Feb. 22, 1634, settled at
Swansea, Mass. before 1658, *m* 1671, Joanna
Esten ; son of Edward Martyn of Ottery St.
Mary, Exeter, Devonshire, *m* June 14, 1632,
Judith Upham, of Bicton, Devon).

Born at Knox, Albany Co., N.Y., April 10, 1823 ;
d June, 1906; admitted to the Bar at Albany,
N.Y., and Washington, D.C., 1840 ; *m* Jan. 31, 1854, Julia Marvin,
d Aug. 28, 1899, da. of Azor Taber of Albany, N.Y. and Sarah, da.
of Maj.-Gen. Paul Todd.

Issue.

i. SUSAN TABER, *m* Sept. 1, 1906, Frederick Allien, of N.Y. City.

Arms—Argent, two bars gules.

Crest—An estoil of sixteen points gules.   *Motto*—Sure and steadfast.

Residence—(Family) South Hill, Riverdale, New York City.

GEORGE, JOSIAS JENKINS,

of Baltimore, Md. (Son of Philip Thomas George, *b* 1815, *m* 1846, Ellen, da. of Josias Jenkins, of Long Green, Md.; son of William E., *b* 1785, *m* Sara Ellicott; son of Robert, *m* Ann Edmondson; son of Joseph; son of Robert George, came from London 1682, of Langford Manor, Kent Co., Md., 1690).

Born at Long Green, Balto. Co., Md., Mar. 9, 1853; Grad. at Rock Hill Coll., 1871; *m* Sept. 25, 1878, Amelia Jenkins, of Kentucky.

Issue.

i. WILLIAM EDMONSON, *b* 1883, *d* 1887.
ii. ANDREW ELLICOTT, *b* Oct. 7, 1889.
i. ELLEN ELIZABETH.   ii. SARAH HARVEY.

Arms—Argent, a fesse gules between three falcons volant azure beaked and membered or.
Crest—A demi-hound sable collared or, ears and legs argent.
Motto—Magna est veritas et prevalebit.

Residence—Ellendale, Long Green, Balto Co., Md.
Clubs—Maryland, Baltimore, Elkridge Fox Hunting, Green Spring Valley Hunt, Baltimore Country, Baltimore Golf, Baltimore Yacht, Bachelors' Cotillion.

PELL, FREDERICK AYCRIGG,

of N.Y. City (Son of John Bogert Pell, of N.Y., sea captain, 1800-82, *m* 1830 Susan Augusta, *d* 1883, da. of Benjamin Aycrigg of N.Y.; son of William 1762-1815, *m* Elizabeth Bogert; son of John 1728-82, *m* Sarah Byranck; son of Samuel, *d* 1695, *m* Margaretta Wessells; son of William, *d* 1747, *m* Elizabeth Van Tuyl; son of Samuel Pell, of New York 1673, *m* Deborah Williams; son of William; son of Alexander of Boothby Pagnal Co. Lincoln; son of John of Huntingdon; son of Thomas; son of Richard of Elkington, Northants; son of John; son of Richard; son of Thomas; son of William Pell of Water Willoughby, Lincolnshire).

Born in N.Y. City May 23, 1840; Counsellor-at-Law; Grad. Princeton Univ. 1871.

Arms—Argent, a bend between two mullets pierced sable.
Crest—On a mural coronet or a mullet pierced sable.

Residence—Lakewood, N.J.
Clubs—University, Princeton, and Reform.
Societies—Colonial Wars, Sons of the Revolution, New York Historical.

COX, JACOB DOLSON,
of Cleveland, Ohio (Eldest son of Hon.
Jacob Dolson Cox, 1828-1900, of Cincinnati, U.S.
Senator, 1860, Brig.-Gen. O.V.I., 1861, Gov. of
Ohio, 1866-68, Sec. of the Interior, 1869-70, Con-
gressman from Toledo, 1876. Dean of Cincinnati
Law Sch., 1880-98, m 1849, Helen, da. of Charles
G. Finney, of Oberlin; son of Jacob Dolson Cox,
who m Thedia, da. of Joseph Kenyon, son of Payne
Kenyon, who m Thedia, da. of Rev. Nathan
Howard, who m Lucy, da. of Clement Minor, who
m Abigail, da. of Ezekiel Turner, son of John
Turner, who m Mary, grand-da. of Elder William
Brewster, 1566-1664).

Born at Warren, Ohio, May 15, 1852; m Oct. 9, 1878, Ellen, da. of
Judge Saml. B. Prentiss, and Jane Atwood Russell, of East
Haddam, Conn.

Issue.

i. SAMUEL HOUGHTON, b July 3, 1880.   i. JEANETTE PRENTISS.
ii. JACOB DOLSON, b Nov. 1, 1881.

Arms—(Brewster) Sable, a chevron ermine between three estoiles argent.
Crest—A bear's head erased azure.   Motto—Verité soyez ma garde.

Residence—925 Euclid Avenue, Cleveland, Ohio.   Clubs—Euclid, Union.
Societies—Am. Soc. of Mech. Engineers, Loyal Legion. Mayflower Descendants.

MANSFIELD, MRS. MAY (née STANSBURY),
of San Francisco, Cal. Da. of John
Skelton (and Mary A. Monaghan) Stansbury,
d June 24, 1879, in Napa City, Cal.—Descended
from Tobias Stanborough, who came from
Norfolk Eng. to Baltimore, Md. 1668, a descendant of Jonas Stanbery, whose tomb is in London.
Also descended from Edward and Eleanor (Hugh)
Foulke, from Wales to Pennsylvania 1698).

Born at Sacramento, Cal., m Walter Damon
Mansfield, a descendant of Sir John
Mansfield, J.P., Master of the Minories, and
Queen's Surveyor, who died in England,
1601.

Arms—(Stansbury or Steynbury) Per pale argent and or, a lion rampant per
fesse gules and sable.
Crest—A lion rampant.
Arms—(Foulke) Vert a chevron between three wolves' heads, erased argent.
Crest—A wolf's head erased.
Mottoes—" Blaidd Rhudd ar y Blaen "; "Consequitur quod cwnque petit."

Residence—California Hotel, San Francisco, California.
Societies—Colonial Dames of Amer., Historic-Genealogical of California, United
Daughters of the Confederacy.

HILL, JOHN PHILIP,
of Baltimore (Son of Chas. E. Hill, of Balto.,
b 1848, Lawyer, Assist. Prof. U.S. Naval Acad.,
1871-75, Lecturer Med. Jur. S. Homœop. College,
Balto., *m* 1875, Kate W. Clayton; son of Rev.
J. Bancroft, 1796-1864; son of Rev. Ebenezer,
1766-1854; son of Samuel, 1716-98; son of Capt.
Samuel, 1671-1755; son of Capt. Ralph, *d* 1695;
son of Ralph Hill, of Plymouth, Mass., 1638).

Born at Annapolis, Md., May 2, 1879; Lawyer;
A.B. Johns Hopkins Univ., 1900; LL.B.
Harvard Univ., 1903; Assist. in Government,
Harvard Univ., 1902-3; Mem. Boston and
Balto. Bars; 2nd Lieutenant, 4th I.M.N.G.

Arms—Gules, a saltire vair between four mullets argent.
Crest—A demi-leopard argent spotted of all colours, ducally gorged or.
Motto—Per Deum et ferrum obtinui.

Residences—2120 North Charles Street, Balto., Md.; "Tamaracks," Temple,
Hillsborough Co., N.H.
Clubs—Maryland, Jr. Cotillion, Harvard of Md., Balto. Country, Athletic,
Union League.
Societies—Maryland Historical, Alpha Delta Phi, Balto.; Phi Delta Phi, Harvard;
Colonial Wars, American Historical Association.

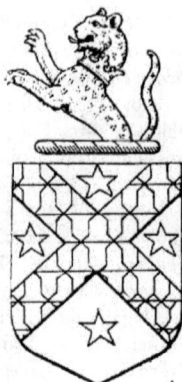

SWIFT, EDWIN ELISHA, M.D.,
of N.Y. City (Son of Edwin D. Swift
1825-1901, Phys. and Health Officer of Hamden,
Ct., *m* Sarah L., 1826-65, da. of Elisha Punderson;
son of Augustus B., 1793-1862; son of Philo
1762-1838; son of Genl. Heman 1733-1814; son
of Jabez 1700-67; son of Jireh 1665-1749; son of
William 1627-1705; son of William Swift of
Sandwich, Mass., *d* 1643; his son Edward was
apprenticed to George Andrews, citizen of London).

Born at Hamden, Ct., Mar. 23, 1855; Assist. Phys.
to Manhattan Eye and Ear Hospital; Grad.
N.Y. Univ. Medical Coll. M.D. 1880; *m* Oct.
28, 1891, Virginie M. Bancroft, da. of Achille
Francois and Elizabeth F. Migeon

Issue

i. ELIZABETH MIGEON.

Arms—Or, a chevron vair between three bucks in full course ppr.
Crest—A demi-buck in the mouth a honeysuckle ppr
Motto—Festina lente.

Residences—112 West 81st Street, N.Y. City; Thousand Islands.
Clubs—Republican, Colonial.
Societies—N.Y. Academy of Medicine, N.Y. County Medical, Medical of Greater
N.Y., Sons of the Revolution.

LOGAN, Major JOHN A., U.S.A. (*deceased*),
of Youngstown, O. (Only son of the Hon.
Maj.-Gen. John Alexander Logan, U.S.V., War of
the Rebellion, U.S. Senator, *b* Feb. 12, 1826,
d Dec. 26, 1886, *m* Mary Simmerson, da. of John
Marion and Elizabeth (Fountain) Cunningham;
son of Dr. John Logan, of Co. Monaghan, Ireland,
m Elizabeth Jenkins, of South Carolina, sister of
Alexander Jenkins, Lieut.-Gov. of Illinois).

Born at Carbondale, Ill., July 24, 1865; late Major
and Assist.-Adj.-Gen. U.S. Volunteers during
the Spanish-American War, May 12, 1898—
May 16, 1899; Major 33rd Inf. U.S.A.;
killed in action while leading his battalion,
Nov. 11, 1899, near San Jacinto, Philippines; *m* Mar. 22, 1887,
Edith, da. of Chauncey H. and Louise (Baldwin) Andrews, of
Youngstown, Ohio.

Issue.

i. John Alexander (3rd), *b* February 9, 1890.
i. Mary Louise.   ii. Edith.

Arms—Or, three passion nails sable, their points in a heart gules.
Crest—A bugle-horn, stringed proper.
Motto—In hoc majorum virtus.

Residence—(Family) Gloan Lodge, Oriole Farms, Youngstown, Ohio.

WORTHINGTON, GEORGE,
of Bennington Centre, Vt. (Son of George
Worthington, 1813-71, of Cleveland, O., *m* 1840,
Maria Cushman, da. of Reuben Harmon and
Amanda (Cushman) Blackmer of Dorset, Vt.;
son of Ralph, 1778-1828, *m* Clarissa Clark; son of
John, 1744-83, *m* Abigail Wright; son of Elijah,
1716-64, *m* Mary Welles; son of William, 1670-1753,
m Mehitable Graver, widow of Richard Morton;
son of Nicholas Worthington from Lancashire,
Eng., to Saybrook, 1649, settled at Hatfield, Ct.,
m (1) Mrs. Sarah Bunce, *m* (2) Susanna).

Born at Cleveland, O., Aug. 8, 1854; Brown Univ.
Providence R.I. Class 1877; *m* Oct. 12, 1880,
Lily Marie, da. of John Wesley and Altia (Downer) Smith of
Albany, N.Y.

Issue.

i. George, *b* July 10, 1890.

Arms—Argent, three dung forks sable.
Crest—A goat statent argent, holding in its mouth an oak branch vert.
Motto—Virtute dignus avorum.

Residences—Bennington Centre, Vt.; Cleveland, Ohio.
Clubs—Union of Cleveland; Ekwanok Country of Manchester Vt., Island Golf
Troy, N.Y.; Mt. Anthony Country of Bennington, Vt.
Societies—Sons of the Am. Revo., Mayflower Descendants, Colonial Wars.

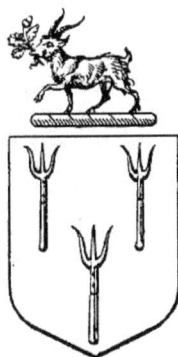

GILBERT, CHARLES PIERREPONT HENRY, of N.Y. City (Only Son of Loring Gilbert, of N.Y. City, and Washington, D.C., *b* 1832, *d* 1895, *m* 1855, Caroline Clementine, da. of Laurence Echebury, and Caroline Monte, his wife.—Descended from John Gilbert, 2nd son of Giles Gilbert, of Bridgewater, Somerset, Eng., being of the same family as Sir Humphrey Gilbert, who was born in Devonshire, 1539, and to whom a patent to colonize North America was granted by Queen Elizabeth. John Gilbert originally settled in Dorchester, Mass., but later moved to Taunton, Mass., where he *d* 1654. He was one of the first two men to represent Taunton at the Great and Genl. Court; Commanded the Yarmouth Military Company, serving in the wars against the Indians; his grandson, Eleazer Gilbert, was an officer in King Philip's War; through his grandmother, Rachel Warner, Mr. Gilbert is descended from Daniel Warner (1666-1754), who served in the expedition against Fort William Henry in 1757, and whose son, Joseph Warner, commanded a company on that expedition; his son, Capt. Elijah Warner, served during the War of the Revolution; Daniel Warner was a grandson of Andrew Warner, who came from England in 1632, and settled in Cambridge, Mass.; Capt. Joseph Warner, *m* Submit Wells (*b* 1742), through whom Mr. Gilbert is descended from Capt. William Allis (*d* 1678), who had a company at the Falls Fight in 1676, and from Capt. William Allis (1642-91), who was in the Deerfield Fight in 1690; Capt. John Allis, *m* Mary, da. of Thomas Meekins, of Braintree, Mass., Deputy to General Court, 1644; he settled in Boston in 1634, having come over in the ship "Griffin"; he is also descended through this line from John Webster, who was *b* in Warwickshire, Eng., and became Colonial Gov. of Con. 1656; later he was one of the founders of Hadley, Mass.).

Born in N.Y. City, Aug. 29, 1861; *m* Sept. 14, 1896, Florence Cecil, da. of Theodore Moss, and Octavia Stephens Ashley, da. of P. V. Husted and Emeline Stephens Ashley.

Issue.

i. DUDLEY PIERREPONT, *b* Mar. 21, 1898.

i. VERA PIERREPONT.

Arms—Argent on a chevron sable three roses of the field.

Crest—A squirrel cracking a nut proper.   *Motto*—Tenax propositi.

Residence—33 Riverside Drive, New York City.

Clubs—Metropolitan, Riding, Racquet, Union League, Ardsley Country, Lawyers

Societies—Colonial Wars, Sons of the Rev., New Eng., Fine Arts, Municipal Arts, Nat. Sculpture, Fel. of Amer. Inst. of Archit., Archit. League, Veteran and Charter Mem. of Squadron A Cav. N.G.S.N.Y., Member of Chamber of Commerce, N.Y. City.

IVES, CHAUNCEY,
of Chambersburg (Son of Chauncey P. Ives,
1807-72, of Lansingburg, N.Y., m Charlotte
Brownell, da. of John Stewart, of Waterford,
N.Y.—Descd. from William Ives, from London on
ship "Truelove," 1635, one of the proprietors of
New Haven, Ct., 1639, d 1648. Also 9th in descent
from Major Simon Willard, 1605-76, one of the
founders of Concord, Mass., Dep. to Gen. Court,
1636-54, Commissioner of Boundary between Mass.
and N.H., 1652, Govr.'s Asst., 1654-76 ; Comdr.-in-
Chief of the Expedition against Ninagret, 1665.
Also 9th from John Whitney, 1589-1673, gt.-
grandson of Sir Robert Whitney).

Born at Lansingburg, N.Y., Sept. 10, 1841 ; m Oct. 2, 1872, Emma S., da.
of Edmund Culbertson, M.D., Pres. Chambersburg Nat. Bank, by
Ellen Harlan, da. of Judge James J. Kennedy.

Issue.
i. CHAUNCEY PELTON, b December 8, 1883.
i. ELLEN CULBERTSON, m Wentworth G. Hare.
ii. CHARLOTTE BROWNELL, m. John Risley Putnam.

Arms—Argent, a chevron between three Moors' heads couped sable.
Crest—A blackamoor's head.

Residence—Brooklyn, New York.

CROMBIE, WILLIAM MURRAY,
of N.Y. City (Eldest son of Wm. Aug.
Crombie, of N.Y., A.D.C., with rank of Colonel, on
staff of Gov. Ormsbee, of Vermont, b April 20,
1844, m 1868, Sarah Elizabeth, da. of Hon. Orlando
Dana Murray, of Nashua, N.H. ; son of Samuel,
b 1814-79, of Concord, N.H. ; son of John, b 1770 ;
son of James, 1st Lt. Baldwin's Reg., N.H. Militia ;
son of John Crombie, from the North of Ireland,
settled in Londonderry, N.H., 1720 ; m 1721,
Joan, da. of Hugh Rankin, from Co. Antrim, who
settled in Londonderry, N.H., 1723).

Born at Burlington, Vt., Nov. 6, 1871, Mem. " Sq.
A," N.G.N.Y., " Troop A," U.S. Vols. in
Spanish-Am. War ; Grad. Univ. of Vermont,
Ph.B., 1893 ; m Dec. 5, 1900, *Harriet Anderson Slade, of N.Y.

Arms—Vert, a cross botonnée argent, on a chief of the last a lion passant gules.
Crest—A demi-lion rampant guardant or, holding a fleur-de-lis gules.
Motto—Labor omnia vincit.

Residences—Bretton Hall, New York City ; Seabright, N.J.
Club—University.
Societies—Sons of the Amer. Rev., Sigma Phi, *Daurs. of the Amer. Rev., Daurs.
of 1812, Daurs. of Founders and Patriots, Nat. of New Eng. Women.

CLOTHIER, ISAAC HALLOWELL,

of Wynnewood, Pa. (Son of Caleb Clothier, of Phila., Pa., 1806-81, *m* Hannah F. Hallowell, 1807-55; son of Caleb, of Mt. Holly, N.J.; son of James; son of Henry Clothier, from Bristol, Eng., 1714, to Burlington, N.J., *m* Abigail Ridgway).

Born at Phila., Pa., Nov. 5, 1837; *m* Sept. 1, 1864, Mary Clapp,* da. of Wm. Jackson, of Phila., and Elizabeth Howe, da. of Enoch Clapp, a desct. of Roger Clapp, 1609-91.

Issue.
i. Morris, L., *b* July 24, 1868, *m* April 26, 1900, Lydia M. Earnshaw.
ii. Walter, *b* July 16, 1874, *m* April 2, 1902, Edith M. Ball.
iii. Isaac H., *b* Nov. 12, 1875, *m* Jan. 7, 1903, Melinda K. Annear.
iv. Wm. Jackson, *b* Sept. 27, 1881, *m* Feb. 21, 1906, Anita Porter.
i. Mary J., *m* Nov. 1, 1892, William Esher Heyl.
ii. Elizabeth J., *m* Apr. 30, 1895, Thomas H. P. Sailer.
iii. Hannah H., *m* Dec. 27, 1898, William Isaac Hull.
iv. Lydia Biddle ; *m* Oct. 24, 1903, John R. Maxwell.   v. Caroline.

Arms—Argent, a chevron betw. three escallop shells gules.
Crest—On a cap of maintenance gules, turned up ermine an escallop shell.
Motto—Pro patria ejusque libertate.

Residences—" Ballytore," Wynnewood, Penna.; Newport, R.I.
Clubs—U. League, Country, Merion Cricket, Radnor Hunt, N. Century*, Acorn.
Societies—Historical of Penna.; *Colonial Dames of America, *Daughters of the American Revolution, *New England Women of Pa.

MARTIN, GEORGE CASTOR,

of N.Y. City (Eldest son of Richard Allen, Martin, M.D., 1858-90, of Phila., *m* 1883, Nellie, da. of George Castor, of Holmesburg, Pa., and Mary E., da. of Joseph Mills and Hannah, da. of Thomas Burrage, 1782-1860, who was son of John, 1755-1822; son of William, *d* 1763; son of John, 1693-1765; son of William, *b* 1657; son of John Burrage, *b* at Norton Subcorse, Norfolk, Eng., 1616, settled in America, 1637, *d* 1685.—Descended from Robert Martin, Mayor of Galway 1621, a direct descendant of Sir Oliver Martin, *viva* 1200).

Born in N.Y. City, March 30, 1885; Graduated at Columbia Institute, 1901; *m* Sept. 22, 1906, Mildred, da. of Henry W. Comegys.

Arms—(For Burrage) Argent, three boars' heads gules.
Crest—A boar's head gules.

Residences—235 W. 108th Street, New York City; Asbury Park. N.J.
Clubs—Deal Lake Boat; 22nd Regt. Engineers, N.G.N.Y.
Societies—N.Y. Zoological, League of Amer. Sportsmen, Sons of the Revolution.

DAVENPORT, WILLIAM BATES,
of Brooklyn, N.Y. (Eldest son of Julius
Davenport, of New York City.—Descended from
Rev. John Davenport, *b* Coventry, Eng., 1597;
B.D., Oxford, 1625; Vicar of St. Stephen's,
Coleman Street, London; Founder and first
Minister of New Haven, Ct.—In descent from
Ormus de Dauneporte, *b* 1086, assumed the local
name in Co. Chester).

Born at New York City, March 10, 1847;
Graduated at Yale University, 1867; Member
of Constitutional Convention, State of New
York, 1894; Public Administrator of Kings
Co., N.Y., 1889-1904; *m* Charlotte Cordelia,
eldest da. of George F. Shepherd.

Issue.

i. EDITH HOXIE, *b* June 8, 1870; *d* June 5, 1872.

ii. FLORENCE, *b* Nov. 1, 1882; *d* May 29, 1884.

Arms—Argent, a chevron sable between three cross crosslets fitchée of the
second.

Crest—A felon's head couped at the neck proper, haltered or.

Motto—Audaces fortuna juvat. _____

Residence—201 Washington Park, Brooklyn, N.Y.

Clubs—University, Manhattan Yacht, Yale (New York), Hamilton (Brooklyn).

GLENN, GARRARD,
of New York (Son of John Thomas Glenn,
1844-99, of Atlanta, Georgia, Lawyer, *m* April 23,
1873, Helen Augusta, da. of William Waters
Garrard, of Hilton, Georgia [6th in descent from
Peter Garrard, of Lille, France, who settled in
England 1687]; son of Luther Judson Glenn, 1818-
86; son of Thomas, 1783-1830; son of Duke; son
of Thomas; son of Dr. John Glen, of North
Carolina; son of Alexander Glen, of "Longcroft,"
Linlithgow, Scotland. Mr. Glenn is descended
on the paternal side from Thos. Reade Rootes, of
Whitemarsh, Va.; Colonel George Reade, who
came to Virginia 1637; General Robt. Lewis, who
came to Virginia 1635, son of Sir Edward Lewis,
Knighted by James I., 1603; also, on the maternal side, from Major
James MacGregor, who fled to Virginia when his clan was proscribed,
d 1724, a descendant of King Robert II. of Scotland).

Born at Atlanta, Georgia, Aug. 7, 1878; Lawyer.

Arms—Argent, a fesse gules between three martlets sable.

Crest—A martlet sable.

Motto—Ad Astra.

Residence—New York City.

M ILLET, JOSIAH BYRAM,
    of Boston Mass. (Son of Dr. Asa Millet
1811-93 of East Bridgewater Mass, *m* 1840 Huldah
Byram.—Descended from Thomas Millet 1605-76,
m 1635 Mary Greenway, settled at Dorchester,
Mass.; son of Henry Millet of Chertsey, Co.
Surrey, gent., Attorney-at-Law in Staples Inn,
Holborn, *m* Joyce, da. of John Chapman of
Chertsey).

Born at Bridgewater, Mass. Sept. 27, 1854; Grad.
    Harvard Univ. B.A. 1877; *m* Oct. 30, 1883,
    Emily Adams, da. of Samuel Foster McCleary,
    B.A., LL.B. Harvard 1841, of Boston and
    Emily Thurston, da. of Capt. James H.
    Barnard.

Issue.

i. HILDA.   ii. ELISABETH FOSTER.

Arms—Argent, a fesse gules between three dragons' heads erased vert.
Crest—Out of a mural coronet an arm in pale habited or, grasping in a glove
    argent a dragon's head erased vert.
Motto—Manus hœc inimica tyrannis.

Residence—77 Mount Vernon Street, Boston, Mass.
Clubs—Tavern, Country.

E DMONDS, RICHARD HATHAWAY,
    of Baltimore, Md. (Second son of Rev.
Richard Henry Edmonds of Norfolk, Virginia,
1831-58, *m* December 1, 1852, Mary Elizabeth,
daughter of William and Mary Elizabeth (Hewitt)
Ashley, of Norfolk, Va.).

Born at Norfolk, Virginia, October 11, 1857;
    President Manufacturers' Record Publishing
    Co.; Editor Manufacturers' Record; Member
    Executive Committee and Director Inter-
    national Trust Co., Baltimore; Director
    Alabama Consolidated Coal and Iron Co.;
    m July 5, 1881, Addie Louise, daughter of
    A. W. and Penelope J. (Healy) Field, of
    Baltimore, Md.

Arms—Or, a chevron azure, on a canton azure a boar's head couped between
    three fleur-de-lis or.
Crest—On a chapeau gules turned up ermine a fleur-de-lis between two wings
    azure.

Residence—Roland Park, Baltimore, Md.
Club—Baltimore Country.
Societies—Maryland Hist., Amer. Statistical Assoc., Southern Hist. Assoc., Amer.
    Assoc. for Advancement of Science.

PORTER, WILLIAM WAGENER (Judge),
of Philadelphia (Son of Wm. Augustus
Porter, Judge of the Supreme Court of Penn., and
of the Court of Alabama Claims; son of David R.
Porter, twice Governor of the Commonwealth of
Pennsylvania, and grandson of General Andrew
Porter, Staff Officer to General George Washington.
—Descended from Robert Porter, of Worcester
Township, Montgomery Co., Pa., 1720).

Born in Philadelphia, Pa., May 5, 1856; ex-Judge
of the Superior Court of the Commonwealth
of Pennsylvania; *m* Mary Augusta, da. of
Charles H. Hobart.

Issue.

i. WILLIAM HOBART.   ii. ANDREW WAGENER.
i. ANITA; *m* February 21, 1906, William J. Clothier.

Arms—Sable, three church bells argent; a canton ermine.
Crest—A portcullis argent chained or.   *Motto*—Vigilentia et virtute.

Residence—2025 Walnut Street, Philadelphia, Pa.
Clubs—Union League, Lawyers, Penn, Merion.
Society—Cincinnati.

SEAMAN, LOUIS L. M.A., M.D., LL.B.,
of N.Y. City (Grandson of Valentine Seaman,
M.D., who introduced vaccination into New York,
1799, seventh in descent from Robert Livingston,
Lord of the Manor).

Born at Newburgh, Oct. 17, 1851; Grad. Cornell
Univ. 1873; Jeff. Med. Coll., M.D., Univ.
Med. Coll., N.Y., M.D.; LL.B., Univ. of
N.Y. Law Dep. 1884; Surg.-Maj. 1st U.S.
Vol. Engrs. in Spanish Am. War; served in
the Philippines 1899-1900, in the Boxer War
1900-1; with the Russians in Manchuria 1904,
with the Japanese 1905; Author of "From
Tokio through Manchuria with the Japanese,"
"The Real Triumph of Japan," "Native
Troops in our Colonial Possessions," "The
Social Waste of a Great City," "Medical Observations on Tropical
Africa," "The Army Canteen"; *m* Fannie Blackstone, *d* 1895, a
gt.-gt.-gd.-da. of Sir W. Blackstone, the eminent Jurist.

Arms—Barry wavy of six argent and azure, a crescent or.
Crest—A demi-seahorse salient argent.   *Motto*—Spectemur agendo.

Residence—247 Fifth Avenue, New York.
Clubs—Calumet, Lotos, Cornell, Players, Authors, Metropolitan, Pilgrims,
Republican, Army and Navy, National Arts.
Societies—Founders and Patriots of Am., Col. Wars, Sons of Revol., N. and M.
order Spanish Am. War, Army of the Philippines, U.S. Mil. Surg's.,
Asiatic Society, Acad. of Medicine, American Assn. Advancement of Sci.

HASKELL, FRANK WALSH,

of Niagara Falls (Son of Benj. Haskell, of Bloomfield, N. J., Mem. of Brooklyn City Guard, 1858, Asst. Adjt.-Genl. 13th Brig. N.G.S.N.Y., 1863, Major in U.S. Service, 1863; Mem. Brooklyn Vet. Assn., *b* 1835; *m* 1861, Harriet Ells, 1840-92, da. of Perez S. Steele, of Brooklyn.—Descd. from Capt. Wm. Haskell, 1617-93, of Beverley, Mass., 1632, Gloucester, Mass., 1643, *m* Mary Tybbot; Dep. Gen. Ct., Mass.).

Born at Brooklyn, N.Y., Dec. 17, 1861; Pres. of the Carborundum Co., Niagara Falls; *m* June 17, 1881, Clara L., da. of John FitzG. and Jane L. (Riggs) Seymour.

Issue.

i. BENJAMIN, *b* Sept. 16, 1901.

i. MAUDE SEYMOUR, *b* 1882; *d* 1887.
ii. GRACE STEELE, *b* 1888; *d* 1895.

Arms—Vaire argent and sable.
Crest—On a mount an apple tree in fruit ppr.   *Motto*—Vincit veritas.

Residence—Niagara Falls, N.Y.
Clubs—Duquesne, Buffalo, Niagara; Niagara Falls Country, Auto. Club of Am.
Societies—Colonial Wars, Sons of the Amer. Revolution, Amer. Electro Chemical, Member of the N.Y. Chamber of Commerce.

RUGGLES, HENRY STODDARD,

of Wakefield, Mass. (Second son Henry Bond Ruggles, of Boston, 1813-97; *m* Mary Goodwin, da. of Jonathan Ross, of Harrison, Me.— Desc'd. from Thos. Ruggles, of Roxbury, Mass., 1637).

Born Oct. 31, 1846; *m* Mary Elizabeth, only child and heiress of the late William Ryan, of Boston.

Issue.

i. HENRY, *b* Feb. 20, 1879; *d* Jan. 24, 1881.
ii. FRANCIS DUNBAR, *b* Aug. 9, 1883.
iii. HORACE CHENEY, *b* June 18, 1887; *d* Feb. 9, 1888.

i. EMMELINE.
ii. MARY ROSAMOND.
iii. MARGUERITE.

iv. MABEL LYMAN.
v. LOUISA KINGSLEY.
vi. ALICIA.

vii. LUCIA DALTON.
viii. JULIA PARKER.

Arms—Quarterly, 1st and 4th argent, a chevron between three roses gules; 2nd and 3rd vert, a cross engr. erm.; on an escutcheon of pretence gules a bend argent, thereon six holly leaves in pairs, erect, ppr.
Crest—A tower or, inflamed proper, and pierced with four arrows in saltire points downward argent.   *Motto*—Struggle.

Residences—Boston, Wakefield, and Rockport, Mass.
Clubs—Quannapowitt, Wakefield Park Golf.
Societies—Sons of the Rev., Sons of the Am. Rev., Essex Inst., Am.-Irish Hist., Roxb'y Mil. Hist., Old Northw. Genea., Am. Art.

SCUDDER, Rev. HENRY TOWNSEND,
of Brooklyn, N.Y. (Son of Henry Joel Scudder,
b at Northport, Suffolk Co., N.Y., Sept. 18, 1825;
d in New York City, Feb. 10, 1886; Counsellor-
at-Law; Member of Congress, 1873-75; great-
grandson of Henry Scudder, 1743-1822; 2nd Lieut.
in Capt. Nathaniel Platt's Company of Minute
Men, raised in Huntington and Smiths Town, L.I.,
April 7, 1776; on Staff of General Talmadge
during Revolutionary War. — Descended from
Thomas Scudder, who came from Kent and settled
at Salem, Mass., 1630; also sixth in descent from Major Moses Mansfield,
1639-1703, of New Haven, Conn.; Deputy at General Court for twenty
years; served with distinction in Indian Wars).

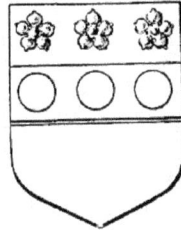

Born in New York City, Sept. 7, 1854; Graduated at Columbia College,
1874; Rector of St. Stephen's Church, Brooklyn; *m* June 5, 1889,
Margaret Mott, daughter of Jacob Weeks.

Issue.

i. HENRY HOLLOWAY, *b* September 24, 1895.

i. EDNA HEWLETT.   ii. DOROTHY WEEKS.

Arms—Gules, on a fesse or, three pellets, in chief as many cinquefoils argent.

Residence—24A, Garden Pl., Brooklyn, N.Y. *Clubs*—University, Grolier, Col. Univ.
Societies—Colonial Wars, Sons of the Rev., Col. Alumni Ass., O. Foreign Wars.

McELROY, CLAYTON,
of Philadelphia (Son of John George
Repplier McElroy, *b* June 30, 1842; *d* Nov. 26,
1890; *m* Nov. 2, 1869, Anna Baldwin, *b* Nov. 2,
1848; *d* Aug. 31, 1897, da. of John Clayton, Esq.,
of Philadelphia.—Descended from Daniel McElroy,
who settled at "The Compass," in Chester Co.,
Penna., 1778; also from Hon. Henry Wolcott,
of Wellington, Somersetshire, Eng., also of Dorchester, Mass., U.S.A., 1578-1635; also from
James Clayton, of Middlewitch, County Chester,
Eng., 1680).

Born in Philadelphia, Pa. Sept. 4, 1872; Graduate
of the University of Pennsylvania, 1893; *m* Nov. 10, 1896, Margaret
Jolliffe, elder da. of Nathaniel Bacon Crenshaw, of Philadelphia.

Issue.

i. CLAYTON, Jr., *b* Jan. 28, 1898.

ii. NATHANIEL CRENSHAW, *b* Sept. 16, 1901.

i. ELIZABETH JOLLIFFE, *b* March 30, 1904.

Arms—(for Wolcott) Argent, a chevron between three cross-rooks ermine.
Crest—A bull's head erased argent, ducally gorged, armed and ringed or.

Residence—2012 Pine Street, Philadelphia, Pa.   *Club*—Merion Cricket.
Societies—Penna. Historical, Sons of the Revolution, Colonial Wars.

SHIPPEN, EDWARD, M.D., U.S. Navy,
of Philadelphia (Son of Richard Shippen of
Burlington, and Anna E. Farmer. — Descended
from Edward Shippen, *b* 1639 at Hillham, Yorks.,
Eng.; Mem. of the Ancient and Hon. Artillery
Co. 1659; Speaker of Assembly 1695; Mem. of
the Prov. Council of Pa. 1696-1712; first Mayor of
Phila., *d* 1712; son of W. Shippen, of Methley,
Yorks).

Born in New Jersey, June 18, 1826; *m* Mary Cath.,
da. of John Rodman Paul; Grad. Princeton
Univ. A.M. 1845; Univ. of Penna. M.D.;
Assist. Surg. U.S.N. 1849, Surg. 1861, Med.
Dir. U.S.N. 1876; Gov. Soc. of Col. Wars
of Pa.; Pres. Geneal. Soc. of Pa.; Comp.
Loyal Legion, U.S.

Issue.

i. ANNA, *m* George Willing.
ii. ELIZABETH, *m* Chas. Wheeler Barnes.
iii. KATHERINE, *m* Frederick A. Packard, M.D.
iv. MARGARET, *m* Edwards S. Dunn.

Arms—Argent, on a chevron gules three oak leaves gules.
Crest—A raven holding an oak leaf gules in the beak.   *Motto*—Vigilans.

Residence—2039 Pine Street, Philadelphia.
Societies—Loyal Legion, Colonial Wars, Genealogical and Historical of Penna.,
Fellow College of Physicians Phila., University Club.

NORRIS, ISAAC,
of Bryn Mawr, Pa. (Eldest son of Isaac
Norris, M.D., *b* 1834; *m* 1862, Clara Victoria, da.
of Lemuel Lamb, and Margaretta Carswell, his
wife.—Descended from Isaac Norris, *b* in London,
Eng., 1671; *d* in Phila., 1735; Provincial Councillor
of Pa.; Speaker of the Assembly; Justice for
Phila. County; Mayor of Philadelphia, &c.;
m 1693, Mary Lloyd [Lloyds of Dolobran, Mont-
gomeryshire, Wales], third da. of Gov. Thomas
Lloyd, Pres. of the Council, Keeper of the Great
Seal, Master of the Rolls, and Lieut-Governor of
the Province).

Born at Philadelphia, 1865; Grad. Yale Univ. Ph.B., 1885; Univ. of
Penna. LL.B., 1888; Mem. of Phila. Bar; *m* April 3, 1902, Harriet
Sears, *d* Aug. 18, 1905, eldest da. of Caspar and Elizabeth Clark
(Greene) Crowinshield.

Issue.

i. MARY LLOYD.

Arms—Argent, on a chevron gules, between three falcons' heads erased sable, a
mullet or.
Crest—A falcon's head erased sable.   *Motto*—Ubique patriam reminisci.

Residence—" Fair Hill," Bryn Mawr, Penna.

A MES, Major AZEL, M.D., of Wakefield Mass. (Son of Dea. Azel Ames of Chelsea Mass. 1813-94; *m* 1837 Louisa 1806-65, da. of Lt. Humphrey Lufkin of Chester N.H.; son of Capt. Azel 1783-1842; son of Job 1752-1827; son of Daniel 1712-78; son of John 1672-1756; son of John, *b* at Bridgewater Mass. 1647-1726; son of William Ames, *b* at Bruton, Somersetshire, Eng. 1605, *d* at Braintree Mass. 1654. Also descended from Peter Browne, Francis Cooke, and Richard Warren, passengers in the "Mayflower" 1620).

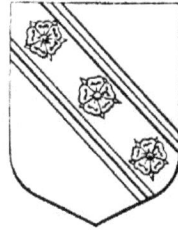

Born at Chelsea Mass. Aug. 16, 1845; Grad. Harvard Univ. Med. School 1871, M.D.; Surg.-Genl. G.A.R.; Mem. Mass. Legislature 1879; Mem. and Secy. Am. Public Health Assn.; Mem. and Secy. Mass. Metrop. Drainage Commission; Editor and publisher Wakefield "Citizen" and Montana "Live-Stock Journal"; Mem. and Secy. U.S. Board Surgeons, Boston, 10 years; 1st Lieut. 2d La. Engineers U.S.A. Civil War; Acting Asst. Surg. U.S.A.; Major and Brigade Surg. U.S.V. Spanish War; Director Vaccination of Porto Rico; Author of "Sex in Industry," "The Work of Local Health Boards," "The 'Mayflower' and her Log," "Elementary Hygiene for the Tropics," "Hist. of the Ames Family," "Some Sanitary Problems of Massachusetts," etc.; *m* 1866 Sarah Dering Thomas, da. of Elijah and Sarah A. (Thomas) Ames of Marshfield Mass.

Issue.

i. Capt. AZEL, *b* Jan. 3, 1871, *m* Bertha Lurene Morrill.

ii. EDWARD WINSLOW, *b* Oct. 29, 1874, *m* Millicent Johnson; U.S. Chargé d'Affaires, Argentine Republic and Chile.

i. LOUISA KIMBALL.

Arms—Argent, on a bend cotised sable three roses of the field.

Motto—Fama candida rosa dulcior.

Residences—24 Yale Ave., Wakefield; and "Rexhame," Marshfield, Mass.

Clubs—Army and Navy, N.Y. City, Army and Navy, Wash D.C., Harvard Union, Cambridge.

Societies—G.A.R., Loyal Legion, Legion Spanish War Veterans, Pilgrim of Plymouth, Amer. Hist. Assn., Webster Hist., N.E. Hist. Geneal., Harvard Univ., Med.-Alumni Assn., Phillips (Andover Mass.) Acad.-Alumni Assn., Assn. Military Surgeons of U.S., Prest. Assn. A. Asst. Surgeons U.S.A., Amer. Public Health Assn., Mass. Med. Soc., Middx. E. Med. Soc., Hon. Mem. Med. Soc. Cal. and Mich., Mem. Amer. Soc. Tropical Med., Natl. Geographic Soc.

D'OYLEY, MARCHIONESS (*née* MACDONALD),
of Paris, France (Eldest da. and co.-h. of
Alastair A. Macdonald, of Keppoch, Inverness,
Scot., *d* Balto., Md., 1858; *m* Annie R., *d* 1849, da.
of Thomas and Margaret (O'Coulter) Walsh, of
Ireland.—Descended from Ivan I., King of the
Isles, who *m* Lady Margaret Stewart, da. of
Robert II., King of Scotland in 1370).

Born at Baltimore; H.I.M. the Sultan of Turkey
conferred, Nov. 7, 1898, the Grand Cross of the
Decoration of the Chefekat : *m* Sept. 8, 1868,
John H. Evans D'Oyley (Marquis D'Oyley), of
Paris. His Holiness Pope Pius IX. conferred
upon her the Grand Cross of the Order of the
Holy Sepulchre.

Issue.

i. REGINALD DONALD, *b* Aug. 9, 1869, *d* May 20, 1889.
ii. GILBERT RAOUL, *b* Feb. 13, 1875; *m* Teresa Agnes Hainsworth.
iii. ALASTAIR IVAN, *b* Feb. 2, 1880, *d* May 26, 1904.

Arms—(For Macdonald) Quarterly, 1st argent, a lion rampant; 2nd or, a hand
in armour holding a cross-crosslet fitchée gules; 3rd or, a lymphad sable
sails furled; 4th vert, a salmon naiant in fesse argent.
Crest—A hand in armour holding a cross-crosslet fitchée gules.
Motto—Air Muir's air Tir.

Residences—Manoir Sans Souci, Bellevue Seine-Oise, France; 25, Rue Franklin,
Paris, France.

OLIVER, CHARLES AUGUSTUS, A.M., M.D.,
of Philadelphia, Pa. (Only son of George
Powell Oliver, A.M., M.D., of Philadelphia,
b February 1, 1824; *d* Feb. 20th, 1884, *m* Maria
Louisa, 1825-99, da. of Don Pedro Nicholas
Suarez, of Corunna, Spain.—Descended from
Nicholas B. Oliver, who settled in the U.S.A.
1778).

Born at Cincinnati, Ohio, December 14, 1853;
Graduate of the University of Pennsylvania;
m June 6, 1888, Mary Schermerhorn, second
daughter of Lewis B. Henry, of New York
City.

Issue.

i. NORRIS SCHERMERHORN, *b* May 19, 1889.
ii. KATHARINE POWELL, *b* April 30, 1892.

Arms—Ermine, on a chief sable three lions rampant argent.
Crest—A lion's head erased ermine, collared and ringed argent.
Motto—Animo et fide.

Residences—1507 Locust St., Phila., "The Elms," Concord, Mass.
Clubs—University, Franklin Inn, National Arts.
Societies—Amer.-Philosophical, Loyal Legion, Foreign Wars.

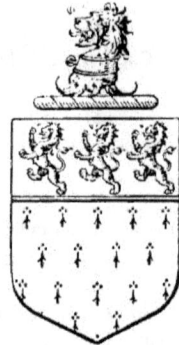

WISTER, RODMAN,
of Phila. (Son of Wm. Wister of "Belfield"
Pa., Sec. N. Pa. R.R., m 1826, Sarah, da. of Wm.
Logan and Mary (Rodman) Fisher of Phila.—Desc.
from Hans Casper Wister, of Hillsbach, Heidelberg; from James Logan 1674-1751 of "Stenton,"
Phila., Sec. to W. Penn, and Acting Gov. 1736-8;
from Owen Jones 1711-93, Col. Sec. and Trea. of Pa.).
Born at "Belfield" Germantown, Aug. 10, 1844;
m Ap. 17, 1872, *Betty, da. of Col. Sam. W.
Black, Gov. of Neb., who m Eliza Ann Irwin,
and gr.-da. of Judge Tho. Mifflin and Eliza
Walker Irwin, and of Dr. John Black, of
Dublin University. Mrs. Rodman Wister is
desc. from John Mackinnon, d 1759, of Mish-
nish, I. of Mull, 14th chief, Clan MacDonald.

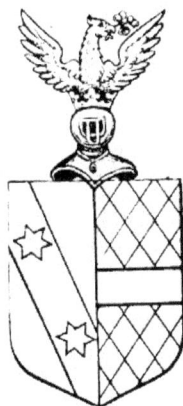

Issue.

i. LANGHORNE HARVEY, b April 12, 1887.   i. EMILY, b 1885, d 1886.
ii. RODMAN MIFFLIN, b June 20, 1890.

Arms—Per pale, dexter argent on a bend azure two mullets of six points argent,
    sinister lozengy argent and sable a bar or.
Crest—Out of a crest coronet or, on a knight's helmet full faced with necklace
    a demi-eagle wings displayed sable, in its mouth a spray of six olives.

Residences—1014 Spruce St., Phila., Pa., and "Shady Hill," Logan, P.O., P.A.
Clubs—Art, Germantown C.C., Milton-on-the-James, Schuylkill Fishing, Belfield
    C.C., Acorn.
Societies—Colonial Wars, Colonial Dames.

BARRY, LLEWELLYN,
of Philadelphia (Son of Llewellyn Fite Barry
of Phila.; adm. Balto. Bar 1850, b 1826, m 1858,
Annie, da. of Joseph Harrison of Phila.—Descended
from John Barry, bro. of Col. Standish Barry of
Maryland, b 1763; in descent from David Barry
of Lemlara co. Cork, Esquire, m Catherine, da. of
Standish Grady, Esq. This family went over to
Ireland with Strongbow, and have been in possession
of Lemlara since the invasion of Henry II. under
the successive Lords Barry, the Viscts. Buttevant
and the Earls of Barrymore).

Born at Paris, France, Jan. 25, 1862; Grad. Univ.
of Penn. B.S. 1884; adm. Phila. Bar July 9,
1887; Mem. 1st Troop Phila. City Cavalry.

Arms—Argent, three bars gamels gules.
Crest—A castle argent, issuing from the top a wolf's head sable.
Motto—Boutez en avant.

Residence—221 South 18th Street, Philadelphia, Penna.
Clubs—Rittenhouse, Phila. Country, Huntingdon Valley Country, Radnor Hunt
    University N.Y., Strollers N.Y.; Kebo Valley; Desert Reading Rooms.
Society—Zeta Psi Fraternity.

TOMPKINS. HAMILTON BULLOCK,
of N.Y. City Son of Tillinghast Tompkins
1795-1860, m Charlotte Merrill 1833-99: son of
Gideon 1761-1837, m Cynthia Brownell: son of
Joseph, b 1712. m Martha Pearce: son of Samuel
1620-1760, m Sarah Coe: son of Nathaniel 1637-
1724. settled at Newport R.I., m 1670 Eliz. Allen.

Born at Brooklyn N.Y. July 30, 1843: Grad.
Hamilton Coll. A.B. 1865. A.M. 1868: N.Y.
Univ. Law Sch. LL.B. 1868; Trustee of
Hamilton Coll.: Dir. Bankers' Loan and In-
vest. Co.: Dir. and Sec. Redwood Lib., New-
port: Vice-Pres. Newport Hist. Soc.: Mem.
Am. Hist. Assoc., &c.: m April 20, 1876, Susan L. Ledyard,
d Oct. 11, 1877.

Arms—Azure, on a chev. betw. three moorcocks close or, three crosses crosslet
sable.
Crest—A unicorn's head erased per fesse argent and or, armed and maned of the
last. gorged with a chaplet of laurel vert.
M.tt—Ne magnum nisi bonum.

———

Residences—1 West 54th Street. N.Y. City: Newport, R.I.
Clubs—University. Grolier. Baltusrol Golf, Newport Reading Room.
Societies—Bar Assoc. N.Y., Am. Bar Assn., Colonial Wars. Colonial Order. Sons
of the Rev'l. Mayflower Descendants. N.Y. Geneal. and biograph. Soc.

DANCY, FRANK BATTLE,
of Atlanta Ga. Son of William Francis Dancy,
1818-60, of Tarborough N.C., m 1 1850, Caroline
Moye, m 2 1858, Mary Eliza Battle: son of
Francis Little, 1770-1848, of Edgecombe Co. N.C.,
m Charlotte Sessums: son of William, d 1776,
m Agatha Little; son of John Dancy of Virginia.

Born at Tarborough N.C. Aug. 4, 1860: Grad. Univ.
of N. Carolina, Class 1881, A.B.; Manager
Georgia Sales Division Virginia-Carolina Chemical Co.; m Dec. 8,
1887, Elizabeth Hanrahan Grimes.

Issue.
i. WILLIAM GRIMES, b Dec. 19, 1889.
ii. FRANK BATTLE, b Nov. 8, 1892.
iii. BRYAN GRIMES, b Oct. 7, 1894.
i. ELIZA BATTLE, b Dec. 25, 1888.

Arms—Argent, on a bend vert three roses or.

———

Residence—63 Ponce de Leon Avenue. Atlanta. Ga.
Clubs—Capital City, Piedmont Driving.
Societies—Amer. Assoc. for the Advancement of Science, Elisha Mitchell Scientific,
Sons of the Revolution. Phi Kappa Sigma Fraternity.

WHEELER, EVERETT PEPPERRELL,

of N.Y. City (Son of David E. Wheeler, 1804-70, Mem. N.Y.S. Legislature; *m* Elizabeth Bartlett,*b* 1811-48, da. of Wm. and Mary Pepperrell (Sparhawk) Jarvis, of Weathersfield, Vt.—Descended from Gen. Sir Wm. Pepperrell, Bt., who com. Colonial forces at Siege of Louisbourg, 1745).

Born in N.Y. City, March 10, 1840; Grad. at N.Y. Coll., B.A., 1856; M.A., 1859; Harvard Univ., B.L., 1859; Chairman N.Y. City C.S. Com.; *m* (1) Nov. 22, 1866, Lydia, L. *d* 1902, da. of Silas H. Hodges, Chairman of B. of Appeal in U.S. Patent Office; *m* (2) April 26, 1904, Alice, da. of Pres. D. C. Gilman.

Issue.

i. David Everett, *b* Nov. 23, 1872; *m* Mabel Blanche Whitney.
i. Annie Lorraine, *m* Gilbert Robert Livingston.
ii. Ethel Jarvis.   iii. Winifred Fay, 1874-96.
iv. Constance Fuller, *m* June 14, 1904, Burges Johnson.

Arms—Pepperrell: Argent, a chevron gules between three pineapples vert; on a canton, azure, a fleur-de-lis or.
Crest—Out of a mural crown argent, with laurel leaves proper in the embrasures, an arm in armour embowed holding a banner argent.
Mottoes—Peperi (above crest); Virtute parta tuemini.

Residences—735 Park Avenue, N.Y. City; New Hamburgh, N.Y.
Clubs—Century, Reform, City, Church, Down Town.
Societies—Alpha Delta Phi, Colonial Wars, New York Historical, East Side House, Civil Service Reform, Phi Beta Kappa.

BLOSS, JAMES ORVILLE,

of N.Y. City (Son of James Orville Bloss, of Rochester, N.Y. 1805-69, *m* 1834 Eliza Ann, 1810-80, da. of Roswell Lockwood; son of Joseph, 1759-1838, *m* Amy Kennedy; son of James, *d* 1776, *m* Elizabeth Clough; son of James, 1702-90; son of Richard, *b* 1659, *m* 1688 Ann Cutler; son of Richard, 1623-65, sailed from Ipswich with his mother Mary in ship "Francis," 1634, *æt.* 11, took the oath at Watertown, Mass., 1652, *m* 1655 Micael, da. of Robert Jennison; his widow *m* John Warren, son of Edmund Blosse, 1587-1681, from England prior to 1634, freeman at Watertown 1639; probably son of Robert Blosse of Reydon, Suffolk [son "Edmund" mentioned in his will pr. Arch. Ipswich 1630], a grandson of Thomas of Reydon, a descendant of Thomas Blosse, of Ipswich, *d* 1342).—*Vide* "Visitation of Suffolk," 1612.

Born at Rochester, N.Y. Sept. 30, 1847.

Arms—Gules, three dragons passant in pale ermine.
Crest—A demi-angel, holding in the dexter hand a griffin's head erased

Residence—912 Fifth Avenue, N.Y. City.
Clubs—Metropolitan, Union League, N.Y.

WARD, REGINALD HENSHAW, Count,
of Twickenham (Son of Andrew H. Ward,
1824-1900; *m* Anna H. W. Field; son of Andrew
H., *b* 1784, *m* Sarah Henshaw, of Leicester, 7th in
desct. from Thomas Henshaw, gent., of L'pool,
1630; son of Thomas, *b* 1758; son of Mj.-Genl.
Artemus, *b* 1727; son of Nahum, *b* 1684; son of
William Ward, *b* 1603, of Sudbury Mass. 1639).

Born at Newton, Mass., April 22, 1862; Hereditary
Count of the Holy Roman Empire; Chancellor-
General, Military Order, French Alliance;
Hereditary Companion Order of the Cincin-
nati; Comp. Mil. Order of Foreign Wars;
Lord of the Manor of North Scarle, Lincoln-
shire; Grand Cross Royal Order of Villa Vicusa of Portugal; Knt.
Comdr. de Numero, R. Order of Carlos III.; Grand Officer Order of
the Sun and Lion; Knt. Comdr., R. Order of Christo; Knt. Comdr.,
R. Order of Takova; Coronation Medal Alphonso XIII.; Jubilee
Medal Carol I. Roumania; Consul General for Roumania; *m* Nov.
26, 1889, Edyth, da. of Horatio Victor Newcomb, of N.Y. City.

Arms—Azure, a cross flory or.
Crest—A wolf's head erased proper, langued gules.
Mottoes—(1) Non nobis solum; (2) Sub cruce salus.

Residence—Fulwell Park, Twickenham, Middlesex, England.
Clubs—Union, Metropolitan of New York City; Country of Boston, Mass.;
Wellington, Bath of London, Travellers of Paris.
Societies—The Mayflower Descendants, Sons of the Revolution, Sons of the
American Revolution.

RUGGLES, Mrs. HENRY STODDARD
(*née* Mary Elizabeth Ryan),
of Boston, Mass. (Only child and heiress of the
late William Ryan, of Boston, Mass., *b* March 7,
1823; *d* March 27, 1848; *m* June 9, 1846, Margaret
Dalton).

Born at Boston, Mass.; *m* Henry Stoddard Ruggles,
of Wakefield, Mass.

Issue.
i. Henry, *b* Feb. 20, 1879; *d* Jan. 24, 1881.
ii. Francis Dunbar, *b* Aug. 9, 1883.
iii. Horace Cheney, *b* June 18, 1887; *d* Feb. 9,
1888.

i. Emmeline.
ii. Mary Rosamond.
iii. Marguerite.
iv. Mabel Lyman.

v. Louisa Kingsley.
vi. Alicia.
vii. Lucia Dalton.
viii. Julia Parker.

Arms—(For Ryan) Gules, on a bend argent six holly leaves in pairs erect proper
Crest—A griffin's head.   *Motto*—Malo mori quam fœdari.

Residences—Boston, Wakefield, and Rochfort, Mass.
Societies—Mary Washington Association, and George Washington Memorial Assn

D E BARY, ADOLPHE,
of N.Y. City (Son of Frederick de Bary,
b Frankfort-on-Main 1815, *d* N.Y. City 1898,
m 1843 Julie Scherpenhausen, *d* 1870, of Crefeldt,
Prussia; son of Christian, *b* 1775, *m* Sophie C. C.
Pilgrim; son of Jean, *b* 1744, *m* Elizabeth A.
de Stockum; son of Issac, *b* 1715; son of Jean,
b 1675; son of François, *b* 1643; son of Israel,
b 1609; son of Pierre; son of Louis, *b* Touray
circa 1530, emigrated to Cologra 1576, settled in
Frankfort 1583; son of Antoine, *b* 1492; son of
Martin 1456; son of Jean; son of Nicolas; son of Gilles;
son of Jacques; son of Jacques; son of Michel; son
of Michel; son of Brice de Bary, Chevalier
Seigneur of Bary, *b* Tournay, Belgium, *circa* 1170).

Born at Crefeldt Oct. 11, 1845, *m* Oct. 30, 1872, Augusta Rawson, da. of
John R. Cecil of N.Y. City.

Issue.

i. FRITZ, *b* Sept. 3, 1888, *d* 1892.

i. LEONIE, *m* George Dillwyn Cross.   ii. MAY.   iii. ANITA.

Arms—Gules, three barbe (fish) heads, two and one argent.

Crest—A star of six points between two eagles' wings argent.

Residence—5 West 52nd Street, N.Y. City.

Clubs—Union League, Riding, N.Y. Athletic, Lawyers, Westchester Country,
Tuxedo, Baltusrol Golf.

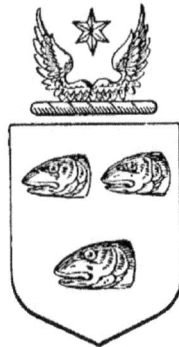

B URNHAM, THOMAS BROWNELL,
of East Grinstead, Sussex (Son of Gordon W.
Burnham, of N.Y. City, 1803-85; *m* (1) 1831, Ann
Griswold Ives, *d* 1847; *m* (2) 1851, Maria Louisa
Brownell, *d* 1883; son of Jedediah 1761-1828; son
of Ebenezer 1722-88; son of Ebenezer, *b* 1691;
son of Josiah 1662-92; son of Deacon John Burnham
1620-94 [brother of Thos. of Hartford, Ct.], settled
at Ipswich, Mass., 1635, a descendant of the
Burnham's of Hatfield Court, Herefordshire).

Born at N.Y. City, Jan. 30, 1866; Director of Am.
Brass Co., Benedict and Burnham Mfg. Co.,
Waterbury Watch Co., and Am. Pin Co., etc.;
Chairman, Farman Auto., Co., Ltd., London;
m (1) 1885, Agnes Havemeyer, 1867-93; *m* (2)
Feb. 9, 1899, Edith, da. of Charles Crosland, of Huddersfield, Yorks.

Issue.
(*By 1st m.*)

i. GORDON LeROY, *b* Dec. 18, 1886.

Arms—Quarterly, 1 and 4 gules, a chevron between three lions' heads erased or;
2 and 3 (Brownell), ermine, on a chevron cotised sa. three escallops or.

Crest—A leopard's head gorged with a coronet ppr.

Motto—Adversis major par secundis.

Residence—Plaw Hatch, East Grinstead, Sussex.

Clubs—Union, N.Y. Yacht, Orleans, Automobile, Sandown, Kempton, Royal
London Yacht, Automobile (France).

EMMONS, SAMUEL FRANKLIN,
of Washington, D.C. (Son of Nathl. H.
Emmons, 1796-1878, of Boston, *m* 1828, Elizth.W.
Wales, 1809-90; son of Samuel, 1755-1836; son of
Samuel, 1733-1816; son of Nathl., Painter, 1703-40;
son of Nathl., 1670-1721 ; son of Samuel, 1635-85 ;
son of Thomas Emmons, of Newport, R.I., 1638 ;
d 1664).

Born at Boston, Mass., March 29, 1841 ; U.S.
Geolog. Sur. ; Gen. Sec. 5th Internl. Cong. of
Geologists, Wash., 1891 ; Grad. Harvard
Univ. A.B., A.M., 1861 ; Ecole Impèriale des
Mines, Paris ; Berg-Akademie Freiberg ; *m* (1)
1876,Weltha A. Steeves, *d* 1888 ; *m* 1889, Sophie
Dallas, *d* 1896, da. of Francis Markoe, Chief
of Diplomatic Bureau S. Dept., U.S.A., and Mary G., da. of Virgil
Maxcy, U.S. Min. to Belgium, Solr. to U.S. Treasury : *m* (2) 1903
Mrs. M. Ogden Jones (Suzanne F. Earle).

Arms—Or, a chevron azure; on a canton of the second a boar's head erased
betw. three fleur-de-lis or.

Crest—A boar's head erased.   *Motto*—Pro Cristo sapiens et fidus.

Residence—1721 "H" Street, N W. Washington, D.C.
Clubs—Century, University, of N.Y.; Metropolitan, Chevy Chase, of Wash.
Societies—Nat. Acad. of Sciences, Am. Philosophical of Phila., Geol of London,
Geol. of Am., Geol. of Wash., Wash. Acad. of Sciences, Am. Inst. of
Mining Engrs., Colorado Scientific, Soc. des Sciences Naturelles.

BRADHURST, AUGUSTUS MAUNSELL,
of N.Y. (Son of Henry M. Bradhurst of
"Pinehurst," N.Y.1822-94, *m* Mrs.Elizabeth Noyes,
da. of Felix Tracy of Oramel, N.Y. ; son of John
Maunsell, 1782-1855, Capt."Bradhurst's Regulars"
War 1812, son of Saml. of Pinehurst 1749-1826,
in N.J. Mil. Rev. War, *m* Mary, da. of Capt. Richard
Smith H.M.S., niece of Gen. John Maunsell and
grand-da. of Richard Stillwell of N.Y. ; son of Sam.
1727-62; son of Samuel 1700-39, *m* Anna, da. of
Hon. Thos. Pell ; son of Jonathan Broadhurst of
Derrington Staffordshire, H. Sheriff of Albany Co.
N.Y. 1700-2).

Born at "Pinehurst," N.Y. Sept. 17, 1865 ; Educated at Christchurch, Oxford ; *m* June 24, 1893,
Minna Evangeline Page, da. of Ch. P. Wood
(son of Sir John Page Wood, Bt., and nephew
of the late Lord Hatherley) of Wakes Colne
Hall, Essex, and Minna, da. of Thos. White of Berechurch, Essex,
and grand-da. of Sir G. H. Smith, Bart. of Upton (extinct).

Issue.

i. CHRISTINE EVANGELINE MINNA ELIZABETH.

Arms—Azure, fretty of eight pieces, raguly or.

Crest—A dexter arm embowed in mail holding in the hand proper a spiked club or.

Motto—Sapere et tacere.

Residence—Rivenhall Place, Essex, England.
Society—Colonial Order of the Acorn

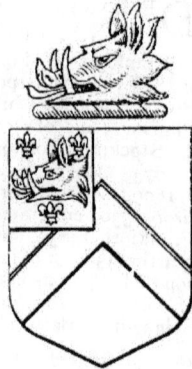

SHUFELDT, ROBERT WILSON, M.D.
of N.Y. City (Son of Rear-Adm. Robert W.
Shufeldt, U.S.N., 1822-85 ; m Oct. 16, 1847, Sarah
Hutchins, d 1872, da. of the Rt. Rev. John
Abercrombie, Rector of Christ Ch. and St. Paul's,
of Phila.—Descended from the family of Zufeld, of
Newburgh, N.Y., 1645).

Born at N.Y. City, Dec. 1, 1850 ; Naturalist and
Author of numerous writings ; Capt.'s Sec.,
U.S. Gunboat, "Proteus," 1864 ; First Lt. Med.
Corps. U.S.A., 1876 ; Capt. 1881 ; Maj., 1904 ;
in Charge of Section, Comparative Anatomy,
Army Med. Mus., 1882 ; Retired 1891 ; Hon.
Curator Smithsonian Inst., Wash. ; Associate
in Comparative Anatomy, U.S. Nat. Mus. ; Judge, Chicago
Exposition ; m (1) Sept. 12, 1876, Catharine, da. of Welles J.
Babcock, of Hartford, Ct. ; (2) Sept. 4, 1895, Florence, da. of John
W. Audubon, of N.Y. City ; (3) Mar. 14, 1898, Alfhild D. Lowum,
da. of Anders M. Evensen, of Christiana.

Issue.
i. ROBERT WILSON, (3rd) b June 7, 1877 ; drowned July 11, 1892.
ii. PERCY WELLES, b Dec. 27, 1879.
i. SARAH ABERCROMBIE.   ii. CATHARINE, d May 5, 1902, Æt. 13.

Arms—Or, a chevron engrailed gules between three boars' heads erased azure.
Crest—A fox's head erased proper.   Motto—Semper vigilans.

Residence—471 West 145th St., New York City, N.Y.
Clubs—Alpha Delta Phi, Cornell Chapter, Cornell University, Ithaca, New York.
Societies—Zoological of London ; L'Alliance Scientifique Universelle de France,
Paris ; Società Italiana d'Antropologia, Etnologia, e Psicologia Comparata,
Florence, Italy ; Fellow Am. Ornithol. Union. U.S. Am. and British for
Psychical Research, Am Naturalists. etc., etc.

BALCH, THOMAS WILLING,
of Philadelphia (Son of Thomas and Emily
(Swift) Balch of Philadelphia.—Descended from
John Balch of Maryland 1658; 6th in descent
from Captain Charles Willing 1710-54, who commanded a Company Associated Regiment of Philadelphia Foot under Colonel Abraham Taylor ; 8th
from Edward Shippen, 1st Mayor of Philadelphia and
Acting Governor of Pennsylvania ; 9th from Acting-
Governor Robert Brooke of Maryland).

Born at Philadelphia, Pa. ; Graduated at Harvard
University 1890 ; Member of the Philadelphia
Bar.

Arms—Barry of six or, and azure ; on a bend engrailed gules three spear heads
argent.
Crest—A demi-griffin proper.   Motto—Ubi libertas, ibi patria.

Residence—1412 Spruce Street, Philadelphia.
Clubs—Philadelphia, Barge.   Societies—The American Philosophical.

BRERETON, THOMAS JOHN,
    of Chambersburg, Pa. (Eldest son of Capt.
Thos. J. Brereton, U.S. O. Corps, distinguished
at West Point and in Mexican War; *m* 1854,
Amelia M., da. of Hon. Harmer Denny of Pittsburgh,
Mem. of Pa. Legislature, M.C., and of the Constitutional Convention, 1837–38, and Elizabeth F.
O'Hara, da. of Gen. James O'Hara, U.S.Q.M.G.
[Ensign, Coldstream Gds., son of Maj. John O'Hara,
of the Irish Brigade in France, and related to the
O'Haras of Tyrawley, Ireland, who traced their
ancestry to the ancient Milesian Kings of Ireland];
gr.-da. of Maj. Ebenezer Denny, original mem. of
the Soc. of the Cincinnati, distinguished in cam-
paigns against the Indians, *m* Nancy, da. of Capt. John Wilkins, of
Carlisle, Pa., a Revol'n. Officer, Aunt of Hon. Wm. Wilkins, Mem. of
Legislature, U.S. Senator, Minr. to Russia, M.C., Sec. of War, and
Judge of the U.S. Dis. Court; and sister of Gen. John Wilkins, an Officer
of the Revol., distinguished during the Whiskey Insurrection, and prominent in the history of Western Pa. Capt. Brereton was son of John A.
Brereton, Surg. U.S.N., who served through War of 1812 on U.S.
frigate "Congress," grandson of Thos. Brereton, who came to America
in 1761 in command of the privateer "Betty," and settled in Baltimore,
Md. [*m* 1781, Sarah, da. of Major Thos. J. Marshall, of Col. Gist's Regt.
of Md. Vols., descended from John Marshall, of Northampton Co., Va.,
1635], gt.-grandson of Thos. Brereton, of Dublin, who was descended
from Sir W. Brereton, Lord High Marshal and Chief Justice of Ireland
under Henry VIII.—Descended from Sir Ralph Brereton, of Brereton,
Cheshire, *temp*. William Rufus, whose ancestor, Gislebert de Venables,
came to England in the retinue of Hugh Lupus, afterwards Earl of
Chester. The parent stem, whose head bore the title Lord Brereton of
Leighlin since the time of Elizabeth, became extinct in 1720; the present
head of the family is Major Wm. R. Brereton, of Co. Kildare, Ireland).

Born at Pittsburg, Pa., Sept. 21, 1858; Grad. at Columbia Coll., 1879;
    Sch. of Mines, Columbia Coll., 1883; *m* Dec. 31, 1884, Frances, da.
    of Wm. H. Lindsay, and Jane Seton, niece of Archbp. Magee, of
    Dublin, and cousin of Archbp. Magee, of York, and descended in the
    eldest line from the family of Seton, one of the most ancient and
    famous of the old Scotch nobility.

Issue.

i. THOMAS, *b* Dec. 2, 1885.	iv. O'HARA DENNY, *b* Aug. 21, 1892.
ii. SETON LINDSAY, *b* Mar. 5, 1889.	i. AMELIA.
iii. FRANCIS MARSHALL, *b* Aug. 19, 1889.	

Arms—Argent, two bars sable.

Crest—Out of a ducal coronet a bear's head proper, muzzled or.

Motto—Opitulante Deo.

Residence—Chambersburg, Penna.

FRENCH, AMOS TUCK,
of Tuxedo Park (Son of Francis Ormond
French, 1837-93 [his two gr.-fathers being Hon.
Dan. French, Atty.-Genl. S.N.H., and Ch. Justice
Wm. M. Richardson, Mem. of Congress, 1811-14];
Grad. Harvard. Univ., 1857, LL.B. 1859; admtd.
N.Y. Bar, 1860; Pres. of Manhattan Trust Co.;
m Ellen, da. of Hon. Amos Tuck, Mem. of Congress,
1847-53. F. O. French had two daurs., Elizth., the
present Lady Cheylesmore, and Ellen, who m Alf.
G. Vanderbilt.—Descended from Edward French,
b Eng., came to Amer. 1636, an original settler of
Salisbury, Mass.).

Born at Boston, Mass., July 20, 1863; Graduated
Harvard Univ., 1885; Vice-Pres. Manhattan
Trust Co., N.Y.; also a Director, Northern Pacific Ry. Co., Northern
Securities Co., and Chicago Burlington and Quincy Ry. Co.; Dir. of C.I.
and L.R.R. Co.; Treas. of Knickerbr. Club; m Dec. 2, 1885, Pauline,
da. of Stuyvesant LeRoy, of N.Y.

Issue.

i. FRANCIS ORMOND, b Nov. 27, 1888.   i. PAULIN LeRoy.

ii. STUYVESANT LeRoy, b Aug. 19, 1895.   ii. JULIA STELL.

iii. EDWARD TUCK, b May 3, 1899. iv. AMOS TUCK, Jr., b Sept. 10, 1901.

Arms—Azure, a chevron between three boars' heads or.

Crest—A boar's head erased.   Motto—Tuebor.

Residences—Tuxedo Park, New York; and Chester, New Hampshire.

Clubs—Union, Knickerbocker, Metropolitan, Tuxedo, Harvard, New York Yacht
Club, Coney Island Jockey Club, Newport Reading Room, etc.

CORNWALL, EDWARD EVERETT,
of Brooklyn N.Y. (Son of Nathaniel Oliver
Cornwall, M.A., M.D., of Portland Ct., m Mary
Ann, da. of Brackett Mortimer and Mary Ann
(Stocking) West [descended from Francis West,
b 1606, from Salisbury, Eng., d Duxbury, Mass.
1692, and George Stocking in New Eng. 1633]:
son of David 1790-1874, m Maria A. Attwood; son
of Nathaniel 1750-1823, m (1) Jerusha Foote, m (2)
Anna Deming; son of William 1727-50, m Sarah
Shepherd; son of William 1692-1755, m Esther
Ranny; son of William 1671-1747, m Esther, gd.-da. of Andrew Ward, Dep.-
Gov. of Conn. 1634; son of William 1641-91, m Mary Bull; son of William,
emigrated to New Eng. before 1633, one of the original proprietors of
Middletown Ct., Representative in the Colonial Legislature 1654-64).

Born at Buenos Aires, S.A., July 2, 1866; Grad. Wesleyan Univ. and
Columbia Univ. Ph.B. 1887, M.D. 1890.

Arms—Ermine, a lion rampant gules crowned or within a bordure engrailed
sable bezantée.

Residence—1239 Pacific Street, Brooklyn, N.Y.

Clubs—University, Invincible.

Societies—Sons of the Am. Revol., L.I. Hist., Chi Psi, Phi Beta Kappa, Am.
Med. Assoc., &c.

B IGELOW, MELVILLE MADISON, LL.D.,
   of Cambridge Mass. (Son of Rev. Wm. Enos
Bigelow of Flint Mich. 1820-1890, *m* Daphne
Florence 1824-1878, da. of Rev. Seth and Lucy
(Hoyt) Mattison of Batavia N.Y.; son of Job
Gardner 1792-1838 ; son of Jabez 1760-1829 ; son of
Jabez 1726-1808 ; son of Gersham 1701-1789 ; son
of Joshua 1654-1745 ; son of John Bigelow of
Watertown Mass. 1617-1703).

*In a deed dat. 1642 he is named " John Bageley," a descendant of
the Baguleys of Baguley Hall, Cheshire; emi. from Wrentham,
Suffolk. (See pedigree through other lines in Her. Coll., Lond.,
" Arundel," vol. iii.).*

Born at Eaton Rapids Mich. Aug. 2, 1846 ; Grad.
   Univ. of Michigan, and Harvard Univ. A.B.,
   LL.B., A.M., Ph.D., LL.D.; *m* Nov. 10, 1898,
   Alice Bradford, da. of Geo. S. Woodman, M.D., and Jane, da. of
Timothy Gridley, Dean of Boston Univ., Law School.

Issue.
(By 1st m.)
i. Leslie Melville, A.B. Harvard, 1895, *b* 1873, *d* 1898.
i. Ada Hawthorn, *b* 1870, *d* 1876.   ii. Charlotte Gray, *b* 1871, *d* 1876.
Arms—Or, three lozenges azure.
Crest—A ram's head erased azure, charged with three lozenges and attired or.

Residences—200 Brattle Street, Cambridge, Mass.; North Woodstock, N.H.
Club—Hon. Mem. Athenæum of London, 1889-94-97, 1906.
Societies—Phi Beta Kappa, Mass. Historical.

S TODDARD, FRANCIS RUSSELL,
   of New York City (Son of Isaac N. Stoddard
1812-91, *m* 1836 Martha Le B. 1816-1900, da.
of Col. John Boies and Mary H. (Le Baron)
Thomas ; son of Col. Elijah, *b* 1785 ; son of Ezekiel,
b 1762 ; son of Jeremiah, *b* 1738 ; son of Jeremiah,
b 1709 ; son of Jeremiah, *b* 1683 ; son of Samuel,
b 1640 ; son of John Stoddard, *d* 1661, of Hingham
Mass. Also from Hon. William Thomas, 1573-1651.
Asst. Gov. of Plymouth Colony 1642).

Born at Plymouth, Mass., Jan. 26, 1844 ; Assessor
   and Cashier of Boston ; Trea. Sherwood
   Manufg. Co.; Banker ; grad. Harvard Univ.,
   A.B. 1866, A.M. 1871 ; *m* April 8, 1868, Mary
F., da. of Jacob Baldwin of Boston.

Issue.
i. Francis Russell, Jr., *b* July 26, 1877.
ii. Mary Baldwin, *m* Oct. 2, 1895, Geo. D. Yeomans, of N.Y.
i. Martha Le Baron, 1870-90.
Arms—Sable, three estoiles within a bordure argent.
Crest—A demi-horse ermine environed round the body with a ducal coronet or.
Motto—Festina lente.
Residences—New York City ; Cedarhurst, L.I.
Clubs—University, Boston; Art, Boston.
Societies—Mayflower Descendants, Colonial Wars, Sons of the American Revolution, Pilgrim of Plymouth.

E LLIOT, DANIEL GIRAUD,
of Chicago (Son of Geo. T. and Rebecca
(Giraud) Elliot.—Desc'd from Henry Elliot, in
K. Philip's War 1675, son of Joseph Elliot, in
Am. 1660; 7th fr. Thos. Welles, Gov. of Ct. 1654,
a desct. of Robt. de Welles of Essex, b 1145, son
of Wm. de Vallibus; 8th fr. Richd. Treat, Gov. of
Ct.; 4th fr. Asa Elliot, of Crown Point 1758; 8th
fr. Matthew Marvin of Hartford Ct.; 7th fr. John
Holliston of Mass. 1644; 7th. fr. William Goodrich,
of Ct. 1660).

Born at N.Y., Mar. 7, 1835; Sc.D., Columbia
University; Ex.-P. Am. Ornithologists'
Union; Hon. Cur. of Zoology Field Mus.
Nat. Hist.; Knt. C. Cr. of Italy, Fredc. of
Wurtemburg, Chas. III. of Spain; Knt. of
Fran. Jos. of Austria, Albert of Saxony, &c.; *m* Nov. 2, 1858, Ann Eliza,
da. of David and Ann Eliza (McIntyre) Henderson of Albany, N.Y.

Issue.

i. MARGARET HENDERSON.   ii. CLARA OGDEN, *m* Kenneth R. Macpherson.

Arms—Azure, a fesse or.

Crest—Out of a ducal coronet or, a griffin's head wings endorsed sable charged
with five hurts. ——— *Motto*—Non sine Deo.

Residences—New York City. N.Y.; Murray Bay, Quebec, Ca.

Club—Century of N.Y.

Societies—Colonial Wars, Fel. Royal Soc. of Edin., Zool. of London and France,
Leopoldina Carolina Acad. Germany, R. Acad. Soc. Lisbon, Acad. Nat.
Soc. Phila., Nat. Hist. Boston, Acad. Nat. Soc. N.Y., Hon. Mem. Linn. Soc.,
N.Y. Zool. Soc., Nutt. Ornith. Club, etc., etc.

F LINT, CHARLES RANLETT,
of N.Y. City (Son of Benjamin, b 1813; son
of Benj., b 1783; son of Jessie, b 1746; son of
Thomas, b 1705; son of Thos., b 1678; son of
Capt. Thos., son of Thos. Flint, from Wales 1642,
settled at Salem, Mass.).

Born at Thomaston, Me., Jan. 24, 1850; Grad.
Polytechnic Inst., Brookline 1868; organised
Gilchrist, Flint & Co. 1871; estd. W. R.
Grace & Co. 1872, of Peru, Chili and San
Francisco; was instrumental in organising Am.
Chicle Co., Natnl. Starch Co., Sloss Sheffield
Steel and Iron Co., Am. Bobbin and Shuttle
Co., Am. Caramel Co., Rubber Goods Mfg.
Co., etc.; Consul for Rep. of Chili 1876; Consul of Nicaragua in N.Y.
1886; Pres. U.S. Elec. Lighting Co. 1880; of Flint & Co. 1885;
U.S. Delegate to the Intern. Conference at Washington 1889-90;
Confidential Agent of the Department of State in negotiating the first
Reciprocity Treaty under the Aldrich Amendment, etc.; *m* Emma
Kate, da. of Joseph Ferris Simmons of N.Y. City.

Arms—Vert, a chevron between three flint stones argent.

Crest—An estoile or.   *Motto*—Sine Manulâ.

Residence—4 East 36th Street, N.Y. City.

Clubs—Century, Union, Metro., Riding, Robbins Island, Liberty Hill, Accomack,
So. Side, N.Y. Yacht, Country, Midday, St. Stephans, London.

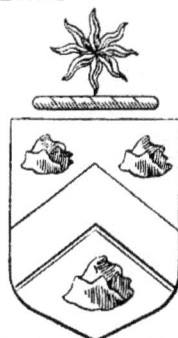

FOULKE, WILLIAM,

of N.Y. City (Eldest son of William Foulke, 1812-88, of N.Y., *b* Curaçao, W.I.; *m* 1846 Mary Elizabeth, 1826-82, da. of Abram Keteltas and Cath. B. (Beekman) Fish; grandson of Joseph Foulke, 1769-1852, and Charlotte, 1785-1846 [da. of Pierre Louis Francis Brion and Maria Detrox, sister to Adml. John P. Louis Brion, Colombia Navy]; gt.-grandson of Foulks, of Piscataway, N.J., mem. of "The N.J. Line" War of Revol., *d* 1799, and Sarah, 1733-99, da. of Joseph and Priscilla (Langstaff) Sutton; gt.-gt.-grandson of John Foulks, of Easton, Talbot Co., and Cecil Co., Md., *d* 1752, and Mary, da. of John Frazier; desc'd. from James Fowke, of Staffordshire—James, and his sons, James, Jr., and Thomas, received grants of land at Accomac, Va., 1664-71—James was a desc'dt. of Roger Fowke and Eliz. Wybaston, of Brewood, Staff., eldest son of William, said to be desc'd. from Fulk-Foulques, Counts of Anjou).

Arms—1st and 4th vert, a fleur-de-lis argent; 2nd and 3rd a chevron gules between three cinquefoils azure.

Crest – A dexter arm embowed vested vert, cuffed argent, in the hand proper an arrow or, feathered of the second, pheoned azure.

Motto—Arma tuentur pacem.

———

Clubs—Union, Seawanhaka Corinthian Yacht, Church.
Societies—St. Nicholas, Colonial Wars.

———

CURRIER, Mrs. NELLIE MAY (*née* Ross),

of Newburyport, Mass. (Daughter of the late Andrew F. Ross, of Newburyport, *b* June 23, 1842, *d* Oct. 26, 1898, *m* Dec. 3, 1865, Jennie, da. of James and Rhoda (Wells) Berry.—Descended from Hugh Ross, of Berwick, Maine, 1725).

Born at Scarboro', Maine; *m* June 23, 1898, Joseph Hilton Allen Currier, of Boston, Mass.

Issue.

i. Ross Hamilton, *b* Dec. 1, 1899.
i. Dorothy, *b* March 23, 1902.

Arms—(for Ross) Within a bordure or, charged with three leopards' faces gules, a field of the second thereon as many lions rampant argent.

Crest—A dexter arm encased in armour wielding a sword proper.

Motto—Constant and true.

———

Residence—174 High Street, Newburyport, Mass.
Society—Daughters of the American Revolution.

BRYANT, WILLIAM SOHIER, M.D., of N.Y. City (3rd son of Henry Bryant, M.D., of Boston Mass. 1820–67, Physician, Naturalist and Surgeon of 20th Mass. Regiment 1861, m Elisabeth Brimmer Sohier of the senior male line of the Counts de Vermandois, in the male line from Charlemagne. The same origin which the illustrious house of Saint Simon has in the female line. This branch of the Sohier family might, by the right of primogeniture, claim the now lapsed but proud title of the Counts de Vermandois, allied in ancient days with the most powerful families of France, and more recently in America with the Lamberts, an ancient (Norman-English and Irish) family, connected through Henry I. of France, with the very ancient descent of Anne of Russia; son of John, merchant, 1786–1865, m Mary Cleveland Smith, daughter of the Rev. John Smith, Prof. of dead languages, Dartmouth College, m Mary Cleveland; son of Capt. (Revolution) John 1742–1816, m Hannah Mason, daughter of Colonel (Revolution) David Mason, m Hannah Symmes; he descended in the female line from Sir James Warr; son of John 1718–58, m Lois Brown; son of John 1689–1722, m Catharine Noakes; son of William 1655–87, settled in Boston; son of Edmund of Barbados, d 1661; son of Thomas Bryant, b in England, d in Barbados, W.I. 1661, m Martha Chaplain).

Born at Boston Mass. May 15, 1861; Grad. Harvard Univ. A.B. 1884, M.A. and M.D. 1888; specialist in ear, nose, and throat diseases; late Major and Brigade-Surgeon of Volunteers; m Sept. 1, 1887, Martha Lyman Cox, descended in the female line from the de Peyster and the Lyman families, the latter allied with the Lamberts, an ancient Norman-English family, connected through Henry I. of France with the very ancient ancesty of Anne of Russia.

Issue.

i. WILLIAM SOHIER, b Dec. 1896.
i. MARY CLEVELAND.
ii. ELIZABETH SOHIER.
iii. ALICE DE VERMANDOIS.
iv. JULIA COX.
v. GLADIS PLANTAGENET.

Arms—(for Sohier) Gules, a mullet argent.
Crest—A cross or, between antlers argent.
Motto—Stella xpi duce.

Residences—57 W. 53rd Street, N.Y.City; Cohasset, Mass. Club—Harvard of N.Y.
Societies—Naval and Military Order of Span.-Amer. War, Order of Foreign Wars

BECKWITH, Mrs. MARGARETTA (*née* PIERREPONT), of N.Y. City (da. of Hon. Edwards Pierrepont, 1813-92, of Hurst Pierrepont, N.Y., U.S. Min. Court of St. James; *m* Margaretta, da. of Saml. Aug. and Margaretta (Duffield) Willoughby of Brooklyn.—Descended from Rev. James Pierrepont, 1659-1714, Minister at New Haven, Ct., *m* Mary Hooker, grand-da. of Rev. Thomas Hooker, one of the founders of Connecticut, 1635).

Born at Brooklyn, N.Y., May 20, 1847; *m* June 1, 1871, Leonard Forbes Beckwith, Chief Engineer of N.Y. City Telephone Company, *b* 1844, *d* 1895, descended from Matthew Beckwith, one of the first settlers of Hartford, Ct., 1642.

Issue.

i. EDWARD, PIERREPONT, *b* April 27, 1877.
ii. SIDNEY FORBES, *b* Feb. 5, 1884.
i. MARGUERITE, *m* June 1, 1894, Prof. Rudolph E. Brunnow.
ii. MARY PIERREPONT.

Arms (Beckwith)—Argent, a chevron gules fretty or, betw. three hinds' heads erased or ; on a chief engr. gules a saltire betw. two roses argent.

Crest—An antelope ppr., in mouth a branch vert.

Motto—Joie en bien.

Residences—Garrison-on-Hudson ; Cazenovia, N.Y.

PIERREPONT, HENRY EVELYN, of Brooklyn (Son of Henry E. Pierrepont, 1808-88, *m* Anna M. Jay; son of Hezekiah B., 1768-1838; son of John, 1740-1805; son of Hezekiah, 1712-41; son of the Rev. James, 1659-1714; son of the Hon. John, 1617-82, of Roxbury, Mass. ; son of James, *d* 1648 ; son of Sir George Pierrepont, of Holme-Pierrepont, Notts., Eng.).

Born at Brooklyn, N.Y., Dec. 9, 1845; Grad. Columbia Coll., B.A., A.M., 1867; *m* Dec. 9, 1869, Ellen, da. of Abiel A. Low, Pres. of N.Y. Chamber of Commerce.

Issue.

i. HENRY E., Jr., *b* Sept. 7, 1873, *d* March 3, 1903.
ii. ROBERT L. *b* Aug. 12, 1876, *m* Kathryn I. Reed.
iii. RUTHERFURD S., *b* July 5, 1882.   iv. SETH L., *b* Dec. 25, 1844.
i. ANNE L., *m* Lea McIlvaine Luquer, of New York.
ii. ELLEN L., *m* R. Burnham Moffat, of New York.

Arms—Argent, semée of cinquefoils gules a lion rampant sable.
Crest—A fox passant proper.   *Motto*—Pie repone te.

Residence—216 Columbia Heights, Brooklyn, N.Y.   *Club*—Hamilton.
Society—Sons of the Revolution.

COOK, HENRY FRANCIS,
of N.Y. City and Sag Harbor N.Y. (Son of Henry Cook of London 1814-87, m Eloise A., da. of Benj. Huntting of Sag Harbor ; son of Harry 1784-1860 ; son of Wm. Ely Cook, b 1756, d at Brighton, Sussex, Eng., 1846, who is supposed to have been descended from Oliver Cooke of South Molton, Devonshire, viva 1620, who was sixth from Walter Cooke of Exeter, 1387).

Born in Brooklyn N.Y. Sept. 11, 1855 ; m Nov. 15, 1883, Lena Marianne, da. of Joseph Fahys of Brooklyn.

Issue.
i. JOSEPH FAHYS, b April 25, 1888.
ii. HENRY, b Mar. 24, 1892.
iii. FRANCIS HOWELL, b Mar. 9, 1899.
  i. EDITH ELOISE. iii. MARIA FAHYS.
  ii. MADELEINE HUNTTING.

Arms—Ermine, on a bend cotised gules three cats-a-mountain argent.
Crest—A demi-leopard guardant or, supporting a branch of oak fructed or.
Motto—Tu ne cede malis sed contra audentior ito (Virgil).

Residences—N.Y. City ; Sag Harbor, N.Y.
Clubs—Union League, Down Town.
Societies—Member N.Y. Chamber of Commerce, Brooklyn Inst. of Arts and Sciences, Colonial Wars. Sons of the Revolution, Pilgrim.

NEWHALL, CHARLES LYMAN,
of Southbridge) Son of Otis Newhall 1798-1886, of Spencer ; son of Reuben 1770-1858 ; son of Allen 1743-94 ; son of John b 1714 ; son of Daniel 1685-1760 ; son of Thomas 1653-1728 ; son of Thomas 1630-87 ; son of Thomas Newhall, d 1674, settled in Lynn, Mass., 1630. Also descd. from Richard Dana, b cir. 1617 ; William Wood, b Matlock, Eng., 1582 ; John Barnard, b 1605 ; Capt. Edwd. Johnson, b 1598 ; Nicholas Shapleigh, about 1600, of Kingsweare, Devon).

Born at Spencer, Mass., Oct. 1, 1834 ; Printer for Admiral in U.S. Navy 1861-67 ; m 1866, Josephine E. Augusta, d 1880, da. of Thomas and Rebecca Robinson, alias José Alessandra, of Pensacola, Fla.

Issue.
i. REBECCA, b and d 1867. ii. MABEL ALICIA, b 1870, d 1871.
iii. FLORENCE DANA, b 1872, m April 25, 1896, Isaac S. Thompson, of N.Y. City.

Arms—Azure, three plates or, on each an ermine spot sable.
Crest—A cross crosslet fitchée azure. Motto—Diligentia ditat.

Residence—Southbridge, Mass.
Societies—G.A.R., Masons, Kearsage Assn. of Naval Veterans, N.E. Hist. Genea., Bostonian. Sons of the Amer. Revol., Nat. Genealogical Society, etc.

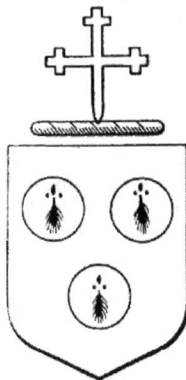

GASTON, WILLIAM ALEXANDER,
of Boston (Son of W. Gaston, 1820-94,
A.M., LL.D., Mem. of Ho. of Rep., Mass., Mem.
Mass. State Senate, Mayor of Roxbury, and
Boston; Gov. of Mass., Pres. Mass. Bar Assn.,
m Louisa A., da. of Laban S. Beecher; son of
Alexander, 1772-1856; son of John, 1750-1805;
son of John, *b* Ireland, 1703, *d* 1783, *m* Jennet, da.
of Rev. Alex. Thompson of Scotland ; son of John,
b Scot., 1650, went to Ireland ; son of Jean Gaston,
b France *cir.* 1600, a Huguenot, settled in Scotland).

Born at Roxbury, May 1, 1859; Grad. Roxbury
Lat. Sch. 1876, Harvard Univ., A.B., 1880;
on Mil. Staff of Gov. Wm. E. Russell,
m April 9, 1892, May Davidson, da. of
Hamilton D. Lockwood of Boston.

Issue.

i. Infant Son, *b* and *d* Aug. 31, 1893.
ii. WILLIAM, *b* Nov. 12, 1896.
iii. JOHN, *b* Dec. 10, 1898.

i. RUTH.
ii. HOPE.

Arms—Chequy, argent and gules, three escallops in bend or.
Crest—An owl sable.   *Motto*—Fama semper vivit.

Residences—97 Bay State Rd, Boston; Fox Islds. Thoroughfare, Nth. Havan, Me.
and Barre, Mass.
Clubs—Somerset, Algonquin, Univ., Exchange, Country, Athletic, Puritan, Tennis
and Racquet, City, Commercial, Curtis, Harvard and Metropolitan of N.Y.
Societies—Bostonian, Roxbury, Military, Mass. Bar Assn., Mass. Horticultural.

BURT, STEPHEN SMITH, M.D.,
of N.Y. City (Eldest son of Oliver Teall Burt,
1824-87, of Syracuse, N.Y., Pres. of the Onondaga
Solar Salt Co., Pres. of the Central City Bank,
Vice-Pres. of the Ontario Steamboat Co., *m* Rebecca,
da. of Edward and Ann (Carr) Johnston ; son of
Aaron, 1792-1848; son of Aaron, 1759-92; son of
Aaron, 1717-92; son of Joseph, 1673-1759; son of
David, 1632 90; son of Henry Burt, who settled
in America, *circa* 1635, *d* 1662, one of the founders
of Springfield, Mass., 1640).

Born at Oneida, N.Y., Nov. 1, 1850; Prof. of Medicine
and Physical Diagnosis, N.Y.; Post Grad. Med.
Schl. Attg. Physician N.Y. Post. Grad. Hospital;
Hon. M.A. Yale Univ., 1890 ; Educated at
Cornell Univ., Coll. of Phy's and Surg's, M.D., 1875, and at Roosevelt
Hospital ; Graduated at Med. Dept. of Columbia Univ., 1875.

Arms—Argent, on a chevron gules, betw. three bugle horns sable stringed of the
second, as many crosses crosslet fitchée or.
Crest—A bugle horn as in Arms. _____
Residences—" Hotel Astor," N.Y. City ; Newport, R.I.
Clubs—Cornell University, Hospital Graduates.
Societies—Colonial Wars, Sons of the Revolution, Founders and Partriots of
America, N.Y. Academy of Medicine, Kappa Alpha.

DUDLEY, EDGAR SWARTWOUT, Col. U.S.A.,
of Johnstown, N.Y. (Son of Hon. James M.
Dudley, 1813-92, Mem. Com'n, Constitutional
Amendment N.Y., *m* Maria, 1820-92, da. of Saml.
and Parthena (Cline) Swartwout.—Desc'd. from
Francis Dudley, 1640, and Roeloff Swartwout,
1635-1715).

Born at Oppenheim, N.Y., June 14, 1845; Grad.
U.S Mil. Acad., W. Point, 1870; Albany Law
Sch., Union Univ. B.L.; LL.D. Univ. of Neb.,
1904; Lt.-Col., Judge Adv., U.S. Vols., 2nd
Army Corps, and Div. of Cuba; Capt., Asst.-
Qt'mr. U.S.A.; P.G. Comdr. Knts. Templar,
Neb.; Dep.-Sup., Council S. Jurisdiction A.A.
Scot. Rite Masonry, U.S.A.; Col. Judge Adv.
U.S.A.; Prof. of Law. U.S. Mil. Acad., West
Point since 1901; *m* June 22, 1870, Mary S.,
da. of Joseph and Mary A. (Sadlier) Hillabrandt.

Arms—Or, a lion rampant vert double queued.
Crest—A lion's head erased.   *Motto*—Nec gladio nec arcu.

Residences—Johnstown, Fulton Co., N.Y.; U.S. Army Stations.
Clubs—Union League: Army and Navy, N.Y.; Ft. Monroe, Va.; Ft. Leaven-
worth, Kan.; Ft. Thomas, Ky.; Columbus, O.; W. Point, N.Y.
Societies—Colonial Wars, Sons of American Revolution, War of 1812, G.A.R. Neb.,
Mil. O. Loyal Legion U.S., Naval and Mil. O. Spanish Am. War.

BLANCHARD, JOSEPH N., Rev., D.D.,
of New York City, (Only son of Justus W.
Blanchard, of Albany, N.Y., Brig.-Gen. U.S. Vols.,
b 1811, *d* 1876, *m* 1837, Olive Baker *d* 1875.—
Descended from Thomas Blanchard, yeoman, from
Penton, Hampshire, Eng., 1639, settled at Braintree,
Will proved April 20, 1654, bequests to wife Mary
and sons Thomas, Samuel, and Nathaniel).

Born at Albany, N.Y., July 1, 1849; Rector of
St. James', Fordham, N.Y., St. John's, Detroit,
Mich., and St. James', Philadelphia; Deputy
to General Convention Episcopal Church,
1886-9, '92, '95; Graduated at Amherst College,
B.A. 1871, M.A. 1874, D.D. 1895; *m* June 3,
1880, Harriet Louise, daughter of William Anderson, Pastor
Reformed (Dutch) Church, Fordham, N.Y. City, and Sarah Louisa,
daughter of Abraham Ryerson.

Arms—Gules, a chevron between three crosses crosslet argent.
Crest—A helmet resting on an eagle's head.

Residence—328, West 57th Street, N.Y. City.
Club—Alpha Delta Phi, of N.Y.
Societies—Alpha Delta Phi Fraternity, Phi Beta Kappa, Loyal Legion

RENWICK, WILLIAM CROSBY,
of N.Y. City (Son of William Rhinelander
Renwick, 1816-83, *m* May 20, 1840, Eliza S., da.
of Wm. B. Crosby, of N.Y., and Harriet A., da. of
Rev. W. Clarkson, D.D., M.D., and Cath., da. of
Gen. Wm. Floyd, signer of the Declaration of
Independence; grandson of James Renwick, founder
of first line of Packets between N.Y. and L'pool.
—Desc'd from the Renwicks, of Roxburghshire,
Scotland).

Born at N.Y. City, May 30, 1845; Dir. of The
    Summit Bank, Summit, N.J., and of Battelle
    and Renwick, N.Y. City; *m* (1) June 19, 1872,
    Harriette McDoual; *m* (2) July 17, 1879,
    Gertrude Camilla Sears.

Issue.
(*By 1st. m.*)
i. MARY WATT, *m* Feb. 7, 1901, Fredc. Kent Dohrman, of Summit, N.J.
(*2nd m*)

i. WILLIAM RHINELANDER.   iii. SUSA EVELYN.
ii. HOWARD CROSBY.

Arms—Gules, two thistles in chief, in base a lion rampant betw. a chevron argent.
Crest—An arm in armour embowed holding a scimitar..
Motto—Contide rete acens.

Residence—Summit, N.J.

COOPER, HENRY DODGE,
of N.Y. City (Son of Matthew H. Cooper,
J.P., 1812-94, of Wantage, N.J., *m* 1835, Emily
Howell, 1815-98, da. of William Coe and Susan
(Howell) Smith, of Sussex Co., N.J.; son of Elias
and Sarah (Dodge) Cooper, of Dutchess Co., N.Y.;
son of Obidiah Cooper, came from Somersetshire,
Eng., *cir.* 1750, settled in Sussex Co., N.J.,
m Mary Van Benschoten, of Holland.—Descended
from Tristram Dodge, who came to America 1700).

Born at Wantage, N.J., Jan. 28, 1853; Capt. 7th
    Regt. N.G.S.N.Y.; *m* Rosalie Martindale,
    da. of Alfred Seaman and Anne Sanford
    (Martindale) Purdy, of N.Y. City.

Issue.
i. DUDLEY MARTINDALE, *b* July 18, 1884.
i. MARION DODGE.

Arms—Argent, three bulls passant sable armed or.
Crest—On a cap of maintenance a bull passant.

Residence—29 West 70th Street, New York City.
Clubs—University, Larchmont Yacht, Merchants.

BLAKE, WILLIAM PHIPPS,
of Mill Rock Ct. and Tucson Arizona (Eldest
son of Elihu Blake of Worcester Co. Mass. 1793–
1875, *m* June 6, 1825, Adeline Nancy 1805–83,
daughter of Captain Jonathan and Mary Elizabeth
(Phipps) Mix of New Haven; son of Elihu,
m Elizabeth Whitney; son of Ebenezer, *m* Tamar
Thompson; son of Ebenezer, *m* Patronella Peck; son
of Jonathan, *m* Elizabeth Candage; son of Edward,
m Patience Pope; son of William 1595–1663 of
Asholt, Co. Somerset, settled at Dorchester Mass.
1630, Mem. Ancient and Hon. Artillery Co.; son
of John of Plainsfield; son of Humphrey Blake
of Tuxwell, *d* 1558, great-grandfather of Admiral
Robert Blake. Also in descent from Deputy Governor Danforth 1622–99
of Massachusetts, and from James Phipps, the father of Sir William
Phipps, Knt., and Governor of Massachusetts Bay Colony).

Born in N.Y. City June 1, 1826; Graduated Yale University 1852; United
States Mineralogist and Geologist Western Surveys 1853; Mining
Engineer and Instructor in Science for the Government of Japan
1861–62; Santo Domingo Commission 1871; Commissioner International Expositions 1867, '73, '76, '78; Director Arizon School of
Mines, Professor of Geology 1896–1904; Chevalier Legion of
Honour, France, 1878; *m* Dec. 25, 1855, Charlotte Haven Lord,
daughter of Hon. Wm. Allen Hayes, of South Berwick Me., Judge
of Probate and many years President of the York County Bar Association, who *m* Susan, daughter of General Lord of South Berwick,
Maine.

Issue.

i. WILLIAM PHIPPS, *b* 1857, *d* 1863.

ii. FRANCIS HAYES, *b* Jan. 30, 1860.

iii. JOSEPH AUGUSTUS, M.D., *b* Aug. 31, 1864, *m* Catharine Ketchum.

iv. THEODORE WHITNEY, *b* May 3, 1866, *m* Lilian Kesley.

v. DANFORTH PHIPPS, *b* 1874, *d* 1896.

i. CONSTANTIA, *m* James Wm. Toumey of Yale Forest School, *d* Jan. 1904.

Arms—Quarterly 1st and 4th (Blake) argent, a chevron between 3 garbs sable;
2nd and 3rd (Phipps) sable, a trefoil within an orle of mullets argent.

Crest—On a chapeau gules, turned up ermine, a martlet argent.

Residences— Mill Rock, New Haven, Ct.; "The Arches," Tucson, Arizona.

Societies—Am. Philosopchial, Geolog.cal of Lond., Geological of Edin., Natnl
Geographic, Am. Inst. of Mining Engineers, Fellow Amer. Assoc. Advct.
Science, Sons of Am. Revoln., Berzelius, Yale; Cosmos, Tucson.

L EARNED, WILLIAM LAW *(deceased)*,
late of Albany, N.Y. (Son of Ebenezer
Learned, 1780-1858, of New London, Ct., *m*
Lydia, 1787-1877, da. of Joshua and Ann Boradil
(Hallam) Coit, of New London.—Descended from
William Learned, of Charlestown, Mass., *circa*
1632).

Born at New London, Ct., July 24, 1821, *d* Sept.
20, 1904 ; Grad. Yale Univ., A.B., 1841, A.M.
1844, LL.D. 1878 ; Justice of Supreme Court,
3rd Jud. Dist., N.Y. State ; Pres., Board of
Public Instruction, Albany ; *m* (1) May 29,
1855, Phebe Rowland, 1830-64, da. of Alex.
and Mary (Pepoon) Marvin, of Albany ; *m* (2)
Jan. 15, 1868, Katherine, da. of Clinton and
Elsie (Van Dyck) De Witt, of New York.

Issue.
(By 1st m.)

i. MARY MARVIN, *b* April 16, 1856; *d* Nov. 23, 1888; *m* John De Witt
Peltz, of Albany, N.Y.

ii. GRACE HALLAM, *b* Oct. 31, 1859; *m* Jan. 3, 1900, Brig-Gen. John H.
Patterson, U.S.A., retired.

iii. MABEL, *b* Jan. 6, 1863, *d* Nov. 25, 1898.

Arms—Azure, a saltire engrailed or, between four lozenges argent.
Crest—A griffin rampant.

Residence—(Mrs. John Henry Patterson), 244 State Street, Albany, N.Y.

K UNKEL, ROBERT SHARP,
of Brooklyn (Son of John Atley Kunkel,
b 1835, Col. in Penna Mil., one of Lincoln's body-
guard from Harrisburg to Balto, *m* 1863, Susan
E. Sharp, 1835-83.—[Desc'd from Capt. James
Sharp, in French and Indian Wars, and from Lt.
Robt. McConnell, Alex. McClintock and George
Eichelberger, Revol. War]; son of Aaron, 1800-78,
m Rebecca, da. of Michael Long, of Lancaster,
Pa.; son of John, 1777-1855, *m* Susanna Coover ;
son of Leonhard, *d* about 1778, of Ephrata,
m Rosina Stumpf; son of John Michael Kunkel,
b Germany, 1727, *d* Lancaster Pa., *cir.* 1780).

Born in Cumberland, Co., June 8, 1864 ; *m* Nov. 5,
1890, Anna, da. of Saml. Read and Ann (Laverty) Hetherington, of
Jersey City.

Issue.

i. JOHN ATLEY, 1894-95.   ii. LORRAINE, *b* June 10, 1898.

Arms—Per fesse or and sable, on mound vert a lion couchant or, supporting a
mullet argent in base. *Crest*—A demi-lion or.

Residences—357 Jefferson Av., Brooklyn, N.Y., Pennington, N.J.
Societies—Colonial Wars, Sons of the Rev., Mercantile Exc., Crescent Club.

FINDLEY, WILLIAM LUTHER,
of N.Y. City (Son of Rev. Wm. Findley, D.D.,
1808-86, of Newcastle, m 1837, Elizabeth, da. of Thos.
Scott and Matilda (Cook) Cunningham, of Mercer,
Pa.—Decended from William Findley; son of John
Findlay, 1773-1855, of Mercer Co., Pa.; son of
William Findley, 1741-1821, b at Londonderry,
Ireland, settled in Pa. 1763, Capt. in Revol.
Army, Mem. U.S. Congress, 1791 to 1817, m 1772,
Mary Cochran. His grandfather, William Findley,
emigrated from Scotland to Londonderry 1682,
assisted in defence of Derry 1689).

Born in Butler Co., Pa., Aug. 23, 1843; Atty. to
   N.Y. Fire Dep., 1880-98; Grad. Westminster
   Coll. A.B. 1863; Law Dep. Columbian Univ.
   1868; Admitted to the Bar of Supreme Court
   State of N.Y. 1869; m Oct. 22, 1877, Carliebel, da. of Lucien B.
   Chase, of N.Y., Mem. Congress, 1845-49, and Julia Anna, da. of John
   F. Delaplaine.

Issue.

i. CHASE DELAPLAINE, b Jan. 21, 1881.

ii. WILLIAM VAN BRUNT, b Sept. 6, 1887.   i. ETHEL ANNA.

Arms —Argent, on a chevron between three roses gules two daggers, chevronways
   points downward of the field hilted or.

Crest—A boar passant argent.   Motto—Fortis in arduis.

Residence—31 East 63rd Street, New York City.
Clubs—Union League, Lawyers, Ardsley, Republican.
Societies—Sons of the Revolution, Pennsylvania of N.Y., Assn. of the Bar.

BELKNAP, HENRY WYCKOFF,
of N.Y. City (Eldest son of Thomas Belknap,
of Hartford, Conn., 1833-83, m 1858, Catherine
Heyer, da. of Henry Suydam and Elizabeth
Brinckeroff (Suydam) Wyckoff, of N.Y.; son of
Thomas 1805-90, m Frances Waterhouse; son of
Joseph 1761-1807, m Sarah Clements; son of
Joseph 1732-1813, m Phoebe —— (?); son of
Thomas 1698-1755, m Sarah Hill, (Wright); son
of Thomas 1670-1755, m Jane Cheney; son of Joseph
1630-1712, m Hannah Meakins; son of Abraham
Belknap, settled Lynn, Mass., 1637, d Lynn 1643,
m Mary —— ?).

Born in New York City, May 18, 1860.

Arms—Azure, on a bend cotised argent three eaglets displayed of the first.
Crest—A dragon statant vert, ducally gorged and lined or.

Residence—40, Chestnut Street, Salem, Mass.
Clubs—Players, National Arts, New York City, Grosvenor Club, London.
Societies—St Paul's School, Concord, N.H., Alumni Association.

FOOTE, JOHN CROCKER,
of Belvidere, Ill. (Son of Hon. John J.
Foote, b 1816, Auditor N.Y.P.O., m 1839, Mary
Crocker; son of Dea. John 1786-1884; son of
Judge Isaac 1746-1842; son of Daniel 1717-1801;
son of Capt. Nathl. 1682-1774; son of Nathl.
1647-1703; son of Nathl. 1620-55; son of Nathl.
Foote, b Eng., 1593, d Wethersfield, Ct. 1644;
? son of Robert Foote of Shalford, Essex).

Born at Hamilton, N.Y., Sept. 20, 1841; Grad.
Colgate Univ. A.B., 1864; m April 24, 1867,
Helen, da. of Saml. B. Garvin, Judge and
Dist. Atty. of N.Y., and Julia M., da. of Hon.
Henry Mitchell, M.D.

Issue.
i. John Garvin, b Feb. 7, 1877; d May 17, 1903; m Mary A. Watrous.
i. Mary Helen, m July 21, 1897, Rev. H. E. Purinton.
ii. Maria Garvin, m June 22, 1905, Alfred A. Engstrom.
iii. Florence Annette, m June 12, 1901, Prof. E. W. Engstrom.

Arms—Argent, a chevron sable in the dexter chief a trefoil slipped.
Crest—An oak tree proper.   Motto—Loyalty and Truth.

Residence—Belvidere, Boone Co., Ill.
Societies—Sons of the Revolution, Colonial Wars, Mayflower Descendants,
    Founders and Patriots, Pilgrim John Howland of Mayflower.

DAWKINS, WALTER I.,
of Baltimore, Md. (Son of Young Parran
Dawkins, Judge, Commissioners and Orphans'
Court, Assessor, etc., b Oct. 3, 1820, d Jan. 23,
1883, m Aleathea Elizabeth, b 1824, d Oct. 25,
1878, daughter of Walter Dorsey, and Ann Ireland,
of Calvert County, Md.—Descended from William
Dawkins, who came from England to America
early in the 18th Century).

Born at Leonardtown, St. Marys Co., Md.,
Oct. 21, 1858; Graduated at St. John's College,
Annapolis, Md., Pr.D., A.M. 1883; admitted
to the Bar 1883.

Arms—Gules, a lion passant guard. or, between two
    roses in pale argent and as many flaunches of
    the second, each charged with a lion ramp. sable.

Crest—A dexter arm couped at the shoulder proper, holding a battleaxe bend-
    ways, on the blade a rose gules.

Residence—St. James Hotel, Baltimore, Md.   Club—University, &c.

Societies—Maryland Historical, Geographical, Art. Amer. Hist., Amer. Bar,
    Amer. Political Science, Nat. Geographic, Municipal Art, Md. State Bar,
    Balto City Bar., &c.

CHOLMELEY-JONES, EDWARD,
of Philadelphia (Son of Edw. Owen Jones,
1808-72. of Nass. and Newnham, Glouc. Eng.,
J.P., D.L., m Cath. S., d 1897, da. of John Fortescue-
Brickdale; son of Rev. Edward, d 1847; son of
Roynon, b 1738; son of William Jones of Nass,
m 1735 Cholmeley, da. of Sir John D'Oyley, of
Cheselhampton, who was 15th in descent from
King Edward III.).

Born at Newnham, Jan. 30, 1852; B.A., Magdalen
Coll., Oxford, 1876, M.A., 1878; m (1) Sept. 29,
1880, Almira Gambault, d 1886, da. of the
Rev. W. H. Gilder, of Flushing, L.I.; m (2)
Oct. 9, 1889, Sarah Teresa, da. of Francis
Haggerty, of Philadelphia.

Issue.

i. EDWIN OWEN NIGEL, b Mar. 10, 1883. i. CATHERINE JEANNETTE.
ii. WILLIAM F. ROYNON, } b Oct. 8, 1884.
iii. RICHARD GILDER, }

(By 2nd m.)

i. REGINALD FORTESCUE, b July 3, 1893, d March 23, 1903.
ii. CHARLES GERALD, b May 16, 1895. i. MABEL FRANCES.
iii. ARTHUR MONTAGU, b Aug. 21, 1897. ii. CONSTANCE HELENA.
iv. EDWIN GROVE, b Sept. 23, 1901. iii. SARAH DOROTHEA.

Arms—Argent, a lion rampant gules.
Crest—A Cornish chough proper.   *Motto*—Ardua peto.

Residence—Broomall, Del. Co., Penna.   *Club*—University.

JUDD, ORRIN REYNOLDS,
of Brooklyn, N.Y. (Son of the Rev. Orrin
Bishop Judd, LL.D., 1816-92, m Susanna, b at
Ryde, I. of W., Eng., da. of Capt. Francis
Reynolds, R.N., son of Rev. Owen Reynolds,
Rector of Aber, Wales; son of Jotham, 1773-1850;
son of Elnathan, 1738-1808; son of Joseph, 1707-
88; son of Joseph, 1672-1757; son of Lieut. John,
1640-1715; son of Thomas Judd, of Cambridge,
Mass., 1633, Deputy for Farmington Ct. 27 years.
Also 8th in descent from Gov. Thomas Welles, 1598-
1660; 7th from Anthony Hawkins, d 1674, Pat. in
Royal Charter of Ct.; 4th from Henry Playford,
b 1740, of London).

Born at Kingston, N.J., Nov. 4, 1870; B.C.S. N.Y. Univ. 1902; LL.B.
1904; Certified Public Accountant; Counsellor-at-Law; Lect. in
N.Y. Univ. School of Commerce, Accounts and Finance; m Oct. 4,
1905, Bertha R., da. of Rev. Julius C. Grimmell, Brooklyn, N.Y.

Arms—Gules, a fesse ragnly between three boars' heads erased argent.
Crest—On a ducal coronet or a cockatrice wings displayed proper.
Motto—Fide sed cui vide.

Residence—Brooklyn, N.Y.   *Society*—Colonial Wars.

DANA, CHARLES, A.M.,
  of N.Y. City (4th son of Hon. Anderson G.
Dana, LL.D., 1791-1861, *m* Eliza A. Fuller, whose
ancestor came to America in the "Mayflower."
Desc'd from Richard Dana, bap. Manchester,
Eng., 1617, to Cambridge, Mass., 1640, *m* Annie
Bullard, grandson of Edward Dana of Kendal,
Westmoreland).

Born Jan. 10, 1824; A.M. Univ. of Vermont;
  came to N.Y. 1845; later he went to St. Louis
  Mo. as a Commission Merchant; in 1854 went
  to San Francisco and Hawaiian Islands, where
  he established the First Bank in the Kingdom;
  returned to N.Y. in 1864; Vice-Pres. of The
  N. Amer. Steamship Co.; Vice-Pres. Des Moines and Fort Dodge
  R.R.; Pres. Standard Gas Co., N.Y.; Dir. of the Erie R.R., N.Y.
  and New Eng. R.R., Indiana and Illinois R.R., New Amsterdam
  Casualty Co.; Woman's Hospital, etc. For forty years the Union
  Club and the Manhattan Chess Club were his favourites; *m* June 5,
  1879, Laura, da. of Dr. J. S. Parkin of N.Y.

Issue.

i. CHARLES A., *b* April 25, 1881, A.M. Columbia Univ., Lawyer.

Arms—Sable, on a bend argent three chevrons vert.
Crest—A bull's head affrontée.

Residence—New York City.

PRUYN, JOHN van SCHAICK L. (dec'd),
  of Albany (Son of Hon. John van S. L.
Pruyn, 1811-77, S. Senator, Mem. 38th and 40th
U.S. Congresses, Chancellor, Univ. of S. of N.Y.,
m 1844, Harriet Corning, da. of Thomas and Mary
R. (Weld) Turner, of Albany.—Descended from
Samuel Pruyn, 1677-1752, Alderman, 1729-31;
son of Frans Pruyn; son of Jan, who came from
Holland and settled in what is now Albany, N.Y.).

Born in Albany, N.Y., Mar. 14, 1859; Grad. at
  Union Coll., B.A., 1880; Albany Law Sch.,
  LL.B., 1882; Alderman of Albany, 1886-90;
  Atty. and Counsellor-at-Law; *m* June 11, 1895,
  Cornelia van Rensselaer, da. of John Erving
  and Cornelia van Rensselaer, da. of Wm.
Paterson van Rensselaer, of Manursing Island, Rye, N.Y.

Issue.

i. JOHN VAN SCHAICK LANSING, Jr., *b* June 6, 1896; *d* May 17, 1897.
ii. ERVING, *b* Oct. 26, 1897.
iii. HENDRIK, *b* Dec. 28, 1900.

Arms—Or, three (Dutch) martlets sable.
Crest—A (Dutch) martlet, sable, with beak and feet, in a vol-à-l'antique or.

Residences—Albany, N.Y.; 70 W. 49th St., N.Y.
Clubs—Fort Orange, of Albany; Union, University, Metropolitan, of N.Y.;
  Reading Room, of Newport, R.I.
Societies—Holland, St. Nicholas, Colonial Wars, Sons of the Revolution.

POOR, Mrs. MARY WELLINGTON (*née* Lane),
of Hackensack, N.J. (Da. of Washington
Jefferson Lane 1807-64, of Arlington, Mass.,
m Cynthia Clark, 1810; son of Ebenezer, 1771-1846;
son of Samuel, *b* 1736; son of James; son of John;
son of Job, 1620-97, settled at Malden, Mass., *cir.*
1650; son of James Lane, of Rickmansworth,
Herts., grandson of Thomas Lane, *d* 1587).

Born at Arlington, Mass.; *m* Jan. 17, 1860, Edward
E. Poor, 1837-1900, of N.Y. and Hackensack;
son of Benj. *b* 1794; son of Benj. *b* 1760; son
of Jeremiah, *b* 1719; son of Benj. *b* 1696;
son of Henry, *b* 1650; son of John Poor,
b 1615, of Darrington, Wiltshire, to New
Eng. 1635.

Issue.

i. Edward E., *b* 1861, *m* 1888 Sarie Grimes.
ii. James H., *b* 1862, *m* 1885 Evelyn Bolton.
iii. Charles L., *b* 1866, *m* 1892 Anna Easton.
iv. Frank B., *b* 1868, *m* 1892 Bessie Hamilton.
v. Horace F., *b* 1878, *m* 1904 Helen Hartshorse.
i. Helen F., *m* 1892 William C. Thomas.
ii. Emily C., *m* 1900 William S. Montgomery.

Arms—(Poor) Or, a fesse azure between three mullets gules.
Crest—A cubit arm erect, vested sable, slashed argent, cuffed ermine, charged
with two mullets in fesse or, grasping an arrow.

Residences—" Polifly," Hackensack, N J.: N.Y. City.

VANN, IRVING GOODWIN,
of Syracuse, N.Y. (Son of Samuel R. Vann, *b* New Brunswick,
N.J., Sept. 4, 1804; *d* Ulysses, N.Y., Oct. 14, 1872; *m* Dec. 24, 1837,
Catherine, da. of Joseph Goodwin, of Ulysses, N.Y.).

Born at Ulysses, Tompkins Co., N.Y., Jan. 3, 1842; Mayor of the City
of Syracuse, N.Y.; Justice of the Supreme Court, N.Y.S., and now
Judge of the Court of Appeals in same State; Graduated B.A. Yale
University, 1863; Albany Law School, LL.B. 1865; M.A. Yale,
1871; LL.D. Hamilton, 1882; LL.D. Syracuse Univ., 1897: LL.D.
Yale, 1898; *m* Oct. 11, 1870, Florence, da. of Henry Augustus
Dillaye, of Syracuse.

Issue.

i. Irving Dillaye, *b* Oct. 17, 1875.
i. Florence Dillaye.

Motto—Otium cum libris.

Residence—316, James Street, Syracuse, N.Y.
Clubs—Century, Citizens (Syracuse, N.Y.), Fort Orange (Albany, N.Y.).
Societies—Onondaga Historical, Albany Historical.

DODGE, WALTER PHELPS,
    of Simsbury, Ct., N.Y., and London (Eldest son of David Stuart Dodge, of Bellehurst, Simsbury, *b* 1836, *m* 1860, Ellen Ada, *b* 1838, *d* 1880, da. of John Jay Phelps, of Bushey Hill, Simsbury, and N.Y.—Descended from William Dodge, of Salem, Mass, 1623).

Born at Beyrout, Syria, June 13, 1869; Barr.-at-Law, Mid. Temple, 1898; Alumnus of Yale, and Oxford Univs.; Author of "The Life of Piers Gaveston," 1899; "From Squire to Prince," 1901; F.R.G.S., 1896; *m* (1) 1888, Ida R. Nelson Cooke, *m* dissolved; *m* (2) Ethel, da. of the late Percy Harmer-Adlard, of Staverton Court, Gloucestershire.

Issue.

i. STUART PHELPS, *b* Feb. 19, 1891.
i. ELLEN ADA PHELPS.
ii. ROSEMARY PHELPS.

Arms—Barry of six or and sable, over all on a pale gules a woman's breast distilling milk all proper.
Crest—A demi-sea dog azure, collared finned and purpled or.
Motto—Leni perfruar otio.

———

Residences—The Grange, Simsbury, Conn.; 46, Green St., Park Lane, London, W.
Clubs—Reform, Wellington, of London; Authors, Racquet, of New York.
Societies—Sons of the Revolution, Royal Geographical, American Geographical.

———

JENKINS, EDMUND FELLOWS,
    of New York City (Son of John Stillwell Jenkins, 1818-52, *m* Minerva Porter Fellows, *d* 1883; grandson of Edmund B. and Polly (Kellogg) Fellows, of Sheffield, Mass., and gt.-grandson of John Fellows, 1733-1808, Capt. Berkshire Militia 1760, Maj.-Genl. 9th Div. Mass. Militia 1789.—Descended from Herman Jenkins, of Coeymans, N.Y., 1st Lieut. 5th N.Y. Militia, 1812-14).

Born at Weedsport, N.Y., July 28, 1844; served throughout the Civil War, 1861-65; 1st Lieut. 126th U.S. Volunteers; Capt. Old Guard of N.Y.; *m* July 11, 1889, Adelaide Eliza, da. of George Montgomery, M.D., of Newburyport, Mass.

Arms—Or, a lion rampant reguardant sable.
Crest—On a ducal coronet or, a lion rampant reguardant sable.

———

Residence—Larchmont, N.Y.
Clubs—N.Y. Athletic, Larchmont Yacht.
Societies—Sons of the Revol., Colonial Wars, Mil. Order of Foreign Wars, Society of the Cayugas, Order of Jamestown 1607, St. Davids, New Eng., New Hampshire Society, Empire State Society Sons of the Revolution, Hotel Association of N.Y., Am. Science and Historic Preservation Society.

R ICE, Mrs. NORA CLAIRE (*née* GRANT),
of Gardiner, Me. (Da. of Wm. Sullivan
Grant, of Gardiner, *b* 1825, by 2nd wife, Ellen C.
Woods; son of Samuel Clinton 1797-1853, of Hallo-
well, Me., *m* Eliz. Frances, da. of Benj. Vaughan,
M.P., *b* 1751, *m* Sarah, da. of Sir Wm. Manning
and aunt to Cardinal Manning, grandson of Benj.
Vaughan of Golden Grove, Wales; son of Maj.
Peter, 1770-1836, of Gardiner, *m* Nancy, da. of
Wm. Barker, of Liverpool, Eng.; son of Capt.
Samuel, 1740-1805, *m* (1) Abigail Jones, *m* (2) Eliz.
Seaward; son of Lieut. Peter 1696-1756, *m* (1)
Lydia Frost, *m* (2) Mary Lord; son of James,
Representative in General Court, 1725-28-32,
m Mary Nason; son of Peter Grant of Boston 1657 of Kittery, Me.
1659, *d* 1718, *m* Joanna, da. of Lieut. George Ingersoll, of Falmouth, Me.
Also from elder Wm. Wentworth, progenitor, of New Hamps. Wentworths.
Also descd. from 1, William Manning, *b* 1702 ; 2, Sir William Manning,
b 1729, *m* Elizabeth Smith, sister of Robt. 1st Baron Carrington ; 3, Sarah
Manning, *b* 1754, *m* Benj. Vaughan ; 4, Eliz. F. Vaughan. Also from
1, Thos. Smith of Nottingham, Ld. of Keyworth ; 2, Abel, *m* Jane
Beaumont ; 3, Abel, Banker of Nottingham, *m* da. of Thos. Bird ;
4, Eliz., *d* 1789, *m* Wm. Manning, Esq. Also from 1, Benj. Vaughan,
b 1679, of Golden Grove, Caermarthen ; 2, Saml. Vaughan, M.P., *b* 1720,
m Sarah, niece of Sir Robt. Hallowell ; 3, Benj. Vaughan, M.P., *b* 1751,
em. to America with wife, Sarah Manning, 1797 ; 4, Eliz. F. Vaughan.
Also from 1, Benj. Hallowell, keeper of the Eng. Customs, Boston ;
2, Sarah Hallowell, *m* Saml. Vaughan ; 3, Benj. Vaughan, *m* Sarah
Manning ; 4, Eliz. F. Vaughan, *m* Saml. C. Grant. Also from Nathan
Lord, of Kittery, Me., 1652. Also from Sampson Woods, War of 1812,
and Maj. Henry Woods of Pepperell, Mass. Served in Amer. Revolution).

Born at Tudor Place, Georgetown, D.C., *m* May 23, 1887, Colonel William
Powell Rice of Washington D.C.

Issue.

i. VAUGHAN MANNING, *b* at Aberdeen Wash., Sept. 12, 1890.

Arms—(Grant) Argent, three lions rampant azure, a chief of the second.

Crest—A demi-lion argent.   *Motto*—Stand sure.

Arms—(Manning) Gu. a cross flory, betw. four trefoils slipped or ; *Crest*—Out of
a ducal coronet an eagle's head sa. betw. two ostrich feathers. *Arms*—
(Smith) Or, on a chev. cotised betw. three demi-griffins the two in chief
respectant ; *Crest*—An elephant's head erased gu., on the neck a fleur-de-lis.
Arms—(Vaughan) Per fesse sa. and arg. a lion ramp. counterchanged, armed
and langued gu. *Arms*—(Hallowell) Arg. on a chev. sa. three annulets of the
field ; *Crest*—A boar's head erect betw. two ostrich feathers.

Residence—Grant Place (Farmingdale), Gardiner, Me.

Societies—Daus. of Am. Revol., Samuel Grant Chapter D.A.R. of Gardiner,
Sons and Daughters Nathan Lord of Kittry, Me. (1632), Maine State
Sanitorium, Paul Jones Chapter D.A.R of Boston, Gardiner Library
Assoc., Grant Family Assoc., of Boston.

PRIME, RALPH EARL,
   of Yonkers (Son of Alanson J. Prime, 1811-64,
m Ruth H. Higbie; son of Nathaniel S.; son of
Benj. Y.; son of Ebenezer; son of James; son of
James Prime, from Yorkshire to New Haven, Ct.,
1638. Also descended from Capt. Ralph Earl,
1600-78, of R.I.; from Rev. John Wheelwright, who
came to Mass. *cir.* 1638; from Edward Howell, of
L.I.; from Henry Pierson and John Higbie).

Born at Matteawan, N.Y., Mar. 29, 1840; Bellevue
   College, D.C.L.; Wooster Univ., LL.D.;
   Lt.-Col. N.Y.S. Vols.; nom. Brig.-Gen. 1863;
   served during Civil War; Trustee of Village
   of Yonkers; City Atty. 1875-76; Dep. Atty.-
   Gen. of N.Y. 1895-96; *m* Aug. 9, 1866, Annie
   Richards-Wolcott.

Issue.

i. RALPH E., Jr., *b* July 9, 1868, *m* Jessie Heermance.
ii. WILLIAM C., *b* Oct. 21, 1870, *m* Charlotte Lovell.
iii. GARDNER W. 1872-90.   iv. EDWARD D.G. 1881-93.
   i. KATHARINE.   iii. JULIA A., *m* Wm. White Knapp.
ii. RUTH H., 1874-1905.   iv. ARABELLA D. (Pansy).

Arms—Argent, a man's leg erased at the thigh gules.
Crest—An owl proper, in mouth a scroll with motto, on a collar two mullets.
Motto—Nil invita minerva.   ———
Residences—63 Hawthorne Av., Yonkers, N.Y.; Fishers Island, Suffolk Co., N.Y.
Societies—Loyal Legion, War 1812, Col. Wars, Sons of the Am. Rev., Frs. and
   Patriots Am. Frs. and Defrs., Army of the Potomac, Am. Bar Ass'n., Met.
   Mus. of Art, Westchester Hist., Huguenot of London, Am. Flag Asso., &c.

JOHNSON, EDWARD (*deceased*),
   of Boston, Mass. (son of Alfred Johnson,
1789-1852, of Belfast, Me., Judge of Probate,
Waldo Co., Me., *m* Nancy Atkinson, of Newbury,
Mass.; descended from son of Rev. Alfred, 1766-
1837; son of Jacob, 1739-40-1816; son of Obediah,
1702-65; son of Obediah, *b* 1664; son of John,
b 1635; son of Capt. Edward Johnson, 1599-1672,
of Herne Hill, Kent, Eng., settled in Mass., 1630).

Born at Belfast, Me., June 30, 1840, *d* Jan. 18, 1906,
   at Boston, Mass., *m* Sept. 15, 1870, Georgiana
   Parker, da. of Erasmus Darwin and Louise
   (Clarke) Miller, M.D., of Dorchester, Mass.
   He was a Mem. of the Somerset and Exchange
   Clubs, Maine Historical and Bostonian Society.

Issue.

i. ALFRED, *b* June 28, 1871.   ii. RALPH, *b* Aug. 25, 1872.
iii. EDWARD, Jr.
iv. LOUISE, *m* Apr. 15, 1902, Lt. Wm. } *b* December 4, 1876.
   V. Pratt, U.S. Navy.

Arms—Gules, three spear heads; a chief ermine.
Crest—A pair of raven's wings sable.
Motto—Servabo fidem.   ———
Residences—(Family), Boston, Mass.; Belfast, Waldo Co., Me.

ISHAM, RALPH,
of Chicago (Son of Ralph N. Isham, M.D.,
1831-1904, of Chicago, m 1856, Kath. E., da. of
George W. and Elizabeth Ann (Manniere) Snow ;
son of Nelson Isham, 1805-95; son of Noah
Isham, 1764-1819; son of John Isham, b 1720;
son of John, b 1681 ; son of John Isham who emigrated from Warwickshire and settled at Barnstaple, Mass., 1670).

Born in Chicago Feb. 13, 1865; Grad. Harvard
Univ., 1889; Sec. and Treasurer of Chicago
Union Transfer Railway Co.; Dir. Natl. Ware-
house and Transfer Co., Chicago Union Transfer
Railway Co.; m (1) Jan. 4, 1893, Lucy Gunn,
1868-94, da. of Albert Keep, Chairman of Board of Directors of
Chicago and N.W. Railway Co., also Director in Merchants' Loan
and Trust Co.; m (2) June 24, 1902, Mary Louise, da. of Major-
Gen. E. S. Otis, U.S.A.

Issue.

i. ALBERT KEEP, b Jan. 9, 1894.

Arms—Gules, a fesse wavy, in chief three piles also wavy, points meeting in
fesse argent.
Crest—A demi-swan, wings endorsed proper.
Motto—Ostendo non ostento. _____
Residences—11 Ritchie Place, Chicago, Ill.; Lake Geneva, Wisconsin.
Clubs—Univ., Athletic, Onwentsia, Saddle and Cycle, Lake Geneva Country,
South Shorn Country.
Societies—Sons of the Revol., Delta Kappa Epsilon, National Geographic Society.

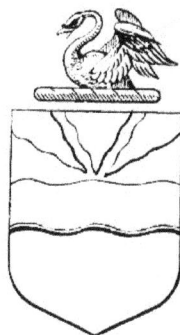

HILL, REV. WILLIAM BANCROFT,
of Poughkeepsie (Son of Rev. Joseph B.
Hill 1796-1864, of Mason N.H., m 1845 Harriet
Brown, g.-gr.-da. of Hope Brown of Sudbury,
soldier in War of Revol.; son of Rev. Ebenezer,
b 1766; son of Samuel, b 1716; son of Capt.
Samuel, b 1676; son of Capt. Ralph, d 1695; son
of Ralph Hill of Plymouth Mass. before 1638).

Born at Colebrook, N.H. Feb. 17, 1857; Prof. of
Biblical Lit., Vassar Coll.; A.B. Harvard
Coll. 1879; admtd. to Balto. Bar 1882; Prof.
of Ethics and Philosophy, Park Coll. 1883;
Grad. at Union Theol. Semy. 1886; Minr.,
Dutch Refd. Ch., Athens and Poughkeepsie
till 1902, when apptd. Prof. at Vassar Coll.;
D.D. Rutgear College, 1905. Author of " Present Problems of New
Testament Study," " Guide to Lives of Christ "; m Dec. 29, 1892,
Elise Weyerhaeuser.

Arms—Gules, a saltire vaire between four mullets argent.
Crest—A demi-leopard argent, spotted of all colours, ducally gorged or.
Motto—Per deum et ferrum obtinui. _____

Residences—Vassar College, Poughkeepsie, N.Y.; Temple, Hillsboro Co., N.H.
Clubs—Phi Beta Kappa, University, Poughkeepsie; Harvard, N.Y.

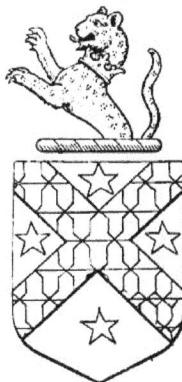

STEVENS, CHARLES E., Rev., LL.D., D.C.L. (*dec'd*), of Philadelphia (Eldest son of James Edward Poole Stevens, of Boston Mass., and heir male of Sir Edward Stephens, Knt., of Sodbury, Co. Gloucester, Member of the Long Parliament, Knighted by King Charles II. 1660; eventual heir of the family of Stephens, of Eastington, Chavenage and other Manors in Gloucestershire, of which family Sir Philip Stephens was created a Baronet 1795; lineal representatives of the Norman house of FitzStephen, through Airard FitzStephen, who came over with the Conqueror and was at Hastings 1066).

Born at Boston Mass. July 5, 1853, *d* Aug. 28, 1906; Ord. Deacon 1875; Priest 1877; Rector of Christ Church, Phila.; Sometime Archdeacon of Brooklyn, N.Y.; Special Lectr. in St. Stephen's Coll., Univ. of Wooster, Univ. of the City of N.Y., and Univ. of Penna; Chaplain-Genl. of the Soc. of Colonial Wars, and of the Order of Foreign Wars of the United States, and Commander of the Penna. Commandery of the latter; author of "Sources of the Constitution of the United States considered in Relation to Colonial and English History," and other works; Hon. Degrees of LL.D. and D.C.L., conferred 1888; received from the King of Portugal the honour of Knight-Commander of the Order of Christ of Portugal 1894, and from the Queen-Regent of Spain, Knight of the Order of Isabella the Catholic of Spain, for rendering distinguished services in Political Science; Officer of the Academy, of France, and other foreign decorations; *m* May 23, 1878, Ella Monteith, eldest da. of Walter Monteith Aikman, F.S.A., and Julia, da. of Robert Aikman, of N.Y. City, descendants of the Aikmans, Lairds of Carney and Brambleton, Scotland.

Issue.

i. Margery Aikman.

Arms—Per chevron azure and argent, in chief two falcons volant or; suspended from shield the decoration of Knight-Commander of the Order of Christ of Portugal.

Crest—A demi-eagle displayed or. *Motto*—Byde Tyme.

Residences—(Mrs. C. E. S.) 62 Willow Street, Brooklyn, New York; "Edgemere," Lake George, N.Y.

Club—(Late mem.) Union League.

Societies—(Late mem.) Fellow Royal Geographical, Am. Geographical, Antiquaries of Scot., Mem Am. Ethnological, Royal Archæological Inst. of Great Britain, Col. Wars, Sons of the Revoln., Mil. Order of Foreign Wars.

WASHINGTON, WILLIAM LANIER,
    of N.Y. (Son of Maj. James B. Wash-
ington 1839-1900 of Virginia, *m* 1864 Mrs. Jane B.
Cabell, da. of Maj. Wm. L. and Virginia (Armisted)
Lanier of New Orleans; son of Col. Lewis Wm.,
1812-71, *m* Mary Ann Barroll; son of Hon.
George C., 1789-1854, *m* Eliza R. Beall; son of
Hon. Wm. Aug., 1757-1810 [*m* his cousin Jane da. of
John Aug. Washington, bro. to Gen. George
Washington]; son of Augustine, *b* 1720, *m* Anne
Aylett; son of Augustine 1694-1743, *m* Jane
Butler; son of Laurence 1661-97, *m* Mildred
Warner; son of Col. John Washington 1627-77.
b at Warton, Lanc., Eng., settled in Bridges Creek,
Va., *m* 2nd wife Anne Pope; son of Leonard,
12th from Robert of Welleburne, Co. Westmoreland 1265, grandson of
Robert de Washington, Lord of Welleburne, *b* 1195. Also desc. from
Lewis Lanier of Bordeaux, France, to America *cir.* 1650).

Born at Montgomery Ala., Mar. 30, 1865; Grad. Western Univ. of Pa. 1886;
    Pres. Elliott-Washington Steel Co.; Chairman Pittsburgh Sheet Steel
    Manuf. Co.; Pres. Laurel Land Co.; Pres. United Oil Cloth Co.

Arms—Argent, two bars gules in chief three mullets of the second.
Crest—A raven with wings endorsed proper issuing out of a ducal coronet or.
Motto—Exitus acta probat.
Residence—The Windsor, 54th St. and Broadway, N.Y. City.
Clubs—Calumet of N.Y., Pittsburgh Golf.

DOUGLAS, CURTIS NOBLE,
    of Albany, N.Y. (Son of John Pettit Douglas
of Theresa N.Y., *m* Henrietta, daughter of Levi
and Elmina (Tucker) Hughson of Pulaski, N.Y.).

Born at Watertown, N.Y., May 28, 1856; Gradu-
    ated Rochester University, A.B. 1877; Member
    of Assembly 4th District Albany County 1894;
    Senator Albany Co. 1899 and 1900; *m* June 24,
    1886, Nancy Sherman, daughter of Lemon
    and Abby G. (Sherman) Thomson, of Albany,
    N.Y.

Issue.

i. THOMSON DOUGLAS, *b* Feb. 26, 1889.
i. DOROTHEA.
ii. GERTRUDE THOMSON.

Arms—Argent, a human heart gules crowned or, on a chief azure three
    mullets or
Crest—A human heart crowned or.   *Motto*—Jamais arrière.

Residences—4 Elk Street, Albany, N.Y.; Thomson, N.Y.
Clubs—Fort Orange, Country, of Albany; Adirondack League, Calumet,
    Democratic, St. Anthony, of N.Y. City.
Society—St Andrews.

MORGAN, JOHN PIERPONT,
    of N Y. City (Son of Junius S. Morgan,
1813-90, m 1836, Juliet, da. of the Rev. John
and Mary Sheldon (Lord) Pierpont, of Litchfield,
Ct., of Boston, Mass.—Descended from Capt.
Miles Morgan 1616-99; grandson of Sir William
Morgan, of Tredegar, S. Wales, settled at West
Springfield 1632; and sixth in descent from the
Rev. James Pierpont 1659-1714, Minister at New
Haven, Ct.).

Born at Hartford, Ct., Apr. 17, 1837; Grad. at
    Gottingen Univ., Germany; m (1) Oct. 6,
    1861, Amelia, da. of Jonathan and Mary P.
    (Cady) Sturges, of N.Y., she d Feb. 17, 1862,
    at Nice; m (2) May 31, 1865, Francis Louisa,
    da. of Charles Tracy, and Louisa, da. of Genl.
    Joseph Kirkland, of Utica.

Issue.
i. John Pierpont, Jr., b Sept. 7, 1867, m Jane Norton Grew.
i. Louisa Pierpont, m Herbert Livingston Satterlee, of N.Y.
ii Juliet Pierpont, m William Pierson Hamilton, of N.Y.
iii. Anne Tracy.

Arms—Or, a griffin segreant sable.
Crest—A reindeer's head couped or, attired gules. Motto—Onward and Upward.

Residences—219 Madison Avenue, N.Y. City; "Cragston," Highland Falls, N.Y.
Clubs—Union, Knickerbocker, Union League. Metropolitan, Century, Lawyers,
    N.Y. Yacht Club, Seawanhaka Corinthian Yacht. Tuxedo, Racquet, Riding,
    Players, Grolier, Jekyl Island, Metropolitan of Washington, Eastern Yacht
    and Somerset of Boston.

LIPPINCOTT, WALTER,
    of Philadelphia, Pa. (Son of Joshua Ballinger
Lippincott, of Phil., 1813-86, m Josephine, 1823-99,
da. of Seth Craige, of Phila.; son of Jacob Wills,
1783-1834; son of Levi, 1749-1813; son of
Jonathan, d 1759; Son of James, 1687-1760; son
of Restore, 1653-1741; son of Richard Lippincott,
of New Jersey, d 1683).

Born at Philadelphia, March 21, 1849; m Oct. 21,
    1879, Elizabeth Trotter, daughter of Sigmund
    H. Hörstmann, of Philadelphia.

Issue.
i. Bertha Hörstmann.

Arms—Per fesse, embattled gules and sable, three leopards passant argent.
Crest—Out of a mural crown gules, five ostrich feathers, alternately arg. and az.
Motto—Secundus dubiisque rectus.

Residences—2101 Walnut St., Philadelphia; "Alscot," Bryn Mawr, Pa.
Clubs—Union League, Rittenhouse, University, Art, Merion, Country, Racquet.
    Radnor Hunt, Franklin Inn.
Societies—Colonial, Mayflower, Penna. Historical.

C ARRITT, JOHN PRICE,
of Islington, Middlesex, Eng. (Eldest son of
Frederick Blasson Carritt and Edith his wife,
dau. and co-heiress of the late John Blount Price
of Islington, J.P. for Middlesex, London and
Westminster, sole heir of his maternal uncle Peter
Clarke Blount of Islington Priory. Great-great-
grandson of Edward and Frances Carritt of Great
Grimsby, Co. Lincoln. Descended also from the
ancient family of Blount and [through more than
one line] from Rhodri-Mawr, Cadwalader and
Beli-Mawr ; Heir presumptive, brother Edgar
Frederick Carritt, M.A., b 1876; next to succeed
latter's son Michael John, b 1906).

Born at Islington Feb. 19, 1872 ; admitted to domi-
cile in France Oct. 10, 1903.

Arms—Quarterly of six :—1 and 6, or on a chief indented sable three roses argent
(for Carritt) ; 2, or, a lion rampant regardant sable (for Price) ; 3, sable,
three scaling-ladders argent, between the upper two a spear-head of the
last, point imbrued proper, on a chief gules a tower triple-towered of the
second (for Lloyd) ; 4, barry nebuly of six, or and sable (for Blount) ;
5, gules, a griffin segreant or, a chief ermine (for Short).

Crest—A two-headed eagle displayed sable, crowned with one four-balled
coronet or.

Residences—France ; and 5, South Grove, Tunbridge Wells, Eng. (temp.).

Clubs and Societies—Several British and Foreign, Learned and other.

B IGELOW, Rev. FRANK HAGAR,
of Washington, D.C. (Son of Francis Edwin
Bigelow, of Concord, Mass, 1809-73, m Ann,
1813-98, da. of Nathan and Sally (Travis) Hagar,
of Weston, Mass. ; son of Converse, d 1858 ; son of
Capt. Converse, d 1829 ; son of Lieut. Josiah,
d 1810 ; son of Lieut. Thomas, d 1756 ; son of
Samuel, d 1731 ; son of John Bigelow [or Bigulah],
of Watertown, Mass., 1617-1703, m Mary Warren.
He served in the Pequot and King Philip's Wars).

Born at Concord, Mass., Aug. 28, 1851 ; Grad. at
Harvard Univ., M.A., B.A., 1873 ; Episcopal
Theological School, Cambridge, Mass., B.D.,
1880 ; Columbian Univ., Wash., D.C., Hon.
L.H.D., 1899 ; Prof. of Meteorology, U.S.
Weather Bureau ; Assist. Min. St. John's Episcopal Church ; and
Prof. of Solar Physics, Columbian Univ., Wash. D.C. ; m Oct. 6,
1881, Mary Ellen, da. of the Rev. Amos Fletcher Spalding, of
Warren, R.I., and Norwich, Conn., and Caroline Elizabeth, da. of
Daniel Saunderson and Almira Stevens.

Issue.

i. MARIAN, b April 29, 1884 ; d June 5, 1884.

Arms—Or, three lozenges azure.

Crest—A ram's head erased azure, charged with three lozenges, attired or.

Residence—1625 Mass. Avenue, Washington, D.C.   *Club*—Cosmos.

Societies—Washington Academy of Sciences, Philosophical, Deutsche Meterol
Gesells, &c., &c.

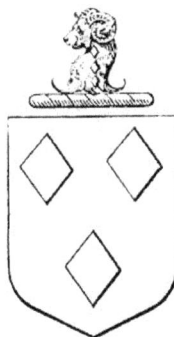

S UMNER, Rear-Admiral GEORGE WATSON, U.S.N.,
S (Retired).
of Washington, D.C. (Only son of Watson Sumner,
M.D., of Constantine, Mich., on Commission to
determine boundary of Mich., *b* 1794. *d* 1847,
m 1841, Hester Ann, *b* 1820, *d* Dec. 14, 1877,
daughter of Samuel Le Page Welling, of New
York and Coldwater, Mich., and Hannah Hussey,
his wife, of Baltimore, Md.—Descended in the
5th gen. from William Sumner, of Bicester,
Oxfordshire, Eng., who came to America in 1636,
and settled at Dorchester, Mass).

Born at Constantine, Mich., December 31, 1841 ;
entered Naval Service in 1858, retired in
1903 ; Educated at Naval Academy, Annapolis,
Md. ; served in the War of the Rebellion ; in the Spanish American
War, and on various sea and shore stations ; Honorary Member of
the Regular Army and Navy Union ; Charter Member Naval and
Military Order, Spanish-American War ; Member of the Associated
Veterans of Farraguts Fleet ; *m* (1stly) Nov., 1868, Henrietta Eliza,
d 1885, daughter of John Ruàn, M.D., of "Hannah's Rest," Santa
Cruz, W.I., and Henrietta Krausé, daughter of William Henry
Krausé, and Eliza Farrington Barnes, his wife ; *m* (2ndly) Feb.,
1886, Maudthilde, daughter of William H. Willis and Joanna (White)
Willis.

Issue.

i. Geo. Albert, *b* Aug 8, 1874, *m* Carrie R. Wanser, *d* Dec. 25, 1899,
m (2ndly) Viola Ketcham.
ii. John Saxton, *b* Sept. 22, 1876 ; *m* Eloise Peckham.
i. Florence Watson, *b* Oct. 4, 1869, *m* Walter Newell Giles.
ii. Alice Blythe, *b* Nov. 29, 1872, *d* April 18, 1905, *m* Clay John
Halverson.
iii. Helen Louise (Georgine L.), *b* Oct. 14, 1881.
iv. Mary Elizabeth (Maude C.), *b* February 20, 1883.

Arms—Ermine, two chevrons gules.
Crest—A lion's head erased argent, ducally gorged or.
Motto—In medio tutissimus ibis.

Residence—"The Pines," Patchogue, Long Island, N.Y.
Societies—Sons of the American Revolution, Regular Army and Navy Union,
Military Order Foreign Wars, Naval and Military Order Spanish-American
War, and Associated Veterans of Farragut's Fleet.

BARCLAY, SACKETT MOORE,
of N.Y. City (Son of Henry Barclay, of
Astoria, L.I., 1794-1865, m Sarah A. Moore,
1809-73, da. of Daniel Sackett and Hannah Moore,
of Newtown, L.I., son of Anthony, of Newtown,
L.I.; son of Rev. Henry, 1714-64, Rector of Trin.
Ch., N.Y.; son of Rev. Thos. Barclay, 1667-1725,
of St. Peters, Albany, Ord. Priest by Bp. of
London, 1707, m 1709, Anna Dorothea, da. of
Rear-Adml. Drauyer and Gertrude Van Schaick).

Born at Astoria, L.I., Dec. 1, 1850; m Oct.
19, 1871, Cornelia, da. of Henry Anthony
Waldburg and Cornelia (Cochrane) Barclay.
Mrs. Barclay descends from Dr. John
Cochrane, 1730-1807, Surg.-Genl. of the Revol.
Army, son of James Cochrane, founder of
Cochranville, Pa.

Issue.

i. HAROLD, b Aug. 14, 1872, m 1906 Helen Fuller Potter of New York.
ii. ROBERT COCHRANE, b Mar. 26, 1874, m 1906 Anita Caldwell
i. BEATRICE WALDBURG, m Stockton Beekman Colt. |Goldsborough.
ii. ETHEL NETHERCLIFT, m Thornton Chard.
iii. CORNELIA COCHRANE.

Arms—Gules, a chevron argent, betw. three crosses pattée of the second.
Crest—A sword in pale ppr.   Motto—Crux Christi nostra corona.
Arms—(Cochrane) ar. a chev. gu. betw. three boars' heads erased az.
Crest—A horse pass.   Motto—Virtute et Labore.

Residences—37 West 46th Street, N.Y. City; Thornfield, Cazenovia, N.Y.
Clubs—Union, St. Nicholas.   Society—Colonial Order.

HOWES, REUBEN, WING, JR., REV.,
of N.Y. City (Son of Reuben Wing Howes
1813-97, founder of Nat. Park Bank N.Y., m 1837
Melissa A. Townsend; son of Daniel 1763-1824;
son of Moody 1724-1806; son of Thomas 1699-1764;
son of Ebenezer, d 1726, m Sarah, grand-da. of
John Gorham the Puritan Captain; son of Jeremiah
1637-1706, m Sarah, da. of Thomas Prence, 4th
Gov. of Plymouth Colony; son of Thomas 1590-1665
of Yarmouth Mass. 1639; son of Thomas; son of
Robert Howes of Carlton Rode, Co. Norfolk, Eng.).

Born at N.Y. City January 31, 1841; A.B.A.M.
Columbia Univ., S.T.D. Racine Coll. Wis-
consin; m Nov. 15, 1864, Emilie, da. of
B. F. Breeden.

Issue.

i. FREDERICK REUBEN, b 1865, d 1900, m 1892 Augusta Schieffelin.
ii. REUBEN WING, b Aug. 12, 1867.
iii. LEANDER TOWNSEND, b July 19, 1872.
i. IRENE HORTON, b 1870, d 1872.

Arms—Argent, a chevron between three griffins' heads erased sable.
Crest—A demi-unicorn issuing out of a ducal crown all proper.
Motto—Stat fortuna domus.
Residence—N.Y. City.   Society—Delta Phi.

CORBUSIER, WILLIAM HENRY,
Lt.-Col., Dep.-Sur.-Gen., U.S.A. (Son of Wm. Morrison Corbusier 1819-80, *m* 1841, Mahala Myers; son of James H. 1795-1846, *m* Eleanor Sloat 1818; son of Thomas Pullein 1761-96 of Harris's Bay, Bermuda, *m* 1782, Alice Peniston ; son of James, *d* 1766, *m* 1748, Ann, da. of Col. Wm. Outerbridge, Chief Justice of Bermuda ; son of Col. Henry Corbusier, mem. of the Assembly and Council, Col. of Colonial Troops, *b* 1700, in Bermuda, *d* April 24, 1764).

Born April 10, 1844; served in War of Rebel'n. 1864-65, in Philippines, Spanish-Amer. War, and Philippine Insurrection ; *m* Mar. 22, 1869, Fanny, da. of the late Geo. Towers Dunbar, Engr. Bd. of Public Wks, and Dep.-Surv.-Gen. of Louisiana, and Surveyor of New Orleans.

Issue.

i. CLAUDE ROMEYN, *b* Aug. 3, 1871.
ii. HAROLD DUNBAR, *b* Jan. 14, 1873, B.S. and M.D., U.S. Army.
iii. PHILIP WORTHINGTON, *b* July 4, 1875, 1st Lt.14th Cavalry U.S. Army.
iv. FRANCIS ADDISON, *b* Mar. 15, 1877. v. WM. TREMAINE, *b* Jan. 31, 1882.
Arms—Vair arg. and az., on a canton a lion ramp. *Crest*—A demi-lion ramp.

Residence—See Army Stations.
Societies—Colonial Wars, Sons of the Am. Rev., War of 1812, Nat. Soc. of the Army of the Philippines, Am Flag Assn., Mil. O. Moro Campaigns.

KNIGHT, EDWARD COLLINGS, JR.,
of Phila. (Son of Edward C. Knight, 1813-1892, Mem. Pa. Constitutional Convention, 1st Pres. Amer. S.S. Co., Pres. Del. and Bound Brook R.R. Co., Pres. N. Pa. R.R. Co., Pres. Guarantee Trust and Safe Deposits Co., *m* 1841, Anna M. Magill ; son of Jonathan, 1788-1823, *m* Rebecca Collings ; son of William, *m* 1784 ; son of Jonathan, *m* 1756 ; son of Isaac, *m* 1728 ; son of Thomas, settled in N. Jersey 1683 ; son of Giles, *m* Eliz'th, da. of Thos. Williams of Whitenhurst, Co. Gloucester ; son of Edward of Woodends ; son of John of Cromehall Manor ; son of John Knight, *b* 1540 ; a Gloucester Recusant 1577).

Born in Phila. Dec. 14, 1863 ; Pres. Dela. and Bound Brook R.R. Co. ; Mem. First Troop Phila. City Cavalry ; Pres. N. Pa. R.R. Co.; *m* June 3, 1886 Clara Waterman, da. of Edmund Parsons Dwight.

Issue.

i. CLARA WATERMAN.

Arms—Sable, a griffin segreant or. *Crest*—A talbot's head erased bezantée.

Residences—1629 Locust Street, Phila.; "Claradon Court," Newport, R.I.
Clubs—Philadelphia, Rittenhouse, Rabbit, Racquet; Union, Brook, New York Yacht.

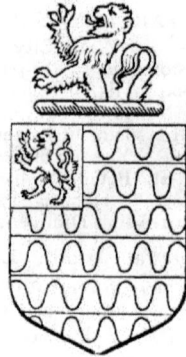

PLYMPTON, GILBERT MOTIER,
    of N.Y. (Son of Col. Joseph Plympton,
U.S.A., 1787-1860, of Sudbury, Mass., m Eliza M.
1801-73, da. of Peter Wm. and Eliza (Beekman)
Livingston; son of Ebenezer 1756-1834; son of
Thomas 1723-89; son of Peter 1666-1743; son of
Thomas Plympton, b Sudbury, Suffolk, Eng., cir.
1620, founded Sudbury, Mass., killed 1676, a
descendant of the Plympton family of Knares-
borough, Yorks., the Eldred de Plympton was a
landowner there temp. Domesday Survey).

Born in N.Y. City, Jan. 15, 1835; Grad. at N.Y.
    Univ. LL.B., 1863; retired from the Law
    1889, entd. Banking, founder of Redmond,
    Kerr & Co.; m May 3, 1864, Mary A., da. of
    Linus W. Stevens of N.Y.

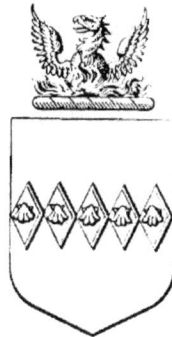

Issue.
i. GILBERT LIVINGSTON, b March 8, 1869, d Dec. 2, 1869.
i. MARY LIVINGSTON, m Robert M. Tarleton.

Arms—Azure, five fusils in fesse or, each charged with an escallop gules.
Crest—A phœnix or, out of flames proper.   *Motto*—Sufficit meruisse.

Residences—30 West 52nd Street, N.Y. City; Wyndtryst, Great Neck, L.I.
Clubs—Metropolitan, Union, St. Nicholas, N.Y. Yacht, Larchmont Yacht, Riding,
    Down Town Association, Westchester Country, Laurentian of Canada.
Societies—Sons of the Rev., Colonial Wars, War of 1812, Colonial Order of the
    Acorn, St. Nicholas, Met. Mus. of Art, Botanical, Zoological, N.Y. Hist.,
    Am. Hist., N.Y. Geneal., M. Ch. of Commerce, Mus. of Nat. Hist., St.
    Andrews.

POND, EDWIN WATSON,
    of Walton, N.Y. (Son of Julius Roswell Pond
    of New Hartford Ct., 1822-91, m Martha A.
Watson 1821-84; son of Roswell 1772-1826; son
of Roswell 1746-76; son of Josiah b 1710; son
of Samuel, b 1679; son of Samuel 1648-1718; son
of Samuel Pond, came with Gov. John Winthrop
1630, m 1642 Sarah Ware, d 1654. Also descd.
from Gov. John Webster, Gov. Thomas Welles,
and John Watson, 1650. Also 12th from John
Warren, of Hadbury, Devonshire, who was 21st
from Rollo, 1st Duke of Normandy, d 927).

Born at New Hartford Ct. June 17, 1853; ex-
    Vestryman of Christ Ch., Walton, N.Y.;
    Pres. of the Village of Walton, N.Y., 1903,
    1904, 1905 and 1906; m Feb. 11, 1886, Florence,
    da. of Samuel Henry St. John, of N.Y.

Issue.
i. SAMUEL HENRY ST. JOHN, b Aug. 24, 1891.
i. MARTHA WATSON, b Dec. 26, 1886, d Apr. 16, 1888.
ii. EMILY ST. JOHN, b Mar. 14, 1888, d Apr. 19, 1888.
iii. SARAH ELIZABETH.

Arms—Argent, a fesse gules between two boars heads, in chief, erased sable,
    and a cross pattée in base of the second.
Crest—A fleur-de-lis gules.   *Motto*—Fide et amore.

Residence—Walton, Delaware Co., N.Y.   *Society*—Colonial Wars.

PARTRIDGE, EDWARD LASELL, M.D.,
of N.Y. City (Son of Joseph. L. Partridge,
1804-1900, m Zibiah N. Willson; son of Cotton,
1765-1846; son of Lieut. Samuel, 1730-1809; son
of Cotton, 1705-33; son of Samuel, 1672-1736;
son of Colonel Samuel, 1645-1740; son of William
Partrigg, of Hartford, Ct., 1640, who came from
Berwick-on-Tweed. Also 7th in desct. from Gov.
Simon Bradstreet.)

Born at Newton, Mass., Sept. 27, 1853; Grad. Coll.
of Physicians and Surgeons (Med. Dep.
Columbia Univ.), 1875; Hon. A.M. Williams'
Coll., 1880; Consulting Phys. N.Y. Hosp.,
N.Y. Inf. Asylum, N.Y. Maternity Hos., and the Sloan Maternity
Hosp.; m Sept. 18, 1884, Gertrude Edwards, da. of Hon. Theodore
W. Dwight, LL.D.

Issue.

i. THEODORE DWIGHT, *b* December 26, 1890.

Arms—(Bradstreet) Argent, a greyhound passant gules, on a chief sable three
crescents or.

Crest—An arm embowed in armour the hand grasping a scimitar.

Motto—Virtute non vi.

———

Residences—19 Fifth Avenue, New York City; "Storm King," Cornwall, N.Y.
Clubs—Century, University, Riding.   *Society*—Colonial Wars, Huguenot.

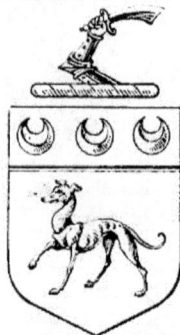

———

THOMAS, DOUGLAS HAMILTON,
of Baltimore (Son of Dr. John Hanson
Thomas), 1813-37, m Annie C. Gordon, 1819-86,
of Falmouth, Va,; son of John Hanson, 1779-1815;
son of Dr. Philip, 1747-1815; son of James, d 1760;
son of James Thomas, *b* in Wales; settled in Kent
Co., Md., 1702; m Elizabeth Hacket).

Born at Balto., Jan. 1, 1847; Capt. and Major
5th Regt. Nat. Guard, 1868-77; Cashier
Marine Nat. Bank, 1878-80; Cashier Merchants Nat. Bank, 1880-86; Pres. 1886 to
present time; Finance Commissioner, 1886-
92; Commissioner, Public Parks, 1886-92;
m Jan. 25, 1870, Alice Lee, da. of Dr. John
Whitridge, of Baltimore.

Issue.

i. DOUGLAS HAMILTON, Jr., *b* Mar. 5, 1872.
ii. JOHN HANSON, *b* Mar. 1, 1876.   i. ALICE LEE.

Arms—Sable, a chevron and canton ermine.
Crest—A demi-unicorn ermine, armed and crined or, supporting a shield sable.
Motto—Virtus invicta gloriosa.

———

Residence—1010 St. Paul Street, Baltimore, Md.   *Club*—Maryland of Baltimore.
Societies—Colonial Wars, Order of Runnemede.

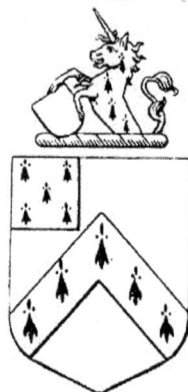

EVANS, JAMES, M.D.,
of Florence, S.C. (Son of Hon. Thomas Evans, of Marion, S.C., State Senator for 12 years, Comr. in Equity, Presidential Elector for S.C., 1832, *b* 1790, *d* 1845, *m* 1816, Jane Beverley, *b* 1795, *d* 1861, da. of George and Martha Daniel, of Oxford, N.C.; son of Lieut. Nathan Evans, 1760-1810, *m* Edith, da. of. Thomas, son of John Godbold, R.N., of Kent, England; son of Nathaniel Evans, of Rydwillin, Caemarthen, came to Pennsylvania 1701-12, joined Society of Baptists under Rev. Thomas Griffiths, removed to "Welch Tract," Cravan Co., S.C., 1735, *m* Ruth Jones, of the Evans family, of Northorpe, Co. Flint, descendants of Ethelystan Glodrydd, Prince of Ferlys, founder of the 4th Royal Tribe of Wales).

Born at Marion, S.C., Sept. 2, 1831; Sec. State Board of Health of South Carolina; late Surgeon 3rd S.C. Reg. C.S.A.; State Engineer of Arkansas, 1856 8; Graduated at Univ. of Penna. M.D., 1861; *m* Jan. 4, 1865, Maria Antoinette, daughter of William Alexander Powell, Esqr., of Leesburg, Va., and Lucy Peachy, daughter of Hon. Daniel Lee, of Winchester, Va.

Issue.

i. POWELL, *m* 1898, Julia Estelle Merchant, of Phila.
ii. WILLIAM ALEXANDER.
iii. JAMES, Jr.
iv. THOMAS.
v. LLEWELLYN STUART (*decd.*)
i. JANE BEVERLEY.
ii. MARIA LEE, *m* 1897, Hon. Frank B. Gary, of Abbeville, S C.
iii. MARIE ANTOINETTE, *m* 1901, Henry Carrington Riely, of Richmond, Va.
iv. LUCY PEACHY, *m* 1904, Rev. Caleb Brecknall Kneaoles Weed (P.E.), of East Orange, New Jersey, Rector of St. John's Church, Fort Smith, Arkansas.

Arms—Argent, a chevron between three boars' heads couped sable.

Crest—On a ducal coronet or, a boar's head fesseways erased sable.

Motto—Libertas.

Residence—"Florence," Florence Co., South Carolina.

Societies—Southern Surg. and Gynl., Am. Med., Am. Med. Congress, Am. Social Science Assn., Instn. of Arts, Sciences, and Letters, late Presdt. S.C. Med. Assn., United Confed. Veterans, Alumni Assn. Univ. of Penna., S.C. Chapter Sons of Amer. Revolution.

STORY, JOSEPH GRAFTON, Col.,
  of Brooklyn, N.Y. (Son of Robert Randall
Story, 1806-74, of Boston, *m* Nov. 5, 1829, Adelia
Ann, 1813-86, da. of Hon. Reuben Munson, of
N.Y. City; son of William, 1782-1812, *m* Anna
Randall; son of William, 1748-1806, *m* Bathsheba
Gray; son of William, 1720-99, Clerk in the Probate
Court and Registrar of the Court of Admiralty,
Boston, *m* Joanna Appleton; son of Elisha Story,
1683-1725, from Cumberland, Eng., to Boston,
Mass., 1700).

Born in Brooklyn, Mar. 18, 1836; Colonel 1880, and
  Asst. Adj.-Genl. S.N.Y. (Brevet Major.-Genl.
  1904); *m* Oct. 28, 1863, Emma, da. of Henry P.
  and Lucy (Kendall) Freeman, of Brooklyn.

Issue.
i. HENRY GRAFTON, *b* Aug. 22, 1869, *m* Marion Massey.
ii. FRANK RANDALL, *b* Dec. 17, 1871.
i. EMMA LOUISE, *b* 1867, *d* 1868.   ii. JOSEPHINE BEATRICE.

Arms— Argent, a lion rampant double queued gules.
Crest—A demi-lion rampant gules.   *Motto*— Fides vincit et veritas custodit.

Residence—21 Herkimer Street, Brooklyn, N.Y.
Societies— Colonial Wars, Sons of the Revolution, War of 1812, Lafayette Post
  No. 140, G.A.R.

JONES, E. CLARENCE,
  of N.Y. City (Son of John Parry Jones, *b* in
Wales, 1830, *d* in New York, 1871, *m* 1885, Ellen
Jane, da. of George Stephenson Hovey, of Nottingham, England.—A descendant of the Jones family
from whom was descended John Parry Jones, of
Llwyn-Oun, Denbighshire, who assumed the additional surname of Parry on his marriage to his
cousin Margaret, da. of Love Parry).

Born in N.Y. City, May 6, 1865; Banker, of the
  firm of E. Clarence Jones and Co., Nassau
  Street, N.Y. City and Philadelphia; *m* Jan. 24,
  1894, divorced 1900, Adelaide Estelle, da. of
  Alfred Storms, of N.Y. City.

Arms—Ermine, a lion rampant sable.
Crest—On a chapeau gules turned up ermine a demi-lion rampant or.
Motto—Gofal dyn duw ai gwerid.

Residence—165 West 58th Street, N.Y. City.
Clubs—Manhattan, Republican, Lawyers, Larchmont Yacht, Indian Harbour
  Yacht, Riverside Yacht, Suburban Riding and Driving, Metropolitan,
  Stock Exchange, N.Y. Riding, Ardsley, Cercle du Bois du Boulogne Paris,

B LOSSOM, BENJAMIN,
of N.Y. (Son of Chas. W. Blossom of
Brooklyn, *b* 1827, *m* Mary Webb, da. of Miles
Cook of Brooklyn, N.Y, [descd. from Francis
Cook, *b* 1577, Blyth, Notts., came in the "Mayflower" 1620]; son of Benjamin 1790-1877; son of
Benjamin 1753-1837; son of Benjamin 1721-1797;
son of Joseph 1673-1749; son of Peter 1627-1700;
son of Thos. Blossom, *b* Eng., em. to Amer. 1629,
d Plymouth Mass.).

Born at Brooklyn, May 20, 1858, *m* (1) Oct. 7, 1886,
Sarah Briggs, 1862-95, da. of Thos. and Ellen
(Masterson) Smith; *m* (2) Nov. 1, 1898, Mrs.
Howard Meyer, da. of Charles and Ellen
Rowena (Pettigrew) Cole.

Arms—Quarterly: 1st and 4th, azure, three wiverns displayed ermine (Blossom);
2nd and 3rd, or, a chevron between two lions passant guardant sable (Cooke).
Crest—Out of a ducal coronet, a hand holding a swan's head and neck erased.

Residences—884 Fifth Avenue, N.Y. City; 955 Orange Grove Boul., Pasadena, Cal.
Clubs—Union League, N.Y. Yacht, Riding, Nassau Co., Suburban Riding and
Driving, N.Y., California, Los Angeles Co., Pasadena Co., Anandale Co.,
Automobile Club of Southern California.
Societies—Sons of the American Revolution, Amer. Museum Natural History,
Veteran Assn. Co. A 23rd Regt. N.G.N.Y., Hon. Mem. Companies A and
J. 23rd Regt. N.G.N.Y. and Veteran Assn. 23rd Regt. N.G.N.Y.

A TKINSON, HENRY M.,
of Atlanta Ga. (Son of George and
Elizabeth (Staigg) Atkinson of Boston, Mass.,
b May 19, 1822; son of Amos, *b* 1792, of Boston;
son of Lt. Amos, *b* 1754, of Newbury; son of
Ichabod, *b* 1714; son of John; son of John
Atkinson, *b* 1640, of Newbury Mass., nephew of
Theodore Atkinson, from Bury St. Edmunds,
Suffolk, to Boston 1634).

Born at Brookline, Mass., Nov. 13, 1862; Banker;
m April 5, 1888, May, da. of Richard Peters.

Issue.
i. HENRY MORRELL, *b* Feb. 23, 1892.
i. MAY PETERS, *b* Oct. 15, 1889.

Arms—Vert, a cross voided between four lions rampant or.
Crest—A dove with wings expanded.
Motto—Nil pacimus non sponte Dei.

Residence—Atlanta, Georgia.
Clubs—Union, Brook, Harvard, of New York; Union, Tennis and Racquet, of
Boston; Capital City Club, Atlanta.
Society—Sons of the Revolution.

D E WOLF, EDWIN ALLIS,
  of St. Louis, Mo. (Second son of
Elisha De Wolf, of Blue Earth, Minn.,
b 1816, *m* 1840, Sabra Sherman; son of
Elisha, 1772-1855; son of Elisha, 1748-
1838; son of Simon, 1718-55; son of
Josiah, 1689-1767; son of Simon, 1648-95;
son of Belthasar De Wolf, one of the first
settlers of Lyme, Conn., 1666, *d* 1696).

Born at Walpole, N.H., Sept. 19, 1844;
    m Oct. 17, 1877, Margaret Harding,
    da. of Hon. John Marshall Krum,
    (Mayor of Alton, Ill., 1837; Mayor of
    St. Louis, Mo., 1848; Judge of the
    Circuit Court), and Mary Ophelia, da.
    of Chester Harding.

Issue.

i. HERBERT, *b* Nov. 14, 1883, *d* Feb. 17, 1903.
i. OPHELIA, *b* May 21, 1881; *d* May 8, 1888.

Arms—Or, three wolves' heads erased sable borne on the breast of an Imperial
    Eagle sable beaked or, the shield surmounted by a Baron's coronet.
Crest—Out of a ducal coronet a demi-wolf gules holding in the dexter paw a
    fleur-de-lis.   *Motto*—Vincit qui patitur.

Residence—5459 Bartmer Avenue, St. Louis, Mo.
Societies—Mayflower Descendants, Colonial Wars, Sons of the Revolution.

B ASCOM, GEORGE JONATHAN,
  of N.Y. City (Son of Jonathan Bascom,
1806-78, *m* Feb. 2, 1842, Mary Ann, 1812-96, da. of
Joseph and Elfrida (Crosby) Holbrook.—Descended
from Thomas and Avis Bascombe (Batiscombe)
from Dorsetshire, England, *circa* 1634, to Windsor,
Conn., probably of Combe Keynes, Dorsetshire,
d 1682).

Born at Brooklyn, N.Y., April 14, 1845; Major
    171st Regiment N.G.S.N.Y.; formerly Captain
    in 71st Regiment N.G.S.N.Y.; *m* Sarah
    Virginia, daughter of Isaac More Tyson, of
    N.Y. City, and Esther, daughter of Timothy
    Ide and Esther Armington.

Arms—Gules, a chevron between three bats displayed sable.
Crest—An olive branch proper.   *Motto*—Non omnis moriar.

Residence—New York City.
Clubs—New York Yacht, Atlantic Yacht, Riverside Yacht of Conn., Mecox Yacht
    of L.I., Saratoga Golf, Saratoga Golf, Army and Navy.
Societies—Colonial Wars, Sons of American Revolution, 71st Reg. Veteran
    Ass'n., A. and H. Artillery of Boston, Old Guard, London Numismatic.

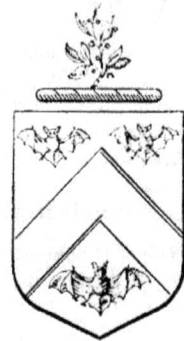

MOSELEY, FRANK,

of Brookline, Mass. (Son of Thomas Edward Moseley of Boston, 1823-90, *m* Mary 1827-97, da. of Edward Crehore of Milton; son of Thomas M., 1796-1877; son of Thomas, *b* 1759; son of Mr. Thomas, 1728-96; son of Ebenezer, *b* 1695; son of Ebenezer, 1673-1740; son of Thomas, 1636-1706; son of John and Cicily Maudesley, of England; *d* 1661).

Born at Roxbury, Mass., March, 1854; *m* April 29, 1880, Martha A.,* da. of Charles H. Hawes, 1828-62, grandson of Deacon Joseph Hawes, 1758-1850, who *m* Thankful, a grand-da. of John Matthews, 1682-1776, of Boston, Mass.

Issue.

i. ELISE.

Arms—Quarterly, 1st and 4th sable, a chevron between three battle-axes argent; 2nd and 3rd or, a fesse between three eagles displayed sable.
Crest—An eagle displayed sable.   *Motto*—Mos legem regit.

Residence—1053 Beacon Street, Boston, Mass.
Clubs—Algonquin. Boston Art.
Societies—Colonial Wars. Bostonian. Sons of the Am. Revol., Bunker Hill Mon. Assn., *Descendants of Colonial Governors, *Mayflower Descdts.

COLLINS, CLARENCE LYMAN,

of N.Y. City (Son of Charles Collins, of Hartford, Conn.—Descended from John Collins, 1616-70, to Boston, Mass., 1644; son of John Collins, of London and Brampton, Co. Suffolk, Eng.—Desc'd. from Richard Lyman, *b* High Ongar, Co. Essex, 1580, to America 1631, related to Sir John Lyman, Knt., Lord Mayor of London 1616. From Thomas Tracy, of Norwich Ct., grandson of Richd. Tracy, of Stanway, Glouc. 1559. From Govr. William Leete, *b* 1612, grandson of Thomas of Ockington, Cambs., and from Govr. William Bradford).

Born at Hartford, Conn., Feb. 22, 1848; *m* Oct. 12, 1870, Marie Louise Clark, daughter of the Hon. Horace F. and Marie Louise (Vanderbilt) Clark, of N.Y. City.

Issue.

i. EDITH LYMAN, *m* Rechid Bey, Count Czaykowski.

Arms—Sable, on a chevron betw. three doves argent, five guttées de sang.
Crest—A dove close argent.   *Motto*—Volabo ut requiescam.

Residence—The Ansonia, New York City.
Clubs—Lambs, Merchants, City, New York Yacht, Suburban Riding and Driving Club, and Gentlemen's Driving Club.
Societies—Colonial Wars, Mayflower Descendants, Mem. Chamber of Commerce, Sons of the Revolution, Metropolitan Museum of Art, Founder and Patriots, New England, Sculptors, Trade and Transportation.

M ANIERRE, WILLIAM REID,
of Chicago (Son of George Manierre,
1817-63, *m* Ann Hamilton, da. of William Reid,
Barrister, of Glasgow, Scot.; son of John, 1782-1823,
m Nancy Lee; son of Louis Manierre, 1757-1794,
b in Normandy, 1757, to America *temp.* French
Revol., settled in New London, Ct., 1785; served
in American Revol. with Genl. La Fayette,
m Rebecca Miner, a descendant of Captain Thomas
Miner, of Pequot, New London, Ct., 1608-90,
Dep.-Gen. Ct., 1650-1, Chief Military at Mystic,
Ct., 1665).

Born in Chicago, April 25, 1847; Grad. of the Union Coll. of Law, 1878,
Chicago Univ.; served in Civil War, 1864; Mem. of the 134th Ill.
Vols.; City Alderman 1883 to 1897; County Commr., 1891-92;
m April 1875, Julia Orr, da. of Cyrus Edson, of Albany, N.Y.

Issue.

i. George, *b* May 15, 1876.
ii. William Reid, *b* Aug. 31, 1885;
 d March 30, 1891.
iii. Edson, *b* Nov. 19, 1892.
iv. Harold, *b* Jan. 22, 1897.

i. Marguerite.
ii. Julie Edson.
iii. Wilhelmine.
iv. Aline.

Arms—D'argent a un pin de sinople a dexter d'une tete de more.

Residence—399 Superior Street, Chicago, Illinois.
Clubs—City, Onwentsia, South Shore Country Club, Saddle and Cycle.
Society—Grand Army of the Republic.

B YINGTON, CHARLES SPERRY,
of Pasadena, Cal. (Son of John Fletcher
Byington, 1832-72; grandson of Justus Byington
1763-1839, who served in Capt. Ambrose Sloper's
Coy. of Conn. Militia 1779.—Descd. from John
Byington (Byntone), weaver, who came from
Dublin to Bradford, Conn., 1699; also from
Robert Hinsdale, *d* 1765; and Joseph Loomis,
1616-87, member of Windsor Troop of Horse, King
Philip's War).

Born at Newton, Michigan, Mar. 14, 1861; Adjut. 10th Battalion (1st
Lieut.) N.G.N.Y., Honourably discharged March 16, 1893; *m* Jennie,
da. of Charles Stanford.

Issue.

i. Chloe Castle, *b* at Albany, N.Y., May 3, 1896.

Arms—Argent, an eagle displayed sable, on a chief vert three roses of the field.

Residences—Pasadena, Calif., and Boston, Mass.
Clubs—The Country Club, Brookline, Mass.; Pasadena Country Club.
Societies—Colonial Wars; Sons of the Revolution: Old Guard, Albany Zouave
 Cadets.

READ, HARMON PUMPELLY, Maj., F.R.G.S., of Albany (Eldest son of His Exc. Gen.
John Meredith Read, 1837-96; Knt. Gr. Cross, O.
of the Redeemer; F.S.A., F.R.I.A.; U.S. Con.-
Gen. to France; U.S. Min. to Greece; Adj.-Gen.
N.Y. State with rank of Brig.-Gen. at outbreak of
the War of the Rebellion, m Delphine Marie, da.
of Harmon Pumpelly, [Pres. Albany Savings Bk.,
Albany Insur. Co., Albany Gas Co.,] and Delphine,
da. of Hon. John R. Drake, County Judge, Mem. of
N.Y. S. Assly. and Mem. of Cong.; son of Hon.
John M. Read, LL.D., 1797-1874, Ch. Just. of Pa.,
m Priscilla. da. of Hon. Josiah Marshall, of Boston;
son of Hon. John Read, 1769-1854, State Senator,
apptd. by Pres. John Adams, Agt.-Gen. U.S.,
m Martha, da. of Brig.-Gen. Saml. Meredith, Mem. Contl. Cong. and First
Trea. of the U.S., and Margaret, da. of Thos. Cadwalader, M.D.,[descd.
from Rhodri-Mawr, King of all Wales, d 876]; son of His Exc. Hon.
Geo. Read, 1733-98, Atty.-Gen., one of the six Signers of the Decl. of
Indep., was also Vice-Pres. of Delaware, became Governor on the capture,
of McKinley during Revol., U.S. Senator, Judge of the Ct. of Admiralty,
m Gertrude, da. of Rev. Geo. Ross, M.A., Rector of Immanuel Ch.
grand-da. David Ross, Laird of Balblair, Scot.; son of Col. John Read,
b in Dublin 1688, d 1756, Proprietor of Kingsley Manor, Md., Comnr. of
Charlestown, Md.; son of Henry Read, Esq., b 1662, of Dublin, m Mary
Molins (MacMollins); son of Sir Charles Read, bap. 1622, of London and
Dublin; son of Richard Read, Esq., 1579-1659, m Helen, da. of Sir Alex.
Cave of Rotherby; son of Thos. Read of Barton Court, H. Sh. of Berks
1581, m Mary Stonhouse; son of Thos. Rede of Barton Ct. Ar., m Anne,
da. of Thos. Hoo, of the Hoo; son of Thomas Hoo, Ar., son of one of the
Knights present at Agincourt; son of Wm. Rede, gent.; son of Edwd.
Rede, Ar.; son of Edwardus Rede, Ar., H. Sh. of Berks 1439).

Born July 13, 1860; former Inspector of Rifle Practice 5th Brig.
N.G.S.N.Y. rank of Major; Pres. of Young Men's Assn. 1886;
Regent of Philip Livingston Chapter, Sons of the Revol.; Gov.-Gen.
Knts. of Albion; m Aug. 24, 1889, Cath. Marguerite, da. of Mons.
Jacques Frederic de Carron d'Allondans.

Arms—Qtly. 1 and 4 gr. qts., qtly. 1 and 4 a saltire betw. four garbs or (Read);
2 and 3 gu. three lions ramp. arg. (Ross); 2 and 3 gr. qts. arg. a lion
ramp. sa. coll. and chained or (Meredith).

Crests—1, on the stump of an oak tree erect a falcon rising ppr. belled and
jessed or (Read); 2, a demi-lion ramp. gu. (Ross); 3, a demi-lion sa. col.
and ch. or (Meredith).

Motto—Cedant arma togæ.

Residence—236 State Street, Albany, N.Y.

Clubs—Fort Orange, Unconditional, Albany.

Societies—Geographical, France; Histl., N.Y.; Knts. of Albion; Delta Psi; 32.
Masonic; Cincinnati of Del.; Sons of the Revl.; Col. Wars. Mayfl'r. Desc's.

JESUP, MORRIS KETCHUM,
of N.Y. (Son of Chas. Jesup, of Saugatuck,
Ct. *m* Abigail, da. of Hon. Saml. B. Sherwood;
son of Major Ebenezer, of Saugatuck, Ct.; son of
Dr. Ebenezer, of Green's Farms; son of
Edward; son of Edward of Green's Farms; son
of Edward Jessup, of Fairfield, Ct., 1639, one of
the two original Patentees of West Farms, Westchester Co., N.Y., 1664, of the Jessops, of Brome-
hall, Sheffield, Yorks., Eng.).

Born at Westport, Ct., June 21, 1830; Hon. A.M.
Williams Coll. and Yale Univ. 1881, A.M.
Columbia Univ. 1900, and LL.D., Princeton
Univ. 1902; Pres. of the Chamber of Com-
merce, N.Y., 1898; Pres. Amer. Museum of Nat. Hist. 1881; *m* April
26, 1854, Maria Van Antwerp, da. of Rev. Thos. De Witt, D.D.,
of N.Y.

Arms—Barry of six argent and azure, nine mullets gules, three three and three.
Crest—A dove standing on an olive branch proper.

Residences—195-7 Madison Avenue, N.Y. City: Lenox, Mass.; Bar Harbor, Me.
Clubs—Century, Metropolitan, University, Jekyl Island, New York Yacht, Metropolitan of Washington, Rittenhouse of Philadelphia.

MACKENZIE, ALEXANDER WILLIAM,
of Columbus, Ohio (Son of Rowland P.
Mackenzie, of Trinidad, 1841-77; son of Lt.-Col.
Alexr. Wm., of London, Eng.; son of Major Alexander, *d* in Canada, 1852; son of Colonel George,
of Murray Keith's Highlanders, present at the
Storming of Seringapatam 1783; son of John,
of Lochend 1741; son of Alexander, of Gairloch,
d 1694; son of Kennith; son of Alexander, *d* 1638;
son of John R; son of John; son of Hector "The
Red"; son of Alexr. Mackenzie, of Kintail, *d* 1488).

Born at Port of Spain, Trinidad, July 15, 1868;
Banker; Ed. at Queen's Royal Coll.; *m* April
5, 1899, Winifred E.*, da. of Capt. Thos. Lee
Brent, of Columbus, Ohio.

Issue.
i. ALEXANDER KENNETH, *b* March 30, 1905.
i. MARGARET LOUISE, *b* March 17, 1900.

Arms—Azure, within a bordure engrailed, chequy of three gules and or, a stag's
head cabossed, attired with ten tyres or.
Crest—A stag's head cabossed as in Arms.   *Motto*—Data fata secutus.

Residence—463 Town Street East, Columbus, Ohio.
Clubs—Ohio, Arlington Country.
Societies—Old N.W. Geneal., *Colonial Dames, *Daughters of the Amer. Revln.

PHELPS, JOHN JAY, U.S.N.,
of Hackensack, N.J. (Son of Hon. Wm. W.
Phelps, 1839-94, of Englewood, N.J., U.S. Min.
to Germany, *m* Ellen Sheffield : Son of John J.,
1810-69 ; son of Alexander, 1769-1802 ; son of
Capt. David, 1733-95 ; son of Lieut. David, 1710-60 ;
son of Captain Joseph, 1667-1750 ; son of William
Phelps, from Tewkesbury, Eng., to America in
ship " Mary and John," 1630, one of five Commissrs.
to govern Colony of Conn).

Born at Paris, France, Sept. 27, 1861 ; Grad. at
Yale Univ., B.A. 1883 ; Chosen Freeholder of
Bergen County, N.J. ; Ensign U.S. Navy ; Capt. U.S. Merchant
Marine, May, 1898 ; *m* April 26, 1883, Rose J. Hutchinson.

Issue.

i. DOROTHY.   ii. ROSE.

Arms—Argent. on a fesse azure, betw. four lions ramp. ppr. three mullets or.
Crest—A fish naiant proper.   *Motto*—Respice finem.

Residences—" Red Towers," Hackensack, N.J.; " Yoncomis." Stony Creek, Conn.
Clubs—Univ., Un. League, New Haven Yt., N.Y. Yacht. Atlantic Yacht, Seawan-
    haka Cor. Yacht. Oritani Field, Englewood Field, Hamilton. Gent's.
    Driving Assn., Sachems Head Yacht.
Societies—U.Sp. War Vets., Psi Upsilon, Scroll and Keys. Military Order of
    Foreign Wars, Founders and Patriots of America, New England, Am.
    Geographical and Am. A.A.

COOKE, JAY, JR.,
of Philadelphia (Son of Jay Cooke of Sandusky
Ohio, settled in Phila. 1837, *b* 1821, *m* 1844, Dorothea
Elizabeth Allen ; son of Eleutheros, *b* 1787, *m* Martha
Carswell ; son of Asaph, 1748-1826, *m* Thankful
Parker ; son of Asaph 1720-92, *m* Sarah Parker ; son
of Samuel, *b* 1668, *m* Hannah Ives ; son of Samuel,
b 1641, *m* Hope Parker ; son of Henry Cooke of
Salem Mass., 1638, *d* 1661, *m* 1639, Judith, da. of
Henry Burdsall of Salem).

Born in Phila., Aug. 10, 1845, *m* April 22, 1868,
Clara Alice, da. of Joel Barlow Moorhead.

Issue.

i. JAY COOKE (3rd), *m* Nina Louise, daughter of
    Edwin North Benson.

i. CAROLINE CLARA, *m* Robert Wilder Bush, of Brooklyn Heights, N.Y.

Arms—Or, a chevron gules between two lions passant guardant sable.
Crest—Out of a mural crown argent, a demi lion guardant issuant sable gorged
    with a mural coronet or.   *Motto*—Tutum monstrat iter.

Residence—2204 St. James Place, Philadelphia, Pa.
Clubs—Union League, Country, Merion Cricket.

VEAZEY, DUNCAN,
     of Baltimore, Md. (Eldest son of George Ross
Veazey of Baltimore, Attorney and Counsellor-at-
Law, *b* 1820, *d* 1856, *m* 1850, Eliza, *b* 1824, *d* 1870,
da. of Rev. John Mason Duncan and Eliza McKim,
of Balto., and grand-da. of John McKim, Jr., of
Balto., and of Capt. Matthew Duncan of Phila.,
and 3rd in desct. from Rev. John Mason of N.Y.,
and 8th in desct. from Cornelis Barentse Van
Wyck, who came from Holland to N.Y., in 1660,
and 6th in desct. from Col. David Provoost, of
N.Y., who was Mayor of N.Y. 1699, Mem. of Genl.
Assembly of N.Y., 1702-11-12, Col. in Colonial
Mil. Force of N.Y. 1718, Mem. of Council 1709-10,
Collector of Duties 1724, and 8th in desct. from
Sergt. David Provoost, who came from Holland to
N.Y. in 1639, and was Comder. of Fort Good Hope 1642-47, Sergt. in
Burgher Corps of New Amsterdam 1653.—Descd. from Col. John Veazey,
Senr., of " Essex Lodge," Cecil Co., Md. 1701-77, Justice for Cecil Co.
1734-57, Col. in Provincial Mil. Force in Cecil Co. 1756-58, Comder. of
Cecil Co. 1755-58, grandson of John Veazey of "Cherry Grove," who
was of the family of Vesey of "Wickes," Essex, derived from the
family of Vesy of Hintlesham, Suffolk, England, and settled in Cecil Co.
in 1687 ; also descd. from Col. John Ward, of Cecil Co. 1673-1747, Col.
in Provincial Mil. Force in Cecil Co. 1717, Mem. of Md. House of
Burgesses 1708-09-11 ; also descd. from William Ward of " Woodlawn,"
Cecil Co. 1727-76, Mem. of Md. House of Burgesses 1762-72, Deputy
from Cecil Co. to Convention of Provl. Deputies of Md. 1774, grandson
of William Ward, who settled in Cecil Co. in 1674 ; also descd. from Rev.
George Ross 1679-1754, the first Rector of Immanuel Church, of Newcastle Del. 1705-54, 2nd son of David Ross, 2nd Laird of Balblair, Co.
Ross, Scotland).

Born at Baltimore, Md., Feb. 16, 1851, Grad. at Univ. of Md. School of
     Law 1877 ; Lawyer ; Mem. of House of Delegates from Cecil Co. in
     Legislature of Md., session of 1882 ; now Auditor of Customs, Balto.
     Md. U.S. Civil Service ; *m* Nov. 24, 1880, Annie Veazey Knight,
     daughter of William and Arabella (Veazey) Knight, of Cecil Co.,
     and grand-daughter of Thomas Brockus and Ann (Ward) Veazey, of
     " Essex Lodge," 5th in desct. from Stephen Knight, of Cecil Co.,
     who was a Mem. of the House of Burgesses of Md. 1720-31, and one
     of the Justices of the Provincial Court of Md. 1738-43.

Issue.

i. GEORGE ROSS, *b* April 19, 1890.

Arms— Ermine, on a cross sable five martlets or.
Crest— An arm embowed couped at the shoulder, erect from the elbow, habited
     gules, cuff ermine, holding in the hand proper five leaves vert.

Residence—2907 St. Paul Street, Baltimore, Md.
Societies—Colonial Wars, Colonial Dames of America.

JUDSON, WILLIAM PIERSON,

of Oswego, N.Y. (Son of Col. John W. Judson, 1810-78, of Ashford, Ct., *m* Emily E., 1820-88, da. of Philo Pierson, of Killingworth, Ct. She was 12th in desc't. from Sir Giles Capel, 1452-1510, and 5th in desc't. from Rector Abraham Pierson, Founder of Yale Coll. 1701. He was 7th in desc't. from Lt. Joseph Judson, 1620-90, of Lancaster, Eng., and Stratford, Ct., from 1634, son of Wm. Judson, *d* New Haven, Ct., 1662 ; and 7th in desc't. from Thos Welles, Gov. of Ct. 1655-58).

Born in Oswego, May 20, 1849 ; Consulting Engr. ; U.S. Civil Engr. on Forts, Harbours, etc., from 1867 ; Dep. State Engr. of N.Y. 1899-1905 ; Mem. Am. Soc. C.E. of N.Y. ; Mem. Inst. of C.E. Lond. ; Asso. Mem. Am. Inst. of Elec. E. ; *m.* Oct. 9, 1888, Mrs. Anna L. McWhorter, *da. of R. H. Thompson, M.D., of Albany, and Anna M. Littlejohn, who was 7th in desc't. from Hon. Richd. Treat, 1584-1669, Deputy Gov.'s Asst. and Mem. Gov.'s Council of Ct., and 7th in desc't. from Hon. Hen. Wolcott, of Tolland, Somersetshire, Eng., and Windsor Ct., Deputy 1639, and Gov'r's.-Assist. 1643-55.

Arms—Per saltire azure and ermine, four lozenges counterchanged.
Crest—Out of a ducal coronet two dexter arms in saltire vested ppr. holding two scimitars in pale.   *Motto*—Vincit que se vincit.

Residences—Oswega, N.Y. ; Broadalbin, Fulton Co. N.Y. ; Punta Gorda, Florida.
Clubs—Fortnightly, Yacht, of Oswego ; Fort Orange of Albany.
Societies—Colonial Wars, Sons of Revol., War 1812, Oswego Hist., Buffalo Hist., N.Y. Genealogical and Biographical, Masonic, National Geographical.
° Colonial Dames.

HYATT, FRANK STANLEY,

of Brooklyn, N.Y. (Son of William Francis Hyatt, *m* (1) Emeline M. Ogden, *m* (2) Julia S. Merrill ; son of Lancelot ; son of Abraham ; son of John ; son of Ebenezer ; son of Thomas ; son of Caleb ; son of Thomas Hyatt, who settled in Stamford, Conn., 1640, served in King Philip's War).

Born at Brooklyn, N.Y., April 1, 1862 ; *m* Oct. 30, 1889, Katharine Estelle, daughter of Eliphalet William and Emma Jane (Smith) Stratton, of New York City.

Issue.

i. Royal Ogden, *b* April 12, 1898, *d* August 22, 1899.
ii. Paul Whitney, *b* February 22, 1901.

Arms—Argent, a lion rampant sable, a chief per fesse indented of the first and second.
Crest—A demi-lion rampant proper. _____.   *Motto*—Fac et spera.
Residence—Brooklyn, N.Y.
Societies—Colonial Wars, Sons of the Revolution.

SMITH, Hon. THOMAS GUILFORD,
of Buffalo, N.Y. (Son of Pemberton Smith,
1816-73, of Phila.; m 1838, Margaretta E., 1817-
1900, da. of Thomas and Hannah (Ogden) Zell.—
Descended from Ralph Smith, of Norfolk, who
settled in Mass. Bay Colony, 1635; at Eastham,
Mass., 1655; his son Ralph, of Eastham, was
father of Ralph, of Burlington, N.J., who m Olive
Clark, and had Ralph, b cir. 1721; m 1749, Marjory,
grand-da. of Jedidiah Allen, member of the N.J.
Colonial Assembly, 1703, the grandson of George
Allen, of Somerset, settled at Lynn, Mass., 1636.
Also descd. from David Ogden, who came to
America with William Penn, 1682, settled in
Chester Co., Pa., d 1705; and descd. from Walter
Newbury, Quaker, at Newport, R.I., 1676, mem.
of Council of Gov. Sir Edmund Andros; also from Henry Howland,
of London, Eng., at Duxbury, Mass., 1633, whose brother John came in
the "Mayflower," 1620; also from Nathaniel Sylvester, of Shelter Island,
N.Y., 1652, who m Grizzel, da. of Thos. Brinley, of Staffordshire, b 1591,
and Auditor of Revenue for Charles I.; and also descd. from William
Swift, of Bocking, Suffolk, came to Mass. 1634; from John Eastwick, of
Boston, 1700; James Lloyd, of Boston, 1675; and from John C. Meng, a
noted German from Mannheim to Germantown, Pa., 1728; also from
Jacob Zell, from Germany to Merion, Pa., 1740; from Wigard Levering,
from Mulheim, Germany, to Penn's Colony, 1685; and from Abraham
Innes and Arent Klincken, founder of Germantown, Phila., Pa., 1685).

Born at Phila. Aug. 27, 1839; Grad. at the Rensselaer Polytechnic Inst.,
Troy, N.Y., C.E., 1861; A.M., LL.D., Hobart Coll. and Alfred
Univ.; Regent of N.Y. Univ.; Pres. Charity Organization Soc.,
Buffalo; Pres. Buffalo Socy. of Natural Sciences; m July 14, 1864,
Mary Stewart, da. of Chauncey P. Ives, of Lansingburgh, N.Y.

Issue.

i. PEMBERTON, C.E., b June 3, 1865; m Edwina W. Winter.

ii. CHAUNCEY PELTON, M.D., b Oct. 27, 1869.

Arms (for Ogden) Gyronny of 8 arg. and gu. in dexter chief an oak branch ppr.

Crest Oak tree ppr., supported by lion ramp. *Motto* Et si ostendo non jacto.

Arms (for Newberry) Ar., three bars az. a chief gu.; *Crest*—Issuant out of a
wreath in full blossom ppr., a Moor's head in profile ppr. *Arms*—(for
Howland) Ar., two bars sa. in chief three lions ramp. of the second; *Crest*
A leopard pass., ducally gorged or. *Arms*—(for Sylvester) Per fesse
dancettee gu. and ar.; *Crest*—Two eagle's wings addorsed. *Arms*—(for
Lloyd) Gu., a lion ramp. or; *Crest* A pelican feeding its young ppr. *Arms*
(for Meng) "Barre contre barre," d'az. et d'ar. de quatre pieces; *Crest*—
Un vol coupe alternativement, d'ar. et d'az. *Arms*—(for Levering) Az.,
three hares in pale ar. *Motto*—Ducit amor patrie.

Residence—489 Delaware Avenue, Buffalo, N.Y.

Clubs—Buffalo, Univ., Buffalo.

Societies—Am. of Civil Engrs., Am. Inst. of Mining Engs., Sons of the Rev.,
Colonial of N.Y., Colonial of Pa., Hist. of Pa., Am. Protective Tariff League,
Buffalo Hist., Buffalo Fine Arts Acad., etc.

LEONARD, WILLIAM A., Rt. Rev. D.D., Bishop of Ohio (Son of W. Boardman Leonard 1820-93, of Brooklyn, N.Y., Presdt. King's Co. Bank and Homœopathic Hospital, m Louisa D. Bulkley 1823-1900 (a descdt. of Rev. Peter Bulkley, of Concord 1636); son of Hon. Stephen B.; son of Silas; son of Joshua; son of Stephen; son of James; son of James; son of Thomas; son of Henry Leonard from Pontypool, Wales, 1626, to Lynn, Mass., later of Taunton).

Born at Southport, Ct., July 15, 1848; Student at St. Stephen's Coll., Annandale; Grad. Berkeley Div. School, Middletown, Ct., 1871; Chaplain of 23rd Regt. N.G.S.N.Y.; Rector Church of the Redeemer, Brooklyn 1872-80; St. John's, Wash. D.C., 1880-89; Consecrated Bishop of Ohio, Oct. 12, 1889; m April 17, 1873, Sarah L., da. of Thos. Sullivan, Presdt. Brooklyn City R.R. Co.

Issue.

i. SARAH LOUISA, d 1887.

Arms—Or, on a fesse azure three fleurs-de-lis argent.
Crest—Out of a ducal crown a wolf's head.   *Motto*—Pour bien desirer.

Residence—840 Euclid Avenue, Cleveland, Ohio.
Clubs—University of Cleveland, Ohio; Church of Cleveland. Ohio.
Societies—Old Colony Historical, American Historical, Sons of Colonial Wars.

EVANS, HENRY, of N.Y. City (Eldest son of Joseph Henry Evans, b in Bledsoe Co., Tenn., Dec. 13, 1835, d Yazo City, Miss., Feb. 3, 1863, Colonel in the Confederate Army and First Aid. on Gen. Wall's staff commanding the Texas Legion, m April 6, 1859, Cora Wilbur, da. of Edward Wyllys Taylor, and Caroline B. Porter, of Houston, Texas.— Descended from Governor John Haynes, of Old Holt, and Copford, Co. Essex, b 1594, d 1653-4; m second wife, Mabel Harlakenden, dau. of Richard, second son of Roger Harlakenden, b 1541, d 1602, who purchased the Earl of Oxford the Manor and Park of Earl's Colne, Essex, 1583. Also eleventh in descent from Governor William Bradford, of Austerfield, England, b 1589, d 1667. He m Alice (Carpenter) Southworth).

Born at Houston, Texas, April 14, 1860; m June 21, 1892, Mary Roland Lopez, of Greensboro, Ala.

Arms—(Harlakenden) Azure, a fesse ermine betw. three lions' heads erased or.
Crest—Between the attires of a stag or, an eagle reguardant with wings expanded.

Residence—20 Fifth Avenue (address, P.O. Box 2038), New York City.
Clubs—Players, Lawyers.
Society—Mayflower Descendants.

JONES, RICHMOND LEGH,

of Reading, Pa. (Son of Hon. J. Glancy Jones
1811-78, U.S. Min. to Austria 1858-61, *m* Anna,
da. of Hon. Wm. Rodman; son of Jehu 1778-1864,
m Sarah Glancy; son of Col. Jonathan, 1740-82,
m Margaret Davis; son of David 1709-84, settled
at Caernarvon Township Pa. 1721, *m* Elizabeth
Davies; son of Rev. William Jones, *b* 1662, of
Llang-wch-llyn, Maesyfallen, Bala, N. Wales,
Rector of Llangower; son of Hugh Jones of
Lllangar, co. Merioneth).

Born at Quincy, Fla., Feb. 17, 1840; Atty. and
Counsellor-at-Law; Capt. of Pa. Vols., War
of the Rebellion 1863; Mem. of Penna. Legislature 1867-69; *m* Nov. 26, 1870, Margaret
E., da. of James and Rebecca (MacVeagh) McCarty.

Issue.

i. ANNA R. JONES, *b* Nov. 24, 1872; *m* June 19, 1895, Nath. Ferguson.

Arms—Or, a lion rampant within a bordure azure.
Crest—A lion rampant azure holding a shield or, within a carved bordure.
Motto—Prorsum et sursum.

Residence—113 North Fifth Street, Reading, Pa.
Societies—Sons of the Revolution, Colonial Wars, Colonial of Penna., War of
1812, Grand Army of the Republic.

PHILLIPS, HENRY BYRON,

of San Francisco (Son of Albert Alex. Phillips,
1827-71, of Scituate, R.I., *m* Almira Rice [a descdt.
of John Rice, of Warwick, R.I., 1650, and wife,
Eliz., g.-gr.-da. of Lewys Lathame, gent., Sergeant-
Falconer to Charles I.]; g.-g.-son of Joseph Phillips,
1773-1852, and wife, Nancy Williams [a descdt. of
Roger Williams, founder of Rhode Island, son of
James Williams, of Conwyl Caro, Carm., and Alice,
gr.-da. of Sir John Pemberton, of Durham, *b* 1599,
and of Wm. Arnold, Esq., of Co. Dorset, emigrated to America, 1635].—
Desc'd. from Michel and Barbara Phelips (or Felipe) who desc'd. from
ancient Israelitish stock of Spain, *via* Portugal and Holland, of Newport,
R.I. 1668).

Born at Summit, R.I., June 5, 1850; *m* Henrietta, da. of Wm. F. Cooper,
Mayor of Santa Cruz.

Issue.

i. STANLEY COOPER, *b* Dec. 10, 1892; *d* March 7, 1901.
i. ALICE WILLETTA.   ii. EDITH HENRIETTA.

Arms—(Williams) Azure, a lion rampant gules surrounded by nine pheons or.
Arms—(Lathame) Or, on a chief indented azure three plates.
Arms—(Arnold) Gules, a chevron ermine between three pheons or.

Residences—Berkeley, and San Francisco, California.
Society—California Genealogical.   *Club*—Union of Berkeley.

MERIWETHER, HUNTER McKEAND,

of Kansas City (Son of James H. Meriwether, M.D., 1814-90, of Todd Co., Ky., m Lucy E., da. of James McClure, of Pa.; son of Dr. Chas. N., 1766-1843; son of Colonel Nicholas, 1736-72; son of Thomas, 1714-56; son of David, 1690-1744; son of Nicholas, 1647-1744; son of Nicholas Meriweather, b Wales, 1631, Clerk of Surrey County Ct. Va., 1655; Judge of Colonial County Ct. 1672, d 1678).

Born at Pecan Grove, Ark., July 21, 1861; Atty. for the Collector of the Revenue; Grad. Vanderbilt Univ., B.S. 1883, B.L. 1885; m Sept. 28, 1887, Lucy U., da. of Capt. Wm. W. Western, Special Envoy to England in behalf of Confederacy, and Juliet B., da. of Warner L. Underwood, U.S. Consul to Scotland.

Issue.

i. WILLIAM WESTERN, b 1888.　　　　i. JULIET B. BLANCHE.

Arms—Or, three martlets sable, on a chief azure a sun in splendour proper.
Crest—An arm embowed in armour garnished or, holding in the hand ppr. a sword entwined round the blade with a snake.　　　*Motto*—Vi et consilio.

Residences—Kansas City, Mo.; Eupedon Farm, Montgomery Co., Tenn.; Pecan Grove Plantation, Arkansas; Macatawa Park, Michigan.
Society—Colonial Wars.

CRANWELL, JAMES HARFORD,

of Baltimore Md. (Son of George W. Cranwell of Baltimore Md. 1830-84, m 1854, Clara B., da. of George C. Halton; son of John, who settled in Baltimore, 1796; son of Patrick, 1740-1828, inherited his father's lands and held in addition part of the townland of Mount Howard in County Wexford, m a sister of Captain Smith of the Camolin Cavalry; son of John Cranwell, 1700-72, who settled in Wexford before 1735, held lands of Ballynamoney and Ballyfin, Wexford, by lease, dated Dec. 12, 1746, m Miss Byrne, of County Wexford, Ireland).

Born at Baltimore, Md., April 3, 1864; m April 8, 1903, Grace, daughter of John and Susan (Clayton) Philips, of Waynesboro, Pennsylvania.

Arms—Gules, three cranes close argent. (Seal on deed dated Dec. 12, 1746.)
Crest—A crane close argent.

Residence—Baltimore, Maryland.　　　*Club*—Green Spring Valley Hunt.
Society—Maryland Historical.

ROGERS, MRS. TALBOT MERCER (*née* J. ELIZABETH SLOCUM),
of Philadelphia (Da. and heiress of James
Slocum, of Brownsville, Pa., *b* Nov. 7, 1811;
d March 15, 1891; *m* Oct. 28, 1833, Caroline
Elizabeth, *b* Nov. 3, 1810, da. and heiress of
Samuel Pitkin, M.D., of Ballston Springs, N.Y.,
Surgeon in the American Army, War of 1812;
great grandson William Pitkin, Attorney-General
of the Colony of Conn., appointed by the King
1676, and grandson of Hon. William Pitkin, Chief
Justice of the Supreme Court of Connecticut, and
also grandson of Colonel Joseph Marsh, Continental
Army, War of the Revolution, first Lieut.-Govr.
of Vermont.—Descended from Giles Slocombe, or
Slocum, of Somersetshire, England, who held lands
in Portsmouth, R.I., *circa* 1638; also 9th in descent from John Webster,
Govr. of Connecticut, 1656, and Thomas Welles, Govr. of Connecticut,
1665, and John Mason, appointed by Charles II. Deputy-Govr. in the
Charter of Connecticut, 1662, Commander of Colonial Troops in the
Pequot War; 9th in descent from Rev. Samuel Whiting, *b* Boston,
England, the seat of his family from time Edward III. Rector of Lynn
Regis, emigrated to America 1638, settled in Lynn, Mass., which is
named in his honour; he entered Emanuel College sizar, 1613, A.B. 1616,
A.M. 1620, *m* 1629 Elizabeth, da. of Sir Oliver St. John, of Cayshoe,
Bedfordshire, 9th Lord Beauchamp of Bletso; created first Lord St.
John of Bletso by his cousin, Queen Elizabeth, Jan. 15, 1559).

Born at Keesville, N.Y., Sept. 3, 1834; *m* Aug. 31, 1858, Talbot Mercer
Rogers, of Philadelphia; educated at Jefferson College; descended
from Robert Rogers, who came from Wales to Pennsylvania, where
he held lands, in the 17th century.

Issue.

i. JAMES SLOCUM, *b* Nov. 21, 1871; B.A. Princeton Coll., 1893; LL.B.
Univ. of Penna., 1896; Attorney-at-Law; *m* April 26, 1904, Agnes
Gertrude, da. of J. George Klemm.

i. CAROLINE PITKIN, *m* Louis Joseph, son and heir of Louis A. J.
Papineau, Lord of the Manor of "Monte Bello," Prov., of Quebec,
Canada.

ii. ELEANOR SLOCUM, *m* Strachan Hallowell Bethune, of Montreal, Ca.,
d Oct. 12, 1906.   iii. MARY MERCER.

Arms—Qtly., 1st and 4th argent, on a fesse gules, betw. three griffins' heads
couped sable, as many sinister wings or (Slocum); 2nd azure, on a bend
argent, betw. two swans of the second, collared and chained or, a crescent
gules, betw. two mullets sable (Pitkin); 3rd per fesse azure and or, a pale
counterchanged, three plates, two and one, each charged with two bars
wavy vert, and as many lions' heads erased, one and two, gules (White).

Crest—A griffin's head gules between two wings expanded or.

———

Residence—3917 Spruce Street, Philadelphia.

Societies—Colonial Dames of America, Historical Soc. Pennsylvania.

G ILMAN, DANIEL COIT, LL.D.,
of Baltimore Md. (Son of Wm. C. Gilman
1795-1863, Mayor of Norwich, Ct., m 1820 Eliza
Coit 1796-1868; son of Benj. C. 1763-1835; son of
Maj. John 1712-70; son of Col. John 1677-1740;
son of Hon. John 1624-1708, a founder of Exeter,
N.H.; son of Edward Gilman, 1587-1681, from
Hingham, Norfolk, to Hingham, Mass., 1638, and
thence to Exeter, N.H.).

Born at Norwich, Ct., July 6, 1831: Pres. of the
Johns Hopkins Univ. 1875-1901, and since
1901 President Emeritus ; Pres. of Carnegie
Inst., Wash. 1902: Grad. Yale Univ. B.A.
1852, A.M. 1855, LL.D. 1889 ; LL.D.
Harvard 1876; St. John's, Md., 1876, Columbia
1887, Princeton 1896, etc. ; Pres. Univ. of
California 1872-5, etc.; President Amer. Civil Service Reform
League since 1901 ; President Amer. Oriental Society 1893-1906;
m (1) 1861 Mary Ketcham, d 1869 ; m (2) 1877 Elisabeth Dwight.
da. of John M. and Jane W. (Andrews) Woolsey of Cleveland, Ohio.

Issue.

i. ALICE, m Hon. Everett P. Wheeler, of N.Y.   ii. ELISABETH.

Arms—Sable, a man's leg couped at the thigh in pale argent.
Crest—A demi-lion issuing from a cap of maintenance.
Motto—Si Deus quis contra.

Residences—614 Park Ave., Baltimore, Md.; North East Harbor, Me.
Clubs—University and Maryland, Baltimore ; University, Century, Authors,
Grolier, N.Y. City: Cosmos, Washington.

W AIT, HORATIO LOOMIS,
of Chicago, Ill. (Son of Joseph Wait, of
N.Y. City, and Harriet H. Whitney : son of Lieut.
Marmaduke, b 1774, 16th U.S. Inf.; son of
Lt.-Col. Joseph, b 1732 ; son of John, of Brookfield, Mass ; son of Joseph; son of Thomas,
b 1641 ; son of Richard Wait, b prob. at Wethersfield, Essex, Eng., 1608, received grants of land at
Watertown, Mass.).

Born at N.Y. City, Aug. 8, 1836: Lieut.-Comdr. Paymaster, U.S.N.,
1862-70 ; Master in Chancery, Circuit Court of Cook Co., Ill., since
1876; m May 7, 1860, Chara Conant, da. of James and Cerusa C.
(Conant) Long, of Chicago, Ill.

Issue.

i. JAMES JOSEPH, m Ada Waldron.   ii. HENRY HEILEMAN.

Arms—Argent, a chevron betw three bugle horns gules stringed sable garnished or.

Residence—4919 Madison Avenue, Chicago, Ill.   *Clubs*—Literary, Church.
Societies—Loyal Legion, Naval Order of the U.S., Colonial Wars, Sons of
American Revolution, Farragut Naval Veteran Association.

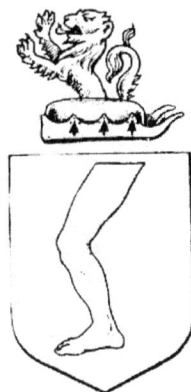

WARNER, JOHN De WITT, Hon.,
of N.Y. City (Son of Danl. De Witt Warner,
1808-88, of Rockstream, Justice of Sess, *m* Charlotte
G., 1831-90, da. of John and Eunice (Taft) Coon, of
Salem, N.Y.; son of Dr. John, 1772-1839, *m* Mary
De Witt; son of Eliphaz 1742-1818, *m* Mercy
Drinkwater; son of Jabez, 1710-87, *m* Hannah
Warner; son of John 1671-1743, Dep.-Gen. Ct. and
mem. Col. Legis., *m* Anna Ward; son of Andrew,
d 1682; son of Andrew, of Cambridge, Mass., 1632,
d Hadley, 1684; son of John Warner, of Hatfield,
Glouc., Eng.).

Born near Watkins, N.Y., 1851; Ph.B., LL.B.
Grad. Cornell Univ. 1872; Union. Univ., 1876;
Mem. of Congress, N.Y. City Dt., 1891-95;
Mem. and Pres. Art Commiss'n. N.Y., 1902-5;
m 1877, Lilian A., da. of Joseph Parshall and Harriet C. (Phelps)
Hudson, of Oneonta, N.Y.

Issue.

i. Joseph De Witt, *b* 1881.   i. Charlotte Lilian.

Arms--Or, a bend engrailed between six roses gules, barbed vert.
Crest—A man's head ppr. couped below the shoulders, habited chequy or and
azure, wreathed or and gules, on the head a cap argent.

Residences—301 W. 109th Street, N.Y. City; "Locust Lodge," Rock Stream, N.Y.
Clubs—Reform, N. Arts, Del. Ka. Epsilon, Cornell, Shakespeare, Playgoers.
Societies—N. Mural Painters, N. Sculp., M. Art, Bar Assn, Met. Art Mus, &c.

KENDALL, WILLIAM BEALS,
of N.Y. City (Son of Isaac Kendall, 1812-67,
of Charlestown and Boston, *m* Mary Elizabeth
Beals; son of Loamin, *b* 1783, *m* Nancy L. Roberts;
son of Jonathan, 1751-1805, *m* Joanna Brooks; son
of Joshua, *b* 1720; son of Joseph, *b* 1688; son of
Jacob, 1660-1743; son of Francis Kendall, Selectman of Woburn, Mass, 1640, *m* 1644, Mary Tidd).

Born at Charlestown, Mass., Jan. 5, 1857; Banker
and Broker, N.Y. Stock Exchange; *m* Feb. 6,
1883, Kate Varnum, [descended from Genl.
James Varnum] da. of Rufus Hayden Whitney,
of Boston.

Issue.

i. William Floyd, *b* Nov. 8, 1883.

i. Katharine Varnum.   ii. Helen Marjorie Stevens.

iii. Elinor Whitney.

Arms—Gules, a fesse chequy, or and azure, between three eagles displayed of
th second.
Crest—An eagle displayed or.   *Motto*—Virtus depressa resurget.

Residence—12 Gramercy Park, New York City.
Clubs—Westchester Co., Players, Racquet.

ATWILL, JAMES WILLIAM,
of St. Joseph Mo. (Eldest son of James W.
Atwill 1823-45, of Boston, Mass., *m* 1843 Sophia
1818-94, da. of Solomon and Sophia (Webb)
Hutchings; son of James; son of Nathan, *b* 1744;
son of Nathan; son of John; son of John Atwill,
from Devonshire, Eng., settled in Casco Bay,
1630-40).

Born at Boston, Mass. Feb. 8, 1844; Lieut.-Col.
1st N. Carolina Infty. during Civil War;
Pres. Free Public Library, St. Joseph, Mo.;
m (1) March 16, 1865, Eliza M. Wiswall,
d April 17, 1867; *m* (2) Sept. 17, 1870, Carrie
Frances, da. of Edward Richard, late Trea.
Inst. for Savings at Roxbury, Mass. for 25
years, and Annetta, da. of Jonas Wallace of
Henniker, N.H.

Issue.
(By *1st m.*)
i. ELIZA M.

(By *2nd m.*)
i. FRANK RUSSELL, *b* Oct. 7, 1872.
ii. HELEN RICHARDS, *b* Feb. 27, 1874; *d* July 24, 1874.
iii. ESTHER W.

Arms—Argent, a pile in point sable and a chevron counterchanged.
Crest—A lion ramp. erminois holding in the paws an annulet.

Residences—St. Joseph, Mo.; Boston, Mass.
Societies—Mayflower Descendants, Mil. Order of Loyal Legion, Colonial Wars,
Sons of the Revolution.

TRUMAN, HENRY HERTEL,
of Orange, N.J. (Son of Daniel H. Truman,
1806-70, of New Haven, Ct., *m* Cordelia Mead, 1822-
96; son of Daniel, 1766-1832, *m* Mary Thompson;
son of Daniel, 1717-91, *m* Deborah Dennis; son of
Joseph, *m* Mary Shapley; son of Joseph Truman,
who settled in New London, 1666, *d* 1697.

Born at Greenwich, Conn., Feb. 7, 1847; Mayor of
Orange, N.J., 1890-92; Warden of St.
Andrew's Parish, So. Orange; *m* Nov. 18
1874, Julie Maria, daughter of Charles Gideon
Judson and Fannie A. Marvin, of N.Y. City.

Issue.
i. EULALIA, *m* Feb. 5, 1902, Percy H. Bradshaw.
ii. GERTRUDE.

Arms—Or, a chevron betw. three human hearts gules ducally crowned of the first.
Crest—A human heart ducally crowned.

Residence—Orange, N.J.   *Club*—Orange Lawn Tennis.
Societies—New England, Mayflower Descendants, Young Men's Christian Assoc.,
Colonial Wars.

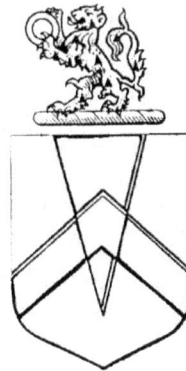

HOWLAND, DANIEL WEBSTER,

of Brookline, Mass. (Son of Henry Prince
Howland, 1820-63, of South Malden, Mass., m Eliza
Townsend, 1821-70, da. of Benj. and Eliza Townsend Britnall, of Malden, Mass.; son of Pelag B.,
1783-1841; son of Prince, 1745-1825; son of Robert,
b 1707; son of Prince, 1685-1713; son of Arthur,
1645-1720; son of Arthur Howland, d 1675, of
Marshfield, Plymouth Colony; son of Humphrey
Howland, Citizen of London, Eng., d 1646, brother
of "Pilgrim" John Howland, 13th Signer of Mayflower Compact, 1620; 6th in descent from Samuel
Sprague, Secy. Plymouth Colony; 7th in descent
from Thomas Prince, Gov. of Plymouth Colony,
and Commissioner of the United Colonies; 8th in
descent from Gov. William Bradford).

Born at South Malden, Mass., Aug. 10, 1856, m June 1, 1892, Maude
Mary, da. of William Charles Dustin Grannis of Chicago, Ill., and
Clarissa Jane Brown, his wife, da. of Lucius and Susannah Brown.

Issue.

i. CLARISSA MARY LOUISE.   ii. ISABELLA BLACKSTONE.

Arms—Argent, two bars sable, in chief three lions rampant of the last.
Crest—A leopard passant sable, ducally gorged or.

Residence – Brookline, Mass.   *Club*—Exchange.
Societies—Colonial Wars, Sons of the American Revolution, Pilgrim, New England
Historic Genealogical.

LEARNED, EDWIN JULIUS,

of Lake Forest Ill. (Son of Samuel Julius
Learned 1823-92, m 1849 (1) Mary A. Gilbert
1850-55, (2) Ann E. da. of Jas. Barr Lowry of
Yorkville Ill., son of George Lowry of Co. Down,
Ireland, and Mayville N.Y.; son of Rev. Erastus
1775-1834 of Westminster Ct.; son of James
1733-1811 of Killingly Ct.; son of William 1688-
1747; son of Isaac, b 1655, of Chelmsford Mass;
son of Isaac, d 1657; son of William Learned of
Bermondsey, Surrey, England, settled at Charlestown Mass, d 1645).

Born at Chicago Ill. Feb. 8, 1858; Treasurer of
Reid Murdoch & Co.

Arms—Azure, a saltire engrailed or between four lozenges argent.
Crest—A griffin rampant.

Residence—Lake Forest, Ill.
Club—Onwentsia.
Society—Chi Psi (Amhurst Coll.)

TODD, HENRY ALFRED,
of N.Y. City (Son of Rev. Richard K. Todd,
M.A., 1814-94, *m* Martha, da. of Lewis P. Clover;
son of Wallingford, *b* 1778, *m* Hannah Todd; son of
Benjamin, *b* 1744, *m* Elizabeth Saunders; son of
John, *b* 1688, *m* Mrs. Abigail (Perley) Jewett; son
of John, *b* 1661, *m* Elizabeth, da. of Capt. Samuel
Brocklebank, who was killed at the battle of
Sudbury 1676; son of John, *b* at Bradford, Yorks,
1621, settled at Rowley Mass. 1643, Mem. of the
Gen. Court of Mass. 1664; son of John, *b* at Pon-
tefract, Yorks., 1594, *m* Alice Clayton of Bradford,
Yorks, 1626; son of William, of Pontefract, Yorks,
m Isabel Rogerson, 1592; probably son of Reginald
Todd, Freeman of York, 1605, and collateral
descdt. of Sir Wm. Todd, Lord Mayor of York, 1487).

Born at Woodstock, Ill., Mar. 13, 1854; B.A. Princeton, 1876, Ph.D.
Johns Hopkins Univ. 1885; sometime Fell. and Tutor of Princeton
Coll.; Prof. of Romance Philology in Columbia Univ.; *m* 1891,
Miriam, da. and co-heiress of John S. Gilman, of Baltimore.

Issue.

i. WALLINGFORD, *b* Aug. 2, 1897.   ii. PAUL W., *b* Nov. 15, 1899.
i. LISA GILMAN.   ii. MARTHA CLOVER.

Arms—Vert, a fox rampant argent.   *Crest*—A dove rising argent.
Mottoes—By cunning not by craft; Astute cum virtute.

Residences—824 West End Avenue, N.Y. City; "Brocklebank," Norfolk, Conn.
Clubs—Century, Independent.
Societies—Pres. Mod. Lang. Assn., Met. Museum of Art, Phi Beta Kappa, Am.
Oriental, Soc. des Anciens Textes Français, Am. Philological Assn.

MOFFAT, R. BURNHAM,
of N.Y. City (Son of Reuben Curtis Moffat, M.D., 1818-94, of
Brooklyn N.Y., *m* Elizabeth Virginia Barclay 1822-92; son of John
Little 1788-1865, of N.Y. City, *m* Hannah Curtis; son of John Little
1753-88, of Goshen N.Y., *m* Mary Yelverton; son of Rev. John Moffat,
b in North of Ireland, settled at Little Britain N.Y., *d* 1788, *m* Margaret
Little).

Born at Brooklyn N.Y. Jan. 7, 1861; Grad. at Harvard Univ. B.A. 1883,
Columbia Univ. LL.B. 1885; *m* June 5, 1895, Ellen Low, da. of
Henry E. and Ellen A. (Low) Pierrepont.

Issue.

i. JAY PIERREPONT, *b* July 18, 1896.
ii. ABBOT LOW, *b* March 12, 1901.
i. ELIZABETH BARCLAY.

Residences—12 East 66th Street, N.Y. City; "Birchwoods," Northeast Harbour, Me.
Clubs—Century, University, Harvard, Down Town, Democratic.
Societies—N.Y. Historical, N.Y. Genealogical and Biographical, Colonial Wars,
N.Y. Bar Association, N.Y. State Bar Association.

D'OYLEY, JOHN EVANS,
    (MARQUIS D'OYLEY),
of Paris, France, heir apparent of the Evans
family and heir presumptive of the D'Oyley family,
(Eldest son of Rudolph H. Evans, of Washington,
D.C., Genl. Commissr. of Deeds for all States and
Territories, &c., *b* 1814, *m* 1836 Elizabeth Josephine,
1818-66, da. of Sir John and Anna M. (Welsh)
D'Oyley, Bart. of Wexford, Ireland, and of Philadelphia, Pa.; son of James Monk Doyley 1732-89;
son of William, *b* 1707; son of Sir John D'Oyley,
d 1746; son of Sir John 1640-1709; son of John
1601-60, Ld. High Sheriff of Oxfordshire; son
of Sir John Cope 1571-1633; son of Sir John
1545-1623; son of John D'Oyley, Ld. H. Sheriff
of Oxfordshire and Berkshire 1560, a direct desct.
of Nigell D'Oyley, Knt., who accompanied William of Normandy to
England 1066).

Born at Phila., June 17, 1838; Grad. Balto. Coll., M.D.S. 1867; name
    D'Oyley assumed at the request of his uncle, Sir Peter D'Oyley,
    legalised by the Court of Common Pleas at Phila. June 4, 1879;
    Hereditary Knt. of the M.O. of the "Cincinnati"; Grand Cross of
    the Most A.M.O. of the "Holy Sepulchre"; Grand Cross of the
    "Lion and Sun" of Persia; Comdr. "Legion of Honour" of the
    Order of "Christ," of "St. Gregory the Great" of "Carlos VII.,"
    &c.; Hereditary Marquis of Rome, 7th Oct. 1879; *m* Sept. 8, 1868,
    Annie Alexis, da. of Alastair Macdonald, of Keppoch, Co. Inverness,
    Scotland.

Issue.

i. REGINALD DONALD, *b* Aug. 9, 1869, *d* May 20, 1889.

ii. RAOUL GILBERT, *b* Feb. 13, 1875, *m* Terry Hainsworth.

iii. ALASTAIR IVAN, *b* Feb. 2, 1880, *d* May 22, 1904.

Arms - Or, two bends azure.

Crest—A demi-dragon proper.

Motto—Ostendo non ostento.

Residences—Manoir Sans Souci, Bellevue Seine-Oise, France ; 25 Rue Franklin,
    Paris, France.

Societies—New England Historical and Genealogical (Boston, Mass.), Literature,
    Science and Art (London, Eng.), Roman Academy of Literature, Science
    and Art (Italy), Honorary President of the Academy of Music (France).

WHIPPLE, Major CHARLES WILLIAM,
of N.Y. City (Son of Major-Gen. Amiel
W. Whipple 1818-63, killed at the battle of Chan-
cellorsville Va., *m* Eleanor M. Sherburne; son of
David Whipple, *b* 1783, *m* Abigail Pepper; son of
David 1759-1842, *m* Arethusia Brooks; son of
James 1732-67, *m* Lydia Powers; son of Jacob
1707-89, *m* Jerusha Leland; son of James 1681-
1766, *m* Mary Fuller; son of Joseph, *d* 1708; son of
Mathew, 1605-47, settled at Ipswich, Mass., 1638;
son of Matthew Whipple of Bocking, co. Essex,
Eng., *d* 1618).

Born at Portsmouth, N.H. Sept. 28, 1846; Major
U.S.A. retired; Grad. West Point 1868; 2nd
Lt. of Artillery, 1874; 1st Lt. Ord. Dept. 1875,
Capt. 1885; Insp.-Gen. of Vols. with rank
Lt.-Col. 1898; *m* April 3, 1877, Josephine K. Jones.

Issue.

i. WALTER JONES, *b* July 17, 1878.

ii. WILLIAM, *b* Jan. 27, 1880.

iii. SHERBURNE, *b* May 2, 1881.

i. ANNETTE BAILEY, *m* November 14, 1906, Arthur Morris Collens, of
Hartford, Connecticut.   ii. ELEANOR SHERBURNE.

Arms—(Sherburne) Quarterly: 1 and 4, vert an eagle displayed argent; 2 and 3,
argent, a lion rampant guardant vert.

Crest—A unicorn's head argent armed or.

Residences—181 Madison Avenue, N.Y. City; Massapequa, L.I.

Clubs—University N.Y., Army and Navy of Washington.

Societies—Sons of the Revolution, Mil. Order of the Loyal Legion.

STONE, JOSEPH,
of Boston Mass. (Son of Phinehas Jones Stone
1810-91 of Boston, *m* Ann Maria Lindsey; son of
Phinehas 1775-1852, *m* Hannah Jones; son of Silas
1742-1827, *m* Eunice Fairbanks; son of Joseph
1702-77, *m* Mary Prescott; son of Simon 1656-1741,
m Sarah Farnsworth; son of Simon 1631-1708,
m Mary Whipple; son of Simon 1585-1665, came
in ship "Increase" from London to Watertown,
Mass. 1635, *m* Joan Clark; son of David and Ursula
Stone of Much Bromley, Essex, England; son of
Simon Stone).

Born at Boston Jan. 4, 1848; B.S. Mass. Institute
of Technology; *m* Feb. 10, 1880, Minnie, da.
of Horatio Harris of Boston.

Issue.

i. HARRIS, *b* 1880, *d* 1881.   i. MARION.

Arms—Argent, three cinquefoils sable, on a chief azure a sun or.

Crest—Out of a ducal coronet or, a griffin's head betw. two wings gules bezantée.

Residence—1731 Beacon St., Brookline, Mass.   *Clubs*—University, Technology.

M INER, CHARLES ABBOTT, Hon. (*deceased*),
    of Wilkes-Barre, Pa. (Son of Robert Miner,
1805-42 ; son of Asher, 1778-1841 ; son of Seth,
1742-1822 ; son of Hugh, 1710-82 ; son of Clement,
1668-1741 ; son of Clement, 1640-1700 ; son of
Thomas Minor, 1608-90, from Bristol, Eng., in
the "Arabella," 1630, to Mass.; son of Clement,
1640 ; son of William Mynor, 1585).

Born at Plains, Pa., Aug. 30, 1830 ; Pres. of
    Wilkes-Barre City Hospital ; Mem. of Pa.
    House of Reprs. ; Comr. of Pa. to World's
    Fair at Vienna ; Vice-Pres. of Wyoming Nat.
    Bank ; *m* Jan. 19, 1853, Eliza R. Atherton ;
    d July 25, 1903.

Issue.
i. ROBERT, 1855-56.   ii. WILLIAM ROSS, 1858-67.
iii. ASHER, *b* Nov. 14, 1860 ; Col. 7th Regt., N.G., Pa. ; *m* Nov. 6, 1889,
     Hetty Lonsdale.
iv. SIDNEY ROBY, A.B., *b* July 28, 1864 ; Counsellor-at-Law.
v. CHARLES HOWARD, S.B., M.D., *b* July 5, 1868 ; Asst.-Surgeon 9th
     Regt. Pa. Vol. Infy., U.S.A.   i. ELIZABETH, 1853-1902.

Arms—Gules, a fesse argent between three plates.
Crest—A mailed hand holding a battle-axe armed at both ends proper.

Residence—(Family), 264 S. Franklin Street, Wilkes-Barre, Pa.

H ART, HENRY GILBERT,
    of Utica, N.Y. (Son of George Washington
Hart, 1814-78, *m* Sarah Jeannett Gay ; son of
Ephraim, 1774-1839 ; son of Thomas, 1749-1811 ;
son of Thomas, 1714-1801 ; son of Lieut. Hawkins,
1677-1735 ; son of Capt. Thomas, 1644-1726 ; son
of Stephen Hart, *b* Braintree, Essex, 1605, of Mass.
Bay Colony, 1632 ; served in Pequot War, 1637 ;
Representative of Farmington, 1647-60).

Born at Utica, N.Y., March 26, 1848 ; *m* Aug. 29,
    Lucy Lord, da. of Reuel Kimball.

Issue.
i. HENRY GILBERT, Jr., *b* Jan. 25, 1879.
ii. MERWIN KIMBALL, *b* June 25, 1881.
iii. RICHARD SEYMOUR, *b* March 13, 1887.

Arms—Gules, a bend between three fleur-de-lis argent.
Crest—A castle triple towered, thereon a flaming heart proper.
Motto Cœur fidele.

Residences—Utica, N.Y.; and Harts Hill, Whitestown, N.Y.
Club—Fort Schuyler, of Utica.
Societies—Sons of the Revolution, Colonial Wars.

BACKUS, CLARENCE WALWORTH, Rev. D.D., of Kansas City (Son of Rev. J. Trumbull Backus, D.D., LL.D. of Schenectady N.Y., *m* Annie E. Walworth, da. of Chancellor R. Hyde Walworth, LL.D. of N.Y. State, Col. in War of 1812 [whose father Benj. Walworth was an officer in War of Revol.; descndt. of Sir Wm. Walworth, Lord Mayor of Lond. *temp.* Rich. II.], and Maria Ketchum Averill, of Plattsburgh N.Y.—Descendant of Lt. Wm. Backus, of Norwich Ct. 1660, whose father Wm. Backus, came from Norwich, Eng. to Saybrook Ct. 1635; gt-gt-grandson of Hon. Joseph Backus, who represented Norwich in the Legislature; and grandson of Major Ebenezer Backus [whose sister Eunice Backus *m* Governor Jonathan Trumbull], who *m* Elizabeth Fitch, da. of Col. Eleazor Fitch, a lineal descendant of Rev. James Fitch, of Norwich Ct., and gt-grand-da. of Rev. Sam. Whiting, of Windsor Ct., whose wife, Elizabeth Adams, was da. of Rev. W. Adams, of Dedham Mass., who *m* Alice Bradford the grand-da. of Gov. Wm. Bradford of the "Mayflower," grandson of Col. John Chester of Wethersfield Ct., a descendant of Leonard Chester, from Lond., Eng., in 1633, a descendant of Sir Wm. Chester, and through his gt-grandfather Rev. James Pierrepont is a descendant of the Duke of Kingston-upon-Hull).

Born at Schenectady N.Y. April 20, 1846; Grad. Union Coll. 1870; Princeton Theol. Sem. 1873; 1st Lt. 97th N.Y. St. Vols. 1864-65, A-de-C. to Gens. Martin D. Hardin and Wesley Merritt; Clergyman in the Presbytn. Ch. 1873-1901, and Congregl. Ch. since; D.D. Univ. of Omaha 1893; *m* April 30, 1873, Susan M. Livingston, da. of James Aug. Washington, M.D. (first cousin three times removed of Gen. Geo. Washington) and Anna White Constable, grand-da. of Gilbert Livingston, of Red Hook Manor N.Y., a descendant of Bp. Livingston who crowned Canute about 1000 A.D., also gt-grand-da. of John Constable, M.D., descendants of Sir Wm. Constable, of Erringham Park and Holderness Manor, Eng.

Issue.

i. ROBERT LIVINGSTON, *b* March 6, 1875, *d* May 3, 1875.
ii. JONATHAN TRUMBULL, *b* Oct. 1, 1878, *m* July 25, 1900, Alma Teresa Dickson (da. of Judge Henry De la Cossette Dickson of Emporia Kansas, and his wife Margaret).
iii. JOHN CHESTER, *b* Oct. 28, 1885, *d* May 24, 1887.
i. ANNA ELIZA, 1874-87.
ii. MARY, 1881-83.

Arms—Azure, a chevron ermine, between three doves argent.
Crest—A dove argent.   *Motto*—Confido in Deo.

Residence— 1900 Central Avenue, Bunker Hill, Kansas City, Kansas.
Societies—Sons of the Revolution, Missouri; Military Order of Foreign Wars, Missouri; Military Order of the Loyal Legion, Missouri; Masonic, N.Y. State.

HENRY, WILLIAM HAMILTON,
    of N.Y. City (Son of Horatio M. Henry,
1820-90, of Phila., Pa., m Sarah Ann, 1820-87, da.
of Richard and Sarah (North) Nugent; Son of
William H., b 1787, m Ann E. Neal; son of Hugh
Henry, b in Coleraine, Ireland, 1744; settled in
Phila., 1765, m Phœba A. Morris; son of John
Henry, of Coleraine, descended of an Ayrshire fam.
of "Henry," who accompanied Sir James Hamilton,
from Scotland to Ireland in 1615).

Born at N.Y. City, Oct. 15, 1845; Business Manager,
    "N.Y. Herald" to 1884; Justice of the
    Peace, New Mexico, 1902; m April 13, 1868,
    Mary A., da. of Garrett and Sarah (Snedeker)
    Sarvent, of Nyack, N.Y.

Issue.

i. James, m Florence Hand.   v. Garrett.
ii William, m Louise Ackerman.   vi. Hamilton.
iii. Richard, m Louise Brockway.   i. Alice, m William T. Hall.
iv. Sterling, m Jessie McQueen.   ii. Maud.

Arms—Azure, a fesse betw. three pelicans argent, vulned ppr.
Crest—A pelican's head erased, vulning ppr.   *Motto*—Fideliter.

Club—(address) New York Press Club.
Societies—Sons of the American Revolution, Scotch-Irish of America, Masonic.

JENNINGS, ALBERT GOULD,
    of N.Y. City (Son of Abraham Gould
Jennings, of N.Y., b Aug. 28, 1821, m April 17,
1851, Cecilia Matilda, d Jan. 6, 1890, da. of John
Post Douglas.—Mr. A. G. J. is 6th in descent
from Lieut.-Govr. Gould, of Conn.; 5th from
Major Peter Burr: Colonel Abraham Gould, killed
in Revol.; 7th from Lt.-Col. Talcott; 6th from
Col. John Burr: 5th from Capt. John Burr).

Born in Brooklyn, N.Y., Oct. 13, 1869; Grad. at
    Princeton Univ., 1890; m Oct. 24, 1894,
    Susie Beatrix, da. of John D. Crimmins, of
    N.Y. City.

Issue.
i Albert Gould, Jr., b Nov. 15, 1897.

Arms—Argent, a chevron gules between three plummets sable.
Crest—A griffin's head or, in the beak a plummet sable in pale.
Motto—Il buon tempo verra.

Residence—2 East 82nd Street, N.Y. City.
Clubs—Union, University, Tuxedo, Country of Westchester, Racquet and Tennis.
Societies—St. Nicholas, Sons of the Revolution, Colonial Wars.

S HIELDS, Rev. CHARLES W., D.D., LL.D., (decd).
  (Only son of James Read Shields 1799-1876,
m Hannah Woodruff, d 1856; son of Patrick Henry,
of Virginia, 1798, m Mary Nance; son of James, of
Virginia, 1772, m Eliz. Graham; son of Thomas,
of Delaware, 1752, m Anne Bayard; son of Archibald
Shields, who emigrated from Scotland 1725).

Born at New Albany, Ind., April 4, 1825; d Aug. 26,
  1904; Grad. Princeton Univ., D.D., Columbia
  Univ. LL.D.; Chaplain, N.J. Soc. of Colonial
  Wars; Prof. in Princeton Univ.; m (1) 1846,
  Charlotte E. Bain, m (2) 1861 Eliz. Kane da. of
  Judge John Kane, of Phila.

Issue.
i. ALBERT J., 1849-60.   ii. CHARLES W., 1853-77.
i. CHARLOTTE J., d 1891, m Bayard Stockton of Princeton.
                (By 2nd m.)
  i. JEAN LEIPER, b 1862, d 1865.   iii. THOS. L. K., b Feb. 25, 1869.
ii. JAMES READ, b Feb. 25, 1867.   i. HELEN HAMILTON, m Bayard Stockton.

Arms— Gules, on a bend or three shields azure.
Crest— A dexter arm embowed in armour holding a shield azure.
Motto— Vincit qui patitur.

Residences—(Family) " Morven," Princeton, N.J.; Ochre Point, Newport, R.I.

B EVAN, HORACE CROMWELL,
  of Baltimore, Md. (Second son of Charles
Frederick Bevan, 1819-85, of Baltimore, Md.,
Captain in State Militia, m 1847, Sarah J. da. of
Elisha and Sarah Carback, of Baltimore, Md.;
Son of Thomas H., 1791-1863; son of Charles,
1756-1829; son of Charles, d 1761; son of Charles;
son of Richard, d 1738; son of Charles Beaven,
who settled in what was then Charles Co., Md.,
afterwards Prince George County, Maryland, 1666,
d 1699, m Mary, da. of Richard Marsham).

Born at Baltimore, Md., September 15, 1854;
  Attorney-at-Law; Student at University of
  Virginia; Graduated at Univ. of Maryland,
  B.L., 1876.

Arms—Azure, a dove arg. beaked and legged gules betw. three gem rings or, in
  chief a mullet charged with a mullet.
Crest—On a mount vert a dove rising, in the beak a gem ring.
Motto—Semper virtute constans.

Residence—1301 Linden Avenue, Baltimore, Md.
Societies—Baltimore Bar Association, Maryland Historical, Sons of the American
  Revolution, Past Master in A. F. & A. Masonry.

SOHIER, WILLIAM DAVIES,
of Boston (Son of William Sohier, of Boston,
1822-94, *m* Susan C. 1823-68, da. of John A.
and Susan (Cabot) Lowell; son of William D.,
b 1787, *m* Elizth. Dexter; son of Edward, *m* Mary
Davies; son of Edward Sohier, *b* 1724, Island of
Jersey, em. to America, *m* Susan Bummer, gr.-da.
of Andre Vigoreux.—Descended from Sohier, sur-
named Roux de Vermandois, 3rd son of Eudes,
7th and last Count of Vermandois, living 1080;
m Adele de Malvoisin, da. of Hugh Seigneure de
Ricardie).

Born at Boston, Oct. 22, 1858; Counsellor-at-Law;
Mem. of the Mass. Legis.; Pres. Rep. Club of Mass. ; Pres. of the
Journal Newspaper Co., Boston; Col. and A.D.C. on the staff of
Gov. Roger Wolcott during the War with Spain; Grad. at Harvard
Law School, 1879; *m* Dec. 13, 1880, Edith F. Alden.

Issue.

i. WILLIAM DAVIES, Jr., *b* Jan. 10, 1889.
i. ELEANOR.   ii. ALICE.

Arms—Gules, a mullet argent.
Crest—Between the antlers of a stag a cross argent.   *Motto*—Stella xpi duce.

Residences—79 Beacon Street, Boston; Beverley, Essex Co., Mass.
Clubs—Republican, Union, Puritan, Boston Athletic Assn., Country, Myopia
Hunt, Essex County, Montserrat Golf, Eastern Yacht.

WHEELOCK, WILLIAM EFNER, M.D.,
of Morristown, N.J. (Son of Wm. Almy
Wheelock, *b* 1825, *m* 1850, Harriet Efner; son of
Joseph, 1788-1857; son of Capt. Moses, 1738-1801;
son of Ephraim, 1696-1785; son of Eleazer, 1654-
1731; son of Rev. Ralph, 1600-83, of Medfield,
Mass., 1645, supposed to be Ralph Wheelock, who
Matric. A.B. at Clare Coll., Cambridge Univ., 1626).

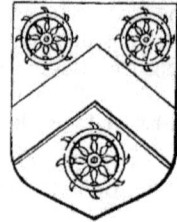

Born at Manchester, Eng., Jan. 26, 1852; Grad.
A.B., Yale College, 1873; M.D. Coll. Phys.
and Surgs., N.Y., 1876; LL.B. Columbia Coll.
Law School, 1885; *m* October 27, 1885, Emily Charlotte, da. of
Rev. John Hall, D.D., of N.Y.

Issue.

i. JOHN HALL, *b* Sept. 9, 1886.
ii. WILLIAM ALMY, *b* May 9, 1888; *d* June 19, 1897.
i. EMILY HALL.

Arms—Argent, a chevron between three catherine wheels sable.
Motto—Non omnis moriar.

Residences—Morris Avenue, Morristown, N.J.; "Wuthering," East Hampton, L.I.
Clubs—Morristown Field Club, Torrey Botanical, N.Y. City.
Societies—N.Y. County Medical, L. M. New Eng., N.Y.; Washington Assn., N.J.

THOMPSON, NORMAN FREDERICK,
of Rockford (Son of Norman C. Thompson,
1828-98, *m* Laura J. Blackmer; son of Norman
Brace, 1801-74, *m* Serefh H. Ruggles; son of Judge
Amos, 1771-1849, *m* Dotha Brace; son of David,
1731-1807, *m* Hannah Griswold; son of Deacon
Gideon, 1704-59, *m* Lydia Punderson; son of Capt.
Samuel, 1669-1749, *m* Rebecca Bishop; son of
John, 1632-1707, *m* Ann Vickers; son of Anthony
Thompson, 1637, settled in New Haven Ct.).

Born at Perry, Georgia, June 27, 1856; A.B. Yale
Univ.; Pres. of The Manufrs. Natl. Bank;
m Jan 10, 1883, Adaline E. Emerson.

Issue.

i. NORMAN FREDERICK, *b* March 14, 1884.
ii. RALPH EMERSON, *b* Feb. 1, 1888.   i. ADALYN.

Arms—Or, on a fesse indented azure, three stars argent; on a canton of the
second the sun in his splendour.
Crest—A cubit arm erect vested gules cuffed argent, holding in the hand five ears
of wheat.   *Motto*—In lumine lucem.

Residence—Rockford, Illinois.
Clubs—Graduates of New Haven Ct., Twentieth Century, Bankers, University of
Chicago, Country, Rockford Automobile, Beefsteak of Rockford.
Societies—Mayflower Descendants, Colonial Wars, Order of Runnemede.

HILLHOUSE, FRANCIS,
of N.Y. City (Son of William Hillhouse,
b 1820, *m* 1854, Frances Julia, da. of Hon. Samuel
Rossiter Betts, Judge U.S. Dist. Court, N.Y.—
Descended from Rev. James Hillhouse, *b* Londonderry, Ireland, 1687, *d* Montville Ct. 1740, M.A.
Glasgow Univ., em. to N.E. 1720, *m* Mary Fitch;
son of John, of Free Hall, Londonderry; son of
Abraham Hillhouse of "Artikelly," served during
the siege of Londonderry).

Born at New Haven, Ct., Sept. 12, 1859; Grad. at
Yale Univ. 1879, *m* July 14, 1897, Sarah
Griswold Fitch, of Norwich, Ct.

Issue.

i. MARY FITCH.
ii. FRANCIS BETTS.

Arms—Sable, a chevron between, in chief, a lion rampant on the dexter side,
and a unicorn on the sinister side, between them a star of five points,
facing each other, in the base a human heart surrounded by three bezants.
Motto—Time deum.

Residence—Mount Kisco, New York.
Clubs—Calumet, St. Anthony, Baltusrol Golf.
Society—Colonial Wars.

R ALLI, PANDIA CONSTANTINE,
    of N.Y. City (Son of Costi Ralli 1824-89 of
Manchester, England, *m* 1851 Xanthippe Frang-
hiadi; son of Pandia Ralli, 1782-1859, *m* Marigo
Schilizzi; son of Ambrose Ralli 1731-1820,
m Despino Maximo; son of Stephen and Julia Ralli.
—Descended from the Ralli family, of Genoese
origin, who settled in the Island of Scio about the
15th century, where they resided until the massacre
of its inhabitants by the Turks in 1821).

Born at Manchester, England, April 28, 1854,
    m April 16, 1884, Daisy Whele.

Issue.

i. CONSTANTINE PANDIA, *b* March 22, 1885.
ii. THEODORE PANDIA, *b* Feb. 21, 1886.
iii. VICTOR PANDIA, *b* Aug. 16, 1889.
i. ELAINE PANDIA.

Arms—Azure, a lion rampant argent semée of lozenges of the field, in chief a
    crescent between two crosses couped of the second.
Crest—A lion rampant argent, semée of lozenges, holding between the paws a
    cross couped azure.

Residence—167 West 88th Street, N.Y. City.
Clubs—Riverside Yacht, Underwriters.   *Society*—Masonic.

B ALDWIN, LE ROY WILBUR,
    of N.Y. City (Son of Warner Horace Baldwin,
of Rutland, Vt., *b* 1837, *m* 1858, Mary Olive, da. of
Philander Barton and Lydia C. (Bryant) Hatch, of
Brandon, Vt.; son of Noah, 1772-1855; son of
David, 1740-1808; son of Moses, 1705-56; son of
James, *b* 1664-8, *d* 1756; son of Joseph, 1640-81; son
of Joseph Baldwin, of Milford, Conn., *d* 1684; son
of Richard Baldwin, of Cholesbury, Co. Bucks.,
Eng., Will proved 1633—Desc'd on the maternal
side from Lieut. Nathaniel Wentworth, Sergt. in
Capt. Jonathan Wentworth's Company, War of
the Revolution).

Born at Rutland, Vt., Oct. 31, 1864; *m* Oct. 10,
    1889, Ettie Lucile, daughter of Lucien W.
    Field, and Etta Wright.

Issue.
i. ETTIE LUCILE.

Arms—Argent, six oak leaves slipped in pairs, two in chief and one in base vert,
    stalks sable, their points downwards.
Crest—A squirrel sejant or.   *Motto*—Vim vi repello.

Residences—8 East 70th Street, N.Y. City; Rutland, Vt.; and Monmouth Beach, N.J.
Clubs—Metropolitan, Turf and Field, Lawyers, Suburban Riding and Driving.

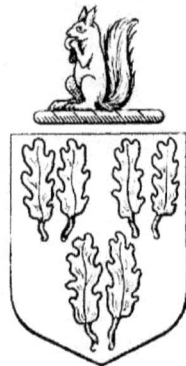

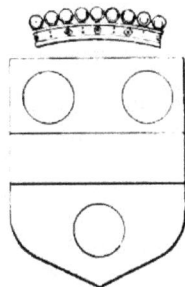

GALLATIN, ALBERT EUGENE,
of N.Y. City. (Only son of Albert Horatio
Gallatin, A.B., M.D., New York Univ., who
never practised medicine, but was Lieut.-Surgeon
in the field during the Civil War; was a well-
known Chemist, studying under best masters
at home and abroad; published some of his dis-
coveries in Chemical Journals; at one time was
Prof. of Chemistry in N.Y. Univ.; *b* March 7,
1839; *d* March 25, 1902; *m* Sept. 11, 1877, Louisa
Belford, da. of Lieut. Maskell Ewing (West Point),
and Cornelia Lansdale, his wife, of Maryland; grandson of Albert Rolaz
Gallatin, *b* 1800; *m* 1837; *d* 1890; and great-grandson of Albert Gallatin,
who came to America in 1780, *b* 1761; *m* 1793; *d* 1849; Secretary of the
Treasury under Jefferson and Madison (two terms); Ambassador to Russia,
took the leading part at Treaty of Ghent; Minister to France for period of
seven years; Minister to England.—Descended through Albert, who was only
son of Jean, *b* 1733, Member of Council of Two Hundred in Geneva;
only son of Abraham, *b* 1706, Auditor; only son of Jean, *b* 1668, Member
of Council of Two Hundred; eldest son of Jean, *b* 1639, Envoy at Venice;
eldest son of Louis, *b* 1612, Member of Council of Two Hundred; son of
Aime, *b* 1577, Member Council of Two Hundred; son of Morin, *b* 1546,
Member Council of Two Hundred; brother of Claude, Seigneur Syndic,
as was his son, grandson, and great-grandson; son of Pierre, *d* 1558; son of
Jean, *d* 1535, Burgess of Geneva, 1510; son of Jean; son of Henri; son of
Guillaume, *d circa* 1360; son of Humbert; son of Guillaume Gallatini,
1319. The Gallatins were a noble family in Savoy in 1258, and settled in
Geneva in 1510. They were officially recognised nobles in Austria in
1710, and the Arms appear in the "Deed of Recognition," confirmed by
d'Hozier de Serigny, Judge-at-Arms of King Louis XV. [Galiffe,
Armorial Genevois, 14. Galiffe, Notices Genealogigues sur les Familles
Genevoisses. Baron le Zur Laubin, Tableaux Pittoresques de la Suisse
11, 534. Etrennes de la Noblesse, ou Etat Actuel des Familles Nobles
de France pour l'annee 1778. Etat de la Noblesse, 1781, 1783.
Encyclopædia Britannica.]

Arms—Azure, a fesse argent between three bezants.

Crest—A French Count's coronet.

Motto—Pro patria devoti.

———

Residence—25 Gramercy Park, New York City.

Clubs—Union; Tuxedo; Automobile; Turf and Field; Strollers; Grolier;
Ardsley; Badminton.

Societies—Colonial Wars; St. Nicholas; N.Y. Historical; Metropolitan Museum
of Art.

HALL, HARRY ALVAN,
of Pittsburgh (Son of Benj. McDowell Hall, 1808-73, of St. Mary's Pa., m 1837, Susannah Geary; son of James Hall, 1765-1826, of Belfast, Ireland, m Margaret Miller).

Born at Karthaus Pa., Oct. 7, 1861; educated at Dickinson Seminary, Lewisburg Univ., Gregory Coll., Yale Univ. A.B. LL.B; Admtd. to the Bar 1881; Mem. Pa. Senate 1890; U.S. Atty. W.D. of Pa., 1893; Capt. Co. H. 16th Pa. Infty. U.S.V. in Spanish-Am. War; Judge-Adv.-Genl. 1st Corps on Staff of Gen. Wilson, promoted Major for gallantry at battle of Coamo, Porto Rico; Genl. Counsel for Austro-Hungary and Italy; President Judge 25th District of Pa., 1906; m June 10, 1886, Currin McNairy, of Nashville, Tenn.

Arms—Azure, a chevron argent between three cranes' heads erased or.
Crest—A crane or standing on a hill vert, a stone in the dexter claw.
Motto—Cura quietem.

Residences—Pittsburg, and Ridgway, Pa.
Clubs—Yale, Players, Manhattan, Lambs and Reform of N.Y. City; Art, Racquet, Penn., of Phila; Duquesne, Univ., Union, Country and Crucible of Pittsburg; Buffalo of Buffalo.
Societies—Past V.C.-in-Chief National Assoc. of Spanish-Am. War Veterans, and Past Comdr.-in-Chief Naval and Mil. Order, Spanish-Am. War, Fellow of Am. Geographical Society, and Member of Archæological Society of Pa., Member of Military Service Institute.

BRADLEY, CYRUS SHERWOOD,
of Southport, Ct. (Son of Lt. John D. Bradley, 1819-1905, Rep. in State Legislature, 1868, m Mary Cath., da. of Capt. Cyrus and Sally Bradley (Hull) Sherwood, of Southport, Ct.; son of Alja, 1782-1861, of Easton, Ct.; son of Levi, 1758-1829; son of Seth, 1735-98, of Greenfield, Ct.; son of John, 1705-47; son of Francis, d 1716, of Fairfield, Ct.; son of Francis and Ruth (Barlow) Bradley, of New Haven, Ct., 1650.—Also descd. from Andrew Warde, d Fairfield, Ct., 1659; son of Richard Warde, of Homersfield and Gorleston, Co. Suffolk, Eng., m Ann, da. of Sir Richard Gunville, 13th from William de Varde, of Givendale, Yorks, 1150. Also descd. from Rev. Peter Bulkley, D.D., of Concord, Mass., 1635, 13th from Robert de Bulkley, 1199-1216).

Born at Southport, Ct., Oct. 21, 1869, late Secy. Soc. of the Sons of the Revolution, State of Connecticut.

Arms—Gules, a chevron argent, between three boars' heads couped or.
Crest—A boar's head couped or.   *Motto*—Liber ac sapiens esto.

Residence—"Westfield," Southport, Connecticut.
Societies—Sons of the Revolution (N.Y. and Ct.), Colonial Wars, War of 1812.

MACKENZIE, GEORGE NORBURY (2ND), of Balto. Md. Barrister-at-Law (Son of George Norbury Mackenzie 1824–87, *m* 1850, Martha Anna, 1829–94, da. of Howell and Hannah (Gorsuch) Downing, of Windham Co., Conn.; son of Thomas of Calvert Co. and Baltimore City, Md., *m* Tacy Burgess Norbury; son of Cosmo of Calvert Co., *m* Sarah Taylor Mackall; son of Thomas of Inverness, Scot., a cadet of the House of Seaforth, and a lineal descendant of Sir Kenneth Mackenzie, 1st Baron of Kintail, who emigrated to Maryland in 1745 and settled in Calvert Co., he *m* (1) Rebecca, sister of Gov. Thomas Johnson, *m* (2) Anne Johns, da. of Richard Johns, Esq., of England and Calvert Co., Md.—Also descended from the Baron Saher de Quincey, one of the Sureties for the observance of the Magna Charta 1215, King Alfred the Great and the Emperor Charlemagne).

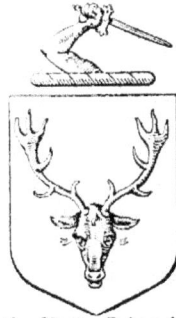

Born in Baltimore May 4, 1851; LL.B. University of Maryland, 1890; Registrar-General, Soc. Colonial Wars; Lieut.-Gov. Maryland Soc. Colonial Wars; Registrar Maryland Soc. Sons of the American Revolution; Grand Marshal Colonial Order; Asst. Historian General Military Order of the French Alliance; Secretary, Maryland Branch American National Red Cross; Vice-President for Maryland, "Old North-West" Genealogical and Historical Society; *m* (1) April 15, 1874, Lucie Tennille, *d* June 27, 1900, da. of Ambrose Maréchal and Mary Jane (Tilyard) Emory, of Baltimore, Md.; *m* (2) June 15, 1902, Mary Elizabeth, da. of William Smithson Forwood and Rebecca Glenn, his wife, of "Glenn Wood," Bel Air, Harford Co., Md.

Issue.
(By 1st m.)

i. GEORGE NORBURY (3rd), *b* April 2, 1875; *m* Dec. 2, 1898, Sara Roberta Maynadier. Issue (1) George Norbury (4th) *b* May 6, 1900, (2) John Moores Maynadier, *b* Sept. 21, 1902, (3) Colin Fitzgerald, *b* May 1, 1904.

ii. COLIN EVAN WILLIAMS, *b* June 11, *d* Oct. 11, 1882.

i. MARY GERTRUDE MACKALL, *m* Sept. 19, 1903, William Louis Jenkins. Issue: Louis William, *b* Aug. 25, 1904; George Kenneth Mackenzie, *b* Nov. 5, 1906.

ii. ANNA VERNON.

iii. KATHARINE TENNILLE, *b* Nov. 22, 1889, *d* July 4, 1890.

(By 2nd m.)

i. THOMAS (4th) *b* Jan 28, *d* July 17, 1906.

i. REBECCA FORWOOD, *b* Jan. 28, *d* July 11, 1906.

Arms—Azure, a stag's head cabossed or.

Crest—A dexter naked arm embowed grasping a sword proper.

Motto—Fide parta fide aucta.

Residence—1808 Park Avenue, Baltimore, Md.

Clubs—University, Baltimore Country, Maryland, Merchants.

Societies—St. Andrews, Colonial Wars, Sons of the American Revolution, Colonial Order, War of 1812, Maryland Historical, Maryland Bar Association, Baltimore Bar Association, Order of Runnemede, Military Order of the French Alliance, National Genealogical, Old North West Genealogical and Historical, American Historical.

BAKER, Rev. WILLIAM OSBORN,
of Haverhill, Mass. (Only living son of Rev.
Alfred Brittin Baker, D.D., b Aug. 11, 1836. Rect.
of Trinity Ch., Princeton, N.J., Dean of the Con-
vocation of New Brunswick, N.J., Pres. of the
Standing Committee of the Dioc. of N.J., m Emilia
Stubbs.—[Desc'd. from Sir Ralph Houghton, Knt.,
1603-98]; son of Elisher, 1802-75; son of Daniel,
1753-1814; son of Henry, 1727-80; son of Daniel,
1692-1740; son of Nathaniel, 1655-1739; son of
Thomas, 1618-1700, of Milford, Ct., 1639; probably
son of Thomas, who m 1589 a da. of Sir Thos. Eng-
ham; son of John Baker, of Battel, Sussex, 1547).

Born at Princeton, N.J., Aug. 18, 1871; Rector of
Trinity Church, Haverhill; Rector of St.
Saviour's Ch., Bar Harbor, Me., 1899-1903;
Grad. M.A. Princeton Univ. 1893; Genl. Theol. Semy., N.Y., 1896;
m Aug. 3, 1899, Elizabeth, da. of Charles Carroll and Maria (Coster)
Jackson, of N.Y. Descended from Charles Carroll of Carrollton,
a Signer of the Declaration of Independence.

Issue.

i. CHARLES CARROLL, b May 15, 1900.   ii. MARY OSBORNE, b Oct. 6, 1906.

Arms—Argent, a tower between three keys erect sable.
Crest—On a tower sable, an arm embowed in armour holding in the hand
a flint stone ppr.

Residences—Trinity Rectory, Haverhill, Mass.; Princeton, N.J.
Club—Princeton of New York.

GRISCOM, CLEMENT ACTON,
of "Dolobran," Haverford, Pa. (Son of John Denn Griscom, M.D.,
b at Salem, N.J., March 25, 1809; d July 23, 1890; m at Salem, N.J.,
Nov. 6, 1839, Margaret Woodnutt, only da. of Clement and Hannah
Acton.—Descended from Andrew Griscom, who is supposed to have come
from Rochdale, Lancashire, probably descended from Francis Griscomb,
of Spotland, Lancs. Settled in Phila. 1680, m 1685 Mary Dole, d 1694).

Born March 15, 1841; Delegate of the U.S. to the International Maritime
Conference, held at Washington, D.C., 1889; m Frances Canby,
da. of W. Canby Biddle, of Phila., June 20, 1862.

Issue.

i. JOHN ACTON, b March 31, 1863; d July 15, 1864.
ii. CLEMENT ACTON, Jr., b June 20, 1868; m Genevieve Ludlow, Sept. 18,
1889.
iii. RODMAN ELLISON, b Oct. 21, 1870, m Anne Starr, Feb. 17, 1897.
iv. LLOYD CARPENTER, b Nov. 4, 1872; m Elizabeth Duer Bronson,
Nov. 2, 1901, at Saint Margaret's, London.
i. HELEN BIDDLE, b Oct. 9, 1866; m Samuel Bettle, June 20, 1889.
ii. FRANCES CANBY, b April 19, 1879.

Residence—"Dolobran," Haverford, Pa.
Clubs—Union, Metropolitan and N.Y. Yacht, of N.Y.; Philadelphia, Rittenhouse,
Union League, Country, Corinthian, Rabbit, Radnor Hunt, of Phila.;
Marlborough and St. James', of London; Metropolitan, of Washington, D.C.
Society—Colonial Wars.

SPENCER, HORATIO NELSON (2ND), M.D.,
of St. Louis, Mo. (Son of Horatio Nelson
Spencer 1798-1876, of Port Gibson, m Sarah
Marshall ; son of Israel S., 1762-1837; son of
Israel, 1732-1813 ; son of Isaac, 1678-1751 ; son
of Samuel, 1648-1705; son of Gerard Spencer,
b in England 1614, d 1685).

Born at Port Gibson, Miss., July 17, 1842 ; Prof. of
Otology, Med. Dept. of Wash. Univ.; Gov.
of Soc. of Colonial Wars, Mo.; Grad. Alabama
Univ. 1862, A.B., A.M.; Coll. of Phys. and
Surg., N.Y.; M.D., 1868 ; Hon. LL.D.,
Westminster Coll., 1897 ; m (1) Sept. 28,
1868, Anna, da. of Isaac B. Kirtland, of N.Y.;
m (2) July 6, 1887, Elizabeth, da. of Isaac
M. Dwight, of South Carolina.

Issue.

i. SELDEN, A.B., M.D., b Mar. 23, 1873.
ii. HORATIO N. (3rd), A.B., b Nov. 28, 1875.
i. LAURA, m Bernard C. Edmunds.
ii. BLANDINA, m Rev. Wm. H. DuBose.　　iii. ANNA, m W. S. Hancock.

Arms—Quarterly, argent and gules, in 2 and 3 a fret or, over all on a bend sable
three escallops of the first.
Crest—Out of a ducal coronet or, a griffin's head argent gorged with a bar
gemella gules between two wings expanded of the second.

Residence—2725 Washington Avenue, St. Louis, Mo.
Clubs—St. Louis, St. Anthony, Missouri Athletic.
Societies—American Otological, Amer. Med. Assn., Colonial Wars, Foreign Wars,
Sons of the Revolution, Confederate Veterans, Delta Psi.

TIERNAN, CHARLES BERNARD,
of Baltimore, Md. (Son of Charles Tiernan,
of Balt., 1797-1886, m Dec. 20, 1836, Gay Robertson, 1817-68, da. of John Hipkins Bernard, of "Gay
Mont," Va., and Jane Gay Robertson, gr.-son of
Luke Tiernan, immigrant, b Co. Meath, Ireland,
1758, d 1839, gr.-gr.-son of Paul Tiernan, who died
in Dublin in 1819.

Born at Baltimore, Md., Sept. 4, 1840; Educated at
St. Mary's and Loyola Colleges, A.B., A.M.;
Johns Hopkins Univ.; Member Baltimore Bar
and Maryland State Bar Assns.; Pres. of
Cathedral Branch, St. Vincent de Paul Society ;
Pres., Cathedral Branch, Young Catholic Friends' Society ; Trustee
of the Cathedral; Vice-Pres. Alumni Assn. of Loyola Coll.

Arms—Azure, a chevron between three leopards' heads, facing, erased or.
Crest—A leopard's head as in Arms; or, a griffin statant gules, wings erect vert.
Motto—Virtute res parvæ crescunt.

Residence—517 North Charles Street, Baltimore, Md.　　Club—Maryland.
Societies—Colonial Wars, Sons of the American Revolution, Hibernian, Maryland
Historical.

WOLCOTT, Hon. ROGER (*deceased*),
Ex-Governor of Massachusetts (Only sur-
viving son (by 1st wife) of Joshua Huntington
Wolcott, who *m* (1stly) Cornelia Frothingham,
and (2ndly) Harriet Frothingham; grandson of
Frederick Wolcott, *b* 1767, Member of the Connecticut Senate; great-grandson of General Oliver
Wolcott, 1726-97, Signer of the Declaration of
Independence, Brigadier-General, 1777, Lieut.-
Governor of Connecticut, 1786-96, Governor, 1797;
great-great grandson of Governor Roger Wolcott,
1679-1767, of Windsor, Conn., Major-General in
Sir William Pepperell's Expedition against Louisburg, Gov. of Connecticut, 1750.—Descended
from John and Agnes Woolcott, of Tolland Co. Somerset, Eng., *d* 1572,
whose grandson, Hon. Henry Wolcott, 1578-1655, sold estates, realising
£8,000, and joined the Dorchester Company, settling at Windsor, Conn.,
1636; *m* Elizabeth (daughter of Thomas Saunders, of Lidyard St.
Lawrence); Member of the Lower House of Assembly, 1637; Deputy,
1639; Magistrate to the Assistant-Governor, 1643-55. His eldest son,
whose male line became extinct, succeeded to the English Property;
his 7th son, Simon, 1625-87, Captain of Fort and Deputy of Simsbury,
m 1661, Martha [sister of William Pitkin, Attorney-General and Treasurer
of Connecticut]; father of Governor Roger Wolcott).

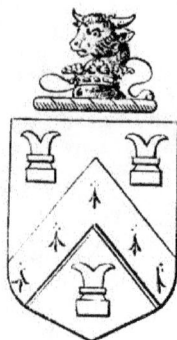

Born in Boston, Mass., July 13, 1847, *d* Dec. 21, 1900; Governor of the
State of Massachusetts, 1897-9; Member of Massachusetts Legislature,
1882-4; Graduated at Harvard University, 1870; Chief Marshal on
the 250th Anniversary of the founding of Harvard College, 1886;
m 1874, Edith Prescott, grand-daughter of the historian of that
name, and a lineal descendant of Colonel William Prescott, of
Bunker's Hill Fame.

Issue.

i. ROGER, *b* 1877.
ii. WILLIAM PRESCOTT, *b* 1880.
iii. SAMUEL HUNTINGTON, *b* 1881.
iv. OLIVER, *b* 1891.
i. CORNELIA FROTHINGHAM.

Arms—Argent, a chevron between three chess-rooks ermine.
Crest—A bull's head erased, argent, ducally gorged, armed, lined and ringed or.
Motto—Nullius addictus jurare in verba magistri.

Residences—(Family) 173 Commonwealth Avenue, Boston, Mass.; " Hill Farm,"
     Readville, Mass.

RHINELANDER, T. J. OAKLEY,
of N.Y. (Eldest son of William Rhinelander, of N.Y., Manager of Family Estates,
b 1827, m Matilda C., da. of Hon. Thomas J.
Oakley, Chief Justice of the Superior Court,
m Matilda C., da. of Henry Cruger, M.P., Mayor
of Bristol, Eng., 1781, and Senator of the State of
N.Y. 1792; son of Lieut. William C., 1790-1870, in
Col. Steven's Regt. War of 1812; son of William,
1753-1825, m Mary, sister of Col. Robert, on
Gen. Washington's Staff, descd. from Daniel Robert
a Huguenot who settled in America 1686; son of
William, 1718-77; son of Philip J. Rhinelander,
b 4 miles from Oberwesel, Germany, a Huguenot
who settled in New Rochelle, N.Y. 1686. The Castle of Schönberg, on
the Rhine, was purchased in 1884 by Mr. T. J. O. R., and his brother
Philip, on account of its propinquity to the land which the family
originally possessed).

Born in N.Y. June 5, 1858; Grad. at Columbia Univ. A.B. LL.B. 1878;
Att. and Counsellor-at-Law; Manager of Family Estates; m June 6,
1894, Edith C., da. of Charles E. and Letitia L. (Campbell) Sands.

Issue

i. PHILIP, b March 16, 1895.

Arms—Argent, two anchors in fesse, flook to flook, between a star of eight points
in chief and three in base, within a bordure azure; the escutcheon surmounted by a crest coronet.

Residences—36 W. 52nd Street, N.Y. City.; Castle Schönberg, Oberwesel-on-Rhine.

Clubs—Union, Metropolitan, Delta Phi, Country, Turf and Field.

Societies—Colonial Wars, Sons of the Revol., War of 1812, St. Nicholas, Colonial
Order, Foreign Wars, Huguenot of America.

SANDS, JAMES THOMAS,
of St. Louis, Mo. (Eldest son of Samuel Gilbert
Sands, 1816-70, m Ann Maria Wright, 1823-74;
son of Col. James, 1785-1825; son of Col. Samuel,
1636-92; son of John, b 1610; son of Capt. James,
1672-1731; son of Capt. James Sandes, b 1622,
settled at Portsmouth, R.I., 1640, prob. son of Col.
John Sandys; son of Sir Samuel Sandys; son of
Edwin Sandes, Archbishop of York, temp. Elizabeth).

Born at St. Louis, Mo., Feb. 22, 1844.

Arms—Or, a fesse dancettée betw. three cross crosslets
fitchée gules.

Crest—A griffin segreant per fesse or and gules.

Motto—Probum non pœnitet.

Residence—St. Louis, Mo.

Clubs—University, Country (St. Louis), Strollers (New York).

Societies—Colonial Wars, War of 1812, Sons of the Revolution, Foreign Wars,
Founders and Patriots, New England, Missouri Historical.

GRANGER, ALFRED HOYT,
of Lake Forest, Ill. (Son of Judge Moses M.
Granger, *b* 1831, of Zanesville, O., Ch. Judge
Supreme C. Commission Ohio, 1883-85, *m* Mary
Hoyt Reese; son of James, *b* 1788; son of Oliver,
b 1747; son of John, *b* 1706; son of Samuel,
b 1668; son of Launcelot Granger, emigrated to
America 1643, *m* Joanna, da. of Robert Adams, of
Newbury, Mass., 1654, 7th in descent from Sir
John Adams, Knt.).

Born at Zanesville, O., May 31, 1867; Class of
1887, Kenyon College, Gambier, O., took a
special course in Architecture at Mass. Inst.
of Technology: studied two years in Paris, under M. Pascal;
m Oct. 4, 1893, Belle, da. of Marvin Hughitt, Prest. Chicago and
N.W.R.

Issue.

i. ELISABETH SHERMAN.　　　iii. MARTHA McCULLOUGH.
ii. BARBARA HUGHITT.

Arms—Gules, a pomegranate slipped or.
Crest—A dexter arm couped and embowed, holding three ears of wheat ppr.
Motto—Honestas optima politia.

Residence—"Woodleigh," Lake Forest, Ill.
Clubs—Univ., Chicago; Caxton, Onwentsia; Rowfant, Cleveland; Grolier, N.Y.

ELDREDGE, MRS. CRESSIDA (*née* PERUZZI DE MEDICI),
of Boston, Mass. (Da. of Marchese Simone
Peruzzi de Medici, of Florence, Italy, Master of
Ceremonies to the late King Humbert of Italy;
Commander of the Order Manriziana and of the
Corona d'Italia; Isabella the Catholic of Spain;
the Red Eagle, and the Crown of Prussia; the
Danebrog of Denmark; St. Stanislaus of Russia;
St. Michael of Bavaria; Officier of the Legion of
Honor of France; Cavalier of Salvatore of Greece;
St. Anne of Russia; the Sun and Lion of Persia,
and of the Ottoman Medjidich, etc.; *m* Feb. 9, 1875,
Edith Marion, da. of Wetmore Story, of Salem,
Mass. (living at Rome, Italy), and Emelyn Eldredge,
of Boston, Mass.).

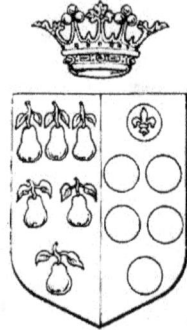

Born at Florence, Italy; *m* November 29, 1900, Major Edward Henry
Eldredge, of Boston, Mass., son of James Thomas Eldredge, and
Ellen Sophia Williams, of Roxbury, Mass.

Arms—(Peruzzi de Medici) Per pale, 1st azure, six pears, stalked and leaved or,
three, two and one; 2nd or, a hurt in chief charged with a fleur-de-lis and
five torteaux, two, two and one.

Residence—Boston, Mass.

IRWIN, BERNARD J. D., General U.S. Army, of Chicago, Ill. (Eldest son of James Irwin 1803-58, of Roundfort, Roscommon, Ireland, and N.Y. City, m Sabina M. Dowling 1803-68, of Rahara, Roscommon; son of William Irwin and Mary Norton, of Linster, Ireland.—Descended from John Irwin, who served in the Parliamentary Army under Cromwell, and settled in Ireland).

Born at Roundfort, June 24, 1828; Grad. N.Y. Med. Coll., M.D. 1851; Assist.-Sur.-Gen. U.S. Army, Medal of Honour for gallantry in action against Apache Indians; m June 20, 1864, Antoinette Elizabeth, da. of Daniel Stahl, M.D., Surg. and Brevet Lt.-Col. U.S. Vols.

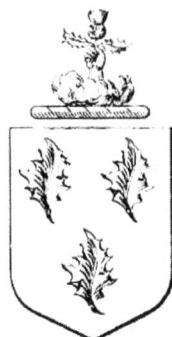

Issue.

i. George le Roy, b Aug. 26, 1868, m Maria Elizabeth Barker.
ii. Stafford Dowling, b Aug. 11, 1874, d May 6, 1875.
i. Ida Stella, m (1) David L. Barnes (2) Arthur A. Small, M.D., of Toronto.
ii. Amie de Houle, m Edward Shields Adams, of Chicago.

Arms—Argent, three holly leaves slipped vert.
Crest—A hand issuing out of a cloud grasping a branch of thistle proper.
Motto—Nemo me impune lacessit.

Residences—575 Division Street, Chicago; Ne-su-na Cottage, Cobourg, Canada.
Clubs—Onwentsia, Winter, Union League (Chicago), Cobourg Golf (Canada).
Societies—Loyal Legion, Army of the Cumberland, Army of the Tennessee.

POMEROY, GEORGE ELTWEED, of Toledo O. (Son of Geo. Eltweed Pomeroy 1807-86, m Helen E. 1816-95, da. of Dr. Gain Robinson of Wayne Co., N.Y.; son of Seth 1777-1861: son of Quartus 1735-1803; son of Gen. Seth 1706-77, a hero of the Louisburg Expedition 1745, Sen. Brig.-Gen. in Rev. War; son of Ebenezer 1669-1754; son of Medad 1638-1716: son of Eltweed, b at Beaminster 1585, m at Crewkerne, Somersetshire, 1629, Marg. Rockett, emigrated to Mass. 1630; son of Richard Pomerye.

Born at Clinton, Mich. Nov. 28, 1848; Pres. first Nat. Bank, Bellevue O.; Pres. Bd. of Trustees of the Sinking Fund of City of Toledo O.; Ex-Gov. O. Soc. Col. Wars; Ex-Pres. Ohio Soc. Sons of the Revol.; Pres. of Geo. E. Pomeroy Co.; m 1883, Matilda, da. of John T. Worthington of Md.

Arms—Or, a lion rampant gules holding in the dexter paw an apple proper, within a bordure engrailed sable.
Crest—A lion rampant gules holding an apple as in Arms.
Motto—Virtutis fortuna comes.

Residences—Toledo, Ohio; Tillula Lake, Michigan.
Clubs—Toledo, Country, Middle Bass, Castalia Trout, Yacht Club.
Societies—Ohio in N.Y., Colonial Wars, Sons of Revolution, Colonial Wars of N.Y., Sons of the Revolution of N.Y., Sons of the American Revolution.

WASHINGTON, JOSEPH EDWIN,
of Wessyngton, Ten. (Son of George
Augustine Washington, 1815-92, mem. of Tenn.
Legislature, 1873, Vice-Prest. L. and N.R.R.,
m Jane, 1830-94, da. of Joseph D. and Mary (Hanna)
Smith, of Florence. Ala.; son of Joseph 1770-1848,
of Southampton, Va.; son of Joseph 1710-60; son
of George 1680-1730, of Surry Co. Va.; son of
Richard 1650-90; son of John 1615-52, of Surry
Co. Va; second son of Sir John Washington of
Thrapston, Eng.).

Born at Wessyngton, Tennessee, Nov. 10, 1851:
Grad. Georgetown Coll., A.B., Hon. A.M.,
1873; mem. General Assembly of Tennessee,
1877; Presidential Elector on Hancock-English
Democratic Ticket, 1880; Mem. of Congress
6th Dist. of Tennessee, 1886-96; m Jan. 15,
1879, Mary, da. of Judge Wyndham Kemp
and Seigniora Peyton, da. of John Peyton and Ann Field (Gilliam)
Bolling, of Petersburg, Va.

Issue.

i. Geo. Augustine, b Oct. 27, 1879.
ii. Joseph Edwin, b Nov. 8, 1883.

i. Anne Bolling.
ii. Bessie Adelaide.

Arms—Argent, two bars gules, in chief three mullets of the second.
Crest—Out of a ducal coronet or, a raven issuant wings endorsed sable.
Mottoes—Virtus sola nobilitas; exitus acta probat.

Residence—Wessyngton, Tennessee.

LUDLOW, BANYER,
of Westchester (Son of Hon. Robert H.
Ludlow, 1802-82, of Black Rock, N.Y., m Cornelia
Le Roy, 1809-86; son of Gabriel 1768-1825; son of
Col. Gabriel 1736-1808; son of Gabriel b 1704; son
of Gabriel, b 1663; son of Gabriel Ludlow b 1634, of
Frome, Somersetshire, emigrated to New York 1694;
son of Thomas; son of Thomas Ludlow, of Dinton
and Baycliffe, Wiltshire, brother of Sir Edmund
Ludlow, Commander-in-Chief of the Forces in
Ireland; of the Ludlows of Hill Deveral, Wilts).

Born at Westchester, N.Y., June 1, 1835; Justice
of the Peace; Vestryman of St. Peter's
Church; Trustee of Public School No. 4, at
Westchester; served in the 71st Regiment
N.Y.S.M. during Civil War; m Oct. 2, 1873, Lydia Cowgill Ellis.

Issue.

i. Cornelia Le Roy, m (1) Arthur Ludlow Clark, d March 12, 1905,
m (2) John S. Gaines, of Virginia.

Arms—Argent, a chevron between three bears' heads sable.
Crest—A lion rampant.   Motto—Spero infestis, metuo secundis.
Residence—"Cedarhurst," Westchester, N.Y.

Club—Westchester Golf.   Societies—St. Nicholas, G.A.R.

CHILDS, DANIEL BREWER,
of New York City (Eldest son by 1st wife of Noadiah Moody Childs, of Syracuse, N.Y.; President of Syracuse Salt Co. and Board of Education; *b* at Stillwater, 1806-96; *m* (1) 1839, Martha, 1821-63, da. of Simeon and Eunice (Macy) Brewer, of Providence, R.I., a " Mayflower " descendant of John Howland 13th Signer of the " Mayflower" Compact; also from Daniel Brewer, who emigrated to America in the " Lion," 1632, and settled at Roxbury, Mass.; *m* (2) 1865, Sarah Elizabeth, da. of Dr. Ebenezer and Sarah Cooke (Shepard) Dawes, of Taunton, Mass.—Descended from Deacon Ephraim Child, who came over with Gov. John Winthrop, 1630; settled at Watertown, Mass.; Deputy, Representative, Selectman and Town Clerk, and from Benjamin Child, Roxbury, Mass. Grandson of Dr. Ephraim Child, Surgeon 41st Saratoga Regt., 1810-12, and great-grandson of Captain Increase Child, soldier in French and English War 1756-8, and Captain in Revolution 1776).

Born at Syracuse, N.Y., May, 5, 1843; Counsellor-at-Law; Graduated at Yale, A.B. 1863; Albany Law University, B.L. 1864; A.M. 1866; admitted to the Bar; Vice-President and one of the projectors of the Law Telegraph Co., 1875-85; Director Manhattan Quotation Telegraph Company, 1874-75, &c.; Director Law Telephone Co.; Attorney and Counsel for these companies and in the Telephone Arbitrations, also for the N.Y. Elevated R.R. in its inception, and Executor, Trustee and Receiver in several large estates; *m* 1888, Kathryn, da. of Dr. Jonathan Cass, Surgeon in the United States Army; Chief on Staff of Alexandria Va. Hospital; served throughout the Civil War, 1861-65, and Mary Peet, of Great Barrington, Mass.; descended from John Cass, of Hampton, N.H., 1644, and John Peet of Stratford Ct., 1635.

Issue.

i. STERLING CASS, *b* May 12, 1889.

ii. HAROLD WINTHROP, *b* October 20, 1891.

i. KATHRYN CASS.

ii. ISABELLA CASS.

Arms—Gules, a chevron engrailed ermine, between three eagles close argent.
Crest—An eagle with wings expanded argent, enveloped round the neck with a snake proper.
Motto—Imitari quam invidere.

Residences—76 East 81st Street, New York; " Cass Cottage," Great Barrington, Mass.
Clubs—University, Lawyers, Locustwood, " Wyantenuck," Berkshire.
Societies—Yale Alumni, Psi Upsilon.

LOWELL, DELMAR RIAL, Rev. A. B., D.D.,
of Middletown (Son of Reuben Lowell,
1812-93; son of Abram, *b* 1774; son of Moses,
b 1726; son of John, *b* 1683; son of Benjamin,
b 1642; son of John; son of Percival, *b* 1591, of
Newbury, Mass, 1639; son of Richard. of Clyvedon,
Somersetshire, 9th in desct. from William Lowle,
of Yardley, Co. Worcester).

Born at South Valley, N.Y., Nov. 29, 1844; served
in Civil War, 1864-65; Chaplain and Major,
U.S.A.; Grad. Wesleyan Univ. 1873; D.D. Ohio
Wes. Univ., 1888; Chaplain Ct. Ho. of Representatives, 1901-3; Alderman of Middletown,
Ct., 1902-3; Chaplain-in-Chief I.A.R.; *m* (1)
1876, Irene E. Maynard, *d* 1877; *m* (2) June
26, 1879, Harriet A. Davis, of Middletown, Ct.

Issue.

i. Roy D., *b* Sept 16, 1884.   ii. Percival D., *b* Mar. 1893.

i. May I., *b* Dec. 16, 1881.

ii. Elsie G.   } *b* 1887 (*decd.*).   iv. Alwilda G., *b* Oct. 14, 1889.
iii. Eloise A.

Arms—Sable, a dexter hand couped at the wrist grasping three darts, one in pale
and two in saltire argent.

Crest—A stag's head cabossed or, between the attires a pheon azure.

Residence—407, University Ave., Syracuse, N.Y.

Societies—New Eng. Hist. Geneal., Mass.; C. M. Oneida Hist., N.Y.; Charter M,
Middx. Co. Hist., Ct.; Charter M. and first Reg. Utah. Sons of the Am.
Revol., Phi Beta Kappa, Delta Kappa Epsilon, I.A.R.

CHASE, WALTER GREENOUGH, M.D.,
of Brookline Mass. (Son of Charles Greenough
Chase of Northfield N.H., 1827-94, *m* 1853, Relief
Judith, 1827-1901, da. of Alvah McQuesten of
Plymouth N.H., descd. from William McQuesten,
who emigrated from Belfast, Ireland, and settled
in Litchfield, N.H., 1745. Descd. from William
Chase, planter, of Roxbury, Mass., who with his
wife Mary and son William came to New England
with Governor Winthrop, sailing from Yarmouth
1630, *d* 1659.

Born in Boston, May 30, 1859; Grad. at Harvard
Univ. 1882, Harvard Med. Sch. 1900; *m* Oct.
20, 1906, Frances Scott Hubbard, of Wiscasset
Maine, da. of Joseph Hubbard and Fannie
Thaxter Scott.

Arms—Gules, four crosses flory or; on a canton azure a lion passant of the second.

Crest—A demi-lion rampant or, holding a cross of the shield.

Motto—Ne cede malis.

Residence—483 Beacon Street, Boston. Mass.

Clubs—University, Country, University of N.Y.

DE LA VERGNE, Colonel HUGUES JULES, of New Orleans La. (Son of Colonel Jules de la Vergne, 1818-87, of New Orleans, Member of the House of the State of La. 1844, Senator in 1856, on Staff of Gov. Alex. Mouton of La. and Lieut.-Col. and A.D.C. on Staff of Gov. Thos. O. Moore of La. during War of Secession, *m* Emma Josephine, da. of Judge Joaquin Bermudez ; son of Colonel Hugues de la Vergne, 1792-1843, Major on Staff of Commanding General at Battle of New Orleans, 1815 ; Secretary of State of La. in 1820; Colonel on Staff of Thos. B. Robertson third Governor of La., *m* Marie Adele de Villeré, da. of Maj.-Gen. J. P. Villeré, second Governor of La. ; son of Count Pierre de la Vergne, Chevalier de St. Louis, *b* at Brive, France, came to New Orleans as an Officer in a Royal Military Company, 1767, *d* 1813, *m* Elizabeth, da. of Guillaume du Verzer ; son of Seigneur Jean de la Vergne, *b* at Brive and descendant of the de la Vergne Seigneur de Juillas, in Limousin. The de la Vergne family is one of ancient chivalry. Castle de la Vergne, cradle of the family is situated at St. Priest-Ligoure, Limousin, now Haute Sienne, France).

Born at New Orleans, La., July 1, 1867 ; Lawyer ; Grad. from Jesuits' Coll., New Orleans, A.B. 1885, A.M. 1887, Ph.B., 1893 ; Grad. Tulane Univ. LL.B., 1888 ; ran for Senate of the State of La., 1904, and Commissioned Major and A.D.C. by Gov. Blanchard of Louisiana July 9, 1904, promoted Lieut.-Colonel March 12, 1905 ; *m* May 2, 1895, Marie Louise, da. of Charles Edouard Schmidt, Lawyer, and Leda Hincks, both of New Orleans.

Issue.

i. MARGUERITE, *b* September 23, 1896.

ii. JUILLAC HUGUES, *b* November 24, 1897.

iii. CHARLES EDOUARD, *b* August 18, 1904.

Arms—D'or à la rose de gueules ; surmounted by a Count's helmet and coronet.

Motto—Honneur et Vaillance.

Residences—823 Esplanade Avenue, New Orleans ; Villa de la Vergne on Bogue Falia, near Covington, La.

Club—Bogne Falia.

Societies—Louisiana Bar Assn., Commercial Law League of Amer., Louisiana Hist. Assn., Jesuits' Alumni, Tulane Alumni, Hon. Mem. Batt. Washington Artillery.

C OSBY, FRANK CARVILL, Rear-Admiral,
Pay Corps, U.S. Navy, (deceased),
of Washington D.C. (4th son of Fortunatus Cosby,
1801-71, of Louisville, Ky., m 1825, Ellen Mary
Blake, 1804-48, of Roxbury; son of Judge Fortunatus
1765-1846, m Mary Ann Fontaine ; son of Charles,
d 1802, m Elizabeth Sydnor ; son of David Cosby,
1700-70, from England, settled in Louisa, Co. Va.,
1720, m Mary Overton, 1705-85, of Louisa Co.).

Born at Louisville Ky. April 10, 1840 ; entered the
Navy 1857 ; commissd. in Pay Corps, Aug. 24,
1861 ; retired April 10, 1902, with increase of
rank for service during Civil and Spanish Wars,
m Dec. 6, 1864, Charlotte M. Spencer, of
Chestertown Md.   He died Feb. 8, 1905.

Issue.

i. Spencer, b Oct. 2, 1867.

ii. Frank Clark, b Oct. 10, 1869, m Carolyn Du Bois.

iii. Arthur Fortunatus, b May 22, 1871, m Virginia Rolette Dousman.

Arms—Argent, a chev. betw. 3 leopards' faces sa. ; on a canton or, a saltire vert
betw. a cross-crosslet in chief gu., a lizard erect in the dexter and a salmon
in the sinister fesse point gu., and a dexter hand couped in the base gu.

Crest—A griffin segreant gu., supporting a broken spear or, headed arg.

Motto—Audaces Fortuna Juvat.

Residence—(Family) 1808 Mass. Ave. Washington D.C.

S ACKETT, HENRY WOODWARD, Col.,
of New York City (Third son of Dr. Solon
Philo Sackett, 1818-93, of Ithaca, N.Y., m Lovedy
K. Woodward; son of Philo, 1788-1863; son of
Major Buel, 1763-1840; son of Benjamin, b 1736;
son of Jonathan, 1696-1773 ; son of William, 1662-
1700; son of John, 1632-1719, of Northampton,
Mass; son of Simon Sackett, from Isle of Ely,
Cambridgeshire, Eng., b 1585, to New Eng., 1630).

Born at Enfield, N.Y., Aug. 31, 1853 ; Grad. Cornell
Univ., 1875; admtd. to the Bar, 1879 ; apptd.
A. de C., Governor Black's Staff N.Y.S., 1896 ;
Pres. of Cornell Univ. Club, N.Y. in 1897-98 ;
Secretary Hudson-Fulton Celebration Com-
mission, 1906 ; m Nov. 17, 1886, Elizabeth Titus ; Senior member of
law firm of Sackett, Chapman & Stevens.

Arms—Argent, a chevron between three mullets of six points sable.

Crest—An eagle's head and neck, erased, or.

Motto—Aut nunquam tentes, aut perfice.

Residences—515 Madison Av., N.Y. City ; and Mamaroneck, Westchester Co., N.Y.

Clubs—University, Cornell University, Republican, National Arts, Hardware,
New York Bar Association, City, Phi Beta Kappa Alumni, St. Nicholas.

Societies—Sons of the American Revolution, Order of Founders and Patriots
of America, St. George's.

FAIRBANKS, HIRAM FRANCIS, Rev.,
of Milwaukee (Son of Rev. Caleb J. Fairbanks, 1821-99, *m* Lydia Franklin, 1822-78 ; son of Caleb, *b* 1798; son of John, *b* 1766 ; son of Lt. Joshua, *b* 1727 ; son of Dr. Jonathan, *b* 1689 ; son of Dr. Jonathan, *b* 1662 ; son of Capt. George, *b* 1619; son of Jonathan Fayerbanke, *m* 1617, at Halifax, Yorks, came to America, 1633.—Descended from John Coolidge, *b* 1604, of Watertown, 7th in descent from Thomas Colynge, of Arrington, Co., Camb., *d* 1495; from John, son of Peter and Marabella Livermore, of Co. Suffolk, *m* 1594 ; and from Jonathan Adams, *b* 1619, son of Henry Adams, ancestor of Presidents John Adams and John Quincey Adams).

Born at Leon, N.Y., May 25, 1845 ; Author of "A Visit to Europe and the Holy Land," &c.
Rector of three different Catholic Churches in the Archdiocese of Milwaukee, Wis., during 34 years ; studied at Lawrence Univ. and St. Louis Univ. ; Graduated at St. Francis Theological Seminary ; ordained Priest, 1868.

Arms—(for Collynge) Vert, a griffin segreant or. *Crest*—A griffin segreant or.

Residence—Rectory of St. Patrick's Church, Milwaukee, Wis.

BRISCOE, WILLIAM DARKE, Capt. C.S.A.,
of Piedmont, W. Va. (Son of Dr. John and Sarah, *m* (Rutherford) Briscoe of Piedmont ; son of Dr. John, 1752-1818, *m* Eleanor Magruder ; son of Dr. John, 1717-88, *m* Elizabeth McMillan, grand-daughter of Burr Harrison, of Chappawamsic Creek, Va. ; son of Dr. John, of St. Mary's Co., Maryland, *m* Elizabeth De Courcy, gr.-grand-da. of Col. Henry De Courcy, of Maryland ; son of Dr. John Briscoe who came to America in the "Dove and Ark," 1634, settled at St. Mary's, Md. ; son of Leonard ; son of Richard of Crofton, Cumberland, Eng. ; son of Robert Briscoe).

Born at Piedmont, W. Va., 1835 ; late Capt. in the Confederate Army ; Planter ; *m* Eva Pendleton Goodloe, of Spottsylvania Co., Virginia.

Issue.

i. John Pendleton.
ii. Frederick.
i. Sallie de Montargis.   ii. Katherine.   iii. Louisa.

Arms—Argent, three greyhounds courant in pale sable.
Crest—A greyhound courant sable, seizing a hare proper.
Mottoes—Grata sume manu ; Alter altero.

Residence—"Piedmont," Jefferson Co., West Virginia.

BOWIE, HOWARD STRAFFORD, M.D. (*deceased*),
late of Baltimore (Son of Allen Perrie Bowie,
1807-56, of Prince George's Co., Md., *m* Melvina
H., da. of Dr. John E. and Rachel W. (Harper)
Berry; son of Capt. Eversfield, 1773-1815, *m* Elizth.,
da. of Capt. and Barbara (Brooke) Lane; son of
Capt. Fielder, 1745-94, *m* Elizath., da. of Rev. John
Eversfield; son of Allen, 1719-83, of Nottingham
Dist., Md., *m* Priscilla, widow of Capt. Wm. Finch;
son of John Bowie, 1688-1759, *b* in Scotland, settled
near Nottingham, P.G.'s Co., Md.).

Born in Prince George's Co., Md., Aug. 10, 1846,
d Feb. 26, 1900; Grad. Med. Univ. of Maryland, 1870; Clinical Assist., later Assist.
Physician Balto. Infirmary; Mem. Medical
and Chirurgical Faculty and Curator; *m* Oct. 7,
1879, Laura Virginia, da. of Edris Berkley,
of Fairfax Co., Va., and Virginia, da. of John Enders of Richmond,
Va.

Issue.

i. EDRIS BERKLEY, *b* May 8, 1882.
ii. ALLEN STRAFFORD, *b* Nov. 13, 1884.

i. VIRGINIA BERKLEY.
ii. ELEANOR HOWARD.

Arms—Argent, on a bend sable three buckles or.
Crest—A demi-lion azure, holding in dexter paw a dagger.
Motto—Quod non pro patria.

Residences—(of Mrs. H. S. B.) 811 Hamilton Terrace, Balto; "An Darach,"
Catonsville, Md.

HUIE, WILLIAM HENRY THOMPSON,
of San Francisco, Cal. (Son of Dr. George
William Huie, of San Francisco, 1824-77, *m* 1848
Sarah Elizabeth, da. of Hon. Robert Augustus
Thompson, Mem. of Congress from Virginia,
m Mary S. Slaughter, of Culpeper, Va.; Son of
James Huie, who came from Dumfries, Scotland,
and settled in Dumfries, Virginia, Master in the
U.S. Navy in 1803, *m* Helen Grant, da. of Judge
Cuthbert Bullitt. Also descd. from Rev. John
Thompson, *b* at Muckamore Abbey, near Belfast,
Ireland, came to Maryland 1740, *m* 1742 the widow
of Governor Spotswood).

Born in Sonoma County, California, March 24,
1855; Merchant.

Arms—Azure, an eagle displayed or.
Crest—A demi-eagle displayed or.

Motto—Respice finem.

Residence—2201 Sacramento Street, San Francisco, Cal.
Societies—Sons of the American Revolution, of Cal.; Cal. Hist. Genealogical;
National Geographic Society.

SHOEMAKER, HENRY FRANCIS,
of N.Y. City (Second son of John Wise
Shoemaker, of Tamaqua, Pa., and his wife, Mary A.,
da. of William Brock; son of Henry, served in
War of 1812; son of John, served in War for
Independence; son of Peter Shoemaker, one of the
founders of Germantown, Penna., 1685, served in
the Indian Wars).

Born in Schuylkill Co., Pa., Mar. 28, 1845; Grad.
from Genessee Seminary, Lima, N.Y.; appointed to U.S. Naval Academy, 1861; Capt.
of Vols. in Union Army during Civil War;
m April 22, 1874, Blanche, only da. of Hon.
James W. Quiggle, LL.D., of Phila., formerly
State Senator and Deputy Atty.-Genl. of Pa.,
and American Consul at Antwerp.

Issue.

i. HENRY WHARTON, b Feb. 24, 1881.
ii. WILLIAM BROCK, b July 29, 1883. d 1906.   i. BLANCHE LE ROY.

Arms—Sable, three chevronels ermine.
Crest—A demi-lion rampant gules, guttée argent, holding in his dexter paw a
regal mace.   Motto—Sapere aude.

Residences—26 West 53rd Street, New York City; "Cedarcliff," Riverside, Conn.
Clubs—Metropolitan, Union League, Riding, Lawyers, Lotos, Riverside Yacht,
Automobile of America, New York Yacht, Army and Navy.
Societies—Sons of the Revol., Pennsylvania, Grand Army of the Republic.

BREWSTER, WADSWORTH J.,
of Detroit Mich. (Son of Silas Wadsworth
Brewster, of Hannibal N.Y., 1813-1882, m 1837,
Mary A. Walden; son of Elias of Mexico N.Y.,
m Lucretia Edgerton; son of Dea. Wadsworth of
Lebanon, Ct.; son of Oliver of Bernardstown,
Mass.; son of William of Lebanon; son of William
of Duxbary, Mass.; son of Love of Duxbary: son
of William Brewster, 1566-1644, Elder of Plymouth
Colony, 1630, drafted "Mayflower" Compact,
Mem. and Chaplain of the 1st Military Company
organised at Plymouth under Capt. Miles Standish.
Also descended from Governor William Bradford).

Born at Hannibal, N.Y., Feb. 10, 1846, m Feb. 10,
1867, Amy da. of William Harrison and Emily
Elmira (Miller) Doud of Brooklyn, Pa.

Issue.

i. A son, b and d 1871.   i. MABEL DOROTHY.
ii. BIRNEY N., b 1873, d 1874.   ii. LUCRETIA EDGERTON.

Arms—Sable, a chevron ermine between three estoiles argent.
Crest—A bear's head erased azure.   Motto—Verité soyez ma garde.

Residence—215 Forest Avenue W., Detroit, Mich.

CURTIS, WILLIAM ELEROY,
    of Washington, D.C. (Second son of Eleroy
Curtis, D.D., 1818-86, m Harriet Eliza, 1822-94,
da. of Rev. Harvey and Deborah (Eddy) Coe, D.D.,
of Hudson, O.—Descended from William Curtis,
from Appledore, Canterbury, Kent, settled at Roxbury, Mass., 1632.

Born at Akron, O., Nov. 5, 1850; Grad. Western
    Reserve Univ. 1871. A.B., B.A., D. Lit.;
    Commr. to the Republics of Central and South
    America; Special Envoy to Spain; Special
    Envoy to the Vatican; Dir., Bureau of the
    American Republics; m Dec. 23, 1874, Cora,
    da. of Simon Peter and Isabella Forbes
    (Liddell) Kepler of Erie, Pa.

Issue.
i. GEORGE KEPLER, *b* June 1, 1877; *d* May 23, 1896.
ii. ELEROY CURTIS, *b* June 1, 1879.   i. ELSIE EVANS.

Arms—Ermine, a chevron sable between three fleurs-de-lis or.
Crest—An arm embowed in armour holding in the hand proper a scimetar, hilt
    and pommel or.
Motto—Velle bene Facere.

Residence 1801 Connecticut Avenue, Washington, D.C.
Clubs—Union League, Alpha Delta Phi, Press, Gridiron, Cosmos.
Societies—Sons of the American Revolution, National Geographic, Americanistas
    (Madrid), Anthropological, Columbia Historical, Association for the
    Advancement of Science, American Historical, &c., &c.

FLOYD, CHARLES HAROLD,
    of Milton, Mass. (Son of Edward Elbridge
Floyd, merchant, of Boston, m (1) Mary Jane
Spalding, m (2) June 6, 1877, Lisbeth Henrietta
Whitney; son of Daniel, 1799-1845; son of Daniel,
1760-1808; son of Daniel, 1728-66; son of Daniel,
1702-48; son of Daniel, 1675-1750; son of Capt.
John Floyd, 1636-1701, of Lynn, Malden and
Rumney Marsh, an officer in King Philip's War,
and Indian and French War of 1690).

Born at Brookline, Mass., Sept. 28, 1878, Grad.
    Harvard S.B., 1903.

Arms—Argent, on a cross sable a rose of the first.
Crest—A griffin sejant vert holding in the dexter paw a
    torch argent, lighted proper.

Residence—"Cedar Ridge," Milton, Mass
Clubs—Hoosick Whisick, Harvard of New York.
Societies—Sons of American Revolution, Bostonian.

LINDSAY, JOHN DOUGLAS,
of New York (Son of Dr. Wm. F. Lindsay, 1826-1900, *m* Sarah A., da. of Aug. Van C. Vredenburgh; son of Rev. John, 1788-1850, of Lynn, Mass.; son of Daniel, 1753-1827; son of Eleazer, 1716-93; son of Ralph, 1684-1747; son of Eleazer, 1644-1716; son of Christopher, em. to America, 1629, settled in Lynn, *d* 1669; son of Christopher of Pitscottie, Scotland, *b* 1571; son of Robert, 1532-78, the chronicler; son of William of Pyetstone, *d* before 1584; son of Sir Patrick Lindsay, 4th Lord of the Byres, *d* 1526, 10th in desct. from Sir William de Lindsay, of Ercildun, Luffness and Crawford, fl. 1161-1200).

Born in New York, Dec. 31, 1865; Admitted to the Bar, 1887; Dep. Asst. Dist. Atty. 1887-93; Asst. Dist. Atty., N.Y. Co., 1894-98; Pres. N.Y. Soc. Prevention of Cruelty to Children, 1903; *m* June 3, 1895, Stella, da. Dr. Elisha Hall and Jael Kavanagh (Smallwood) Gregory, of St. Louis.

Arms—Gules, a fesse chequy argent and azure, three stars in chief and a mascle in base argent.

Crest—A swan with wings expanded proper. *Motto*—Love but dried.

Residence—34 West 11th Street New York.
Clubs—Calumet, Manhattan of N.Y., Fort Orange of Albany.
Societies—St. Nicholas, N.Y. Bar Assn., N.Y. State Bar Assn., N.Y. Historical, Alumni N.Y. Univ., Colonial Wars, Sons of the Revol., etc., etc.

CARTER, OSCAR CHARLES SUMNER,
of Phila. (Son of Oscar C. B. Carter, 1809-63, of Nashua, N.H., *m* 1856, Mary L., da. of Daniel R. Brower, of Norristown, Pa.; son of Oscar C. B., of Nashua, N.H., *b* 1809; son of Charles, of Keene, N.H., *b* 1788; son of Elijah, of Lancaster, Mass., *b* 1764; son of Ephraim, *b* 1713; son of Samuel, of Woburn, Mass., *b* 1677; son of Samuel, of Watertown, Mass.; son of Rev. Thomas Carter, *b* 1610, of Watertown, Mass., 1635, brother of James Carter, of Hinderclay, Suffolk, he is supposed to have matriculated at Cambridge Univ., A.B., 1629, A.M., 1633).

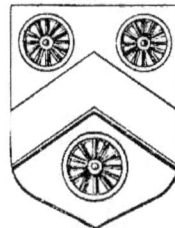

Born in Phila., March 1, 1857; Prof. of Geology and Mineralogy, Central High School, Phila; *m* Oct. 23, 1882, Elenora da. of John L. Martin, of Harrisburg, Pa.

Issue.

i Oscar Sedgewick, *b* Nov. 14, 1884.

Arms—Argent, a chevron between three cartwheels vert.

Crest—On a mount vert, a greyhound sejant argent, sustaining a shield of the last, charged with a cartwheel vert.

Residence—1930 Chestnut Street, Philadelphia.
Clubs—Priestly Chemical of Univ. of Penna., Verein der Bohrtechniker, Vienna.
Societies—Section Geology and Mineralogy Acad. of Nat. Sciences, National Geographic of Washington, Geographical of Phila.

DE PEYSTER, JOHN WATTS, Brig.-Gen., S.N.Y., Brev. Major.-Gen., N.Y.,

of Rose Hill (Son of the late Frederic de Peyster, LL.D., 1796-1882, Pres. of the N.Y. Hist. Soc., etc. "Probably connected as an active officer with more societies than any other New Yorker who ever lived," *m* Mary Justina, 1801-21, da. of the Hon. John Watts, *d* 1836; Speaker of the Assembly, N.Y., 1791-94; Mem. of Congress, 1793-95; first Judge of Westchester Co., 1806, etc.; last Royal Recorder of N.Y., Founder of the Leake and Watts Orphan House).

Born at N.Y. City, March 9, 1821; Brev. Major-Gen. N.Y. by "Concurrent resolution," or "Special Law," N.Y. State Legislature, April, 1866, "for meritorious services rendered to the Nat. Guard and to the U.S. prior to and during the Rebellion," first and only General officer receiving such an honour from S.N.Y., and only officer thus brevetted (Major-Gen.) in the U.S.; M.A., Litt.D., LL.D., F.R.H.S.G.B., Lond.; Hon. F.S.S.L. and A., Lond.; Hon. Pres. of the Colonial Soc. of Am.; Hon. Vice-Pres. of the Numismatic and Antiquarian Soc. of Phila.; M. Maatsschappij der Nederlandsche Letterkunde, Leyden, Holland, etc., and Honorary, Corresponding, Life Mem. of the Amer. Mus. of Nat. Hist., Life Mem. and Mem. or Fell. of over fifty Hist., Literary, and Scientific Societies and Institutions.

Issue.

i. John Watts, Jr., Brev.-Col. U.S. Vol. and Col. N.Y. Vol.; Major of 1st N.Y. Vol. Artillery; *b* Dec. 2, 1841, *d* April 12, 1873.

ii. Frederic, Jr., Brev.-Col. N.Y.V., and Major U.S.V., *b* Dec. 12, 1842, *d* Oct. 30, 1874.

i. Estelle Elizabeth (Prudence), *b* June 7, 1843, *d* Dec. 12, 1889.

ii. Maria (Beata), *b* July 7, 1852, *d* Sept. 27, 1857.

Arms—(for de Peyster) Argent, a tree eradicated proper surmounted by a Netherland Count's helmet.

Arms—(for Watts) Argent, on a mount an oak tree all proper; debruised of a fesse azure charged with a crescent between two mullets argent.

Crest—A dexter hand issuing from a cloud holding a branch of laurel all proper.

Motto—Forti non deficit telum.

Residence—Rose Hill, near Tivoli, P.O. Township of Red Hook, Duchess Co., N.Y.

Club—Century.

Societies—Military Order of the Loyal Legion of the U.S., St. Nicholas, Holland, Hon. Corresponding, Life or Regular, Fellow or Member of numerous Societies in the United States and abroad.

FITZGERALD, DESMOND,
  of Brookline, Mass. (Son of Captain Lionel Charles William Henry Fitzgerald, K.T.S. 1812-94, m Sarah Caroline, d 1856, daughter of Hon. Patrick Brown, President of Her Britannic Majesty's Council of the Bahama Islands ; son of Lieut.-Colonel Edward Thomas Fitzgerald, b 1784, served with the Guards at the battle of Waterloo, m Emma Green, d 1845 ; son of Charles Lionel Fitzgerald, Lieut.-Colonel North Mayo Militia, m 1777, Dorothea, daughter of Sir Thomas Butler, Baronet ; son of George Fitzgerald, m Lady Mary Hervey ; son of Thomas Fitzgerald, of Turlough, 1661-1747 ; son of John Fitzgerald, of Gurteens, Co. Waterford, m the widow of General Harrison, by whom he acquired the estates of Turlough, Co. Mayo. This ancient family descended from the Barons of Burnchurch, also reputed to be descended from Strongbow-Desmond line of Fitzgerald.

Born at Nassau N.P., May 20, 1846 ; Consulting Civil Engineer ; Past Department Engineer Metropolitan Water Board of Boston ; Past Chairman Massachusetts Topographical Survey Commission ; Chairman Brookline Park Commission, etc. ; Past President Boston Society Civil Engineers ; Past President American Society Civil Engineers ; Past President New England Water Works Association ; m June 21, 1870, Elizabeth P.C. Salisbury, daughter of Stephen Salisbury, M.D., of Brookline, Mass.

Issue.

i. HAROLD, b May 19, 1877, m Oct. 3, 1903, Eleanor Fitzgerald.

ii. STEPHEN SALISBURY, b Sept. 19, 1879, m Sept. 9, 1906, Agnes Blake.

i. CAROLINE ELIZABETH, m Chas. Augustus Van Rensselaer.

ii. HARRIOT, m Robert Jones Clark of Boston.

Arms—Ermine, a saltire gules.

Crest—A boar passant.

Motto—Honor probataque virtus.

———

Residence—Brookline, Mass.

Clubs—Union, Country, St. Botolph.

Societies—Am. Civil Engrs. N.Y., Boston Civil Engrs., Colonial Wars, Sons of the Revol. ; Descendants of Colonial Governors, etc.

HUIDEKOPER, FREDERIC WOLTERS,

of Washington, D.C. (Son of Edgar Huidekoper, 1812-62, *m* Frances Shippen, 1818-97. —
Descended from Harm Jan, son of Anne and
Gesiena F. Wolters Huidekoper, Hogeveen, Holland, 1776, to America, 1796, 7th from Wm. Shippen,
of Methley, Yorks, Armiger).

Born at Meadville, Pa., Sept. 12, 1840; Grad.
Harvard Univ. A.B., '62, A.M., '71; Capt.
Co. F, 58th Pa. Mil. 1863; Pres. C. and E.
Ill. R.R., '77-'82; Pres. E. and T. H. R. R.,
'81-82; 1st Vice-Pres. R. and D. R. R., and
Vice-Pres. R. and W. P. T. Ry. and Ware-
house Co.; Pres. Va. Mid. R.R., '86-'87;
Pres. and Receiver, P., S., and L. E. R. R., '89-'91; Pres. S. A.
and O. R. R. '90-'92; Governor of the Society of Colonial Wars (D.C.)
1901-2; *m* Jan. 22, 1867, Anna Virginia*, da. of FitzJames Christie,
of Erie, Pa.

Issue.

i. FREDERIC LOUIS, *b* March 8, 1874.
ii. REGINALD SHIPPEN, *b* May 24, 1876.
i. GRACIE, *b* July 5; *d* July 6, 1872.

Arms—Party per pale, azure and argent, 1st, a sword ppr., hilted or, in pale, a
mullet of six points in chief of the last; 2nd, three arbalets all ppr.
surmounted by a Ritter's coronet (Friesland).

Residence—1614 Eighteenth Street, Washington, D.C.
Clubs—Metropolitan, Country (Washington), University, Harvard, (N.Y. City).
Societies— Sons of the Revolution, Colonial Wars, *Huguenot (N.Y.), *Colonel
Dames, *Daughters of the American Revolution.

STRYKER, THOMAS HUBBARD,

of Rome, N.Y. (Son of John Stryker, 1808-85,
of Orange, N.J., *m* Frances E. Hubbard; son of
Daniel P., 1783-1816; son of John, 1740-86; son
of Pieter, 1705-74; son of Jan, 1684-1770; son of
Pieter, 1653-1741; son of Jan Van Strÿcker,
1615-97, from Holland to Flatbush, L.I., 1653).

Born in Rome, N.Y., Nov. 14, 1847; Grad. A.B.
and A.M. Hobart Coll., Geneva, N.Y. 1868;
Chairman Bd. of Fire and Police Commissrs.,
Rome, 1894; Pres. Rome Locomotive and
Machine Works; Director in various Local
Companies and Institutions.

Arms—Paly of four or and gules three boars' heads sable armed argent.
Crest—Out of a ducal coronet or, a griffin's head sable between two palm branches
in orle, vert. *Motto*—In extremis terribilis.

Residence—112 E. Liberty Street, Rome, New York.
Clubs—Rome, University, New York City.
Societies—Colonial Wars, Founders and Patriots, Sons of the American Revolu-
tion, Sigma Phi.

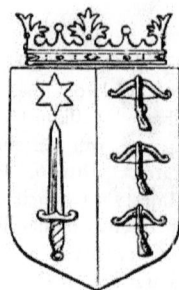

SHIRLEY, RUFUS GEORGE,

of New York (Only son of William Fearclo Shirley, 1833-1903, *m* Caroline Chester Sidell, 1848-1903; son of Wm. Wright, 1797-1865, *m* Elizbth. G. Coddington ; son of William, *d* in London 1827, *m* Augusta, da. of Sir George Hastings ; son of William, *d* 1780, *m* Margaret, da. of Sir Alexander Bathurst, Bt. ; son of Laurence, 1693-1743, *m* Ann, da. of Sir Walter Clarges, Bt. ; son of Sir Robert, Bt., 1650-1717, created Viscount Tamworth and Earl Ferrers 1711, *m* Elizth. Washington ; son of Sir Robert, Bt., 1629-56, Lord of Eatington, *m* Kath. da. of Sir Humph. Ockeover ; son of Sir Henry, Bt., 1588-1632, Ld. of Eatington, *m* Lady Dorothy, da. of Sir Robt. Devereux, E. of Sussex ; son of Sir George, Bt., 1559-1622, Ld. of Eatington, *m* Frances, da. of Henry, Lord Berkeley ; son of John, 1535-70, of Staunton Harolde, Esq., *m* Jane da. of Thomas, Lord Lovett ; son of Francis, 1515-70, of Staunton Harolde, Esq., *m* Dorothy da. of Sir John Gifford ; son of Sir Ralph, Knt., 1487-1516, *m* (4th wife) Jane, da. of Sir Robert Sheffield ; son of John, *d* 1486, Ld. of Eatington, *m* Elianor da. of Hugh, Lord Willoughby ; son of Ralph, *d* 1466, Ld. of E., *m* Margaret da. of Thomas Staunton of Staunton Harolde, Esq. ; son of Sir Ralph, Knt., of Eatington, *m* Jane (Joyce) da. of Thomas Bassett, Esq., of Brailesford ; son of Sir Hugh, Ld. of E., Chief Warden of Hingham Ferrers, Constable of Donnington Castle 1399, *m* Beatrice da. of Sir Peter Broase ; son of Sir Thomas, Knt., *d* 1363, *m* Isabell da. of Ralph Bassett : son of Sir Ralph, Knt., Ld. of E., *d* 1326, gov. of Horston Castle, *m* Margaret da. of Walter de Waldershef ; son of Sir James de Eatington, living 1278, adopted the name Shirley being Lord of Sirlai, co. Derby, *m* Agnes de Waunton : son of Sir Sewallis de Eatington, Knt., living 1251, *m* Isabell da. of Robert Meysnl ; son of Henry, Lord Eatington, 1205 ; son of Sewallis de Scyrle, Ld. of Eatington, living 1192, *m* Matilda Ridel ; son of Fulcher, held land in Shirley, *d* 1169 ; son of Susunalo, Ld. of E., living 1079-86, the first recorded owner of Nether Eatenden, the original seat of the "ancient family of Shirley."—On the maternal line Mr. R. G. S. is descended from Hester, *b* in Canterbury, Eng., da. of Pierre du Bois of Artois, France, who *m* 1652 Glaude De La Maistre).

Born in N.Y. City Aug. 7, 1873 ; late Naval Cadet U.S. Navy, Class of 1895 ; Veteran 4th Division 1st N.B.N.Y. ; 1st Lieut. Company H, 9th Regiment N.G.N.Y.

Arms—Paly of six or and azure : a canton ermine.

Crest—A Saracen's head couped ppr. wreathed about the temples or and azure.

Motto—Honor virtutis præmium.

Residence—716 Madison Avenue, New York City.

Clubs—North Lake Fish and Game of Montreal, Delta Chi of New York.

Societies—St. George's of N.Y. Veteran Corps of Artill., N.Y. Hist., New Eng., War of 1812, St. Nicholas, Sons of the Revol., Sons of the Amer Revol., Colonial Wars, Huguenot, Met. Mus. of Art, Amer. Mus. of Nat. Hist., Veteran Vol. Firemen, Co. of Richmond, N.Y. Athletic, Delta Chi.

GALLAHER, WILLIAM BOWEN,
of Waynesboro', Va. (Son of Hugh Laffert
Gallaher, 1812-86, of Shepardstown, W. Va.,
m April 19, 1837, Elizabeth Catherine, da. of
Wm. Bowen, of Jefferson Co., Va.; son of Hugh
Gallaher, who settled at Lebanon, Penna., 1798,
m Sarah, da. of Hugh Lafferty, of Donegal, Ireland ;
son of John O'Gallagher, of Clagneely, Donegal,
Ireland).

Born at Shepherdstown, W. Va., Feb., 10, 1840;
Educ. at Georgetown and Virginia Mil. Inst. ;
Lieut. Co. E. 1st Virginia Cavalry under
General Joseph E. Johnston, C.S.A.; *m* Aug. 8,
1864, Amelia Frances, da. of Maj. Thos.
Briscoe, of Jefferson Co., Virginia.

Issue.
i. THOMAS BRISCOE, *b* Nov. 27, 1865.
ii. CHARLES JAMES, *b* Aug. 17, 1868.
iii. WM. BOWEN, *b* Sept. 22, 1880.
i. JULIET HITE.   ii. ELEANOR MAGRUDER.   iii. FRANCES AMELIA.

Arms—Argent, a lion ramp. sable, treading on a serpent in fesse proper, between
eight trefoils slipped vert.

Crest—A crescent gules, out of the horns a serpent erect proper.

Residence—" Springdale," near Waynesboro', Augusta Co., Virginia.

JACKSON, JAMES HATHAWAY, M.D.,
of Dansville, N.Y. (Second son of James Caleb
Jackson, 1811-95, *m* Lucretia E., 1810-90, da. of
Elias Brewster [a descendant of Elder William
Brewster, of the "Mayflower"]; son of James,
b 1778; son of Col. Giles, *b* 1732; son of John,
b 1703; son of Lieut. John Jackson, 1645-95, of
Cambridge, Mass., from Stepney, London, nephew
of Richard Jackson, whose lands at Cambridge,
Mass., he inherited).

Born at Peterboro', N.Y., June 11, 1841; Grad.
from Bellevue Hospital Med. Coll. M.D. 1876;
Proprietor of the Jackson Health Resort;
m Sept. 13, 1864, Kate, da. of Hon. Emerson
and Hannah (Arnold) Johnson, Mem. of Mass.
Senate, 1865, of Sturbridge, Mass.

Issue.
i. JAMES ARTHUR, M.D., *b* May 4, 1868, *m* Ethelwyn McMullen.

Arms—(For Brewster) Azure, a chevron ermine between three estoils argent.
Crest—A leopard's head erased sable.   *Motto*—Verité soyez ma garde.

Residence—Jackson Health Resort, Dansville, N.Y.
Societies—Sons of the Amer. Revolution, Mayflower Descendants, Colonial Wars.

L EONARD, CLARENCE ETTIENNE,
of Caryl-Yonkers N.Y.(Son of Ephraim Wilkes
Leonard, 1823-82, of Taunton, Mass. ; *m* Melancie
D. Godfrey, of Taunton, Mass. ; son of James,
1797-1875 ; son of Ephraim, 1764-1819 ; son of
Philip, 1718-85 ; son of Joseph, 1692-1775 ; son of
Benjamin, *b* 1643 ; son of James Leonard, *d* 1691,
of Providence, R.I., 1645, built the first Iron
Works in Plymouth Colony.—Descended from
Edward III., through the Dacre family in two
lines).

Born at New Bedford, Mass., Feb. 10, 1854 ;
   m Oct. 6, 1875, Lizzie Standish, da. of Joseph
   and Ann M. (Hathaway) Wright, of Taunton.

Issue.
i. CLARENCE A., 1877.
ii. RALPH M., *b* June 28, 1881.
iii. CLARENCE T., *b* Sept. 8, 1887.
i. NINA E., 1878-85.
ii. PEARL M., *b* Jan. 25, 1880.
iii. FAYE A., *b* Feb. 15, 1883.
iv. LOLA I., 1885-1902.

Arms—Or, on a fesse azure three fleurs-de-lis argent.
Crest—Out of a ducal coronet or, a tiger's head argent.
Motto—Memor et fidelis.

Residence—Caryl-Yonkers, New York.
Societies—Sons of the Revol., Mayflower Descendants, Founders and Patriots of
   Am., Sons of the Am. Revol., Old Colony Hist., New Eng., Long Island
   Hist., N.Y. Genealogical, etc.

H OLMES, EDWIN BRADFORD,
of Brookline, Mass. (Son of Bradford Reed
Holmes, *b* 1825, *m* 1848, Mary Elizabeth, da. of
Noah Perry Ford, of North Abington, Mass. ; son
of Jonathan, *b* 1794 ; son of Jonathan, *b* 1755 ; son
of Job, *b* 1728 ; son of Eleazer, *b* 1688 ; son of
Nathaniel, *b* 1643 ; son of John, who settled in
Plymouth, Mass. ; son of Thomas Holmes, of
Colchester, Essex, Eng., Will proved 1637).

Born at N. Abington, Mass., Jan. 3, 1853 ; Most Worshipful G. M. of
   A. F. and A. M. of the Commonwealth of Mass., 1895-96, *m* Jan. 12,
   1880, Sarah Frances, da. of Isaac Reed Pratt, of N. Abington, Mass.

Issue.
i. EDWIN PRATT, *b* Feb. 9, 1886.
ii. FRANCIS BRADFORD, *b* Dec. 27, 1887.
i. MARY FRANCES.

Arms—Barry of six or and gules ; on a canton of the second a chaplet of the first.

Residences—33 Winthrop Road, Brookline ; and Nantasket Beach, Hull, Mass.
Club—Exchange, of Boston.

McCLURE, ALEXANDER KELLY,

of Philadelphia, Pa. (Second son of Alexander McClure, of Centre, Pa., *d* 1855, *m* Isabella, *d* 1867, da. of William Anderson, of Andersonsburg, Perry County, Pa., who *m* Miss Johnson, of Andersonsburg.—Descended from John McClure, of Carlisle, Pennsylvania, *b* N. of Ireland, *d* in Mifflin, Penna., *circa* 1795, a cadet of the McClures of Balmagie, Scotland, a branch of which family settled in County Down after the battle of the Boyne).

Born at Centre, Penna., Jan. 9, 1828 ; LL.D., Washington and Lee Univ., 1883 ; State Supt. of Printing, 1855 ; State Representative, 1858-9,65 ; State Senator from Franklin, 1860-2, from Philadelphia, 1872-4 ; Asst. Adj. Gen. U.S. 1862-3 ; Prothonotary of Supreme Court, 1903 ; *m* Feb. 10, 1852, Matilda S. Grey, *d* 1877 ; *m* (2ndly) 1879, Cora M. Gratz.

Issue.

i. WILLIAM A., *b* Dec. 24, 1852.

Arms—Argent, on a chevron engr. azure, betw. two roses in chief and a sword in base point down of the second, a mullet or.
Crest—A tower domed ppr. from the top a flag arg. thereon a rose crowned or.
Motto—Spectemur agendo.

Residences—1828 Spruce St., Philadelphia ; Wallingford, Pa.
Clubs—Philadelphia, Union League, Clover, Penna., Lawyers, Pen and Pencil.

DOTY, PAUL AARON LANGEVIN,

of St. Paul, Minnesota (Only son of Wm. Henry Harrison Doty, 1839-98, of Dover, N.J., *m* 1861, Anna Bergevin, da. of Paul Bergevin de Langevin, of Quebec, and Margaret Bruyere, of Montreal.—Descended from Edward Doty, *b* in London, Eng., 1599, *d* Aug. 23, 1655, Pilgrim passenger of the "Mayflower," Signer of the "Compact," took part in "first encounter," Dec. 8, 1620).

Born at Hoboken, N.J., May 30, 1869 ; Dep. Gov.-Gen. Soc. of Mayflower Descendants ; Graduated at Stevens Inst. of Technology, 1888, M.E. ; *m* Feb. 10, 1892, Theodosia, da. of Israel Newton and Jeanette M. W. (Coney) Stiles, Brig.-Gen. U.S.V., 1861-65, of Chicago.

Arms—Argent, two bars between as many mullets sable pierced or.
Crest—A mullet sable.   *Motto*—Palma non sine pulvere.

Residence—286 Laurel Ave., St. Paul, Minn.
Clubs—Minnesota, Town and Country.
Societies—Amer. Soc. Mech. Engrs., Amer. Assn. Adv. Science, American Gas Institute, Mayflower Descendants, Colonial Wars.

HURRY, EDMUND ABDY,
of N. Y. City (Son of Edmd. Hurry, 1807-75, *m* Elizabeth, 1818-82, da. of James Flanagan, Counsellor-at-law, J.P. ; son of Saml. Hurry, 1778-1820, agent between U.S. and Eng. Shipowners in the adjusting Claims, War of 1812, third son of John Hurry, of Liverpool.—Descd. from the Hurrys of Gt. Yarmouth, Eng., who descended from the Cliftons, Ives, Coopers, Bracy, Winn, Watts, of Norfolk).

Born at N.Y. City, Aug. 8, 1839; Grad. Columbia Coll. 1860; Columbia Law Sch. 1862, M.A., LL.B.. U.S.N., 1863-64 ; *m* Nov. 17, 1868, Emily Ashton, da. of Wm. Rhinelander Renwick, of N.Y. and Eliza S., da. of Wm. Bedlow Crosby, of N.Y. City.

Issue.

i. RENWICK CLIFTON, *b* Sept. 7, 1874, *m* 1904, Lucy Washington Morss.
ii. RUTGERS IVES, *b* Nov. 17, 1883.

i. EDITH RENWICK.   ii. BESSIE CROSBY.
iii. HELEN SCHUYLER, *m* 1893, Wm. Vandervoort Draper.
iv. MARY CROSBY, *m* 1899, Walton C. Peckham.
v. EMILY ASHTON, *m* 1904, Louis Gross Smith.

Arms—Argent, in chief a lion ramp. gules, in base two mullets voided azure.
Crest—A harpy proper.   *Mottoes*—1, Sans tache ; 2, Nec arrogo, nec dubito.

Residences—" Clifton." Barclay Hts., Saugerties-on-H.; 122 E. 39th St., N.Y. City.
Clubs—University, Union League, Church, Saugerties.
Societies—New York Genealogical and Biographical, St. Nicholas, American Geographical, St. George's, Alumni of Columbia Univ. N.Y.

BROCKETT, MRS. HATTIE FOSTER (*née* NOURSE).
of Alexandria, Virginia (Daughter of Rev. James H. and Sarah F. (Blackman) Nourse, of Washington, D.C. ; son of James, 1805-54, of Washington, D.C., *m* Sarah North Harvey ; son of Michael, 1778-1860, *m* Mary Rittenhouse ; son of James, 1731-84, who settled at Charleston, West Virginia ; son of John and Eliza (Gregory) Nourse, of Hereford, England).

Born at Charleston, West Virginia, *m* Albert Doyle Brockett, of Alexandria, Virginia, son of Edgar Longden Brockett and Georgiana Katherine Seymour.

Arms—(for Nourse) Gules, a fesse between two chevrons argent.
Crest—An arm embowed, vested azure, cuffed argent, grasping in the hand proper a snake of the last, environed round the arm.
Motto—By courage, not by cunning.

Residence—" Aspen Grove," 318 Washington Street, North Alexandria, Virginia.

SHAFFER, NEWTON MELMAN, M.D.,
   of N.Y. City (Son of Rev. James Newton
Shaffer, 1811-1901, *m* Jane E. Hale, 1814-66; son
of William 1773-1823; son of William Shaffer, who
came from Holland to New York in 1760, *d* 1778).

Born at Kinderhook, N.Y., Feb. 14, 1846; Asst.
   Res. Surg. Hosp. for Ruptured and Crippled,
   1867-68 ; Surg.-in-Chief N.Y. Orthopædic
   Disp. and Hosp. 1876-98; Orthopædic Surg.
   St. Luke's Hosp. 1873-88; Prof. Orthop. Surg.
   N.Y. Univ. 1882-86, and 1896-98; now Con-
   sulting Orthopædic Surg. St. Luke's and
   Presbyterian Hosp.; Prof. of Orthopædic Surg.
   Cornell Univ. Med. Coll.; Surg.-in-Chief N.Y.
   State Hosp. for Crippled and Deformed
   Children; Grad. N.Y. Univ. Med. Dept. M.D., 1867; *m* Oct. 15, 1873,
   Margaret H. da. of Wm. Perkins, Mem. of Maine State Legislature,
   and Mayor of Gardiner, Me.

Issue.

i. NEWTON MELMAN, Jr., *b* May 2, 1878.

Arms (For Hale) Gules, three broad arrows or, feathered and barbed argent.
Crest—A dexter arm embowed in armour ppr. garnished or, bound with a ribbon
   gules, holding an arrow.

Residences—28 E. 38th Street, N.Y. City; Beacon Hill Cottage, Ridgefield, Conn.
Clubs—Century, University, Ridgefield Country, Ardsley.
Societies—Academy of Medicine, Congress of Amer. Physicians and Surgeons,
   Amer. Orthopædic Assn., etc.

TYLER, EDWARD ROYALL,
   of Boston, Mass. (Son of John Tyler, 1813-81,
of Boston, *m* Martha Willis Alger; son of John,
1788-1853, *m* Elizth. Thompson; son of John Steel,
1754-1813, *m* Sarah Whitwell; son of Royall, 1724-
71, Mem. of King's Council, *m* Mary Steel; son of
William, 1688-1754, *m* (1) Sarah Royall, *m* (2) Jane
Pepperell; son of Thomas Tyler, *d* 1703, from
Budleigh, Devonshire, to Boston, Mass., 1680,
m Miriam, 1663-1730, da. of Pilgrim Simpkins.

Born at Boston, Sept. 26, 1854; *m* Jan. 20, 1881,
   Jennie Louise, *b* Mar. 14, 1852, *d* May 4, 1892,
   da. of Barney and Eliza A. (Glynn) Cory.

Issue.

i. EDITH ROYALL, *b* at Boston, March 4, 1882, *m* Jan. 31, 1903, Herbert
   Thorn King, of N.Y. City.

Arms—(Granted 21st November, 1771, to the descendants of Andrew and William Tyler, of
   Boston, New Eng.)—Sable, on a fesse erminois, between three cats passant
   guardant ermine, a cross moline enclosed by two crescents gules.
Crest—A demi-cat rampant guardant ermine.   *Motto*—Nec aspera terrent.

Residences—Cimiez, Nice, France, and Boston, Mass.   *Club*—Algonquin.
Societies—Mayflower Desedts., Colonial Wars, The Cincinnati, Sons of the Am.
   Revol., N.E. Hist. and Geneal., Bostonian, Harvard Musical Assn.,
   St. Bernard Commandery, Knights Templar.

HOWE, HERBERT MARSHALL, M.D.,
of Philadelphia (Son of Rt. Rev. Mark
Anthony De Wolf Howe, D.D., 1808-95, of
Reading, Pa., by his 2nd wife Elizabeth Smith,
1822-55, da. of Rev. Herbert and Ann (Smith)
Marshall, of Middleburgh, Va.; son of John, 1783-
1864, of Killingly, Ct.; son of Capt. Perley,
1742-93; son of Rev. Perley, 1710-53, of Killingly,
Ct.; son of Capt. Sampson, 1683-1736; son of
Abraham, 1649-1718, of Ipswich; son of James,
1607-1702, of Roxbury, Mass.; son of Robert
Howe, of Broad Oak, Essex, Eng., *b circa* 1580).

Born at Roxbury, Mass., July 16, 1844; Grad.
Penna. Univ., 1865; Prest. Allentown Rolling
Mills Co., Ogden Mine R.R. Co., Cranbury
Furnace Co., etc.; *m* Nov. 28, 1871, Mary
Wilson Fell.

Issue.

i. JOHN FELL, *b* December 3, 1875, *d* December 31, 1895.
i. MARY HERBERT.   ii. EDITH.   iii. GRACE.
iv. RHODA, *m* April 19, 1902, William Gilman Low, Jr., of Brooklyn, N.Y.
v. ELIZABETH AMANDA.

Arms—Argent, a chevron between three wolves' heads couped sable.
Crest—Out of a ducal coronet or a unicorn's head gules.

Residences—1622 Locust St., Phila., Pa.; Ferrycliffe Farm, Bristol, R.I.
Clubs—Union League, Rittenhouse, Country, of Phila.; N.Y. Yacht, Squantum.
Societies—Colonial Wars, Sons of the Revolution.

DODGE, JOHN H. PRENTISS, LL.B. (*deceased*),
of Manchester-by-the-Sea, Mass. (Only son
of John Crowninshield Dodge, 1809-89, First Sec.
of the Board of Trade, and Alderman of Chicago
in 1852, *m* Catharine Lucretia, 1817-1901, da. of
Col. John Holmes Prentiss, of Cooperstown, N.Y.;
son of John, 1784-1820; son of Joshua, 1752-1814;
son of George, 1726-1808, of Beverly; son of Joshua,
1694-1771; son of Joshua, 1669-95; son of William,
1640-1720; son of William Dodge, who came from
England, 1629, on the " Lyon's Whelp," and
settled at Beverly, Mass.).

Born at Chicago, Ill., Oct. 13, 1850, *d* Feb. 19, 1904;
Grad. Columbia Coll. Law School, Columbia
Univ., N.Y. City, LL.B., 1870; Counsellor-
at-Law; Mem. of the N.Y. Bar and Boston
Bar, Counsellor of Supreme Court, U.S.A.

Arms—Barry of six or, and sable, on a pale gules a woman's breast gouttant.
Crest—A demi-lion maryn sable, langued and armed gules. about his neck a
gemel gold.   *Motto*—Veritas.
(In 1306 King Edward I. gave to Pierre Dodge the Coat of Arms. In 1526 King Henry VIII.
gave the Crest to John Dodge, of Wrotham, Kent.)

Residence—(Family), Manchester-by-the-Sea, Essex Co., Mass.

WILLOUGHBY, HUGH DE LAUSSAT, Lieut., U.S.N.R., of Newport R.I. (Son of Samuel Aug. and Estelle (de Laussat) Willoughby of Brooklyn, N.Y.; son of Augustus, *b* at Cornwallis, Nova Scotia; son of Samuel Willoughby who went to Cornwallis from Virginia; probably desc'd from Thomas Willoughby, who settled in Virginia 1626; son of Thomas of Wateringham, Kent; son of Thomas Willoughby, Dean of Rochester, 1581).

Born at Solitude, Del. Co., N.Y.; Grad. at Pa. Univ.; Lt. Comdg. the R.I. Naval Reserve, U.S.N.R; *m* 1878 Augusta de Peyster, da. of James B. and Jane (McClelland) Harrison of Derbyshire, Eng.

Issue.
i. Hugh de Laussat, Jr., *b* May 19, 1895.
i. Estelle de Laussat.   ii. Kate.

Arms—Or, a fretty azure.
Crest—The bust of a man, couped at the shoulders, and affrontée proper.
Motto—Vérité sans peur.
Residence—"The Chalet," Newport, R.I.
Clubs—N.Y. Yacht, St. Augustine Yacht, Biscayne Bay Yacht, Newport Golf, St. Augustine Golf.
Societies—Alumni University of Penna, Academy of Nat. Science.

LOCKWOOD, HANFORD NICHOLS, of Asheville (Son of Thomas W. Lockwood, 1811-95, of Troy, N.Y., *m* Mary Scott, 1817-85, da. of Fred. S. and Mary Bruen (Goble) Thomas, of Newark, N.J.; son of Handford N., *m* Rachel Wildman; son of Isaac, 1761-1838, *m* Aner Nichols; son of Isaac, *m* Ruth Whitney; son of Joseph, *m* Mary Wood; son of Ephraim Lockwood and Mercy St. John, of Watertown, Mass., 1630, in descent from Rev. Richard Lockwood, Rector of Dingley, Co. Northampton, 1530).

Born at Troy N.Y. Oct. 2, 1859; Grad. Union Univ. LL.B. 1883, *m* April 30, 1889, Isabel Dwight, da. of Daniel Wesley and Marian (Ward) Ingersoll, of St. Paul, Minn.

Issue.
i. Hanford Nichols, Jr., *b* Nov. 9, 1895.
i. Isabel Wildman.   ii. Mary Thomas.   iii. Marian Dwight.

Arms—Argent, a fesse between three martlets sable.
Crest—On the stump of an oak tree erased proper a martlet sable.
Motto—Tutus in undis.

Residences—Asheville, N.C.; La Jolla, California.
Societies—Founders and Patriots, Sons of the American Revolution.

S UTTON, Rev. JOSEPH FORD, D.D.,*
of N.Y. City (Son of Michael Rorick Sutton 1797-1881, of Hardyston, N.J., m 1822 Elizabeth Forrester: son of Jacob 1773-1852,
m Hannah Rorick; son of Capt. Jonathan 1735-1818 of Revolutionary
Army, m Rachel Collier; son of Zebulon of Bernard Township N.J.,
b 1707; son of Daniel of Piscataway N.J., b 1681, m (1) 1704 Patience
Martin, m (2) 1724 Lydia Collier; son of William Sutton, m 1666 at
Eastham Mass. Damaris, da. of Richard and Alice Bishop, d at Piscataway 1715).

Born at Hardyston N.J. July 15, 1827; Grad. Rutgers Coll. 1852,
A.M. 1855; Grad. B.D. 1857, D.D. Marysville Coll. 1881; Chaplain
102nd Regt. N.Y. Vols. 1862, m (1) April 10, 1859, Eliza Storrs,
da. of Horace Holden, who served on Staff of Gen. Colfax in War of
1812; son of Lieut. Levi Holden of Gen. Washington's Body
Guard, m (2) April 10, 1866, Kate Judson Holden, m (3) Mrs. Joanna
Bates Sutton.

Issue.

i. HORACE HOLDEN, b 1867, d 1874.
ii. JOSEPH HOLDEN, b 1869, d 1902, A.B. 1890, A.M. and LL.B. 1903
Princeton Univ.
iii. DANIEL JUDSON, b 1872, d 1874.
iv. EDWARD FORRESTER HOLDEN, b Feb. 15, 1874, A.B. Princeton 1895,
M.D. Columbia Univ. 1899.
v. FREDERICK JUDSON HOLDEN, b June 3, 1876, A.B. Princeton 1898.

Residence—Orange, New Jersey.
Clubs—The Presbyterian Union, Rutgers Coll., N.Y. Alumni, Zeta Psi.
Societies—American Geographical, Comrade of the Loyal Legion of the U.S.
* (By mistake this record was published in a former Edition in incorrect form.)

B REWSTER, SAMUEL DWIGHT,
of New York City (Son of Sydney Lyman
Brewster, of Bowling Green, Ohio, m Oct. 10,
1850, Mrs. Catherine Smith (widow).—Descended
from William Brewster, 1566-1654, Elder of
Plymouth Colony, 1630, who drafted the "Mayflower" Compact; Member and Chaplain of the
1st Military Company organised at Plymouth under
Captain Myles Standish. He served against the
Indians).

Born at Bowling Green, Ohio, Aug. 6, 1851,
m April 19, 1893, Isabel Erskine, da. of Robert
Hall Parks, and Isabel Beecher, his wife, da.
of Colonel John Erskine.

Issue.

i. SYDNEY ERSKINE.   ii. WARREN DWIGHT.

Arms—Sable, a chevron ermine between three estoiles argent.
Crest—A bear's head erased sable.   *Motto*—Verité soyez ma garde.

Residence—45 West 49th Street, New York City.
Clubs—Union League, Merchants, N. Y. Yacht, N. Y. Athletic, Nassau Country.
Societies—Mayflower Descendants, Huguenot, Colonial Wars, New Eng., Sons of
the Revolution, New York Historical.

WILSON, HAROLD,
of Clermont (Son of Wm. Henry Wilson,
1791-1884, M.D., A.B., Grad. Union Coll. Schenectady, 1810, Coll. of Phys. and Surgs. N.Y., 1812,
Surg. U.S. Army, War of 1812, *m* 1829 Anne, da.
of Thomas and Alice (Cunliffe) Hulme, of Lancashire, England ; son of William Wilson, 1756-1828,
M.D., Glasgow Univ., from Berwick, Eng.,
m Mary Howey, of Northumberland, Eng., settled
at Clermont, N.Y., 1784).

Born at Clermont, N.Y., Jan. 7, 1836, *m* June 25,
    1863, Mary Elizabeth Livingston, da. of Judge
    John Sanders, of Schenectady, N.Y., and
    Jane, da. of Walter Tryon and Elizabeth
    (McKinstry) Livingston of Clermont.

Issue.
i. WILLIAM HENRY, *b* Dec. 26, 1875.   ii. HAROLD, *b* Nov. 6, 1881.
i. ANNE HULME.   ii. JANE LIVINGSTON.
iii. SARAH HULME, *m* Sept. 7, 1905, Wm. Ten Broeck, son of Barent A.
    Mynderse and Albertina S. Ten Broeck.

Arms—Sable, a wolf salient or, ducally gorged and chained gules, in chief a
    mullet of the second between two mullets argent.
Crest—A wolf's head erased erminois gorged with a collar sable charged with
    three mullets argent,
Motto—Ego de meo sensu judico.

Residence—Clermont, Columbia Co., N.Y.   *Society*—War of 1812.

NOYES, JAMES ATKINS,
of Cambridge (2nd son of James S. Noyes
1816-93, *m* Mary B., da. of Robert Ball and Sarah
(Barker) Edes of Charlestown, Mass.—Descended
from Nicholas Noyes, of Newbury, Mass., 1634).

Born at Brooklyn, N.Y., Oct. 2, 1857; Ph. B.
    School of Mines, Columbia Univ., 1878; A. B.
    Harvard Univ. 1883; Editor Harvard Quin-
    quennial Catalogue ; Mem. Harvard Univ.
    Council ; *m* Feb. 4, 1890, Constance, *d* Jan. 1,
    1895, only child of Justin Winsor, LL.D.,
    Librarian of Harvard Univ.

Issue.
i. PENELOPE BARKER.

Arms—Azure, three crosses botony in bend argent.
Crest—On a chapeau azure, turned up ermine, a dove argent, in the beak an
    olive branch vert.

Residence—71 Sparks Street, Cambridge, Mass.
Clubs—University, Harvard of N.Y.; Union of Boston ; Oakley Country of
    Watertown ; Hasty Pudding, Institute of 1770, D. K. E. of Harvard Univ.;
    Phi Beta Kappa, Harvard.
Societies—Colonial Wars, Sons of Revol., Mayflower Descdts., Colonial of Mass.,
    Colonial Dames of America.

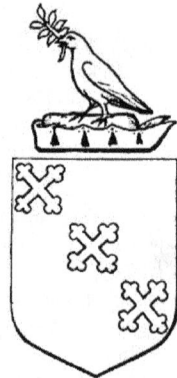

HUME, ROBERT DENISTON,
of San Francisco, Cal. (Son of Capt. William
Hume 1794-1868, of Augusta, Me., *m* (1) Harriet
Hunter, *m* (2) Elizabeth F., 1809-89, da. of
Jeremiah Webber, of Vassalboro, Me.; son of John
1770-1830, *m* Nancy Webb; son of John Hume,
m Helinor Manson, of Aberdeen, Scotland, served in
the Revol. War; son of George Hume, who settled at
Culpepper, Va., 1721, second son of Sir George
Hume of Wedderburn, who was engaged in Rebellion of 1715).

Born at Augusta, Me., Oct, 31, 1845; Mem. House
of Representatives for Oregon, 1900, Mem.
elect of same 1902; *m* (1) Cecilia Ann Bryont;
m (2) 1877, Mary Ann, da. of George Duncan, Provisional Treasurer
under Sir Julius Vogel, of N.Z., and Elspeh Wilson, of Aberdeen,
Scotland.

Issue.
(*By 1st m.*)

i. ROBERT DENISTON, *d s.p.*   ii. AMELIA, *d* in infancy.

Arms—Vert, a lion rampant argent.   *Crest*—A lion's head erased or.

Residences—2421 Pierce Street, San Francisco, Cal.; Wedderburn, Oregon.
Societies—Sons of the American Revolution, Masonic.

LINNARD, GEORGE BROWN,
of Philadelphia (Son of Henry Mifflin Linnard,
1848-84, of Phila., *m* Harriet Elizabeth Brown; son
of Eugene, *m* Maria Amelia Gibbs. [*See* Gibbs
family, of Warwickshire, beginning from Thomas
Gybbys, *temp.* Richard II. to Sir Henry Gibbs,
living 1612, whose son Robert came to Boston
1658]; son of Thomas Mifflin, *m* Adelaide Tauzin;
son of Colonel William Linnard, 1749-1835, Officer
in Artillery during Revolution, served as Colonel
in War 1812).

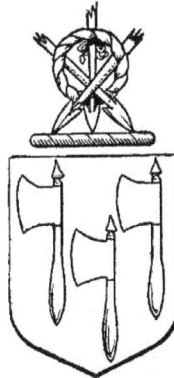

Born at Philadelphia July 27, 1873; Grad. Prince-
ton Univ. A.B., Univ. of Penna. LL.B., Mem.
Phila. Bar, and of the firm Graham & Co.,
Bankers; *m* Oct. 16, 1901, Mary Wallace
Audenried of Phila.

Issue.
i. ANNA LOUISE.

Arms—(Gibbs) Sable, three battleaxes in pale argent.
Crest—Three broken tilting spears or, two in saltire and one in pale, enfiled with
a wreath argent and sable.

Residences—7721 St. Martin's Lane, Philadelphia; Castine, Me.
Clubs—University, Union League, Philadelphia Cricket.
Society—Sons of the Revolution.

POWEL, ROBERT JOHNSTON HARE-
of New York (Son of Samuel Powel, 1818-85,
m Mary, da. of Robert, gr.-da. of Dr. Alex. Johnston,
whose wife, Elizabeth, was da. of Capt. John
Gilbert, R.N., killed 1756; son of Col. John Hare
Powel, 1786-1856, his maternal aunt, Mrs. Elizth.
(Willing) Powel, wife of Sam'l. Powel, "Patriot
Mayor" of Phila., 1775 and 1789, adopted him,
transposing his name from John Powel Hare, he
succeeded to entailed estate including Powelton in
Phila.; Secy. of Legation at Court of St. James,
1808-11; Insp. General U.S. Army, 1814-15;
Penna. Senator, 1827-30; sold Powelton in 1853,
built and resided in the present Hist. Soc. building,
Phila., *m* Julia, da. of Col. Andrew de Veaux, who
m Anna M., da. of Philip, son of Philip ver Planck of Manor of Courtlandt,
N.Y.; son of Robert Hare, *b* at Woolwich, Kent, Eng., 1752, settled at
Phila., 1773, a framer of the first Constitution, and Speaker of the first
Senate of Penna., *m* Margaret, da. of Chas. Willing, who *m* Anne, da. of
Joseph, son of Edward Shippen, 1639-1712, the first Mayor of Phila.
son of Richard and Martha (Harford) Hare, Esquire, 1700-76, of Lime-
house, London).

Born at Newport, R,I., May 4, 1855; Grad. Harvard Univ. B.A. 1878;
Mem. of Phila. Bar, 1882, and N.Y. 1886; Trustee of Estates;
Director and Counsel for Manhattan Eye, Ear and Throat Hospital,
N.Y., since 1898; *m* June 1, 1887, Elisabeth Butler, da. of John
Player Crosby, who *m* Margaret Barker, da. of Benj. Franklin Butler,
of N.Y.; Atty. Gen. for U.S. 1833-38, Acting Secy. of War, 1837.

Issue.

i. JOHN HARE- *b* and *d* July, 1893.

ii. ROBERT JOHNSTON HARE- *b* Nov. 23, 1895.

i. ELISABETH HARE- *b* Nov. 11, 1889.

Arms—Per fesse, argent and or, a lion rampant gules.

Crest—On a cloud argent an estoile of eight points each point divided gules and
argent.

Motto—Proprium decus et patrum.

Additional Bearings—(Hare) Gu. two bars and a chief indented or; *Crest*, a demi-lion ramp.
arg. holding a cross crosslet fitchée gules; *Motto*, Non Videri sed esse. (Johnston)
Arg. a saltire sa. on a chief gu. three cushions or; *Crest*, a spur erect or, winged arg.;
Motto, Nunquam non paratus. (Gilbert) Arg., on a chev. az. three roses seeded and
leaved ar.; in base an eagle displ., a chief erm.; *Crest*, a squirrel sejant gu.; *Motto*,
Mallem mori quam mutare)

———

Residences—Dobbs Ferry, N.Y.; Newport, R.I.

Clubs—Harvard D.K.E. (Apha) and Rifle Club, formerly of the Rittenhouse,
Germantown Cricket and Phila. Barge, of Phila.; Ardsley, N.Y.

Societies—New York Bar Assn., Pennsylvania Hist. Society of Phila.

SCHIEFFELIN, GEORGE RICHARD,
of N.Y. (Son of Richard L. Schieffelin,
1801-89, m Margaret H. McKay, b Aug. 2, 1813;
son of Jacob, 1757-1835; son of Jacob, 1734-69;
son of Jacob, d 1750, from Weilheim-an-der-Teck,
in Wurtemberg, to Penna, 1735; son of John
George Schieffelin, 1666-1725).

Born in N.Y. July 27, 1836; Counsellor at Law :
Columbia Graduate 1855; m May 19, 1866,
Julia M., da. of the Hon. Isaac C. Delaplaine,
of N.Y.

Issue.
i. GEORGE R. D., b Feb. 20, 1884, m April 5, 1904,
Louisa Scribner, of N.Y.
i. JULIA F., m Dec. 4, 1888, Joseph B. Ismay, of Liverpool, Eng.
ii. MARGARET H., m Dec. 10, 1890, Henry G. Trevor, of N.Y.
iii. MATILDA CONSTANCE, m Jan. 13, 1900, Charles Bower Ismay, of
Yorkshire, Eng.   iv. SARAH DOROTHY.

Arms—Tiercé per fesse sable and or, on three piles, two conjoined with one betw..
transposed invected counterchanged, as many cross crosslets sable.
Crest—A holy lamb passant bearing cross staff and pennon proper.
Motto—Per fidem et constantiam.

_____

Residences—22 W. 52nd Street, N.Y. City ; " Plas-ar-Llyn," Southampton, L.I.
Clubs—Union, Century, Riding, Down Town (N.Y. City), Shinnecock Golf,
Meadow of Southampton, L.I.
Societies—Colonial Wars, St. Nicholas, New York Historical, New York Geo-
graphical, War of 1812, Colonial Order.

_____

WHISTLER, GARLAND NELSON, LIEUT.-COL. U.S. ARMY,
of Fort Totten, N.Y. (Son of Brevet-
Brigadier-General Joseph Nelson Garland Whistler,
U.S.A., grandson of Col.Wm. Whistler and gt.-grand-
son of Major John Whistler, a soldier in the
British Army which surrendered at Saratoga
under Burgoyne; after the Revolutionary War he
remained in America and served, with great
distinction, in the U.S. Army, he m Anna, da. of
Sir Edward Bishop).

Born at Schenectady, N.Y., August 10, 1847 :
Lieut.-Col. Artillery Corps U.S. Army ; m Ellen
Wharton, da. of Dr. Stirling B. Everitt, of
Wilmington, N.C.

Arms—Gules, a bend of five mascles betwe en two lions
passant argent.
Crest—A harp or, stringed sable.
Motto—Honor et fidelitas.

_____

Residence—Fort Totten, N.Y.
Clubs—Army and Navy (N.Y. City), Artillery (Fort Munroe, Va.).
Societies—Loyal Legion, Spanish-American War, War of 1812, Colonial Wars.

CALVERT, CHARLES BALTIMORE (*deceased*), of College Park, Md. (Son of Charles Benedict Calvert, 1808-64, of Riversdale, Prince George's Co., Md.; Mem. of the State Legislature, 1839, of Congress, 1862; 1st Pres. of Md. State Agr'l. Society, and Mem. of U.S. Agr'l. Society, *m* 1839, Charlotte Augusta, 1816-76, da. of William Norris, of Baltimore, by Sarah Martin, his wife, of Worcester Co. Md.—Descended from Charles Calvert, 5th Baron Baltimore).

Born at Riversdale, Md., Feb. 5, 1843, *d* Aug. 31, 1906; Grad. at Maryland Agricultural College A.B., June 26, 1863; elected to the State Legislature, 1864, served in the Special Session, 1866, re-elected 1867; Trustee of State Agricultural College; *m* June 14, 1866, Eleanor,* da. of Richard Creagh Mackubin, M.D., Member of the State Legislature, of Strawberry Hill, Ann Arundel Co., Md., by Hester Ann, da. of Brice John and Ann Lee (Fitzhugh) Worthington. Mrs. Calvert is 6th in descent from Zachariah Maccubbin, 1756, High Sheriff of Ann Arundel Co., Md.; 6th from Charles Carroll, 1691-1755; 9th from Capt. James Neale, 1615-84, Mem. Prov. Council, Md., Atty. of Lord Baltimore; 9th from Edward Lloyd, 1695, Burgess from Lower Norfolk Co., Va.; 6th from Capt. John Worthington, 1650-1701, &c.

Issue.

i. CHARLES BENEDICT, *b* November 8, 1871; *d* July 2, 1872.

ii. RICHARD CREAGH MACKUBIN, *b* Dec. 31, 1872., *m* Zoe Ammen Davis.

iii. GEORGE HENRY, *b* Oct. 2, 1874, *m* Cornelia Russell Knight.

iv. CHARLES BALTIMORE, *b* October 9, 1878.

i. ELEANOR, *m* W. Gibson Carey.

ii. HESTER VIRGINIA, *m* Dr. Henry Walter Lilly.

iii. CHARLOTTE AUGUSTA, *m* Thomas Humphrey Spence.

iv. ROSALIE EUGENIA STIER.

v. ELIZABETH STEUART, *m* William Douglas N. Thomas.

Arms—Paly of six or, and sable a bend counterchanged; quartering (Crossland) Quarterly, argent and gules a cross flory counterchanged.

Crest—Out of a ducal coronet or, two pennons the dexter of the first the other sable, staves gules.

Motto—Fatti maschi, parole femine.

———

Residence—" MacAlpine," College Park, Md.

Societies—Colonial Dames, Daughters of the American Revolution, Daughters of the Confederacy.

CONE, ROBERT BUCKLAND,
of N.Y. City (Eldest son of Joseph Wm.
Cone, of Hartford, Ct., *b* 1841, *m* 1864, Julia-
ette C., 1841, da. of William and Maria (Clark)
Buckland, of Hartford, Ct.; son of Cyrenius O.,
1820-58; son of Joseph W., 1775-1848; son of
Sylvanus, 1731-1812; son of Lt. James, 1698-1775;
son of Nathaniel, 1675-1730; son of Daniel Cone,
b in Edinburgh, 1626, *d* 1706; Freeman of Hartford, 1669; one of the purchasers of a 30 mile tract,
now comprising part of Middx. Co., Ct. Also
descd. from Stephen Hopkins, 14th Signer "Mayflower" Compact, 1620).

Born at Hartford, Ct., Nov. 8, 1865; Veteran, Co.
"K" 1st Regt. Ct. Nat. Guard; Secy. N.Y.
Soc. of the Order of Founders and Patriots of America; Grad.
Hartford Public High School, 1884.

Arms—Gules, a fesse engr. betw. a cinquefoil in chief and crescent in base argent.

Crest—A pine cone.   *Motto*—Truth with trust.

Residence—61 West 50th Street, New York City.

Club—Calumet.

Societies—Mayflower Descendants, Order of Founders and Patriots of America,
Sons of the American Revolution, New England, of New York.

BOORAEM, ROBERT ELMER,
of New York City (Son of Henry Augustus
Booraem, 1815-89; *m* 1838, Cornelia Van Vorst,
1818-90, a descendt. of Cornelis Van Vorst, who
settled in New Netherlands 1636, apptd. Superin-
tendent of the Colony.—Descd. from W. Jacobse
Van Boerum, who emigrated from Amsterdam
1649, settled in Flatbush L.I., Magistrate there
1657-62-63. Also descd. from John Aylmer, Ld.
Bp. of London under Q. Elizabeth).

Born at Jersey City, March 28, 1856; Engineer of
Mines; Columbia Graduate, 1878.

Arms—Or, a moor's head sable wreathed about the head argent, between three
trefoils slipped vert.

Crest—A helmet of nobility, round the neck an order of Knighthood.

Residence—19 West 31st Street, New York City.

Club—Union.

Societies—St. Nicholas, Colonial Wars, American Institute Mining Engineers,
Sons of the Revolution.

TISDALL, Mrs. FLORENCE VICTOIRE (*née* RODRIGUE),
of N.Y. City (Da. of Aman T. M. A. Rodrigue,
M.D. [Baron de Curzay], 1809-57; of Phila., Pa.,
m 1835, Ann Caroline, 1811-88, da. of Hugh Bellas,
Esq., 1780-1853, of Sunbury, Northumberland Co.,
Pa., *m* Esther Anthony, 1786-1869.—Desc. from
the celebrated Don Rodrigo Diaz de Bivar, "the
Cid," of Spain, and Rodriguez del Fuente, through
the Sieur Michel Rodrigue, Baron and Comte de
Curzay, of Quebec, Ca., and La Rochelle, France
(recorded at his decease, 1777, "Chevalier Conseiller du Roi, Pres. Tresorier de France, Seigneur
de Curzay," etc., the family being borne on the
rolls of "La Noblesse convoquée pour les Etats-Généraux, du Départ-
ment de la Charente Inférieure, 1789"), and his wife, Marguerite,
da. of the Seiur Jacques L'Artigue, of La Rochelle, whose son,
André Jacques Rodrigue, of La Rochelle, 1759-1845, *m* 1798, Marie
Jeanne Françoise, 1782-1874, da. of the Sieur Marie Dominique
Jacques d'Orlic, of Bordeaux, France, and Fort Dauphin, San
Domingo, W.I. 1748-1825 (styled "Ancien gendarme de la Garde du
Roi," serving under Monseigneur le Mareschal de Rohan, Prince de
Soubise, 1770-77, and afterwards Capt. of Dragoons at Fort Dauphin,
1783), and of Dame Marie Lorraine Carrere, of San Domingo, his wife,
grand-da. of the Chevalier Jacques Gratian Benoist d'Orlic, styled
"Ecuyer, et Avocat au Parlemenr de Bordeaux," and of Dame Marie de
Caillan, his wife (*m* 1747), and 7th in descent from the Sieur Jehan d'Orlic,
of Guyenne, who in 1602 had Letters Patent issued appointing him
"Conseiller Secretaire du Roy et Controlleur en la Chancellerie de
Bordeaux." The family was ennobled five times in the 18th century.
André Jacques and Marie Jeanne Françoise Rodrigue were parents of Aman
Theodore Michel Aristide Rodrigue as above, being emigrées of the
French Revol. to San Domingo, W.I., and thence to the U.S., 1793.
Also fourth in descent from Hugh Bellas, Esq., Co. Antrim, 1717-89, of
the noble family of Bellasis of Bellasis (anciently written Bellasys,
Belasise, and Belasyse), originally of Normandy, and of Co. Pal. Durham,
in 11th century, and afterwards of Cos. York and Westmoreland, Eng.,
and of Antrim and Londonderry Cos., Ireland (the latter of "Ulster
Plantation" in reign of James I.); created Barons Bellasis and Barons,
Viscounts, and Earls Fauconberg, *temp.* Charles I.).

Born in Hollidaysburg, Pa.; *m* Dec. 23, 1885, FitzGerald Tisdall, Ph.D.,
of New York City.

Arms—(Rodrigue) Argent a fesse gules between three leopards' heads couped gules
two in chief and one in base, a crescent for mark of cadency.
Crest—A baron's coronet.
Motto—Intaminatis.
Supporters—Two lions rampant proper.
Arms—(d'Orlic) Azure, three lilies ppr., a crescent for difference.

Residences—"The Buckingham," New York City; "Bellasylva," Woodbridge, N.J.
Club—Quid Nunc, of New York City.
Societies—Harlem Philharmonic, Ladies' Auxiliary of Harlem Eye, Ear, and
Throat Infirmary. Salmagundi of Woodbridge.

BALDWIN, ORVILLE DWIGHT,
of San Francisco, Cal. (Son of Orrin Calkins
Baldwin, 1809-61, of Amsterdam, N.Y.; son of Dr.
Harvey, 1784-1852, of Lexington, N.Y., m Nellie
Calkins; son of Samuel, 1755-1818, of Goshen Ct.;
son of Samuel, 1725-1804; son of Hon. Nathaniel,
1693-1760, of Guildford; son of Samuel, 1655-96,
of Guildford Ct.; son of Nathaniel, b Cholesbury,
Co. Bucks, Eng., settled in Milford Ct., 1639,
m 2nd wife Mrs. Joanna Westcoat; son of Richard,
of Cholesbury, d 1630; son of Richard; son of
Richard Baldwin, 1500-52, of Aston Clinton, Bucks,
nephew of Chief Justice Sir John Baldwin).

Born at Renslaerville, N.Y., Aug. 18, 1843, Banker;
m Millie Eva, da. of Chas. Fredk. Wehn [son
of Charles and Dorothea (von Glöde) Wehn,
of Prussia] and Eva Catherine, da. of Michael
Rohé, of Alsace Lorraine.

Issue.
i. ORVILLE RAYMOND, b Feb. 6, 1876, m Anna Deuprey.
i. BLANCHE EVELYN, m John McGaw, of England.

Arms—Qtly. 1 and 4, arg. six oak leaves in pairs vert (Baldwin) ; 2, chequy or
and az. (Warren), Wm. de Warren, 1st Earl of Surrey ; 3, ar. an eagle
displ. sa. (Bruen).
Crest—A squirrel sejeant holding hazel sprig.
Mottoes—Vim vi repello ; ex vide fortis.

Residence—"Beaumont," 1000 Green St., San Francisco, Cal.
Societies—Sons of Amer. Revol., Colonial Wars, Barons of Runnymede, etc.

WOODWARD, WILLIAM,
of N.Y. City (Son of William Woodward,
1835-89, one of the founders of the N.Y. Cotton
Exchange, m 1865, Sarah Abigail, da. of Hon. Saml.
and Mary Peckham Rodman; son of Henry
Williams, 1803-41, m Mary Edge Webb; son of
Capt. Henry, 1770-1822, m Eleanor Williams
Turner, Wid.; son of William, 1742-1807, m Jane
Ridgeley; son of William, m Alice Ridgeley; son
of Abraham, m Priscilla Ruley; son of William
Woodward, of London, England).

Born in New York City, April 7, 1876; Grad.
Harvard Univ., A.B. 1898; A.M. 1899;
LL.B. Harvard Law School, 1901, m Oct. 24,
1904, Eliz. Ogden, da. of Duncan and Eliz.
(Ogden) Cryder, of New York.

Issue.
i. EDITH, b October 8, 1905.

Arms—Argent, two bars azure ; over all three bucks' heads cabossed or.
Crest—On a ducal coronet a boar's head couped argent.
Motto—Virtus semper viret.

Residence—11 West 51st Street, New York City.
Clubs—Union, Knickerbocker, Coaching, Racquet, (N.Y. City), Bachelor's,
St. James' (London)

C HENOWETH, ALEXANDER C.,
of N.Y. City (Son of Rev. George D. Chenoweth, 1811-80, m Francis A., da. of Capt. Wm.
Bradford Crawford ; son of John, 1770-1865 ; son
of John, 1728-1820 ; son of Arthur Chenoweth,
of Maryland, 1700, who was descd. from John
Chenoweth of Mogion, Cornwall, living 1620 ; also
6th in desct. from William Cromwell, 1671 ; 6th
from Mary Calvert, gr-da. of Lord Baltimore ; and
5th from John Davenport).

Born at Baltimore, Md., June 5, 1849 ; Engineer in
charge of the Croton Aqueduct, 1890 to 1896 ; Grad. Dickenson
Coll ; m April 19, 1876, Catharine R., da. of Hon. Fernando Wood.

Issue.

i. ALEXANDER FERNANDO WOOD, *b* Oct. 8, 1883.
i. MAUD, *b* March 24, 1881 ; *d* Aug. 22, 1882.
ii. KATHARINE, *b* Sept. 22, 1886 ; *d* May 5, 1892.

Arms—Sable, on a fesse or three Corrish choughs' heads of the first.
Motto—Might makes right.

Residence—41 East 59th Street, New York City.   *Club*—Manhattan.
Societies—Member of N.Y. City Chamber of Commerce, Colonial Wars, War of
the American Revolution, War of 1812, Veteran Artillery Corps, Veteran
Washington Continental Guard.

R OCKWOOD, CHARLES GREENE, Jr., A.M., Ph.D.,
of Princeton (Son of Charles G. Rock-
wood, *b* July 19, 1814, *d* July 17, 1904, m Sarah
Smith, 1812-93; son of Ebenezer, 1781-1815; son
of Dr. Ebenezer, 1746-1830; son of Lieut. Elisha,
1716-88; son of Nathaniel, 1665-1721; son of
Nicholas, *d* 1680, of Dorchester, Mass.; 7th in
descent from Roger Rokewood, of Euston, Suffolk).

Born at N.Y. City, Jan. 11, 1843 ; Grad. Yale Coll.,
1864; Prof. of Mathematics, Bowdoin Coll.
1868-73; Rutgers Coll., 1873-77; Princeton
Univ., 1877; Emeritus, 1905; m June 13,
1867, Hettie Hosford, da. of Simeon P. Smith
of N.Y.

Issue.

i. KATHARINE CHAUNCEY.

Arms—Argent, three chess rooks sable, two and one, a chief of the last.
Crest—A lion sejant guardant, argent.

Residences—34 Bayard Lane, Princeton, N.J.; "Sunset Hill," Durham Centre, Conn.
Clubs—Nassau, Princeton, N.J.: University, Yale, and Princeton of New York.
Societies—St. Nicholas, Sons of the Revoln., Colonial Wars, Fel. Am. Assn. Adv.
Science, Am. Mathematical. Nat. Geograph. N.J. Hist., Am. Metrological,
Seismol., Italy.

SALTER, WILLIAM MACKINTIRE,
of Chicago, Ill. (Son of Rev. Wm. Salter,
D.D., of Burlington, Iowa, *b* 1821, *m* Mary Ann
Mackintire, 1824-93 ; son of William F., 1787-1849,
son of John Salter, 1740-1814, of Portsmouth, N.H.,
m Jane, da. of Joseph Frost, 1717-66 ; son of Joseph
Frost, 1681-1732, *m* Mary, sister of Sir Wm.
Pepperrell : son of Charles Frost, 1631-97 ; son of
Nicholas Frost, 1585-1663, of Tiverton, Devon-
shire).

Born at Burlington, Iowa, Jan. 30, 1853 ; Lecturer
of the Society for Ethical Culture, Chicago ;
Grad. Knox Coll., A.B. 1871 ; Harvard Univ.,
B.D. 1876 ; Göttingen Univ., 1876-7 ; Co-
lumbia Univ., 1881-2, *m* Dec. 2, 1885, Mary
Gibbens.

Issue.
i. JOHN RANDALL (adopted), *b* April 16, 1898.
i. ELIZA WEBB, *b* Jan. 20, 1888, *d* Dec. 2, 1889.

Arms—(Pepperrell) Argent, a chevron gules betw. three pineapples vert; on a
canton gules a fleur-de-lis argent.
Crest—Issuing from a mural coronet or, an arm embowed between two laurel
branches, grasping a staff, thereon a flag argent.
Mottos—Peperi ; Fortiter et fideliter.

Residences—Chicago, Ill.; Silver Lake, N.H.
Club—Chicago Literary.
Society—The Pepperrell Association of Kittery Point, Me.

CHURCHILL, WILLIAM HUNTER,
of N.Y. City (Eldest son of Richard Cuyler
Churchill, 1st Lt. 4th Artillery, U.S.A., 1845-79,
m 1866, Josephine, da. of Henry Young ; son of
William II., *b* 1819, *m* Elizabeth M., da. of Richd.
Cuyler ; son of Brig.-Gen. Sylvester, *b* 1783,
m Lucy da. of William Hunter ; son of Joseph,
1748, of Woodstock Vt.; son of Joseph, *b* 1712 ;
son of Barnabas, *m* 1711 Lydia Cushman ; son of
Joseph ; son of John who settled in Plymouth,
Mass., *m* 1644, Hannah, da. of William Pontus,
Grantee of Plymouth ; son of Jasper Churchill, of
London, 1628, who supplied Gov. Endicott, of
Mass. Bay, with arms ; 18th in des. from Gitto de
Leon, 1055).

Born at Fort Delaware, Sept. 12, 1867 ; Graduated
at Princeton University, 1888.

Arms—Sable, a lion rampant argent, debruised with a bendlet gules.
Crest—Out of a ducal coronet or, a demi-lion rampant argent.
Motto—Dieu defend le droit.

Residence—"A Dieu Vale," Dinard, France .
Clubs—Calumet, Racquet and Tennis, of N.Y. City.

TAYLOR, WASHINGTON IRVING, Capt.,
of Brooklyn, N.Y. (son of Stephen G. Taylor,
A.M., Ph.D., 1819-84, of Sanbornton, N.H.,
m 1856, Mary A., da. of Robert and Sarah (Wilson)
Cobb, of Portland, Me.: grandson of Jonathan
Taylor, 1739-1816, of Stratham, N.H.; son of
Edward Taylor, grantee of Sanbornton.—Descd.
from Gov. Simon Bradstreet, 1603-97, Secy. Mass.
Bay Colony. Also 8th in desct. from Gov. Thomas
Dudley, of Mass., and from Gov. Thomas Wiggin,
first Gov. of Maine and N.H. under Lord Saye and
Sele and Lord Brooke).

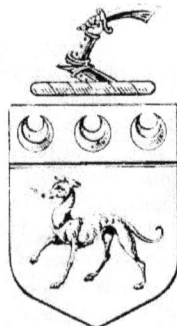

Born in Brooklyn, N.Y., Dec. 13, 1864; Grad. at Columbia Coll., A.B.
1887; A.M. 1888; LL.B. *cum laude*, 1888; Ph.D. 1889; Capt. and
Inspector of Small Arms Practice 13th Regt. Coast Artillery,
National Guard, State of New York.

Arms—(For Bradstreet) Argent, a greyhound passant gules, on a chief sable
three crescents or.
Crest—An arm embowed in armour holding in the hand a scimitar proper.
Motto—Virtute et non vi.

Residence—40 Wall Street, N.Y. City.
Societies—Colonial Wars, Sons of the Revolution, Military Order of 1812, Veteran
Corps of Artillery, Military Service Institute of U.S.

COLES, EDWARD OLIVER,
of N.Y. City (Eldest son of the late Edward
Coles, 1809-1900, *m* Hester Bussing, da. of Wm.
White and Elizabeth Mesier Moulton, tenth in
descent from Robert Moulton, of Salem, Mass.;
27th in descent from Roger de Coigneries, *temp.*
William the Conqueror; 14th from Fulk Woodhull,
15th Baron of Woodhull Castle, Bedford; 13th
from William Underhill, of Wolverhampton, Co.
Stafford; 15th from Ri'cus Colles, of Powick, 1442.
—Descended from Robert Cole, of Suffolk, England,
to America with Gov. Winthrop, 1630, one of the
first settlers of Ipswich, Mass., and Providence,
R.I.).

Born at Dosoris, L.I., June 30, 1843; *m* Jan. 23,
1867, Helen Blanchard, da. of Louis B. and
Emma (Manning) Brown.

Issue.
i. LILLIAN.   ii. GERTRUDE SCHERMERHORN.

Arms—Quarterly, 1st and 4th argent, a bull passant gules armed or, within a
bordure sable bezantée (Coles); 2nd argent, a chevron sable between
three trefoils slipped vert (Underhill); 3rd sable, three bells argent, a
canton ermine (Porter).
Crest—A demi-dragon vert, holding in the dexter paw an arrow or, headed and
feathered argent.   *Motto*—Deum Cole regem serva.

Residences—73 West 55th Street, New York City; Elberon, New Jersey.

WETMORE, WILLIAM BOERUM, Major,
of Allenhurst N.J. (Son of Samuel
Wetmore 1812-85, m Sarah T. Boerum 1820-99;
son of Samuel, 1775-1851, m Eliz. W. Warner; son
of Seth, 1744-90, m Mary Wright; son of Judge
Seth, 1700-44, m Hannah Whitmore; son of
Izrahiah, 1657-1702; son of Thomas 1615-81, to
Boston, Mass. 1642; son of Sir Wm. Whitmore,
Bt., who descended from Sir John, Lord of
Whytemere, b circa 1185).

Born at London, Eng., Dec. 7, 1849, Cadet at U.S.
Mil. Acad. West Point 1867-72, Grad. June 14,
1872, and promoted to 2nd Lt. 6th Cavalry;
served on Staff of Gen. Pope 1873-76, A.D.C.
to Gen. Miles in Indian War of 1874 and battle
of Red River, recommended for brevets of 1st
Lt. and Capt., resigned Dec. 1, 1876, Major 9th Regt. N.G.S.N.Y.
1879-82, m (2) Kath. B. Havercamp.

Issue. *(By 1st m)*

i. Louis H., b Sept. 19, 1889.   i. Wenonah.   ii. Dagmar.

Arms—Argent, on a fesse azure three martlets or.
Crest—A falcon close proper belled or.   *Motto*—Virtus, libertas et patria.

Residence—Allenhurst, N.J.
Clubs—Union, University, N.Y. Yacht, Larchmont Yacht, Manhattan, Army and
Navy N.Y., Aero, N.Y., Newport, R.I., Army and Navy of Washington.
Societies—Cincinnati, War of 1812, Naval Order, Order of Veterans Indian Wars
of U.S., New Eng., Chamber of Commerce N.Y., Am. Geographical, Am.
Numismatic, Nat. Acad. of Design, Metropolitan Mus. of Art, U S, Mil.
Service Inst., U.S. Naval Inst., Navy League, U.S. Cavly. Assn.

JONES, WALTER R. T.,
of N.Y. City (Son of John H. Jones, 1785-
1859, of Cold Spring Harbor L.I., m Loretta
Hewlett, 1791-1838; son of John, 1755-1819,
m Hannah Hewlett; son of William, 1708-79, of
S. Oyster Bay L.I., m Phebe Jackson; son of
Thomas Jones, 1665-1713 [tradition says that he
participated in the Battle of the Boyne], Major
Queen's Co. Regt., High Sheriff and Ranger-General
of L.I., from Strabane, Ireland, to South Oyster
Bay L.I., 1692, m Freelove Townsend, 1674-1726).

Born at Cold Spring Harbor Feb. 20, 1830; Grad.
Columbia Coll. 1850; m Oct. 10, 1854, Anna
Pierson, 1831-82, da. of Rear-Adml. Theodorus
Bailey, U.S. Navy.

Issue.

i. Theodorus Bailey, b Oct. 11, 1863, d March 27, 1879.
i. Josephine Katherine, m 1877, Lieut. Charles William Whipple, U.S.A.

Arms— Gules, a lion rampant within a bordure or.
Crest—A demi-lion rampant.   *Motto*—Trust in God.
Residences—181 Madison Avenue, N.Y.City; Masapequa, L.I.
Clubs—Union League, University, Seawanhaka Corinthian Yacht.
Societies—St. Nicholas, Geographical, Assn. of the Bar of N.Y. City.

DYER, LOUIS,
    of Oxford (Second surviving son of the Hon.
Charles Volney Dyer, M.D.--son of Daniel Dyer,
b W. Greenwich R.I. Oct. 16, 1764, *d* Brattleboro'
Vt. Feb. 14, 1842; son of Geo. Dyer, *b* W. Green-
wich R.I. Dec. 26, 1736, *d* Clarendon Springs Vt.
Jan. 18, 1817; son of Samuel Dyre [the eldest great-
great-grandson of Roger and Mary Williams], *b* S.
Kingston R.I. 1670, *d* W. Greenwich, R.I. soon
after March 25, 1760; son of Edward Dyre [name-
sake and grandson to Capt. Edward Hutchinson,
Mrs. Ann Hutchinson's eldest son], *b* S. Kingston
R.I. 1670, *d* W. Greenwich R.I. after 1760; son of
Samuel Dyer, *b* Boston Mass. 1635, *d* Newport R.I.
1678; son of William Dyre [great-nephew of Sir James Dier, J.C.B., and
a founder (1638) of Portsmouth R.I. and (1639) of Newport R.I., where he
was the first "Clerk" of the Colony, and in 1653 "Commander-in-Chief
upon Sea" against the Dutch], *b* Co. Somerset 1587, *d* Newport 1676;
son of George Dyer of Bratton Seymour, Co. Somerset, *d* before 1639 and
after 1623, son of John Dyer of Roundhill (Wincanton, Somerset); son of
Richard of Wincanton, *d* 1623 --a founder (1836) of Chicago Ill., Judge
(1863-65) of the International Mixed Court at Sierra Leone and Rome,
b Clarendon Springs Vt. June 12, 1808, *d* Chicago Ill. April 24, 1878,
m Nov. 7, 1837, Louisa Maria [a great-great-granddau. of Stephen Gifford,
the youngest of the founders (1660) of Norwich Ct., and a gt.-gt.-gt.-
grand-dau. of Capt. Samuel Talcott, who was graduated at Harvard in
1658, and whose father, John Talcott, one of the founders of Hartford Ct.,
came from Braintree, Eng., 1632, to Boston] *b* Sherburn N.Y. Sept. 20,
1812, *d* Chicago April 5, 1875).

Born at Chicago Ill. Sept. 30, 1851; Grad. A.B. Harvard Univ. 1874;
    B.A. Oxon, 1878; M.A. Oxon, 1893; Asst. Prof. of Greek at Harvard
    Univ. 1878-87; Acting Prof. of Greek at Cornell Univ. 1895-96;
    Hearst Lecturer at the Univ. of California 1900-01; Lecturer in
    Modern Languages at Balliol Coll., Oxford Univ. 1893-96; on
    Machiavelli at the Royal Institution in 1898; on Council of Hellenic
    Soc. since 1891; since 1901 Mem. for America of the London
    Committee of the Egypt Exploration Fund; *m* Nov. 23, 1889,
    Margaret Ann, da. of the late Alexander Macmillan, Hon. M.A.
    Oxon (Joint Founder with his brother Daniel of Macmillan and Co.),
    of Portland Place, London, and Bramshott Chase, Hants., and
    Caroline Brimley, of Cambridge, Eng.

Issue.

i. CHARLES VOLNEY, *b* Dec. 22, 1890.   i. RACHAEL MARGARET.
ii. CECIL MACMILLAN, *b* Jan. 17, 1894.

Arms—Sable, on a fesse between three goats passant argent, a martlet.
Crest—A Saracen's head in profile proper, on the head a cap or, verged round the
    temples chequy argent and azure.   *Motto*—Terrere nolo, timere nescio.

Residence—Sunbury Lodge, Banbury Road, Oxford, England.
Club—Royal Societies. *Societies*—Society of Col. Wars, Hellenic, Dante Society.

HIRST, BARTON COOKE, M.D.,
of Phila, (Son by 2nd w. of Judge Wm.
Lucas Hirst, 1804-76 and Lydia Barton, 1837-95,
da. of Barton and Sarah Emily (Camac) Cooke.
—Descended from John Hirst, who came from
Mirfield, Yorks., Eng., 1749, to the Moravian
Colony at Bethlehem, Pa., to teach German
Moravians the methods of manufacturing woollen
cloth; son of Joshua and Elizth. Hirst of Mirfield),

Born at Chestnut Hill, Pa., July 20, 1861; Grad.
Univ. of Pa., M.D., 1883, Prof. of Obstetrics
1889; m April 22, 1890, Elizabeth H. Dupuy,
da. of Thomas and Elizth. H. (Dupuy)
Graham of (Graham Bros.) Glasgow, Liverpool and N.Y.

Issue.

i. BARTON COOKE, Jr., b May 13, 1891.   i. ELIZABETH GRAHAM,
ii. THOMAS GRAHAM, b July 23, 1892.   b July 19, 1900.
iii. JOHN COOKE, b April 13, 1894.

Arms—Gules. a sun in splendour or.
Crest—A hurst of trees proper.   Motto—Efflorescent.

Residence—1821 Spruce Street, Philadelphia, Pa.
Clubs—University, Philadelphia Cricket.
Societies—American Gynecological, College of Physicians.

TALLANT, MRS. JENNIE. S. (née STILWELL),
of Butte Montana (Da. of John Thomas
Stilwell 1819-95, m Nancy Beaumont 1825-87, da.
of Truman Abraham Warren 1800-25; son of
Lyman, b 1771; son of Abraham, b 1747; son of
Abraham, b 1717; son of Benjamin 1670-1745; son
of Joseph, b 1626; son of Richard Warren, who
came to Plymouth, Mass., in the "Mayflower"
1620; son of Christopher Warren, of Heads-
borough).

Elected State Regent of the Daughters of the
American Revolution of Montana in 1901,
serving four years, then elected Honorary
State Regent by the 13th Continental Congress
of the D.A.R.; m Feb. 4, 1880, Walter Stout
Tallant.

Issue.

i. HENRY STILWELL, b Nov. 28, 1880; Graduated from State School of
Mines in Butte, Montana, 1904.

Arms—(Warren) Gules, a lion rampant argent, a chief chequy, or and azure.
Crest—Out of ducal coronet a demi-eagle.

Residence—Butte, Montana.   Society—Daus. of the American Revolution.

GRIFFITH, WILLIAM HERRICK,
of Albany, N.Y. (Son of the late Edwin
Henry Griffith, *b* 1830, *d* 1875, and Mary Louisa
Knowlton, his wife, *b* 1833, of Albany and Castleton-on-Hudson, N.Y.; tenth in descent from Capt.
Wm. Knowlton, of Cheswick, Eng., 1584-1632;
grandson of Smith Griffith, 1793-1878, of Nassau,
N.Y., *m* Lemira Herrick, 1793-1859, seventh in
descent from Sir William Herrick, of London,
Leicester, and Beau Manor Park, and eighteenth in
descent from Eric, King of Danes; great-grandson
of Major Joshua Griffith, 1763-1830, served in War
of 1812, *m* Ruth Paine, sixth in descent from Hon.
Stephen Paine, of Rehoboth, Mass., subscriber to
King Philip's War, a descendent of Hugh de Payen; great-great-
grandson of William Griffith, who came to America from Cardigan,
Wales, 1731, with his wife, Ruth, served in the War of the Revolution,
settled in Oneida Co., N.Y., a lineal descendant of Llewellyn, Prince of
North Wales).

Born at Castleton-on-Hudson, N.Y., January 27, 1866; Secretary and
  Treasurer of the Knowlton Association of America; Past Regent,
  Philip Livingston Chapter, Sons of the Revolution; Registrar-
  General and Genealogist of the Heraldic and Chivalric Order of
  Albion; *m* February 3, 1892, Grace Elizabeth Clute, *b* June 12, 1865,
  daughter of the Hon. Matthew Henry Robertson, of Albany, N.Y.,
  and Elizabeth Clute, his wife (both deceased).

Issue.

i. MARGARET FRANCES, *b* December 27, 1892.

Arms—Quarterly, 1st and 6th gules, three lions passant argent in pale, armed
    azure (for Griffith); 2nd argent, a fesse vaire or, and gules (for Herrick);
    3rd argent, a chevron gules, between three ducal coronets sable (for
    Knowlton); 4th azure, three lozenges or (for Freeman); 5th argent, a
    chevron between three cross-crosslets sable (for Southworth).

Crests—1. A bull's head couped argent horned and eared sable, gorged with a
    chaplet of roses. 2. A demi-lion rampant sable, armed gules.

Motto—Virtus omnia nobilitat.

Residence—445 State Street, Albany, New York.

Societies—Sons of the Revolution, Baronial Order of Runnymede, Order of
    Founders and Patriots, Colonial Wars, Mayflower Descendants, Order of
    Colonial Governors, Order of Old Guard of Illinois, War of 1812, New
    England Historic Genealogical, Albany Institute, Albany Historical and
    Art, 32nd degree Ancient Accepted Scottish Rite, N.Y. State Historical
    Association, Old North-west Genealogical Society, Knowlton Association
    of America, Order of Albion.

BLAKE, JOSEPH AUGUSTUS, M.D.,
of N.Y. City (3rd son of Professor Wm.
Phipps Blake, of Mill Rock, near New Haven,
Conn.—Descended from William Blake, 1595-1663,
of Asholt, Somersetshire).

Born at San Francisco, Cal., August 31, 1864;
Graduated at Yale University, B.A., 1885;
Ph.B., 1886; Columbia University, M.D.,
1889; Surgeon St. Luke's Hospital;
Surgeon Roosevelt Hospital; Professor of
Surgery, Columbia University; *m* Dec. 17,
1890, Catharine, da. of Landon Ketchum and
Ann Augusta Burrit, of New York City, a
lineal descendant of the family of Gov. Lewis
Morris, Governor of N.J., 1738-46; Chief Justice New York; and
one of the Signers of the Declaration of Independence; and of James
Graham, Attorney-General of Province of New York in 1685.

Issue.

i. JOSEPH AUGUSTUS, *b* Oct. 29, 1891.
ii. FRANCIS HAYES, *b* Nov. 11, 1900.

Arms—Quarterly, 1st and 4th argent, a chevron between three garbs sable
(Blake); 2nd and 3rd sable, a trefoil within an orle of mullets argent
(Phipps).
Crest—On a chapeau gules, turned up ermine, a martlet argent.

Residence—601 Madison Av., New York City.
Clubs—University, Yale, Riding.
Societies—Fellow of the New York Academy of Sciences, Amer. Surg. Assn.,
Academy of Medicine, Member various Medical Societies.

HALSEY, FREDERIC ROBERT,
of N.Y. City (Son of Robert Halsey, of
Ithaca, N.Y.—Descended from Thomas Halsey,
1592-1681, *b* in Hertfordshire, England, settled at
Southampton, L.I., served in Indian Wars,
Deputy to General Court, Colony of Conn., 1664).

Born at Ithaca, N.Y., March 28, 1847; Graduated
at Harvard University, A.B. 1868; Paymaster-
General of the State of N.Y.; *m* April 24,
1872, Emma Gertrude, da. of Henry Keep and
Emma A. Woodruff, his wife, of Watertown,
N.Y.

Arms—Argent, on a pile sable, three griffins' heads
erased of the first.
Crest—A cubit arm gules, cuff argent, holding in the hand a griffin's leg erased or.
Motto—Nescit vox missa reverti.

Residences—22 West 53rd Street, N.Y. City; "Egeria," Tuxedo Park, N.Y.
Clubs—Union, University, Racquet, Grolier, Harvard, Manhattan, Westminster
Kennel, N.Y. Athletic, Tuxedo, Automobile of America, Automobile de
France; Cercle de l'Isle de Puteaux, Paris; Royal Societies Club,
St. James' Street, London.
Societies—St. Nicholas, N.Y. Historical Society.

NICOLL, DE LANCEY,
of N.Y. City (Son of Solomon Townsend
Nicoll 1813-65; son of Edward H., *b* 1784; son
of Henry, *b* 1756; son of Benj., *b* 1718; son of
Benj., *b* 1694; son of William, *b* 1657; son of
Matthias Nicoll, *b* 1631, M. of Inner Temple,
appted. Secry. of Commission to N. E. Colonies,
1664; son of Rev. Matthias, of Plymouth, Devonshire; son of John; son of William; son of John;
son of Henry; son of John Nicoll, of Islip,
Northants, who died 1467).

Born at Shelter Island, N.Y., June 24, 1854; Grad.
Princeton Univ., 1874, B.A., M.A., Columbia
Law School, 1876; Dist. Att., N.Y. City,
1890-93; Mem. of Constitutional Convention,
1887; *m* Dec. 11, 1890, Maud, da. of Lt.
Richard Cuyler Churchill, U.S. Army.

Issue.

i. DE LANCEY, Jr., *b* May 19, 1892.   i. JOSEPHINE CHURCHILL.

Arms—Azure, three eagles displayed in bend, between two cotises engrailed and
    crosses crosslet fitchée or,
Crest—An eagle rising or, holding a cross-crosslet, crosslet again, fitchée of the last.
Motto—Fide sed cui vide.
Residences—23 East 39th Street, N.Y. City; " Windymere," Southampton, L.I.
Clubs—Union, Metropolitan, University, Manhattan, Calumet, Tuxedo, Rockaway
    Hunt, Down Town, Riding, Lawyers, Ardsley, etc.
Societies—St. Nicholas, Bar Association.

HALL, GEORGE ELI,
of San Francisco (Son of Chas. O. Hall,
1832-93, of Boston, *m* Mary A. Dale; son of Eli,
1785-1856; son of Timothy, 1758-97; son of
Timothy, *b* 1732; son of Preserved, *b* 1706; son of
Benj., *b* 1668; son of Edward, *b* 1670, of Reho-
bath, Mass.; son of Francis, *d* 1621, of Henbury,
Glouc., Eng.; son of Francis, *d* 1611, of Bromyard,
Heref.; son of Thomas, of Ledbury, *d* 1611; son
of Anthony Hall, of Henwick, Worc., Eng.).

Born at Nice, France, Mar. 17, 1863; Grad. Univ.
of Leipzig, 1882; Consul Gen. of Turkey;
Comdr., Orders of Lion and Sun, Persia,
Osmanié and Medjidié, Turkey; Order of
Christ, Portugal; Pres. San Francisco
Chapter, Soc. of Colonial Wars.

Arms—Argent, three talbots' heads erased sable betw. nine cross crosslets azure.
Crest—A dragon's head couped azure, collared argent.

Residences—Pacific Union Club, San Francisco.
Clubs—Pacific, Union.
Societies—Colonial Wars, Sons of the Amer. Revolution, Soc. of the Cincinnati.

A NABLE, ELIPHALET, NOTT (*deceased*), of N.Y. City (Son of Henry Sheldon Anable of Long Island City N.Y. 1815-87, *m* 1855, Rosanna Frick of Williamsville, N.Y. 1831-1901; son of Joseph 1773-1831; son of John 1744-1815; son of Cornelius, *b* 1704; son of John, *b* 1673; son of Samuel 1646-78; son of Anthony Annable, *b* 1599, of Plymouth 1623, represented Barnstable for 14 years as delegate to the General Court of Mass., *d* Barnstable Mass. 1674, probably son of John Annable of Bury St. Edmunds, Co. Suffolk, England, whose ancestor, William Annable, of Dunstable, used the arms for a seal to a deed dated 1396).

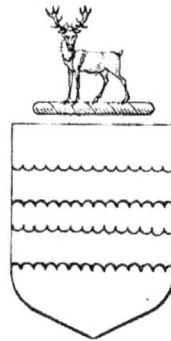

Born at Newtown L.I. Sept. 1, 1857, *d* Oct. 18, 1904; Grad. Union Coll. A.B. 1878; Columbia Univ. Law School LL.B. 1880; *m* Dec. 22. 1891, Annie Housel, da. of the late William G. Schenck of N.Y. City.

Issue.

i. ANTHONY, *b* Jan. 11, 1897.

Arms—Argent, two bars engrailed gules.
Crest—A stag at gaze proper.

Residence—(Mrs. Eliphalet Nott Anable) Morristown, N.J.

H AMILTON, EZEKIEL BRADDIN, of N.Y. City (Fourth son of James Hamilton, of Silver Hill, Enniskillen, Ireland, who settled at Stratford, Ontario, Ca., 1845; son of Douglas; son of John James; grandson of James, 7th Earl of Abercorn, *d* 1743; son of James, Baron of Montcastle and Visct. Strabane, 1701, 5th in desct. from Sir Claude Hamilton, Lord Paisley 1587).

Born at Stratford-on-Avon, Ca., Nov. 20, 1861; Graduate Trinity Univ., Toronto; Western Univ., London, Ontario; Trinity Coll., Cambridge, Eng.; Minister for N.Y. City Gov., Department of Charities and Corrections; became a Member of N.Y. State Bar, 1900; *m* June 24, 1896, Augusta Rosalie Stevenson.

Arms—Qtly., 1 and 4 gules, three cinquefoils pierced ermine (Hamilton); 2 and 3 argent, a ship with sails furled and oars, sable (Earls of Arran).

Crest—Out of a ducal coronet or, an oak tree penetrated transversely in stem by a frame saw proper, inscribed " through," frame gold.

Motto—Sola nobilitas virtus.

Residences—61 East 55th Street, New York City; Newport, R.I.

L EWIS, SILAS WEIR (*deceased*),
of Phila. (Son of John Fredk. Lewis, 1791-
1858, *m* Eliza, 1788-1865, da. of Jacob and Esther
(Zebley) Mower.—Descended from the patrician
family of Ludewig, who in 13th century were
citizens in the Free Imperial City of Hall, Suabia,
and of the Holy Rom. Emp.; fourth in desct. from
Johann D. Ludewig, Impl. Notary of Germany,
was Johann Andreas P. Ludewig, who was father
of John F. Lewis; came to America from Crailsheim
1777, and upon his settlement in Phila., 1783,
Anglicised his name to Lewis).

Born in Phila., 1819-88; *m* 1850, Caroline A.,
1831-91, da. of Lewis and Sarah L. (Hynson)
Kalbfus; Treasr. Pa. Inst. for Deaf and
Dumb, Northern Home for Friendless Child-
ren, The Athenæum Un. Benev. Assn., and St. John's Evangelical
Luth. Church; Sec. Southern Home for Destitute Children; Dir.
Farmers' and Mechanics' Bank.

Issue.

i. Rev. Louis K., *b* July 8, 1851, *m* Amy Lewis.
ii. R. Howard W., *b* Sept. 8, 1855, *m* Mabel Potter.
iii. John Frederick, *b* Sept. 10, 1860, *m* Anne H. R. Baker.
i. Caroline L. J., *m* Edward S. Sayres.
ii. Mary Adele, *m* J. Franklin McFadden.

Arms—Or, three bars azure interlaced by a pike in pale, sable, head downwards.
Crest—An eagle's wing or, charged as in Arms.   *Motto*—Unbestechlich.

Residence—(Of issue) Philadelphia, Penna.

G AZZAM, EDWIN VAN DEUSEN, M.D.,
of Utica, N.Y. (Son of Audley W.
Gazzam 1836-84, Maj. 103rd Regt. Pa. Vols.,
Brev. Brig.-Genl., Atty.-at-Law, *m* Mary E. Van
Deusen *b* 1841, *d* 1871 [8th in desct. from Abraham-
son Van Deursen, of N. Brabant, who came to
America 1650]; son of Dr. Edward D., *m* Elizabeth
A. de Beelen, a descendant of Baron Fredc. E. F.
de Beelen Bertholff; son of William; son of
William Gazzam, Jr., an English Journalist, *b* in
Cambridge, who espoused the American cause,
arrived in Philadelphia, and went thence to Pitts-
burgh, of which port he was appointed first
Collector by Pres. Madison; *d* in Pittsburgh 1811).

Born at Utica, N.Y., Feb. 5, 1866; Grad. at Univ. of Pa. M.D. 1892;
Mem. of the Empire State Soc., Sons of the Amer. Revolution.

Arms—(de Beelen Bertholff) Per fesse argent and sable, in chief a bull's head
caboshed thereon three rooks sable, in base a wheel supported by two
billets or.   *Motto*—Deus major columna.

Residence—8 Rutger Street, Utica, N.Y.   *Club*—Utica Medical.
Societies—Sons of the Amer. Revol., Wash.-Continental Guard, Metropolitan
Mus. of Art, Amer. Art, N.Y. Med. League, Phys. Mutual Aid, Masonic,
A.A.A. of S., Alumni of N.Y., Post Grad. Hospital, Alpha Mu Pi Omega
Med. Fraternity, Alumni of the Univ. of Pa., Med. Soc. County of Oneida,
N.Y. State Med. Soc., Am. Med. Assn., The Penn. Soc. of N.Y., &c., &c.

S EWELL, ROBERT VAN VORST,
of N.Y. City (Eldest son of Robert Sewell
1833-98, Attorney and Councillor-at-Law, of N.Y.
[brother of the late Major General William Sewell,
thrice returned a Member of the U.S. Senate],
m 1860 Sarah, da. of Cornelius Van Vorst, of Van
Vorst, Jersey City, N.J., and Elizabeth Brower of
Jersey City, and grandson of Thomas Sewell,
Collector of Inland Revenue for County Mayo,
Ireland, 1838-40).

Born in N.Y. City May 9, 1861 ; Associate Nat.
Acad. of Design, 1901 ; Nat. Soc. Mural
Painters, 1896; 1st Acad., Prize 1890 ; Silver
Medal Pan Amer. Exposition, 1902, etc. ;
Grad. Columbia Univ. B.A., 1880; *m* April 12, 1889, Lydia Amanda,
da. of Benjamin and Julia A. (Washburne) Brewster.

Issue.

i. ROBERT BREWSTER, *b* 1896.   ii. WILLIAM JOYCE, *b* 1902.

Arms—Sable, a chevron betw. three butterflies argent ; quartering (Van Vorst)
or, a ram rampant sable, horned argent.
Crest—An arm embowed in armour holding a staff surmounted by a cap of liberty.
Motto—Scattered we endure.

Residences—25 W. 67th St., New York City ; "Dar el gebel," Tangier, Morocco.
Clubs—Century, Union League, Lotos.
Societies—Architectural League. Nat. Academy of Design. Mural Painters.

W HITNEY, DRAKE,
of Niagara Falls, N.Y. (Son of Major Solon
M. W. Whitney, *b* 1815, *m* Frances E. Drake,
1822-83.—Descended from John Whitney, of Isleworth, Middx., 1589-1673, settled in Watertown,
Mass., 1635; son of Thomas, gent., *d* 1637 ; son of
Robert ; son of Sir Robert Whitney, *d* 1567, 6th in
descent from Sir Robert, of Castle Clifford, *d* 1441,
who was 7th in descent from Eustace de Whitney,
of Whitney-on-the-Wye, 1200; gt-grandson of
Thursten the Fleming, who came with William the
Conqueror, 1066).

Born at Niagara Falls, N.Y., Aug. 23, 1843 ; Grad.
C.E., Troy Polytechnic, 1864 ; Goethingen
Univ., 1866, Hanover, and Freiberg Mining
Acad., 1868 ; Ecole des Mines, Paris, 1869 ;
Corporation Engineer, *m* Oct. 15, 1896, Grace
Virginia (Oatman) Whitney.

Arms—Azure, a cross chequy or, and gules.
Crest—A bull's head couped sable, armed or, the points gules.
Motto—Magnanimeter crucem sustine.

Residence—Niagara Falls, N.Y.
Clubs—Civic, Theta Delta Chi, Graduate of New York.
Societies—Colonial Wars, Sons of the Revolution, Mayflower Descendants.

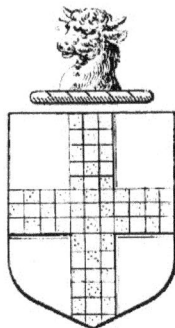

FRANCINE, ALBERT PHILIP,
of Phila. (Son of Albert Philip Francine
1841-79, *m* Anne French Hollingshead, a descd. of
John Hollingshead, Mem. of Assembly, N.J., 1683,
and Richd. Stockton of L.I. 1665; son of Jacques
Louis de Francine, Seigneur de Grandmaison,
Comte de Villepreux, *b* in France Feb. 29, 1786,
d Dec. 10, 1866, settled in New Jersey, *m* Catherine
Lohra; gt.-gt.-gt.-grandson of Francois de Francine, Seigneur de Grandmaison, Comte de Villepreux, who was successively Comisiare Genl. des
Guerres, Marechal de Bataille (1658), Major de la
ville de Paris (1660), Conseiller d'Etat, etc., and 9th in decent from
Giovanni Francini, of Florence, one of the " Prieurs de la Liberte,"
Florence. 1318).

Born at Phila. Dec. 8, 1873; A.B. Pa. Univ. 1894, A.M. Harvard Univ.
1895, M.D. Pa. Univ. 1898; Instructor in Medicine Pa. Univ., &c.

Arms—Azure, issuing from the sinister side an arm in armour holding in the
hand a cone between three fleur-de-lis or, an estoile of seven points in chief,
surmounted by a count's coronet of nine balls.

Residence—218 South 15th Street, Philadelphia, Pa.
Clubs—Rittenhouse, Huntingdon Valley Country.
Societies—Fellow Coll. of Physicians of Phila., Colonial Wars, Pennsylvania
Historical.

MORSE, WALDO GRANT,
of Yonkers, N.Y. (Son of Adolphus Morse,
of Rochester, New York, and Mary E. Grant,
sixth in descent from Christopher Grant, one
of the founders of Watertown, Massachusetts.—
Descended from Samuel Morse, who settled at
Dedham, Massachusetts, 1635; son of Rev. Thomas
Morse of Foxearth, Co. Essex, Will proved in
London, 1597).

Born at Rochester, New York, March 13, 1859;
Councillor-at-Law; Palisade Commissioner,
State of New York; *m* Adelaide, da. of
Albert Cook, of Seneca Falls, N.Y.

Arms—Argent, a battle-axe in pale proper between three pellets.
Crest—Two battle-axes in saltire proper banded with a chaplet of roses.
Motto—In Deo non armis fido.

Residence—Yonkers, New York.
Clubs—Lawyers, Reform, Quill, of New York City; Amackassin, Saegkill Golf,
of Yonkers.
Societies—Morse, Am. Academy of Political and Social Science, Am. Bar Assn.,
N.Y.S. Bar Assn., Bar Assn. of the City of New York, Colonial Wars, Sons
of the Revol., New Eng., Genesee, Rochester Alumni.

R HINELANDER, PHILIP,

of N.Y. City (Son of William Rhinelander, of N.Y., *b* Sept. 20, 1827, *m* Matilda C., da. of Hon. Thomas J. Oakley, Justice of the Superior Court, *m* Matilda C., da. of Henry Cruger, M.P., Mayor of Bristol, Eng., 1781; son of Lieut. William Christopher, 1790-1878, in Col. Steven's Regt. War 1812; son of William, 1753-1825, *m* Mary, sister of Col. Robert, on Gen. Washington's Staff, descd. from Daniel Robert a Huguenot who settled in America 1686 on the Revocation of the Edict of Nantes; son of William, 1718-77; son of Philip Jacob Rhinelander, *b* near Oberwesel, Germany, settled at New Rochelle, N.Y., 1686).

Born at Greenfield Hill, Ct., Oct. 8, 1864; Grad. Columbia Grammar School, 1882; *m* April 11, 1888, Adelaide B. Kip.

Issue.

i. Isaac L. Kip, *b* 1895, *d* infant.   iii. T. J. Oakley, *b* Sept. 20, 1898.
ii. Philip Kip, *b* Aug. 11, 1896.   iv. Leonard Kip, *b* May 9, 1903.
i. Adelaide Kip.

Arms—Argent, two anchors in fesse, flcok to flook, between a star of eight points in chief and three in base, within a bordure azure; the escutcheon surmounted by a crest coronet, a distinction granted to a few landed proprietors of the Rhine provinces.

Residence—32 East 39th Street, N.Y. City.   *Clubs*—Union, Delta Phi, Country. *Societies*—Colonial Wars, Sons of the Revol., War of 1812, St. Nicholas, Foreign Wars, Huguenot.

T HOMAS, ISAAC RAND,

of Boston (Son of Arthur Malcolm Thomas 1844-79, *m* Mary S. Sargent of Boston; son of Alexander 1802-74; son of Thomas K. 1771-1849; son of Alexander 1747-1800; son of Elias 1718-88; son of Peter, *b* 1682, *m* Elizabeth Burrows; son of George Thomas of Boston, 1660-70, *m* Rebecca Maverick).

Born at Dorchester, Mass., Oct. 5, 1864; *m* June 12, 1889, Gertrude Stuart, da. of George Francis Fabyan of Boston.

Issue.

i. Arthur Malcolm, *b* March 25, 1890.
i. Elizabeth Whitwell, *b* June 21, 1891.

Arms—Or, on a cross sable five crescents argent.
Crest—A greyhound's head couped argent.   *Motto*—Nec elatus, nec dejectus.

Residence—Boston, Massachusetts.
Clubs—Eastern Yacht, Union, Tennis and Racquet.

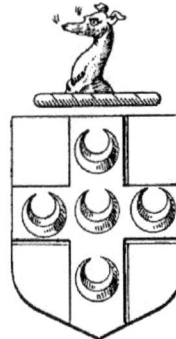

RUGGLES, CHARLES HERMAN,
of Milwaukee, Wis. (Son of Genl. George D.
Ruggles, Adj.-Genl. U.S.A., *b* Sept. 11, 1833, *m*
Jan. 1867 Alma H., da. of Stephen Satterlee and
Alma (Hammond) L'Hommedieu, of Cincinnati;
son of David, *b* 1783; son of Joseph, *b* 1757; son
of Capt. Lazarus 1730-97; son of Joseph, *b* 1701;
son of Rev. Benjamin 1676-1708; son of John of
Roxbury; son of John of Nasing, Essex, settled at
Roxbury, Mass., 1635; son of Thomas; son of
Nicholas; son of Thomas Ruggles of Sudbury,
Norfolk, Eng., *d* 1547).

Born at Omaha, Neb., Dec. 1, 1870; Grad. Ren.
Polytechnic Inst. C.E. 1892; *m* Dec. 3, 1895,
Virginia Cath., widow of Benj. H. Tyson, and
da. of Dr. R. H. and Cath. E. (Bailey) Cabell, of Richmond, Va.

Issue.

i. ANNA CHRISTIE. ii. ALMA L'HOMMEDIEU.

Arms—Argent, a chevron between three roses gules.

Crest—A tower or, inflamed ppr., transpierced with four arrows in saltire, points
downwards., argent. *Mottoes*—Struggle; Nec forte nec fato.

Residence—Milwaukee, Wis.

Societies—Colonial Wars, Descendants of Colonial Governors, Order of Runnemede, Order of The Constitution, Theta Zeta.

BENNETT, DANIEL COLLINS,
of Albany (Son of Thomas D. Bennett, of
Albany Co., N.Y., *b* 1812, and grandson of Daniel
Bennett, of Falfield, Gloucestershire, England,
came to America Feb. 14, 1782).

Born at Albany, N.Y., February 29, 1848;
m Eleanor, da. of Noel Earl Sisson.

Issue.

i. NOEL SISSON, *b* 1878.
i. EMELINE SISSON,
ii. ELIZABETH CAMPBELL.
iii. ELEANOR MARGARET.

Arms—Per bend dancettée argent and sable, a bend between two martlets
counterchanged.

Residence—88 Lancaster Street, Albany, N.Y.

Club—Fort Orange, Albany, N.Y.

RICHARDS, JEREMIAH,
of New York (Son of Jeremiah Richards,
1818-44, of Boston, Mass., *m* Lydia A. Peck; son of
John, 1781-1829; son of Ebenezer, 1744-84; son of
Ebenezer, 1718-99; son of James, 1683-1760; son
of Nathaniel, 1648-1726; son of Edward Richards,
from London to Boston in 1632, *d* Dedham, 1684,
m Susan Hunting. Also descd. from Degory Priest,
of London, who came in the " Mayflower," 1620).

Born at Boston, Mass., Oct. 1, 1844; *m* May 30, 1871,
Susan A., da. of Jacob Monfort, a descendant
of Peter Monfort, of Long Island, 1635.

Issue.

i. CHARLES SPIELMANN, *b* June 11, 1876, *m* Lida C. Darrah.
ii. WILLIAM STIGER, *b* Sept. 12, 1881.
i. ANNA, 1872-97, *m* Forest H. Parker, Jr. (*decd.*).
ii. HARRIET MONTFORT, *m* Geo. Stillman Ryer.
iii. ETHEL ADELAIDE.

Arms—Sable, a chevron between three fleurs-de-lis argent.
Crest—A griffin's head erased argent.

Residence—352 West 87th Street, N.Y. City.
Clubs—Un. Lea., Merchts., N.Y. Athletic, Columbia Yacht, Megantic Fish & Game.
Societies—Mayflower Descendants, Colonial Wars, War 1812, Sons of the Revo-
lution, American, New York, Long Island, and New Eng. Historical Socs.

TALCOTT, MARY KINGSBURY,
of Hartford, C. (Da. of Russell G. Talcott,
1818-63, Dir., Hartford Bank and Aetna Fire Ins.
Co., *m* 1846, Mary Seymour; son of Russell, 1788-
1818; son of George, 1755-1813; son of Col. Elezur,
1709-97; son of Ensign Benjamin, 1674-1727; son
of Capt. Samuel, *b* 1635; son of John Talcott, of
Cambridge, Mass., 1632; son of John, *d* 1604, of
Braintree, Essex, Eng.; son of John Talcott, of
Colchester, *d* 1606).

Born at Hartford; Registrar of the Connecticut
Society of the Colonial Dames of America;
Registrar of the Ruth Wyllys Chap. Daughters
of the American Revolution.

Arms—Argent, on a pale sable three roses of the field.
Crest—A demi-griffin argent, wing endorsed, gorged with a collar sable, charged
with three roses.

Residence—815 Asylum Avenue, Hartford, Connecticut.
Societies—Colonial Dames of America, Daughters of the American Revolution,
Connecticut Historical, American Historical, Mayflower Descendants,
Descendants of Colonial Governors of Connecticut.

BONNER, ROBERT EDWIN,
of New York (Eldest living son of Robert
Bonner, *b* Ramelton, Ireland, 1824, *d* 1899, Founder
and Editor of the *New York Ledger*, Pres. of the
Scotch-Irish Society, *m* Jane, 1829-78, da. of Adam
McCanlis; son of Andrew, 1783-1843, *m* Marian
Allen; son of William Bonner, of Castleshannon,
Donegal, Ireland).

Born at N.Y. City, July 26, 1854; Grad. at
Princeton Univ., A.B., A.M., 1876; *m* Oct. 20,
1880, Kate Helena, da. of Edward Griffith
by Anne, da. of Alfred Thomas, all of N.Y. City.

Issue.
i. GRIFFITH.
ii. COURTLANDT, *b* June, 1887, *d* June, 1889.
iii. HAMPTON.   iv. KENNETH.   i. KATE D'ANTERROCHES.

Arms—Quarterly, gules and sable, a cross pattée quarterly ermine and or; on a
chief of the last a demi-rose streaming rays, between two pelicans vulning
themselves of the first.
Crest—A talbot's head argent collared azure, studded edged and ringed or.
Motto—Semper fidelis.

Residence—563 Madison Avenue, N.Y. City.
Clubs—University, Metropolitan, Lotos, Princeton.

LATHROP, BRYAN,
of Chicago, Ill. (Son of Jedediah Hyde
Lathrop, *b* July 3, 1806, *d* 1889, *m* 1843,
Mariana, daughter of Daniel Bryan, of Alexandria,
Va., she died 1893.—Descended from Rev. John
Lathrop, Queen's College, Cambridge, 1605,
Clergyman of the Church of England, later
renounced his Orders and became Pastor of the
First Independent Church of London, 1623, was
subsequently imprisoned by Archbishop Laud, on
being released settled in New England, 1634, and
became the Minister of Barnstaple, Mass., 1639).

Born at Alexandria, Virginia, August 6, 1844;
m April 21, 1876, Helen, da. of Judge Asa
Owen Aldis, of Washington, D.C.

Arms—Gyronny of eight azure and gules, an eagle displayed argent.
Crest—A game cock proper.

Residences—77 Bellevue Place, Chicago; York Harbour, Maine.
Clubs—Century of New York: University, Chicago, Union, Washington Park,
Athletic, Onwentsia, Literary, Chicago Golf, Metropolitan, of Wash.

ALBRO, ADDIS, Rev., M.S., LL.B., DD.,
of Detroit, Mich. (Son of William Bliss
Albro, *b* May 2, 1800, *d* Aug. 31, 1879, *m* March 28,
1854, Ann Elizabeth Wood, *b* May 1, 1819, *d* Feb. 3
1878.—Descended from Major John Albro,
b England, 1617; *d* Portsmouth, Rhode Island,
Dec. 14, 1712; Colonial Militia, 1644-76; Member
Sir Edmund Andros' Council, 1686; Member
Council of War, 1676; in charge of Rhode Island
during King Philip's War, 1676; Member of
Committee 1679, to give true account to His
Majesty the King of the territory of Mt. Hope, and
of the late war with the Indians; also from Benedict
Arnold (Eldest son of William Arnold), first Gov.
of the Colony of Rhode Island, 1663-78; Member of Council of War, 1676;
m Dec. 17, 1640, Damaris, da. of Stukely Wescott; and from Hugh le
Bigod and Roger le Bigod, Sureties for the Observance of the Magna
Carta of King John, dated at Runnemede, June 15, O.S., 1215. Name
variously spelled in England, Aldborough, Aldburg, &c.).

Born at Middleburgh, N.Y., Feb. 18, 1855; Educator and Lecturer;
Clergyman Methodist Episcopal Ch.; *m* Feb. 19, 1878, Mary Alice
Scribner *b* April 6, 1859, *d* Aug. 12, 1905, daughter of Myron Eugene
and Mary (Kromer) Scribner, Schoharie, N.Y.; Coll. Pres. and Prof.,
1879-86; Pastor 1887-1900; Chaplain Michigan Military Academy,
1901-3; General Secretary American Reform Association since 1896;
Chaplain New York State Senate, 1893-94; Delegate to National
Republican Conventions in 1880 and 1900; Editor American Reform
Magazine.

Issue.

i. ADDIS BLISS, *b* March 22, 1879; Graduated from Wesleyan Univ.,
Middletown, Conn. (A.B.), 1899; *m* Elizabeth Alice Atkeison,
Dec. 19, 1901.

ii. AMES SCRIBNER, *b* Oct. 7, 1882; Sophomore (1902), in Wesleyan
Univ., Middletown, Conn.

iii. WARD SLOAN, *b* Sept. 27, 1889; Cadet Michigan Military Acad.,
Orchard Lake, Mich.

i. IVA DELL, *b* April 20, 1881; *d* May 24, 1883.

ii. RUTH.

Arms—Azure, a fesse argent between three cross-crosslets or.

Crest—An ibex passant or.

Residence—Detroit, Mich.

Club—Michigan.

Societies—Order of Runnemede, Colonial Wars, Sons of the Amer. Revolution,
Founders and Patriots of America, Mayflower Descendants, Descendants
of Colonial Governors, Mason, Knights Templar, A.A.S.R., Supreme
Council, 33°.

K ÜHNE, PERCIVAL,
of N.Y. City (Son of Frederick Kühne, *b* at
Magdeburg, Germany, a prominent banker of N.Y.
City, and for over sixteen years representative as
Consul-General of most of the German States,
m Josephine, da. of George J. Miller, of N.Y. Ci'y).

Born April 6, 1861 ; Mem. of Knauth, Nachod &
Kühne, Bankers ; Trustee and Mem. Exec.
Com., Colonial Trust Co., N.Y. ; Trustee,
Mutual Alliance Trust Co. ; Palisade Guaranty
and Trust Co. ; Citizens' Savings Bank ;
Lincoln Safe Deposit Company ; Colonial Safe
Deposit Company ; Empire Trust Company ;
Vice-Pres. and Dir. Regina Music Box Co. ;
Mem. N.Y. Chamber of Com'ce. ; *m* Jan. 31, 1893, Lillian Middleton,
da. of Hamilton Robinson and Emilie W. (Smith) Kerr.

Arms—Per fesse or and azure two cross swords in saltire points downwards and
an arrow in pale point upwards
Crest—Between a pair of eagle's wings cross swords and arrow as in Arms.

Residence—7 East 78th Street, N.Y. City.
Clubs—Union, Metropolitan, Union League, Calumet, Down Town Association.
Societies—Veteran Co. " K " 7th Regt. N.G.N.Y., Holland Lodge No. 8, F.A.M.,
N.Y. Botanical, N.Y. Zoological, Amer. Acad Political and Social Science,
Metropolitan Museum of Art.

H ENDRICK, Mrs. ELIZ'TH W. (*née* CAMPBELL),
of Washington, D.C. (Da. of Rev. Alex. W.
Campbell, 1803 - 48, of Chesterfield Co., Va.,
m Mary, 1805-45, da. of Dr. Bennett W'mson and
Eliz'th (Winston) Moseley, of Bedford Co., Va. ;
son of James Campbell, 1751-1814, of Tornavy,
Dunnen, Scot., *m* Marie Jean Victoire, 1769 1839,
da. of Colonel Pierre de la Porte [served in Wars of
Louis XV. and XVI.], of Toulouse, by Marianne, da.
of Count Francois Tu Bouef, of Normandy, France.
Also descd. from Lieut. William Winston, 1707-99,
son of Isaac and Mary D'Aubigne).

Born in Woodford Co., Ky., March 14, 1841 ;
m Aug. 7, 1861, Rev. Calvin Styles Hendrick,
of Bourbon Co., Ky., *b* March, 1838, *d* Sept.
14, 1865, son of the Rev. John Thilman and
Jane Elizabeth (Bigelow) Hendrick, of Richmond, Va.

Issue.
i. CALVIN WHEELER, *b* June 21, 1865, *m* Sarah Rebecca Herring.

Arms—(Campbell) Gyronny of eight or and sable, within a bordure of the first.
Crest—A lymphad with oars in action sable.
Motto—Set on.

Residence—1619 New Hampshire Avenue, N.W., Washington, D.C.
Societies—Daughters of the American Revolution, Colonial Dames of Virginia.

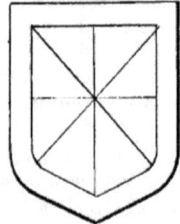

DAVIES, WILLIAM GILBERT,
of N.Y. City (Son of Judge Henry Ebenezer
Davies, 1805-81, *m* 1835, Rebecca Waldo, 1812-84,
da. of John Tappan, of Boston, Mass.—Descended
from John Davies, of Litchfield, Conn., 1735).

Born at N.Y. City, March 21, 1842 ; Counsellor at
Law ; Trinity Coll., Hartford, 1860 ; admitted
to the Bar 1863 ; LL.D., 1906 ; Lecturer of
Life Insurance Law in the University of the
City of New York ; *m* Dec. 15, 1870, Lucie
Carter, da. of the Hon. Alexander Hamilton
Rice, of Boston, Mass.

Issue.
i. Augusta McKim, *m* April 25, 1900, Louis Marsfield Ogden.

Arms—Quarterly, 1st and 4th, gules, on a bend argent a lion passant sable armed
and langued gules ; 2nd, argent, a lion rampant sable armed and langued
gules ; 3rd, or, a lion rampant gules armed and langued of the first.
Crest—A lion's head erased quarterly argent and sable langued gules.
Motto—Heb Dhuw heb ddym Dhuw a digon.

Residence—Tuxedo Park, New York.
Clubs—Union, Century, University, Liederkranz, Grolier, Tuxedo, Lawyers,
Manhattan, Democratic, Church, St. Nicholas.
Societies—Sons of Revolution, Colonial Wars, Colonial Order, New England,
Friendly Sons of St. Patrick ; Am. Bar Assn., N.Y.S. Bar Assn., etc.

SCHINDEL SAMUEL J. BAYARD, Capt. U.S.A.
(Son of Capt. Jeremiah P. Schindel 1839-94,
6th U.S. Infantry, *m* Martha Pintard da. of
Samuel John Bayard [descd. from Rev. Nicholas
Bayard of the Univ. de Paris, fled from Rochelle·
to Holland after the Revocation of the Edict of
Nantes, Cadet of the House of Bayard of
Picardie] ; son of Rev. Jeremiah Schindel 1807-
70, Chaplain in Mexican War 1845-47, and 110th
Regiment Pa. Vols. in Civil War ; son of Rev.
John Peter 1787-1853, in War of 1812 ; son of
Johann Peter 1766-1829 of Lebanon Pa. ; son
of Johann Peter 1732-84, from Airlebach, Prov.
Erbach Germany 1751, settled at Lebanon
Pa. ; son of Johann C., 1685-1752 ; son of Conrad
Von Schindel, 1678).

Born at Camden N.J., June 3, 1871 ; Grad. U.S. Mil. Academy West
Point (Artillery) 1893 ; 6th U.S. Infy. 1895 ; *m* Nov. 11, 1903, Isa
Urquhart, da. of John Thomas Glenn. of Atlanta Ga.

Arms—Gules, three shingles argent set in the form of a triangle.
Crest—Out of a crown or three shingles as in Arms within a wreath vert between
two wings gules.

Address—War Dept., Washington, D.C.
Societies—Society of Santiago, National Geographical.

FOWLER, THOMAS POWELL,

of N.Y. City (Son of Isaac S. Fowler, *b* 1822, *m* 1847, Mary Ludlow Powell--Descd. from Wm. Fowler, from London, Eng. to Boston, with Rev. John Davenport 1637, *d* 1660, 1st Magistrate of New Haven Ct.).

Born at Newburgh, N.Y., Oct. 26, 1851; Grad. Columbia Coll. Law Sch. LL.B. 1874; Pres. N.Y., O. and W.R.R.; Dir. A. T. and Santa Fe R.R.; Dir. Trust Co., N.Y.; Dir. N.Y. Life Insur. Co., &c.; *m* April 20, 1876 Isabelle Dunning.

Issue.

i. Benjamin D., *b* Oct. 26, 1892.   i. Ruth D.   iv. Alice D.
ii. Thomas P., Jr., *b* Feb. 24, 1893.   ii. Louisa O.   v. Katharine S.
iii. Augustus L., *b* July 20, 1896.   iii. Isabel W.   vi. Eleanor G.R.

Arms—Qtly., 1, az., on a chev. betw. three lions pass. guardt. as many crosses formée sa.; 2, per fesse arg. and sa., a lion rampt. counter-changed; 3, arg., a chev. betw. three bears' heads erased sa.; 4, arg., a fesse gu., in chief a label of four points az.

Crest—An owl argent ducally gorged or.   *Motto*—Watch and pray.

Residences—39 East 68th Street, New York City; Belair, Warwick, N.Y.
Clubs—Metropolitan, Grolier, Down Town, Tuxedo.
Society—Sons of the Revolution.

SOUTHER, CHARLES EDWARD,

of Montrose, S. Orange, N.J. (Son of Elbridge H. Souther, *b* 1813, *m* Mary D. Whittier; son of Moses, *b* 1788; son of Jonathan, *b* 1761; son of Samuel, *b* 1730; son of Samuel, *b* 1696; son of John, *b* 1660; son of Joseph Souther, of Boston, nephew of Nathaniel Souther [Souter], of Scrooby, Lincolnshire, Eng.; settled in New Eng., Clerk of Plymouth Colony, 1635-46).

Born at Haverhill, Mass., Aug. 16, 1844; Counsellor-at-Law, S.N.Y.; Grad. A.B. Harvard Univ. 1865; Columbia Law School, LL.B. 1869; Mem. Executive Committee, N.Y. Law Inst., elected Treasurer 1898; *m* June 30, 1877, Mary, da. of Tristam Burges, of Providence, R.I.

Issue.

i. Tristam Burges.
i. Marion Page.   ii. Eleanor Moore.

Arms—Azure, a chevron cotised argent.
Crest—A harpy guardant, wings displayed proper.

Residence—Montrose, South Orange, New Jersey.
Clubs—Union League, Essex County, Country of Orange, N.J.
Societies—New Eng. of N.Y., New Eng. of Orange, Down Town Assn. Bar Assn. of N.Y., American Economic Assn.

McLEAN, GEORGE HAMMOND,
of N.Y. City (Son of James Monroe McLean,
1818-90, *m* 1840 Louisa Theresa Williams; son
of Cornelius, *b* 1787, *m* Hannah Hammond; son
of Charles 1757-94; son of Charles 1714-59; son
of William McLean, 1679-1749, of McLean Island,
Stamford, Conn).

Born at N.Y. City, Nov. 24, 1849; Vice-Pres. of
Citizens' Insurance Co.; Director Manhattan
Life Ins. Co.; Trustee Manhattan Savings
Institution, &c.; Captain in the Old Guard;
m Nov. 21, 1878, Harriet Amelia, da. of Henry
Dater, of N.Y.

Issue.

i. JAMES CLARENCE HAMMOND, *b* Nov. 6, 1879.
ii. ALAN DATER, *b* Sept. 11, 1889.

Arms—Quarterly, 1st, argent, a lion rampant gules; 2nd, azure, a castle triple-
towered argent with flags displayed gules; 3rd, or, a dexter hand couped
fesseways gules holding a crosslet fitchée azure; 4th, or, a galley her sails
furled sable flag gules, on a sea vert a salmon naiant argent.
Crest—A battle-axe erect in pale, crossed by a branch of laurel and cypress in
saltire all proper.
Motto—Altera merces.
Residences—126 West 57th Street, N.Y.; McLean Island, on the Sound, near
Stamford, Ct.
Clubs—Metropolitan, Calumet, Players, N.Y. Athletic, Lambs, Suburban, Atlantic
Yacht.
Societies—St. Nicholas, S.A.R., M.M.A., A.M.N.H., S.P.C.A., Delta Psi.

BALDWIN, TOWNSEND BURNET,
of N.Y. City (Son of Hon. Harvey Baldwin,
b Ovid, N.Y., Feb. 4, 1797; *d* Syracuse, N.Y.,
Aug. 22, 1863; Grad. Clinton Coll.; Officer in War
of 1812; *m* Feb. 12, 1833, Ann Sarah, *b* Johnstown,
N.Y., Sept. 28, 1816, *d* Brooklyn, N.Y., Dec. 20,
1886, da. of Col. William Dodge, of Johnstown,
N.Y., and niece of Washington Irving.—Descended
from Captain Samuel Baldwin, of Windsor, Mass.,
1639).

Born at Syracuse, N.Y., July 2, 1846; served in
War of the Rebellion; Major on Major-General
Mott's Staff, N.G.S.N.J.; Hon. Mem. of the
Phila. City Troop and 7th Regt., N.G.S.N.Y.; Gov. of the Soc. of
Colonial Wars of N.J.; *m* Feb. 6, 1872, Mary Nismith, da. of Robert
James and Sarah (Parish) Dillon, of N.Y. City.

Arms—Gules, a griffin segreant or.
Crest—A lion rampant azure holding in the paws a cross crosslet fitchée, or.

Residence—Edgewater Park, N.J.
Clubs—Union, New York Yacht.
Societies—Colonial Wars of N.J., Sons of the Revolution of N.Y., Yorktown
Battalion of N.J., American Geographical Society.

G EER, WALTER,
of N.Y. City (Son of Asahel Clarke Geer of
Washington, D.C., 1823-1902, *m* 1856 Augusta,
da. of Keyes and Mary (Bushnell) Danforth, of
Williamstown, Mass. ; son of Walter, *b* 1792,
m Henrietta Van Buren, a cousin of Pres. Martin
Van Buren; son of Walter ; descendant of Thomas,
b 1623 ; son of Jonathan Geere, of Heavitree, Co.
Devon, Eng., came to Boston, 1635).

Born at Williamstown Aug. 19, 1857 ; Grad. at
Williams Coll. A.M. 1878 ; Law Sch., Nat.
Univ. LL.M. 1882 ; *m* Sept. 26, 1883, Mary,
da. of Orlando B. and Martha G. (Wiley)
Potter, of N.Y.

Issue.

i. OLIN POTTER, *b* Feb. 5, 1886.   i. MARTHA WILEY, 1887-88.
ii. WALTER, *b* May 27, 1889.   ii. HELEN DANFORTH.
iii. JOSEPH WHITE, *b* Jan. 9, 1892.

Arms—Gules, two bars argent each charged with three mascles of the first, on a
canton or a leopard's face azure.
Crest—A leopard's head erased proper ducally gorged or, langued gules between
two wings gules.   *Motto*—Non sans cause.

Residences—246 West 72nd Street, N.Y. City : "Crow's Nest," Ossining, N.Y.
Clubs—University, Manhattan. Lawyers, Strollers, Arts, Puritan (Boston), Art
(Philadelphia), Maryland (Baltimore).
Societies—New England, National Sculpture, Williams Alumni, Sons of the
Revol.. Municipal Art, Genealogical and Biographical, N.Y. Historical.

B REWSTER, HARRY LANGDON,
of Rochester, N.Y. (Son of William W.
Brewster, of New York City, and Julia Ann Noyes,
d Aug. 27, 1869.— Descended from William
Brewster, 1566-1644, Elder of Plymouth Colony,
1630, who drafted the Mayflower Compact).

Born at N.Y. City, Jan. 5, 1850 ; *m* June 29, 1875,
Harriet Augusta, daughter of Junius Judson, of
Rochester, N.Y., and Lavenda, daughter of
Thomas Bushnell and Nancy Blood.

Issue.

i. GWENDOLYN LAVENDA JUDSON.

Arms—Sable, a chevron ermine between three estoils
argent ; impaling (for Judson) per saltire azure and ermine four lozenges
counterchanged.
Crest—A bear's head erased sable.
Motto—Verité soyez ma garde.
Arms—(BUSHNELL)—Argent, five fusils in fesse gules, in chief three mullets sable.
Crest—On a ducal coronet a wivern sans feet.   *Motto*—Dum spiro spero.

Residence—408 East Avenue, Rochester, N.Y.
Clubs—Genesee Valley, Country (Rochester), Republican (N.Y. City).
Society— Sons of the American Revolution.

PELL, HOWLAND,
of N. Y. City (Son of Wm. Howland Pell, b
1833, m Adelaide, da. of Benj. and Anna M.
(Schieffelin) Ferris, of N. Y.; son of Morris Ship-
ley Pell, 1810-81; son of Wm. Ferris Pell, 1779-
1841; son of Benjamin, d 1828; son of Joshua, d
1781; son of Thomas, d 1739; son of Major John
Pell, 1643-1702, 2nd Lord of Pelham Manor, N.Y.,
1669, styled Sir John Pell in the New Rochelle
Town Records, and of Rachael Pinckney; First
Justice C. of Comm. Pleas, 1688, and First Mem.
of the Genl. Assly., 1691-95, for Westchester Co.,
N.Y., on Comm. for Defence of frontier and Chairman of the Grand Comm., Capt. of Horse, 1684,
Maj. 1692, French Ind. War. Only son of Rev.
and Rt. Hon. John Pell, D.D., F.R.S. [1611-85;
Grad. Trinity Coll., Camb., 1630, and Ithamar Reginoills. Dr. Pell
invented the sign ÷ for division, was apptd. Profr. at Breda by Prince of
Orange, and coat-of-arms placed in City Hall of Harlaem; Cromwell
apptd. him Min. Res. to Switzerland, 1654-58; at the Restoration took
Holy Orders, 1661, and held the livings of Fobbing, Laindon, and Orset
in Essex. Was one of the first F.R.S., Eng., 1663; took deg. D.D.,
Lambeth, being Domestic Chap. to Archbp. Canterbury; his private and
public papers are preserved in the "Pell Papers" British Museum; used
coat-of-arms borne by his American descdts.; was son of Rev. John Pell,
d 1616, Rector of Southwick, Sussex, and Mary Holland, and he in turn
of another John Pell, descended from the ancient Lincolnshire family
[Biog. Brit. Dic. Natl. Biog., Lee, London, 1895; Woods Fasti, Oxon,
1691, Bolton's Hist. Westchester Co., N.Y. State Records, &c.]).

Born at Flushing, L.I., Mar. 19, 1856; Stud. Sch. Mines, Columbia
Coll., 1876; Vet. Comps. "I," "K," 7th Regt. N.G.S.N.Y.; 2nd
Lt. Co. "E"; 1st Lt. Co. "G"; Capt. Co. "A" 12th Regt.
N.G.S.N.Y.; Dep. Gov. Gen. Soc. Colonial Wars; m Apr. 12, 1887,
Almy Goelet*, da. of Fred. and Almy G. (Gerry) Gallatin, of N.Y.

Issue,

i. HOWLAND GALLATIN, b Aug. 17, 1889.

i. GLADYS AMY HOWLAND.

Arms—Ermine, on a canton azure a pelican or, vulned gules.

Crest—On a chaplet vert flowered or, a pelican of the last vulned gules.

Motto—Deus amici et nos.

(Arms granted October 19 1594.—Richard Lee, Clarenceux.)

Residence—450 Madison Avenue, New York City.

Clubs—Union Tuxedo, New York Yacht.

Societies—Colonial Wars, War of 1812, St. Nicholas, New York Historical,
*Colonial Dames of America.

PORTER, ALEXANDER SYLVANUS.
 of Boston (Son of John K. Porter, 1808-85, *m*
Mary P. Robertson, *d* 1848; son of Sylvanus
1778-1821; son of Jonathan 1732-91; son of
Joseph *d* 1750; son of Thomas 1671/2-1754; son
of Thomas, *d* 1671-2; son of Richard Porter, from
Weymouth, Eng., to New Eng. 1635. Also descd.
on the maternal side from Duncan de Atholia 1st
Laird of Strowan, *b* 1275).

Born at Coalsmouth, Va., Aug. 25, 1840; Pres. of
   Boston Real Estate Exchange; Boston Lease-
   hold Co.; Vice-Pres. Beacon Society; *m* (1)
   April 27, 1865, Mary O. Cushing; *m* (2) April
   24, 1879, Frances W. Cushing.

Issue.
i. James O., *b* Feb. 25, 1870, *m* Mabel Ballou.
ii. Alexander S., Jr., *b* Feb. 6, 1873.
i. Mary O.   ii. Katharine C.   iii. Elizabeth S.   iv. Frances R.

Arms—Argent, on a fesse sable between two barrulets or, three bells of the first.
Crest—A portcullis argent chained or.   *Motto*—Vigilantia et virtute.

Residences—22 Brimmer Street, Boston, Mass., and Campobello, N.B.
Clubs—Union, Algonquin Country, Essex County, Chestnut Hill Golf, Salem
   Athletic, Exchange, Eastern Yacht, Campobello Golf.
Societies—Bostonian, Beacon, Associated Board of Trade.

BOARDMAN, ALBERT BARNES,
 of N.Y. City (Only son of Norman Boardman,
of N.Y. City, *d* 1873, *m* Anne Waldron, da. of
Thomas and Elizabeth (Waldron) Williams, of
New York City; son of Capt. Jason, of Rocky
Hill Ct.; son of Capt. John; son of Lieut. Johnathan; son of Lieut. Johnaihan Boreman, of
Weathersfield Ct.; son of Samuel Boreman (Boardman), of Claydon, near Banbury, Oxford, Eng.,
settled at Ipswich, Mass., 1641).

Born at New York City, Feb. 26, 1853; Lawyer;
   Graduated at Yale Univ. B.A., 1873; *m* 1876,
   Georgina Gertrude, da. of John and Mary
   (Sewell) Bonner.

Issue.
i. Sydney Sewell, *b* 1878.   i. Mary Cecil.
ii. Philip Waldron, *b* 1883.   ii. Geraldine May.

Arms—Argent, a chevron vert bordured gules.
Crest—A lion sejant, collared and lined or.

Residences—40 West 53rd Street, N.Y. City; "Idle Wild," Southampton, L.I.
Clubs—University, Union League, Manhattan, N.Y. Athletic, Garden City of
   Southampton.

CLINTON, CHARLES WILLIAM,
　　of New York City (Son of Alexander
Clinton, M.D., Lt. U.S.A. War of 1812, m
Adeline A., da. of Capt. Alex. J. Hamilton, of
Innerwick, Scot., 18th in descent from John, son
of Sir Wm. de Hamilton, *temp.* King David
Bruce ; son of Charles ; son of Brig.-Gen.
Jaures, in War of Revol., whose bro. George
was Brig.-Gen., 1st Gov. of N.Y., and twice
Vice-Prest. of U.S.; sons of Charles Clinton,
who came to America, 1729, whose ancestor,
William, was descd. from Sir Henry Clinton, son
of the 2nd Earl of Lincoln).

Born at N.Y. City, Nov. 9, 1836; Vice-Pres. N.Y.
　　Chap., American Inst. of Archts. ; 1st Sergt.
　　" K " Co. 7th Regt. N.Y.S.N.G. 1863 ; vet. of " K " Co. 7th Regt. :
　　m Aug. 25, 1886, Emily de Silver Gorsuch.

Issue.

i. CHARLES KENNETH, *b* Nov. 18, 1889.　　　i. MARGERY HAMILTON.
ii. DE WITT, 1893-96.

Arms—Argent, six crosses crosslet fitchée sable ; on a chief azure two mullets
　　pierced or.
Crest—Out of a coronet gules five ostrich feathers argent, banded azure.
Motto—Patria cara carior libertas.

Residence—39 East 57th Street, New York City.
Clubs—Century, New York Yacht, Tuxedo, Rockaway Hunt, etc.
Societies—Amer. Inst. of Architects, Soc. of Amer. Artists, Architectural League,
　　Municipal Art. Soc.

WEED, JOHN,
　　of New York City (2nd son of Rufus Weed,
of Noroton, Conn., *b* March 7, 1802, *d* May 30, 1883,
m Feb. 25, 1831, Phebe, *b* Nov. 10, 1805, *d* April 10,
1867, da. of John and Sarah (Fancher) Clock, of
Noroton, Conn. ; son of Benjamin Weed, soldier in
War of the Revolution.—Descended from Jonas
Weed, *b* at Stanwich, Northamptonshire, England,
settled at Watertown, Mass., 1631, and Wethersfield, Ct., 1635).

Born at Noroton, Conn., Jan. 27, 1839.

Arms—Argent, two bars gules in chief three martlets
　　sable.
Crest—A martlet sable.

Residences—4th Avenue and 17th Street, New York City ; Noroton, Conn.
Club—New England.

DRAPER, WILLIAM FRANKLIN,
of Washington, D.C. (Son of George Draper,
of Hopedale, Mass., 1817-87, by Hannah, 1817-83,
da. of Benj. and Anna (Mowry) Thwing, of
Uxbridge, Mass.; son of Ira; son of Major Abijah;
Revol. War; son of Capt. James, French and Ind.
Wars; son of James Draper; son of Thomas
Draper, of Heptonstall, Yorks., to America 1647).

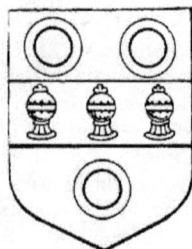

Born at Lowell, Mass., April 9, 1842; served in
U.S.A. from 2nd Lt. to Brig.-Gen. inclusive;
wounded in Battle of the Wilderness; Mem. of Congress, Foreign
Affairs Committee; U.S Ambassador to Italy; Hon. D.L. Washington
and Lee Univs.; Grand Cordon of St. Maurice and Lazare; *m* (2)
May 22, 1890, Susan, da. of Maj.-Gen. Wm. Preston, Co. Army, Mem.
of Congress, U.S. Min. to Spain, of Lexington, Ky.

Issue.
(*By 1st m.*)
i. WILLIAM FRANKLIN Jr., *b* Dec. 17, 1865.
ii. GEORGE OTIS, *b* July 14, 1867.
iii. ARTHUR JOY, *b* Apl. 28, 1876, *m* Lily Duncan Voorhies.
iv. CLARE HILL, *b* Oct. 4, 1876.   i. EDITH *m* Montgomery Blair.
(*By 2nd m.*)   i. MARGARET PRESTON.

Arms—Or, on a fesse betw. three annulets gules, as many covered cups of the field.

Residences—" K " Street and Conn. Ave., Washington, D.C.; Hopedale, Mass.
Clubs—Metropolitan, Chevy Chase, Army and Navy (Washington), Union,
      Athletic, New Algonquin (Boston).
Societies—Sons of the Revol., Founders and Patriots, Loyal Legion, Colonial Wars.

SHEPARD, CHARLES NELSON,
of Grand Rapids, Michigan (Son of Ralph
Shepard.—Descended from the Rev. Thomas
Shepard, *b* at Towcester, Northants, England, 1605,
matriculated at Emanuel Coll., Cambridge Univ.,
Minister at Earl's Colne, Co. Essex, settled in
Cambridge, Mass.).

Born at Herkemer, New York, Nov 13, 1836;
m Helen Anna, daughter of William Bell
Ledyard.

i. CHARLES WILLIAM.
ii. HARRY LEDYARD.
i. HELEN LOUISE.

Arms—Gules, three battle-axes or, a chief ermine.
Crest—Two battle-axes in saltire or.   *Motto*—Nec timeo, nec sperno.

Residence—Grand Rapids, Michigan.

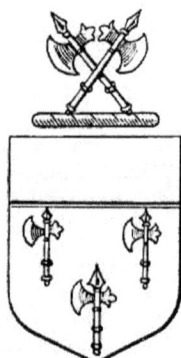

LIVINGSTON, PHILIP,
of Morristown (Son of Livingston Livingston,
d 1872, m Mary Celia Livingston ; son of Philip ;
son of Philip P. ; son of Philip [Signer of Declaration of Independence] ; son of Philip ; son of Col.
Philip [2nd Lord of Livingston Manor] ; son of
Col. Robert [1st Ld. of L.M.] ; son of Rev. John of
Ancrum, Scotland ; son of Rev. William and Agnes
Livingston, of Mony-a-brook).

Born at N.Y. City, Nov. 9, 1861 ; Grad. Harvard
Univ. A.B., 1884 ; LL.B. Columbia Law Sch.,
1887 ; Vice-Comdr. Harvard Canoe Club, 1883 ;
Comdr. Mt. Desert Canoe Club, 1891-95, 1896 ;
Veteran and Hon. Mem. Co. " K " 7th Regt.
N.G.N.Y. ; Lieut. of 10th Co. 7th Regt. Veterans, 1899 ; Gov.
Soc. of Colonial Wars, 1893 ; Steward, 1899, etc. ; m April 16,
1890, Juliet B. Morris.

Arms—Qrtly., 1 and 4 arg., three gilly flowers gu. within a dble. tres. flory co.-flory ;
2, qtly., 1 and 4 gu., on a chev. arg. a rose betw. two lions pass. combat.
arg. ; 2 and 3 az., three martlets or ; 3, sa., a bend betw. six billets or.
Crest—A demi-savage ppr., wreathed head and middle with laurel, in the dexter
hand a club, and in sinister a serpent vert.   Motto—Si je puis.

Residences—992 Fifth Av., N.Y. City ; "Oak Dell," Madison Av., Morristown, N.J.
Clubs—Metropolitan of New York, Morristown, Morris County Golf.
Societies—Colonial Wars, St. Nicholas, Sons of the Revolution, St. Andrews.

HILLHOUSE, JAMES,
of N.Y. City (Son of William Hillhouse,
b Nov. 22, 1820, and Francis Julia, m Jan. 18,
1854, da. of Hon. Samuel Rossiter Betts, Judge
U.S. District Court for S. Dist., N.Y., and Caroline
Abigail Dewey, his wife.—Descended from Rev.
James Hillhouse, b 1687, of Montville, Conn.,
1721, d 1740, M.A. Glasgow Univ., Ordained
1717, m Mary, da. of Capt. Daniel Fitch ; son of
John Hillhouse, of Free Hall, Co. Londonderry,
Ireland, and grandson of Abraham Hillhouse, of " Artikelly," who was
in the City of Londonderry during the siege).

Born at New Haven, Conn., Nov. 19, 1854 ; Graduated at Yale Univ.,
1875 ; m Oct. 3, 1894, Hildegarde, da. of Albert Speyers, of N.Y. City.

Arms—Sable, a chevron between, in chief a lion rampant on the dexter side, and
a unicorn on the sinister, between them a star of five points facing each
other in the base a human heart surrounded by three bezants.

Motto—Time Deum.

Residence—Sachem's Wood, New Haven, Conn.

Clubs—University, Church. Association of the Bar of N.Y. City, Country Club,
Quinnipiack, Graduates' Club of New Haven.

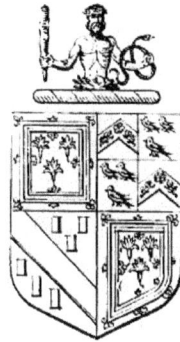

HAYES, HARRY E.,
of Cleveland, O. (Son of William J. Hayes,
b Oct. 11, 1837, Banker, *m* Sarah J., 1840-87, da.
of George P. Burwell 1817-91, one of the original
" Prohibitionists of Ohio," nominated for Governor
of Ohio, descended from John Burwell, who came
to America from Hemel Hempsted, Herts, Eng.,
and was made a Free Planter, settled in Wepawang
(now Milford), Ct., 1639. A part of the township
is known by the name of " Burwell's Farm." Also
descended from John Hayes, the discoverer of copper in the Lake
Superior region, and Manager of the first Copper Mine, " Cliff ").

Born at Cleveland, O., June 6, 1860 ; Vice-Pres., Nat. Arts Club, N.Y. ;
m Nov. 27, 1888, Grace Lucretia, da. of Hoyt H. and Julia (Moore)
Green, of St. Louis.

Issue.

i. HOYT ELMORE, *b* Feb. 27, 1890.   i. HELEN.
ii. WARWICK JAMES, *b* Nov. 17, 1892.
iii. KENNETH LINTON, *b* Sept. 16, 1894.

Arms—(Burwell) Argent, a lion rampant sable, ducally crowned or, charged with
eight roundels argent.

Residence—1500 Euclid Avenue, Cleveland, Ohio.
Clubs—National Arts of N.Y., Union, Roadside, Golf, Tippecanoe, Political.
Societies—Sons of the American Revolution, Arts Societies of Cleveland, Ohio.

ALDIS, OWEN FRANKLIN,
of Chicago, Illinois (Son of the late Judge Asa Owen Aldis, of
Washington, D.C.—Descended from John Aldis, who was born in England,
came to America with his father, married Sarah Eliot, daughter of Philip
Eliot, from Nazing, Co. Essex, in ship " Hopewell." and niece of the
" Apostle " Eliot ; son of Deacon Nathan (and Mary) Aldis, yeoman,
supposed to have come from Norwich, Co. Norfolk, England, 1636, settled
in Dedham, Mass., 1638, *d* 1676).

Born at St. Alban's, Vt., June 6, 1853 ; Graduated at Yale University,
1874 ; Director of the World's Columbia Exposition, Chicago, 1892-93 ;
m Leila, *d* April 10, 1887, daughter of William Dezang Houghteling.

Issue.

i. OWEN WILLIAM.

Residences—77 Bellevue Place, Chicago ; York Harbour, Maine.

Clubs—Union, Chicago Athletic, Chicago University, Literary, Chicago Golf,
Union League, Ontwentsia, Caxton, University of N.Y., Century of N.Y.,
Metropolitan of Washington.

A MORY, CHARLES WALTER,
of Boston, Mass. (Second Son of William
Amory 1804-88, of Boston, *m* Anna Powell Grant,
1813-95, da. of Hon. David and Miriam (Mason)
Sears of Boston; son of Thomas C. 1767-1812,
m Hannah R. Lingee; son of Thomas 1722-84,
m Elizabeth Coffen; son of Thomas Amory
1682-1728, who settled in Boston 1720, *m* 1721
Rebecca Holmes).

Born in Boston, Mass., Oct. 16, 1842; Grad.
Harvard Univ., A.B., 1863; served as Captain,
2nd Mass. Cavalry, War of the Rebellion;
Trea. of the Amoskeag Cotton Mills, Manchester, N.H.; *m* Oct. 23, 1867, Elizabeth,
da. of George and Helen M. (Read) Gardner of Boston.

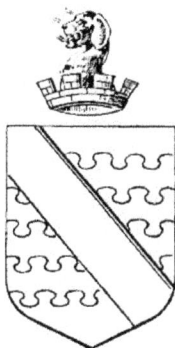

Issue.

i. WILLIAM (2nd), *b* Sept. 19, 1869.
ii. GEORGE GARDNER, *b* June 22, 1874.
i. CLARA, *m* Thomas Jefferson Coolidge, Jr.   ii. DOROTHY.

Arms—Barry nebuly of six argent and gules, a bend azure.
Crest—Out of a mural coronet or, a talbot's head azure, eared of the first.
Motto—Tu ne cede malis.

Residences—278 Beacon Street, Boston, Mass.; "Mosquito Hut," Wareham, Mass.
Clubs—Somerset, Country, Eastern Yacht, Exchange.
Societies—Army of the Potomac, Military Order of the Loyal Legion, Humane.

C HRYSTIE, WILLIAM FEW,
of Hastings-on-H., N.Y. (Son of Albert
Chrystie, *m* 1822, Frances, da. of Col. William
Few, of N.Y., U.S. Sen. from Geogia, one of the
framers of the U.S. Constitution, and grand-da. of
Capt. James Nicholson, 1737-1804, Senior Officer
U.S. Navy, War of Revol.; son of Major James
Chrystie, *b* in Edinburgh, Scotland, 1750, Lieut. in
U.S. Army in Revol. War, *d* 1807).

Born at Fishkill Landing, N.Y., July 5, 1823;
Columbia Coll., 1839-40; Harvard Law Sch.,
Mass., 1842; *m* Jan. 11, 1855, Emily Harvey,
da. of Western B. Thomas, of Augusta, Ga.

Issue.

i. WILLIAM, *b* July 6, 1859.
ii. FRANCIS FEW.
i. EMILY, *m* Oct. 23, 1884, Prof. M.M. Curtis, of Cleveland, O.
ii. MARY CATH., *m* Oct. 7, 1896, C. de Witt Cochrane, of N.Y.

Arms—Argent, a chevron between three wells sable.
Crest—A phoenix rising out of flames proper.   *Motto*—Malo mori quam foedari.

Residences—Hastings-on-Hudson, N.Y.; Sand Hills, Ga.; and Greenport, L.I.
Clubs—Union, N.Y. City; Ardsley Country, Town Ridge Yacht, Hastings.

PLUMB, HENRY BLACKMAN,
of Warrior Run, Pa. (Son of Charles Plumb, 1802-31, *m* Julia A., 1806-89, da. of Elisha and Anna (Hurlbut) Blackman ; son of Jacob ; son of Jacob ; son of Waitstill J. ; son of Joseph ; son of John ; son of Robert ; son of John, of Ridgewell Hall, Essex, Eng., one of the first settlers of Wethersfield, Conn., 1635 ; son of Robert, gent., *d* 1628 ; son of Robert, yeo., *d* 1613 ; son of John Plumbe, of Gt. Yeldham, Essex, England).

Born at Hanover, Pa., Nov. 13, 1829 ; Counsellor-at-Law ; *m* (1) 1851, Emma L., 1835-59, da. of Ashbel and Angelina (Bennett) Ruggles ; *m* (2) April 24, 1900, Edith M., da. of William G. and Elizabeth (Selby) Green.

Issue.

i. GEORGE H. R., *b* June 12, 1854, *m* 1887, Mary E. Van Buskirk.
i. MARTHA, *b* and *d* Dec. 12, 1852.

Arms—Ermine, a bend vairé or and gules cotised vert.
Crest—Out of a ducal coronet or, a plume of four ostrich feathers argent.

Residence—Warrior Run, Luzerne Co., Penna. (P.O., Peely).
Societies—Mayflower, Colonial Wars, Sons of the American Revolution.

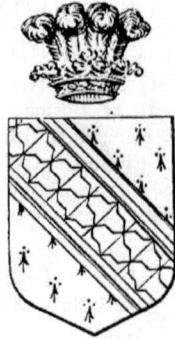

STOCKBRIDGE, HENRY,
of Baltimore (Son of Henry S. Stockbridge 1822-95, *m* 1852, Fanny E., da. of Caleb Montague of Sunderland Mass ; son of Jason 1780-1860, *m* Abigail Montague ; son of David 1749-1832, *m* Patience Bartlett ; son of Samuel, *b* 1711, *m* Sarah Tilden ; son of Samuel, *b* 1679, *m* Lydia Barrell ; son of Charles 1634-84 ; son of John Stockbridge, 1608-57, in ship " Blessing " to New Eng., 1635).

Born at Baltimore Sept 18, 1856 ; Grad. Amherst Coll. 1877 ; Law Dep. Maryland, Univ. 1878 ; Mem. of Congress 1889-91 ; Commissioner Immigration 1891-93 ; Assoc. Judge Supreme Bench Balto. 1896 ; *m* Jan. 5, 1882, Helen Maria, da. of Chester Smith of Hadley Mass.

Issue.

i. HENRY, *b* Dec. 21, 1885.　　　　ii. ENOS SMITH, *b* May 3, 1888.

Arms—Argent, on a chevron azure three crescents or.
Crest—Out of a cloud two dexter hands in armour conjoined, holding up a heart inflamed all proper.

Residence—11 N. Calhoun Street, Baltimore, Md.
Societies—Md. Hist., Am. Hist., Col. Wars, Sons of the Revolution, etc.

CROSS, ARTHUR DUDLEY,
of San Francisco (Son of Wm. Berry Cross
1826-91 of San F., *m* 1858 Mary A. 1829-95, da. of
George and Abigial (Ricker) Hilton of Parsonfield,
Me.; son of Samuel, *b* 1789, *m* (1) Abigial Richardson, *m* (2) Hannah Barrey; son of Abijah 1758-1848,
served in Rev. War, *m* (1) Elizabeth Parker, *m* (2)
Hannah Foster; son of Wm. of Metheun; son of
William; son of John Cross of Metheun, Mass.,
from England in "Elizabeth" of Ipswich 1634, one
of the proprietors of Hampton Mass. 1638).

Born at Sacramento Cal. Dec. 14, 1864; Grad.
Univ. of Cal. B.S. Class of 1887; *m* May 15,
1893, Elsie Chapline, da. of Thos. Bailey and
Josephine I. (Chapline) Pheby of Oakland, Cal.

Issue.

i. ARTHUR D., *b* April 24, 1898.
i. ELSIE HILTON.

Arms—Sable, a fesse between three mullets argent pierced gules.
Crest—A tower argent from the top flames of fire issuing.

Residence—1719 Broderick Street, San Francisco, Cal.
Societies—Colonial Governors, Sons of the American Revolution.
Club—Zeta Psi Fraternity.

DAVIS, JOSEPH,
of Denver, Col. (Eldest son of William
Davis, of Boston, 1801-65, *m* (2), 1839, Maria,
1817-70, da. of Charles and Harriet (Fellowes)
Davis, of Roxbury, Massachusetts; son of William,
1770-1850; son of Moses, 1744-1823; son of Aaron,
1709-77; son of Ebenezer, 1678-1712; son of
William Davis, of Roxbury, Mass., *d* 1683, aged
66 years).

Born at Boston, Nov. 24, 1840; 1st Lieut. and
Adjt. 30th Regt. Mass. Vet. Infy. Vols; Chair-
man of Council of City of Trinidad, Col.; Pres.
of Bank of Southern Colorado; Chancellor of
Commandery of State of Col., Mil. Order,
Loyal Legion of U.S.; Grad. at English High Sch., Boston, 1858;
m Sept. 4, 1874, Sarah Aug., da. of Abijah Davis, of Middlesex Co.,
N. J., and Jerseyville, Ill.

Issue.

i. JOSEPH SWALLOW, *b*. Sept. 10, 1875, *m* June 6, 1900, Edith Wight.

Arms—Gules, a griffin segreant or.   *Crest*—A griffin segreant or.

Residences—Boston, Roxbury and W. Medford, Mass.; Trinidad, and Denver, Col.
Societies—Loyal Legion, Sons of the Revolution, Army of the Potomac, 19th
Army Corps, Grand Army of the Republic.

S PITZER, CEILAN MILO, Brig.-Gen.,
of Toledo, O. (Son of Aaron B. Spitzer
1823-92, m (1) Laura M. Perkins, m (2) Anna M.
Collins; son of Dr. Nicholas de Spitzer 1783-1868,
m Nancy Bovee; son of Dr. Garret de Spitzer
1758-1801, m Annatje Sixbury; son of Dr. Er-
nestus, 1709-89, from Heilbronn, Wurtemburg, to
Phila. 1747, settled in Schenectady, served in
French and Indian War, m Barbara Wilfelin.—
Descended from the knightly family of Von
Spitzers in Lower Steiermarke, Germany).

Born at Batavia, N.Y. Nov. 2, 1849; estab. 1871
the Seville Exch. Bank, 1878 German-Amer.
Bank of Cleveland, 1881 Spitzer & Co.
(Bankers) Toledo and N.Y.; Director Ohio
Savings Bank and Trust Co., Security Trust
Co., W. and L.E.R.R. Co.; Pres. of Spitzer
Bdg. Co.; Quartermaster-Gen. of Ohio 1900; m 1884 Lilian Cortez,
da. of Alex. McDowell, cousin of Gen. Irvine McDowell.

Arms—Party per pale azure and or, a nude woman ppr. on a mound vert in the
dexter hand a star or, the sinister on her hip; impaling (McDowell) azure,
a lion ramp. argent crowned or, on a canton arg. three piles gules.
Crest—A nude woman affronté holding two proboscides couped issuing from a
helmet crowned.   *Motto*—Ingenio ac labore.

Residence—Toledo, Ohio.   *Clubs*—Toledo, Country, Middle Bass.
Society—Ohio of N.Y.

R ICHMOND, ADELBERT GILLETT (*deceased*),
of Canajoharie (Son of Roswell Wells,
Richmond, 1813-72, m Caroline D. Hart; son of
Roswell, b 1787; son of Rev. Benjamin, b 1750;
son of Edward, b 1723; son of Benjamin, b 1695;
son of Edward, b 1658; son of Capt. Edward,
b 1632; son of John Richmond, 1594-1664, from
Ashton Keynes, Wilts., Eng., to Taunton, Mass.,
1635).

Born at De Ruyter, N.Y., 1838; Pres. Canajoharie
Nat. Bank and Farmers' and Mechanics' Bank,
Fort Plain, N.Y.; Hon. Curator of Archæo-
logical Dept., Univ. N.Y., m March 15, 1883,
Helen A. Weaver. He died Nov. 13, 1899.

Issue.

i. Emily Adele.

Arms—Argent, a cross patonce azure between four mullets gules.
Crest—A tilting spear argent headed or broken in three parts one piece erect,
the other two in saltire, enfiled with a ducal coronet of the last.
Motto—Resolve well and persevere.

Residences—(Family) Syracuse, New Woodstock, Chittenango, Mohawk, Canajoharie, of New York State; and Washington D.C.

ONDERDONK, ANDREW JOSEPH,
of Brooklyn (Son of Hon. Horatio G.
Onderdonk, 1808-86, Judge of the Court of
Common Pleas under the former Constitution of
the State of N.Y., of N. Hempstead, L.I., *m* 1830,
Elizth. Schenck Onderdonk; son of Joseph of N.
Hempstead, L.I., 1766-1852, *m* Dorothy Montfort;
son of Adrian, 1726-94, *m* Maria Hegeman; son of
Andries, 1686-1758, *m* Gertrude Lott; son of
Andries, *m* Maria Van Der Vliet; son of Dr. Adrian
Van Der Donk *b* in Holland (Province of Breda),
resident of Amsterdam 1656, Grad. LL.D. Univ.
of Leiden, came to the New Netherlands, 1656,
wrote "History of the New Netherlands ").

Born at Manhasset, L.I., March 23, 1847; Grad. of Albany Law School;
called to the Bar May 4, 1868; *m* Oct. 12, 1880 Annie L., da. of
Saml. H. and Louise (Ketteltas) Frost, State Senator, 1870-71, of
Staten Island N.Y.

Arms—Argent, a lion rampant sable.
Crest—A royal helmet proper wreathed argent and sable.

Residences—171 Park Place, Brooklyn, N.Y.; and Manhasset, L.I.
Clubs—Lawyers, Riding and Driving, Atlantic Yacht, Manhasset Yacht.
Societies—St. Nicholas, Holland, Long Island Historical, N.Y. Genealogical.

PARSONS, ALBERT ROSS,
of Garden City, L.I., N.Y. (Son of Brev
Lt.-Col. and Elder John J. Parsons, 1827-94, of
N.Y., *m* 1846, Sarah Volinda Averill, of Buffalo;
son of Aaron, 1797-1866; son of Aaron, 1761-1815;
son of Aaron, 1736-99; son of Aaron, 1712-95; son
of Daniel, 1685-1774; son of Capt. Joseph, 1647-
1729; son of Cornet Joseph Parsons, 1618-83, of
Springfield, Mass., *m* Mary Bliss, of Hartford, Ct.).

Born at Sandusky, O., Sept. 16, 1847; Studied at
Leipsic and Berlin, 1867-72; Pres. Am. Coll.
of Musicians, Univ. of N.Y.; elected at the
International Congress of Musicians, Colum-
bian World's Fair, Chicago, 1893; author of
" Parsifal, or the Finding of Christ through
Art"; Wagner's " Beethoven," " New Light
from the Great Pyramid," etc.; *m* April 23, 1874, Alice E. da. of
Cornelius H. Van Ness, of N.Y.

Arms—Gules, a leopard's head between three crosses pattée fitchée argent.
Crest—A halbert, headed argent, embrued gules.

Residence—Garden City, Long Island, N.Y.   Club—National Arts.
Societies—N.Y. Historical, Garden City Casino Assn., Sons of the Revolution,
Colonial Wars, Wars of 1812, Soc. of the Cincinnati.

HOLDER, CHARLES FREDERICK, LL.D., of Pasadena, Cal. (Son of Joseph Bassett Holder, M.D., of N.Y. City, 1824-88; Surg. U.S. Army, 1860-69; Curator of Zoology, Amer. Mus. of Nat. History, N.Y., etc.; *m* 1849, Emily, da. of John Chase Gove, of Wash., D.C., descendant of Edward Gove, N.H. Assembly, 1683.—Descended from Christopher Holder, 1630-88, Missionary, founder of Quaker Societies in America, 1657, relative of Dr. William Holder, 1616, and Sir Christopher Wren).

Born at Lynn, Mass., Aug. 5, 1851; entered U.S. Naval Acad., 1869; Asst. Curator Zoology, Am. Mus. of Nat. Hist., N.Y., 1875; Author of "Elements of Zoology," "Life of Charles Darwin," "Stories of Animal Life," "Big Game Fishes," etc.; late Trustee, Throop Univ., State Normal Coll., Pasadena Pub. Lib.; Pres. Bd. of Education; *m* Nov. 8, 1879, Sarah E. Ufford, of Brooklyn, a descendant of the Huguenot, William Provost, of Paris, 1534.

Issue.

i. EMILY EATON.

Arms—Sable, a chevron between three anchors argent.
Crest—Out of a five-leaved ducal coronet gules a lion sejant or.

Residence—475 Bellefontaine Street, Pasadena, Cal.
Clubs—Valley Hunt, Country, Sunset, Tuna Club.
Societies—Fel. N.Y. Acad. of Sciences, National Geographical, Pioneer Quakers.

STANLEY, JAMES GORDON, of Baltimore (Son of Rev. Harvey Stanley, 1809-85, *m* Mary A. Kinney; son of Hon. John W., *d* 1830, Pres. State Senate of N.C.; son of John, of Charles City, Va.; son of Dancy; son of Major John, Surveyor-Gen. of Maryland, Mem. Lower House of Assembly, *d* 1698; son of William Stanley, of Canterbury, Kent, Eng.).

Born at Princess Ann, Md., Sept. 22, 1845; *m* Nov. 13, 1873, Caroline H., da. of Edward and Mary Jane (Cox) Schwartze, M.D., of Baltimore.

Issue.

i. EDWARD SCHWARTZE, *b* Sept. 12, 1874.
i. MARY.   ii. SARAH HANDY.

Arms—Argent, on a bend azure three bucks' heads cabossed or.
Crest—On a chapeau gules turned up ermine an eagle, wings endorsed or, feeding on an infant in its nest ppr. swaddled azure, banded of the third.
Motto—Sans changer.
Residence—1318 N. Charles Street, Baltimore, Md.
Clubs—University, Baltimore Country.   *Society*—Colonial Wars.

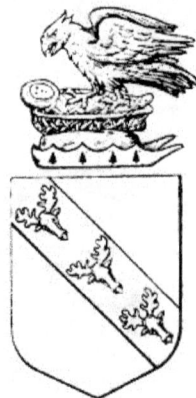

DUKE, RICHARD THOMAS WALKER, Jr.,
of Charlottesville (Son of Col. Richard T.
Walker Duke 1822-98, Col. 46th Va. Regt. C.S.A.,
Mem. 41st and 42nd Congress U.S.A., m 1846
Eliz. S. 1820-96, da. of Wm. Scott and Marg. F.
(Brown) Eskridge of Staunton Va.; son of Richard
of Albemarle; son of Clivears; son of Clivears of
Hanover; son of Clivears; son of Henry of York;
son of Col. Henry Duke, Mem. Ho. of Burg's. Va.
1696, descendant of George and Cath. (Braham)
Duke, of Wandsworth, Surrey, England).

Born at Charlottesville Aug. 27, 1853; Grad. Univ.
of Va. 1874; Judge Corporation (Hustings)
Court, Charlottesville; G. M. of Masons, Va.;
m Oct. 1, 1884, Edith Ridgway, da. of John F.
and Mary H. (Harker) Slaughter of Lynch-
burg Va.

Issue.
i. RICHARD THOMAS WALKER, b June 19, 1887.
ii. JOHN FLAVEL SLAUGHTER, b Feb. 11, 1889.
iii. WILLIAM ESKRIDGE, b Feb. 23, 1893.

i. MARY A.
ii. HELEN RISDON.

Arms—Azure, a chevron between three birds close argent membered gules.
Crest—On a plume of five ostrich feathers, two argent three azure a sword argent
    hilt or.   Motto—In adversis idem.

Residences—546 Park Street, Charlottesville, Va.; Sunny Side, Albemarle Co., Va.
Club—Democratic, N.Y. City.
Societies—Colonial Wars, Sons of the Revolution, Zeta Psi, Phi Beta Kappa.

SNELLING, RODMAN PAUL,
of Dedham (Son of Samuel G. Snelling, of
Boston, b Nov. 9, 1824, m Eleanora E. Paul;
son of Samuel, b 1798; son of Samuel, b 1765; son
of Col. Jonathan, b 1734; son of Capt. Jonathan,
b 1696; son of Joseph, b 1667; son of John, b 1625,
who came to New Eng. with his uncle, Dr. Wm.
Snelling, 1647; son of John Snelling, gent., of
Chaddlewood, Devonshire, England).

Born at Forest Hills, Boston, 1861; Grad. Harvard Univ. B.A. 1881;
    m June 12, 1900, Eva B., da. of Richard de Treville, of Charleston,
    S.C.

Issue.
i. ELLA DE TREVILLE.

Arms—Gules, three griffins' heads erased argent, a chief indented ermine.
Motto—Ma force d'en haut.

Residence—"Chaddlewood," Dedham, Mass.
Clubs—University, Country, Eastern Yacht, Norfolk Country.

G LIDDEN, JOHN MURRAY, Lieut.-Col.,
of Newcastle, Me. (Son of Wm. T. Glidden,
of Newcastle, *m* Catharine Cottrell; son of Col.
John, 1785-1864; son of Joseph, 1759-1810; son of
Joseph, 1734-1829; son of Lt. Charles, 1713-1802;
son of Capt. Richard, 1660-1728; son of Charles
Glidden, of "Glidden," Hants., Eng., *b* 1630,
settled in N. Hampshire 1656).

Born at Liverpool, Eng., July 4, 1843; *m* Oct. 21,
1896, *Anna, da. of Hon. J. M. Warren, of
Troy N.Y. (9th from Gov.. William Bradford).

Issue.

i. Joseph Warren, Capt. U.S.A.   iii. John Montfichet.
ii. Wm. Gernon, (*decd.*).   iv. Arthur Boynton.
i. Mary Warren, *m* Geo. Scott Winslow of Boston.
ii. Amy Gardner.
iii. Susan A., *m* H. W. Clifford, of Newcastle.   iv. Anna Warren.

Arms—Or, on a bend azure three escallops of the field.
Crest—A wolf's head couped azure collared and ringed or.
Motto—Spe.

_____

Residence—"Gladisfen," Newcastle. Lincoln Co., Me.
Clubs—Union N.Y., Phila., Cumberland Portland, Me., Lennox, Atlantic. &c.
Societies—Cincinnati, Colonial Wars, (Depy. Gov. General) Sons of the American
Revolution, Maine Hist., Hist. of Penna,* Colonial Dames.

_____

W ILKINSON, OGDEN DUNGAN,
of Phila. (Son of Fredk. R. Wilkinson
1837-83, *m* Harriet S. Folwell; son of Col. Ogden D.,
1805 66; son of Col. Elisha, 1772-1846; son of
Lt.-Col. John, 1711-82; son of John, 1677-1751;
Son of Capt. Samuel, *d* 1727; son of Lt. Lawrence,
d 1692; son of William and Mary (Conyers) Wilkinson of Harperly House, Lanchester, Eng.).

Born at Trenton, N.J., May 2, 1863; late Capt. and
Quartermaster N.G.P., *m* Ap. 4, 1883, Sarah
Jane, da. of Robert and Sarah J. (Corscaden)
Taylor.

Issue.

i. Sarah Dill.   ii. Elizabeth.

Arms—Azure, a fesse erminois between three unicorns passant argent.
Crest—Out of a mural coronet gules a demi-unicorn erminois erased of the first,
armed and maned of the second.
Motto—Nec rege nec populo, sed utroque.

_____

Residence—2031 Walnut Street, Philadelphia.
Clubs—Union League, Corinthian Yacht (Philadelphia), New York Yacht.
Societies—Penna. Historical, Penna. Genealogical, Bucks Co. Historical, Penna.
Colonial, Founders and Patriots, Foreign Wars, War of 1812, Sons of the
Revolution, Order of Albion, Descendants of Colonial Governors.

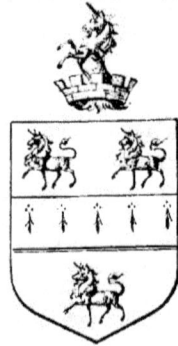

TROWBRIDGE, SAMUEL BRECK PARKMAN,
of N.Y. City (Son of Gen. W. P. Trowbridge
1828-92, LL.D., Ph.D., M.A., *m* Lucy Parkman ;
son of Stephen van R., 1794-1859, *m* Eliz. Conklin ;
son of Maj. Luther 1756-1802, *m* Eliz. Tillman ;
son of Capt. Thos., *m* Hannah Perry; son of
Col. John, 1701-72, *m* Mehetable Eaton ; son of
Thos., *b* 1677; son of Lt. James 1636-1717, Rep.
of Dorchester at Gen. Ct., *m* Margt. Jackson ; son
of Thos., settled at Dorchester 1634, *m* Eliz.
Marshall ; son of Edmund of Taunton, Co. Somerset; son of Thos.,
d 1620; son of John Trowbridge, *d* 1576, descd. from Peter de Trowbridge of the Peverils of Sandford 24 Ed. I.).

Born at N.Y. City May 20, 1862 ; Grad. Trinity Coll. 1883 M.A.; Columbia
Univ. 1886 Ph.B.; School of Classical Studies Athens, Greece, 1887,
Ecole des Beaux Arts, Paris 1890; Troop A 1st Cavalry N.G.N.Y.
1890; 2nd Lt. 12th Infy. 1894, 1st Lt. 1895 N.G.N.Y.; Pres. Soc. of
Beaux Arts Architects 1903-04; Vice-Pres. Alliance Francaise N.Y.
1904; Mem. Correspondant de la Société des Architects Diplomés
par le Govt. Francais; Hon. Mem. British Inst. of Archaeology,
Athens ; *m* Jan. 16, 1896, Sophia Pennington Tailer.

Arms—Or, a bridge of three arches, towered embattled in fesse gules masoned
sable, three streams transfluent proper.

Residence—123 East 70th Street, N.Y. City.

Clubs—Union, Century, Racquet and Tennis, St. Anthony, Ardsley.

Societies—Colonial Wars, Sons of the Rev., Archae., Inst. of Am., Am. Inst.
of Archts.

SEWELL, WYNN REEVES (*decd.*),
of Allegheny, Penna. (Son of James Harrison
Sewell, 1813-85, *m* Matilda, *d* 1892, da. of Thomas
(Segrave) Reeves, and Hannah of Phila.; son of
James H., *d* 1842; son of John, *d* 1805; son of
Charles, *d* 1742; son of Nicholas, 1655-1737; son
of Henry Sewell, from London to Maryland, 1661,
Councillor and Secty. of Md., *m* Jane, da. of
Vincent Lowe of Derby, Eng., she afterwards
m Charles Calvert 3rd Lord Baltimore).

Born in Allegheny, Sept. 27, 1854; *d* Dec. 9, 1899;
A.B., A.M., Lafayette Coll., 1876 ; Vice-Pres.
of Pa. Soc. of Sons of the Am. Revol.; Councillor-at-Law ; admitted to the Bar, 1879 ;
m Oct. 27, 1881; Martha, da. of Mark W. Watson, of Pittsburgh.

Arms—Sable, a chevron between three bees volant argent.

Crest—A dexter arm embowed in armour proper garnished or, holding an acorn.

Motto—Frangas non flectes.

Residence—(Mrs. W. R. Sewell) 709 Ridge Avenue, Allegheny, Pennsylvania.

CORLIES, MRS. CAROLINE (*née* ATLEE), of Phila. (Dau. of Edwin Pitt Atlee, M.D. 1799-1836, *m* Margaret C. Bullock: son of Edwin Aug. 1776-1852, M.D., *m* Margaret Snyder, niece of Gov. Simon Snyder; son of Wm. Aug. 1735-93, Pres. Judge 1st Dis. Ct. of Pa., *m* Esther Bowes: son of William Atlee of Ford Hook House, Acton, Middx., Secty. to Lord Howe, he *d* April 24, 1744).

Born in Philadelphia; Mem. of the Penna. Soc. Colonial Dames of Am.; *m* Sept. 25, 1851, Samuel Fisher Corlies, *d* 1888.

Issue.

i. SAMUEL ROWLAND, 1855-56.
i. CLARA, 1852-56.
ii. SARAH FISHER, *m* April 30, 1874, John Buck Morgan.
iii. MARGARET LONGSTRETH.
iv. CAROLINE ATLEE, *m* April 10, 1884, Fred. Lang Baily.
v. EDITH ATLEE, *m* Nov. 9, 1887, Samuel F. Houston, *d* 1895.
vi. FLORENCE, 1866-68.

Arms—(For Atlee) Azure, a lion rampant argent.
Crest—Two lions' heads erased addorced.

Residence—264 S. 21st Street, Philadelphia.
Clubs—Acorn, Germantown Cricket, Sedgeley, New Century.
Societies—Browning, Colonial Dames.

ROWLAND, HENRY JAMES, REV., of Philadelphia (Eldest son of William Rowland, 1813-72, *m* Elizabeth Harvey, 1816-80, descdt. of Benjamin Harvey, of Derbyshire, who came to Penna with Wm. Penn; son of Benjamin, *b* 1777, *m* Elizabeth Brittian; son of Captain Jonathan, *b.* 1751, *m* Sarah Maxwell; son of John. *m* Anne Smith; son of John, who came to Penna. 1699; son of William and Kath. Rowland, of Rhosybayvil, a farm in the parish of Bayvil, Pembrokeshire, Wales. These Rowlands were at one time Lords of the Manor Llantood).

Born at Frankfort, Pa., July 5, 1843; Univ. of Penna, 1865; Divinity School of the Prot. Epis. Ch., 1868; Asst. Minister of St. James'; late Chaplain of the Educational Home and the Ch. Home; *m* Feb. 14, 1878, Anne, da. of Hon. John Cadwalader, of Philadelphia.

Issue.

i. JOHN CADWALADER, *b.* Feb. 10, 1879.
i. ELIZABETH CADWALADER, *b.* May 7, 1888.

Arms—A fesse between three Saxon heads.   *Crest*—A lion rampant.

Residences—1607 Locust Street, Philadelphia; Bryn Mawr, Pennsylvania.

GILBERT, JAMES HARRIS,
of Chicago Ill. (Son of Elisha B. Gilbert,
m Jane Harris of Monaghan, Ireland; son of Benj.
b 1770; son of Nathl. b 1750; son of Capt. Nathl.
1723-87; son of Lt. Nathl. 1689-1756; son of
Jonathan 1648-98; son of Jonathan 1618-82; son
of John of Little Ellington, Norfolk; son of
Thomas; son of Richard, Lord of the Manor
of Walcote, Norfolk; son of William; son of Otis,
H. Sheriff of Devon. 1475; son of William of
Compton; son of William Gilbert of Compton,
m Eliz. Champernon).

Born at Toronto, Can. June 30, 1844; Sheriff,
Alderman and Acting Mayor of Chicago;
admt. Barrister-at-Law at Toronto 1865; in
1867 admtd. to practice in Illinois, later in
U.S. Dist. Courts, and in 1879 State of Kansas;
Delegate at large to Rep. Convention at Minneapolis in 1892,
from Illinois; Presdt. of the Met. Trust and Savings Bank; m June
15, 1870, Ella K., da. of Silas Huntley of Chicago.

Issue.
i. HUNTLEY HARRIS, b Feb. 10, 1887.   i. HELEN RICHMOND.

Arms—Argent, on a chevron sable three roses of the field.
Crest—A squirrel cracking a nut proper.   Motto—Mallem mori quam mutare.

Residence—2628 Prairie Avenue, Chicago, Ill.
Clubs—Union League, Bankers, Athletic and Ontwensia.
Societies—Sons of the Am. Revo., Colonial Wars, Mil. Order of Foreign Wars.

NEILL, Hon. RICHARD RENSHAW,
U.S. Secy. of Legation, Lima, Peru (Son of
Major James Patriot Wilson Neill, U.S. Army
1821-99, m Alice 1819-56, da. of Richard Renshaw
and Mary Irwin Johnston of Phila. and grand-da.
of Col. Francis Johnston 1748-1815.—Descended
from John Neill, Attorney, from Tyrone, Ireland,
1739, his son Henry, by an act of the General
Assembly of Del. June 21, 1780, commanded the
2nd "Continental Regt. No. 38 ").

Born at Phila. Oct. 20, 1845; served in Civil War
in Light Artillery, Phila., 2nd Lt. U.S. Marines
1865, resigned 1st Lieut. 1873; Appd. 1884
Secy. U.S. Leg. Lima; m Nov. 2, 1870, Mary
Cox of Chester Co., Pa.

Issue.
i. RICHARD RENSHAW, b Nov. 12, 1876.
ii. WALTER HERBERT, b Aug. 21, 1882, Lieut. 13th U.S. Cavalry.
i. ALICE JOHNSTON, 1872-97, m R. F. Mackenzie.
ii. NADINE CAMAC, m Edward John Prew, d 1897.

Arms—Azure, on a fesse argent three mullets gules.
Crest—A demi-lion holding between the paws a mullet.   Motto—Fortiter et recte.

Residence—U.S. Legation, Lima, Peru, S. America.
Societies—Cincinnati of Del., Order of Albion, Sons of the Rev., Lima Geo., etc.

DORCY, BEN HOLLADAY, Lieut.,
U.S. Army (Eldest son of John Chipman
Dorcy, *b* at N.Y. City, 1833; son of Laurence
D'Arcy, *b* in Ireland, 1796, *m* Eliza Symmes, da. of
Capt. Nathl. Holmes Downe, of Boston, grandson
of Col. William Downe, one of H.M.'s Justices for
Co. Suffolk).

Born at Portland, Or., Oct. 28, 1869; Mem. of U.S.
Classified C.S. Treasury, Interior and War
Depts., 1891-8; Lt. and Adjt. 3rd Regt. of Infty.
Pa. Vols., Spanish Am.-War, 1898; 2nd Lieut.
4th Regt. of Cavalry, U.S.A., to rank from
April 5, 1899; promoted 1st Lieut., Feb. 2,
1901; *m* June 1, 1899, Linda, da. of Ben. and
Lydia E. (Campbell) Holladay, of Kentucky, and half-sister of the
late Comptesse Arthur de Pourtales-Gorgier, and the late Baronne
Henri Renouard de Bussierre).

Issue.
i. BEN HOLLADAY, Jr., *b* Aug. 23, 1900.
ii. JOHN BIDDLE, *b* May 9, 1902.

Arms—Azure semée de crosses crosslet and three cinquefoils argent.
Crest—A bull sable, horns and hoofs or.   *Motto*—Un Dieu, un Roi.

Residences—Portland, Oregon; Philadelphia, Pa.
Club—Pen and Pencil of Philadelphia.
Societies—Sons of the Revolution, Penna. Commandery, Naval Order of the U.S.,
War of 1812, Veterans of Indian Wars of the U.S.

HURD, CHARLES RUSSELL,
of Milton, Mass. (Son of Charles Henry
Hurd, Captain and Assistant - Adjutant - General
during Civil War, 1861-65.—Descended from John
Hurd, 1613-81, of Windsor, Conn., Deputy to
General Court, 1657-58).

Born at Charlestown, Mass., Sept. 30, 1864, Mem.
of Dudley, Battell & Hurd of Boston; *m* Mary
Claflin, daughter of George A. Newell.

Issue.
i. GEORGE NEWELL, *b* July 15, 1891.
ii. EDMUND A., *b* May 23, 1895.
i. DOROTHY.

Arms—Gules, a lion rampant or.
Crest—On a garb of wheat a crow proper.
Motto—Bona bonis.

Residence—Milton, Mass.
Clubs—Reform of New York, N.Y. Athletic.
Societies—Colonial Wars, Sons of the Revolution, Military Order of Loyal Legion.

MAGRUDER, HON. BENJAMIN DRAKE, of Chicago (Son of Wm. H. N. Magruder, A.B., LL.D., of Baton Rouge, La. ; son of Captain James Truman Magruder, *d* 1831, of Magruder, Prince George's Co., Md., a naval officer, presented at Court of George III., 1790, *m* his 2nd cousin, Elizabeth Magruder. He was 1st cousin of Geo. Fraser Magruder, of Virginia, to whom the arms were confirmed).

Born at Mount Ararat, Miss., Sept. 27, 1838 ; Chief Justice of Supreme Court of Ill. since 1885, representing the Northern Dist. ; A.M., LL.B., and LL.D. of Yale Univ. ; *m* Julia, da. of Phillip Clayton Latham, of Kentucky, son of Hon. James Latham, of London, Eng., and Culpepper, Va.

Issue.

i. HENRY LATHAM, *b* Dec. 25, 1866.
i. ELLEN LATHAM, *b* May 26, 1865 ; *d* Sept. 26, 1896.

Arms—Argent, a fir-tree on a mount vert, surmounted of a sword bendways, on its point an Imperial Crown proper ; a canton azure.
Crest—A lion's head erased proper crowned with an antique crown.
Mottoes—Srioghail mo dhream ; E'en do bot spair nocht.

Residences—7 Washington Place, Chicago, and Springfield, Ill.
Clubs—University, Union, and Union League.

PETERS, WILLIAM RICHMOND, of N.Y. City (Son of Rev. Thos. McC. Peters, 1821-93, *m* 1847, Alice, da. of Rev. William Richmond, of N.Y. City.—Descended from Andrew Peters, who settled in Andover, Mass., 1657, probably related to Rev. Hugh Peters, who came to New Eng. with John Winthrop, Jr., 1646, son of Thomas Dikewood Peters, Merchant of Fowey, Cornwall, England).

Born in New York City April 13, 1850 ; *m* 1879, Helen, da. of Henry Anthon Heiser, of New York City.

Issue.

i. WILLIAM RICHMOND, *b* 1888.　　i. ISABEL MERCIEN.
ii. THOMAS McCLURE, *b* 1889.　　ii. ALICE RICHMOND.

Arms—Gules, on a bend or, between two escallops argent, a Cornish chough proper between two cinquefoils azure.
Crest—Two lions' heads erased and endorsed. the first or the second azure, gorged with a plain collar counterchanged.
Motto—Sans Dieu rien.

Residences—23 West 73rd Street, N.Y. City ; Oyster Bay, Long Island.
Clubs—Century, Reform, Down Town.

FERRIS, MORRIS PATTERSON,
of Dobbs' Ferry, N.Y. (Son of the Rev. Isaac
Ferris, D.D., LL.D.; *b* October 9, 1798; *d* June
13, 1873; *m* Letitia Storm, *d* February 4, 1902;
Graduated at Columbia College, 1816; Theo-
logical Seminary, 1820; Union College D.D., 1833;
Columbia College LL.D., 1853; Chancellor of the
University of New York, 1852; Chancellor Emeritus,
1870; Pastor of the Middle Dutch Church, Albany,
1824-36; Market Street Church, N.Y., 1836-40.
Descended from John Ferris, of Leicestershire,
England, settled in Fairfield, Connecticut, *circa*
1640; one of the Proprietors of Throckmorton's
Neck, in Westchester Co., N.Y.).

Born at New York City, Oct. 3, 1855; Graduated at the University of
New York City, 1874; University Law School, 1876; Admitted to
the Bar, 1876; Member of the Advisory Council of the Society of
the Daughters of the Cincinnati; Registrar of the Society of War
of 1812; President Yonkers Historical and Library Association;
Treasurer Society of American Authors; Secretary, Sons of
Revolution; Secretary, N.Y. State Historical Association;
Attorney-General of the Order of Founders and Patriots; Secretary,
Colonial War Lake George Monumental Committee; *m* Sept. 4,
1879, Mary Lanman, daughter of Colonel John de Peyster Douw,
and Marianne Chandler Lamann, his wife, of Poughkeepsie, N.Y.

Issue.

i. MORRIS DOUW, *b* February 12, 1884.

ii. VAN WYCK, *b* May 28, 1890.

i. MARY VAN RENSSELAER.

Arms—Azure, on a chevron or three horseshoes of the first, between three
cinquefoils argent.

Crest—Out of a ducal coronet a hand proper between two wings.

Motto—Multum in florius artae.

Residence—Dobbs' Ferry, Westchester Co , N.Y.

Clubs—St. Andrew's Golf, Lawyers', Delta Phi, Ardsley.

Societies—Foreign Wars, Colonial Wars, Sons of the Revolution, War of 1812,
Founders and Patriots, Huguenot, Westchester Bar Ass'n., American
Historical, Yonkers Historical, Long Island Historical, N.Y. Genealogical
and Biographical, Society of American Authors, N.Y. State Historical.

FREEMAN, GEORGE WENTWORTH,
of Portland, O. (Son of Franklin Freeman, 1824-86, of Dover, N.H., State Rep., Magistrate, and City Treas., *m* 1847, Hannah Stevens, 1823-59, da. of Samuel and Phebe (Wentworth) Dame, of Dover, N.H.; son of James, *b* 1790; son of Benjamin, *b* 1762; son of Isaac, *b* 1733; son of Ebenezer, *b* 1687; son of Edmund, *b* 1657; son of Major John Freeman, 1627-1719, served against the Indians, 1677, Major of Barnstable Troop, 1685, etc.).

Born at Dover, N.H., Feb. 22, 1859; Educated at Cornell Univ.; Capt. 2nd Regt. U.S. Vol. Engrs.; U.S. Assist. Engr.; served in Spanish-American War; *m* Dec. 16, 1886, Mattie, da. of James Hearst and Martha J. (Gray) Foster of Albany, Oregon.

Issue.

i. George Foster, *b* Sept. 20, 1887.

ii. James Wentworth, *b* Oct. 13, 1894.   i. Martha Gray.

Arms—Azure, three lozenges or.

Crest—A demi-lion rampant gules holding in the paws a lozenge or.

Motto—Liber et audax.

Residence—314 N. Grand Avenue, Portland, Oregon.

Societies—Colonial Wars, Sons of the American Revolution, Mayflower.

SCHIEFFELIN, EUGENE.
of New York City (Youngest son of Henry Hamilton Schieffelin and Maria Theresa, his wife, second da. of Samuel Bradhurst, M.D., of New York. —Descended from Jacob Schieffelin, of Weilheim, under Deck, Germany, who came to Philadelphia in 1746, bringing with him the family Bible printed in 1560, which is still in the possession of the family resident in New York).

Born in New York City, January 29, 1827; *m*. Catherine Tonnelé, second daughter of Valentine Gill Hall, of New York City.

Arms—Tiercé per fesse sable and or. On three piles (two conjoined with one between, transposed) invected counterchanged, as many cross-crosslets of the first.

Crest—A holy lamb passant crowned with glory and bearing cross staff and pennon proper.

Motto—Per fidem et constantiam.

Residences—865 Maddison Avenue, New York City; "Dryburn," Tivoli on Hudson, New York.

Clubs—Union, St. Nicholas, City.

Societies—Colonial Wars, St. Nicholas, Colonial Order.

H ENDRICK, CALVIN WHEELER,
of East Orange, N.J. (Son of Rev. Calvin S.
Hendrick, 1838-65, *m* Elizabeth W., da. of Rev.
Alex. Wheeler and Mary (Moseley) Campbell, of
Bedford Co., Va.; son of Rev. John S. 1811-98,
m Jane E. Bigelow, of Richmond Va.; son of Joseph
W., of Hanover Co., Va., *m* Mary D. Shilman; son
of William Hendrick, of Holland, settled in Hanover
Co., Va., 1750-60. Also descd. from Lieut. Wm.
Winston and Sarah Dabney, grand-da. of Cornelius
D'Aubigné, a refugee from France, after the
Revocation of the Edict of Nantes).

Born at Puducah, Ky., June 21, 1865; Assist.
Chf. Engr., G.S. and F.R.R.; City Engr. of
Macon, Ga.; Engr. in Charge of Sewers;
Rapid Transit R. R. Comm., N.Y.; *m* Nov. 29, 1892, Sarah R., da. of
Wm. F. and Chloe P. (Conyers) Herring of N.Y.

Issue.
i. CALVIN WHEELER, Jr., *b* Oct. 19, 1893.
ii. HERRING-DE-LA-PORTE, *b* Jan. 13, 1896.

Arms—Argent, a hind standing in a forest.
Crest—Out of a ducal coronet a hind's head.

Residence— 129 Glenwood Avenue, East Orange, N.J.
Societies—Colonial Wars, Am. Soc. Civil Engineers, N.Y.

L EGGETT, FRANCIS HOWARD,
of N.Y. City (Son of Abraham Leggett, of
N.Y. City, *b* 1805; son of Abraham; son of
Ezekiel; son of William, *b* 1715; son of Capt.
William, *b* 1691; son of Gabriel Leggett, proprietor
of an estate in Westchester Co., now the 23rd Ward
of N.Y. City; son of Hebmingius Leggett, High
Sheriff of Essex, Eng., settled in America, 1640,
viâ Barbadoes, W.I.).

Born in N.Y. City, March 27, 1840; *m* Mrs. Besse
Sturges, da. of John David L. Macleod.

Issue.
i. FRANCES HOWARD.
(*Children of Mrs. Leggett by 1st m.*)
i. HOLLISTER STURGES.   ii. ALBERTA STURGES.

Arms—Ermine, a lion rampant gules.
Crest—Two lions' gambs erect gules supporting a mitre or.

Residences—21 West 34th Street, N.Y. City; Ridgely Manor, Stone Ridge,
Ulster Co., N.Y.
Clubs—Metropolitan, Union League, Tuxedo, Riding, Grolier, Merchants,
National Arts.

READ, Mrs. MARGUERITE (*née* De Carron d'Allondans), and Mademoiselle Louise Catherine de Carron d'Allondans, daughters of Monsieur Jacques Frederic de Carron d'Allondans, Municipal Councillor, *b* 1835, *d* 1870, and Catherine Marguerite, his wife, da. of Frederick Pillard, 7th in descent (last of the line) from le Sieur Pierre Carron, who held some minor office under the Princes of Montbéliard about 1650, he *m* Johanne Marthelot d'Allondans ; his father, Jehan Carron de Presentevilliers, was the brother of the learned Monsieur Pierre Carron, Maistre des Escholes Francaises à Montbeliard, and they both were sons of honorable homme Jacques Carron de Verroreille (a man of wealth in the city of Montbeliard) and this last was grandson of noble homme Jean de Carron, Lord of the Manor of Carron, 1521, who was enobled by Francis I., April 29, 1539, and whose father, le Sieur Antoine Carron, has been claimed as an ancestor by the Carrons, Counts of Cessens, and other notable families of the name).

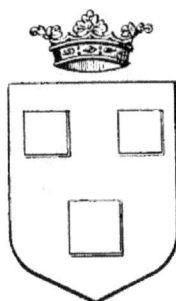

Born in France ; *m* Aug. 24, 1889, Major Harmon Pumpelly Read, F.R.G.S., of Albany, N.Y., son of General John Meredith and Delphine Marie (Pumpelly) Read, G.C.R.

Arms— (de Carron d'Allondans) Azure, three tiles or, surmounted by a ducal coronet.
Motto—Loyauté.
Residence—236 State Street, Albany, N.Y.

WEED, HENRY FRANK, of N.Y. City (Fourth son of Rufus Weed, of Noroton, Ct., *b* Mar. 7, 1802, *d* May 30, 1883, *m* Feb. 25, 1831, Phebe, *b* Nov. 10, 1805, *d* Apl. 10, 1867, da. of John and Sarah (Fancher) Clock, of Noroton, Ct. ; son of Benjamin Weed, soldier in War of the Revolution.—Descd. from Jonas Weed, *b* at Stanwick, Northamptonshire, Eng., settled at Watertown, Mass., 1631, and Wethersfield, Ct., 1635).

Born at Noroton, Ct., Feb. 6, 1844, *m* Apl. 11, 1872, Adeline, *b* May 27, 1845, da. of James Waterbury and Louisa J. (Wood) Stanton, of Stamford, Conn.

Issue.
i. WALTON F., *b* Feb. 26, 1875.   i. FLORENCE L.   ii. LOUISA S.

Arms—Argent, two bars gules in chief three martlets sable.
Crest—A martlet sable.

Residences—17th Street and 4th Avenue, New York City ; Noroton, Conn.
Club—New York Athletic.   *Society*—Sons of the Revolution

FREEMAN, ALDEN,
of New York City (Eldest son of Joel Francis
Freeman, of East Orange, N.J., late Treas. Stand-
ard Oil Coy., and Chairman of the Board of the
Missouri, Kansas and Texas R.R., *b* Oct. 12,
1836, *m* Dec. 5, 1860, Francis M., da. of
Judge Seth Alden and Mercy (Hunt) Abbey, of
Cleveland, O.—Descended from Henry Freeman
1670-1763, of Woodbridge, N.J., *m* Elizabeth
Bonue 1695. Descended, on the maternal side,
from John Abbey, from England in ship " Bona-
venture," 1634 ; one of the early settlers of Salem.
His son, Thomas Abbey, fought in King Philip's
War, and was wounded at the taking of the Indians' Fort at Narragansett, 1675 ; in 1683 Thomas Abbey became one of the founders of Enfield,
Conn. His grandson, Thomas Abbey, was Ensign and Lieut. in French
and Indian Wars, 1758-61 ; became the noted Captain Abbey of the
American Revol., serving throughout the entire conflict with distinction. In 1861, his grandson, Judge Seth Alden Abbey, of Cleveland,
Ohio, at the age of 63 years was made 1st Lieut. of the 2nd Ohio Cavalry,
and served throughout the Civil War, part of the time as Brig. Quartermaster. The mother of Judge Abbey was Hannah Alden, gt.-gt.-grand-da.
of Dep.-Gov. John Alden, 1599-1687, of Plymouth Colony, the 7th Signer
of the Mayflower Compact. Other ancestors were William Vassall, Asst.
Gov. of Mass. Bay Colony, son of John Vassall, Alderman of London ;
William Harvey, Clarenceux King of Arms ; Capt. Miles Morgan, the
" Hero of Springfield," grandson of Sir William Morgan, of Tredegar,
Wales).

Born at Cleveland, O., May 25, 1862 ; Grad. N.Y. Univ. B.S., 1882,
M.S., 1887 ; one of the founders and incorporators of the Hereditary
Patriotic Order of "Settlers and Defenders of Amer."; M. of Councils
Soc. of Colonial Wars, and Order of Founders and Patriots, N.J.

Arms—(Abbey) Gules, five fusils conjoined in fesse, betw. three escallops argent.

Crest—An eagle's head erased proper.   *Motto*—Alte fert aquila.

——— ———

Residences—Metropolitan Club, N.Y. City ; Elm Gate, East Orange, N.J.

Clubs—Metropolitan, Players, National Arts, Church, New York Yacht, Reform,
Opera, Psi Upsilon, Nineteenth Century, Twilight, Baltusrol Golf, Essex
County, Country, Riding and Driving (Orange N.J.), Republican.

Societies—Mayflower Descendants, Founders and Patriots, Colonial Wars, Sons
of the Revol., St. Nicholas, Ohio, Phi Beta Kappa, National Steeplechase
and Hunt Assn., N.J. Historical ; New Eng. of Orange, N.J., Huguenot,
Sons of Amer. Revol., Revol. Memorial of N.J., Colonial Governors.

GOULD, CHARLES ALBERT,
of N.Y. City (Son of Wm. W. Gould, of
Woodstock, Ct., *b* 1826, *m* 1847, Electa Moulton
Pratt; son of Jedediah; son of Ophir; son of
Bezaleel; son of Eliezer; son of Zaccheus; son of
Capt. John Gould, 1635-1710, of Great Messenden,
Bucks., Eng., chosen Selectman of Topsfield in
1663, served in King Philip's War).

Born at Batavia, N.Y., Jan. 13, 1849; Collector of
Customs Buffalo Dist. 1881-85; Pres. Gould
Coupler Co., Gould Steel Co., of Anderson;
founder of Depew; Commodore Amer. Yacht
Club; *m* Julia Adelaide Stocking.

Issue.
i. HENRY COLTON, 1869-92, *m* Lillian Augusta Rockwell.
ii. CHARLES MOULTON, *b* Sept. 7, 1873, *m* Lillie Bell.
iii. WILLIAM STOCKING, *b* Sept. 4, 1875, *m* Ethel Blanch Sanders.
i. CELIA ADELAIDE, *m* George G. Milne.

Arms—Per saltire, azure and or, a lion rampant counterchanged.
Crest—A demi-lion rampant or, holding a scroll argent.
Motto—Probitate et labore.

Residences—714 Fifth Avenue, New York City; "Greystone," Rye, N.Y.
Clubs—Union League, Republican, Engrs., Lawyers, Larchmont Yacht, Amer.
    Yacht, N.Y. Yacht, Atlantic Yacht, N.Y. Athletic, Lotus, Reform.
Societies—Colonial Wars, Sons of the American Revolution.

PECK, WILLIAM EMERSON,
of N.Y. (Son of Charles Peck, 1830-1903,
m Mary Folger Davis; son of Elnathan 1803-65,
m Mary Dewey; son of Michael, 1773-1861,
m Mary Marshall; son of Samuel, 1736-1822,
m Mehitable Smith; son of Samuel, *b* 1716,
m Hannah Jennings; son of Samuel, *b* 1690,
m Martha Clark; son of Joseph, *b* 1653, *m* Mary
Camp; son of Joseph, of Conn. 1635; son of
Robert Peck, of Beccles, Suffolk, England).

Born at New Britain Ct. June 30, 1858; Grad. Yale
Univ. B.A. 1881; *m* Jan. 30, 1884, Bertha T.,
da. of Edward Napoleon Pierce, of Plainville
Ct.

Issue.
i. ELENA MARJORIE.

Arms—Or, on a chevron gules three crosses formée of the field.
Crest—Two lances in saltire or, headed argent, with pennons of the first, each
    charged with a cross formée gules, entiled with a chaplet vert.
Mottoes—(1) Crux Christi salus mea; (2) Probitatem quam divitias.

Residences—12 East 58th Street, N.Y. City; Sachem's Head, Conn.
Clubs—Fulton, Barnard, University, N.Y. Yacht, Montclair Golf, Sachem's Head
    Yacht, Grads. of N.H., Maple Hill Golf.
Societies—New England, Sons of the Revolution.

E LLICOTT, EUGENE,
of Phila., Pa. (Son of Benj. Ellicott 1796-1869, of Ellicott City and Balto., Md., *m* Mary 1819-54, da. of Wm. Carroll, of " Rock Creek," Md., a descendant of Charles Carroll, Atty-Genl. of Md., 1689, who was in descent from the O'Carroll's of King's Co., Ireland.—Descended from Andrew Ellicott, from Devonshire *circa.* 1700).

Born at Balto., Md., Dec. 8, 1846 ; U.S. Coast and Geodetic Surv. 1864-90 ; Asst. to Prov. Univ. of Pa. 1895-1901 ; Capt. 1st Regt. U.S. Vol. Engrs. 1898-99, served in Porto Rico and Cuba ; *m* (1) Jan. 17, 1877 Margt. Ingersoll, da. of Richd. W. and Annie (Smith) Tyson ; *m* (2) June 6, 1895, Eleanor C., da. of Joseph Patterson and Jane, da. of Rev. Cornelius C. Cuyler, of Phila.

Issue.

i. Daniel, *decd.*
i. Mary Carroll.   ii. Ruth Clement, *decd.*   iii. Margaret Tyson.

Arms—Lozengy or and azure, a bordure argent.
Crest—A hawk with wings expanded and belled ppr.
Motto—Esto super vias antiquas.

Residence—2031 Locust Street, Philadelphia, Penna.
Clubs—Faculty, Phila. ; Metropolitan, Wash. ; University, Balto.
Societies—Sons of Revol. ; Spanish-Am. War ; Pa. His. ; D. of Columbia Hist.

Q UINCY, MARY PERKINS,
of New Haven, Ct. (Da. of John Williams Quincy of N.Y., 1813-83, *m* (2) Lucretia D. Perkins, 1832-83 ; gt.-grandson of Judge Edmund Quincy, father of Dorothy, who *m* John Hancock, Pres. of the Continental Congress, 1776, and Govr. of Mass. ; son of Judge Edmund Quincy, Colonial Envoy to Court of St. James's ; son of Colonel Edmund Quincy, whose descdt., Abigail Smith, *m* John Adams, 2nd U.S. Prest., whose son, John Quincy Adams, was 5th Prest. ; son of Edmund Quincy, 1602-35, of Mass. Bay Colony, 1633 ; son of Edmund and Ann (Palmer) Quincy of Wigsthorpe, Northamptonshire, Eng.—Also descd. from Govr. John Haynes, 1594-1654, and Govr. George Wyllys, of Connecticut, 1642).

Arms—Gules, seven mascles conjoined three, three, and one or.
Crest—Three ostrich feathers argent.   *Motto*—Sine maculâ macla.

Residences—47 Hillhouse Avenue, New Haven, Conn. ; New York City.
Societies—Colonial Dames, Colonial Governors.

THOMAS, RONALD,
of Santa Barbara Cal. (Second son of Col.
John Addison Thomas, U.S.A. [son of Isaac Jeton
Thomas], Adjut.-Genl. State of N.Y., Asst. Sec.
of State 1855-57, *b* 1810, *d* Paris, France, 1858,
m Catherine, *d* Paris, France, 1885, da. of Thomas
A. Ronalds, 1783-1832, *m* 1815, Maria D. Lorillard;
son of James Ronald, *b* at Paisley, Scotland, 1752,
d 1812, emigrated to America, *m* Margaret Ritchie
of Paisley; son of Alexander Ronald, *b* Paisley
1692, *d* 1784, a descendant of the Earl of Orkney).

Born in N.Y. City Nov. 3, 1848, *m* (1) April 1881,
Daisy, *d* May 1900, da. of John C. and Mary
(Potter) Richards, M.D. ; Physician and
Surgeon in Civil War ; *m* (2) April 1902, Julia, da. of the late Thomas
Trowbridge and Adelia (Edson) Hayes, of N.Y. City.

Arms—Sable, a chevron and canton ermine.
Crest—A unicorn's head erased.   *Motto*—Virtus invicta gloriosa.

Residence—" The Roses," 1926 Santa Barbara Street, Santa Barbara, Cal.
Clubs—N.Y. Union League, N.Y. Athletic, Country of Westchester Co., Santa
Barbara Country.
Societies—Life Mem. Holland Lodge F. and A.M., Mem. 7th Regt. Veteran Assn.

MORGAN, JAMES LANCASTER (3RD),
of New York City (Son of James Lancaster
Morgan (2nd), *b* 1845, *m* Alice M., da. of John J.
Hill, of Albany, N.Y. ; son of Abijah, 1783-1869 ;
son of Charles, 1756-1833 ; son of Charles, 1720-60 ;
son of James, 1683-1764 ; son of Charles and
Elizabeth Morgan, of Flushing, Long Island, 1683).

Born in Brooklyn, N.Y., April 27, 1867 ; Grad.
Ph.B. School of Mines, Columbia Univ., N.Y.,
1888 ; *m* November 2, 1892, Maria Letitia, da.
of Hon. Alex. T. Goodwin, of Utica, N.Y.

Issue.
i. JAMES LANCASTER (4th), *b* July 24, 1893,
d Sept. 14, 1894.
i. HELEN RIDGLEY, *b* May 26, 1896.

Arms—Vert, a lion rampant or; impaling (Goodwin) or, a lion passant guard.
sable, on a chief gules three lozenges vairé.
Crest—A reindeer's head cabossed proper.   *Motto*—Dum spiro spero.

Residences—201 West 55th Street, N.Y. City ; "Lanmore," Larchmont Manor, N.Y.
Clubs—University, Larchmont Yacht, Chemists'.
Societies—Colonial Wars, Psi Upsilon.

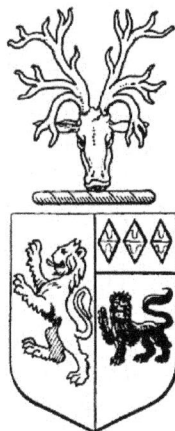

MAPES, CHARLES VICTOR,
    of N.Y. City (Son of Prof. James J. Mapes,
A.M., LL.D., 1806-66, one of the Founders of the
National Agricultural Society, m Sophia, d 1885,
da. of Judge Garrett Furman, of N.Y. City.—
Descended from Thomas Mapes, of Mape's Neck,
Southold, Long Island, N.Y., 1649, a descendant
of John Mapes, of Feltham, Co. Norfolk, Eng.,
who m Joice, grand-da. of Sir Hugh Blount).

Born at N.Y. City, July 4, 1836; A.B. Harvard
    University, 1857; m Martha Meeker, da. of
    Oliver Spencer Halsted.

Issue.

i. CHARLES HALSTED, b June 8, 1864.
ii. JAMES J., b Jan. 19, 1866, d April 10, 1896.
iii. HERBERT, b February 28, 1868, d August 23, 1891.
iv. VICTOR, b March 10, 1870.   v. CLIVE SPENCER, b Sept. 9, 1878.

Arms—Sable, four fusils in fesse or.
Crest—An arm embowed in armour or, holding in the gauntlet a spur argent
    leathered sable.
Motto—Fortis in arduis.

Residence—60 West 40th Street, New York City.
Clubs—University, Lawyers, Players, City, Barnard, Harvard, Suburban Riding
    and Driving.

COLGATE, BOWLES,
    of N.Y. City (Eldest son of Charles C.
Colgate, b August 22, 1822, d January 7, 1880,
m March 4, 1845, Frances Eliza, b March 21, 1826,
d June 8, 1888, daughter of Ira Perego; grandson
of Bowles Colgate, and great-grandson of Robert
Colgate, of Filston, Seven Oaks, Kent, b Sept. 11,
1758, d in America, July 20, 1826, grandson of
Steven Colgate, of Horsham, Sussex, 1703-64).

Born at Brooklyn, N.Y., Jan. 13, 1846; m Oct. 21,
    1869, Annie A., daughter of Charles Shields
    and Mary M., daughter of Rev. Merritt
    Haviland Smith.

Issue.

i. LATHROP, b February 2, 1877.
i. FLORENCE.

Arms—Argent, a chevron between three escallops sable.
Crest—A demi-wolf rampant holding in the dexter paw a sword.
Motto—Omne bonum desuper.

Residences—50 East 57th St., N.Y. City; "Shorcham," Monmouth Beach, N.J.

THAYER, WILLIAM HOLBROOK,
of Brookline Mass. (Son of Charles Edward
Thayer 1828-98 of Boston, *m* Mary Orr Hersey;
son of Dr. Joel F., *b* 1797, *m* Elizabeth Fessenden;
son of Johnathan, *b* 1760, *m* Betsy Faxon; son of
Capt. Johnathan, 1725-1805, *m* Dorcas Hayden;
son of Shadrach, 1701-83, *m* Rachael White; son
of Ephraim, 1669-1757, *m* Sarah Bass; son of
Shadrach, 1629-78, *m* (1) Mary Barrett, (2)
Deliverance Priest; son of Thomas Thayer, *b* at
Thornbury, Glouc., Eng., *m* Margerie Wheeler,
settled at Braintree, Mass., *d* 1665).

Born at Boston, Oct. 11, 1865; Grad. Harvard
Univ. A.B. 1889; *m* March 23, 1892, Lucy
R. Bouvé.

Issue.

i. CHARLES EDWARD, *b* Feb. 18, 1896.   i. ADÈLE BOUVÉ.
ii. ROBERT FESSENDEN, *b* May 24, 1899.

Arms—Per pale ermine and gules, three talbots' heads erased counterchanged.
Crest—A talbot's head erased or.   *Motto*—Foecundi galices.

Residence—Brookline, Mass.   *Clubs*—University, Boston Yacht.
Society—Sons of the Revolution.

BURCH, THOMAS HAMILTON, M.D.,
of N.Y. City (Son of Thos. Hamilton Burch,
of Alabama, *b* 1820, *m* 1848, Charlotte Clancy, da.
of Patrick Gray, of Dublin, of the Grays of Belfast,
Ireland, *m* Edith Bird of Alabama; son of Girard
Birch, of Girard, Ala., descd. from Rev. Peter
Birch, D.D., Canon of Westminster Abbey, 1710).

Born at Girard, Russell Co., Ala., Sept. 23, 1857;
Grad. M.D. Univ. City of N.Y., 1880; Surg.
of New Amsterdam Hospital; *m* Sept. 13,
1883, Martha Ann, 1862-92, da. of John and
Matilda (Gieger) Slonaker, of Jersey Shore,
Lycoming Co., Pa.

Issue.

i. THOMAS HAMILTON, Jr., *b* Sept. 8, 1884.

Arms—Azure, three fleurs-de-lis or.
Crest—A fleur-de-lis argent entwined with a serpent proper.
Motto—Prudentiâ simplicitate.

Residence—68 West 45th Street, New York City.
Clubs—New York Yacht, New York Athletic, Atlantic Yacht.
Societies—N.Y.Co. Medical, Fellow Academy of Medicine, Medical Jurisprudence,
Physicians' Mutual Aid Association, 32° Scottish Rite, Mystic Shrine.

LYMAN, HENRY DARIUS,
of N.Y. City (Son of Darius Lyman 1821-92,
Chief Nav. Div. Trea. Dept., U.S.A., m Betsy C.
Converse 1819-82; son of Hon. Darius Lyman, Judge
of Probate 1789-1865; son of Col. Moses Lyman,
son of Dea. Moses Lyman 1713-68; son of Captain
Moses Lyman 1689-1762; son of Moses Lyman
1662-1701; son of Lieut. John Lyman, b at High
Ongar, Essex, Eng., 1623, d at Northampton,
Mass. 1690; son of Richard Lyman 1580-1642 of
High Ongar, m Sarah Osborne of Halstead, Kent,
4th in descent from Thomas Lyman of Navistoke,
who m Elizabeth Lambert, gt.-grand-da. of Sir
William Lambert of Owlton).

Born at Parkman, O., April 12, 1852; 2nd Assist. Postmaster-General
U.S.; Pres. of Am. Surety Co. of N.Y.; m Jan. 13, 1887, Laura
McAllister; d Dec. 31, 1902, da. of the late John Alexander Stevens, M.D.

Arms —Qtly, 1 and 4, per chevron gules and argent, in base an annulet of the first
2, gules, a chevron betw. three sheep; 3, qtly. ermine and gules, a cross or
Crest —A demi-bull argent attired and hoofed or, langued gules.
Motto —Quod verum tutum.

Residence —41 West 73rd Street, New York City.
Clubs —Union League and Lotos, New York.

CADWALADER, CHARLES EVERT, M.D.,
of Philadelphia (Son of Hon. John Cadwalader
1805-79, Judge, U.S. Dist. Court, m (1) 1828, Mary
Binney, of Phila., m (2) 1833, Henrietta Maria,
1806-89, da. of Charles N. and Sarah Upshur
(Teackle) Bancker; son of Thomas, d 1841, Maj.-
Gen. 1st Div. Pa. Mil.; son of Gen. John, d 1786,
son of Dr. Thomas, Prov. Councillor, Chairman
of the Great Tea Meeting, Phila., 1733; son of John
Cadwalader, came from Wales to Penna. 1697,
settled in Merion).

Born in Phila., Nov. 5, 1839; Grad. Penna Univ., B.A. 1858, M.A. 1851,
M.D. 1861; Capt. 6th Pa. Cavalry (Lancers), and A.-de-C. on Staff of
Generals Hooker and Meade in command of Army of Potomac in
Civil War, with rank of Lt.-Col.; m July 15, 1897, Mary Bridget,
da. of Michael and Mary A. Ryan, of Limerick, Ireland.

Arms —Gules, a lion rampant argent, armed and langued azure.

Residence —240 South 4th Street, Philadelphia, Penna.
Clubs —University, United Service, Germantown Cricket.

Societies —Cincinnati, Sons of the Revol., Colonial Wars, War of 1812, Aztec
Army of Potomac, Loyal Legion, "Coll. of Physicians," Phila. Co. Medical
Am. Med. Assn., Grand Army of the Rep., Historical.

DAVIS, CHARLES H., Rear-Admiral, U.S.N.,
of Washington, D.C. (Son of Rear-Adml.
Chas. H. Davis, U.S.N., 1807-77, *m* Harriette
Blake Mills, *d* 1892; son of Daniel, 1762-1835,
Solr.-Genl. Mass.; son of Judge Daniel, 1713-99;
son of Joseph, 1662-1729; son of Robert, *d* 1693;
son of Dolor Davis, from Benefield, Northants.,
Eng., who settled at Cambridge, Mass., 1634, *m* at
E. Fairleigh, Kent, 1624, Margery Willard of
Horsemonden).

Born at Cambridge, Mass., Aug. 28, 1845; Midshipman, Nov. 29, 1861, Civil War; Capt.
U.S.N.; War with Spain; Comendador de
numero of the Royal Order of Isabella the
Catholic, of Spain; *m* Mar. 31, 1875, Louisa
M., da. of Surg.-Genl. John Van Pelt and Elizabeth (Wright) Quackenbush, M.D., of Albany.

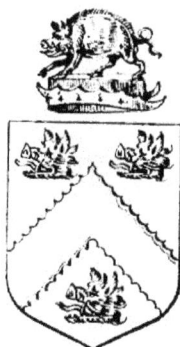

Issue.

i. CHARLES HENRY, *b* April 23, 1885. i. ELIZABETH.
ii. DANIEL, *b* Nov. 20, 1886.

Arms—Gules, a chevron engrailed between three boars' heads erased argent.
Crest—On a chapeau gules, turned up ermine, a boar statant.
Motto—Virtute duce comite fortuna.

Residences—Naval Observatory, Wash. D.C.; Conanicut Island, Narragansett
Bay, R.I.
Clubs—University, Knickerbocker, New York Yacht.
Societies—Cincinnati, Military Order of Foreign Wars.

O'DONNELL, JOHN CHARLES,
of Washington, D.C. (Eldest son of
Charles Oliver O'Donnell 1823-77, *m* Helen Sophia
Carroll 1840-86; son of Gen. Columbus O'Donnell,
m Eleanor C. Pascault; son of John; son of John
1715-80; son of Jacob, *d* 1765; son of John; son
of Jacob, *d* 1680; son of Edward, *d* 1651; son of
Hugh, *d* 1610; son of John, *d* 1581, 8th in desct.
from Aledh, 1333).

Born at Baltimore, Md., May 15, 1868; *m* April 8,
1896, Julia, da. of Major John Rufus N.Y.
Ordnance Corps, of Washington, D.C. and
Julia (McCauley) Edie.

Arms—Sable, two lions rampant, supporting a sinister hand between three
mullets argent.
Crest—Out of a ducal coronet or, a dexter arm embowed holding a javelin proper.
Motto—In hoc signo vinces.

Residence—1629 16th Street, Washington, D.C.
Clubs—Metropolitan (Washington), Baltimore, Chevy Chase (Baltimore),
Knickerbocker (N.Y.).

DODGE, WILLIAM EARL,
    of N.Y. City (Son of Wm. Earl Dodge, 1805-83
M. of Congress, *in* 1828, Melissa Phelps, of N.Y.; son
of David Low, 1774-1852; son of David, 1742-1807;
son of David, 1723-82; son of Daniel, 1677-1740;
son of Richard, 1643-1705; son of Richard of
Salem, Mass., 1638; son of John Dodge, of
Somersetshire, Eng.).

Born at N.Y. City, Feb. 15, 1832; Hon. A.M. Yale
    Univ.; Pres. N. E. Soc.; Pres. Nat. Arbitra-
    tion Soc.; Vice-P. N.Y. Chamber of Com.;
    Chairman Exec. Com. Met. Mus. of Art; Vice-
    P. Am. Mus. of Nat. Hist.; Dir. N.Y. Botanic
    Garden; Dir. U.S. Steel Corporation, etc.,
    m April 5, 1854, Sarah, da. of David Hoadley,
    Pres. Panama R.R. Co.

                    Issue.
i. WILLIAM EARL (3rd), *b* Oct. 17, 1858, *d* Sept. 14, 1884.
ii. CLEVELAND HOADLEY, *b* Jan. 16, 1860, *m* Grace Parish.
i. GRACE C.   ii. MARY M. H.   iii. ALICE HOADLEY, *m* W. H. Osborn.

Arms—Barry of six or and sable, on a pale gules a woman's breast guttant.
Crest—A demi sea-lion azure, collared finned and purfled or.
Motto—Leni perfruar otio.

_____

Residences—262 Madison Avenue, N.Y. City; "Greyston," Riverdale-on-Hudson.
Clubs—Century, Metropolitan, City, Reform, Union League, Country.
Societies—New England, Amer. Historical, Geographical, Continental Wars.

_____

CHUMASERO, WILLIAM (JUDGE), *deceased*,
    of Helena, Montana (Son of Isaac Chumasero,
1786-1833, of Nottingham, England, *m* Frances
Chamberlain 1792-1845.—Descended from Vasco
Yanez Chumacero, who *m* Catalina Gonzalis, of
Estramaduro, Spain, whose ancestor Don Juan
de Chumacero, Count de Guara, President of the
Council of Castile, and Ambassador to Rome, was
tortured in the Spanish Inquisition.)

Born at Nottingham, England, July 9, 1818;
    d in California Feb. 25, 1893; *m* Jan. 30,
    1845, Mary Elizabeth, *b* Feb. 25, 1824, da. of
    Amos Denison and Cornelia (Leonard) Brown.

                    Issue.
i. MARY ELIZABETH, widow of J. K. P. Miller.
ii. JULIA KATE, widow of C. A. Broadwater.
iii. ANTOINETTE.

Arms—Azure, two arms in armour argent issuing from the dexter side holding a
    budding club all within a bordure or, charged with seven suns in splendour
    gules and seven crosses of St. Anthony azure alternately.

_____

Family Residence—520 Benton Avenue, Helena, Montana.

DUNNELL, WILLIAM NICHOLS, Rev.,
of N.Y. City (Son of Elbridge G. Dunnell,
M.D., 1791-1827, of N. Y. City, m Sarah S.
Nichols, 1793-1868, of Waterbury, Ct.—Descd.
from Michail Dunnell, a French Huguenot, settled
in America 1653).

Born in N.Y. City, Feb. 3, 1825; S.T.D., Griswold
Coll.; Rect. Trinity Ch., Red Bank, N.J.,
1859-1871; Rect. All Saint's Ch., N.Y., since
1871; Chaplain 22nd Reg. N.G.S.N.Y.; Chaplain Nat. Guard Ass., S.N.Y.; Pres. Church-
man's Assn. of N.Y.: Prelate Palestine Commandery No. 18; Chaplain of Phoenix Chapter
F. and A.M., and Roome Lodge F. and A.M.;
m Harriet Hartland; da. of Rev. Benj. Evans
(Rect. Ch. of the Holy Evangelist, afterwards
in charge of St. George's Chapel, N.Y.), and Harriet Hartland, of N.Y.

Issue.

i. WILLIAM WARREN, 1860-80.   i. HARRIET HARTLAND, 1858-75.

Crest—Issuing from a castle in clouds an arm in armour holding in the hand
proper a plain cross argent.   Motto—Nec temere nec timide.

Residences—292 Henry Street, N.Y. City.   Club—Clericus.
Societies—Sons of the Revolution, Colonial Wars, Knight Templars, Masonic.

MORTON, HENRY SAMUEL,
of Hoboken N.J. (Son of Henry Morton
1836-1902 of Hoboken, N.Y., Pres. of the Stevens
Inst. of Technology, m Clara Whiting 1837-1901,
da. of Samuel N. and Clara (Whiting) Dodge;
son of Henry Jackson 1807-90, m Helen McFarlon;
son of Jacob 1761-1836, m Catherine Ludlow; son
of John, who came to America with the British
Army 1760, settled in N.Y. 1761, m Maria Sophia
Kemper; son of John Morton, of Dawson's Bridge,
Castledawson, Co. Antrim, Ireland; son of John
Morton, of Morton Hill, Ballynogher, Par. of Mayherafelt, Co. Londonderry,
where he settled after the Restoration of Chas. II.).

Born at Hoboken May 24, 1874; Patent Lawyer; Degree (M.E.)
Mechanical Engineer, Stevens Inst. of Technology 1837; m April 23,
1902, Sarah C., da. of Wm. White Bronson, Jr., of Phila. and
gt.-gt.-grand-daughter of Rt. Rev. William White, 1st Episcopal
Bishop of the U.S.

Issue.

i. HENRY, b January 27, 1906.

Arms—Or, a lion rampant sable.

Residences—529 River Street, Hoboken, N.J.; "Upenuff," Pine Hill, N.Y.
Clubs—St. Nicholas, Baltusrol Golf, New York Yacht, Underwriters.

CARTER, CHARLES SHIRLEY, M.D.,
of Washington, D.C. (Youngest son of
Thomas Nelson Carter, 1800-84, of Annefield, Va.,
m 1836, Anne Willing, da. of John Page, of Page
Brook, Va., and Evelyn Byrd Nelson, of York
Town, Va.; son of Dr. Robert, b 1774; son of
Charles, b 1732; son of John, b 1690; son of
Robert, 1663-1732, called "King Carter"; son of
Colonel John Carter, Member of Burgesses for
Virginia, 1649-58, Council 1668, d 1669).

Born at Annefield, Va., 1840; Surg., Confed. Army
in Civil War; Dir. and Vice-Pres., Peoples
Nat. Bank, Leesburg; Grad. Penna. Univ.,
M.D., 1861; m Oct. 22, 1867, Mary Mercer, da. of Gov. Thos. and
Elizabeth G. (Sherlock) Swann, of Md.

Issue.
i. CHARLES SHIRLEY, Jr., b Dec. 22, 1870, m Elizabeth Bentley.
ii. WILLIAM PAGE, b Mar. 6, 1884.
i. ANNE PAGE, m Dr. W. J. S. Stewart.   ii. LOUISE SHERLOCK (decd.).

Arms—Argent, a chevron betw. three cart wheels vert.
Crest—On a mount vert a greyhound sejant argent, sustaining a shield of the last
charged with a cart wheel vert.   *Motto*—Purus excelleris.

Residences—1430 "N" St., N.W. Washington, D.C.; Bellegrove, London Co., Va.
Clubs—Metropolitan, Washington Golf.
Societies—Sons of the Revolution, Soc. of the District of Columbia.

VEASEY, ISAAC PARKER,
of Great Falls Montana (3rd son of George
Ross Veazey, 1820-56, m 1850 Eliza, 1824-70, da. of
Rev. John Mason Duncan; son of Dr. John; son
of Dr. Thomas, of "Essex Lodge," Md.; son of
Col. John; son of Edward, of Essex Lodge; son
of John Veazey, of Cherry Grove, Md., 1687).

Born at Baltimore, Md. Feb. 13, 1854; admitted to
the Bar 1875; Pres. of 1st Branch of City
Council 1881-82; City Solicitor 1883; Post-
master of Baltimore 1885; m April 13, 1875,
Grace, d Feb. 24, 1900, da. of Thomas
Stockton Gaddess of Baltimore, Md.

Issue.
i. THOMAS STOCKTON, b Oct. 13, 1877.
ii. ISAAC PARKER, Jr., b Jan. 9, 1882.
i. ELIZA, b 1878, d in infancy.   iii. SARAH WARD, b 1881, d in infancy.
ii. ELIZABETH REVELY.   iv. GRACE GADDESS, b 1883, d in infancy.

Arms—Ermine, on a cross sable five martlets or.
Crest—An arm embowed couped at the shoulder, erect from the elbow, habited
gules, cuff ermine, holding in the hand proper four leaves vert.

Residence—Great Falls, Montana.

BROOKE, GEORGE SMITH,
of Spokane (Son of Rev. Robert D. Brooke,
of Md., 1824-98, *m* Mary W. Smith; son of Thomas,
d 1824; son of Thomas, *d* 1785; son of Thomas,
d 1768; son of Walter, *d* 1740; son of Thomas,
d 1744; son of Col. Thomas, *d* 1730; son of Major
Thomas, *d* 1676; son of Robert Brooke, of Manor of
" De la Brooke," Md., *b* Whitchurch, Hants, 1602,
M.A. Oxford, 1618-24, grandson of Richard Brooke,
of Whitchurch, and Southampton, Hants, *d* 1594).

Born at Dubuque, Iowa, Feb. 12, 1855; Mayor of
Sprague, Wash., three terms; Pres. of the
Fidelity Nat. Bank, Spokane; Sen. Warden
All Saints' Cathedral; Grad. A.B. Griswold
Coll., Davenport, Iowa, 1872; *m* 1882, Julia
Isabella, da. of Joseph W. Hill, of Westport, Conn.

Issue.

i. ROBERT DUNBAR, *b* 1882.
ii. PHILIP SLAUGHTER, *b* 1892.
iii. GEORGE MAGRUDER, *b* 1898.

i. REBECCA.
ii. JULIA ELTINGE.
iii. MARY WATSON.

Arms—Chequy or and azure, on a bend gules a lion passant of the first.
Crest—A demi-lion rampant erased or.

Residence—Spokane, Washington.
Societies—Colonial Wars, Sons of the American Revolution.

HOLLINGSWORTH, ELLIS,
of Boston (Son of Ellis A. Hollingsworth,
1819-82, of S. Braintree, Mass., *m* 1844 Susan J.,
da. of Rufus and Susan (Kingsbury) Sumner of
Milton, Mass.; son of Mark, 1777-1855; son of
Amor, 1739-1826; son of Thomas, 1698-1753; son
of Thomas, *d* Winchester Va. 1732; son of Valentine
Hollingsworth, came to America with William
Penn in 1682, *m* Catherine Cornish, da. of the
High Sheriff of London).

Born at South Braintree, Mass., Feb. 9, 1860;
m Oct. 2, 1895, Elsie Madeline, da. of John
Henry Littlefield of Dorchester, Mass., by
Susan Jane, da. of Joseph and Madeline
Robinson.

Arms—Azure, on a bend argent three holly leaves vert.
Crest—A stag couchant argent.
Motto—Disce ferenda pati.

Residences—38 Fairfield Street Boston; " Edgemere," Vineyard Haven, Mass.
Clubs—Union, Athletic, New Riding.

M ORRIS, ROBERT CLARK,
    of N.Y. City (Son of Col. Dwight Morris
1816-94, Consul-Gen. to France, Sec. of State of
Conn., *m* 1868 Grace J. 1844-84, da. of Lewis W.
Clark of Chicago Ill.; son of James 1754-1817;
son of James; son of James; son of Eleazar; son
of Thomas Morris, Morris Cove N.H., 1637, signed
the "Plantation Covenant"; son of Thomas; son
of Roger; son of Hugh; son of Rees ap Ieven;
son of Ievan ap Philip of Carmarthen; son of Philip
ap David; son of Philip Dorddu ap Howel; son
of Howel ap Madoc; son of Cadwgan ap Elystan).

Born at Bridgeport, Ct., Nov. 19, 1969; Atty. and
    Counsellor-ot-Law; Lecturer in Law Dep.
    Yale Univ.; Grad. at Yale Univ. 1890;
    Master of Laws 1892; Doctor of Civil Law 1893; Counsel for the
    U.S. and Venezuelan Claims Commission 1903; *m* June 24, 1890,
    Alice A., da. of Andrew Y. Parmelee, of New Haven, Ct.

Arms—Quarterly, 1 and 4 gules, a lion rampant, guardant or; 2 and 3 argent,
    three boars' heads couped sable.
Crest—A lion rampant guardant, or.
Mottoes—1. Gwell angau na chwlydd. 2. Marte et mare faventibus.

———

Residences—767 Fifth Avenue, N.Y. City; Lakewood, N.J.
Clubs—Yale, Republican, Tuxedo, Metropolitan, Lakewood Country.
Societies—Cincinnati, Loyal Legion, Sons of the Revolution, Bar Association,
    International Law Association, Society of Medical Jurisprudence.

———

M OTT, ROBERT GAYOSA,
    of N.Y. City (Son of James Mason Mott,
1800-86, of Balto., Md., *m* 1830, Caroline Jeannette
Mècanger, 1816-99, of Balto.; son of Joshua,
d 1832; son of Gershom, 1726-87; son of Gershom,
1698-1758; son of Charles, *d* 1741; son of Adam
Mott, came from Co. Essex, England to New York
1645, *d* 1690, *m* Elizabeth Redman).

Born at Baltimore, Md., March 29, 1841; Mem.
    N.Y. Stock Exchange; *m* 1871, Agnes Mary,
    da. of Joseph Marin Cooper, President of
    Chatham National Bank, of N.Y. City, and
    Agnes, da. of Hood Gibson.

Issue.

i. Joseph Cooper, *b* Feb. 25, 1872.
i. Jeannette Le Brun, *m* W. Eugene Parsons.

Arms—Sable, a crescent argent.
Crest—An estoil of eight points argent.   *Motto*—Spectemur agendo.

———

Residence—20 East 55th Street, New York City.

GLENN, Mrs. HELEN AUGUSTUS (*née* GARRARD).

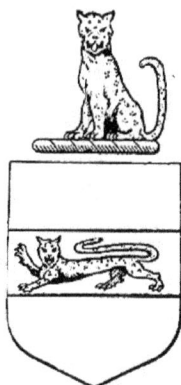

of Atlanta, Ga. (da. of William W. Garrard, 1818-66, of Columbus, m Frances J. G. Urquhart : son of Jacob ; son of Anthony, 1756-1807 ; son of Jacob, came to Virginia 1741 ; son of Jacob Antoine ; son of Peter Garrard, of Lille, France, who settled in Eng. 1687).

Born at Garrard, Ga., m April 23, 1873, John Thos. Glenn, 1844-99, son of Col. Luther J. Glenn, [descended from the Glens of Bar, Linlithgow, Scotland], who m Mildred Lewis R., da. of John A. Cobb, who m Sarah R., da. of Thomas Reade Rootes, of " White Marble," Va., grandson of Major Philip Rootes, of " Rosewall," Va., who m Mildred Read, grand-da. of Col. Geo. Reade, who came to Virginia 1637, grandson of Andrew Reade, of " Faccombe," Hampshire, Eng., 1585.

Issue.

i. JOHN THOMAS, d inf. 1876.   iii. LUTHER JUDSON, d inf. 1881.
ii. GARRARD, b Aug. 17, 1878.   iv. WILLIAM L., b April 16, 1887.
i. ISA URQUHART, m Capt. S. J. B. Schindel, U.S.A.
ii. HELEN M.

Arms—(Garrard) Argent, on a fesse sable a lion léopardé of the field.
Crest—A leopard assis proper.

Residence—33 Forest Avenue, Atlanta, Ga.
Societies—Colonial Dames of America, Order of the Crown in America.

EDDY, CHARLES HENRY,
    of Boston, Mass. (Second son of Henry W.

Eddy, b Oct. 17, 1826, m Jan. 3, 1850, Julia A. Foster, b Aug. 28, 1828, d April 6, 1883.— Descended from John Eddy, came to Plymouth in the " Handmaid," Oct. 29, 1630, removed to Watertown, Mass., d Oct. 12, 1684, m (1) Amy, m (2) Joanna, who d Aug. 25, 1683, æt. 80 ; son of Rev. William Eddy, Vicar of St. Dunstan's Church, Cranbrook, Kent, England, a native of the City of Bristol, Gloucestershire).

Born at Worcester, Mass., October 5, 1860.

Arms—Sable, three old men's heads couped at the shoulders argent, crined proper.
Crest—A cross-crosslet fitchée sable, and a dagger argent, hilt or, in saltire.
Motto—Crux mihi grata quies.

Residences—The Berkeley, Boston, Mass.; Sutherland Road, Aberdeen.
Club—Puritan.

CHURCHILL, WINSTON,
of Cornish N.H. (Son of Edward Spalding
Churchill of Portland Me., *b* 1846, *m* 1871 Emma
Bell Blaine of St. Louis; son of Edwin 1812-75,
m Mary Phipps Carter; son of James Creighton
1787-1865, *m* Eliza Walker Osborne; son of Thomas
1762-1807, *m* Alice Creighton; son of Thomas,
m Mary Stuart Ewes; son of Barnabas, *m* Lydia
Harlow; son of Joseph, *m* Sarah Hicks; son of
John, settled at Plymouth Mass. 1643, *d* 1662,
m Hannah Pontus; son of Jasper Churchill of
London, Eng., 1628, 18th in descent from Gitto de
Leon, 1055).

Born at St. Louis Mo., Nov. 10, 1871; Grad. U.S.N.
Acad. Annapolis 1894; Hon. A.M. Dartmouth
1903; Author; Mem. N.H. Legislature 1903-4;
m Oct. 22, 1895, Mabel Harlakenden Hall.

Issue.

i. John Dwight Winston, *b* Dec. 21, 1903.   i. Mabel Harlakenden.

Arms—Sable, a lion rampant argent debruised with a bendlet gules.
Crest—Out of a ducal coronet or, a demi-lion rampant argent.
Motto—Robur ex parvo.

Residences—Harlakenden House, Cornish, N.H.; 28 The Fenway, Boston, Mass.
Clubs—Tennis and Racquet, Boston, Century N.Y., New York, Union N.Y.,
Univ. St. Louis, Blue Mountain Forest Game, Tavern Boston, Pilgrims
of London, &c.

THOMPSON, FREDERICK DIODATI,
of Islip L.I. (Son of David Thompson
1798-1871, *m* Sarah Diodati Gardiner 1807-91; son
of Hon. Jonathan 1773-1846; son of Judge Isaac
1743-1816; son of Jonathan 1710-86; son of Samuel
1668-1749; son of John, one of the original Proprietors of Brookhaven, *d* 1688; son of Rev.
William Thompson, Grad. of Brazenose Coll.,
Oxford, 1619, settled in New Eng. 1634).

Born Dec. 17, 1850; Grad. LL.B. Columbia
Coll.; Turkish Commissioner to the Chicago
Exposition, decorated by the Sultan with the
Orders of Medjidieh and Osmanlieh; Chevalier
of the Holy Sepulchre of Jerusalem; Chevalier
of St. Maurice and St. Lazare; Comdr. Crown
of Italy, created Italian Count 1902.

Arms—Or, on a fesse dancette azure three etoiles argent, on a canton of the
second the sun in his splendour.
Crest—A cubit arm erect vested gules cuffed argent, holding in the hand five ears
of wheat or.   *Motto*—In lumine lucem.

Residence—Sagtikos Manor, Apple Tree Wick, West Islip, L.I., New York.
Clubs—Union, Knickerbocker, Metropolitan of New York.
Societies—St. George, Colonial Wars, Sons of the Rev., Misencordia of Lucca,
Italy, N.Y. Hist., L.I. Hist., Acad. of Design, Delta Psi, the Cincinnati.

HYDE, JAMES NEVINS, M.D.,
of Chicago, Ill. (Eldest son of Edward
Goodrich Hyde, of New Orleans, La., *b* Sept. 20,
1811, *d* Sept. 4, 1888, *m* Nov. 9, 1836, Hannah
Huntington, da. of Henry Thomas, of Norwich,
Conn.—Descended from William Hyde, of Hartford,
Conn., 1616, *d* 1681, and from John Alden,
1599-1687, who *m* Prescilla Mullins).

> *Born* at Norwich, Ct., June 21, 1840, passed
> Assist. Surg., U.S. Navy; Prof. of Derma-
> tology, Rush Med. Coll., Chicago; Grad.
> Yale Univ. A.B. 1861, A.M. 1865; Univ. of
> Penn. M.D. 1869; *m* July 31, 1871, *Alice
> Louise, da. of Alexander Griswold.

Issue.

i. CHARLES CHENEY, *b* May 22, 1872.

Arms—Azure, a chevron between three lozenges or.
Crest—An eagle, with wings endorsed sable beaked and membered or.
Motto—Deus nobis haec otia fecit.

Residences—2409 Michigan Av., Chicago; "The Barnacle," Prouts Neck, Me.
Clubs—The Onwentsia, Lake Forest, University, Athletic, Chicago.
Societies—Military Order of the Loyal Legion, Colonial Wars, Mayflower
    Descendants, *Colonial Dames, *Daughters of the American Revolution.

FISKE, LOUIS SAMUEL,
of Philadelphia (Son of Samuel Lyon Fiske
1815-69, *m* Maria Louise Hodges; son of Major
Samuel 1773-1833; son of Deacon Daniel 1709-78
of Sturbridge Mass.; son of Nathan 1672-1723 of
Watertown; son of Lieut. Nathan 1642-96; son of
Nathan, *b* at Weybread, Co. Suffolk, Eng., settled
at Watertown, Mass., 1640; son of Jeffery Fiske,
who was descended from Symond Fiske, Lord of
the Manor of Stadhaugh, Suffolk, *temp.* Hen. viii.).

> *Born* at Southbridge, Mass., Feb. 14, 1844, *m* (1)
> April 23, 1883, Mary, da. of Capt. John Dobson
> of Phila., *m* (2) May 10, 1894, Mrs. Katharine
> H. Tucker.

Issue.

i. SARAH DOBSON, *b* Feb. 11, 1886.

Arms—Chequy argent and gules, on a pale sable three mullets pierced or.
Crest—On a triangle argent an estoile or.

Residence—2042 Locust Street, Philadelphia.
Clubs—Union League, Phila., Country, Radnor Hunt, Rose Tree Fox Hunting,
    Germantown Cricket.
Societies—Pennsylvania Historical, New England of Pa.

K EMPER, ANDREW CARR, M.D. (*deceased*),
of Cincinnati (Son of David R. Kemper,
1793-1849, *m* Sarah Hall, 1799-1868, da. of Hugh
Fulton, of Kentucky, who *m* Jane Rogers of Dublin.
—Descd. from John Kemper, of Virginia, 1714; son
of Johann von Kemper, an Oberst in Palatinate
Army, Com'dr of Stahleck Castle, Bacharach on
Rhine, 1712).

Born at "E. Walnut Hills," O., July 11, 1832, *d* Aug.
15, 1905; Grad. Centre Coll., Ky., 1855;
Univ. of Louisville, 1866, B.A., M.A., M.D.;
Asst. Adj.-Gen., Capt. on Staff of Maj.-Gen.
H. W. Halleck, 1861-65; *m* Jan. 10, 1865,
Louisa A., da. of James and Caroline (Brown)
Anderson, Jr., of Louisville.

Issue.

i. CARR LAWSON, 1867-74.
ii. JAS. BROWN, Capt. U.S.A., *b* Jan. 6, 1876, *m* 1903, Mercer Mason.
i. CAROLINE, *m* Louis Carlton Bulkley, of Bossier, Louisiana.
ii. SARAH HALL, 1870-74.

Arms—Party per pale gules and azure, on the 1st a griffin rampant argent, on
the 2nd a griffin rampant or, facing each other.
Crest—A demi-griffin or, langued gules, holding a hammer or, headed argent.
Motto—Die Kemper.

———

Residence—(Mrs. A. C. K.) c/o L. C. Bulkley, Alden Bridge, Bossier Pa., La.

C ORNING, HENRY WICK,
of Cleveland, O. (Son of Warren H. Corning,
b 1841, *m* 1864, Mary Helen, da. of Henry Wick,
of Cleveland.—Descended from Ensign Samuel
Corning, Freeman of Boston, Mass., 1641).

Born at Cleveland, Jan. 13, 1869; at St. Paul's Sch.,
Concord, N.H. 1882-87; Grad. of Harvard
Univ., 1891; 1st Lt., Troop A, Ohio, N.G.,
1896; Capt. 1st Ohio Vol. Cavalry 1898;
Commd. Troop B during Spanish-Am. War;
m Nov. 2, 1897, Edith, da. of William and
Sarah (Bushnell) Warden, of Philadelphia."

sue.

i. WARREN HOLMES, *b* Feb. 25, 1902.   i. MARY.

Arms—Argent, a saltire sable.
Crest—A bugle-horn stringed gules.   *Motto*—Crede cornu.

———

Residence—1147 Prospect Street, Cleveland, Ohio.
Clubs—Knickerbocker of N.Y. City, Union, Country, Roadside, Tavern of
Cleveland, Hasty Pudding, A.D., Harvard Univ.

A VERY, FRANK MONTGOMERY,
of Brooklyn, N.Y. (Eldest son of Lieut.
Irving Montgomery Avery, of Brooklyn, N.Y.;
Lieut. 48th Regt. N.Y.S. Vols., 1861-64; Brigade
Quartermaster 2nd Brigade 10th Army Corps;
b Scipio, N.Y., July 1, 1832; *m* Auburn, N.Y.,
April 10, 1856, Jane Sabrina, *b* Dec. 18, 1835;
d Oct. 11, 1894, daughter of the Hon. Garret V.
Orton, Judge, &c., and Rosamond Cooke, his wife,
of Auburn, N.Y.—Descended from (1) Christopher
Avery, *b* in England *circa* 1590; settled at
Gloucester, Mass., 1630; removed to New Lon-
don, Conn., 1663; Freeman of the Colony, 1669;
d March 12, 1679; (2) Captain James Avery, 1620–
1704; served in King Philip's and Frontier Wars;
Judge, and Deputy to General Court; (3) Captain James Avery, Jr.,
1646-1732; Guardian Pequot Indians; Judge; Deputy; (4) Captain
James Avery, 3rd, 1673-1754; Guardian Pequot Indians; Judge;
Deputy; (5) Lieut.-Col. Ebenezer Avery, 1704-80; Ensign, Lieut. and
Capt., and Lieut.-Col. 8th, Conn.; Deputy; (6) Lieut. Ebenezer Avery,
Jr., 1732-81; Ensign and Lieut. 8th, Conn., killed in action, Fort
Griswold, Sept. 6, 1781; (7) Col. Ebenezer Avery, 3rd, 1762-1842;
served in War 1812; (8) Rev. Charles Eldredge Avery, 1794-1854.
Also descended from Elder William Brewster, 1561-1644, who drafted
the Mayflower Compact, and from Captain George Denison, 1619-94,
wounded at the Battle of Naseby, served in King Philip's War and other
Indian Wars in Connecticut).

Born in Brooklyn, Nov. 22, 1857; Counsellor-at-Law; Educated at
University of Heidelberg, Germany; Graduated LL.B., University
of the City of New York, June, 1882; Judge Advocate General of
the Military Order of Foreign Wars of the United States; *m* at
Mannheim, Germany, Sept. 7, 1880, Therese Marie, daughter of
George Craddock, of Philadelphia.

Issue.

i. IRVING MONTGOMERY, *b* June 8, 1881.

ii. HENRY CRADDOCK, *b* Aug. 10, 1885.

i. MARION FRANCES.

Arms – Gules, a fesse between three bezants or.
Crest—Two lion's gambs or, supporting a bezant.
Motto—Fidelis.

Residence—108 Lincoln Place, Brooklyn, New York City.
Club—Montauk.
Societies—Colonial Wars, Sons of the Revolution, War of 1812, Sons of the
American Revolution, Conn. Military Order of Foreign Wars, Military
Order of the Loyal Legion, Bar Association, Fellow of the American
Geographical Society.

DALL, HORACE HOLLEY,
of N.Y. City (Son of Austin Dall 1819-99,
m 1851, Mary A., da. of W. M. and Harriette
W. (Holley) Brand of Lexington Ky.; grandson of
James Dall of Boston, who m Henrietta, da. of
Elijah and Esther (Phelps) Austin, of New Haven,
Ct., a member of the Austin family which received
grant of land in Texas, prominently identified with
its settlement, after whom the capital was named.
Esther Phelps was da. of Judge John Phelps of
Stafford, Ct., officer in Am. Rev., a Delegate to
Convention at Hartford, Ct., that, 1788, ratified the
U.S. Constitution. The wife of Judge John Phelps
(and mother of Esther), Lady Mary Richardson,
was a lineal descendant of Sir Thomas Richardson, Speaker of House of
Com. *temp.* James I., L. C. Justice of Eng. under Charles I., buried in
Westminster Abbey.—Descended from W. Dall of Boston 1760, *b* in
Forfar, Co. Angus, Scotland 1716, *m* Elizabeth Bradford 1751, *d* 1803).

Born at Baltimore Md. May 21, 1860.

Crest—On a chapeau gules, turned up ermine, a lion passant crowned with a
ducal coronet or. *Motto*—Coronat fides.

Residence—40 Garden Place, Brooklyn, N.Y.
Clubs—Crescent Athletic (Brooklyn), Church of the Diocese of L.I.
Societies—New Eng.; 7th Regt. Vetn. Assn., Southern, N.Y.; Maryland, N.Y.

COLES, HENRY RUTGERS REMSEN,
of East Hampton L.I. (Eldest son of Isaac
Underhill Coles, and Catherine S. Remsen, his
wife.—Descended from Robert Cole, of Suffolk,
Eng., who emigrated to America in 1630).

Born at Tarrytown, Westchester Co., N.Y.,
July 15, 1873, *m* at Geneva, Switzerland,
Margaret Miller, da. of Sylvanus Miller
Davidson, 9th in descent from Malcolm
Davidson, of Dingwall, Scotland.

Issue.

i. HENRY RUTGERS REMSEN, *b* May 28, 1897.

Arms—Qtly., 1 and 4, argent, a bull passant gules
armed or, within a bordure sable bezantée;
2 and 3, argent, a chevron sable between three
trefoils slipped vert.
Crest—A demi-dragon vert, holding in the dexter paw an arrow or, headed and
feathered argent.
Motto—Deum cole regem serva.

Residences—126 East 34th Street, New York City; East Hampton, L.I.
Clubs—Union, N.Y. Athletic.
Societies—Sons of the Revolution, Colonial Wars, Old Guard of Chicago,
Huguenot, Genealogical Biographical and Historical.

WEBB, WILLIAM SEWARD, M.D.
of Shelburne Farms, Vt. (Son of James W.
and Laura V. (Cram) Webb, grandson of Gen.
Saml. B. Webb 1753-1807, who served as Lt.-Col.
and A.-de-C., Staff of Gen. George Washington,
a founder of the Soc. of the Cincinnati.—Descd.
from Richard and Eliz. Webb, from Gloucestershire, Eng., with Rev. Thos. Hooker, settled at
Hartford, Ct., 1635).

Born in N.Y. City, Jan 31, 1851 ; Grad. Columbia
Univ., M.D. 1875 ; Col. and A.-de-C. Staff of
Gov. of Vt. ; Mem. of Vt. Legislature ; Chair-
man and President, Rutland R.R. Co. ; Pres.
St. Lawrence and Adirondack R.R. ; *m* Dec.
20, 1881, Lila O., da. of Wm. H. and Louisa
(Kissam) Vanderbilt.

Issue.
i. JAMES WATSON, *b* July 1, 1884.
ii. WILLIAM SEWARD, Jr., *b* May 11, 1887.
iii. VANDERBILT, *b* April 23, 1891.   i. FREDERICA VANDERBILT.

Arms—Gules, a cross engrailed humettée between four falcons or.
Crest—Out of a ducal coronet a demi-eagle displayed or.

Residences—Shelburne Farms, Shelburne, Vt. ; 680 Fifth Avenue, New York City.
Clubs—Metrop., Un. League, Univ., Tuxedo, Racquet, Country, N.Y. Yacht, West-
minster Kennel, Riding, Church, Grolier, Turf & Field, Somerset, St. James.
Societies—St. Nicholas, Sons of the Am. Revol., Colonial Wars, Foreign Wars.

PLACE, BARKER,
of N.Y. City (Son of James Keyes Place
1815-97, State Commissioner Public Works, Mem.
Coffee Exchange, Director Mercantile Library
Association N.Y. City, *m* Susan Angévine, da. of
Nathaniel and Hannah (Angévine) Barker of N.Y.
City ; son of Dr. Charles 1793-1858, *m* Dorothy
Keyes ; son of Ephriam, 1774-1840, *m* Ann McIvor ;
son of James 1753-93, *m* Mary Golden ; son of
Aaron Place 1682-1770, born at Bristol, England,
m Mary Burtis).

Born at N.Y. City July 1, 1849; 7th Regt. Veteran ;
m Nov. 19, 1872, Grace, da. of Samuel
Newhall and Nannie Norwood Fenno (Bailey)
Fuller of Boston.

Issue.
i. MARIAN, *m* June 8, 1904, Percy S. Hildreth.

Arms—Per pale or and gules a lion passant guardant counterchanged.
Crest—A tree proper.   *Motto*—Vive revicturus.

Residence—127 East 26th Street, N.Y. City.

TISDALL, FITZGERALD, Ph.D.,
of N.Y. City (Son of FitzGerald Tisdall of
Greenwich, L.I., *b* 1813, *d* 1878, *m* April 11, 1837,
Elizabeth Ann Clute, *b* 1820, *d* 1858, da. of Jacob
Didymus Clute of Schenectady N.Y., a family of
Dutch descent, settled there for over 250 years;
grandson of Michael Tisdall of Cork, Ireland, and
Bristol, England, a cousin of the Rt. Hon. George
Canning, First Lord of the Treasury and Premier
of Great Britain in reign of George IV., and whose
son, Viscount Canning, was Governor-General of
India during time of Sepoy Mutiny; great-grandson
of Rev. FitzGerald Tisdall of Cork, Ireland, who
was descended from the Tisdalls of Mount Tisdall
and the Manor of Martry, county Meath, a branch
of the ancient family of the same name in England which bore Arms
" three pheons argent on a shield sable," which Arms, Richard St. George
Ulster King-of-Arms in 1679, ratified and confirmed to Michael Tisdall,
Esq., J.P., of county Meath, and his brothers, adding "a thistle or, for
distinction," as is stated in the original certificate in Ulster's office. Also
great-great-grandson of Colonel Robert Magaw of the Pennsylvania Line
in the American Revolution, and great-great-great-grandson of Colonel
Cluert van Brunt of the New York Assembly during the same period.)

Born at Greenwich, N.Y., March 15, 1840; Grad. N.Y. City College 1859;
appointed Director of Cooper Union Schools of Science and Art
1870; received honorary degree of Doctor of Philosophy, N.Y
University, 1874; appointed Professor of Greek Language and
Literature in College of City of New York 1879; J.P. of Woodbridge
N.J.; *m* Dec. 23, 1885, Florence Victoire, da. of Aman Theodore
Michel Aristide Rodrigue, M.D. (Baron de Curzay), of Philadelphia
Penna. and of Ann Caroline, da. of Hugh Bellas, Esq., of Sunbury
Northumberland Co. Penna., his wife; descended from Hugh
Bellas, Esq., of Co. Antrim, Ireland (1717-89), of the noble family
of Bellasis of Bellasis, Co's. Durham and York, of peerage of Great
Britain, *temp.* Charles I.

Arms—Sable, a thistle or, between three pheons, points downwards, argent.
Crest—Out of a crest coronet or, an armed hand erect holding in the hand an
arrow, all proper.
Motto—Tutantur tela coronam.

Residences—" Lladsit Wold" (" Bellasylva"), Woodbridge, N.J.; 80 Convent
Avenue, Hamilton Grange, N.Y. City.
Clubs—University, City College, Delta Kappa Epsilon and Schoolmaster's of
New York City.
Societies—American Institute of Archæology, Phi Beta Kappa Alumni Association,
American Philological (all of New York City), Salmigundi of Woodbridge.
N.J., and Member of Managing Committee of American School of Athens,
Greece.

BENJAMIN, Mrs. JULIA KEAN (*née* FISH), of Garrison, N.Y. (Da. of Hon. Hamilton Fish, 1808-93, Mem. of Congress, Gov. State of N.Y., U.S. Senator, U.S. Sec. of State 8 years, during Gen. Grant's Admin., Mem. Soc. of the Cincinnati, 40 yrs. its Pres.-Gen., *m* Julia, *d* 1887, da. of Peter Philip Kean; son of John Kean, of S. Carolina, Mem. 1st C. Congress; son of Col. Nicholas, 1758-1833; son of Jonathan, 1728-79; son of Samuel, 1704-67; son of Jonathan, 1680-1723; son of Nathan; son of Jonathan Fish, of Mespat, Newtown, L.I., 1653).

Born at N.Y. City, *m* Dec. 8, 1868, Maj. Saml. Nicoll Benjamin, 1839-86; Maj. and Asst. Adj.-Gen., Brev. Lt.-Col. U.S.A.; Grad. W. Point, 2nd Lt. Artillery 1861; served through Civil War, twice brevetted; apptd. Ch. of Artillery 9th A. C. 1864; son of Wm. Massena and Sarah J. (Turk) Benjamin, of N.Y. City.

Issue.

i. WILLIAM MASSENA, *b* March 9, 1874.

ii. HAMILTON FISH, }

iii. JULIAN ARNOLD, } *b* Jan. 21, 1877.

Arms—(Fish) Sable, a chevron wavy between three fleurs-de-lis argent.

Crest—A tiger's head erased ermine, maned and tusked or.

Residence—" Ienia " Garrison, Putnam County, New York.

SMITH, JAMES CLINCH, of Smithtown, Suffolk Co., New York (Son of John Lawrence Smith *b* Sept. 16, 1816, *deceased*, and Sarah Nicoll, his wife, *deceased*, daughter of James Clinch, of New York.—Descended from Richard Smythe, "the Bull rider," of Myreshaw, Bradford, Yorkshire, Eng., Patentee, of Smithtown, L.I., 1650).

Born at Smithtown, Long Island, New York, April 3, 1856, Counsellor-at-Law; Graduated Columbia College, LL.B., 1878; *m* June 5, 1895, Bertha Ludington, daughter of Charles J. and Mary (Ludington) Barnes, of Chic., Ill.

Arms—Sable. six fleurs-de-lis argent three two and one.

Crest—Out of a ducal coronet or a demi-bull salient argent armed of the first.

Motto—Nec timeo, nec sperno.

Residence—Smithtown, Suffolk Co., New York.

Clubs—Union, Calumet, Metropolitan, New York Yacht, Sewanhaka Corinthian Yacht, Country, Riding, Larchmont Yacht, Meadow Brook Hunt.

Society—Delta Psi.

PAGET, ALMERIC HUGH,
of New York City (Sixth son of the late General Lord Alfred Henry Paget, C.B., Member of Parliament, Chief Marshal of the Royal Household, *b* June 29, 1816, *d* Aug. 24, 1888, *m* April 8, 1847, Cecilia, second da. of G. T. Wyndham, of Cromer Hall, Norfolk, by Maria, his wife, Countess of Listowel.—Descended from Henry, 1st Earl of Uxbridge, who in the lifetime of his father, 1711, was created Baron Burton of Burton, in Staffordshire, and Earl of Uxbridge, 1714.—He was descended from (1st Lord) Sir William Paget, who in the 4th of Edward VI. was sent Ambassador to the Emperor Charles VI. and was created Baron Paget of Beaudesert).

Born in London, England, March 14, 1861 ; *m* Pauline, da. of the Honble. William C. Whitney, of New York City.

Arms—Sable, on a cross engrailed between four eagles displayed argent, five lions passant guardant of the field.
Crest—A demi-heraldic tiger sable, maned ducally gorged and tufted argent.
Motto—Per il suo contrario.

Residences—11 East 61st Street, New York City ; Great Neck, L.I.
Clubs—Metropolitan, Racquet, Lawyers ; Turf, and White's (of London).

TRENCHARD, EDWARD,
of N.Y. City (Son of Rear-Adml. Stephen D. Trenchard, U.S.N., 1818-83, *m* Ann O'Connor Braclay, 1819-78; son of Capt. Edward, 1787-1824, U.S.N.; son of Curtis, *b* 1745; son of George, *b* 1706, Attorney-General under the Crown ; son of George, 1686-1728; son of George Trenchard, 1535-1715, to W. Jersey in Wm. Penn's Company, kinsman of Sir John Trenchard).

Born at Phila., Pa., Aug. 17, 1850 ; Recorder, Naval Order of U.S., N.Y. Com.; Companion, Order of Bolivar, 3rd class, conferred in recognition of service rendered the Republic of Venezuela ; *m* June 11, 1878, Mary, da. of William B. Stafford, Pres. of N. River Bank, N.Y.

Issue.

i. EDITH ISABEL.

Arms—Per pale argent and azure ; in the first three palets sable.
Crest—A cubit arm erect vested azure cuff argent, holding in the hand proper a sword of the second, hilt and pommel or.
Motto—Nosce te ipsum.

Residence 50 W. 92nd Street, N.Y. City.
Societies—Colonial Wars, Mil. Order, Naval Order, Mil. Order Loyal Legion.

MERRICK, JOHN VAUGHAN,

of Roxborough (Son of Samuel V. Merrick, 1801-70, of Hallowell Me., *m* Sarah Thomas; son of John Merrick 1766-1861, of Hallowell, *m* Rebecca Vaughan; son of Samuel Merrick 1726-67 of London, Middx., Eng., *m* Mary Riley).

Born at Phila. Aug. 30, 1828; Vice-Pres. Phila. Zoological Soc.; Pres. Free and Open Church Assn.; Trustee Pa. Univ.; Pres. Franklin Inst. 1867-70; *m* Oct. 23, 1855, Mary S. W., 1834-97, da. of Samuel O'Brie.

Issue.

i. JOHN VAUGHAN, *b* July 4, 1864, *m* Anne Harter.
ii. JAMES HARTLEY, *b* Sept. 5, 1869, *m* Edith Lovering.
i. EMILIE DUVAL, *m* George A. Bostwick.
ii. MARY VAUGHAN, *m* David E. Williams.

Arms—Qtly:—1 and 4 (Merrick) sable, on a chevron argent betw. three staves raguly or, inflamed ppr., a fleur-de-lis azure betw. two Cornish choughs ppr.; 2, gules, two porcupines in pale argent; 3 (Vaughan) azure three boys' heads couped at shoulders, snakes about necks ppr.

Crests—(1) On a tower or a Cornish chough ppr., in the dexter foot a fleur-de-lis azure; (2) a lion's head erased pierced through the neck with a spear.

Motto—Christi servitus vera libertas.

————

Residence—Roxborough, Philadelphia, Pa.

Clubs—Philadelphia, Union League Phila.

Societies—Amer. Philosophical, Franklin Institute, Amer. Soc. of Mechanical Engineers, Phila. Zoological Society.

WELLS, EDWARD,

of Burlington, Vermont (Son of William Wellington Wells, *b* Oct. 28, 1805, *d* April 9, 1869, *m* Jan. 13, 1831, Eliza, *d* Aug. 5, 1873, da. of Dan Carpenter, and Betsey Partridge, his wife, of Waterbury, Vermont.—Descended from Hugh Welles, who settled in Massachusetts, 1635; son of Thomas Welles, merchant, of London, and co. Essex, Eng., a branch of Welles of Lincolnshire).

Born at Waterbury, Vt., Oct. 30, 1835; City Representative of Legislature 1890-91; *m* (1stly) April 26, 1858, Martha Frances, *d* Nov. 25, 1876; *m* (2ndly) Oct. 14, 1879, Effie E., both daughters of Lucius Parmelee, of Waterbury, Vt.

Issue.

i. ANNA PARMELEE, (by 1st m.).

Residence—61 Summit Street, Burlington, Vermont.

Clubs—Algonquin, Ethan Allen, Nineteenth Century.

Society—Colonial Wars.

A GNEW, Honble. PARK,
of Alexandria, Va. (Son of John Park Agnew,
1819-92, *m* Matilda E., da. of John L. Thomas of
Lebanon, Pa. and Matilda E. Seeley of Vergennes
Vt., a desdt. of Robert Seeley, founder New Haven
Ct. 1630; son of John 1777-1849, *m* Elizabeth, da.
of Dr. Robert Park; son of David 1743-97, *m* Mary
Irwin; son of Capt. James Agnew, *b* 1711,
m Rebecca Scott, from the Agnews of Lochnaw,
presumably of Galdenoch, Scotland. Also from
Christopher B. Mayer *b* Carlsruhe, Germany, 1702).

Born at Cumberland Md. July 3, 1847; Collector
of Internal Revenue for 6th Dist., Va.; Chairman State of Va. Republican Committee;
Pres. and Director of several Corporations;
m Oct. 26, 1871, Laura Richards, da. of Robert Bell of Alexandria.

Issue.

i. John Park.

i. Matilda Bell, *m* Nov. 15, 1899, Walter Goodman Rogers.

ii. Mary Bell.   iii. Laura Thomas, *decd.*   iv. Margaretta Linton.

Arms—Argent, a chevron between two cinquefoils in chief gules, and a saltire
couped in base azure.

Crest—An eagle issuant and regardant proper.   *Motto*—Consilio non impetu.

Residence—Pitt Street, Alexandria, Va.

S TONER, STANLEY,
St. Louis Mo. (Son of Eben Rickart Stoner,
of Ohio, *b* Jan. 11, 1827, *m* Ann E. Whitaker, a
direct descendant of George Salisbury, to whom
George IV. gave a grant of land in Catskill Co.,
N.Y.; son of Joseph Stoner, 1795-1852, *m* Margaret
Fred; son of Philip, 1758-1838, of Penna. and
Ohio; son of Joseph Stoner, 1695-1770, settled in
Pennsylvania).

Born in Illinois, Jan. 19, 1865; Grad. B.S. Cornell
Univ., 1886; LL.B. Washington Univ., 1891;
Attorney-at-Law; *m* 1902, Evadne Gaty
Rumsey.

Arms—Per fesse sable and or, a pale engrailed between three eagles counterchanged.

Crest—Out of a ducal coronet sable a demi-eagle displayed or.

Motto—Robur atque fides.

Residence—5273 Westminster Place, St. Louis, Mo.

Clubs—St. Louis, University, &c.

Societies—Kappa Alpha, Cornell.

B ARTHOLOMEW, JAMES H. SHERMAN,
of Guerneville, Cal. (Son of Sherman Willard
Bartholomew 1825-62, of Sangerfield, N.Y.,
m Mary Eliza, da. of Stanton K. and Frances H.
Kingsbury) Parke, of Hebron, Ct.; son of Ira
1798-1830; son of Ira 1753-1828; son of Joseph
1721-81 son of Andrew, d 1755; son of Lieut.
William, 1640-97, served in King Philip's War;
son of William, d 1681; son of William, d 1634;
son of John Bartholomew of Burghursh).

Born at Sangerfield, N.Y., May 23, 1848; Grad. Eastman Coll., Poughkeepsie, N.Y., 1865; Iowa Wesleyan Univ. 1877; Charter Trustee
of Dakota Coll.; Atty-at-Law; U.S. Commr.; Trea. Lt. Wm. Bartholomew Assn.; Naval Lt.-Comdr. armed cable Ship, " C. H. Tupper,"
in Wilcox Rebellion; m Dec. 17, 1885, Helen Severance.

Issue.
i. SHERMAN BURGHURSH, *b* May 28, 1894.
i. MAY SEVERANCE.   ii. YULA DRURY.   iii. STELLA EMILY.

Arms—Argent, a chevron engrailed between three lions rampant sable.

Residence—Guerneville, Sonoma Co., California.
Societies—Colonial Wars, Sons of American Revolution, Mayflower Descendants,
Lieut. William Bartholomew Association.

D AVIDSON, SYLVANUS MILLER,
of Fishkill Landing, N.Y. (Fourth son of
Morris Miller Davidson, 1810-54, m 1840, Elizabeth
Shrimpton, *b* at Beaconsfield, Eng., da. of Dr. John
Stratford, Physician in charge of the London
Hospital.—Ninth in descent from Malcolm
Davidson, of Dingwall, Scotland).

Born at N.Y. City, Jan. 12, 1849; served in War
of the Rebellion; m at Yokohama, Japan
Jan. 30, 1871, Angelica Malcolm, da. of William
Ryan, of Phila., and Angelica Gilbert Malcolm,
da. of Joseph Gibbons and Angelica (Gilbert)
Malcolm.

Issue.
i. MALCOLM, *b* March 24, 1882.
i. MARGARET MILLER, *m* Henry Rutgers Remsen Coles, of N.Y. City.

Arms—Azure, on a fesse between three pheons argent a stag couchant gules,
attired with ten tynes or.
Crest—A falcon's head couped proper.
Motto—Sapienter in cinere virtus.

Residence—Fishkill Landing, New York.
Society—Sons of the Revolution.

DENNIS, RODNEY STRONG,
of N.Y. City(Son of Rodney Dennis of Hartford
Ct., *b* Jan. 14, 1826, *m* June 6, 1854, Clara 1831-88,
da. of Wm. Strong; son of Rev. Rodney Gove,
1791-1865, *m* Mary Parker 1793-1877; son of
Arthur 1745-1825, *m* Mary Goodhue 1749-1819;
son of Rev. John 1708-73, *m* 1736, Martha
Wilcomb; son of John 1673-171 2, *m* 1699, Lydia
White, 1673-1712; son of Thomas Dennis,
b Eng. *cir.* 1638, *d* 1706, *m* Grace Searle).

Born at Hartford Ct., Dec. 17, 1868 ; *m* May 9, 1890,
    Cecile, da. of Adolph and Barbara (Dix)
    Miellez, of Springfield, Mass.

Issue.

i. RODNEY GOVE.
i. DOROTHY, *d* April 25, 1896.   ii. FAITH.

Arms—Ermine, three battleaxes in pale gules.
Crest—A tiger's head erased ermine.

Residence—148 West 95th Street, N.Y. City.
Clubs—Calumet, Lawyers, N.Y.; Exchange, Boston; Baltimore, Germania, and
    Baltimore Country, Baltimore; Columbus Club, Columbus, Ohio.
Societies—Sons of the Revolution, Sons of the American Revolution, Colonial
    Wars, Mayflower Descendants, New England, &c.

BELLOWS, JOHNSON McCLURE, REV.,
of Norwalk, Ct. (Son of Geo. Gates Bellows,
b Boston 1827, *m* 1864, Mary White, da. of Josiah
E. and Harriet (Johnson) McClure, of Brookfield,
Mass.; son of John; son of Col. Joseph; son of
Col. Benjamin, the founder of Walpole, N.H.; son
of Benjamin; son of John Bellows, of Marlborough,
Mass., 1635, *d* 1682, *m* Mary Wood, of Concord).

Born at N.Y. City, Mar. 19, 1870; Grad. of Genl.
    Theol. Seminary, N.Y., 1893; Rector of Grace
    Church, Norwalk, Ct.; *m* June 1, 1896,
    Katharine Gaillard, da. of Charles and Harriet
    (Cleveland) Hammond, of Cleveland, O.

Arms—Sable, fretty or, on a chevron azure three lions' heads erased of the second.
Crest—An arm embowed habited, the hand proper grasping a chalice pouring
    water into a basin also proper.   *Motto*—Tout d'en haut.
Arms—(McClure) Arg. on a chev. engr., betw. two roses in chief and a sword in
    base, a mullet or.
Crest—A tower domed ppr. from the top a flag, thereon a rose crowned or.

Residences—The Rectory, Norwalk, Conn.; 267 Fifth Avenue , New York City.
Clubs—Calumet, N.Y. Clericus, Norwalk, Fairfield Clericus.

DOUGHTY, FRANCIS EDWARD M.D.,
of N.Y. City (Son of Samuel G. Doughty
1818-69, *m* 1844, Jane Rebecca 1824-61, da. of
Hon. Richard P. and Betsey A. (Howard) Hart,
of Troy, N.Y.; son of David S. 1786-1822; son of
Joseph, *b* 1763; son of Joseph 1730-1807; son of
Joseph 1692-1733; son of Elias 1664-1744; son of
Elias, *b* 1633, *d* at Flushing L.I., 1688; son
of Francis Doughty, *b* 1605, at Hempstead, Glouc.,
Eng., *m* Bridget Stone, of Earlhouse, Bedfordshire).

Born at Troy, N.Y., Aug. 14, 1847; Grad. at Coll.
of Phys. and Surgs., 1869, M.D.; *m* Oct. 12,
1868, Hannah, da. of Nathaniel Winthrop Starr.

Issue.

i. AUGUSTUS DURKEE, *b* April 2, 1875, *d* Dec. 21, 1875.

ii. NATHANIEL WINTHROP, *b* Sept. 11, 1879, *d* July 2, 1883.

i. FRANCES EDNA, *m* May 20, 1900, Frederic A. Lund, M.D.

Arms—Argent, two bars between three mullets of six points sable, pierced or.
Crest—A cubit arm erect, vested per pale crenelle or and azure, cuffed argent
holding in the hand proper a mullet as in Arms.

Residences—512, Madison Avenue, New York City; Eastern Point, Groton, Conn.
Clubs—Fencers, N.Y. Yacht Club.
Societies—St. Nicholas, Colonial Wars, Sons of the Revol., Mayflower Descdts.

BROWN, EDWARD MARSH,
of New York City (Eldest son of Edward
Brown, *b* June 2, 1815, *d* May 27, 1898, *m* March 11,
1837 Eliza James Marsh, *d* Dec. 18, 1883; son
of Robert and Sarah (Cox) Brown; son of Robert
Brown).

Born in New York City, Aug. 17, 1838, Commodore
of the New York Yacht Club; *m* Nov. 22,
1860, Adelaide Eugénie, da. of John Mayher,
and Jane Elizabeth McNally, his wife, of New
York City.

Issue.

i. CLARENCE EUGENE.

i. EMILY LOUISE.

Arms—Per pale, argent and sable, a double-headed eagle displayed counter-
changed.
Crest—An eagle displayed vert.
Motto—Suivez la raison.

Residence—45 West 46th Street, New York City.
Clubs—Union, Union League, Manhattan, New York Yacht, Larchmont, Players,
Church.

B ROOME, GEORGE COCHRAN,
of Binghamton, N.Y. (Son of Lt.-Col. John
L. Broome 1824-98, served with the Bombay Vols.
1842, India, Mexican War 1847, Civil War,
m Mary Cochran; son of John L. 1766-1835, Capt.
N.Y. Mil., War of 1812, *m* Mrs. F. A. Justic; son
of John 1734-1810, Lt.-Col. 2nd Regt., N.Y. War
of Revol., Lt.-Govr. State of N.Y., Broome Co.,
named in his honour, family Arms made its seal,
m Rebecca Lloyd of Lloyds Neck, L.I.; son of
John, *m* Marie, da. of Count de la Tourette).

Born at N.Y. City Dec. 7, 1866; Capt. N.Y. Militia
1890; Capt. Hawaiian Army 1895; Capt. 4th
U.S. Infy. Span.-Am. War; *m* April 12, 1898, Mary Orme Keyworth.

Issue.

i. MARY JOSEPHINE KEYWORTH.

Arms—Sable, on a chevron or three slips of broom vert.
Crest—A demi-eagle or, wings sable, in the beak a slip of broom vert.

Residence—Mount Broome, Binghamton, N.Y.
Club—Metropolitan of Washington, D.C.
Societies—Loyal Legion, Sons of the Revolution. St. Nicholas, Colonial Wars.

E LDREDGE, EDWARD HENRY, MAJOR,
of Boston, Mass. (Second son of James
Thomas Eldredge, of Boston, Mass., *b* June 1,
1828, *d* Dec. 18, 1889, *m* Oct. 24, 1855, Ellen
Sophia, da. of John D. W. Williams, of Roxbury,
Mass., and Ellen Sophia Bigelow, of Boston,
Mass.; son of Oliver 1789-1857, of Boston;
son of James 1745-1811, of Brooklyn Ct.; son of
Charles, 1720-95; son of Daniel Eldredge, of
Groton, Conn., *m* June 26, 1711, Abigail Fish, of
Groton. He is supposed to have been descended from John Eldred
(Eldredge), of Buckinghamshire, *b* 1592, afterwards known as John
Eldredge, of London, gentleman).

Born at Roxbury, Mass., Sept. 13, 1866; Major 8th Massachusetts
Infantry, U.S.V.; *m* Nov. 29, 1900, Mira Cressida Perruzzi de
Medici, daughter of Marchese Simone Perruzzi de Medici, of
Florence, Italy, and Edith Marion, his wife, daughter of William
Wetmore Story.

Arms—Per chief, a lion rampant (Harl. MS. 506).

Residence—Boston, Mass.
Clubs—Somerset, Country, Kennel of Boston, Army and Navy of N.Y. City.
Societies—Sons of Amer. Revol., War of 1812, Foreign Wars, Spanish-Amer. War.

A LMEY WILLEY HENRY,
of Rochester, N.Y. (Second son of Philip
Greene Almy 1818-73, of Rochester, N.Y., m Mary
Elizabeth 1828-97, da. of Nehemiah and Sarah
Ann (Van Schuyver) Osburn; son of Dr. Job
1782-1854; son of Thomas, b 1735; son of Job
1696-1717; son of William 1665-1747; son of
Christopher 1632-1713, Deputy from Portsmouth,
R.I. and Assistant to Gov. Andros; son of William
Almy, b 1601, from Benenden, Kent, Eng., settled
in Portsmouth, R.I., 1635, admitted a Freeman 1655, d 1677).

Born at Rochester, N.Y. May 15, 1858; m April 23, 1887, Jessie Louise,
da. of Hartwell Start, of Rochester, N.Y., and Ellen Augusta, da.
of George W. Moon.

Issue.
i. CHARLES OSBURN, b March 4, 1888.
ii. HERBERT EUGENE, b May 3, 1890.
iii. PHILIP GIRARD, b May 29, 1892.
iv. HARTWELL START, b Aug. 11, 1895.

Arms—Or, a turret in chief and crosskeys in base.

Residences—36 Oxford St., Rochester, N.Y.; Beach Avenue, Ontario Beach, N.Y.
Society—Sons of the American Revolution.

C OPE, PORTER FARQUHARSON,
of Philadelphia, Pa. (Son of Caleb Fredk.
Cope, 1797-1888, of Phila., m Josephine Porter;
son of William, b 1766; son of Caleb 1736-1824;
son of John 1691-1773; son of Oliver Cope and his
wife Rebecca, of Auburn, Co. Wilts., Eng., land
granted to him by William Penn 1681; son of
John, d 1649, of Marden, Wilts, who was 6th in
descent from Sir William Cope, of Banbury,
Oxfordshire, Eng., d 1513).

Born in Phila., June 15, 1869, m June 14, 1900,
Henrietta Bunting.

Issue.
i. MILLICENT SYNG BUNTING.
ii. LORETTA PORTER.

Arms—Argent, on a chevron azure, between three roses gules slipped proper, as
many fleurs-de-lis or.
Crest—A fleur-de-lis or, issuing from the top thereof a dragon's head gules.
Motto—Æquo adeste animo.

Residence—4806 Chester Ave., Philadelphia, Pa.
Societies—Tenn. Hist., Pa. Hist., Colonial of Pa., Hist. Geneal. of Pa., Am.
Branch (London) for Physical Research, &c.

GROSS, SAMUEL EBERLY, Capt. U.S.A.,
of Chicago (Son of John Custer Gross,
1819-95, of Dauphin Co., Pa., m 1843, Elizabeth
Eberly 1821-97; son of Christian 1788-1843; son of
Capt. John 1749-1823; son of John Gross, b at
Manheim, Germany, 1712, of Montgomery Co., Pa.,
1745; grandson of John Christoph Gross, Electoral
Magistrate of Böhl, a desct. of Seigneur Jean de
Gros, of Dijon, France, d 1456. Also of Huguenot
and Holland Dutch descent).

Born at the Mansion Farm, Pa., Nov. 11, 1843;
Capt. Co. "K" 20th Pa. Cavalry during the
Civil War; Capt. Chicago Contl. Gd.; Comdr.
Ill. Comdy. Mil. Order Foreign Wars; Vice-
Pres. Gen., Sons of the Am. Revol.; Pres. Ill. Soc. Sons of the Am.
Revol.; Dep.-Gov. Soc. of Colonial Wars; Govr. Chicago Art
Inst.; m Jan. 15, 1874, Emily Brown.

Arms— Qtly., 1 and 5, azure, a chevron betw. three saltires argent ; 2 and 6, argent
three bends azure ; 3 and 4. argent a lion ramp. sable armed gules.
Crest—A raven volant sable.   *Motto*—Teneo tenuere majores.

Residence—48 Lake Shore Drive, Chicago, Ill.
Clubs—Chicago, Union League, Union, Chicago Athletic, 20th Century, Caxton,
Press, Iroquois. Marquette, Washington Park, Union Veteran.
Societies—U.S. Grand Post No. 28 G.A.R., Pres. Soc. Western Army of the
Potomac, Huguenot of Am., Foreign Wars of the U.S., Sons of the Am.
Revol., Colonial Wars, Am. Wars, Pres. Holland Soc. of Chicago.

RULON-MILLER, JOHN,
of Bryn Mawr, Pa. (Son of William Henry Miller, b Dec. 1, 1824,
d May 18, 1868, m Elizabeth Archer, b Aug. 10, 1825, d March 25,
1866, daughter of John West Rulon, of Philadelphia; son of Daniel
Leeds Miller, 1788-1858, of Philadelphia; son of Andrew Miller, b 1760;
son of Andrew Miller, 1732-69; son of Ebenezer Miller, 1702-74; son of
Joseph Miller, who came from the State of Connecticut to Fenwick
Colony, New Jersey, 1698).

Born at Philadelphia, Nov. 6, 1850; assumed the additional name of
Rulon by decree of the Court, July 9, 1895; m Margaret Hansell,
daughter of Clayton French, of Philadelphia.

Issue.

i. John, b March 11, 1883.
ii. Sumner, b March 16, 1885.

i. Emily Spring   iii. Caroline French.
ii. Margaret Hansell.   iv. Mary Irvins.

Residences—2124 Pine Street, Phila.; Wyola Mawr, Newtown Square, Penna.
Clubs— Rittenhouse, Art, Country, Radnor Hunt, Merion Cricket, Bachelors.
Society—Colonial.

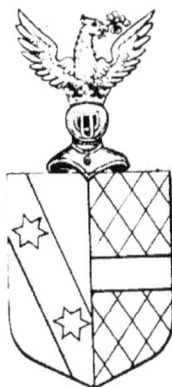

WISTAR, ISAAC JONES, General,
of Philadelphia, Pa. (Eldest son of Caspar
Wistar, M.D., of Philadelphia, 1801-67, *m* Lydia
Cooper Jones, 1804-78; son of Thomas; son of
Richard; son of Caspar Wister; son of Johannes
Caspar Wister, *b* 1696, at Wald Hilsbach, near
Heidelberg, Germany; settled in Phila. 1717).

Born at Phila. Nov. 14, 1827; Brig.-Gen. Vols.
U.S.A.; Pres. of Natl. Acad. of Natl. Sciences
of Phila., 1892-96; Pres. Am. Philosophical
Soc. of Phila.; Manager of Phila. Library
Co.; Founder of the Wistar Inst. of Anatomy
and Biology; Educated at Haverford Coll.,
1841-3; Sc.D. Univ. of Phila.; *m* July 9, 1862,
Sarah, da. of Robert and Rebecca Price
Toland, of Phila.

Arms—Per pale, dexter, argent, on a bend azure two mullets of six points argent;
sinister, lozengy argent and sable, a bar or.

Crest—Out of a crest coronet or, on a Knight's helmet full-faced with necklace, a
demi-eagle wings displayed sable, in its mouth a spray of six olives.

Residences—17th and Spruce Sts., Phila., Pa.; "Stockdale," Claymont, Delaware.

Clubs—Rittenhouse, University, Reform, of N.Y. City.

Societies—American Philosophical, National Academy of National Sciences.

SMITH, ROBERT HOBART,
of N.Y. City (Son of Wm. Alex. Smith,
b 1820, *m* 1847, Clara M. Bull, 1827-57; son of
Robert, *b* 1792; son of Capt. Robert, *b* 1752,
m Rebecca Hobart [6th in descent from Edmund
Hobart, *b* in Hingham Norf. 1570, one of the
founders of Hingham, Mass.]; son of William
Smith, *b* at Dumfries, Scotland, 1717, *d* N.Y. 1768).

Born at N.Y. City Feb. 22, 1848; Trinity Grad.
1869; *m* July 5, 1873, Dinah Watson, da. of
Josias Dunn, of "Airfield," Co. Dublin
Ireland.

Issue.

i. Robert William Hobart, *b* March 30, 1876.

Arms—(Hobart)—Sable, an estoile of eight points or between two flaunches
ermine.

Crest—A bull passant per pale sable and gules bezantée, in the nostrils a ring or.

Residence—542 West 150th Street, New York City.

Club—Century.

FAIRBANKS, ROBERT NOYES,
of N.Y. City (2nd son of Rev. Henry
Fairbanks, Ph.D., of St. Johnsbury, Vt., Prof. of
Natural Philosophy at, and Trustee of, Dartmouth
Coll., *b* 1830, *m* Annie Noyes, 1845-72; son
of Thaddeus, 1796-1886; son of Joseph, 1763-
1846; son of Ebenezer, 1734-1818; son of
Eleasur, 1690-1741; son of Eliesur, *b* 1655; son of
George, *d* 1682: son of Jonathan Fairbanks, of
Dedham, Mass., 1633, mentioned in the will of his
cousin, George Fairbanke, of Somerby, Yorks.,
Eng., 1650).

Born at Hampshire, N.H., Nov. 19, 1866; Grad. at
Dartmouth Coll., 1888; *m* Jan. 1, 1890, Camilla,
da. of W. II. Van. Kleeck, of N.Y.

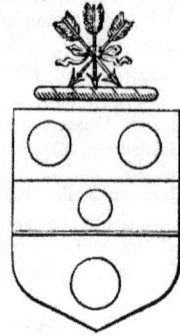

Issue.

1. SYDNEY VAN KLEECK, *b* June 8, 1895.   i. BEATRICE HELEN.

Arms—Argent, on a fesse azure between three hurts a bezant.

Crest—Three arrows tied together, one in pale and two in saltire, points
downwards.   *Motto*—Finem respice.

Residence—"Oaken Eaves" Hornsey Lane, Highgate, London, Eng.

Clubs—Engineers of N.Y., Automobile and Whitefriars of London.

Societies—"D.K.E.," Am. Mech. Eng'rs., Fell. R. Geographical Soc., American
Society in London.

PARSONS, MRS. JEANNETTE LE BRUN (*née* MOTT),
of N.Y. City, daughter of Robert Gayoza
Mott, who *m* 1871 Mary Agnes, daughter of Joseph
Marin Cooper, 1813-77, who *m* Agnes Gibson; son
of Joseph Cooper, of England, who *m* Charlotte,
daughter of Marin Le Brun, 1777-1863, of France,
who *m* Charlotte De Beaumont; son of Marin
Le Brun, Magistrate of the Royal Valliage of
Saint Sauveur Landelin and "Charge Conseiller
du Roi Maison de France," 1690).

Born at N.Y. City, *m* Oct. 28, 1893, William Eugene
Parsons of N.Y. City, son of William Chancery
and Emeline (Booth) Parsons of Northampton, Mass.

Issue.

i. LE BRUN.

Arms—(Le Brun) Per fesse azure and sable, in chief ten bees or, in base two
squares and a wolf or.

Residence—715 Park Avenue, New York City.

Society—St. Margarets, N.Y.

MERRILL, FREDERICK JAMES H.,
of Albany, N.Y. (Son of Maj. Hamilton
W. Merrill, 1814-92, U.S., Dragoons, *m* Louisa
Kauffman, 1820-97; son of Asa, 1785-1873; son of
Jared, 1754-1832; son of Israel, *b* 1716; son of
Daniel, 1673-1750; son of John, 1635-1712; son
of Nathaniel Merrill of Newbury, Mass., 1635).

Born in N.Y. City, April 30, 1861; Fellow in
Geology Columbia Univ.; Assist. Geologist
Geol. Sur. of N.J.; Dir. N.Y. Scientific
Exhibit, Chicago Exposition; State Geol. of
N.Y.; Dir. N.Y. State Mus.; *m* Sept. 1, 1888,
Winifred, da. of Emmet Edgerton, of N.Y.

Issue.

i. HAMILTON, *b* Dec. 21, 1890.   i. LOUISE EDGERTON.
ii. EDGERTON, *b* Apr. 21, 1901.   ii. WINIFRED.

Arms—Argent. a bar azure between three peacocks' heads erased proper.

Crest—A peacock's head erased proper.

Residences—" Kushaqua Farms," Altamont, N.Y.; 95 Washngtn. Ave., Albany, N.Y.

Clubs—Fort Orange, University, Reform, N.Y. Athletic, Larchmont Yacht. &c.

Societies—Acad. of Sciences, Am. Fisheries, N.E. Hist. and Geneal. Albany Hist.,
Colonial Wars, Sons of the Revol., Mil. O. of Foreign Wars, &c.

PECK, GEORGE, M.D., CAPT. U.S. NAVY (*deceased*),
of Elizabeth (Son of Aaron Peck, of Orange,
N.J., 1798-1865, *m* Miranda Pierson, 1800-63.—
Descended from Henry Peck, who came to Bosto
with Gov. Eaton, 1637, settled in New Haven, Ct.,
signed the Compact, June 4, 1639, *d* 1651; son of
Robert Peck of Beccles, Suffolk. Eng.).

Born at Orange, N.J., July 9, 1826; Coll. of Phys.
and Surg. N.Y., M.D., 1847; Hon. A.M.
Princeton; Commissd. Asst. Surg. U.S.N.,
Feb. 25, 1851; passed Asst. Surg. 1856; Surg.,
1861; Med. Insp., 1871; Med. Dir. and
Capt., 1878; retired, 1888; *m* Sept. 20, 1847,
Eliza A. Brewster, 1829-99. He *d* July 26,
1906, at Mohonk Lake, N.Y.

Arms—Or, on a chevron gules three crosses formée of the field.

Crest—Two lances or, in saltire, headed argent with pennons or, each charged
with a cross formée gules, enfiled with a chaplet vert.

Motto—Crux Christi salus mea.

Residence—(Mrs. G. P.), 926 North Broad Street, Elizabeth, N.J.

SULLIVAN, ARTHUR THOMAS,
   of N.Y. (Eldest son of Thos. Sullivan, 1817-80,
of Brooklyn, Pres. Brooklyn City R.R., m 1839,
Phebe S., 1812-1901, da. of Jarvis and Deborah
(Saxton) Powell, of Bettspage, L.I.; grandson of
Arthur Bull Sullivan, b at Waterford, Ireland,
1786; son of Thomas Sullivan, of Waterford).

Born at Brooklyn, N.Y., Jan. 15, 1842; m April
   23, 1867, Isabel, da. of James Keyes Place
   [5th in desct. from Aaron Place, b Bristol,
   Eng., 1682, d Hempstead, L.I., 1770],
   by Suzanne A., da. of Nathaniel Barker, and
   Hannah Angévine, of N.Y., a desct. of Andrée
   Augevine from Poitiers, France, 1685, to New
   Rochelle.
                          Issue.
i. ARTHUR BULL, b Feb. 25, 1873.   i. FLORENCE S.
ii. LEONARD, b Mar. 11, 1886.

Arms—Per fesse, the base per pale, in chief or, a dexter hand couped at the wrist,
   grasping a sword gu. entwined with a serpent ppr. betw. two lions ramp.
   respecting each other, gu.; the dexter base vert, charged with a buck trippant
   or; on the sinister base, per pale arg. and sa. a boar pass. counterchanged.
Crest—On a ducal coronet or, a robin, in the beak a sprig of laurel ppr.
Motto—Lamh foisdin-each an uachtar.

Residence—584 5th Avenue, New York City.
Clubs—Union League, New York Yacht, Metropolitan.

THOMPSON, HENRY BURLING,
   of Wilmington, Delaware (Son of Lucius Peters Thompson, b 1833,
m Caroline, da. of Benjamin Sands Burling; son of Newcomb B., b 1799,
m Harriett L. Peters; son of Samuel, b 1766, m Ruth Forster; son of
Benjamin, b 1735, m Phebe Davis; son of Benjamin Thompson, of
Bridgeton, N.J., b 1705, m Amy Newcomb).

Born 1857; Grad. at Princeton Univ., 1877; m 1891, Mary, da. of Major-
   Genl. James H. Wilson, b 1837, in command of the 1st Army Corps,
   U.S.A., Macon, Georgia; son of Capt. Harrison, Mem. of Govs.
   Council, Illinois, 1808-14, son of Sergt. Isaac G. Wilson, of Front
   Royal, Va., 9th Regt. Va. Line Continental Army, War of Rev.

                          Issue.
i. HENRY BURLING, JR., b 1897.
i. MARY.
ii. KATHARINE.
iii. MARGARET.

Residence—1305 Rodney Street, Wilmington, Delaware.
Clubs—University of New York, Philadelphia, Manheim Cricket, Delaware Field.
Society—Historical of Delaware.

CALHOUN, JOHN CALDWELL,
of New York City (Son of Andrew Pickens
Calhoun, 1812-65, of "Fort Hill," Pickens Co.,
S.C., Cotton Planter and Commissioner from South
Carolina to Alabama, 1860, at the beginning of
Civil War, m 1836 Margaret Maria, 1816-91, da.
of Duff Green, of Kentucky and Washington, D.C.,
by Lucretia Edwards, of Kentucky, sister of Ninian
Edwards, first Governor of Illinois ; grandson of
John Caldwell Calhoun, Secretary of War under
President Monroe ; Vice-President of the United
States under Presidents John Quincy Adams and
Andrew Jackson ; Secretary of State under Presi-
dent Tyler ; m Floride Calhoun, sister of John
Ewing Calhoun, first Senator from the up country
of South Carolina.—Descended from James Calhoun
(Colquhoun), and Catherine Montgomery, of Donegal, Ireland, who came
to America, 1733, with his son Patrick, who married Martha Caldwell,
grandson of Sir James Colquhoun, Principal Clerk of Sessions, who
m Mary Falconer of Edinburgh, a descendant of Sir John Colquhoun,
Governor of Dumbarton Castle, temp. James II.).

Born at Marengo Co., Alabama, July 9, 1843 ; left South Carolina College
(Sophomore year), 1861, to enter Civil War; Captain during the
Civil War with brevet rank of Colonel ; Chairman of Dobbs Ferry
Monumental Committee, 1894 ; Special Ambassador of Empire State
Society, Sons of the American Revolution, to France, 1897, on the
occasion of International Celebration of Franco-American Alliance,
Feb. 6, 1778 ; m Dec. 8, 1870, Linnie, da. of David Adams, of
Lexington, Kentucky, by Elizabeth Johnson, da. of Joel Johnson, a
brother of Richard M. Johnson, Vice-President of the United States.

Issue.

i. JAMES EDWARDS, b May 1, 1878, Captain U.S. Army.

ii. DAVID ADAMS, b January 14, 1881.

iii. JOHN CALDWELL, Jr., b April 22, 1887.

i. JULIA JOHNSON.

Arms—Argent, a saltire engrailed sable.

Crest—A hart's head couped gules.

Supporters—Two greyhounds, collared sa.

Mottoes—Si je puis ; Cnock elachan.

Residences—617 West End Avenue, New York City ; Hague, Lake George, N.Y.

Clubs—Manhattan, Lawyers, Reform, Democratic.

Societies—Southern, Sons of the American Revolution, Confederate Veterans.

DELCAMBRE, ALFRED PIERRE,
of N.Y. City (Eldest son of Major Alfred
Pierre Delcambre, of Mt. Vernon, N.Y., formerly
Judge of Westchester Co., N.Y., and for 24 years
an Officer of the 8th and 71st Regts., N.G.S.N.Y.,
b 1850, m 1877, Grace Margaret, b 1856, d 1901,
da. of Thomas and Margaret Lane).

Born at N.Y. City, 1878; Mem. of the 71st Regt.
U.S. Vols., and served with the Regiment
during Spanish-American War; Graduated at
St. Francis Xavier Coll., 1898: m Dec. 2, 1899,
Eugenia Gabrielle, da. of Count Louis Palma
di Cesnola, late Gen. U.S. Army, Director-in-
Chief of Metropolitan Museum of Art, N.Y.
City, and Marie Isabel, Countess di Cesnola,
da. of Admiral Samuel Chester Reid, U.S.
Navy, a lineal descendant of Henry Reid, Earl of Orkney, and Lord
High Admiral to Robert III. (Bruce), King of Scotland, 1393.

Crest—An arm in chain armour embowed holding a flaming sword.
Motto—Adhæreo virtute.

Residences—829 Park Avenue, N.Y. City; "Shady Dell," Mount Kisco, Westchester Co., N.Y.

GRISWOLD, GEORGE,
of Tuxedo Park, N.Y. (Eldest son of George
and Lydia (Alley) Griswold, of N.Y. City; son of
George, b 1777; son of George, b 1726; son of
Rev. George, b 1692, grad. Yale College, 1717; son
of Matthew, Dep. Gen. Court; son of Matthew,
1620-98, Black Hall, Lyme, Ct., first Magistrate of
Saybrook Colony, and agent for its Governor,
Colonel Fenwick, the regicide, m Anna Wolcott;
son of George Griswold, of Kennilworth, Warwickshire, Eng).

Born in New York City, April 3, 1857; Grad.
Harvard Univ., B.A., 1880; m May 4, 1886,
Emily O., da. of Edwin A. Post, of N.Y.,
and Margarett O., da. of Robert Oliver
Gibbes, of Charleston, S.C.

Issue.

i. GEORGE, b. October 8, 1896.

Arms—Argent, a fesse gules between two greyhounds courant sable.
Crest—A greyhound passant proper.
Motto—Volando reptilia sperno.

Residence—Tuxedo Park, Tuxedo, N.Y.
Clubs—Union, Metropolitan, Tuxedo, Porcellian of Cambridge, Mass.

R HODES, JOHN FOSTER,
of Chicago, Ill. (Fourth son of the Rev. Daniel
Rhodes, 1808-91, *m* (1) 1830, Elizabeth, 1810-53,
da. of John and Mary Lowry, *m* (2) 1855, Louisa,
da. of John and Nancy Cunnard; son of Henry
Rhodes, *m* Sarah Willard; son of John Henry
Rhodes, *m* Catherine Dofler; son of Henry Rhodes,
who left Frankfort-on-the-Main, 1750, for America,
and died on the way over, a descendant of
Huges I., Count de Rodez, brother of Willemus
Rode, of Rode, Co. Chester, England).

Born at Brownsville, Pa., Sept, 14, 1850; knighted
by the King of Portugal, and received the Royal
Military Order of Christ, 1895; *m* Sept. 12, 1878, Margaret White,
da. of John Paterson and Cornelia White of Portland, Ct.

Issue.
i. JOSEPH FOSTER, *b* November 18, 1881.
i. MARGARET ELIZABETH.
ii. NELLIE, *b* April 8, 1886, *d* May 8, 1887.

Arms—Quarterly, 1st and 4th gules, a lion rampant or; 2nd and 3rd argent, two
    bends gules, on a chief azure a label of three points or.
Crest—A double-headed eagle displayed sable.   *Motto*—Cœlum non animum.

Residences—Hotel Metropole, Chicago, Ill. ; Woodstock, Vt.
Clubs—Chicago, Chicago Athletic, Washington Park, Parmacheene of Maine,
    Lakota of Woodstock. Vt., Woodstock Country.

M ESIER, LOUIS (*deceased*),
of New York City (Son of Edward Sebring,
Mesier, 1803-54, by his second wife Georgianna
K., da. of Robert Hyslop, of Kelso, Scotland; son
of Peter A., 1773-1847, *m* Mary Van Wyck; son of
Abraham, 1726-74, *m* Eliz. Robbins; son of
Peter J., 1698-1784, *m* Jannitji Wessels; son of
Abraham, *b* 1663, *m* Eliz. van Cowenhoven; son
of Peter Jansen Mesier, *b* in Normandy, France,
1631, and Maritje Willems, of New York, 1660).

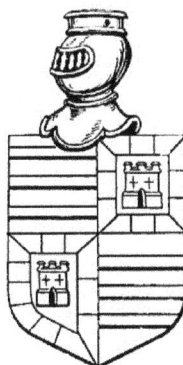

Born in N. Y. City, July 26, 1844, *d* 1904, *m* Dec. 4,
    1878, Maria Louise, da. of Josiah H. Gautier,
    of New York.

Arms—Quarterly, 1st and 4th, or, three bars azure, 2nd
    and 3rd, gules a castle or, within a bordure gobony of twelve argent
    and gules.

Crest—A helmet crowned proper.   *Motto*—Tiens à ta foy.

Residence—(Mrs. L. M.), 24 West 21st Street, New York City.

MOORE, Mrs. EVA (*née* CARLETON),
of Annapolis, Md. (Da. of Major-General
James H. Carleton, U.S.A., 1813-73, *m* Sophia
Garland, 1829-1880, da. of Samuel and Maria A.
(Garland) Wolfe; son of John; son of John; son of
Jonathan; son of John; son of John; son of Lieut.
John; son of Edward Carleton, *b* England, 1605,
of Rowley, Mass., 1639, Deputy in the General
Court of Mass. Bay, 1642-45; great gr.-son of
John Carleton, of London, who was 15th in
descent from Baldwin de Carleton, *viva* 1066).

Born at Fort Leavenworth, Kansas *m* Oct. 2, 1877,
Edwin King Moore, *b* July 24, 1847, Commander United States Navy, son of Joseph A.
and Nancy J. Moore.

i. MAUDE CARLETON, *b* May 12, 1884, *d* May 13, 1885.

Arms—(Carleton) Argent, on a bend sable three mascles of the field.
Crest—Out of a ducal coronet or, a unicorn's head sable, the horn twisted of the
first and second.
Motto—Quærere verum.

Residence—Naval Academy, Annapolis, Md.
Societies—Colonial Dames, Daughters of the American Revolution.

SEYMOUR, GEORGE FRANKLIN, Rt.
Rev., D.D., LL.D., D.C.L.,
Bishop of Springfield, Ill. (Only surviving son of
Isaac Newton and Elvira (Belknap) Seymour.—
Descended from Richard Seymour, of Hartford,
Conn., 1640).

Born at N.Y. City, Jan. 5, 1829; Grad. from Columbia Coll., 1850; Racine Coll. D.D.; Columbia
Univ. LL.D.; D.C.L. Univ. of the South,
Sewanee, Ten.; Founder and First Warden
of St. Stephen's Coll., Annandale, Dutchess
Co., N.Y.; Prof. of Ecclesiastical History in
the General Theological Seminary, N.Y. City;
Dean of the same; Consecrated Bishop of
Springfield, Ill., June 11, 1878; *m* July 23,
1889, Harriet Atwood, da. of John Jay Downe,
and Sarah Wentworth, of Strafford, N.H.

Arms—Gules, two wings conjoined in lure, the tips downwards or.
Crest—Out of a ducal coronet or, a phœnix in flames proper with wings
expanded or.
Motto—Foy pour devoir.

Residence—Bishop's House, Springfield, Ill.

RUGGLES, Mrs. VIRGINIA (*née* CABELL), of Milwaukee, Wis. (Da. of Dr. Robert H. Cabell, *d* 1876, of Richmond, Va., by 2nd w Cath. Eyre Pelham; son of Landon Cabell, *m* Judith Scott, da. of Col. Hugh Rose, *b* 1743, by Caroline M., da. of Col. Sam. Jordan and 2nd w. Judith S. Ware; son of Rev. Robert Rose of Richmond, Va. 1725, *b* at Wester Alves, Scot., *m* Ann, da. of Col. Hen. Fitzhugh of Va., 8th from Hugh Rose of Kilravock and Lady Margaret Seaton, da. of Earl of Huntley. Landon Cabell was son of Col. Wm. Cabell of Union Hill, Va.; son of Capt. Wm. Cabell of Liberty Hall, Va. and Bugley, Warminster, Wilts, Eng.).

Born at Richmond, Va., *m* (1) B. Howard Tyson of Balto., Md., *m* (2) Dec. 3, 1895, Charles Herman Ruggles of Milwaukee, Wis.

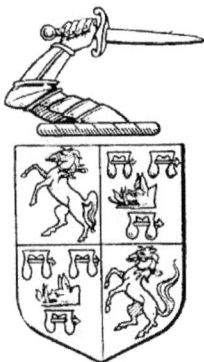

Issue.

(1st *m*)

i. B. HOWARD, *b* 1887, *d* 1888.
i. VIRGINIA.
ii. JULIA SCOTT.

(2nd *m*)

i. ANNA CRYSTIE.
ii. ALMA HAMMOND L'HOMMEDIEU.

Arms—(Cabell) Qrtly.; 1st and 4th sa., a horse ramp. ar. bitted and bridled or; 2nd and 3rd (Rose) or, a boar's head couped gu. betw. three water bougets sa.
Crest—An arm in armour embowed grasping a sword all ppr. *Motto*—Impavide.

Residence—Milwaukee, Wisconsin. *Clubs*—Acorn and Country of Phila.
Societies—Va. Hist., Daus. of the Am. Rev., Daus. of 1812, Daus. of the Confederacy, Councillor for Wis. "Order of the Crown," Founder "Order of the Constitution," "Colonial Dames."

SARGENT, Mrs. ELIA (*née* LEDYARD), of West Newton, Mass. (Youngest da. of the late William Stuart Ledyard and Frances Lavinia Worthington).

Born at Brooklyn, N.Y., *m* April 7, 1880, Prof. Dudley Allen Sargent, *b* Sept. 28, 1849, son of Benjamin Sargent, a desct. of William Sargent who came from Northampton, Eng., settled at Charlestown, N.E. 1639.

Issue.
i. LEDYARD WORTHINGTON, *b* June 29, 1882.

Arms—(For Ledyard) Ermine, on a chevron or three mullets pierced gules.
Crest—A demi-lion rampant argent, holding in the dexter paw a mullet gules.
Motto—Per crucem ad stellas.

Residence—Cambridge, Mass. *Club*—Newton Women Suffrage League.
Societies—Mayflower Descendants, Daughters of the American Revolution, United States Daughters of 1812, Browning.

CUSHING, HARRY COOKE, JR.,

of N.Y. City (Son of Major Harry Cooke Cushing, U.S.A., *b* 1841, *m* Martha W. Budd; son of George W., *b* 1809; son of Daniel, *b* 1783; son of Benj. 1735-86; son of Benj., *b* 1706; son of John 1660-1738; son of John 1627-1708; son of Matthew 1589-1616, came in ship "Diligent" 1638, settled at Hingham, Mass.; son of Peter, *d* 1596; son of Thomas, *d* 1588; son of John of Hardingham 1531; son of William, of Hingham 1492; son of Thos. Cushing, of Hardingham, Norfolk).

Born at Fort Foote Md. May 14, 1869, Grad. Cornell Univ. 1891, *m* Adelaide B., da. of I. Albert Connfelt of N.Y.

Issue.

i. HARRY COOKE 3rd, *b* June 10, 1895.
ii. LEONARD JARVIS, *b* Oct. 20, 1900.

Arms—Qtly., 1 and 4 gules, an eagle displ. argent; 2 and 3 gules, three dexter hands coupel argent, a canton chequy or and azure.
Crest—Two bears' gambs erased sable supporting a ducal coronet or, from which is suspended a human heart.

Residence—102 Waverly Place, N.Y. City.
Clubs—Westchester Country, Cornell University, Strollers.
Societies—American Institute of Electrical Engineers, Colonial Wars.

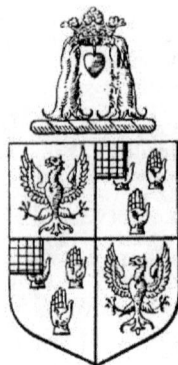

EARLE, HENRY MONTAGUE,

of N.W. City (Eldest son of Wm. Edward Earle, 1841-94, of Greenville, S.C., Captain and Major of Artillery, War of the Secession, Assistant U.S. Attorney of S.C., *m* Elizabeth Price, *d* 1878; son of Henry M., 1802-90; son of Aspasio; son of Baylis, 1795-1844; son of Samuel, 1692-1771; son of Samuel, 1670-1746; son of Samuel, 1638-99; son of John Earle, a Royalist, who came from Somersetshire, Eng., to Northumberland Co., Va., 1649, *d* 1697, related to Sir Walter Earle, Knt., Mem. Board of Managers, Virginia Coy., London).

Born in Greenville Co., S.C., March 28, 1870; Grad. at Georgetown Univ. L.B., 1893; *m* April 19, 1897, Mary Louise, da. of Elmore Frank Coe, of N.Y. City.

Arms—Gules, three escallops within a bordure engrailed argent.
Crest—A lion's head erased or, transpierced by a broken spear.
Motto—Vulneritus non victus.

Residence—239 Madison Avenue, New York City.
Clubs—City, Lawyers, Country, of New York; Metropolitan, of Washington.

WARD ANDREW HENSHAW, Jr.,
of Milton, Mass. (4th son of Andrew H.
Ward, of Allston, Boston, Mass., *b* 1824, *m* 1852
Anna H. Walcott, da. of Isaac and Sarah A.
(Walcott) Field, of Providence, R.I.; son of Andrew
H., *b* 1784; son of Thomas W., *b* 1758; son of
Maj.-Gen. Artemas Ward, 1727-1800, Chief Justice
of the Common Pleas Court, 1776, Comder. of the
Army of New Eng. under Gen. George Washing-
ton; son of Nahum, *b* 1684; son of William Ward,
b 1603, settled in Sudbury, Mass., 1639).

Born at Newton, Mass., April 18, 1864; Graduated
Harvard Univ., A.B. 1885, LL.B. 1892;
m July 3, 1899, Margaret, da. of Geo. Stowe
May, of Atlanta, Georgia.

Arms—Azure, a cross flory or.

Crest—A wolf's head erased proper
langued gules.

Mottoes—1. Non nobis solum.
2. Sub cruce salus.

Residence—Milton, Mass.

SALTONSTALL, DUDLEY WINTHROP,
of New York City (Son of Dudley E. Saltonstall, *b* 1846, of Toledo, O., *m* Annie Parmelia
Satterlee; son of Dudley G., *b* 1808; son of
Joshua; son of Dudley, *b* 1738, Commodore of the
American Fleet, Penobscot, 1779; son of Gurdon,
b 1708; son of Gurdon, *b* 1666; son of Nathaniel,
b 1639; son of Richard, *b* 1610; son of Sir
Richard Saltonstall of Huntwicke, *b* 1586, settled
in New Eng. 1630).

Born at New York City, June 22, 1874; Graduated
at Peekskill Military Academy.

Arms—Or, a bend between two eaglets displayed sable.

Crest—Out of a ducal coronet or a pelican's head azure.

Motto—Teneo tenuere majores.

Residence—Rye, N.Y.

Societies—Sons of the American Revolution, Naval Reserve Association.

E LKINS, STEPHEN BENTON, Honble.,
of Elkins, West Virginia (Eldest son of
Philip Duncan Elkins, *b* July 4, 1812, *m* Oct. 5,
1840, Sarah Pickett Withers, *b* November 15, 1814,
d November 10, 1865, daughter of Charles Withers,
and Jane Pickett, his wife, of Fauquier Co.,
Virginia ; son of Philip Elkins, *b* 1772.—Descended
from Ralph Elkins, who received from Governor
Francis Moryson, January 13, 1661, a patent of
land in York Co., Virginia, but located shortly
afterwards in what was then known as Westmoreland, but later King George Co., Va., between the
Potomac and Rappahanock Rivers. He was one
of the leading men of Virginia, and founder of the Elkins' family in
Virginia).

Born in Perry Co., Ohio, September 26, 1841 ; Graduated at Missouri
University, A.M., 1860 ; admitted to the Missouri Bar 1863 ; Member
of the Territorial Legislature 1864-5 ; U.S. Senator for West
Virginia, elected 1895 for six years ; U.S. Secretary of War, 1890-92 ;
Attorney-General and U.S. District Attorney for New Mexico ;
Member of Congress, two terms, 1873-77 ; Vice-President of West
Virginia Central and Pittsburg Railway ; *m* April 14, 1875, Hallie L.
Davis, daughter of Honble. Henry Gassaway Davis, who served
twelve years in the U.S. Senate, from West Virginia, by Katharine
Bantz, his wife, of Elkins, West Virginia.

Issue.

i. DAVIS, *b* January 24, 1876.

ii. STEPHEN BENTON, Jr., *b* October 20, 1877.

iii. RICHARD, *b* March 6, 1879.

iv. BLAINE, *b* September 14, 1881.

i. KATHARINE.

Arms—Per cross or and gules, a cross vairé between four tigers passant counterchanged, armed and langued azure, all within a bordure quarterly of the
second and first charged with fleurs-de-lis and roundels counterchanged.

Crest—A demi-tiger rampant quarterly ermine and erminois, armed and langued
gules holding between the paws a bezant.

———

Residences—1626 " K " Street, Washington, D.C.; 46 West 58th Street, New
York City ; " Hallichurst " Elkins, West Va.

Clubs—Chevy Chase, Washington, Metropolitan ; Republican, Union League
(N.Y. City).

MICKEL-SALTONSTALL, ANDREW H.
of Berkeley Springs, W. Va., who by
judicial decree assumed the name and arms of
Saltonstall (Son of Geo. B. Mickle 1830-90, of
Bayside, L.I., m Isabel, da. and co.-h. of Thomas
M. Beare and Mary Susan, da. of Wm. Saltonstall
of N.Y.; son of Hon. Andrew H. Mickle, Mayor of
N.Y. 1846; son of James Mickle, of Orange Co.,
N.Y., b Scotland, 1760; son of Archibald; son of
Robert; son of James viz. 1640, whose son Rev.
Alexander was father of Wm. Julius Mickle, R.A.,
of Portugal, translator of the "Luciad" of Camoens.
—Descended also from Sir Richard Saltonstal
1586-1660, of Yorkshire, came to Watertown Mass.
1628; m Grace, da. of Robt. Kaye of Yorkshire [9th in lineal descent from
Edward III.]; Proprietory Patentee and First Assist. Genl. Court Mass.
Bay Colony, Chairman Committee to arrange transfer of Government of
the Compy. to the Colony, 1629; original Patentee of Connecticut with
Lords Say and Sele, Brooke, and others; whose son Richard, b 1610,
m Muriel, da. of Brampton and Muriel S. Gurdo; Serg.-Maj. in Colonel
Endicott's Regt. 1641; Asst. and Depy.-Genl. Court. Mass 1635-49, whose
eldest son, Col. Nathl. 1647-1707, was in command of troops sent against
Gov. Andros 1680; whose son Gurdon 1666-1724 was Gov. of Conn. 1708;
whose son Gurdon of New London, 1708-85, m Rebecca Winthrop
[gt.-gr.-da. of Maj.-Gen. Wait Still Winthrop, and gt.-gt.-gr.-da. of Gov.
John Winthrop of Mass.; and gt.-gr.-da. of Gov. and Maj.-Gen. Thomas
Dudley, of Mass. 1576-1653], whose son Rosewell had William of N.Y.,
whose da. was Mary Saltonstall aforementioned).

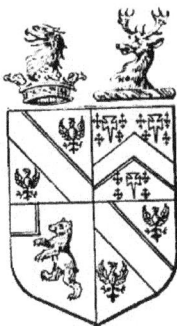

Born at "Bay Lawn," Bayside, L.I., N.Y., Oct. 5, 1856; m June 9, 1892,
Susan, da. of Dr. John Harrison and Sophie (Forrest) Hunter, of
Berkeley Springs, W. Va., of the Hunters of Hunterstown.

Issue.

i. Sophie Forrest.   ii. Muriel Winthrop.

Arms—Qtly. 1 and 4, or, a bend betw. two eaglets displ. sable (Saltonstall);
2, gules, a chevron betw. three crosses pattée fitchée each cantoned with
four cross-crosslets argent (Mickle); 3, argent, a bear rampant sable, a
canton gules (Beare).

Crest—Out of a ducal coronet or, an eaglet's head azure, (Saltonstall); a stag's
head, couped at the neck or (Mickle).

Motto—Teneo tennere majores.

———

Residence—"Dalmeny," Berkeley Springs, West Virginia.

Societies—N.Y. Genealogical and Biographical, Colonial Wars, Sons of the
Revolution, Order of Runnemede.

B ARTON, EDWARD RITTENHOUSE,
of Englewood, N.J. (Son of Rev. John G.
Barton, LL.D., 1813-77, Pres. of St. Paul's
Coll., L.I., m Anna Maria, 1824-94, da. of Captain
George and Sarah (Graeff) Musser, of Lancaster,
Pa.; son of Rev. David Rittenhouse Barton; son
of Rev. Thomas Barton, b Co. Monaghan, Ireland,
1730, studied at Dublin Univ., came to Phila.
1751, returned to England 1755 and was ordained
by the Bp. of Chester, m Esther Rittenhouse,
d 1780).

Born at College Point, L.I., July 24, 1847;
m May 25, 1870, Elizabeth Blanche, da. of Rev.
Alfred Hinsdale and Elizabeth B. (Dominick) Partridge, Rector of
St. Matthew's, Bedford, N.Y., 1838-55, Rector of Christ Church,
Brooklyn, N.Y., 1855-83.

Issue.
i. HOWARD RITTENHOUSE, b Sept. 28, 1871.
ii. ALFRED GRAEFF, b June 4, 1873, d Oct. 14, 1881.
i ELEANOR GRAEFF.   ii. ETHEL LOUISE.

Arms—Argent, three boars' heads couped gules, armed of the first.
Crest—A boar's head as in arms.   *Motto*—Crescit sub pondere virtus.

Residence—Lydecker Street, Englewood, Bergen, Co., N.J.
Club—Englewood.

S KINNER, HENRY WHIPPLE,
of Detroit (Son of Lieut. Edwin A. Skinner,
U.S.A., 1822-76, Lieut. and Quartermaster of 10th
Mich. Inft. Regt., m Catherine S., 1830-81, da. of
Major John Whipple; son of Richard, of Ohio,
m Cath. C. Hurin; son of Daniel, m 1789, Elizabeth
Todd; J., prob. son of Richard, d New Jersey,
1772; son of John Skinner, of Hoodbridge, N.J.).
Born June 8, 1852; L.S. Sp., Harvard Univ., 1891;
6 years' service Detroit Light Guard, Co. "A"
3rd Regt. Mich. State Militia; m June 25, 1892,
Henrietta C. da. of Richard H. Dana, of
Boston.

Issue.
i. RICHARD DANA, b April 21, 1893.

Arms—Sable, a chevron or between three griffins' heads erased argent.
Crest—A griffin's head erased argent, holding in its mouth a dexter gauntlet.
Motto—Nunquam non paratus.

Residence—360 Jefferson Avenue, Detroit, Mich.
Clubs—University, Institute of 1770, Harvard Glee Club. Hasty Pudding, Harvard
Univ., of Cambridge, Mass.
Societies—Founders and Patriots of Am., Colonial Gov., Colonial Wars, Sons of
the Am. Revol., War of 1812, Mil. Order of the Loyal Legion.

SUSE, FREDERICK EDWARD,

of N.Y. City (Eldest son of Theodore H. W. Suse, 1823-91, of Hamburg, Ger., *m* Anna L. E., 1828-83, da. of John E. and Christiane (Becker) Weber of Hamburg; son of Frederick H., 1789-1857, firm Suse & Co., Hamburg, Oberalter, St. Michaelis, *m* Sophia Magdalena, da. of Senator Claus H. and Jane (Hitchcock) Sonntag; son of Hieronymus J. B., 1745-1809, Procurator judicialis and advocati, of Hamburg, *m* (1) Maria Catharina and (2) Anna Lucia, both daus. of Hans H. and Maria (Moller) Willigmann; son of Berend Suse, 1715-45, Advocati, *m* Catharina Rebecca Willigmann; son of Berend Suse, 1675-1726, Imperial Notary and Advocate of Hamburg, *m* Anna Moller; son of Bernd Suse, of Hamburg, 1645).

Born at Hamburg, Germany, May 12, 1852; *m* Oct. 31, 1883, Léontine, Catherine, da. of Philipp Emile Sauer and Léontine, da. Jean Baptist Marié of N.Y. City.

Issue.

i. KATARINA ELISE.

ii. LÉONTINE MARIÉ.

Arms—Sable, a fesse argent.

Crest—A pair of eagles' wings sable, each charged with a fesse as in Arms.

Residence—N.Y. City.

LEWIS, CLIFFORD,

of Phila. (Son of David Lewis, 1800-95, *m* Camilla Phillips, *d* 1887; son of David, *b* 1776; son of Ellis, *b* 1734; son of Robert; son of Ellis ap Lewis (Ellis Lewis), *b* Wales *cir.* 1680, of Kennett Township, Pa., 1708; son of Lewis ap Robert by his wife Mary, who *m* (2) Owen Robert Robert and settled in Gwynedd, Pa., where he *d* 1722).

Born in Philadelphia June 18, 1843; Treasurer of the Mutual Assurance Co., *m* Feb. 9, 1869, Ellen E., da. of William Burn N. Cozens, of Philadelphia.

Issue.

i. DAVID, *b* Dec. 12, 1869.

ii. CLIFFORD, JR., *b* Mar. 28, 1871.

iii. WILLIAM BURN NASH, *b* Dec. 29, 1872.

i. ELEANOR.

Arms—Or, a lion rampant azure.

Residences—313 S. 12th Street, Philadelphia; Lakewood, N.J.; Cape May, N.J.

WARREN, CHARLES ELLIOT,
of N.Y. City (Son of George Wm. Warren,
1828-1902, Mus. Doc., Prof. of Columbia Univ.,
N.Y., m Mary E. Pease, 1839-91 ; son of George,
1789-1858; son of William, 1751-1831; son of
Phineas, 1718-97 ; son of Joshua, 1668-1760 ; son
of Caleb, b 1642 ; son of Richard, 1608-70 ; son of
Richard Warren, Signer of the Mayflower
Compact, 1620 ; son of Christopher Warren of
Headbury, England, a direct desct. of William de
Warrenne, 1st Earl of Warren and Surrey.

Born at Brooklyn, N.Y., April, 9, 1864 ; Major and
Ordnance Officer ; Inspector Small Arms, 5th
Brigade, N.Y.; m April 19, 1892, Anna M.
Geissenhainer.

Issue.
i. GEORGE WILLIAM, b June 24, 1899.
i. SUSANNE ELIZABETH. ii. MARGARET RESSLEAR.

Arms—Gules, a lion rampant argent, a chief chequy or and azure.
Crest—Out of a coronet a demi-eagle displayed. Motto—Pro patria mori.

Residences—326 89th Street, N.Y. City ; Oyster Bay, L.I.
Clubs—St. Nicholas, Union League. Lotos, Army and Navy, Seawanhaka.
Corinthian Yacht, Columbia Yacht, Knollwood Country, Westchester
Automobile.
Societies—7th Veteran, Sons of the Revolution, Colonial Wars, Mayflower
Descendants, Mil. Order of Foreign Wars, War of 1812.

CHRISTMAS, CHARLES HENRY,
of Brooklyn, N.Y. (Son of Charles Christmas,
of Manchester, England, and Brooklyn, N.Y., by
Harriett Andrews).

Born in Brooklyn, N.Y., 1826 ; m 1849, Emily,
da. of Captain Henry Davis and Abigail
Robinson, his wife, of Southport, Ct.

Issue.
i. CHARLES WAKEMAN, b Dec. 24, 1851, d Oct. 1895.
i. FLORENCE EMILY, b Sept. 9, 1855, d June, 1868.
ii. HARRIET ANDREWS, m Nov. 23, 1875, John
Chester Eno, of New York City, and
Simsbury, Conn., a descendant of James
Eno, who came from England and settled in Windsor, Conn.,
1646, d 1682.

Arms—Gules, on a fesse or, between three hares argent, a crescent of the second
between two martlets of the first.
Crest—An arm erect charged with two bars, one or, the other gules, holding in
the hand a double branch of roses proper.

Residences—Brooklyn, N.Y.; New York City; Bridgeport, Conn.
Club—Union League.

FRAZER, PERSIFOR, Dr.,
of Philadelphia, Pa. (Son of John Fries
Frazer 1812-72, of Phila., Vice-Provost Univ.
of Penna, one of the Founders of the National
Academy of Sciences, m 1838, Charlotte Jeffers,
da. of Thomas and Sarah Hollingshead (Cave).
—Descd. from John Frazer of Phila., 1735-65).

Born at Philadelphia, July 24, 1844; B.A. Univ. of
Penna, 1862; Acting Ensign U.S. Navy, War
1861-5; Prof. of Chemistry, Univ. Penna,
1872-4; Vice-Pres., U.S. Inter. Geol. Congresses, London, 1885, St. Petersburg, 1897;
Docteurès-Sciences Naturelles, Univ. de France, 1882, etc.;
m Sept. 2, 1871, Isabella N., da. of Edward Siddons Whelen.

Issue.

i. Persifor (Junr.), m Mary, da. of John Lowber Welsh.

ii. Laurence, *deceased.*   iii. John.   i. Charlotte.

Arms—Azure three cinquefoils argent.

Crest—Out of a ducal coronet or an ostrich's head and neck, between wings,
holding in the beak a horseshoe.   *Motto*—Je suis prest.

Residences—928 Spruce Street, Philadelphia; "Ardlie," near Milford, Penna.

Clubs—University, Philadelphia Cricket.

Societies—Cincinnati, N.J., Sons of the Revolution, War of 1812, Colonial Wars,
Military Order of the Loyal Legion, Naval Veteran Ass'n., Penna Hist.,
Am. Phil., Am. Inst. of M.E., Géologique de Belgique, Géologique du
Nord, Life Fellow A.A.A.S., Life Mem. B.A.A.S., etc.

BREWSTER HENRY COLVIN,
of Rochester N.Y. (Son of Simon Latham
Brewster, of Rochester, N.Y.—Descended from
Elder William Brewster, 1566-1644, who drafted the
Mayflower Compact, Member and Chaplain of the
1st Military Company organised at Plymouth, under
Captain Myles Standish, and served against
the Indians).

Born at Rochester, N.Y., Sept. 7, 1845; Representative in Congress for 31st District of New
York; m Alice, da. of Louis Chapin.

Issue.

i. Rachel Alice.   ii. Editha Colvin.

Arms—Azure, a chevron ermine between three estoils argent.

Crest—A leopard's head, erased, sable.

Motto—Verité soyez ma garde.

Residence—353 East Avenue, Rochester, N.Y.

Clubs—Genesse Valley, Country of Rochester; Union League, New York City.

WHEELER, JOSEPH, Gen. U.S. Army (*deceased*),
of Wheeler, Ala. (Son of Joseph Wheeler
1787-1866, of Augusta Ga., *m* (1) Sally Bradley,
m (2) Julia Knox Hull; son of Joseph 1748-1804;
son of Capt. James 1716-68; son of Samuel 1681-
1721; son of Moses 1651-1724; son of Moses
Wheeler, *b* in Kent, England, 1598, settled in New
Haven, Ct. 1638, *d* 1698 *ætat* 100).

Born at Augusta, Ga., Sept. 10, 1836; *d* Jan.,
1906; Grad. West Point 1859; LL.D. George-
town Coll. 1899; Gen. commanding Army
Corps of Confederate Cavalry 1861-65; Mem.
U.S. Congress 1880-1900; Major-Gen. U.S.
Cavalry Divisions and Senior Mem. of Com-
mission which negotiated surrender of Santiago;
Regent Smithsonian Institute 1886-1900; Pres.
Board of Visitors to Military Academy 1895; *m* Feb. 8, 1866,
Daneilla Ellen, *d* 1896, da. of Richard Jones of Courtlandt Ala.

Issue.
i. JOSEPH, *b* March 23, 1872, Capt. U.S.A.
ii. THOMAS H., U.S.N., drowned Sept. 7, 1898.
i. LUCY LOUISE.   iii. JULIA KNOX.
ii. ANNIE EARLY.   iv. ELLA, *d* 1872.   v. CARRIE PEYTON.

Arms—Vert, on a fesse or three lions rampant of the first.
Crest—Out of a mural crown or a griffin's head issuant argent.

Residence—(Family) Wheeler, Lawrence Co., Alabama.

GILES, STEPHEN WEART,
of Flatbush, N.Y. (Son of John Christie
Giles, 1825-93, Captain on General Spicer's Staff
of N.Y.C., *m* Isabella, 1825-90, da. of Stephen and
M. J. (Lee) Weart, of New York City.—Descended
from William Giles, *b* in the parish of St. Giles-in-
the-Fields, London, *d* in New York, Aug. 13,
1702).

Born in New York City, May 29, 1849, *m* Virginia,
da. of George Watson Walker, of Portsmouth,
N.H.

Issue.
i. JOHN CHRISTIE, *b* 1880.

Arms—Gules, a cross between four uncovered cups or, on a chief of the last
three pelicans sable.
Crest—A cup or, out of it three pansy flowers proper.

Residence—Newkirk Avenue, Flatbush, N.Y. City.
Club—The Brooklyn League.
Societies—Colonial Wars, New York Historical, Sons of the Revolution, St.
Nicholas, Daughters Am. Revolution, The Brooklyn of New England
Women, Colonial Daughters of the 17th Century.

HORWITZ, Miss CAROLYN NORRIS,
of Baltimore, Md. (Daughter of Theophilus
B. Horwitz, of Baltimore, Counsellor-at-Law, who
d April 5, 1895 ; g.-da. of Dr. J. Horwitz, M.D., of
Berlin, Germany, who settled in Baltimore. On
maternal side, da. of Mary Rebecca Barroll, g.-da.
of James Edmondson Barroll, distinguished lawyer
of Chestertown, Md., gt.-g.-da. of Wm. Barroll,
Counsellor-at-Law ; gt.-gt.-g.-da. of Rev. William
Barroll, b near Hereford, Eng., 1734, B.A. Cambridge Univ. 1757 ; Ordained Priest, 1759 ; Rector
of St. Stephen's Ch., N. Sassafras Parish, Md.,
1760 ; m Anne, da. of Rev. Alex. Williamson,
d 1778. Rev. Wm. Barroll was gr.-son of Sir
James Barroll, Mayor of Hereford, Eng., a Colonel in British Army,
killed in battle 1647. His pedigree and arms, granted 1585, were
entered at Herald College 1642. Miss Horwitz is a gt.-gt.-gt. niece of
Judge Gunning Bedford, of Delaware, one of the framers of the Declaration of Independence, but was prevented from signing by serious illness.

Born at Holly Hall, Cecil Co., Md. ; Authoress of " Swanhilde," " Fairy
Lure," and " Twentieth Century Chronology of the World," &c. 1212

Arms —Per chevron argent and azure, a chevron or, in base a lion rampant
holding a staff.
Crest —An eagle rising proper.   Motto —Veritate Victoria.

Residence —830 Hamilton Terrace, Baltimore, Md.

STOCKTON, RICHARD,
of Newark, N.J. (Son of Richard Stockton,
1824-76, of " Springdale," Princeton, N.J., Treasurer of Camden and Amboy R.R., m Oct. 4, 1860,
Susan, da. of Albert Baldwin and Caroline (Bayard)
Dod, of Princeton, N.J. ; son of Robert F. ; son of
Richard ; son of Richard, Signer of Declaration of
Independence ; son of John ; son of Richard ; son
of Richard and Abigail Stockton, came to America
1656, in desct. from David de Stockton, of Chester,
1250).

Born at Princeton, N.J., June 6, 1870 ; Midshipman, U.S.N. Acad.,
Annapolis, 1885-86, class of 1889, served in Cuba with Troop K,
1st U.S. Vol. Cav. (Roosevelt's Rough Riders), 1898 ; 1st Troop
N.G.N.J., 1898-1905 ; m Mar. 5, 1900, Mary Hampton Keen.

Arms —Gules, a chevron vairé sable and argent betw. three mullets of the last.
Crest —A lion rampant supporting an Ionic column.   Motto—Omnia Deo pendent.

Residence —26 James Street, Newark, N.J.
Society—Army of Santiago.

OTIS, EDWARD OSGOOD, M.D.,
    of Boston, Mass. (Third son of the Rev.
Israel Taintor Otis 1805-89, of Exeter, N.H.,
m Olive Morgan, *b* 1810, *d* Oct 6, 1906, da. of
Erastus and Martha (Morgan) Osgood, of Lebanon,
Conn.—Descended from John Otis, 1620-83, *b* at
Glastonbury, Co. Somerset, *m* Mary Jacob, settled
at Hingham, Mass., 1635, the ancestor of the great
patriot James Otis, and of Harrison Gray Otis, the
third Mayor of Boston).

Born at Rye, N.H., Oct. 29, 1848; Grad. at
    Harvard College, 1871, A.B., M.D.; ex-Presi-
    dent American Climatological Association;
    m June 6, 1894, Marion, da. of William
    Faxon, of Boston, Mass.

Issue.

i. JOHN FAXON, *b* Jan. 29, 1898.

ii. EDWARD OSGOOD, Jr., *b* Aug. 16, 1899.   i. OLIVE.

iii. WILLIAM FAXON, *b* Oct. 12, 1903.

Arms—Argent, a saltire engrailed, between four cross-crosslets fitchée azure.
Crest—An arm embowed vested gules, the hand holding a laurel branch.
Motto—Sapiens qui vigilat

Residence—381, Beacon Street, Boston, Mass.   *Club*—University.
Societies—American Climatological Association, Sons of the American Revolution.

MAY, JAMES RUNDLET, M.D.,
    of Portsmouth, N.H. (Son of George Hall
May, of Savannah, Ga., *b* Sept. 2, 1815, *d* Oct. 3,
1858, *m* Oct. 6, 1840, Louisa Catherine, *b* Nov. 7,
1817, *d* Feb. 10, 1895, da. of James Rundlet, and
Jane Hill, his wife, of Portsmouth, N.H.—Descd.
from John May, who came from Mayfield, Sussex,
Eng., settled at Roxbury, Mass., 1640).

Born at Portsmouth, N.H., Nov. 2, 1841; Grad.
    at Harvard University, 1861, A.M., M.D.;
    m April 26, 1881, Mary, da. of Horace Morison,
    of Baltimore, Md., and Mary Elizabeth, da. of
    Samuel Lord, of Portsmouth, N.H.

Issue.

i. RALPH, *b* June 22, 1882.

Arms—Gules, a fesse between eight billets or.
Crest—Out of a ducal coronet or, a leopard's head couped proper.
Motto—Vigilo.

Residence—Portsmouth, N.H.
Clubs—University of Boston, Harvard of New York.

ROGERS, JAMES SLOCUM,

of Phila. (Only son of Talbot Mercer Rogers, of Phila., *m* J. Eliz., da. and h. of James Slocum, of Brownsville, Pa.—Descd. from Robert Rogers, who came from Wales to Penna. in the 17th cent.; 10th in desct. from William Pitkin, Atty.-Gen. of Conn., 1664-74; 9th in desct. from William Pitkin 2nd, Chief Justice of Conn., 1713-23; also 10th in desct. from Thomas Welles, Gov. of Conn. 1655; John Webster, Gov. of Conn. 1656; John Mason, apptd. by Charles II.; Dep.-Gov. of Conn., 1662; 13th in desct. from Oliver St. John, ninth Lord Beauchamp of Bletso).

Born Nov. 21, 1871; Grad. at Princeton Univ., B.A. 1893; Univ. of Pa., LL.B. 1896; Attorney-at-Law; *m* April 26, 1904, Agnes Gertrude, da. of J. George Klemm, of Phila.

Issue.

i. ELEANOR EASTWICK ROGERS.

Arms—Qtly., 1 ar. on a chev. vert. betw. three stags courant sa., five ermine spots or, a crescent sa. for diff. (Rogers); 2 ar. on a fesse gu. betw. three griffins' heads couped sa., as many sinister wings or (Slocum); 3 az. on a bend ar., betw. two swans of the second collared and chained or, a crescent betw. two mullets sa. (Pitkin); 4 per fesse az. and or, a pale counterchanged, three plates two and one, each charged with two bars wavy vert, and as many lions' heads erased, one and two, gu. (White).

Crest—A stag's head erased sa. thereon 3 ermine spots and attired or.

Residence—Haverford, Penna.

Clubs—University, Princeton of Philadelphia.   *Society*—Colonial Wars.

FISKE, STEPHEN,

of New York City (Son of William Henry Fiske, of New Brunswick, N.J.—Descended from Nathan Fiske, of Watertown, Mass., 1643; Daniel Fiske, of Laxfield, Co. Suffolk, 1208).

Born at New Brunswick, N.J., Nov. 22, 1840; Graduated at Rutger's College, 1861; admitted to the New York Bar, 1865.

Arms—Chequy argent and gules, on a pale sable three mullets pierced or.

Crest—On a triangle argent an estoile or.

Residences—47 West Ninety-third Street, New York City; Netherwood, N.J.

Clubs—Lotos, Rutger's, Dramatists, Penn. Press.

Societies—American Authors, Foresters, Metropolitan Art.

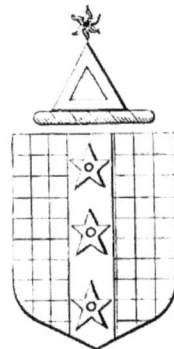

HOWARD, GEORGE,
of Washington, D.C. (Eldest son of Sir Henry Howard, C.B., K.C.M.G.; H.B.M. Secty. of Legation, Athens 1885, Copenhagen 1886, Pekin 1887, Minister at the Hague; *b* Corby Castle, Eng., Aug. 11, 1843, *m* Oct. 2, 1867, Cecilia, da. of George W. Riggs, of Washington, D.C.; grandson of Sir Henry Francis Howard, G.C.B., K.C.M.G., *m* (1) Hon. Sevilla Erskine, da. of Lord Erskine: *m* (2) Baroness Von der Schulenburg.—Descended from Sir Francis Howard, of Corby Castle, Cumberland, son of Thos. Howard, 4th Duke of Norfolk).

Born at Munich, Bavaria, Nov. 26, 1869; *m* Nov. 5, 1902, Mary, da. of Wm. H. Clagett, of Washington, D.C.

Arms—Qtly., 1, gu. on a bend betw. six crosses-crosslet fitchée ar. an escutcheon or, charged with a demi-lion ramp. pierced through the mouth with an arrow, within a double tressure flory counter-flory of the first (Howard); 2, gu. three lions pass. guard. in pale or, in chief a label of three points ar. (Brotherton); 3, chequy or, and az. (Warren); 4, gu. a lion ramp. ar. armed and langued az. (Mowbray); 5, gu. three escallops ar. (Dacre); 6, barry of six ar. and az. three chaplets ppr. (Greystoke).

Crest—On a chapeau gu. turned up erm. a lion statant guard, the tail extended or, gorged with a ducal coronet ar.   *Motto*—Sola virtus invicta.

Residence—1008 16th Street, Washington, D.C.
Clubs—Metropolitan, Chevy Chase, Alibi.

CARPENTER, JAMES EDWARD (*deceased*),
of Phila. (Son of Edward Carpenter, 1813-89, *m* Anna Maria, da. of Benjamin M. Howey.—Descended from Samuel Carpenter, of Philadelphia, 1683-1714, First Treasurer of the Province of Pennsylvania; Member of Colonial or Governor's Council).

Born at Kent Co., Md., March 6, 1841, *d* at Newburyport, Mass., Aug. 16, 1901; thirty years Treasurer of the Historical Society of Pennsylvania; Chairman Pa. Soc. Sons of the Revolution; Capt. 8th Pa. Cavalry; Brevet-Major of Vols. on Staff of Brevet Major-Genl. David McM. Gregg, Army of the Potomac; eight years Officer of 1st Troop Phila. City Cavalry; *m* Harriet Odin Dorr.

Issue.

i. EDWARD, Capt. Artillery Corps, U.S. Army.
ii. WILLIAM DORR.   i. HELEN DALTON, *m* Fred. S. Moseley, of Boston.
iii. LLOYD PRESTON.   ii. GRACE, *deceased*.

Arms—Azure, a greyhound passant a chief sable.
Crest—A greyhound's head erased per fesse sable and argent.
Motto—Audaces fortuna juvat.

Residence—(Family) " Pine Bank," Salisbury Point, Amesbury, Mass.

AUSTIN, EUGENE K., COLONEL,
of N.Y. City (Son of Stephen F. Austin,
1837-91, of N.Y. City, *m* 1860 Cecelia Kelly ; son
of John Phelps, 1791-1842, *m* Louisa S., da. of
Luke Kip ; son of Elijah, 1751-94, *m* Esther, da. of
Judge John Phelps; son of Elias, 1718-76 ; son of
Capt. Richard, 1666-1733 ; son of Capt. Anthony,
d at Sheffield Ct. 1708; son of Richard Austin,
1598-1638, who settled at Charlestown, Mass., 1638).

Born at Dresden, Germany, Feb. 17, 1872 ; Banker ;
late Colonel 108th Inf. N.G.N.Y.; *m* Dec. 28,
1897, Mabel Grant, da. of Roswell D. Hatch.

Issue.

i. EUGENIE VAN VOORHEES, *b* 1906,
i. EDITH HATCH, 1899-1900.
ii. CECILIA KIP, *b* 1899.
iii. CONSTANCE MABEL PHELPS, *b* 1902.

Arms—(*Used by Elijah A.* 1775) Argent, on a fesse between two chevrons sable
three cross-crosslets of the first, within a bordure of the same charged with
a wreath of laurel and roses proper.

Crest—A cross or between wings argent.

Residences—257 West 74th Street, N.Y. City ; "Hearthstone," New Rochelle, N.Y.
Societies—Sons of the Revolution, Vet. Assn. 1st Signal Corps, Colonial Wars,
St. Nicholas.

CARROLL, WILLIAM STERETT (*deceased*),
of Baltimore Co. Md. (Son of Henry Carroll
1796-1877, of "Clynmalyra," Balto. Co., *m* Mary,
da. of Col. Samuel Sterett ; son of Henry Hill,
1768-1805, of "Litterluna," Md., *m* Sarah Rogers ;
son of Charles, 1729-73, of "Duddington," Wash.
D.C., *m* Mary Hill ; son of Daniel, 1707-34, *m* Ann
Rozier ; son of Charles, 1660-1720, of "Doug-
horegan Manor," Maryland ; son of Daniel Carroll
of "Litterluna," Kings Co., Ireland).

Born at "Clynmalyra," Balto. Co., Nov. 5, 1837,
d Mar. 21, 1906; *m* 1867, Louisa, da. of Henry
Cooke Tilghman, a descdt. of Richard Tilghman of "The Hermitage," Queen Anne's Co., Md., 1660.

Issue.

i. HENRY, *b* Feb. 4, 1875, *m* Nov. 16, 1905, Anne Merryman.
ii. WILLIAM STERETT, *b* Oct. 13, 1877, *m* Nov. 21, 1906, Grace Harris.
i. MARY BORDIEU STERETT.
ii. LOUISA TILGHMAN, *m* Alfred Pleasants.

Arms—Arg., two lions combattant gu. supporting a sword arg. hilt and pommel or.
Crest—On stump of oak tree, sprouting, a hawk proper belled or.
Motto—In fide et in bello forte.

Residence—(Mrs. W. S. C.), "Duddington," Baltimore Co., Md.

SPENCER, SELDEN PALMER,
of St. Louis, Mo. (Eldest son of Samuel
Selden Spencer, of Erie, Pa., *b* 1826, *m* Eliza D.
Palmer; son of William, 1784-1871; son of Israel,
1762-1837; son of Israel, 1732-1813; son of Isaac,
1678-1751; son of Samuel, *d* 1705; son of Gerard
Spencer, *b* in England, 1614, *d* 1685).

Born at Erie, Pa., Sept. 16, 1862; Mem. of Legislature of Missouri, 1895-96; Judge, Circuit
Court, for the 8th Judicial Circuit of Missouri,
1897-1903; Grad. Yale Univ., 1884; M.A.
Ph.D. Westminster Coll.; LL.B. Wash.
Univ.; Hon. M.D. Missouri Med. Col.;
m Dec. 8, 1886, Susan Brookes.

Issue.

i. JAMES BROOKES.   iii. OLIVER McLEAN.
ii. SELDEN MARVIN.   i. SUSAN PALMER.

Arms—Quarterly, argent and gules, in 2 and 3 a fret or. over all on a bend sable
three escallops of the first.

Crest—Out of a ducal coronet or, a griffin's head argent, gorged with a bar
gemella gules between two wings expanded of the second.

Residence—4457 Washington Boulevard, St. Louis, Missouri.

Clubs—St. Louis, Mercantile, Field, Missouri Athletic.

Societies—Phi Beta Kappa, Delta Kappa Epsilon, Nu Sigma Nu, Phi Delta Phi
Sons of the Revolution, Colonial Wars, New England, Foreign Wars.

BROOKS, JAMES GORDON CARTER,
of Chicago, Ill. (Son of William Hathorne
Brooks, and Sarah Carter, his wife.—Descended
from Henry Brooks, *b circa* 1625, by Susanna
Richardson, his wife).

Born at Salem, Mass., Aug. 25, 1837; *m* Rose,
daughter of Samuel Thomas Hambleton, of
Maryland.

Issue.

i. CHARLES RICHARDSON (*deceased*).
ii. JAMES HAMBLETON.
i. ALICE HAWTHORNE, *m* George J. Farnsworth.
ii. EDITH GORDON, *m* Henry Blaksley Collins.

Arms—Sable, three escallops or.

Crest—A beaver passant.   *Motto*—Perseverando.

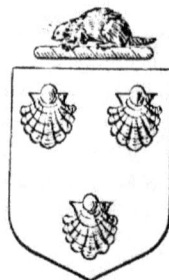

Residence—87 Cass Street, Chicago, Ill.
Clubs—Union, Athletic, Union League.

Armorial Addenda.

" Helpe then, O holy virgin! chiefe of nyne,

    Thy weaker Novice to performe thy will;

Lay forth out of thine everlasting scryne

    The antique rolls, which there lye hidden still,

Of Faerie knights, and fayrest Tanaquill."

(SPENSER'S " FAERIE QUEENE.")

Armorial Addenda.

ADAMS.

HENRY ADAMS, of Braintree, Mass., 1630, d 1646, ancestor of Pres. John Adams.

Arms—Argent, on a cross gules five mullets or.

Crest—Out of a ducal coronet a demi-lion.

AIKMAN.

JOHN AIKMAN, of New York, 1783, and "Newhouse" Co. Stirling, Scotland.

Arms—Argent, a sinister hand in base issuing out of a cloud fesseways, holding an oaken baton paleways ppr. with a branch sprouting out at the tip, over all a bend engr. gules.

Crest—An oak tree ppr.

AKERLY.

ROBERT AKERLY, of Brookhaven, L.I., 1655, from Lancashire, Eng.

Arms—On a mound the stump of a tree, thereon a dove holding in the beak a branch of laurel betw. two pine trees.

ALDEN.

JOHN ALDEN, 1599-1687, of Duxbury, Mass. Came in the "Mayflower," 1620, from Dorking, Surrey, Eng.

Arms—Gules, a bezant betw. three crescents within a bordure engr. ermine.

Crest—Out of a ducal coronet, per pale gules and sable, a demi-lion or.

ALLERTON.

Isaac Allerton, 1583-1659, of New Haven, Ct. Came in the "Mayflower," 1620.

Arms—Argent, a chevron betw. three lions' heads erased sable.

Crest—A lion's head collared.

ALLING.

Roger Alling, of New Haven Ct., 1639.

Arms—Per bend rompu, argent and sable, six martlets counterchanged.

Crest—An eagle argent holding in the beak an acorn or, leaved vert.

ALSOPP.

Joseph Alsopp, came in ship "Elizabeth and Ann," 1635, settled at New Haven, Ct., brother of John Alsopp, of Bonsall, Derbyshire, Eng.

Arms—Sable, three doves rising argent, legged and beaked gules.

Crest—A dove rising holding in the beak an ear of wheat.

AMBLER.

Richard Ambler, settled in Yorktown, Va., 1730; son of John Ambler, Sheriff of Yorks, Eng., 1721.

Arms—Sable, on a fesse or, between three pheons argent, a lion pass. guard. gules.

Crest—Two dexter hands conjoined, holding a crown.

AMORY.

Jonathan Amory, of South Carolina, 1685, b at St. Annes, Somersetshire, Eng.

Arms—Azure, on a bend or, three eagles displayed gules, within a bordure of the second.

ANDREWS.

John Andrews, who came from Wales to Boston, Mass., *circa* 1663.

Arms—Argent, two keys endorsed in bend or, a sword interposed between them in bend sinister azure.

Crest—A lion's head erased.

ANDREWS.

JOHN ANDREWS, came from Co. Essex, Eng., to New England, 1643.

Arms—Gules, a saltire or surmounted by another vert.

Crest—A blackamoor's head in profile, couped at the shoulders and wreathed about the temples ppr.

ANDRUS.

JOHN ANDRUS, "The Settler" of Framington, Conn., 1635.

Arms—Argent, on a chevron engrailed gules, between three mullets vert, as many quartrefoils pierced or.

Crest—A greyhound's head couped per pale or and sable, on the neck a saltire counterchanged between a pellet and a bezant.

APPLETON.

SAMUEL APPLETON, of Ipswich, Mass., 1635, son of Thomas Appleton, of Little Waldingfield, Suffolk, Eng.

Arms—Argent, a fesse sable between three apples, stalked and leaved vert.

Crest—An elephant's head couped sable, eared or, in the mouth a snake vert wreathed about the trunk.

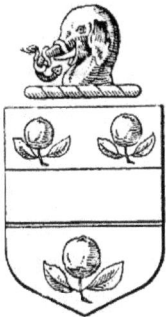

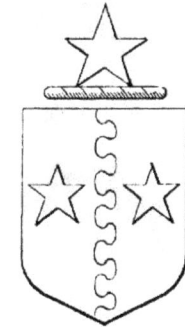

APTHORP.

CHARLES APTHORP, son of John and Susan (Ward) Apthorp, of Bexley, Kent, Eng., b 1698, d Boston, Mass.

Arms—Per pale nebulée argent and azure, two mullets counterchanged.

Crest—A mullet argent.

ASHHURST.

RICHARD ASHHURST, of Philadelphia, b 1784, grandson of Richard Lewis Ashhurst, who m Miss Clitheroe, of Lancashire, Eng.

Arms—Gules, a cross between four fleurs-de-lis or.

Crest—A fox statant proper.

ATHERTON.

Maj.-Gen. HUMPHREY ATHERTON, of Dorchester, Mass., 1637, from Winwick, Lancashire. Capt. of the A. and H. Artillery Company.

Arms—Gules, three sparrow-hawks argent, belled and jessed or.

Crest—A hawk proper, legged and beaked or.

AUSTIN.

RICHARD AUSTIN, of Bishopstoke, Hampshire, Eng., settled at Charlestown, Mass., 1638.

Arms—Argent, on a fesse, between two chevrons sable, three cross crosslets of the first, within a bordure of the same charged with a wreath of laurel and roses proper.

Crest—A cross between wings argent.

BAGLEY.

JOHN BAGLEY, settled in New England, 1750.

Arms—Or, three lozenges azure.

Crest—On the top of a spear issuing a wivern, sans legs, tail nowed.

BAINBRIDGE.

CHRISTOPHER BAINBRIDGE, to New Eng., 1635, probably a grandson of Anthony Bainbrigg, ranger of Teesdale Forest, 1557.

Arms—Argent, a chevron embattled between three battleaxes sable.

Crest—A goat sable, horned and unguled argent, around the neck a collar of the last, standing on a mount vert.

BALDWIN.

EDWARD BALDWIN, of Brogdens, Maryland, *d* 1759.

Arms—Argent, a chevron ermines betw. three hazel sprigs vert.

Crest—A squirrel sejant or, holding a hazle sprig vert.

BANGS.

EDWARD BANGS, *b* Chichester, Co. Sussex, Eng., 1592, to Plymouth, Mass., 1623.

Arms—Sable, a cross engrailed ermine, between four fleurs-de-lis or.

Crest—A Moor's head full-faced couped at the shoulders ppr. on the head a cap of maintenance gules, turned up ermine, adorned with a crescent whence issues a fleur-de-lis.

BANKS.

JAMES BANKS, *b* 1709, Northfield, Yorkshire, Eng., of Newark, New Jersey, 1729.

Arms—Sable, a cross engrailed or, between four fleurs-de-lis argent.

Crest—A griffin segreant, implumed or, holding a cross formée fitchée gules.

BARCLAY.

James Barclay, of Bucks Co., Penna., *d* 1792, an officer of the Crown under the Proprietary Government.

Arms—Azure, a chevron between three crosses pattée argent.

Crest—A bishop's mitre.

BARLOW.

Joel Barlow, poet, politician and miscellaneous writer, *b* in Connecticut, 1756.

Arms—Argent, on a chevron engrailed, between three crosses-crosslet fitchée sable, two lions passant facing each other of the first.

Crest—A demi-lion argent, holding a cross-crosslet fitchée sable.

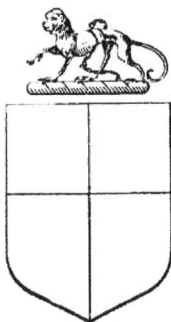

BARNES.

Stephen Barnes, of Southampton, Long Island, and Branford, Conn. 1700.

Arms—Quarterly or and vert.

Crest—An ape proper with broken chain.

BARTLETT.

Robert Bartlett, *b* England, 1603, *d* Plymouth, Mass., 1676.

Arms—Azure, three doves with wings expanded argent.

Crest—A dove rising argent, in the beak an olive branch.

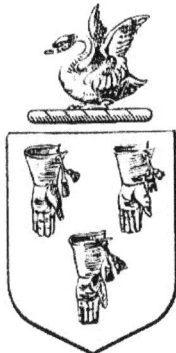

BARTLETT.

Richard Bartlett, from Ernely, Co. Sussex, Eng., to Newbury, Mass., 1634.

Arms—Sable, three falconers' sinister gloves pendent argent, tasseled or.

Crest—A swan couched argent, with wings expanded.

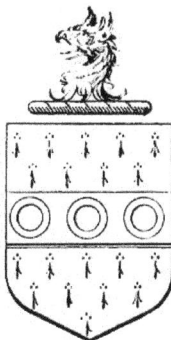

BARTON.

Dr. John Barton, of Salem, Mass., 1672.

Arms—Ermine, on a fesse gules three annulets or.

Crest—A griffin's head erased proper.

BATT.

WILLIAM and THOMAS BATT, of
Virginia, 1667.
Arms—Argent, a chevron between
three reremice displayed sable.

BAYARD.

PETER BAYARD, of New York, 1674.
Arms—Azure, A chevron between
three escallops or
Crest—A demi-unicorn argent.

BEALL.

Colonel NINIAN BEALL, 1650-1717,
Commander-in-Chief of the Provincial Forces in Maryland.
Arms—Sable, a chevron between
three woolves' heads erased
argent.
Crest—A demi-wolf sable, sustaining
a half spear in pale tasseled or.

BEEKMAN.

Lieut. WILHELMUS BEEKMAN,
1623,
1707, from Hasselt Oberyssel,
Netherlands, to New York, 1647.
Arms—Azure, a bend wavy argent
between two roses or.
Crest—Two wings endorsed.

BELCHER.

ANDREW BELCHER, of Sudbury,
Mass., 1639; son of Thomas, of
London; son of Robert Belcher,
of Kingswood, Wiltshire.
Arms—Or, three pales gules, a chief
vairé.
Crest—A greyhound's head erased
ermine, gorged with a collar gules
rimmed and ringed or.

BELLINGHAM.

Governor RICHARD BELLINGHAM,
to New England, 1634; son of
William Bellingham, gent., of
Brombe Wood, Lincolnshire,
Eng., living 1592.
Arms—Argent, three bugle horns
sable, garnished or.
Crest—A stag's head couped argent,
attired or, gorged with a chaplet.

BENHAM.

JOHN BENHAM, gent , who settled in
Dorchester, Mass., 1630, of Benham Ho., Berkshire.

Arms—Ermine, a fesse dancettée
sable.

Crest—A chart proper.

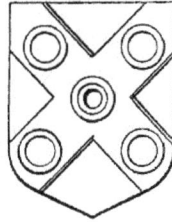

BENJAMIN.

JOHN BENJAMIN, 1598-1645, from
Bristol, Eng., in the ship "Lion,"
1632, settled at Cambridge, Mass.

Arms—Or, on a saltire quarterly,
pierced sable five annulets counterchanged.

Crest—On a chapeau turned up
ermine a flame of fire proper.

BERNARD.

Governor FRANCIS BERNARD, 1705.

Arms—Argent, a bear rampant sable,
muzzled and collared or.

Crest—A demi-bear muzzled and
collared or.

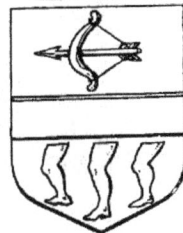

BIRNIE.

JAMES BIRNIE, 1705-1864, of Aberdeen, Scotland, came to America
1816, served in North West Fur
Co.

Arms—Gules, a fesse argent between
a bow and arrow, in full draught,
in chief, and three legs couped at
thigh paleways of the second in
base.

Crest—A lion's head erased proper.

BETTS.

THOMAS BETTS, from England 1639,
founder of Guilford, Connecticut.

Arms—Sable, on a bend argent, three
cinquefoils gules.

Crest—Out of a ducal coronet or, a
buck's head gules attired or,
collared argent.

BIBBY.

THOMAS BIBBY, *b* Dublin 1740, Capt.
7th regt. of foot, settled in New
York, 1760.

Arms—Azure, three eagles displayed
double-headed or.

Crest—An eagle displayed as in arms.

BIDDLE.

WILLIAM BIDDLE, 1630-1712, Mem. of Council, Genl. Assembly, New Jersey, son of Michael Biddle of Elmshurst, Staffordshire.

Arms—Argent, three double brackets sable.

Crest—A demi-heraldic tiger rampant, ducally gorged.

BLAKE.

WILLIAM BLAKE, from Little Baddow, Co. Essex, to New Eng., 1630, settled at Dorchester Neck. He was grandson of John Blake, of Over Stowey, Gloucestershire.

Arms—Argent, a pale sable, over all a bend gules charged with three martlets or.

Crest—A dragon's head erased argent pellettée.

BLEECKER.

JAN JANSEN BLEEKER, b 1642, at Meppel, in Province of Oberyssel, Netherlands, to New York, 1658.

Arms—Per pale azure and argent, 1st two chevronels embattled counter embattled or, 2nd a sprig of roses vert flowered gules.

Crest—A pheon or.

BLIVEN.

EDWARD (Edmon) BLIVEN, of Westerly, Rhode Island, 1685.

Arms—Gules, a lion rampant surmounted by a bendlet argent.

BOERUM.

Capt. WILLIAM BOERUM, who served with the Continental Army under Maj.-Gen. Nathaniel Green.

Arms—Gules, three boars' heads or.

Crest—Out of a mural coronet gules a snake entwined vert.

BOLLES.

JOSEPH BOLLES, of Wells, Mass., 1665, from Nottinghamshire, England, brother of John Bolles of Clerkenwell, Middx., Eng.

Arms—Azure, out of three cups or as many boars' heads argent.

Crest—A demi-boar wounded in the breast with a broken spear.

BONYTHON.

RICHARD BONYTHON, son of John Bonython, Co. Cornwall, Eng., settled on the Saco River, New Eng., 1631.

Arms—Argent, a chevron between three fleurs-de-lis sable.

BOSTON.

JACOB BOSTON, of Accomac County, Virginia, and Jefferson Co., Connecticut, 1800.

Arms—Vert, a lion rampant argent, crowned or.

Crest—A horse's head in armour proper.

BOSTWICK.

ARTHUR BOSTWICK, settled at Stratford, Connecticut, 1641, son of Arthur Bostwick of Tarporly, Cheshire, Eng.

Arms—Sable, a fesse humettée argent.

Crest—On the stump of a tree eradicated argent, a bear's head erased sable, muzzled or.

BOUTELLE.

JAMES BOUTELLE (Boutwell), settled at Lynn, Mass., 1632.

Arms—Per pale gules and sable, an estoil of eight points issuing from a crescent or.

BOWEN.

RICHARD BOWEN, 1600-75, of Kittle Hill, Glamorganshire, Wales, came to New Eng. 1640, Deputy to Plymouth General Court.

Arms—Azure, a stag argent, vulned in the back with an arrow, attired or.

Crest—A stag as in Arms proper.

BOWES.

NICHOLAS BOWES, M.A., Harvard Coll., b 1706, of Boston, Mass.

Arms—Ermine, three bows in pale gules, stringed sable, on a chief azure a swan between two leopards' heads argent.

Crest—A demi-lion rampant holding a bundle of arrows banded vert.

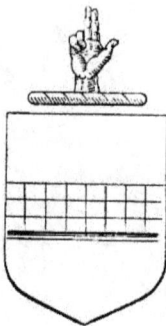

BOYD.

JOHN BOYD, from Coleraine, Co. Londonderry, Ireland, to Newcastle, Delaware, 1791.

Arms—Azure, a fesse chequy or and gules.

Crest—A dexter hand erect pointing with the thumb and two fingers proper.

BRADFORD.

WILLIAM BRADFORD, first Governor of Mass., came in the "Mayflower" 1620, son of William Bradford, of Austerfield, Yorkshire.

Arms—Argent, on a fesse sable three stags' heads erased or.

Crest—A stag's head erased or.

BRADSTREET.

SIMON BRADSTREET, Governor of Massachusetts, 1679-86, *b* at Horbling, Lincolnshire, 1603, *d* 1697.

Arms—Argent, a greyhound passant gules, on a chief sable three crescents or.

Crest—An arm embowed in armour holding in the hand a scimitar proper.

BREESE.

SYDNEY BREESE, *b* at Shrewsbury, 1709, settled in New York 1733.

Arms—Argent, on a fesse azure three boars' heads couped or, in chief a lion passant gules.

Crest—A boar's head argent pellettée between two oak branches vert, fructed or.

BRENT.

GILES BRENT, Lieut.-Governor of Maryland 1643, son of Richard Brent of Stoke, Sheriff of Gloucestershire 1615.

Arms—Gules, a wyvern or.

Crest—A wyvern's head between two wings expanded or.

BRENTON.

WILLIAM BRENTON, Governor of Rhode Island, and Providence Plantations, 1666 to 1669.

Arms—Argent, two bars gules, on a canton of the second a cross of the first.

Crest—A semi-savage affrontée handcuffed proper.

BRETT.

Francis Brett, of New York, 1707-66, son of Captain Roger Brett of H.M. Army.

Arms—Argent, a lion rampant between nine cross-crosslets fitchée gules.

Crest—On a chapeau gules, turned up ermine, a lion passant of the first.

BREWER.

Daniel Brewer, of Roxburg, Mass., 1632.

Arms—Gules, two bends wavy, first argent, second or.

Crest—A mermaid with mirror and comb proper.

BRICE.

John Brice, from Haversham, Buckinghamshire, Eng. (originally of Donnington, Somersetshire), to Annapolis, Maryland, *circa* 1700.

Arms—Sable, a griffin passant or.

Crest—A lion's head erased ermine, pierced through the neck with an arrow or.

BRIGGS.

Walter Briggs, from Norfolk, Eng., to Scituate, Mass., 1643.

Arms—Gules, three bars gemelles or, a canton ermine.

Crest On the stump of a tree a pelican or, vulning herself proper.

BRIGHT.

Henry Bright, *b* 1602, of Watertown, Mass., 1630; son of Henry Bright, of Bury St. Edmunds, Co. Suffolk.

Arms—Sable, a fesse argent between three escallops or.

Crest—A dragon's head gules, vomiting flames proper, collared and lined or.

BROMFIELD.

Edward Bromfield, *b* 1648, at South Stoneham, Hampshire, *d* in Boston, Mass., 1734; grandson of Arthur Bromfield, of Haywood House, New Forest, Hants.

Arms Sable, on a chevron argent three branches of brome vert, budded or, on a canton or a spear's head azure, embrued gules.

Crest—A demi-tiger azure armed and tufted or, holding erect a broken sword argent, hilted of the second.

BROOKS.

HENRY BROOKS, *b* in Cheshire, Eng.,
  settled in New England, 1660.
Arms—Sable, three escallops or.
Crest—A beaver passant.

BROUGHTON.

JOHN BROUGHTON, merchant, of
  Marblehead, Mass., 1720.
Arms—Argent, a chevron between
  three mullets gules.
Crest—An eagle's head erased sable,
  holding a snake argent, on the
  breast two chevrons of the last.

BROWNE.

JOHN BROWNE, planter, of Talbot
  County, Maryland, *d* 1698.
Arms—Gules, a chevron between three
  fleurs-de-lis or.
Crest—A demi-lion rampant, chained.

BROWNE.

NATHANIEL BROWNE, of Hartford,
  Conn., 1654, grandson of Sir
  William Browne, Lt.-Gov. of
  Flushing, Holland.
Arms—Sable, three lions passant in
  bend between two cotises argent,
  in chief a trefoil slipped ermine.
Crest—A griffin's head erased vert,
  eared beaked and collared or,
  charged on the neck with a trefoil
  slipped ermine.

BRUEN.

OBADIAH BRUEN of Plymouth Colony,
  1640, son of John Bruen of Stapleford, Cheshire, England.
Arms—Argent, an eagle displayed
  sable.
Crest—A fisherman per pale argent
  and sable each article of the attire
  counterchanged, in the dexter
  hand a staff, in the sinister a net
  thrown over the shoulder or.

BRUNE.

FREDERICK WM. BRUNE, from
  Bremen, Germany, 1776, *d* in
  Baltimore, Md.
Arms—Argent, issuing from a wood,
  on the sinister side, a stag courant
  proper.
Crest—A pair of antlers proper.

BULKLEY.

Rev. PETER BULKLEY, of Concord, Mass., came from Odell, Bedford-fordshire, England, 1635.

Arms—Sable, a chevron between three bulls' heads cabossed argent.

Crest—Out of a ducal coronet a bull's head argent.

BURLEIGH.

GEORGE WM. BURLEIGH, of Somers-worth, New Hampshire.

Arms—Paly of six argent and gules, on a chief paly six crescents all counterchanged.

Crest—A stag's head erased gules.

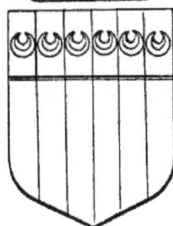

BURRAGE.

JOHN BURRAGE, b Norton Subcorse, Norfolk, England, 1616, settled in Charlestown, Mass., 1637.

Arms—Argent, a crescent between three boars' heads gules.

Crest—A boar's head gules.

BURROWES.

WILLIAM BURROWES, Treasurer of the "Worshipful Company of Merchants Adventurers," Ham-burg, 1728.

Arms—Argent, the stump of a laurel tree eradicated proper.

Crest—A lion passant.

BURWELL.

Major LEWIS BURWELL, b Harting-ton, Co. Bedford, Eng., settled at Carter's Creek, Virginia, 1640.

Arms—A saltire between four griffins' heads erased.

Crest—A griffin's claw grasping a twig of three leaves.

BUSH.

JOHN BUSH, from London to Boston, Mass., 1634.

Arms—Azure, a wolf rampant argent, collared and chained or, in chief three crosses pattée fitchée of the second.

Crest—A goat's head erased argent.

BUSHNELL.

FRANCIS BUSHNELL, from Horsted, Co. Sussex, Eng., of Guilford, Conneticut, 1639.

Arms—Argent, five fusils in fesse gules, in chief three mullets sable.

Crest—On a ducal coronet a wivern, sans feet.

BUSSEY.

GEORGE BUSSEY, settled in Virginia, 1635, later of Calvert County, Maryland.

Arms—Argent, three bars sable.

Crest—A sea dragon sans wings and legs the tail nowed, barry argent and sable.

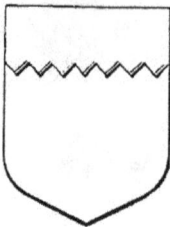

BUTLER.

THOMAS BUTLER, b in Ireland 1674, settled at Berwick, Maine, 1692.

Arms—Or, a chief indented azure.

Crest—Out of a ducal coronet or, a plume of five ostrich feathers argent, thereon a falcon rising of the last.

BUTLER.

THOMAS BUTLER, b Dublin, Ireland, 1720, settled in Lancaster Co., Pa., 1748, grandson of Edward Butler, 8th Bart., of Dunboyne.

Arms—Or, a chief indented azure and three escallops in bend counterchanged.

Crest—Out of a ducal coronet or, a plume of five ostrich feathers argent, a falcon rising of the last.

CABELL.

Captain WILLIAM CABELL, of Richmond, Virginia, 1744.

Arms—Sable, a horse rampant argent, bitted and bridled or.

Crest—An arm in armour embowed grasping a sword all proper.

CAMPBELL.

DUNCAN CAMPBELL, of Boston, Mass., 1688, Postmaster of the Colonies.

Arms—Gyrony of eight or, and sable.

Crest—A boar's head couped.

CANDEE.

Zaccheus Candee, 1640-1720, of New Haven, Connecticut, 1670, grandson of Jean de Candé.

Arms—Argent, a lion rampant azure holding an escallop shell or, in chief three golphs.

Crest—A stag's head erased ermine, horned or.

CANFIELD.

Thomas Canfield, of New Haven, Connecticut, 1639.

Arms—Sable, a fret engrailed, in chief dexter corner a cinquefoil argent.

Crest—A cinquefoil argent.

CAPEN.

Bernard Capen, *b* 1552, at Dorchester, Eng., Deacon of the first church at Dorchester, Mass., 1632, *d* 1638.

Arms—Sable, a chevron between three mullets or.

Crest—A demi-lion gules.

CAREY.

Samuel Thomas Carey, of New York, *b* 1800, 5th in descent from Patrick Carey, *b* 1622, 4th son of Sir Henry Carey, 1st Viscount Falkland.

Arms—Argent, on a bend sable three roses of the field.

Crest—A swan with wings addorsed proper, beaked gules, membered sable.

CARLETON.

Edward Carleton, *b* in England, 1605, settled at Rowley, Mass., 1638.

Arms—Ermine, on a bend sable three pheons argent.

Crest—A dexter arm embowed proper, vested to the elbow gules, doubled ermine, holding a javelin argent.

CARPENTER.

Timothy Carpenter, *b* Wales, 1665, Emigrated to America, 1678; son of Ephraim, *b* 1623, a gt.-grandson of Caleb Carpenter, of Prussia, 1540, who settled in Wales.

Arms—Paly of six azure and gules.

Crest—A coney sejant argent.

CARPENTER.

WILLIAM CARPENTER, *b* 1576, Harwell, Berkshire, Eng., to Weymouth, N.E., 1638.

SAMUEL CARPENTER, *b* 1649, Eng., 1st Treasurer of Prov. of Pennsylvania.

Arms—Argent, a greyhound passant, a chief sable.

Crest—A greyhound's head erased, per fesse sable and argent.

CARR.

WILLIAM CARR (Kerr), came from Antrim, Ireland, to Pennsylvania, buried in Neshaminy Presbyterian Cemetery, 1788.

Arms—Qtly. 1st and 4th azure, the sun in full splendour or; 2nd and 3rd gules, on a chevron argent three mullets of the field.

Crest—A unicorn's head erased argent.

CARROLL.

CHARLES CARROLL, Attorney-General to Lord Baltimore, settled in Maryland 1688, son of Daniel Carroll, of Litterluna, King's Co., Ireland.

Arms—Argent, two lions combatant gules supporting a sword argent, hilt and pommel or.

Crest—On the stump of an oak tree, sprouting new branches proper, a hawk of the last belled or.

CHAFFEE.

THOMAS CHAFFEE, came from England to Hingham, Mass., 1637.

Arms—Azure, a fesse lozengy argent.

Crest—A peacock in pride proper.

CHAMBERLAIN.

R. CHAMBERLAIN, of New Hampshire, Justice of the Peace, 1684.

Arms—Gules, an inescutcheon argent within an orle of mullets or.

Crest—Out of a ducal coronet or, an ass's head argent.

CHANCELLOR.

Captain RICHARD CHANCELLOR, who served in army of Charles II., settled in Westmoreland Co., Virginia, 1682.

Arms—Or, a lion rampant sable, armed and langued gules, on a chief of the last three mullets of the first.

Crest—An eagle displayed sable.

CHANDLER.

Major Job Chandler, Receiver-
General of Province of Maryland
1651-6, descendant of Thomas
Chandler of Cubbington, Worcestershire, Eng.

Arms—Per chevron azure and sable,
three cherubs or.

Crest—Out of clouds proper a cherub
as in arms.

CHANDLER.

William Chandler, proprietor, of
Roxbury, Mass., freeman 1640.

Arms—Chequy argent and azure, on
a bend sable three lions passant
or.

Crest—A pelican in her piety proper.

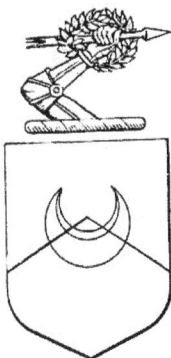

CHAPMAN.

Robert Chapman, 1616-87, of Saybrook, Connecticut, 1635.

Arms—Per chevron argent and gules,
a crescent counterchanged.

Crest—An arm embowed in armour
holding a broken spear encircled
with a wreath proper.

CHASE.

Aquala Chase, *b* at Chesham, Buckinghamshire, Eng., 1618, settled at
Hampton, Mass., 1646.

Arms—Gules, four crosses patonce
argent, on a canton azure a lion
passant or.

Crest—A lion rampant or, holding a
cross patonce gules.

CHASE.

William Chase, planter, of Roxbury, Mass., 1630.

Arms—Gules, four cross-crosslets
argent, on a canton azure a lion
passant or.

Crest—A griffin's head erased holding
in the beak a key.

CHAUNCEY.

Rev. Charles Chauncey, *b* 1589,
Yardley, Hertfordshire, England,
B.A. Trinity Col., Cambridge, 2nd
President of Harvard College,
Massachussets.

Arms—Gules, a cross patonce argent,
on a chief azure a lion passant or.

Crest—Out of a ducal coronet or, a
griffin's head between wings gules.

CHECKLEY.

Col. SAMUEL CHECKLEY, b 1653, son of William Checkley, of Preston-Capes, Northamptonshire, Eng., settled at Boston, Mass.

Arms—Argent, a chevron between three mullets sable.

Crest—A mullet sable.

CHESTER.

LEONARD CHESTER, b 1610, at Blaby, Lancashire, Eng., came to Water-town, Mass., 1633.

Arms—Ermine, on a chief sable, a griffin passant with wings en-dorsed argent.

Crest—A dragon passant argent.

CHEW.

JOHN CHEW, member of Virginia House of Assembly, 1623-42, descended from the Chews of Chewton, Somersetshire, Eng.

Arms—Gules, a chevron argent, on a chief azure three leopards' faces or.

CHUTE.

LIONEL CHUTE, of Ipswich, Mass., 1635, descended from Chewte of Taunton, Somersetshire, Eng.

Arms—Gules, semée of mullets or, three swords barways proper, the middle one encountering the other two ; on a canton per fesse argent and vert a lion passant.

Crest—A dexter hand couped at the wrist holding a broken sword proper.

CLARK.

JOHN CLARK, of Great Munden, Hertfordshire, England, to New-ton, Mass., 1630, one of the Founders of Hartford, Ct., 1636.

Arms—Gules, two bars argent, in chief three escallops or.

Crest—An escallop quarterly gules and or.

CLARKE.

GEORGE CLARKE, of Swanswick, near Bath, Somersetshire, Eng., came to Colonial Office of New York in 1710, Governor of the Colony 1737-44.

Arms—Azure, three escallops in pale or, between two flaunches ermine—Quartering "Hyde."

Crest—A pheon proper.

CLARKSON.

MATTHEW CLARKSON, commissioned 1689, by William III., Secretary of the Colony of New York.

Arms—Argent, on a bend engrailed sable three annulets or.

Crest—A griffin's head between two wings sable.

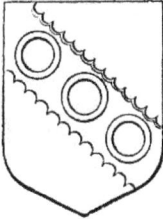

CLAIBORNE.

Colonel WILLIAM CLAIBORNE, Secretary and Treasurer of Virginia, King's Surveyor of the Dominion 1620, son of Sir Edmund Cliburne, of Cliburne Hall, Westmoreland.

Arms—Argent, three chevronels interlaced sable, a chief of the last—Quartering, a cross engrailed vert (Bassingwerke).

Crest—A demi-wolf reguardant proper.

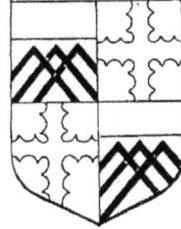

CLAY.

ROBERT CLAY, b 1688, son of Robert Clay of Chesterfield, Derbyshire, Eng., settled in Philadelphia, 1710.

Arms—Argent, a chevron engrailed between three trefoils slipped sable.

Crest—A pair of wings argent, semée of trefoils sable.

CLEVELAND.

MOSES CLEVELAND, from Ipswich, Co. Suffolk, Eng., to New Eng. 1635, settled at Woburn, Mass., 1649; son of Samuel Cleveland, son of William Cleiveland of Hinckley, Yorks, d 1630.

Arms—Per chevron sable and ermine, a chevron engrailed counterchanged.

Crest—A demi-old man habited azure, on his head a cap gules, turned up with hair front, in dexter hand a spear from which a line passing behind and coiled-up in sinister hand.

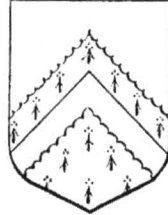

CLINTON.

Colonel CHARLES CLINTON, of Little Britain, Ulster Co., New York, 1729, son of James Clinton, of Longford, Ireland, a grandson of Sir Henry Clinton.

Arms—Argent, six cross-crosslets fitchée sable, on a chief azure two mullets or, pierced gules.

Crest—Out of a ducal crown gules five ostrich feathers argent, banded azures.

COAKLEY.

Dr. COAKLEY, of Richmond, Virginia.

Arms—Ermine, on a chief sable a lion's head erased between two eagles displayed or.

Crest—A lion passant or, in dexter paw an eagle's leg erased gules.

COCHRAN.

Thomas and John Cochran from Coleraine, Ireland, 1750.

Arms—Argent, a chevron between three boars' heads erased sable within a bordure of the second.

Crest—A horse passant argent.

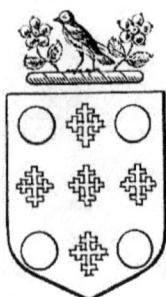

COFFIN.

Tristram Coffin, *b* 1609, Brixham nr. Plymouth, Devonshire, Eng., settled at Haverhill, Mass., 1642.

Arms—Azure, four bezants within five cross-crosslets or.

Crest—A bird or, between two cinquefoils argent, stalked and leaved vert.

COLEY.

Samuel Cooley, settled at Milford, Connecticut, 1639.

Arms—Or, a lion rampant gules.

Crest—A dexter arm in armour proper holding a scimetar, hilt and pommel or.

COLLINS.

Edward Collins, merchant, gent. of Cambridge, Mass, 1636.

Arms - Argent, a dexter hand gauntleted in sinister base grasping a sword in bend proper, pommel and hilt or.

Crest—An owl argent.

COMSTOCK.

Christopher Comstock, settled in Connecticut, 1635-40, son of Frederick Komstohk of Frankfort-on-Maine.

Arms—Or, a sword point downwards, issuing from a crescent in base gules, between two bears rampant sable.

Crest—An elephant rampant proper.

COOK.

Edward Cook, 1800-50, of Stafford, England, settled in New York.

Arms—Or, a chevron engrailed gules between three cinquefoils azure, on a chief of the second a lion passant argent.

Crest—An antelope's head or.

COOKE.

GEORGE COOKE, of Cambridge, Mass.,
1679, grandson of Thomas Cooke
of Pebmarsh, Essex.

Arms—Sable, three bends argent.

Crest—A demi-lion rampant.

CRADOCK.

Rev. THOMAS CRADOCK, *b* Bedfordshire, England, came to Maryland, 1744, brother of Rt. Rev.
John Cradock, Archbishop of
Dublin.

Arms—Argent, on a chevron azure
three garbs or.

Crest A bear's head erased sable,
billetée and muzzled or.

CRANE.

JASPER CRANE, 1605-81, from Co.
Suffolk, England, to New Haven,
Connecticut, 1639.

Arms—Gules, on a fesse between
three crosses pattée fitchée or, a
crane between two annulets azure.

Crest—A demi-hind or, ducally gorged
azure.

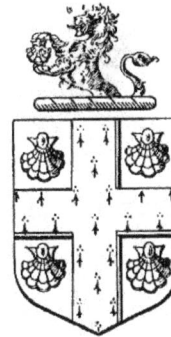

CROSSMAN.

ROBERT CROSSMAN, of Taunton,
Mass., 1645.

Arms—Argent, a cross ermine
between four escallops sable.

Crest—A demi-lion ermine holding
an escallop sable.

CROWNINSHIELD.

JOHAN RICHTAS CASPER VON
CROWNENSCHILD, from Germany
to New York, 1680, originally
from Sweden.

Arms—Azure, a crown argent.

CUNNINGHAM.

ANDREW CUNNINGHAM, of Boston,
Mass., 1660-1715.

Arms—Argent, a shake fork between
three mullets sable.

Crest — A unicorn's head couped
gules, horned or.

CURWEN.

Captain George Curwen, 1610-84, of Salem, Mass.

Arms—.Argent, fretty gules, a chief azure.

Crest—A unicorn's head erased.

CUTHBERT.

Thomas Cuthbert, of Philadelphia, Pa., 1759.

Arms—Vert, a fesse engrailed betwn. four mullets argent, an arrow in pale surmounting the fesse, point downwards proper.

Crest—A demi-lion rampant azure.

CUTLER.

John Cutler, from Spranston, Co. Norfolk, England, settled at Hingham, Mass., 1637.

Arms—Azure, three dragons' heads erased or, langued gules, a chief argent.

Crest—A dragon's head erased azure, gorged with a mural coronet or, holding in the mouth a laurel branch.

DAGGETT.

Aaron Daggett, of Greene Corner, Maine, Justice of the Peace, d 1842.

Arms—Argent, on a chief azure three crescents or.

Crest—An eagle displayed gules charged with a bezant.

DAVIE.

John Davie, grad. of Harvard, 1681, son of Humphrey Davie, merchant of Boston, from Creedy, Devonshire, Eng., son of Sir John Davie, Bart., 1641.

Arms—Argent, a chevron between three mullets pierced sable.

Crest—A holy lamb proper.

DAY.

Robert Day, b 1604, settled at Hartford, Conn., 1636.

Arms—Per chevron or and azure, three mullets counterchanged.

Crest—Two hands conjoined proper fixed to a pair of wings, the dexter or, the sinister azure, each charged with a mullet counterchanged.

DELAFIELD.

JOHN DELAFIELD, settled in New York, 1783, Count of the Holy Roman Empire.

Arms—Sable, a cross patonce or, borne on the breast of the Imperial Eagle of Germany.

Crest—A dove displayed, holding in the beak an olive branch proper.

DELANO.

PHILIPPE DE LA NOYE, from Leyden, Holland, to Plymouth, Mass., 1621. His grandson Jonathan de Lano settled at Tolland, Conn., 1722.

Arms—Argent, fretty gules, on a chief of the second, three wolves' heads erased or.

DE LUZE.

LOUIS PHILIPPE DE LUZE, b Frankfort, Germany, 1793, of New York, 1821.

Arms—Quarterly 1st and 4th argent, two eagles' wings endorsed sable; 2nd and 3rd azure, a chevron or, in base a fleur-de-lis of the last.

Crest—Out of a ducal crown or, a spear head of the same between two eagles' wings sable.

DENISON.

WILLIAM DENISON, b at Bishop's Stortford, Hertfordshire, Eng., settled at Roxbury, Mass., 1632.

Arms—Argent, on a chevron engrailed gules, between three torteaux, an annulet or.

Crest—A dexter arm embowed, vested vert, the hand proper grasping a scimitar.

DEVOTION

EDWARD DEVOTION (De Vaution), a Huguenot, from New Rochelle, France, of Brooklyn, Mass., 1650, founder of the Edward Devotion School Fund.

Arms—Argent, on a bend azure between two martlets sable three escallops or.

DE ZENG.

FREDERICK AUGUSTUS DE ZENG, of Red Hook, Dutchess Co., New York, 1784, son of Baron de Zeng of Rückerswalde - Walkenstein, Saxony.

Arms—Sable, an Ionic column in bend imperially crowned or.

Crest—Out of a crest-coronet two spears coupée, addorsed or, pennons gules, three cocks' feathers sable arising with each spear, between the spears an Ionic column imperially crowned in bend sinister of the first, base on the foot of the dexter spear.

DIGGES.

EDWARD DIGGES, Governor of Virginia, 1656, son of Sir Dudley Digges of Chilham, Kent, England.

Arms—Gules, on a cross argent five eagles displayed sable, armed gules.

Crests—1st an eagle's leg couped, from the thigh sable three ostrich feathers argent ; 2nd an eagle's head sable.

DIODATI.

WILLIAM DIODATI, of New Haven, Conn., 1717.

Arms—Party per pale, 1st gules, a lion rampant or, 2nd barry or and gules.

Crest—A demi-lion rampant.

DISBROW.

SAMUEL DISBROW, of Guilford, Conn., 1639, son of James Disbrow of Ettisley, Cambridgeshire.

Arms—Argent, a fesse between three bears' heads and necks couped sable, muzzled or.

Crest—A bear's head as in Arms.

DODD.

EDWARD DODD, of Hartford, Conn., 1683, son of John Dodd of Northamptonshire, England.

Arms—Argent, on a fesse gules between two cotises wavy sable, three crescents or.

Crest—A serpent vert issuing from and piercing a garb or.

DONGAN.

THOMAS DONGAN, Governor of New York, 1684.

Arms—Argent, a fesse or between three fleurs-de-lis.

Crest—Out of a baron's coronet a demi-lion rampant.

DORR.

EDWARD DORR, 1648-1734, of Boston and Roxbury, Mass.

Arms—Per pale gules and azure, three stag-beetles' with wings extended or.

Crest—A demi-tiger azure holding between the feet an escallop or.

DRAKE.

JOHN DRAKE of Boston, Mass., 1635, son of William Drake, of Wyscomb, Devonshire, and grandson of John Drake, sheriff of Dover, England.

Arms—Argent, a wivern wings displayed and tail nowed gules.

Crest—A dexter arm erect couped at elbow proper holding a battle-axe sable.

DRAPER.

Captain JAMES DRAPER, 1654-98, of Dedham, Mass., son of James Draper, of Roxbury.

Arms—Argent, on a fesse engrailed between three annulets gules as many covered cups or.

Crest—A stag's head gules, attired or, charged on the neck with a fesse between three annulets of the last.

DUANE.

ANTHONY DUANE, b 1682, at Cong, Co. Galway, Ireland, Purser in English Navy, settled in New York, 1702.

Arms—Ermine, a wild cat passant, in chief two crescents sable.

Crest—A demi-wolf.

DU BOIS.

LOUIS DU BOIS, French-Huguenot, founder of New Platz, served in the Colonial forces, 1670.

Arms—Argent, a lion rampant sable armed and langued gules.

Crest—A lion rampant sable, between two tree stumps vert.

DUER.

Major-General WILLIAM DUER, 1747-99, on the Committee Government of New York, 1777.

Arms—Ermine, a bend gules.

Crest—A dove rising, holding an olive branch.

DUFFIELD.

GEORGE DUFFIELD, of Ballymena, Co. Antrim, Ireland, settled at Pequea, Lancaster County, Penna, 1730.

Arms—Sable, a chevron between three doves argent.

Crest—A dove, in the beak an olive branch proper.

DUMARESQUE.

Captain Phillip Dumaresque, *d* at Boston, Mass., 1775; son of Elias and Frances de Carteret Dumaresque, of Jersey, C.I.

Arms—Gules, three escallops or.

Crest—A bull passant guardant.

DUMMER.

Lieut.-Governor William Dummer, 1723.

Arms—Azure, three fleurs-de-lis or, on a chief of the second a demi-lion of the first.

Crest—A demi-lion azure holding in the dexter paw a fleur-de-lis.

DUNMORE.

Larry Dunmore, came from the North of Ireland and settled in Pennsylvania, 1760.

Arms—Vert, three Garbs or.

DWIGHT.

John Dwight, from Dedham, Co. Essex, England, to Watertown, Mass., 1635.

Arms—Ermine, a lion passant or, on a chief gules a crescent of the second, in base a cross crosslet fitchée.

Crest—A demi-lion rampant.

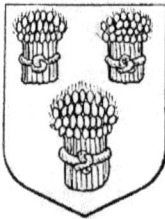

EAGER.

William Eager (Eger), settled at Cambridge, Mass., 1630.

Arms—Azure, a lion rampant or, armed and langued gules, gorged with an antique crown, a chief ermine.

Crest—A demi-lion rampant azure, gorged with an antique crown and charged on the shoulder with a mullet.

EAMES.

Thomas Eames, 1618-80, came from Cornwall, England, settled at Framingham, Mass., served in Pequot War.

Arms—Argent, out of a fesse azure a demi-lion rampant issuant gules.

Crest—A lion rampant sable.

EARDELEY.

DANIEL EARDELEY, 1812-84, of New York, son of John Eardeley of Staffordshire, England.

Arms—Argent, on a chevron azure three garbs or, a canton charged with a fret of the third.

Crest—A stag in full course or.

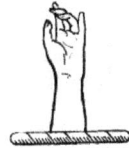

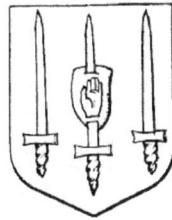

ECKLEY.

REV. JOSEPH ECKLEY, D.D., *b* in London, Eng., 1750, came with his father to New Jersey, 1767.

Arms—Three swords proper, the centre sword piercing an inescutcheon charged with the bloody hand of Ulster.

Crest—An arm couped at the elbow, hand open.

EELLES.

MAJOR SAMUEL EELLS, of Milford, Conn., 1603, son of John Eells of Barnstaple, Devonshire, England, who settled at Dorchester, Mass., 1630.

Arms—Argent, three eels naiant azure.

Crest—A dexter arm in armour fesseways, holding a sword enfield with a boar's head couped proper.

EGERTON.

TOMAS EGERTON, 1540-1616, ancestor of the Egertons of Albany, New York.

Arms—Argent, a lion rampant gules between three pheons sable.

Crest—On a chapeau gules turned up ermine a lion rampant of the first supporting an arrow or.

EGLESTON.

BAGOT EGLESTON, *b* in England, 1500, *d* at Windsor, Connecticut, 1674.

Arms—Argent, a cross sable, in the first quarter a fleur-de-lis of the second.

Crest—A talbot's head erased sable collared argent.

ELY.

JOSHUA ELY, of Dunham, Nottinghamshire, England, settled in New Jersey, 1685.

Arms—Argent, a fesse engrailed between six fleurs-de-lis gules.

Crest—A pheon point upwards gules.

ELIOT.

JOHN ELIOT, baptized at Widford, 1604, settled at Roxbury, Mass., 1631, son of Bennett Elliott of Nasing, Essex. Eng.

Arms—Argent, a fesse gules between two bars gemelle wavy sable.

Crest—An elephant's head argent, collared gules.

ELLIMAN.

JAMES B. ELLIMAN, from Coventry, Warwickshire, England, to New York, 1820.

Arms—Argent, a fesse gules between three eagles displayed.

Crest—An eagle displayed.

ELWOOD.

RICHARD ELWOOD, came from England 1748, settled at Minden, New York.

Arms—Azure, a chevron argent between in chief two roundles or, in base a buck's head cabossed of the second attired of the third.

Crest—A dexter arm embowed in armour, in the hand a battle-axe.

EMERSON.

THOMAS EMERSON, of Ipswich, Mass., 1650, probably from Lincolnshire, England.

Arms—Per fesse indented or and vert, on a bend engrailed azure three lions passant.

Crest—A lion rampant vert bezantée, holding a battle-axe gules headed argent.

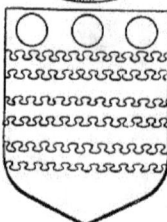

EMERY.

JOHN EMERY, of Romsey, Hampshire, England, to Newbury, Mass., 1635.

Arms—Argent, three bars nebulée gules, in chief as many torteaux.

Crest—Out of a mural crown a demi-horse argent maned or, collared gules studded of the first.

EMMET.

Dr. THOMAS EMMET, LL.D., *d* in New York, 1827; grandson of Dr. Christopher Emmet, 1701-43, of Tipperary, Ireland.

Arms—Azure, a fesse engrailed ermine between three bulls' heads cabossed proper.

Crest—Out of a ducal coronet or, a demi-bull proper.

EVANS.

LOTT EVANS, emigrated to Pennsylvania with William Penn, 1681.

Arms—Argent, three boars' heads couped sable, quartering gules, a lion rampant reguardant argent.

Crest—A demi-lion rampant reguardant holding between the paws a boar's head couped sable.

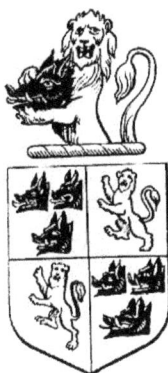

EYRE.

GEORGE EYRE, from Nottinghamshire, England, 1727, to Burlington, New Jersey, gt.-grandson of Sir Gervase Eyre, of Hope, Derbyshire.

Arms—Argent, on a chevron sable three quatrefoils or.

Crest—On a cap of maintenance proper, a booted armed leg couped at the thigh, quarterly argent and sable, spur gold.

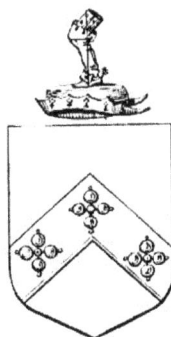

FAIRFAX.

Rev. BRYAN FAIRFAX, 1737-1802, 8th Baron, title confirmed by House of Lords, May 4th, 1800, grandson of Colonel William Fairfax, of Virginia, 1720.

Arms—Or, three bars gemelles gules, surmounted of a lion rampant sable.

Crest—A lion passant guardant sable.

FAIRFIELD.

JOHN FAIRFIELD, one of the original proprietors of Wenham, Mass., 1643.

Arms—Gules, a lion rampant crowned or.

Crest—On a mound vert two doves billing proper.

FALLS.

ALEXANDER FALLS, served in the First Colonial Regiment from New York, 1738, son of Alexander McFall, of New York, 1735.

Arms—Or, a fesse sable between two eagles displayed in chief and a stag's head cabossed in base of the last.

Crest—An eagle's head erased.

FARMER.

ROBERT ADOLPH FARMER, of Pennsylvania, 1790; son of Major-Gen. Robert Farmer, Governor of Florida.

Arms—Argent, a fesse sable between three lions' heads erased gules.

Crest—Out of a ducal coronet or a cock's head gules.

FARWELL.

HENRY FARWELL, of Concord, Mass., 1635.

Arms—Sable, a chevron engrailed argent, between three leopard's heads or.

Crest—Two oak branches orleways vert.

FAUNTLEROY.

THOMAS WARING FAUNTLEROY, of Virginia, 1636.

Arms—Gules, three infant's heads argent, crined or.

Crest—A fleur-de-lis or, between two wings expanded azure.

FAWCONER.

EDWARD FAWCONER, of Andover, Mass., 1648, from Kingsclere, Hampshire.

Arms—Sable, three falcons argent, belled or.

Crest—A garb of wheat or, banded argent.

FEARN.

JOHN FEARN, of Pitsylvania Co., Virginia, 1780.

Arms—Per bend or and gules, two lions' heads erased and counterchanged.

Crest—A talbot's head argent, eared and collared gules, garnished and ringed or, issuing out of a ferne proper.

FENNER.

Captain ARTHUR FENNER, of Providence, R.I., 1646, served as Lieutenant in Cromwell's Army.

Arms—Vert, on a cross argent, between four eagles displayed gules, a cross formée of the last.

Crest—An eagle displayed argent, membered or.

FENWICK.

GEORGE FENWICK, of Gray's Inn, London, and Co. Northumberland, England, to Boston, Mass., 1636, of Saybrook, Conn., 1656.

Arms—Per fesse gules and argent six martlets counterchanged.

Crest—A phœnix in flames proper, gorged with a mural crown.

FERGUSON.

JAMES FERGUSON, of South Carolina, 1700.

Arms—Argent, a lion rampant azure, on a chief gules a star between a cross-crosslet fitchée and a rose of the field.

Crest—A dexter hand grasping a broken spear bendways proper.

FIELD.

ROBERT FEILD, *b* 1605, son of William Feilde, of Sowerby, Yorkshire, Eng., came to New England, 1645.

Arms—Sable, a chevron between three garbs argent.

Crest—A dexter arm issuing out of a cloud fesseways, in the hand a sphere or.

FITCH.

Captain THOMAS FITCH, 1630-90, of Norwalk, Conn., Deputy Governor.

Arms—Vert, a chevron between three lions' heads erased or.

Crest—A leopard's head cabossed or, in the mouth a sword proper hilted gules.

FONTAINE, DE LA.

Rev. PETER DE LA FONTAINE, Chaplain to the Virginia Commission, 1716.

Arms—Argent, a fesse embattled between two elephants' heads erased with tusks depressed in chief, in base a three-masted ship with sails spread and flying a pennant.

Crest—An elephant's head erased with tusks elevated.

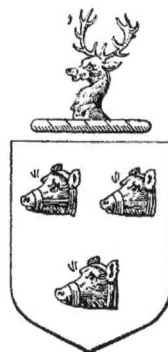

FORBUSH.

DANIEL FORBES (Forbush), *b* 1620, at Kinella, Aberdeen, Scotland, served under Leslie at Dunbar, *d* at Cambridge, Mass., 1693.

Arms—Azure, three bears' heads couped argent, muzzled gules.

Crest—A stag's head proper.

FORSYTH.

JOHN FORSYTH, Newburgh, New York, *b* 1784, Aberdeen, Scotland.

Arms—Argent, a chevron engrailed gules between three griffins segreant vert, armed and membered sable.

Crest—A demi-griffin segreant vert.

FOSTER.

James Foster, of Dorchester, Mass., 1688.

Arms—Argent, a chevron gules between three bugle horns vert, on a chief of the second as many leopards' heads or.

Crest—An arm embowed in armour holding a spear proper.

FRANKLIN.

Dr. Benjamin Franklin, 1758.

Arms—Argent, on a bend engrailed, between two lions' heads erased gules, a dolphin between two martlets or.

Crest—The head of a fish erased gules between two sprigs vert.

FRAZER.

John Frazer, of Philadelphia, 1735, b in Glasslough, Co. Monaghan, Ireland, 1700.

Arms—Azure, three cinquefoils argent.

Crest—Out of a ducal coronet or, an ostrich's head and neck between wings, holding a horseshoe.

FRY.

John Frye, came from Devonshire, settled in Buck's County, Pennsylvania 1700.

Arms—Gules, two horses courant argent.

Crest—An arm embowed in armour holding in the hand, a sword proper.

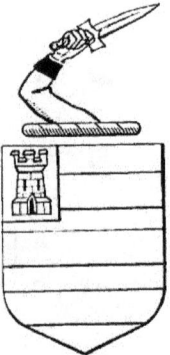

FULLER.

Lieut. Thomas Fuller, of Dedham, Mass., 1635, son of Ralph Fuller, of Wortwell, Co. Norfolk, Eng.

Arms—Argent, three bars gules, on a canton of the second a castle or.

Crest—A dexter arm embowed vested argent, cuff sable, holding a sword proper.

GARDINER.

Lion Gardiner, 1599-1663, first Lord of the Manor of Gardiner's Island, New York.

Arms—Argent, a chevron between three bugle horns stringed gules.

Crest—An arm in armour grasping in the hand a broken shaft of a lance.

GAY.

JOHN GAY, settled at Dedham, Mass.,
1630, *d* 1688.

Arms—Gules, crusily or, three lions
rampant argent.

Crest—A demi-greyhound rampant
sable or.

GAYER.

WILLIAM GAYER, came from Cornwall, England, to Nantucket, 1692.

Arms—Ermine, a fleur-de-lis sable.

Crest—A lion rampant supporting a
spear.

GEDNEY.

JOHN GEDNEY, from Norwich, Co.
Norfolk, England, to Salem,
Mass., 1637.

Arms—Or, three eagles displayed
purple.

Crest—An eagle as in arms.

GERRISH.

Captain WILLIAM GERRISH, *b* at
Bristol, Gloucestershire, Eng.,
1617, *d* at Salem, Mass., 1687.

Arms—Gules, between three escallop
shells argent an arrow fesseways
or.

Crest—A bird rising holding in the
beak an escallop shell.

GIBSON.

JOHN GIBSON, of Cambridge, Mass.,
1634, *d* 1604, *æt* 93.

Arms—Gules, a stork between three
crescents ; quartering Davis.

Crest—On an embattled tower a stork
rising gules, beaked and membered or.

GILPIN.

JOSEPH GILPIN, 1664-1741, settled at
Chads Ford, Chester Co., Penna.,
son of Thomas Gilpin of War-
borough, Oxfordshire, Eng.

Arms—Or, a boar statent sable.

Crest—A dexter arm embowed in
armour holding in the hand a
sprig of laurel vert.

GOODRICH.

WILLIAM GOODRICH, *b* at Bury St. Edmunds, Co. Suffolk, Eng., settled at Wethersfield, Mass., 1635.

Arms—Azure, semée of cross-crosslets, a lion rampant argent.

Crest—A demi-lion rampant, couped argent, holding in the dexter paw a cross-crosslet fitchée.

GOOKIN.

Colonel CHARLES GOOKIN, Governor of Pennsylvania, 1708, grandson of Sir Vincent Gookin, *temp* James I.

DANIEL GOOKIN, of Virginia, 1621, *b* in Kent, Eng., brother of Sir Vincent Gookin.

Arms—Gules, a chevron ermine between three cocks or.

Crest—On a mural crown gules a cock proper or, beaked and legged azure, combed and wattled gules.

GORDON.

GORDON, of Brandon, Virginia and Louisville, Kentucky.

Arms—Azure, on a fesse argent, between three boars' heads couped or, a wolf's head couped sable.

Crest—A hart's head affrontée proper.

GORGE.

Sir FERDINANDO GORGE, Governor of New England, 1623.

Arms—Argent, a whirlpool azure.

Crest—A greyhound's head erased argent, collared gules.

GOVE.

EDWARD GOVE, *b* in London, 1630, settled at Hampton, New Hampshire, 1668.

Arms—Argent, a cross lozengy between four eagles displayed sable.

Crest—Out of a mural coronet or, a demi-monkey sable.

GREENE.

JOHN GREENE, from Southampton, Eng. to Boston, Mass., 1635, grandson of Robert Greene of Bowridge Hill, near Gillingham, Dorsetshire.

Arms—Azure, three bucks trippant or.

Crest—A buck's head or.

GREENLEES.

WILLIAM GREENLEES, of Cincinnati, Ohio, 1800, b 1776 at Cambleton, Argylshire, Scotland.

Arms—Argent, a fleur-de-lis vert, between three mullets gules, within a bordure engrailed of the last.

Crest—A sprig growing out of a mount proper.

GREENWOOD.

MILES GREENWOOD, of Norwich, Mass., 1627, son of Miles Greenwood, of Greenwood, Yorkshire, and Nerwich, Co. Norfolk, Eng.

Arms—Argent, a fesse sable between three mullets in chief and as many ducks in base of the second.

Crest—A mullet sable between wings of the last.

GREGORY.

HENRY GREGORY, of Springfield, Mass., 1640, son of Thomas Gregory, gent., of Nottingham, England.

Arms—Per pale argent and azure, two lions rampant endorsed counterchanged.

Crest—Two lions' heads endorsed erased, azure and argent, collared or.

GUILD.

JOHN GUILD, of Dedham, Mass., 1636, served in King Philip's war.

Arms—Azure, a lion rampant or.

Crest - A dexter hand holding a scimitar.

HALE.

Ensign ROBERT HALE, of Charlestown, Mass., 1630.

Arms—Gules, three broad arrows reversed or, feathered and barbed argent.

Crest—A dexter arm embowed in armour proper, garnished or, bound with a ribbon gules, holding an arrow.

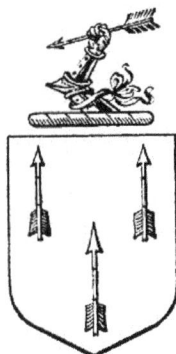

HANBURY.

WILLIAM HANBURY, Merchant, of Plymouth, Mass., 1642, came from Wolverhampton, Staffordshire, Eng.

Arms—Or, a bend engrailed vert cotised sable.

Crest - Out of a mural crown sable a demi-lion rampant or, in the paw a battle-axe.

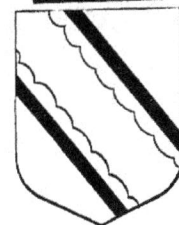

HAMERSLEY.

WILLIAM HAMERSLEY, 1687-1752, an officer in H.M.S. "Valeur," stationed in New York, 1714-16, where he settled.

Arms Gules, three rams' heads couped or.

Crest—A demi-griffin or, holding a cross-crosslet fitchée gules.

HAMILTON.

Captain JOHN HAMILTON, of Charlestown, Massachusetts, 1651.

Arms—Quarterly 1 and 4, gules, a mullet argent between three cinquefoils ermine; 2 and 3, gules, a heart proper, between three cinquefoils ermine.

Crest—A boar's head erased proper.

HAMBLETON.

WILLIAM HAMBLETON, from Poole, Dorsetshire, Eng., to Talbot County, Maryland, 1640.

Arms Gules, three cinquefoils ermine.

HANCOCK.

WILLIAM HANCOCK, Proprietor, of Cambridge, Mass., 1634.

Arms—Gules, a plate, on a chief argent three cocks of the first.

Crest—A cock's head erminois combed wattled and ducally gorged gules.

HAND.

JOHN HAND, from Stanstead, Kent, England, one of the nine patentees of East Hampton, Long Island, 1648.

Arms—Argent, a chevron azure between three dexter hands gules.

Crest—A stag trippant.

HARE.

ROBERT HARE, *b* at Woolwich, Kent, England, 1752, settled in Philadelphia 1773, son of Richard Hare, Esq., of Limehouse, Middx.

Arms—Gules, two bars and a chief indented or.

Crest—A demi-lion rampant holding a cross-crosslet fitchée gules.

HARRISON.

NATHANIEL HARRISON, Clerk of the
Provincial Council of Virginia,
d 1727.

Arms—Sable, three lozenges conjoined
in fesse ermine.

Crest—A demi-lion rampant proper,
holding in the paws a lozenge.

HARWOOD.

JOHN HARWOOD, of Boston, Mass.,
1645. Will proved in London, 1685.

Arms—Argent, a chevron between
three stags' heads cabossed sable.

Crest—A stag's head cabossed sable,
holding in its mouth an oak bough
proper, acorned or,

HASBROUCK.

ABRAHAM HASBROUCK, from Manheim, Germany, settled at Kingston, New York, 1675.

Arms—Purple, a chevron between
three hand-lamps or, in flame
proper.

Crest—A demi-negro wreathed, in the
dexter hand an arrow, in the
sinister a lamp, as in arms, held
across the body.

HASTINGS.

THOMAS HASTINGS, of Watertown,
Mass., 1634, supposed to have
descended from the Earl of
Huntington.

Arms—Argent, a maunch sable.

Crest—A bull's head erased sable
gorged with a ducal coronet, and
armed or.

HAWES.

EDMUND HAWS, b at Yarmouth, Co.
Norfolk, came from London,
England, 1835, to Plymouth,
Mass., d 1693.

Arms—Azure, a fesse wavy between
three lions passant or, armed and
langued gules.

Crest—Out of a mural coronet azure
a lion's head or.

HAWKES.

GEORGE WRIGHT HAWKES, came
from Dudley, Worcestershire,
England, to New York, 1798.

Arms—Azure, three bends or, a chief
ermine; quartering (Wright) sable,
on a chevron, between three unicorns' heads or, as many spear-
heads gules.

HAWLEY.

JOSEPH HAWLEY, *b* at Parwich, Derbyshire, England, 1609, settled at Stratford, Conn., 1630, *d* 1690.

Arms — Vert, a saltire engrailed argent.

Crest — A dexter arm embowed in armour proper, garnished or, holding in the hand a spear pointing downwards.

HAYNES.

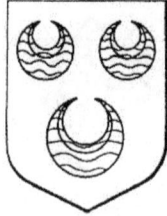

JOHN HAYNES, Governor of Mass., came to Boston, Mass., 1633, son of John Haynes, of Old Holt and Copford Hall, Essex, England.

Arms — Argent, three crescents, barry undée azure and gules.

Crest — A heron volent proper.

HAZARD.

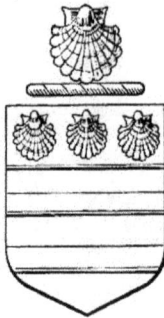

THOMAS HAZARD, came from Wales to Boston, Mass., 1636.

Arms — Azure, two bars argent, on a chief or three escallops gules.

Crest — An escallop gules.

HENSHAW.

JOSHUA HENSHAW, of Dorchester, Mass., 1653, son of William Henshaw of Toxteth Park, Lancashire, England.

Arms — Argent, a chevron sable between three heronshaws of the second.

Crest — A hawk close or, preying on a mallard's wing of the first, erased gules.

HERNDON.

WILLIAM HERNDON, *m* 1677 Catherine, da. of Governor Edward Digges of Virginia, son of Sir Dudley Digges.

Arms — Argent, a heron volant between three escallops sable.

Crest — An escallop shell.

HERRICK.

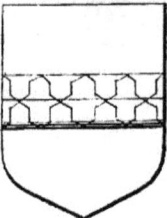

HENRY HERRICK, *b* in London, Middx., 1604, son of Sir William Herrick, settled at Salem, Mass.

Arms — Argent, a fesse vaire or and gules.

Crest — A bull's head couped argent, horned and eared sable.

HIGGINSON.

CHARLES H. HIGGINSON, of New Jersey, son of Henry T. Higginson of Cornelia House, County Down, Ireland, whose ancestor, Colonel Higginson, fought at the battle of the Boyne.

Arms—Sable, three towers in fesse argent, between six trefoils slipped or.

Crest—Out of a tower proper a demi-griffin segreant vert, armed and beaked or.

HILL.

WILLIAM HILL, of Boston, Mass., 1750.

Arms—Gules, two bars ermine, in chief a lion passant per pale or and azure.

Crest—A lion passant or, supporting a cross gules. (Sometimes a boar's head sable, in the mouth a broken spear.)

HINCKLEY.

SAMUEL HINCKLEY, of Tenterden, Co. Kent, England, to New England, 1634, of Barnstaple, Mass., 1638.

Arms—Gules, a chevron engrailed sable.

Crest—A lion's head erased proper.

HINTON.

THOMAS HINTON, *b* at Leydon, Holland, 1640, came to Baltimore, Md., 1665, son of Sir John Hinton, Physician to Charles I. and II.

Arms—Per fesse indented sable and or, six fleurs-de-lis counterchanged.

Crest—An eagle's leg erased encircled by a serpent proper.

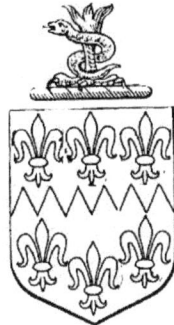

HITCHCOCK.

LUKE HITCHCOCK, of Weathersfield, Massachusetts, 1650.

Arms—Argent, on a cross azure five fleurs-de-lis or, in the first quarter a lion rampant gules.

Crest—A lion's head erased or, in the mouth a round buckle argent.

HOADLEY.

WILLIAM HOADLEY, 1630-1709, of Bradford, Conn., brother of John Hoadley, who received Letters Patent from Charles II., and aided in bringing about his Restoration in lending Gen. Monk £300.

Arms—Quarterly azure and or, in the first quarter a pelican of the second vulning itself proper.

Crest—On a terrestial orb or a dove rising proper, in the beak an olive branch.

HOARE.

JOHN HOARE, b 1632, of Scituate and Concord, Mass., son of Charles Hoare, High Sheriff of Gloucester, England.

Arms—Sable, an eagle displayed with two heads, within a bordure engrailed of the first.

Crest—A deer's head erased.

HODGE.

WILLIAM HODGE, who d in Pennsylvania, 1723.

Arms—Argent, on a bend gules three roses of the first.

Crest—A crescent resting on a crescent reversed.

HOFFMAN.

Colonel MARTINUS HOFFMAN, 1707-72, Justice of the Peace and a distinguished officer in the Colonial and Revolutionary Armies.

Arms—Argent, on a mount vert three pine trees proper.

Crest—A cock proper.

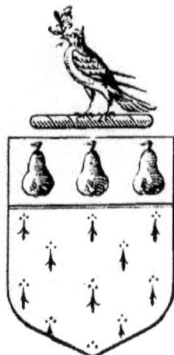

HOLDEN.

JUSTINIAN HOLDEN, 1613-91, from Cranbrook, Kent, England, settled in Watertown, Mass.

Arms—Ermine, on a chief gules three pears or.

Crest—A dove close holding in the beak an olive branch proper.

HOLLINS.

WILLIAM HOLLINS, of Baltimore, Maryland, 1797-1810, son of William Hollins of Newcastle-under-Lyme, Staffordshire, England, d 1769.

Arms—Argent, a chevron azure, in chief four crosses formée fitchée of the second.

Crest—A dexter hand pointing with two fingers to a star proper.

HOLYOKE.

Rev. EDWARD HOLYOKE, of Lynn, Mass., 1638, d at Chelsea, Mass. 1660, came from Tamworth, Staffordshire, England.

Arms—Azure, a chevron argent cotised or between three crescents of the second.

Crest—A cubit arm erect habited gules, cuff argent, holding in the hand an oak branch vert, fructed or.

HOPKINS.

Mr. STEPHEN HOPKINS, gent., of London, came in the "Mayflower" 1620, settled at Plymouth, Mass.

Arms—Sable, on a chevron, between three pistols or, as many roses gules.

Crest—A tower per bend indented argent and gules, in flames proper.

HORWITZ.

Dr. JONATHAN HORWITZ, of Berlin, a student of Goettingen Univ., came to Baltimore the latter part of the 18th century.

Arms—Per chevron argent and azure, a chevron or, in base a lion rampant holding a staff.

Crest—An eagle rising proper.

HOUGH.

RICHARD HOUGH, came from Macclesfield, Cheshire, England, 1683, settled in Bucks County, Penn.

Arms—Argent, a bend sable.

Crest—A wolf's head erased sable.

HOUGHTON.

RALPH HOUGHTON, 1603-98, knighted by Charles I., fought under Cromwell, fled to America and became Recording Officer of Lancashire, Mass.

Arms—Sable, three bars argent.

Crest—A bull passant argent.

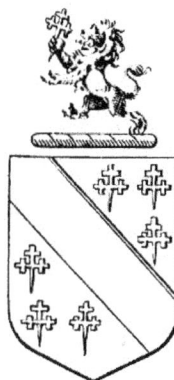

HOWARD.

ABRAHAM HOWARD, *b* in England, came to New England with son James *circa* 1730, settled at Marblehead, Mass.

Arms—Gules, a bend between six cross-crosslets fitchée argent.

Crest—A lion rampant argent, holding a cross of the shield.

HOWELL.

EDWARD HOWELL, of Marsh Gibbon, Buckinghamshire, England, sold the manor of Westbury, came to Boston, Mass., 1639.

Arms—Gules, three towers triple towered argent.

Crest—Out of a ducal crown or a rose gules, stalked and leaved vert, between two wings endorsed of the last.

HOWARD.

THOMAS HOWARD, of Boston, Mass.. 1746.

Arms—Per cross argent and sable, on a bend gules three lions rampant or.

Crest—A lion's head erased or.

HUBBARD.

"HUBBARD tomb" in the Granery burial ground, Boston, 1746.

Arms—Quarterly argent and sable, on a bend gules three lions passant or.

Crest—A lion's head erased.

HUBBELL.

RICHARD HUBBELL, of New Haven, Conn., 1647, said to have come from Ipsley, Warwickshire, Eng.

Arms—Sable, three leopards' heads jessant fleur-de-lis or.

Crest—A wolf passant.

HULL.

GEORGE HULL, who came to New England *circa* 1700, m Esther Bulkeley

Arms—Azure, an eagle displayed or.

Crest—A hunting horn azure, garnished or.

HUNLOCK.

Of Boston, Massachusetts, 1700, came from Wingerworth, Derbyshire, England.

Arms—Azure, a fesse between three tigers' heads erased or.

Crest—On a chapeau azure, turned up ermine, a cockatrice with wings expanded proper.

HUNTER.

Captain DAVID HUNTER, *b* 1728, of York Co., Penna., and Martensburg, Virginia, descended from the Hunters of Hunterston, Ayrshire, Scotland.

Arms—Vert, three dogs of the chase courant argent, collared or, on a chief of the second as many hunting horns of the first, stringed gules.

Crest—A greyhound sejant argent collared or.

HUNTINGTON.

SIMON HUNTINGTON, came from Norwich, Norfolk, England, settled at Norwich, Connecticut, 1660.

Arms—Argent, fretty sable, on a chief gules three mullets or.

Crest—A griffin's head erased or, between two wings gules.

HUTCHINS.

JOHN HUTCHINS, from Southampton, Hampshire, England, settled at Newbury, Mass., 1642.

Arms—Argent, three lions passant sable.

Crest—A lion passant guardant sable.

HUTCHINSON.

RICHARD HUTCHINSON, of Salem, Mass., 1647, son of Thomas Hutchinson, of Arnold, near Nottingham, England.

Arms—Per pale gules and azure, semée of cross-crosslets or, a lion rampant argent.

Crest—Out of a ducal crown or a cockatrice with wings endorsed azure, armed gules.

JAFFREY.

GEORGE JAFFREY, of Portsmouth, New Hampshire, 1762, Judge of the Supreme Court of N. H.

Arms—Paly of six argent and sable, on a fesse of the first three mullets sable.

JANES.

WILLIAM JANES, from Kirkland, Cambridgeshire, England, to New England, 1637.

Arms—Argent, a lion rampant azure between three escallops gules.

Crest—Out of a coronet or a demi-lion rampant azure, holding an escallop gules.

JAUDON.

PETER JAUDON, a French Huguenot who fled to England on the Revocation of the Edict of Nantes, and later settled in Bucks County, Pennsylvania.

Arms—Argent, on a mount vert a grape vine in fruit and leaf all proper, on a chief azure three mullets of the first.

Crest—A phœnix proper rising from fleur-de-lis argent.

JEFFRIES.

DAVID JEFFRIES of Boston, Mass., 1718, son of David Jeffries of Taunton, Somersetshire, Eng., to New England, 1677.

Arms—Sable, a lion rampant or, between three scaling ladders of the second.

Crest—A castle or, towers domed.

JEFFREY.

WILLIAM JEFFREY, of Newport, Rhode Island, 1670, came from Sussex, England.

Arms—Azure, fretty or, on a chief argent a lion passant gules.

JOCELYN or JOSSILYN.

HENRY JOCELYN, Chief Magistrate of Maine, to New England, 1635, son of Sir Thomas Jocelyn, of Co. Kent, England.

Arms—Chequy gules and azure, on a fesse of the first an annulet or.

Crest—A bear's head couped at the neck sable, muzzled gold.

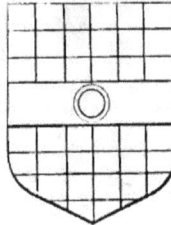

JOHNS.

RICHARD JOHNS, b Bristol, Gloucestershire, 1645, came to America 1675, settled at The Cliffs, Maryland.

Arms—Argent, on a cross raguly azure, between four pheons gules, five bezants.

JOHNSON.

JOHN JOHNSON, of New England, 1637, came to America with John Winthrop.

Arms—Gules, three spear heads argent, a chief ermine.

Crest—A spear head argent, between two branches of laurel vert.

JOHNSON.

ROBERT JOHNSON, who came from Kingston-on-Hull, Yorkshire, Eng., to New Haven, Conn., 1637.

Arms—Argent, a chevron sable between three lions' heads gules, crowned or.

Crest—An eagle rising proper.

JOHNSON.

Dr. John Johnson, son of the Marquis of Annandale, b in Edinboro' Scotland, 1661, settled at Perth Amboy, New Jersey, 1685.

Arms—Argent, a cross of St. Andrew sable, on a chief gules three wool bags or.

Crest—A winged spur or.

KASSON.

Adam Kasson, from Belfast, Ireland, to Boston, Mass., 1722, later of Connecticut.

Arms—Argent, three chevrons and a canton gules, on each a mullet of the field.

Crest—On a tower a dove rising proper.

KANE or KEAYNE.

Captain Robert Keayne, Citizen of London, of Boston, Mass., 1635, founder of the Ancient and Hon. Artillery Company of Boston.

Arms—Azure, an eagle displayed argent.

Crest—A demi-griffin with wings endorsed.

KAY.

Nathaniel Kay, of Newport, Rhode Island, 1727.

Arms—Argent, two bendlets sable.

Crest—A goldfinch proper.

KELLEY.

Thomas Kelley, came from Ireland to Pennsylvania, 1664, proprietor of a plantation called Ruffland.

Arms—Gules, a tower triple-towered supported by two lions rampant or.

Crest—A greyhound statent proper.

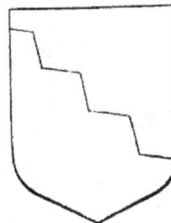

KENDALL.

Thomas Kendall, came from Settle, Yorkshire, England, settled in Pennsylvania, 1700.

Arms—Per bend dancettée argent and sable.

KIMBALL.

RICHARD KIMBALL, from Rattlesden, Suffolk, Eng., settled at Watertown, Mass., 1634.

Arms—Argent, a fesse within a bordure engrailed sable.

Crest—A mermaid proper.

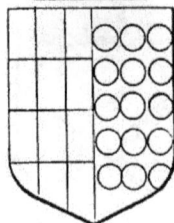

KITTELLE.

JOACHIM VON KETEL (Ketelshuyn), settled at Rensselaerswyck (now Albany), New York, 1642.

Arms—Per pale 1, chequy sable and or, in four rows of three each: 2, or, fifteen hurts in five rows of three each.

Crest—Three lilies of the field argent.

KING.

Major RUFUS KING, LL.D., United States Senator, U.S. Minister to England, 1796.

Arms—Sable, a lion rampant guardant ermine, between three crosses pattée fitchée at foot or.

Crest—A lion's gamb erect and erased sable, holding a cross pattée fitchée or.

KIP.

HENDRICK HENDRICKSEN KIP, came to New Amsterdam from Holland prior to 1643, Member of Governor Stuyvesant's Council.

Arms—Azure, a chevron or, between two griffins sejant and confrontée in chief, and a dexter hand couped in point argent.

Crest—A demi-griffin argent, holding in the paws a cross gules.

KNOWLTON.

Colonel THOMAS KNOWLTON, of Connecticut, 1740.

Arms—Argent, a chevron gules between three crowns sable.

Crest—A demi-lion rampant sable, armed gules.

LANE.

GEORGE LANE, of Rye, Westchester Co., New York, 1666.

Arms—Or, a chevron ermines between three mullets pierced azure.

Crest—A dexter cubit-arm erect vested ermines turned up indented argent, holding in the hand proper a mullet azure.

LANSING.

GARRIT FREDERICK LANSING, of Albany, New York, 1650.

Arms—Or, three increscents azure two and one.

Crest—Three ostrich feathers azure.

LA SERRE.

JEAN PIERRE LA SERRE, fled from France at the Revocation of the Edict of Nantes, 1685.

Arms—Or, a mountain vert issuant from the base, on a chief invected azure three estoils of the field.

Crest—A stag proper attired or, semée of estoils, resting the dexter hoof upon a bezant.

LATTING.

RICHARD LATTING, of Lattingtown, Long Island, *d* 1670, son of John Latting, of Norwich, Co. Norfolk, England.

Arms—Argent, three chevronels between three estoils vert.

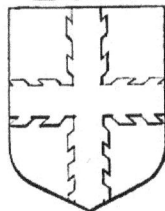

LAWRENCE.

HENRY LAWRENCE, came to New England from Wissett and Holton, Co. Suffolk, England, 1630, settled at Charlestown, Mass, grandson of John Lawrence of Rumburgh, 13th in descent from Sir Robert Lawrence.

Arms—Argent, a cross raguly gules.

Crest—A demi-turbot, tail upwards.

LAWTON.

THOMAS LAWTON, of Portsmouth, Rhode Island, 1638, from Cheshire, England.

Arms—Argent, on a fesse, between three cross-crosslets fitchée sable, a cinquefoil of the first pierced of the second.

Crest—A demi-wolf salient reguardant argent, vulned in the back gules, and licking the wound.

LEDYARD.

JOHN LEDYARD, *b* in England, 1700, Justice of New London Court, Connecticut.

Arms—Ermine, on a chevron or three mullets pierced gules.

Crest—A demi-lion rampant argent, holding in the dexter paw a mullet gules.

LEE.

Colonel RICHARD LEE, Secretary of
State in Virginia, 1659, of Strat-
ford Hall, Virginia, and Cotton
Hall, Shropshire, England.

Arms—Gules, a fesse chequy or and
azure, between ten billets argent
four in chief and six in base.

Crest—On a staff raguly lying fesseways a squirrel sejant proper
cracking a nut, from the dexter
end of the staff a hazel branch
vert, fructed or.

LEEDS.

RICHARD LEEDS, 1595-1693, came
from Great Yarmouth, Co. No-
folk, England, settled at Dorchester, Mass.

Arms—Argent, a fesse sable between
three eagles displayed gules.

LEETE.

Governor WILLIAM LEETE, of Guildford, Conn., *b* 1639, son of John
Leete, of Dodington, Huntingdonshire, England.

Arms—Argent, on a fesse gules, between two rolls of matches sable
fired proper, a martlet or.

Crest—On a ducal crown an antique
lamp or, fired proper.

LINDLY.

FRANCIS LINLY, one of the founders
of Newark, New Jersey, 1655.

Arms—Sable, a lion rampant between
eight crosses patée fitchée argent.

LITTLE.

THOMAS LITTLE, from County Essex,
England, 1633, settled at Marshfield, Mass., 1650.

Arms—Sable, a pillar crowned between
two wings joined at the base or.

Crest—Standing on an arrow a cock
or, beaked and wattled gules.

LIVINGSTON.

WILLIAM LIVINGSTON, Governor of
New Jersey, 1776-90.

Arms—Argent, three cinquefoils gules
within a double treasure flory
counterflory vert.

Crest—A ship in distress.

LORD.

THOMAS LORD, b 1585, came to New England, 1635, probably from Sudbury, Co. Suffolk, England.

Arms—Argent, on a fesse gules, between three cinquefoils azure, a hind passant betw. two pheons or.

Crest—A demi-bird sable on the head two small horns or, wings expanded.

LOWNDES.

CHARLES LOWNDES, of South Carolina, 1730, descended from Lowndes, of Legh Hall, Cheshire, England.

Arms—Argent, fretty azure, on a canton gules a lion's head erased or.

Crest—A lion's head erased or, gorged with a chaplet vert.

LUDLOW.

ROGER LUDLOW, of New England, 1639, son of Thomas Ludlow, of Dinton, Wiltshire, England.

Arms—Argent, a chevron between three bears' heads erased sable.

Crest—A demi-bear, rampant sable.

LUDWELL.

PHILIP LUDWELL, of Green Spring, Virginia, Proprietory Governor of North Carolina, 1693-97, son of Philip Ludwell, of Bruton, Somersetshire.

Arms—Gules, on a bend argent, between two castles of the second, three eagles displayed sable.

M'CALLA.

JOHN M'CALLA, of Isle of Isla, Scotland, settled in Pennsylvania, having a grant of land from the Crown, 1750.

Arms—Gules, two arrows in saltire ar. surmounted by a fesse chequy of the second and first, between three buckles, within a bordure indented or.

Crest—A boot couped at the ancle thereon a spur proper.

McCLARY.

ANDREW McCLARY, from Gardin, Scotland, settled at Epsom, New Hampshire, 1726.

Arms—Or, a chevron azure between three roses gules.

McCLELLAND.

ROBERT McCLELLAN, Laird of Bar-
magachan, Bourge, Kirkcud-
bright, Scotland, settled at Woodbridge, New Jersey, 1685.

Arms—Argent, two chevrons sable.

Crest—A naked hand supporting a
Moor's head on the point of a
sword.

McCULLOUGH.

Captain BENJAMIN McCULLOUGH,
emigrated from the north of Ireland to New Jersey, 1720.

Arms—Argent, on a cross azure five
pheons.

Crest—A cubit arm, in the hand a
dart.

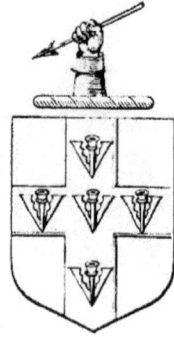

MacDUFFIE.

DANIEL MacDUFFIE, came from
Londonderry, Ireland, settled in
Nutfield, New Hampshire, 1720,
son of Rufus MacDuffie of
Londonderry.

Arms—Or, a lion rampant gules.

Crest—A demi-lion rampant gules
holding a sword in pale proper.

McGUIRE.

— McGUIRE, from Fermanagh, Ireland, settled in Maryland, 1750.

Arms—Vert, a horse thereon a man in
complete armour in the dexter
hand a sword proper.

Crest—A stag statant proper, collared
and lined or.

MAITLAND.

DAVID MAITLAND, of New York,
d 1792, son of Rev. Alexander
Maitland, of Tongland, Kirkcud-
brightshire, Scotland.

Arms—Or, a lion rampant within a
double tressure flory counter-
flory gules.

Crest—A lion sejant affrontée gules,
ducally crowned, in the dexter
paw a sword, in the sinister a
fleur-de-lis azure.

MANN.

EDWARD MANN, of Ipswich, Suffolk,
England, came to New England,
1625.

Arms—Sable, on a fesse embattled,
counter embattled, between three
goats passant, as many pellets.

Crest—A demi-dragon, wings endorsed argent, guttée sable.

MANNING.

WILLIAM MANNING, came from Kent, England, to Cambridge, Mass., 1630.

Arms—Gules, a cross flory between four trefoils slipped or.

Crest—An eagle's head sable between two ostrich feathers argent all issuing out of a ducal crown or.

MARKHAM.

Deacon DANIEL MARKHAM, came to New England, 1666, settled at Middletown, Conn., 1676, grandson of Sir Robert Markham, of Nottinghamshire, England.

Arms—Azure, on a chief or a demilion rampant issuant gules.

Crest—A lion of St. Mark sejant winged or, circled round the head argent, supporting a lyre or.

MASCAREN.

JEAN PAUL MASCAREN, 1684-1760, of Boston, Mass., 1706, *b* at Castras in Languedoc, France.

Arms—Argent, a lion rampant gules, on a chief azure three mullets or.

Crest—A mullet or.

MATHER

Rev. RICHARD MATHER, *b* 1596 at Lowton, par. Winwick, Lancashire, settled in New England, 1635.

Arms—Ermine, on a fesse wavy azure three lions rampant or.

Crest—On the trunk of a tree lying fesseways vert a lion sejant or.

MAYE.

JOHN MAYE, of Mayfield, Sussex, England, settled at Roxbury, Mass., 1640.

Arms—Gules, a fesse between eight billets or.

Crest—Out of a ducal coronet or a leopard's head proper.

MESSINGER.

HENRY MESSINGER, settled in Boston prior to 1640, Member of the Ancient and Hon. Artillery Company of Boston, 1658.

Arms—Argent, a chevron between three close helmets sable.

Crest—A pegasus courant ducally gorged and chained or.

METCALF.

MICHAEL METCALF, *b* 1586, settled in New England, 1637, son of Leonard Metcalf, of Tatterford, Co. Norfolk, England.

Arms—Argent, on a fesse wavy, between three calves passant sable, a sword fesseways.

Crest—A talbot sejant sable the dexter paw supporting a shield or, thereon a hand issuing from clouds, holding a pen.

MILHAU.

Comte CÆSAR MICHAEL DE MILHAU, *b* at St. Dominque, F.W.I., 1762, Citizen of the United States 1803, *d* at Baltimore 1813.

Arms—Argent, a fesse azure, in chief rising from the fesse the sun proper surrounded by three stars, in base a dove close holding in the beak an olive branch.

MILNE.

DAVID MILNE, of Aberdeen, Scotland, settled in Philadelphia, 1827.

Arms—Or, a cross moline azure, pierced ovalways, between three mullets sable, within a bordure wavy of the second.

Crest—A galley with oars erect in saltire proper.

MILNER.

THOMAS MILNER, of Nansemond County, Mass., Clerk of the House of Burgesses, 1681-4, from Appleton, Yorkshire, England.

Arms—Per pale or and sable, a chevron between three horses' bits counterchanged.

Crest—A horse's head couped bridled and maned or.

MOFFETT.

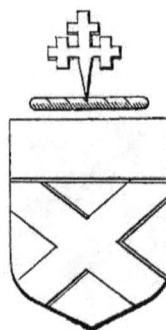

JOSEPH MOFFATT, M.D., of Brimfield, Mass., 1762, descended from Thomas Moffatt, of Exeter, Eng.

Arms—Argent, a saltire azure, a chief gules.

Crest—A cross-crosslet fitchée gules.

MONTGOMERY.

WILLIAM MONTGOMERY, of Brigend, Ayrshire, Scotland, settled in New Jersey, 1706.

Arms—Gules, three fleurs-de-lis or,; quartering—Azure, three annulets or, stoned gules, all within a bordure engrailed of the second.

Crest—A female figure, attired azure, in dexter hand an anchor or, in sinister a head.

MORRIS.

ANTHONY MORRIS, baptized, 1654, at
St. Dunstans, Stepney, London,
Mem. of Provincial Council of
Pennsylvania, Justice of the Su-
preme Court, 1694, son of Captain
Anthony Morris of Stepney.

Arms—Sable, a lion passant between
three scaling ladders or.

MORRIS.

RICHARD MORRIS, of Morrisania
Manor, New Jersey, 1660, son of
William Morris of Tintern, Mon-
mouthshire, S. Wales.

Arms—Gules, a lion rampant or.

Crest—A tower argent, in flames
proper.

MORTON.

GEORGE MORTON, *b* 1585, at Austerfield, Yorkshire, England, *d* at
Plymouth, Mass., 1624.

Arms—Argent, a chevron between
three lozenges sable.

MOSELEY.

Rev. SAMUEL MOSELEY, 1708-91,
Chaplain to Governor Belcher.

Arms—Sable, on a chevron, between
three mill pricks argent, three
mullets gules.

Crest—An eagle displayed ermine.

MUMFORD.

THOMAS MUMFORD, planter, Magistrate of Rhode Island, *d* 1692.

Arms—Or, semée of cross-crosslets
azure a lion rampant of the last.

Crest—A demi-cat guardant proper.

NELSON.

THOMAS NELSON, 1677-1745, of York-
town, Virginia, son of Hugh
Nelson of Penrith, Cumberland,
England.

Arms—Per pale argent and sable, a
chevron between three fleurs-de-lis
counterchanged.

Crest—A fleur-de-lis per pale argent
and sable.

NEWTON.

THOMAS NEWTON, Attorney-General, Judge of Admiralty, Secretary of New Hampshire, 1689.

Arms—Sable, two shinbones in saltire argent.

Crest—An arm embowed holding a shinbone.

NICHOLAS.

Dr. GEORGE NICHOLAS, Surgeon in the British Navy, *b* in Lancashire, England, settled in Virginia, 1722.

Arms—Azure, a chevron engrailed between three owls or.

Crest—On a chapeau azure, turned up ermine, an owl with wings expanded or.

NICHOLSON.

CHRISTOPHER NICHOLSON, of Maryland, 1750.

Arms—Azure, two bars ermine, on a chief argent three suns proper.

Crest—Out of a ducal coronet or, a lion's head erased gules.

NICHOLSON.

ROBERT NICHOLSON, of Charles City County, Virginia, 1655.

Arms—Azure, on a cross argent, between four suns or, a cathedral church gules.

Crest—A demi-man habited in a close coat azure, the buttons, and cuffs turned up or, armed with a headpiece and gorget argent, the beaver open, holding in the dexter hand a sword erect and in the sinister a bible open clasps argent.

NICHOLSON.

WILLIAM NICHOLSON, *b* at Berwick-on-Tweed, England, settled at Annapolis, Maryland, *d* 1719.

Arms—Ermine, on a pale sable three martlets or.

Crest—A demi-lion issuing from a castle triple towered proper.

NORTON.

GEORGE NORTON, came to Boston, Mass., 1629, grandson of Thomas Norton, Esquire, of Sharpenhow, Bedfordshire, England. Also used by the descendants of Rev. John Norton, *b* at Bishops Stortford, Herts, 1606, settled in New Eng., 1634.

Arms—Gules, a fret argent, over all a bend vairé.

Crest—A griffin sejant proper, winged gules, beak and forelegs or.

OAKLEY.

SAMUEL OAKLEY, of New York, 1772, son of John Oakley.

Arms—Argent, on a fesse, between three crescents gules, as many fleurs-de-lis or.

Crest—A dexter arm embowed in armour proper, in the hand a scimetar of the last hilt or.

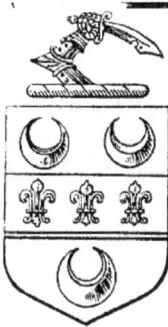

OFFLEY.

DAVID OFFLEY, Mem. of the Ancient and Hon. Artillery Company of Boston, 1638, a descendant of Sir Thomas Offley, Lord Mayor of London, 1556.

Arms—Argent, on a cross flory azure, between four Cornish choughs proper, a lion passant guardant or.

Crest—A demi-lion rampant per pale or and azure, collared per pale counterchanged, holding an olive branch.

OLMSTEAD.

JAMES OLMSTEAD, b. 1580, of New Eng., 1632, son of James Olmsted of Leighs Magna, Essex, Eng.

Arms—Sable, a pheon between three crescents argent.

Crest—A stag's head gules, armed or.

O'NEILL.

JOHN O'NEILL, of Bradford, New Hampshire 1796, from Antrim, Ireland.

Arms—Per fesse wavy, the chief argent charged with a sinister hand gules, in base waves of the sea proper thereon a pike fish naiant of the last.

Crest—An arm embowed in armour proper, garnished or, grasping a sword of the first.

OSGOOD.

Captain JOHN OSGOOD, 1630-93, of Andover, Mass., served in King Philip's War.

Arms—Argent, three garbs within a tressure flory counter flory gules.

Crest—A lion rampant gules holding in the paws a garb of the last.

OTIS.

JOHN OTIS, planter, of Hingham, Mass., b at Glastonbury, Somersetshire, Eng., 1581, came to New England 1635.

Arms—Argent, a saltire engrailed between four cross crosslets fitchée azure.

Crest—An arm embowed vested gules, in the hand a bunch of laurel proper.

OVERTON.

Isaac Overton, of Southold, New York, d 1688.

Arms—Azure, a bend within a bordure or.

Crest—On a chapeau gules turned up ermine a martlet sable.

OWSLEY.

Captain Thomas Owsley, 1663-1700, settled in Stafford County, Virginia, 1690, son of Rev. John Owsley, of Glooston, Leicestershire, England.

Arms—Or, a chevron sable between three holly leaves vert, on a chief of the second a lion passant or, between two fleurs-de-lis argent.

Crest—A demi-lion rampant or, holding a branch of holly vert.

PAGE.

Colonel John Page, 1627-92, from Co. Middlesex, England, settled at Williamsburg, Virginia, 1650.

Arms—Or, a fesse dancettée between three martlets azure within a bordure of the last.

Crest—A demi-horse per pale dancettée or and azure.

PAINE or PAYNE.

William Paine, of Ipswich, Mass., 1635, son of William Paine, of Nowton, Co. Suffolk, England.

Arms—Argent, on a fesse engrailed gules, between three martlets sable, as many mascles or, all within a bordure engrailed of the second bezantée.

Crest—A wolf's head erased azure charged with five bezants.

PAINE.

Moses Paine, of Braintree in New England, gent., d 1643.

Arms—Azure, on a bend gules three arrow-heads, between a lion's head cabossed, and an eagle's leg couped holding a torteau.

Crest—A demi-man couped in profile, in the dexter hand an arrow.

PALMER.

Thomas Palmer, of Boston, Mass., 1650, son of William Palmer of Wanslip, Leicestershire, Eng.

Arms—Argent, two bars sable charged with three trefoils slipped of the field; in chief a greyhound courant of the second.

Crest—On a mount vert a greyhound sejant sable gorged with a collar or, rimmed gules, on the shoulder with a trefoil slipped vert.

PALMER.

WALTER PALMER, Deputy to the General Court, Plymouth, Mass., 1645.

Arms — Or, two bars gules, each charged with three trefoils slipped vert, in chief a greyhound courant.

Crest — A demi-panther rampant guardant, flame issuing from ears and mouth proper, supporting a palm branch

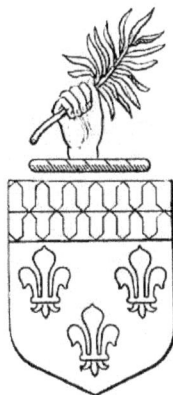

PALMES.

EDWARD PALMES, in New England 1681, son of Andrew Palmes of Sherborn, Hampshire, England, who died at Stapleford, Notts., 1666, aged 73.

Arms — Gules, three fleurs-de-lis argent, a chief vairé.

Crest—A hand holding a palm branch proper.

PARKER.

WILLIAM PARKER, *b* in England, *d* at Portsmouth, New Hampshire, 1736, son of Philip Parker.

Arms—Argent, a chevron between three bucks' heads caboosed gules.

Crest –A buck's head erased.

PARMELE.

JOHN PARMELIN, one of the founders of Guilford, Connecticut, 1639.

Arms—Gules, two bars wavy argent, in chief three mullets of six points or.

Crest—A covered cup or, between two wings sable each charged with a mullet of the third.

PARSONS.

WILLIAM PARSONS, of New York, 1794.

Arms Per chevron azure and or, in chief two crosses pattée, in base a sea-lion sejant guardant counter-changed.

Crest—A sword erect proper, pommel and hilt or, between two crosses pattée of the last.

PARSONS.

JOSEPH PARSONS, of Springfield, Massachusetts, 1646, *d* 1683.— ENOCH PARSONS, *b* 1769, son of Rev. Jonathan Parsons, of Lyme, Connecticut.

Arms—Gules, two chevrons ermine between three eagles displayed or.

Crest—An eagle's leg erased at the thigh or, standing on a leopard's head gules.

PEABODY.

Lieut. FRANCIS PEABODY, b at St. Albans, Hertfordshire, England, 1614, settled at Topsfield, Mass., 1635.

Arms—Per fesse nebuly gules and azure, in chief two suns in splendour, in base a garb or.

Crest—An eagle rising or.

PEASE.

ROBERT PEASE, came from Ipswich, Suffolk, Eng., to Boston, Mass., 1634, son of Robert Pease of Great Baddow, Co. Essex, England.

Arms—Per fesse argent and gules, an eagle displayed counterchanged.

Crest—An eagle's head erased, in the beak a stalk of pea-haulm proper.

PELHAM.

HERBERT PELHAM, of Cambridge, Mass., 1635, grandson of Anthony Pelham, of Laughton, Co. Suffolk, England.

Arms—Azure, three pelicans argent, vulning themselves proper.

Crest—A peacock in its pride proper.

PEMBERTON.

Rev. D. EBENEZER PEMBERTON, 1672-1718, of Pennsylvania. PHINEAS PEMBERTON came from Boulton-le-Moors, Lancashire, England, 1682.

Arms—Argent, a chevron between three buckets sable, hooped and handled or.

Crest—Upon a coney argent an eagle proper.

PENHALLOW.

SAMUEL PENHALLOW, 1665-1726, settled at Portsmouth, Hampshire, 1686, son of Chamond Penhallow, of St. Mabyn, Co. Cornwall, England.

Arms—Vert, a cony argent.

Crest—A goat passant azure, hoofed and attired or.

PENROSE.

BARTHOLOMEW PENROSE, who settled in Pennsylvania, 1702.

Arms—Argent, three bends sable each charged with as many roses of the field.

Crest—A trout naiant or.

PERKINS.

John Perkins, *b* 1590, Freeman of Newent, Gloucestershire, Eng., 1630, settled in Ipswich, Mass., 1654.

Arms—Or, a fesse dancettée between ten billets ermine.

Crest—A pineapple proper stalked and leaved vert.

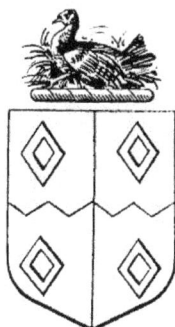

PEROT.

Jacques Perot, *b* at Georgetown, Bermuda, settled in Pennsylvania, 1730.

Arms—Quarterly per fesse dancettée, 1st and 4th or a mascle azure 2nd and 3rd azure, a mascle or.

Crest—A hen on a nest proper.

PERRINE.

William Perrine, *b* 1743, served in Capt. Peter Perrine's Company Middx., Co. Militia, in Revolutionary War, descended from the Perrines of Island of Jersey.

Arms—Argent, on a chevron, between three escallops sable, as many crosses pattée or.

Crest—Out of a ducal coronet or a peacock's head proper.

PETER.

Robert Peter, 1726-1806, from Glasgow, Scotland, settled at Georgetown, Maryland, son of Thomas Peter of "Crossbasket," Glasgow.

Arms—Argent, a lion passant gules surmounted of a sword paleways, on a chief sable a boar's head couped between a mullet and a crescent argent.

PHIPPEN.

David Phippen, of Hingham, Mass., 1635, son of Robert Phippen of Weymouth, Dorsetshire, and brother of George Phippen of Truro, Cornwall, England.

Arms—Argent, two bars sable, in chief three escallops of the last.

Crest—A bee volant in pale or winged vert.

PIATT.

John Piatt, *b* at Dauphine, France, emigrated from Holland to New Jersey, 1740.

Arms—Azure, on a fesse argent a lion passant, in chief three spheres argent.

PINCHON or PYNCHON.

WILLIAM PINCHON, founder of Springfield, Mass., came in the "Arabella," 1630, son of John Pynchon, gent., of Wrattle, Co. Essex, England.

Arms—Per bend argent and sable three roundles within a bordure engrailed counterchanged.

Crest—A tiger's head erased argent.

PITCHER.

ANDREW PITCHER, of Kenton, Devonshire, England, proprietor of Dorchester, Mass., 1641.

Arms—Or, a bend gules surmounted by another azure.

Crest—A demi-man in military habit holding a flag displayed azure.

PITT.

MARY PITT, daughter of Peter Pitt, sheriff of Bristol, England, 1650, *m* Andrew Newell of Charlestown, Mass.

Arms—Sable, a fesse chequy argent and azure between three bezants.

Crest—A stork proper.

POE.

JOHN POE, of Donegal, Ireland, settled in Maryland, 1743.

Arms—Argent, a fesse between three crescents azure issuing flames proper.

Crest—A boar's head pierced by a spear.

POLE.

Captain WILLIAM POLE, of Dorchester, Mass., 1630, son of Sir William Pole, of Colcombe, Devonshire, who *d* 1635, son of William Pole, of Shute, Devonshire, Eng., who *d* 1587.

Arms—Azure, semée of fleurs-de-lis, a lion rampant argent.

Crest—A lion's gamb erased gules, armed or.

POLLOCK.

CHARLES POLLOCK, 1732-1795, settled in Northumberland County, Pennsylvania, son of Dr. Thomas Pollock, M.D., of Coleraine, Ireland.

Arms—Vert, a saltire or between three bugle-horns.

Crest—A boar passant, quarterly or and vert, transpierced with an arrow proper.

POOLE.

Captain EDWARD POOLE, *b* 1609, Weymouth, Dorsetshire, Eng., founder of Weymouth, Mass., 1635.

Arms—Azure, a lion rampant argent, between eight fleurs-de-lis or.

Crest—A stag's head cabossed gules the attires barry of six or and azure.

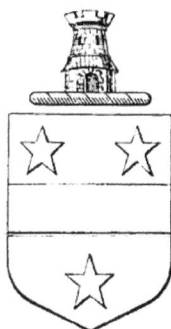

POORE.

JOHN POORE came from Wiltshire, England, 1635, settled at Newbury, Mass., 1652.

Arms—Argent, a fesse azure between three mullets, gules.

Crest—A tower sable masoned argent.

POPHAM.

GEORGE POPHAM, *d* in New England, 1698, a kinsman of Chief Justice Sir John Popham.—Descended from Popham, of Huntworth, Somersetshire, England.

Arms—Argent, on a chief, gules two bucks' heads carbossed.

Crest—A buck's head erased.

PRATT.

Lieut. WILLIAM PRATT, 1622-78, of Saybrook, Mass., served in the Pequot War, son of Rev. William Pratt, of Stevenage, Hertfordshire, England.

Arms—Vert, a fesse dancettée argent, in chief two lions rampant of the last.

Crest—A lion rampant between a branch of oak and another of pine.

PREBLE.

ABRAHAM PREBLE, from County Kent, England, to Scituate, Mass., 1636, *m* Judith, da. of Nathaniel Tilden, of Kent.

Arms—Gules, on a pale or, between four lions' heads erased argent, three lozenges sable.

Crest—A lion's head erased or.

PRESTON.

JAMES PRESTON, of Maryland, 1760.

Arms—Argent, three unicorns' heads erased sable.

Crest—Out of a ducal coronet a unicorn's head proper.

PROVOOST.

David Provoost, a French Hugue-
not, who came from Holland to
Amsterdam, 1639, in the Dutch
West India Company.

Arms—Party per pale, 1st argent,
three arrows' points upwards,
each enfiled through a mullet
sable, 2nd azure, a bar between
two chevrons or.

Crest—An arm embowed in armour
in the hand an arrow fesseways.

PUMPELLY.

Jean Pompilie, a French Huguenot
refugee to America from Avignon,
France, originally from Spoletto,
Italy.

Arms—Argent, chaussé azure, a pale
gules, charged with a fleur-de-lis
or between two roses of the last
on the azure, on a chief or an
eagle displayed sable.

PUTNAM.

John Putnam, from Abbots Aston,
Buckinghamshire, Eng., 1634, *d* at
Danvers, Mass., 1662.

Arms—Sable, crusily fitchée argent,
a stork of the last.

Crest—A wolf's head gules.

PYNE.

John Pyne, planter, of Charlestown,
South Carolina, *b* in Ireland 1766.

Arms—Gules, a chevron ermine between three pine-apples or.

Crest—A pine-tree proper.

RANDOLPH.

Colonel William Randolph, *b* 1651,
settled in "Turkey Island," Vir-
ginia, 1674, grandson of William
Randolph, 1572-1660, of Little
Houghton, Northamptonshire,
Eng.

Arms—Gules, on a cross or five
mullets of the first.

Crest—An antelope's head erased or,
in the mouth a baton.

RANKIN.

b at Kilsyth, Stirlingshire, Scotland,
1773, settled in New York 1792.

Arms—Gules, three boars' heads
erased argent between a lance
and a lochabar-axe of the second.

Crest—A lance erect proper.

RHOADS.

JOHN RHOADS (Rodes), from Waingrove, par. Pentrick, Derbyshire, England, settled in Penn., 1680.

Arms—Argent, a lion passant guardant between two acorns azure, cotised ermine.

Crest—A cubit arm holding a branch of oak, fructed proper.

RICH.

THOMAS RICH, of Springfield, Mass., 1696, whose ancestor settled at Cape Cod, 1625.

Arms—Gules, a chevron between three crosses botonnée or.

Crest—On a mount vert a wivern ar.

RICHARDS.

JOHANN FREDERICH REICHERT, of Philadelphia, 1679, came from Augsburg, Wurtemburg.

Arms—Quarterly 1 and 4, gules, an ostrich argent in the beak a horseshoe, the ostrich in first quarter contourné; 2 and 3, Per fesse azure and or, on a fesse argent three mullets gules, in chief a lion rampant issuing or royally crowned, and in base three stalks of wheat.

Crest—Issuing out of a crest coronet three stalks of wheat proper.

RICHARDSON.

THOMAS RICHARDSON, of Dublin, Ireland, and New York, 1830.

Arms—Or, on a fesse azure, between a bull's head couped in chief and a lymphad in base sable, a saltire couped argent.

Crest—A lion rampant argent, holding between the paws a garland.

RIDGELEY.

HENRY RIDGELEY, came from Devonshire, England, 1659, took up 6,000 acres of land near Annapolis, Maryland.—ROBERT RIDGELEY, of St. Mijoes Creek, Md., 1670.

Arms—Argent, on a chevron sable three mullets pierced of the first.

Crest—A stag's head erased.

RIDGWAY.

RICHARD RIDGWAY, from Wallford, Berkshire, England, who arrived in the Delaware River, 1679, settled in Bucks County, Penna.

Arms—Argent, on a chevron engrailed gules, between three peacocks' heads erased azure ducally gorged or, as many trefoils slipped.

Crest—A hawk proper.

ROBBINS.

JOHN ROBBINS, of Theddingworth, Leicestershire, England, settled at Weathersfield, Connecticut, d 1660.

Arms—Per pale sable and argent, two flaunches and three fleurs-de-lis in fesse all counterchanged.

Crest—Between two dolphins haurient respecting each other or a fleur-de-lis per pale argent and sable.

ROBINSON.

GEORGE ROBINSON settled in Kent County, Delaware, 1685.

Arms—Vert, on a chevron, between three bucks trippant or, as many cinquefoils gules.

Crest—A buck trippant or.

ROBINSON.

ROWLAND ROBINSON, b at Lay Bluff, Cumberland, England, 1654, settled in Rhode Island.

Arms—Or, on a chevron gules, between three stags trippant, three mullets pierced.

Crest—A buck trippant.

ROGERS.

JAMES ROGERS, b in England, 1615, arrived in New London, Conn., in the ship "Increase," 1635.

Arms—Argent, a chevron between three bucks trippant sable.

Crest—A buck as in Arms.

ROLLINS.

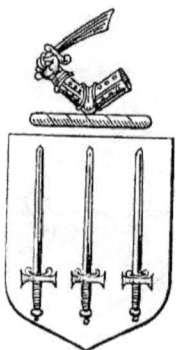

JAMES ROLLINS (Rawlins) came from Cornwall, England, 1632, settled at Ipswich, Mass.

Arms—Sable, three swords paleways points upwards argent, hilts and pommels or.

Crest—An arm embowed in armour holding in the gauntlet a falchion argent.

ROSSE.

Rev. JOHN ROSSE, M.A., Glasgow University, 1754, Rector of All-hallows, Worcester, Maryland, son of Andrew Rosse, Professor of Humanity at Glasgow University, 1706-35.

Arms—Or, a chevron chequy sable and argent between three water bougets sable.

Crest—A hawk's head erased proper.

ROYSTER.

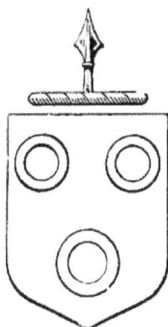

Jacob Royster (Roster), b in England, settled at Clarksville, Virginia, circa 1760.

Arms—Argent, three annulets gules, two and one.

Crest—A spear head proper.

RUSSELL.

Caleb Russell, President of Morristown Academy, 1792-97.

Arms—Argent, a lion rampant gules, on a chief sable three escallops of the first.

Crest—A demi-lion rampant gules.

SANDERS.

Thomas Saunders, b at Amsterdam, Holland, came to New Amsterdam, 1636, great grandson of the Rev. Lawrence Saunders, M.A., the Martyr, burned at Coventry, 1555.

Arms—Sable, a chevron ermine between three bulls' heads carbossed argent.

Crest—A demi-bull erased gules.

SARGENT.

William Sargent, of Charlestown, Mass.,1639, son of Roger Sargent, of Northampton, who was son of Hugh Sargent, 1530-95, of Courteenhall, Northampton, England.

Arms—Argent, a chevron between three dolphins embowed sable.

Crest—A dolphin embowed sable.

SATTERLEE.

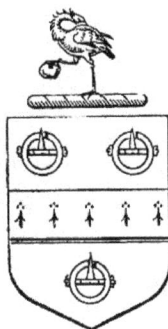

Captain William Satterlee, English Navy, settled in New London, Connecticut, 1682, son of Rev. William Satterlee, Vicar of St. Ide, near Exeter, Devonshire, England.

Arms—Gules, a fesse ermine between three round buckles or.

Crest—A stork resting, holding in the dexter claw a stone proper.

SAVAGE.

Captain Thomas Savage, came from St. Albans, Hertfordshire, settled at Boston, Mass., 1635.

Arms—Argent, six lions rampant, sable.

Crest—Out of a ducal coronet or a lion's gamb erect sable.

SCHENCK.

Roelof and Jan Martense Schenck, came from Utrecht, Holland, 1650, settled at New Amersfoort, Long Island.

Arms—Sable, a lion rampant or.

Crest—A demi-lion or langued gules armed azure, issuing from a German Baron's Coronet or.

SCHUYLER.

Philip Piterse Van Schuyler, *b* in Holland, 1628, *d* at Albany, New York, 1684.

Arms—Vert, an arm clothed or issuing from the dexter side holding in the hand a falcon proper, hooded of the second.

Crest—A falcon as in Arms.

SCREVEN.

Rev. William Screven, *b* 1620, Somersetshire, England, founder of Georgetown, South Carolina, came to Boston, Mass., 1665.

Arms—Argent, guttée de sang, a lion rampant sable.

Crest—A buck at gaze proper attired or.

SEARS.

Richard Sears, *b* 1590, member of Robinson's Leyden Congregation, came to Plymouth, Mass., 1630, son of John Bouchier Sayers, of Amsterdam, Holland.

Arms—Gules, a chevron argent between three pewits proper.

Crest—A dexter arm embowed in armour proper, garnished or, grasping a griffin's head erased or.

SHAPLEIGH.

Major Nicholas Shapleigh, came from Kingsweare, Devonshire, England, to Kittery, Maine, 1650.

Arms—Vert, a chevron between three escallops argent.

Crest—An arm vested gules, turned up argent, in the hand proper a chaplet vert garnished with roses of the first.

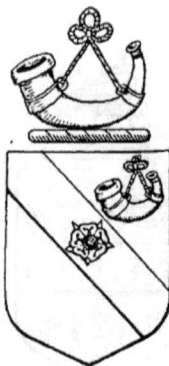

SHED.

Daniel Shed (Sherd), 1620-1708, settled at Braintree, Massachusetts, 1646.

Arms—Argent, on a bend sable a rose of the field, in the sinister canton a bugle-horn strung of the second.

Crest—A bugle-horn argent strung and garnished sable.

SHELDON.

Isaac Sheldon, b 1629, in Co. Essex, England, Founder of Northampton, Massachusetts, 1660.

Arms—Sable, a fesse between three sheldrakes argent.

Crest—A sheldrake proper.

SHERMAN.

John Sherman, of Watertown, Mass., Representative to the General Court, 1660, of the Shermans of Yaxley, Suffolk, England.— Hon. Philip Sherman, b at Dedham, Essex, England, 1610, d at Portsmouth, R.I., 1687.

Arms—Or, a lion rampant sable between three oak leaves vert.

Crest—A sea-lion sejant sable, charged on the shoulder with three bezants.

SHORT.

Clement Short, came from England, settled at Boston, Mass., removed to Berwick, Mass., 1666.

Arms—Azure, a griffin segreant between three estoils or.

Crest—A griffin's head or between wings azure charged with estoils.

SILL.

John Sill, b 1610, probably at Newcastle-on-Tyne, Northumberland, England, settled in Cambridge, Mass., 1637.

Arms—Argent, a fesse engrailed sable fretty or, in chief a lion passant gules.

Crest—A demi-griffin proper collared argent.

SKELTON.

Rev. Samuel Skelton, Rector of Sempringham, Lincolnshire, came to Salem, Massachusetts, 1629.

Arms—Vert, a fesse between three fleurs-de-lis or.

Crest—A pea-hen's head erased sable, in the beak an acorn or, stalked and leaved vert.

SLAUGHTER.

Francis and William Slaughter, of Essex County, Virginia, 1660-80.

Arms—Argent, a saltire azure.

Crest—Out of a ducal coronet or an eagle's head argent between two wings endorsed sable.

SLOCUM.

Anthony Slocome, of Barnstaple, Devonshire, England, settled at Taunton, Massachusetts, 1643.

Arms—Argent on a fesse gules, between three griffins' heads couped sable, as many wings or.

Crest—A griffin's head gules between two wings expanded or.

SMITH.

George Smith, of Old Haugh, Cheshire, England, to Dover, Massachusetts, 1645, claimed that he was son of Captain John Smith of Pocahontas fame.

Arms—Vert, a chevron gules between three Turks' heads couped proper turbaned or.

Crest—An ostrich or, holding in the beak a horse-shoe argent.

SPOTSWOOD.

Major-General Alexander Spotswood, 1676-1740, Governor of Virginia.

Arms—Argent, a chevron gules between three oak trees eradicated vert.

Crest—An eagle displayed looking to the Sun in splendour.

STANDISH.

Captain Myles Standish, came in the "Mayflower," 1620, of the House of Standish of Standish, Lancashire, England.

Arms—Azure, three standing dishes two and one argent.

Crest—An owl with a rat in its talons proper.

STEARNS.

Isaac Stearns, came from England, 1630, with Gov. Winthrop and Sir Richard Saltonstall, settled at Watertown, Mass.

Arms—Or, a chevron between three crosses flory sable.

Crest—A cock starling proper.

STEBBING.

Rowland Stebbing, came from Ipswich, Suffolk, England, to Springfield, Mass., 1634.

Arms—Quarterly or and gules, on a bend sable five bezants.

Crest—A lion's head erased or.

STEELE.

GEORGE STEELE, came from Essex, England, 1630, settled at Cambridge, Mass., d at Hartford, Conn., 1663.

Arms—Argent, a bend chequy sable and ermine between two lions' heads erased gules a chief azure (sometimes charged with three billets or).

Crest—Out of a ducal coronet or a demi-ostrich with wings endorsed or.

STERLING.

DAVID STERLING, born 1622, settled at Charlestown, Massachusetts, son of James Sterling, of Hertfordshire, England.

Arms—Argent, on a bend engrailed azure three round buckles or, in chief a lion's head erased gules.

Crest—A lion passant proper.

STETSON.

ROBERT STETSON, 1613-1703, came from Kent, England, settled in Scituate, Massachusetts, 1634.

Arms—Argent, a bend azure between two griffins sable.

Crest—A demi-griffin or.

STEVENS.

BENJAMIN STEVENS, of Falmouth (now Portland), Maine, 1700.

Arms—Gules, a sword erect between three mullets argent.

Crest—Out of a ducal coronet a cubit arm vested, holding a book expanded.

STEVENS.

JOHN STEVENS (Stephens) of Guilford, Connecticut, 1640, cadet of the family of Stephens, of Eastington, Alkerton, and other manors, in Gloucestershire, England.

Arms—Per chevron azure and argent, in chief two falcons with wings expanded or.

Crest—A demi-eagle displayed or charged on the breast with a mullet sable.

STOCKTON.

Lieut. RICHARD STOCKTON, 1606-1707, of Flushing, L.I., purchased 6,500 acres of land in New Jersey.

Arms—Gules, a chevron vairé and argent between three mullets of the last.

Crest—A lion rampant proper, supporting an Ionic column.

STOKES.

James Stokes, of Boston, Massachusetts, 1642.

Arms—Sable, a lion rampant double queued ermine.

Crest—A dove with wings expanded, in the beak an olive branch.

STONE.

William Stone, Governor of Maryland, 1648-55, nephew of Thomas Stone, merchant and citizen of London, England.

Arms—Per pale or and sable a lion rampant counterchanged.

Crest—A unicorn's head sable, issuing from rays or, maned and armed of the last, between two wings displayed of the first.

STORRS.

Samuel Storrs, *b* 1640, settled at Barnstaple, Mass., 1663, son of Thomas Storrs, of Sutton-cum-Lound, Nottinghamshire, England.

Arms—Or, a fesse dancettée gules between three mullets of six points azure.

Crest—A unicorn's head erased argent, armed and maned or.

STOWE.

John Stowe, came from Co. Middlesex, England, to Roxbury, Mass., 1654, Member of the Ancient and Hon. Artillery Company of Boston.

Arms—Vert, a cross raguly between four leopards' faces or.

Crest—On a ducal coronet or a leopard's face or between wings vert.

STRONG.

John Strong, came to New England, 1630, settled at Dorchester, Mass., son of Richard Strong of Taunton, Somersetshire, England.

Arms—Gules, an eagle displayed or within a bordure engrailed of the last.

Crest—Out of a mural coronet or a demi-eagle with wings displayed of the last.

STUMPF.

John Stumpf, of Stafford, Harford County, Maryland, 1650.

Arms—Per chevron argent and sable, three griffins' heads erased counterchanged.

Crest—A griffin's head erased per chevron argent and sable.

STURGIS.

Edward Sturgis, came from Harmington, Northamptonshire, Eng.
settled at Sandwich, Mass., 1635.

Arms—Azure, a chevron between
three cross-crosslets fitchée within
a bordure engrailed or.

Crest—A talbot's head couped or eared
sable.

SUYDAM.

Heyndrycke Reycke Van Suytdam, came from Holland, settled
at New Amsterdam (New York),
1663.

Arms—Argent, a chevron azure between two crescents and a mullet
gules.

Crest—A swan in water among reeds
proper.

SWARTWOUT.

Tomys Swartwout, settled on Long
Island, 1652, son of Rolof Swartwout of Groningen, Holland.

Arms—A stag rampant guardant in
an enclosure of a forest sable.

Crest—A demi-stag guardant.

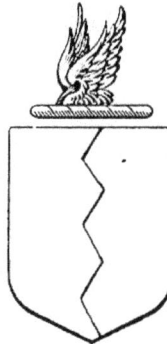

SYLVESTER.

Nathaniel Sylvester, who married
Grissell, da. of Thomas Brinley,
Auditor to Charles I., settled at
Shelter Island, N.Y., 1652.

Arms—Per fesse dancettée gules and
argent.

Crest—Two eagles' wings addorsed.

SYMONDS.

Samuel Symonds, gent., of Ipswich,
Mass., 1637, came from Yeldham
Magna, Essex, England.

Arms—Azure, a chevron engrailed
between three trefoils slipped or.

Crest—Out of a mural coronet, chequy
argent and azure, a boar's head
of the first, crined sable.

TABER.

Philip Taber, 1605-72, came from
England, settled in Watertown,
Mass., 1633.

Arms—Azure, on a chevron engrailed,
between three lions' heads erased
or, as many leopards passant
collared.

Crest—A lion's head erased or.

TAINTOR.

CHARLES TAINTOR, came from South
Wales to New England 1643,
settled at Fairfield, Connecticut,
1643.

Arms—Sable, three tents argent.

TALMAGE.

THOMAS TALMAGE, settled at East
Hampton, Long Island, 1630.

Arms—Argent, a fret sable.

Crest—A horse's head erased argent
between wings or pellettée.

TEACKLE.

Rev. THOMAS TEACKLE, *b* in Gloucestershire, England, 1624, *d* in Virginia, 1695.

Arms—Gules, a maunch argent.

Crest—An arm erect couped at the
elbow, habited gules, charged
with three fleurs-de-lis argent,
holding in the hand proper a
fleur-de-lis or.

TEMPLE.

ROBERT TEMPLE, an officer in the
British Army, who settled in
Boston, Mass., 1717, and whose
third son, (Sir) John, succeeded
to the Baronetcy of Stowe, 1786.

Arms—Quarterly 1 and 4, or, an eagle
displayed sable (Arms of the
Heptarch Kingdom of Mercia);
2 and 3, argent, two bars sable
each charged with three martlets
or.

Crest—On a ducal coronet or a martlet of the same.

TEN BROECK.

Major DIRCK WESSELSE TEN
BROECK, 1638-1717, first Recorder
of Albany, N.Y.

Arms—Azure, a bull between a bear
and a horse argent; on a fesse
or two apple-trees proper.

Crest—A demi-horse rampant.

THACHER.

TOMAS and ANTONY THACHER, 1595-
1667, of Yarmouth, Mass., sons
of Rev. Peter Thacher, Vicar of
Queen Camel, Somersetshire,
England, 1574-1624.

Arms—Gules, on a fesse or, between
three lozenges ermine, a trefoil
slipped azure between two eagles'
heads erased of the field, beaked
argent, and about their necks a
leash of the last.

Crest—A bittern sitting among reeds
proper.

THEOBALD.

CLEMENT THEOBALD, of Lower Norfolk County, Virginia, 1641, d at Charles Co., Maryland, 1678.

Arms—Gules, six crosses crosslet fitchée or.

Crest—A phoenix with wings expanded sable in flames proper.

THOMAS.

JOHN THOMAS, of Portsmouth, Rhode Island, 1688-1728.

Arms—Argent, a chevron lozengy or and sable between three ravens.

Crest—On the branch of a tree lying fesseways, and sprouting from the dexter end proper, a raven with wings expanded of the last.

THOMPSON.

Rev. JOHN THOMPSON, *b* at Muckamore Abbey, Belfast, Ireland, M.A. of Edinburgh University, Minister at York, Maryland, 1740.

Arms—Argent, three towers triple towered gules.

Crest—An arm embowed in armour holding a sword.

THORNDIKE.

JOHN THORNDIKE, of Beverly, Mass., 1668, brother of Rev. Herbert Thorndike, Prebend of Westminster, sons of Francis Thorndike, of Scamblesby, Lincolnshire, Eng.

Arms—Argent, six gouttes, three, two, and one gules, on a chief of the last three leopards' faces or.

Crest—A demi-lion rampant guardant holding a chaplet of laurel vert.

TICKNOR.

WILLIAM TICKNOR, of Boston, 1646, and Scituate, Mass., 1656, served in King Philip's war, 1676.

Arms—A chevron between three escallops in chief and in base a boar's head erased.

Crest—A demi-lion holding a sword.

TILDEN.

NATHANIEL TILDEN, of Tenterden, Kent, England, settled at Scituate, Mass, 1634, brother of Joseph Tilden, merchant and citizen of London.

Arms—Azure, a saltire ermine between four pheons or.

Crest—A battle-axe erect entwined by a serpent proper.

TILGHMAN.

Dr. RICHARD TILGHMAN, Surgeon in the British Navy, purchased the Manor of Canterbury, Maryland, 1659, son of Oswald Tilghman, of Holloway Court, Kent, England.

Arms—Per fesse sable and argent, a lion rampant reguardant double-queued counterchanged and crowned or.

Crest—A demi-lion sable crowned or.

TIMPSON.

THOMAS TIMPSON, of New York, 1765.

Arms—Per chevron gules and argent, in chief two lions rampant of the second, in base an oak tree fructed or.

Crest—A piece of battlement argent, thereon an eagle rising proper, in the beak an oak branch fructed or

TODD.

CHRISTOPHER TODD, came to New Haven, Connecticut, 1639, son of Willam Todd, 1593-1617, of Pontefract, Yorkshire, England.

Arms—Argent, within a bordure vert three foxs' heads couped gules.

Crest—On a cap of maintenance gules turned up ermine a fox sejant proper.

TOWNE.

WILLIAM TOWNE, b 1599, settled at Salem, Mass., 1635, son of Nicholas Towne of Yarmouth, Norfolk, England.

Arms—Argent, on a chevron gules three cross-crosslets of the first.

Crest—An oak tree proper.

TOWNSEND.

THOMAS TOWNSEND, baptized at Bracon Ash, Norfolk, 1594, settled at Lynn, Mass., 1635, son of Henry Townsend and Margaret Forth, a cousin of Gov. John Winthrop. —JOHN TOWNSEND, from Norwich, Norfolk, England, to New England, 1635.

Arms—Azure, a chevron ermine between three escallops or.

Crest—A stag trippant.

TRACY.

THOMAS TRACY, of Salem, Mass., 1636, grandson of Richard Tracy, of Stanway, Gloucestershire, England.

Arms—Or, an escallop in dexter chief point sable between two bendlets gules.

Crest—On a chapeau gules, turned up ermine, an escallop sable between two wings or.

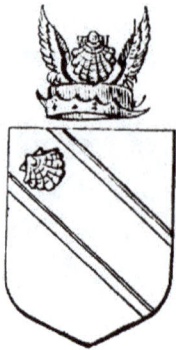

TUCK.

ROBERT TUCK, settled at Watertown, Mass., 1635, came from Gorleston, Co. Suffolk, England.

Arms—Argent, a chevron between three greyhounds' heads erased sable.

Crest—Three mullets in chevron or.

TUTTLE.

JOHN TUTTLE, of Dover, New Hampshire, 1640, *d* at Carrickfergus, Ireland, 1656.

Arms—Azure, on a bend cotised or a lion passant sable.

Crest—On a mount vert a Cornish chough proper in the beak an olive branch.

TYNG.

EDWARD TYNG, *b* 1600, at Dunstable, Bedfordshire, England, came to Boston, Mass., 1639.

Arms—Argent, on a bend sable three martlets or.

Crest—A wolf's head erased sable.

UNDERHILL.

Captain JOHN UNDERHILL, 1597-1672, of Boston, 1630, Governor of Piscataqua Plantation. He had previously served in the British Army in the Netherlands, in Ireland, and at Cadiz.

Arms—Argent, on a chevron sable, between three trefoils slipped vert, as many bezants.

Crest—On a mound vert a hind lodged or.

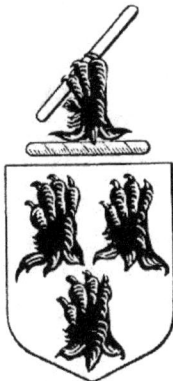

USHER.

Colonel JOHN USHER, Lieut.-Governor of New Hampshire, 1692.

Arms—Argent, three lions' gambs sable.

Crest—A lion's gamb sable holding a wand argent.

VAN CORTLANDT.

Colonel OLOFF STEVENSON VAN CORTLANDT, *b* 1610, who came to the New Netherlands 1636, the last Burgomaster of New Amsterdam before the English took possession of the city.

Arms—Argent, four windmill wings conjoined in saltire sable, voided gules, between five stars placed crosswise of the last.

Crest—A star gules.

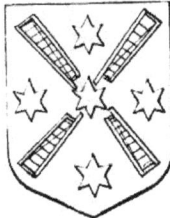

VAN RENSSELAER.

KILIAEN VAN RENSSELAER, of Nykerk and Amsterdam, Holland, first Patron and Founder of Rensselaerwick, in New Netherlands, *m* 1627, Ann Van Weeley.

Arms—Gules, a cross molin argent.

Crest—An iron fire basket from which issue flames proper.

VAN WYCK.

CORNELIUS BARENTSE VAN WYCK, who emigrated from Holland, 1660, settled at Long Island.

Arms—Sable, a cross or between eight thistles argent two in each quarter.

Crest—A ducal coronet uplifted by two griffins proper.

VASSALL.

WILLIAM VASSALL, *b* 1590, came to Salem, Mass., 1627, son of John Vassall, Alderman and merchant of London, 1588.

Arms—Azure, in chief a sun in base a chalice or.

Crest—A ship with masts and shrouds proper.

VERNON.

DANIEL VERNON, of Newport, Rhode Island, 1666, son of Samuel Vernon, merchant, of London, England.

Arms—Or, on a fesse argent three garbs of the field.

Crest—A demi-Ceres affrontée proper, vested vert, holding three ears of wheat over her shoulder, in the right hand a sickle proper.

VON SAHLER.

ABRAHAM VON DER SAHLE, came from Saxony, bought an estate on the Perkiomen, near Philadelphia, 1778

Arms—Sable, a female bust habited or, crowned, issuing from a reversed crown.

Crest—A female bust as in arms.

VOSE.

ROBERT VOSE, settled at Dorchester, Massachusetts, 1636.

Arms—Ermine, a chevron gules between three roses.

Crest—A demi-lion rampant holding a rose.

WADSWORTH.

CHRISTOPHER WADSWORTH, of Dux-
bury, Mass., 1632.—WILLIAM
WADSWORTH, of Cambridge,
Mass., 1632.

Arms—Gules, three fleurs-de-lis argent.

Crest—On a globe of the world, winged
proper, an eagle rising or.

WALDRON.

RICHARD WALDRON (Walderne),
b 1615, at Alcester, Warwickshire,
England, settled in New England,
1635, son of William Walderne.

Arms—Argent, a chevron ermines
between three bulls' heads sable
armed gules.

WALMSLEY.

THOMAS WALMSLEY, came from
Settle, Yorkshire, England, *temp.*
William Penn, settled on Neshaminy Creek, Bucks Co., Pennsylvania.

Arms—Gules, on a chief ermine a
trefoil slipped between two hurts.

Crest—A lion statant guardant ermine
ducally crowned or, charged on
the side with a trefoil slipped.

WALTER.

THOMAS WALTER, from Youghal, Co.
Cork, Ireland, to Boston, Mass.,
1679, originally of Lancashire,
England.

Arms—Azure, a fesse dancettée or
between three eagles displayed
argent.

Crest—A lion's head erased argent.

WALTON.

Captain WILLIAM WALTON, merchant, of New York, trading with
the West Indies and the Spanish
Main, 1760.

Arms—Argent, a chevron gules between three hawks' heads erased
sable.

Crest—A wild man, wreathed about
the middle and temples proper,
holding in the dexter hand a
trefoil slipped or, in the sinister
hand a spiked club or reclining
on his shoulder.

WALWORTH.

WILLIAM WALWORTH, who came
from England and settled in New
England, 1680.

Arms—Gules, a bend engrailed between two garbs or.

Crest—A cubit arm erect holding a
dagger.

WARREN.

ARTHUR WARREN, of Weymouth, Massachusetts, 1638.

Arms—Chequy or and azure, on a canton gules a lion ramp. argent.

Crest—On a chapeau gules, turned up ermine, a wivern argent wings expanded, chequy or and azure.

WASHBURN.

JOHN WASHBURN, came from Evesham, Worcestershire, England, to Duxbury, Massachusetts, 1632,

Arms—Argent, on a fesse, between six martlets gules, three cinquefoils argent.

Crest—A coil of flax surmounted with a wreath, argent and gules thereon flames of fire proper.

WEAVER.

THOMAS WEAVER, Attorney-General in the Leeward Islands, settled in New York, 1701.

Arms—Sable, two bars argent, on a canton of the last a garb of the second.

Crest—A ram's head erased argent, armed or.

WEBSTER.

Governor JOHN WEBSTER, *b* in Warwickshire, England, *d* at Hadley, Mass., 1661, said to be a gt. grandson of John Webster, of Cambridge, and Huntingdonshire, *temp.* Henry VIII.

Arms—Azure, on a bend argent cotised or, between two demi-lions rampant ermine, a rose gules seeded and leaved proper between two boars' heads couped sable.

Crest—A dragon's head couped reguardant, quarterly per fesse embattled or and vert, flames issuing from the mouth.

WEIR.

ROBERT WEIR, settled in New Rochelle, N.Y., 1790, son of Walter Weir, of Paisley, Scotland, son of William Weir, Magistrate, of Stirling, 1745.

Arms—Argent, on a fesse azure three mullets of the field.

Crest—A demi-horse in armour proper, bridled and saddled gules.

WELD.

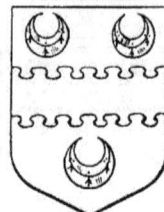

Captain JOSEPH WELD, 1595-1646, came from Sudbury, Co. Suffolk, England, of Roxbury, Mass., 1635.

Arms—Azure, a fesse nebulée between three crescents ermine.

Crest—A wivern sable guttée, ducally gorged and chained or.

WELLES.

Governor THOMAS WELLES, 1598-1660, of Westersfield, Conn., 1635, son of Thomas Welles, Merchant, of London, and of Essex, England.

Arms—Or, a lion rampant double queued sable, on a chief gules two annulets interlaced of the field.

Crest—Out of a mural crown a demi-lion, double queued sable, holding between the paws two annulets interlaced.

WELLS.

EBENEZER WELLS, of Brattleboro', Vermont, 1750.

Arms—Or, on a cross sable a sun in full splendour, in the first quarter a lion rampant of the second.

Crest—A unicorn's head erased azure, crined armed and ducally crowned or, between two wings of the last.

WENDEL.

GIVERT JANSEN WENDEL, of East Friesland, Netherlands, served in the Dutch East India Company, settled at Albany, N.Y., 1640.

Arms—Per fesse azure and argent, in chief a ship in full sail of the second, in base two anchors in saltire rings downwards sable.

Crest—A ship in full sail proper.

WENTWORTH.

Elder WILLIAM WENTWORTH, 1615-96, of Exeter, New Hampshire, son of William Wentworth, of Alford, Lincolnshire, who was descended from Oliver Wentworth, of Elmsall, Yorkshire, 1522.

Arms—Sable, a chevron between three leopards' faces or.

Crest—A griffin passant argent.

WEST.

ROBERT WEST, of Providence, R.I., 1645, Monmouth, N.J., 1667, a cadet of the family of West, Lords De La Warr.

Arms—Quarterly, 1 and 4, argent, a fesse dancettée sable; 2 and 3, gules, three leopards' faces reversed jessant-de-lis or.

Crest—Out of a ducal coronet or a griffin's head azure beaked and eared or.

WESTERVELT.

LUBBERT LUBBERTSEN VAN WESTERVELT, came from Meppel, Dreuthe, Holland, 1662, settled at Flatbush, L.I.

Arms—Vert, three fleurs-de-lis argent.

Crest—Out of a coronet or two arms in armour proper holding between them a fleur-de-lis.

WHARTON.

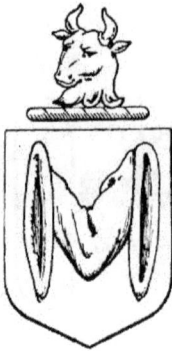

THOMAS WHARTON, of Philadelphia, 1688, son of Richard Wharton, of Orton, Co. Westmoreland, England.

Arms—Sable, a maunch argent.

Crest—A bull's head erased argent armed or.

WHEELER.

MOSES WHEELER, born in Kent, England, 1598, settled in New Haven, Conn., 1638.

Arms—Vert, on a fesse or three lions rampant of the first.

Crest—Out of a mural crown or a griffin's head argent.

WHEELWRIGHT.

Rev. JOHN WHEELWRIGHT, founder of Exeter, Mass., 1638, son of Robert Wheelwright of Saleby, near Alford, Lincolnshire, England.

Arms—Ermine, on a fesse or, between three lions' heads erased, three plates.

Crest—A lion's head erased.

WHISTLER.

Major JOHN WHISTLER, officer in the British army which surrendered at Saratoga under Burgoyne, he settled in America.

Arms—Gules, a bend lozengy between two lions passant argent.

Crest—A harp or stringed sable.

WHITE.

JOHN WHITE, of Canterbury, Kent, came to Philadelphia, Pa. with William Penn.

Arms—Argent, a chevron engrailed between three roses gules.

Crest—A demi-lion rampant gules holding a flag of St. George.

WHITE.

Elder JOHN WHITE, b 1596, in Co. Essex, England, came to New England 1632, settled at Cambridge, Mass.

Arms—Argent, a chevron between three popinjays vert, beaked legged and collared of the second, within a bordure azure charged with eight bezants.

Crest—Between two wings argent a popinjay's head vert, collared gules, holding in the beak a rose gules, slipped and leaved of the second.

WHITELEY.

Arthur Whiteley, came from Northamptonshire, England, settled in America 1676.

Arms—Argent, on a chief gules three garbs or.

Crest—A buck's head erased proper.

WHITING.

Francis Whiting, 1779-1826, of Elmington, Gloucester County, Virginia.

Arms—A chevron between three wolves heads erased.

Crest—A wolf's head erased.

WHITON.

Thomas Whiton, of Hingham, Mass., 1635.

Arms—Gyronny of four azure and ermine, a leopard's head or, in chief three bezants.

Crest—A lion rampant.

WILBUR.

Samuel Wilbur (Wildbore), merchant, of Boston, Mass., 1633, one of the incorporators of Providence, R.I.

Arms—Sable, on a fesse, between two boars' heads passant, a javelin head of the field.

Crest—A boar's head erased, pierced by a spear argent.

WILGUS.

Samuel Wilgus, of Monmouth, New Jersey, 1755.

Arms—Or, on a chevron sable, between three lions' heads erased of the second, as many quatrefoils of the field.

WILKINS.

John Wilkins, of Frome, Somersetshire, settled in Baltimore, Maryland, 1846.

Arms—Argent, on a pale engrailed, between two plain cotises sable, three martlets or.

Crest—A martlet as in arms.

WILLARD.

Major SIMON WILLARD, b 1605, of Cambridge, Mass., 1634, son of Richard Willard of Horsmonden, Kent, England.

Arms—Argent, a chevron ermine between three flasks proper.

Crest—A griffin's head erased.

WILLET.

Captain THOMAS WILLET, merchant, came from Leyden, Holland to Plymouth, Mass., 1630.—JOHN WILLET, from Wales to Boston, *circa* 1660.

Arms—Argent, three bars gemelles sable, in chief as many lions rampant of the second.

Crest—On a ducal coronet or a moorcock with wings expanded sable, combed and wattled gules.

WILLIAMS.

Bragadier-General OTHO HOLLAND WILLIAMS, who served during the American Revolution, son of Joseph Williams who came to America 1730.

Arms—Argent, a chevron between three boars' heads, couped gules.

Crest—A boar's head couped argent pierced with an arrow.

WILLIAMS.

ROBERT WILLIAMS, 1600-90, settled at Roxbury, Mass., 1638, son of Stephen Williams, of Great Yarmouth, Norfolk, England.

Arms—Sable, a lion rampant argent armed and langued gules.

Crest—A fighting cock proper.

WILLIS.

GEORGE WILLIS, from Fenny Compton, Warwickshire, England, settled at Hartford Conn., 1638. —HENRY WILLIS, from Wiltshire, England, 1675.

Arms—Per fesse gules and argent, three lions rampant counterchanged within a bordure ermine.

Crest—Two lions' gambs erased, the dexter argent the sinister gules, supporting an escutcheon or.

WILSON.

Dr. ROBERT WILSON, born at Cupar, Fifeshire, Scotland, 1736, settled in Charleston, South Carolina, 1755.

Arms—Gules, a chevron counter embattled between three mullets argent.

Crest—A talbot's head erased argent.

Armorial Addenda.

WILSON.

Colonel WILLIAM WILSON, 1646-1713, of Hampton, Virginia, naval officer of the lower district of James River.

Arms—Sable, on a cross engrailed, between four cherubims or, a human heart of the first wounded on the left side proper and crowned with a crown of thorns vert.

WILSON.

Rev. JOHN WILSON, of Boston, Mass., son of Rev. William Wilson, D.D., Canon of Windsor, d 1587.

Arms—Per pale argent and azure, three lions' gambs erased fesseways in pale counterchanged.

Crest—A lion's head erased argent guttée de sang.

WOLVERTON.

CHARLES WOLVERTON, of New Jersey, 1780.

Arms—Sable, a fesse wavy or between three wolves heads erased argent.

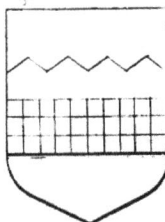

WOODBURY.

ANDREW WOODBURY, of Manchester, Mass., 1731, Deputy to Spanish Convention, 1774.—HUMPHREY WOODBERY, of Beverley, Mass., 1680, son of John Woodberye, of Somersetshire, England.

Arms—Or, a fesse chequy sable and gules, a chief dancettée azure.

WOODFORD.

THOMAS WOODFORD, came from Lincolnshire, England, to Plymouth, Mass., 1632.

Arms—Sable, three leopards' heads reversed jessant as many fleurs-de-lis gules.

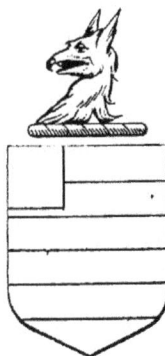

WOODWARD.

CHARLES WOODWARD, born 1775, in London, England, settled in Philadelphia, 1800.

Arms—Barry of six or and sable, a canton gules.

Crest—An heraldic tiger's head erased argent.

WORTHINGTON.

NICHOLAS WORTHINGTON from Lancashire, England, settled in New England 1649.

Arms—Argent, three dung forks sable.

Crest—A goat statant argent holding in its mouth an oak branch vert.

WRIGHT.

WILLIAM WRIGHT, U.S. Senator for New Jersey, 1829, descended from Edward Wright, of Saybrook, Connecticut, 1630.

Arms—Or, a fesse chequy argent and azure between three eagles' heads erased of the third.

Crest—A unicorn passant reguardant the dexter paw resting on a mullet or.

WRIGHT.

Deacon SAMUEL WRIGHT, born in London, England, settled at Springfield, Mass., 1641.

Arms—Azure, two bars argent, in chief three leopards' heads or.

Crest—Out of a ducal coronet or a dragon's head proper.

WYATT.

JAMES WYATT, of Baltimore, Maryland, born 1748 at Bristol, Gloucestershire.

Arms—Sable, a fesse dancettée argent between three eagles displayed or, a chief of the last.

Crest—Out of park pales argent and sable, charged with escallops in fesse or, a pine-tree fructed proper.

YOUNG.

General ROBERT YOUNG, of Guilford Township, now Franklin Co., Pennsylvania, 1768.

Arms—Argent, on a chevron azure three bezants, on a chief gules two cinquefoils or.

Crest—Out of a mural coronet gules a goat's head or.

YOUNG.

BRIDGET, daughter of William Young, of Kenton, Warwickshire, Shropshire, married Gov. George Wyllis, of Hartford, Conn., 1642.

Arms—Or, three roses gules.

Crest—A wolf passant sable.

Royal Warrant Holders

... to ...

His Majesty King Edward the Seventh.

Her Majesty Queen Alexandra.

Her late Majesty Queen Victoria.

T. R. H. The Prince and Princess of Wales.

H. R. H. The late Duke of Saxe-Coburg and Gotha.

T. R. H. The late Duke and Duchess of Teck.

A permanent record of many leading houses of Business enjoying Royal Patronage, the possession of a Warrant from Royalty to use and display the Royal Arms, and in this way indicate the excellence of their work.

———

Although these Appointments to Royalty are of ancient origin, the attendant privilege of thus using the Royal Arms is now protected by the Patents, Designs, and Trade Marks Act, 1883.

[46 AND 47 VICTORIA, C. 57, S. 106].

Royal Warrant Holders.

ANTIQUE FURNITURE DEALERS.

BARBER & SONS, 12, High Street, Windsor, Berks, Eng.

By Special Appointment to Her Majesty the Queen, also to Her late Majesty Queen Victoria.

London Depot: 5, Pickering Place, St, James' Street, London, W.

WARING & GILLOW, Ltd., 164–180, Oxford St., W., London, Eng.

Upholsterers and Decorators to H.M. King Edward VII.; Double Grand Prix, Paris, 1900; Two Grand Prizes, St. Louis, 1904; Grand Prix, Milan, 1906.
Also at Liverpool, Manchester, Lancaster, Paris, Johannesburg.

ANTIQUE AND MODERN SILVER PLATE.

LAMBERT, 10, 11 and 12, Coventry Street, Piccadilly, W., London, Eng.

Jewellers and Silversmiths to His Majesty King Edward VII.

Antique and Modern Table, Decorative and Ecclesiastical
Silver Plate. Diamond Work and Pearls.

ARCHERY, POLO, GOLF AND SPORTING GOODS.

BUCHANAN, Ltd., 15, Pall Mall, London, S.W., Eng.

Telephone 5194 Gerrard.

To His Majesty King Edward VII.; His Majesty the King of Portugal.

ART FABRICS.

LIBERTY & Co., Ltd., Regent Street, W., London, Eng., Manufacturers of Art Fabrics.

To His Majesty King Edward VII.

Also at Paris, Manchester, Bristol, Birmingham.

ART PUBLISHERS AND PICTURE DEALERS.

THOS. McLEAN, 7, Haymarket, W., London, Eng., Printseller and Publisher.

(Established in the Haymarket 1811).

To His Majesty King Edward VII.; Her late Majesty Queen Victoria; also H.R.H. the Prince of Wales, &c.

THE FINE ART SOCIETY, 148, New Bond Street, London, Eng.,

Publishers to His Majesty The King. Printsellers to Her Majesty The Queen.

Continuous Exhibitions of First-Class Water Colours throughout the year.

ART PUBLISHERS AND PRINTSELLERS.

ARTHUR ACKERMANN & SON, 191, Regent St., W., London, Eng.

To Her Majesty Queen Alexandra; Her late Majesty Queen Victoria.

Genuine Old and Modern Sporting Print Experts.

P. & D. COLNAGHI & Co., 13 and 14, Pall Mall East, S.W., London, Eng.

Printsellers and Publishers to His Majesty King Edward VII.

"Royal Warrant Holders since H.M. King George III."

THE FINE ART SOCIETY, 148, New Bond Street, London, Eng.,

Publishers to His Majesty The King. Printsellers to Her Majesty The Queen.

Special Collections of the works of Axel Haig, Haden, Meissonier, Whistler, Lord Leighton, &c.

AUCTIONEERS, ESTATE AGENTS.

HOLLAND & SONS, 9, Mount Street, Grosvenor Square, W., London, Eng., also Sanitary Engineers.

Upholsterers to His Majesty King Edward VII.; Her late Majesty Queen Victoria.

BAG AND DRESSING CASE MANUFACTURERS.

EDWARDS & SONS, 161, Regent Street, W., London, Eng.

To His Majesty The King; Her Majesty The Queen; Her late Majesty Queen Victoria; T.R.H. The Prince and Princess of Wales.

BOOKSELLERS.

JOHN & E. BUMPUS, Ltd., 350, Oxford Street, W., London, Eng., Booksellers.

To H.M. King Edward VII.; also to H.R.H. The Duchess of Fife; H.I.M. The Empress of Russia; Her late Majesty Queen Victoria.

BOW MAKERS AND EXPERTS IN VIOLINS.

W. E. HILL & SONS, 140, New Bond Street, W., London, Eng. Workshops: London and Hanwell, Middx.

Sole Violin and Bow Manufacturers to H.M. King Edward VII.; also to H.M. The Queen Regent of Spain; H.M. Queen Maria Pia of Portugal; H.M. The late Queen Victoria; H.R.H. The late Duke of Saxe-Coburg and Gotha.

(Mentioned in Pepys Diary, A.D. 1660.)

BRANDY SHIPPERS.

J. DENIS, HENRY MOUNIÉ & Co., Cognac, France.

(Established in 1838).

To His Majesty King Edward VII.

BRIDLE-BIT, STIRRUP AND SPUR MAKERS.

LATCHFORD & Co., 59, St. Martin's Lane, W.C., London, Eng.

To His Majesty King Edward VII. ; H.R.H. The Prince of Wales, K.G. ; Her late Majesty Queen Victoria.

"Royal Warrant Holders since H.M. King George III."

BRONZE MANUFACTURERS.

ELKINGTON & Co. Ltd., 22, Regent St., S.W., & 73, Cheapside, E.C., London, Eng., Goldsmiths, Silversmiths & Bronze Manufacturers.

To His Majesty King Edward VII. ; Her late Majesty Queen Victoria ; H.R.H. The Prince of Wales; H.R.H. The late Duke of Saxe-Coburg & Gotha ; H.M. The King of Spain ; H.M. The King of Italy; H.M. The King of the Belgians ; and the I. and R. Court of Austria.

Also at Glasgow, Liverpool, Manchester, Newcastle-on-Tyne and Birmingham. And at Calcutta, Rangoon, Montreal, &c.

BRUSH AND COMB MAKER.

J. FLORIS, 89, Jermyn Street, St. James', London, S.W., Eng.

To His Majesty The King; H.R.H. The Prince of Wales; Her late Majesty Queen Victoria ; T.R.H. The late Duke and Duchess of Teck.

CARPET MANUFACTURERS.

WARING & GILLOW, Ltd., 164-180, Oxford St., W., London, Eng.

Upholsterers and Decorators to H.M. King Edward VII. ; Double Grand Prix, Paris, 1900 ; Two Grand Prizes, St. Louis, 1904 ; Grand Prix, Milan, 1906.

Also at Liverpool, Manchester, Lancaster, Paris, Johannesburg.

CHAMPAGNE SHIPPERS.

CHARLES HEIDSIECK, of Reims, France, and 110, Fenchurch Street, E.C., London, Eng.

To His Majesty King Edward VII.

VEUVE, POMMERY, FILS & Cie, Reims, France.

To His Majesty King Edward VII.; Her late Majesty Queen Victoria ; H.R.H. The Prince of Wales.

LANSON PÈRE & FILS, Reims, France.

(Established in 1760).

To His Majesty King Edward VII., and Her late Majesty Queen Victoria.

CHEMISTS.

SQUIRE & SONS, 413, Oxford Street, London, W., Eng. (the only address).

Chemists on the Establishment of His Majesty The King, and of H.R.H. The Prince of Wales.

CHIMNEY PIECES.

M. FEETHAM & Co., 9, Clifford St., Bond Street, W., London, Eng.

To His Majesty King Edward VII.; Her late Majesty Queen Victoria.

Chimney Pieces of all periods in Marble. Wood and Stone.

CHRONOMETERS.

E. DENT & Co., Ltd., 61, Strand, W.C., and 4, Royal Exchange, E.C., London, Eng.

To His Majesty King Edward VII.; Her late Majesty Queen Victoria; to the Principal Governments and Observatories throughout the world. Makers of the Great Westminster Clock, " Big Ben," and sole custodians since its erection.

M. F. DENT & Co., 34, Cockspur Street, S.W., London, Eng.

Chronometer, Watch and Clock Makers to Her late Majesty Queen Victoria; H.R.H. The Prince of Wales; H.I.M. The Emperor of Japan; The Principal Courts of Europe.

CLOCK, WATCH AND CHRONOMETER MAKERS.

S. SMITH & SON, Ltd., 9, Strand, W.C., London, Eng. Speedometer and Motor Watch Makers.

To His Majesty King Edward VII.

(Established Half-a-Century).

Chronometer Makers to the Indian Government, etc. Watchmakers to the Admiralty, and Imperial Japanese Navy.

COACHMAKERS.

BARKER & Co., 66, Chandos Street, 10, 11 and 12, Bedford Street, Charing Cross, W.C., and 67, Newington Causeway, S.E., London, Eng., Coachmakers.

To His Majesty King Edward VII.; H.R.H. The Prince of Wales; Her late Majesty Queen Victoria.

HOLMES & Co., 37, Margaret St., Cavendish Sq., W., London; and at Derby, Lichfield, Sheffield, Burton-on-Trent, Eng.

To His Majesty King Edward VII.; Her late Majesty Queen Victoria.

STOCKEN & Co., 144, Fulham Road, S.W., London, Eng.

To His Majesty King Edward VII.; H.R.H. The Prince of Wales.

COURT FLORIST AND FRUITERER.

J. BUTLER, 171 and 172, Sloane Street, Belgravia, S.W., London, Eng.

Telephone: 665 Ken.   (Established 1827).

To H.R.H. The Princess Christian.

Hampers of Fruit in different stages of ripeness packed and delivered on board the American Liners at Southampton and Liverpool by our own Agents.

CRICKET, LAWN TENNIS, GOLF, POLO, RACKETS.

JOHN WISDEN & Co., 21, Cranbourn Street, W.C., London, Eng.

Telephone: 2120 Gerrard. Telegrams: "Wisden, London."

To H.R.H. The Prince of Wales.

CUSTOM HOUSE AGENTS.

WOOLLEY & COWLEY, 36, Seething Lane, E.C., London, Eng.

To His Majesty King Edward VII.; Her late Majesty Queen Victoria ; H.R.H. The Prince of Wales.

(Royal Warrant Holders since 1848).

DECORATORS.

WARING & GILLOW, Ltd., 164–180, Oxford St., W., London, Eng.

Upholsterers and Decorators to H.M. King Edward VII.; Double Grand Prix, Paris, 1900 ; Two Grand Prizes, St. Louis, 1904 ; Grand Prix, Milan, 1906.

Also at Liverpool, Manchester, Lancaster, Paris, Johannesburg.

DIAMOND WORK AND PEARLS.

LAMBERT, 10, 11 and 12, Coventry Street, Piccadilly, W., London, Eng.

Jewellers and Silversmiths to His Majesty King Edward VII.

Antique and Modern Table, Decorative and Ecclesiastical Silver Plate. Diamond Work and Pearls.

DOG BISCUITS, GAME AND POULTRY FOODS, INCUBATORS, Etc.

SPRATT'S PATENT, Ltd., 24 and 25, Fenchurch Street, London, Eng.

Also at Paris, Newark U.S.A., and Berlin (Germany).

Purveyors to His Majesty King Edward VII.

Of Dog Biscuits, Game Foods and Incubators.

DRESSMAKING.

REDFERN, Ltd., 26 & 27, Conduit Street, and 27, New Bond Street, W., London, Eng.; also at Paris, 242, Rue de Rivoli; New York, 568 Fifth Avenue; Edinburgh; Monte Carlo; Nice.

To H.M. The Queen; Her late Majesty Queen Victoria; H.R.H. The Princess of Wales; H.I.M. The late Empress Frederick of Germany; H.I.M. The Empress Alexandra Feodorovna of Russia; The Dowager Empress of Russia; H.M. The Queen of Denmark; H.M. The Queen of the Hellenes; H.M. Queen Mary of Portugal; The Grand Duchess Vladimir.

DRESSING AND SUIT CASE MANUFACTURERS.

J. C. VICKERY, 179, 181 and 183, Regent Street, W., London, Eng.

To H.M. The King; H.M. Queen Alexandra; H.M. The King of Portugal; T.M. The King and Queen of Denmark; T.R.H. The Prince and Princess of Wales; T.R.H. The Prince and Princess Christian of Schleswig-Holstein.

DYERS AND CLEANERS.

DAINTREE & Co., 95, Mount St., Grosvenor Sq., W., London, Eng.

Telephone No. 2625 Gerrard.

To T.R.H. The Prince and Princess Christian.

Speciality—Court Dresses chemically cleaned.

ELECTRIC FITTINGS.

WARING & GILLOW, Ltd., 164-180, Oxford St., W., London, Eng.

Upholsterers and Decorators to His Majesty, King Edward VII.; Double Grand Prix, Paris, 1900; Two Grand Prizes, St. Louis, 1904; Grand Prix, Milan, 1906.

Also at Liverpool, Manchester, Lancaster, Paris, Johannesburg.

FIREPLACE MAKERS.

M. FEETHAM & Co., 9, Clifford Street, Bond St., W., London, Eng.

To His Majesty King Edward VII.; Her late Majesty Queen Victoria.
Speciality. Reproductions from Original Models in all styles.

FISHING ROD AND TACKLE MANUFACTURERS..

HARDY BROTHERS, London & North-British Works, Alnwick, Eng.

Makers to H.R.H. The Prince of Wales; H.M. The King of Italy; and patronized by Her Majesty Queen Alexandra, Princess Royal, Princess Victoria, etc., etc.
And the leading authorities in the Angling World.

41 Highest Awards for Cane-built Steel Centre, Cane-built and Greenheart Rods and Tackle.

Branches: LONDON, 61, Pall Mall; EDINBURGH, 5, South St. David Street; MANCHESTER, 12, Moult Street.

Catalogues and "Hints to Anglers" free, 300 Illustrations.

FITTED MOTOR BAG MANUFACTURERS.

J. C. VICKERY, 179, 181 and 183, Regent Street, W., London, Eng.

To H.M. The King; H.M. Queen Alexandra; H.M. The King of Portugal; T.M. The King and Queen of Denmark; T.R.H. The Prince and Princess of Wales; T.R.H. The Prince and Princess Christian of Schleswig-Holstein.

FLORAL EXPERT AND GROWER.

FELTON & SONS (Principal R. F. FELTON, F.R.H.S., F.Z.S.), 7, 8 and 9, Hanover Court, Hanover Square, W., London, Eng.

Telephone: 908 Mayfair: 4998 Gerrard: 666 Mayfair.

To His Majesty King Edward VII.

In addition to holding perhaps the largest stock of fresh flowers in London, Mr. Felton is prepared to supply plants and pack same for export of every variety shown at their London establishments.

FORWARDING AND SHIPPING AGENTS.

ROSENBERG, LOEWE & Co., Succrs., 109, Fenchurch Street, E.C., London, Eng.

To H.H. The Duke of Saxe-Meiningen; H.R.H. The late Duke of Edinburgh and Saxe-Coburg-Gotha.

FRUITERERS AND FLORISTS.

G. ADAM & Co., 39, New Bond Street, W., London, Eng.; also Halles Centrales, Paris, France.

To His Majesty The King.

Hampers of carefully selected Fruits in different stages of ripeness, packed and placed on board the American Steamers by our own Agents at Southampton and Liverpool.

FURNITURE MAKERS AND DESIGNERS.

WARING & GILLOW, Ltd., 164–180, Oxford St., W., London, Eng.

Upholsterers and Decorators to H.M. King Edward VII.; Double Grand Prix, Paris, 1900; Two Grand Prizes, St. Louis, 1904; Grand Prix, Milan, 1906.

Also at Liverpool, Manchester, Lancaster, Paris, Johannesburg.

FURRIERS.

REDFERN, Ltd., 26 & 27, Conduit Street, and 27, New Bond Street, London, Eng.; also at Paris, 242, Rue de Rivoli; New York, 568 Fifth Avenue; Edinburgh; Monte Carlo; Nice.

To H.M. The Queen; Her late Majesty Queen Victoria; H.R.H. The Princess of Wales; Her late Majesty The Empress Frederick of Germany; H.I.M. The Empress Alexandra Feodorovna of Russia; The Dowager Empress of Russia; H.M. The Queen of Denmark; H.M. The Queen of the Hellenes; H.M. Queen Mary of Portugal; The Grand Duchess Vladimir.

GLASS PAINTERS.

HEATON, BUTLER & BAYNE, 14, Garrick Street, Covent Garden, W.C., London, Eng.

Artists in Stained Glass to His Majesty King Edward VII.

Agents in New York—THE GORHAM COMPANY, NEW YORK CITY.
„ in Chicago—SPAULDING & COMPANY.

GOLDSMITHS.

BARKENTIN & KRALL, 289 and 291, Regent St., W., London, Eng.

To H.R.H. The Princess of Wales (now Her Majesty Queen Alexandra).

ELKINGTON & Co. Ltd., 22, Regent St., S.W., & 73, Cheapside, E.C., London, Eng., Goldsmiths, Silversmiths & Bronze Manufacturers.

To His Majesty King Edward VII.; Her late Majesty Queen Victoria; H.R.H. The Prince of Wales; H.R.H. The late Duke of Saxe-Coburg & Gotha; H.M. The King of Spain; H.M. The King of Italy; H.M. The King of the Belgians; and the I. and R. Court of Austria.

Also at Glasgow, Liverpool, Manchester, Newcastle-on-Tyne and Birmingham.
And at Calcutta, Rangoon, Montreal, &c.

LAMBERT, 10, 11 and 12, Coventry Street, Piccadilly, W., London, Eng.

Jewellers and Silversmiths to His Majesty King Edward VII.

Antique and Modern Table, Decorative and Ecclesiastical
Silver Plate. Diamond Work and Pearls.

J. C. VICKERY, 179, 181 and 183, Regent Street, W., London, Eng.

To H.M. The King; H.M. Queen Alexandra; H.M. The King of Portugal; T.M. The King and Queen of Denmark; T.R.H. The Prince and Princess of Wales; T.R.H. The Prince and Princess Christian of Schleswig-Holstein.

GUN AND RIFLE MANUFACTURERS.

STEPHEN GRANT & SONS, 67A, St. James' St., S.W., London, Eng.

To His Majesty King Edward VII.; Her late Majesty Queen Victoria; H.R.H. The Prince of Wales; H.R.H. The late Duke of Saxe-Coburg-Gotha.

HATTERS.

ROBERT HEATH, Ltd., 37 and 39, Knightsbridge, S.W., London, England (only address).

To Her late Majesty Queen Victoria; Her Majesty Queen Alexandra; H.I.M. The Empress of Russia; The Court of Greece; H.M. The Queen of Norway; The Principal Courts of Europe.

JOHNSON & Co., 111, Regent Street, W., London, Eng.

To Her late Majesty Queen Victoria; H.R.H. The Prince of Wales.

HATTERS —*continued.*

LINCOLN BENNETT & Co., Ltd., 1, 2 and 3, Sackville St., and 40, Piccadilly, W., London, Eng., Gentlemen's Hats and Caps.

To His Majesty The King; H.M. The Queen; H.R.H. The Prince of Wales; The Royal Family; The Sovereigns and Royal Courts of Europe.

Gold Medals and Diplomas—London, 1851; Philadelphia, 1876; Paris, 1878 and 1889; Sydney, 1879; Melbourne, 1880; London, 1884; Calcutta, 1884; Adelaide, 1887; Chicago, 1893; Grand Prix, Paris, 1900.

HOSIERS, GLOVERS, OUTFITTERS.

SWEARS & WELLS, Ltd., 190 and 192, Regent St., W., London, Eng.

To Her Majesty The Queen; Her late Majesty Queen Victoria; T.R.H. The Prince and Princess of Wales; H.I.M. The late Empress Frederick of Germany; H.R.H. The Princess Royal; H.R. & I.H. The Duchess of Edinburgh; H.M. The King of Spain; H.I.M. The Empress of Russia; H.I.M. The German Empress; H.M. The Queen of Sweden; H.M. The Queen of Denmark; H.M. The Queen of Greece; T.M. The King & Queen of Norway.

HUNTING BOOTS.

H. MAXWELL & Co., 161, Piccadilly, W., London, Eng., Spur Makers. (Temporary Premises, 8, Dover Street, Piccadilly).

To His Majesty King Edward VII.; Her late Majesty Queen Victoria; H.R.H. The Prince of Wales; Their late Majesties King George IV., King William IV.; His Majesty the King of Portugal.

IRISH LINENS AND DAMASKS.

ROBINSON & CLEAVER, Ltd., Belfast, Ireland; and 156 to 170, Regent Street, W., and 101, 102, Cheapside, E.C., London, Eng., Damask and Cambric Manufacturers.

To His Majesty King Edward VII.; Her late Majesty Queen Victoria; H.M. The King of Spain; H.R.H. The Princess of Wales; H.I.M. The late Empress Frederick of Germany.

FAULDING, STRATTON & Co., 67, New Bond St., W., London, Eng. Table Damask and Cambric Handkerchief Manufacturers.

To His Majesty King Edward VII.; Her late Majesty Queen Victoria; H.R.H. The Prince of Wales; His late Majesty King William IV.

Table Linen and all Linen of the choicest character.

JEWELLERS.

ELKINGTON & Co. Ltd., 22, Regent St., S.W., & 73, Cheapside, E.C., London, Eng., Goldsmiths, Silversmiths & Bronze Manufacturers.

To His Majesty King Edward VII.; H.R.H. The Prince of Wales; Her late Majesty Queen Victoria; H.R.H. The late Duke of Saxe-Coburg & Gotha; H.M. The King of Spain; H.M. The King of Italy; H.M. The King of the Belgians; and the I. and R. Court of Austria.

Also at Glasgow, Liverpool, Manchester, Newcastle-on-Tyne and Birmingham. And at Calcutta, Rangoon, Montreal, &c.

JEWELLERS *continued*

LAMBERT, 10, 11 and 12, Coventry Street, Piccadilly, W., London, Eng.

Jewellers and Silversmiths to His Majesty King Edward VII.

Antique and Modern Table, Decorative and Ecclesiastical
Silver Plate. Diamond Work and Pearls.

LIBERTY & Co. Ltd., Regent Street, W., London, Eng., Goldsmiths and Silversmiths.

To Her Majesty Queen Alexandra.

Also at Paris, Manchester, Bristol, Birmingham.

LONGMAN & STRONGI'TH'ARM, 1, Waterloo Place, Pall Mall, S.W., London, Eng.

To His Majesty The King; Her late Majesty Queen Victoria; H.R.H. The Prince of Wales; The Prince Regent.

J. C. VICKERY, 179, 181 and 183, Regent Street, W., London, Eng.

To H.M. The King; H.M. Queen Alexandra; H.M. The King of Portugal; T.M. The King and Queen of Denmark; T.R.H. The Prince and Princess of Wales; T.R.H. The Prince and Princess Christian of Schleswig-Holstein.

LADIES', GIRLS' AND BOYS' TAILORS.

SWEARS & WELLS, Ltd., 190 and 192, Regent St., W., London, Eng.

To Her Majesty The Queen; Her late Majesty Queen Victoria; T.R.H. The Prince and Princess of Wales; H.I.M. The late Empress Frederick of Germany; H.R.H. The Princess Royal; H.R. & I.H. The Duchess of Edinburgh; H.M. The King of Spain; H.I.M. The Empress of Russia; H.I.M. The German Empress; H.M. The Queen of Sweden; H.M. The Queen of Denmark; H.M. The Queen of Greece; T.M. The King & Queen of Norway.

LEATHER GOODS MANUFACTURERS.

J. C. VICKERY, 179, 181 and 183, Regent Street, W., London, Eng.

To H.M. The King; H.M. Queen Alexandra; H.M. The King of Portugal; T.M. The King and Queen of Denmark; T.R.H. The Prince and Princess of Wales; T.R.H. The Prince and Princess Christian of Schleswig-Holstein.

MEDALLISTS.

ELKINGTON & Co. Ltd., 22, Regent St., S.W., & 73, Cheapside, E.C., London, Eng., Goldsmiths, Silversmiths & Bronze Manufacturers.

To His Majesty King Edward VII; Her late Majesty Queen Victoria; H.R.H. The Prince of Wales; H.R.H. The late Duke of Saxe-Coburg & Gotha; H M. The King of Spain; H.M. The King of Italy; H.M. The King of the Belgians; and the I. and R. Court of Austria.

Also at Glasgow, Liverpool, Manchester, Newcastle-on-Tyne and Birmingham.
And at Calcutta, Rangoon, Montreal, &c.

MEMORIAL BRASSES.

BARKENTIN & KRALL, 289 and 291, Regent St., W., London, Eng., Goldsmiths.

To H.R.H. The Princess of Wales (now Her Majesty Queen Alexandra).

MEMORIALS.

GAWTHORP & SONS, 16, Long Acre, W.C., London, Eng., Art Metal Workers

By Appointment to His Majesty The King.

Have executed Memorials, Church Fittings, and Wrought Iron Work for Their Majesties King Edward VII.; Queen Alexandra, and the late Queen Victoria. Memorials in " Latten " Brass, Marble, Alabaster, Bronze, Copper, Etc.

MILLINERS

ROBERT HEATH, Ltd., 37 and 39, Knightsbridge, S.W., London, England (only address).

To Her late Majesty Queen Victoria ; Her Majesty Queen Alexandra ; H.I.M. The Empress of Russia ; The Court of Greece ; H.M. The Queen of Norway ; The Principal Courts of Europe.

LINCOLN BENNETT & Co., Ltd., 1, 2 and 3, Sackville Street, and 40, Piccadilly, London, Eng.

To His Majesty The King ; H.M. The Queen ; H.R.H. The Prince of Wales ; The Royal Family ; The Sovereigns and Royal Courts of Europe.

Gold Medals and Diplomas— London, 1851 ; Philadelphia, 1876 ; Paris, 1878 and 1889 ; Sydney, 1879 ; Melbourne, 1880 ; London, 1884 ; Calcutta, 1884 ; Adelaide, 1887 ; Chicago, 1893 ; Grand Prix, Paris, 1900.

MOTOR BODY BUILDERS.

BARKER & Co., 66, Chandos Street, 10, 11 and 12, Bedford Street, Charing Cross, W.C., and 67, Newington Causeway, S.E., London, Eng., Coachmakers.

To His Majesty King Edward VII. ; Her late Majesty Queen Victoria ; H.R.H. The Prince of Wales.

HOLMES & Co., 37, Margaret Street, Cavendish Square, W., London, and at Derby, Lichfield, Sheffield, Burton-on-Trent, Eng.

To His Majesty King Edward VII.; Her late Majesty Queen Victoria.

STOCKEN & Co., 144, Fulham Rd., S.W., London, Eng., Coachmakers.

To His Majesty King Edward VII.; H.R.H. The Prince of Wales.

Garage: 97a, Drayton Gardens, S.W.

MOTOR CAR MANUFACTURERS.

THE DAIMLER MOTOR Co. (1904) Ltd., Daimler Works, Coventry; also London, Manchester, Nottingham, Bristol, Eng., Motor Car Manufacturers.

To H.M. King Edward VII.; T.R.H. The Prince and Princess of Wales.
The English Daimler Co., 1473 Broadway, corner of 56th Street, New York City.

NATURAL MINERAL TABLE WATERS.

THE GODES-BERGER COMPANY, 17 and 18, St. Dunstan's Hill, E.C., London, Eng.

To H.M. King Edward VII.; Her late Majesty Queen Victoria since 1860.
"Godes-berger" Natural Mineral Table Water from the Spring
at Godesberg, a Rhein, Germany.

OBJECTS OF ART (Italian, Ancient and Modern).

WARING & GILLOW, Ltd., 164-180, Oxford St., W., London, Eng.

Upholsterers and Decorators to H.M. King Edward VII.; Double Grand Prix, Paris, 1900; Two Grand Prizes, St. Louis, 1904; Grand Prix, Milan, 1906.
Also at Liverpool, Manchester, Lancaster, Paris, Johannesburg.

OBJECTS OF ART AND TROPHIES IN BRONZE AND PRECIOUS METALS.

ELKINGTON & Co. Ltd., 22, Regent St., S.W., & 73, Cheapside, E.C., London, Eng., Goldsmiths, Silversmiths & Bronze Manufacturers.

To His Majesty King Edward VII.; Her late Majesty Queen Victoria; H.R.H. The Prince of Wales; H.R.H. The late Duke of Saxe-Coburg & Gotha; H.M. The King of Spain; H.M. The King of Italy; H.M. The King of the Belgians; and the I. and R. Court of Austria.

Also at Glasgow, Liverpool, Manchester, Newcastle-on-Tyne and Birmingham.
And at Calcutta, Rangoon, Montreal, &c.

PERFUMER.

J. FLORIS, 89, Jermyn Street, St. James', London, S.W., Eng.

To His Majesty The King; H.R.H. The Prince of Wales; Her late Majesty Queen Victoria; T.R.H. The late Duke and Duchess of Teck.

PICTURE DEALERS AND PRINTSELLERS.

ARTHUR ACKERMANN & SON, 191, Regent St., W., London, Eng.

To Her Majesty Queen Alexandra; Her late Majesty Queen Victoria.
Old and Modern Sporting Prints always on view.

P. & D. COLNAGHI & Co., 13 and 14, Pall Mall East, S.W. London, Eng.

Printsellers and Publishers to His Majesty King Edward VII.

"Royal Warrant Holders since H.M. King George III."

PUBLISHERS AND BOOKSELLERS.

JOHN & E. BUMPUS, Ltd., 350, Oxford Street, W., London, Eng. Booksellers.

To H.M. King Edward VII.; also to H.R.H. The Duchess of Fife; H.I.M. The Empress of Russia; Her late Majesty Queen Victoria.

RIFLE MANUFACTURERS.

STEPHEN GRANT & SONS, 67A, St. James's Street, S.W., London, Eng.

To His Majesty King Edward VII.; Her late Majesty Queen Victoria; H.R.H. The Prince of Wales; H.R.H. The late Duke of Saxe-Coburg-Gotha.

SAFE DEPOSIT.

THE PALL MALL DEPOSIT AND FORWARDING CO., LTD., Carlton Street, Regent Street, London, S.W. City Agents, ROSENBERG, LOEWE & Co., SUCCRS., 109, Fenchurch Street, E.C., Forwarding Agents.

To H.H. The Duke of Saxe-Meiningen; H.R.H. The late Duke of Edinburgh and Saxe-Coburg-Gotha.

SANITARY ENGINEERS.

DENT & HELLYER, 35, Red Lion Square, W.C., London, Eng.

(Established 1730). The Originators of the Modern System of Sanitation.

To His Majesty King Edward VII.; Her late Majesty Queen Victoria.

All the Royal Palaces are fitted with Messrs. Dent & Hellyer's Sanitary Appliances.

SCOTCH WHISKY DISTILLERS.

JAMES BUCHANAN & CO., Ltd., 26, Holborn, E.C., London; and at Glasgow, Bristol, Manchester, Birmingham, Leeds, &c., Eng.

To His Majesty The King; H.R.H. The Prince of Wales.

Also at Paris, 217, Rue St. Honoré; Hamburg, 16 Neueberg; New York, 29 Broadway.

SEAL ENGRAVERS.

LONGMAN & STRONGI'TH'ARM, 1, Waterloo Place, Pall Mall, S.W., London, Eng.

To His Majesty the King; Her late Majesty Queen Victoria; H.R.H. The Prince of Wales; The Prince Regent.

Book Plates, Antique Seals, Die Sinking, Portraits of Animals engraved and painted in Crystal.

SEEDSMEN.

SUTTON & SONS, Reading, Eng., Seedsmen.

To His Majesty King Edward VII.

"Consult Sutton's Guide and Catalogue for 1907."

SILKS.

LIBERTY & Co., Ltd., Regent Street, W., London, Eng., Silk Mercers.

To H.R.H. The Princess of Wales.

Also at Paris. Manchester. Bristol. Birmingham.

SILVERSMITHS.

EDWARDS & SONS, 161, Regent Street, W., London, Eng.

To His Majesty The King; Her Majesty The Queen; Her late Majesty Queen Victoria; T.R.H. The Prince and Princess of Wales.

ELKINGTON & Co. Ltd., 22, Regent St., S.W., & 73, Cheapside, E.C., London, Eng., Goldsmiths, Silversmiths & Bronze Manufacturers.

To His Majesty King Edward VII; Her late Majesty Queen Victoria; H.R.H. The Prince of Wales; H.R.H. The late Duke of Saxe-Coburg & Gotha; H.M. The King of Spain; H.M. The King of Italy; H.M. The King of the Belgians; and the I. and R. Court of Austria.

Also at Glasgow, Liverpool, Manchester, Newcastle-on-Tyne and Birmingham. And at Calcutta, Rangoon, Montreal, &c.

LAMBERT, 10, 11 and 12, Coventry Street, Piccadilly, W., London, Eng.

Jewellers and Silversmiths to His Majesty King Edward VII.

Antique and Modern Table, Decorative and Ecclesiastical Silver Plate. Diamond Work and Pearls.

J. C. VICKERY, 179, 181 and 183, Regent Street, W., London, Eng.

To H.M. The King; H.M. Queen Alexandra; H.M. The King of Portugal; T.M. The King and Queen of Denmark; T.R.H. The Prince and Princess of Wales; T.R.H. The Prince and Princess Christian of Schleswig-Holstein.

SOAP MAKERS.

A. & F. PEARS, Ltd., 71-75, New Oxford Street, W.C., London, and Isleworth, Middlesex, Eng.

To His Majesty King Edward VII.; Her Majesty Queen Alexandra; Their Majesties the King and Queen of Spain.

SPEEDOMETER AND MOTOR WATCH MAKERS.

S. SMITH & SON, Ltd., 9, Strand, W.C., London, Eng.

(Established Half-a-Century).

By Appointment to His Majesty The King.

See Special Catalogue for these Instruments and other Motor Accessories.

SPURS AND WHIPS.

H. MAXWELL & Co., 161, Piccadilly, W., London, Eng., Spur Makers. (Temporary Premises, 8, Dover Street, Piccadilly).

To His Majesty King Edward VII.; Her late Majesty Queen Victoria; H.R.H. The Prince of Wales; Their late Majesties King George IV., King William IV.; His Majesty The King of Portugal.

STAINED GLASS MEMORIAL WINDOWS.

HEATON, BUTLER & BAYNE, 14, Garrick Street, Covent Garden, W.C., London, Eng.

Artists in Stained Glass to His Majesty King Edward VII.

Agents in New York—THE GORHAM COMPANY, NEW YORK CITY.
   ,,   in Chicago—SPAULDING & COMPANY.

STATIONERS, AND FANCY LEATHER MANUFACTURERS.

EDWARDS & SONS, 161, Regent Street, W., London, Eng.

To His Majesty The King; Her Majesty The Queen; Her late Majesty Queen Victoria; T.R.H. The Prince and Princess of Wales.

TAILORS AND ROBE MAKERS.

EDE, SON & RAVENSCROFT, 93 and 94, Chancery Lane, W.C., London, Eng.

To His Majesty King Edward VII.; H.M. Queen Alexandra; H.R.H. The Prince of Wales; H.R.H. The Princess of Wales.

Robe Makers and Tailors to Corporate Bodies, Legal, Clerical, and for all Universities.

TEA MERCHANTS.

RIDGWAYS Ltd., 6 & 7, King William Street, City, and 182, Oxford Street, W., London, Eng. Sole Agent for U.S.A. LOUIS SHERRY, Fifth Av., New York.

To Her late Majesty Queen Victoria.

TROUSSEAUX AND IRISH LINENS.

ROBINSON & CLEAVER, Ltd., Belfast, Ireland; and 156 to 170, Regent Street, W., and 101, 102, Cheapside, E.C., London, Eng., Trousseaux and Irish Linen Manufacturers.

To His Majesty King Edward VII.; Her late Majesty Queen Victoria; H.M. The King of Spain; H.R.H. The Princess of Wales; H.I.M. The late Empress Frederick of Germany.

UPHOLSTERERS, CABINET MAKERS, DECORATORS.

HOLLAND & SONS, 9, Mount St., Grosvenor Square, W., London, Eng.

To His Majesty King Edward VII.; Her late Majesty Queen Victoria; The Royal Academy of Arts.

VIOLIN AND BOW MAKERS.

W. E. HILL & SONS, 140, New Bond Street, W., London, Eng.
Workshops: London, and Hanwell, Middlesex.

Sole Violin and Bow Manufacturers to H.M. King Edward VII.; also to H.M. The Queen Regent of Spain; H.M. Queen Maria Pia of Portugal; H.M. The late Queen Victoria; and H.R.H. The late Duke of Saxe-Coburg and Gotha.

(Mentioned in Pepy's Diary, A.D. 1660).

WATCH & CLOCK MAKERS.

E. DENT & Co., Ltd., 61, Strand, W.C., and 4, Royal Exchange, London, E.C., Eng.

To His Majesty King Edward VII.; Her late Majesty Queen Victoria; to the Principal Governments and Observatories throughout the world. Makers of the Great Westminster Clock, "Big Ben," and sole custodians since its erection.

M. F. DENT & Co., 34, Cockspur Street, S.W., London, Eng.

Chronometer, Watch and Clock Makers to Her late Majesty Queen Victoria; H.R.H. The Prince of Wales; H.I.M. The Emperor of Japan; The Principal Courts of Europe.

WINE, SPIRIT, AND LIQUEUR MERCHANTS.

BERRY BROTHERS & Co., 3, St. James's Street, S.W., London, Eng.

To His Majesty King Edward VII., and H.R.H. The Prince of Wales.

(Established at the above address in the XVII. Century.)

GEORGE TANQUERAY & Co., 5, Pall Mall East, S.W., London, Eng.

Telegraphic Address: "Tanqueray, London." Telephone: 3778 Gerrard.

To H.R.H. The Prince of Wales.

WRITING, CARD, AND LIQUEUR TABLE MFRS.

J. C. VICKERY, 179, 181 and 183, Regent Street, W., London, Eng.

To H.M. The King; H.M. Queen Alexandra; H.M. The King of Portugal; T.M. The King and Queen of Denmark; T.R.H. The Prince and Princess of Wales; T.R.H. The Prince and Princess Christian of Schleswig-Holstein.

YACHT FITTERS.

WARING & GILLOW, Ltd., 164–180, Oxford St., W., London, Eng.

Upholsterers and Decorators to H.M. King Edward VII.; Double Grand Prix, Paris, 1900; Two Grand Prizes, St. Louis, 1904; Grand Prix, Milan, 1906.

Also at Liverpool, Manchester, Lancaster, Paris, Johannesburg.

www.armorial-register.com

www.ingramcontent.com/pod-product-compliance
Lightning Source LLC
Chambersburg PA
CBHW060326100426
42812CB00003B/889